Gisela Holfter, Horst Dickel
An Irish Sanctuary

Gisela Holfter, Horst Dickel
An Irish Sanctuary

German-speaking Refugees in Ireland 1933–1945

DE GRUYTER
OLDENBOURG

ISBN 978-3-11-063467-9
e-ISBN (PDF) 978-3-11-035145-3
e-ISBN (EPUB 978-3-11-039575-4

Library of Congress Cataloging-in-Publication Data
A CIP catalog record for this book has been applied for at the Library of Congress.

Bibliographic information published by the Deutsche Nationalbibliothek
The Deutsche Nationalbibliothek lists this publication in the Deutsche
Nationalbibliografie; detailed bibliographic data are available on the Internet
at http://dnb.dnb.de.

© 2018 Walter de Gruyter GmbH, Berlin/Boston
This volume is text- and page-identical with the hardback published in 2016.
Cover image: *Irish Times*, 21 January 1939
Typesetting: Konvertus, Haarlem
Printing: CPI books GmbH, Leck

♾ Printed on acid free paper
Printed in Germany

www.degruyter.com

For Annelie and Glenn

Contents

List of Images —— X
Tables —— XI
Acknowledgements —— XII

Introduction —— 1

Part I **Passages To Ireland**

Chapter 1
The Distant Option – German Refugees to Ireland, 1933–1938 —— 13
    The students —— 18
    The businessmen —— 25
    The Lisowski story —— 27

Chapter 2
"Those days in Vienna…" —— 31
    Georg Klaar/George Clare —— 31
    Social profiles —— 32
    "Those days in Vienna…" —— 35
    Economics of the dispossessed —— 39
    Ribbons and zip fasteners —— 41
    Getting out —— 49
    The Kagran Group —— 50
    Protestant helpers —— 52
    Catholic attempts —— 57
    … and the Jews? —— 60

Chapter 3
The Jews of Komotau —— 63

Chapter 4
The German Pogrom and After —— 76
    The capital and the concentration camp —— 77
    Out of Saxony —— 85
    Out of the Rhineland —— 89

Chapter 5
The Routes of the Refugees: Italian Passages to Ireland —— 92

Part II Exiled in Wartime Ireland

Chapter 6
The State, the Helpers and the Refugees —— 99
"A certain degree of confusion ..." – New challenges in 1938 —— 108
The Irish Co-ordinating Committee for Refugees —— 119
The aid organisations and the new policy —— 132
Doors shut tight —— 140
Care and control —— 144
Assessment and comparison —— 145

Chapter 7
Uncharted Terrain – German-speaking Refugees in the Irish Provinces —— 153
Continental urbanites in Irish fields —— 153
Times at the demesnes and other places: workers, sojourners and their hosts —— 164
Students and teachers in the Irish provinces —— 173
"It was all right when foreigners came along to start industries and give employment but [...]" – Exiles in provincial economies —— 181
Les Modes Modernes, Wings and the exile community in Galway —— 184
Happy exile in Cork? —— 194
The exiles of Co. Tipperary —— 196
Longford Ribbons —— 203
Under Western Hats —— 210
On Europe's fringe —— 220

Chapter 8
Continental Dubliners —— 228
"Only entrepreneurial partnership or agony"? Business ventures in exile —— 230
Settled employees —— 234
Job-seekers —— 236
Dependants —— 240
New homes —— 245
The lure of the city —— 256

Chapter 9
Academics in Exile —— 270
At Irish universities —— 275
Trinity College —— 277

Germany's leading serologist – Hans Sachs —— 282
Ludwig Hopf – Einstein's first assistant —— 289
University College Dublin and the National University of Ireland in Cork, Galway and Maynooth —— 300
Ernst Lewy – a linguist with rare abilities —— 304
A brief interlude —— 310
"Certain distinguished Austrian Professors" —— 310
Academics who did not come —— 317
The Dublin Institute of Advanced Studies (DIAS) —— 323
Overall assessment —— 344

Chapter 10
Transit Lives —— 348
Exit Great Britain —— 356
Exit Northern Ireland? —— 361

Part III After the War

Chapter 11
Refugees Revisited —— 365
Educated in Ireland —— 365
Growing old – in Ireland? —— 371
Women in exile —— 374
Leaving the outposts —— 377
Restitution and compensation —— 383
Home and identity —— 384
Brokers of modernity? —— 390
And the academics? —— 398

Bibliography —— 407
A Primary sources —— 407
B Literature —— 415
1 Secondary literature —— 415
2 Personal recollections and autobiographies —— 434

Index of Names —— 438

Index of Places —— 448

List of Images

Chapter 1 – The Distant Option
Image 1 Advertisement for Irish and Danish folksong evening – Eden Archive, Oranienburg
Image 2 Dr Käte Müller-Lisowski – courtesy Beatrix Färber, CELT Project, UCC

Chapter 2 – "Those days in Vienna ..."
Image 1 Emil Hirsch's ribbon factory, Göpfritz – courtesy Jenny Kenny and Desmond Hirsch
Image 2 Emil Hirsch and staff in Vienna – courtesy Jenny Kenny and Desmond Hirsch

Chapter 3 – The Jews of Komotau
Image 1 Reiniger & Co. factory, Komotau – courtesy Alice Hlavackova

Chapter 4 – The German Pogrom
Image 1 Passport Else Brandenburg – courtesy Denis Henderson
Image 2 Herbert Unger in Berlin 1938 – courtesy Klaus Unger

Chapter 6 – The State, the Helpers and the Refugees
Image 1 Newspaper article 'Irish Sanctuary for Refugees', *Irish Press*, 23 November 1938 – courtesy *Irish Press*
Image 2 Gerhard Rosenberg – courtesy Entschädigungsamt, Berlin
Image 3 Lists of refugee appeal (in different Irish newspapers, here from *Irish Times*) – courtesy *Irish Times*
Image 4 Newspaper article 'Dancing the Austrian Way', *Irish Independent*, 7 August 1939 – courtesy *Irish Independent*

Chapter 7 – Uncharted Terrain
Image 1 Refugees and helpers in Ardmore, *Irish Times*, 21 January 1939 – courtesy *Irish Times*
Image 2 Fritz Hirsch in Ardmore – courtesy Mary Casey
Image 3 Gerhard Hirschberg – courtesy Theffania Everett
Image 4 James Forrest drawn by Herbert Unger – courtesy Klaus Unger
Image 5 Herbert Unger feeding pigs in Kingsfort – courtesy Klaus Unger
Image 6 Kurt Staudt in Kingsfort – courtesy Klaus Unger
Image 7 Rugby 1934/1935 (Jürgen 'George' Holländer and Kurt Böhm) – courtesy Newtown School Waterford Archive
Image 8 Cricket 1940s (Jochen Hengstenberg & Kurt Schwarz) – courtesy Newtown School Waterford Archive
Image 9 Tipperary 1939 – courtesy Peter Kingshill and Sophia Kingshill
Image 10 Staff ribbon factory Longford – courtesy Jenny Kenny and Desmond Hirsch, names supplied by George Clare
Image 11 Kurt and Isabella Hainbach – courtesy Mark Hainbach
Image 12 Anselm Horwitz – courtesy Jo Sorochinsky

Chapter 8 – Continental Dubliners
Image 1   Ernst von Glasersfeld ploughing his farm – courtesy Ernst von Glasersfeld
Image 2   Newspaper article 'Sammy has a trainer', *Irish Times*, 26 January 1942, courtesy *Irish Times*
Image 3   Map of Rathmines – Google maps (in accordance with their "fair use" guidelines)
Image 4   Claire, Gabriele and Monica Hennig – courtesy Monica Schefold
Image 5   Claire and John Hennig – courtesy Monica Schefold

Chapter 9 – Academics in Exile
Image 1   Hans Motz – courtesy Anna Motz
Image 2   Hans Sachs – courtesy John Cooke
Image 3   Ludwig Hopf – courtesy Deutsches Museum, Munich
Image 4   Ernst Lewy – courtesy Peggy Moore-Lewy
Image 5   Schrödinger portrait by Seán Keating – courtesy School of Theoretical Physics, Dublin Institute of Advanced Studies
Image 6   Paul Ewald, Max Born, Walter Heitler, Erwin Schrödinger in Dublin – courtesy Dublin Institute of Advanced Studies

Chapter 10 – Transit Lives
Image 1   Stiegwardts in Argentina – courtesy Julia Crampton

Chapter 11 – Refugees Revisited
Image 1   Frank Drechsler – courtesy Mary Drechsler
Image 2   Peter Schwarz and his mother Berta – courtesy Peter Schwarz
Image 3   Einhart, Maria and Sigurd Kawerau (left to right) – courtesy Klaus Unger
Image 4   Ottilie Heitler – unknown artist, courtesy Denis Henderson
Image 5   Lisa Fischer – courtesy Margaret Wynne
Image 6   Dielenz return to Nuremberg – courtesy Anni Zakon, Amberg
Image 7   Graves Ernst and Marie Scheyer – photo by authors
Image 8   Wedding Robert Weil and Renate Scheyer – courtesy Stephen Weil

Tables

Chapter 8 – Continental Dubliners
Table 1   Exiles' residences in greater Rathmines
Table 2   Exiles and places of tertiary education in Dublin, 1939 – 1945

Chapter 10 – Transit Lives
Table 1   Transmigrants, 1933–1938, 1939 to 1945

Acknowledgements

This volume would not have been possible without the support and ongoing encouragement of many former refugees and their family members. We are immensely grateful for this. Sadly a considerable number of former refugees and helpers to whom we spoke are no longer alive to see the result. Hopefully this book contributes to their recognition and the recognition of the Irish people who helped them.

We would like to thank a number of institutions for their support, especially the Irish Research Council, the University of Limerick, the Royal Irish Academy, the German Academic Exchange Service (DAAD), the Austrian Academy of Science and also the Zentrum für Antisemitismusforschung (TU Berlin), the Research Centre for German and Austrian Exile Studies and the Leo Baeck Institute, London. Archivists in numerous libraries and archives around the world have been very supportive and helpful, as were many Irish local historians. The permission from the Department of Justice to allow us access to closed files was of great importance (and hospitality in the Irish Naturalisation and Immigration Service by John Brady and his colleagues was much appreciated).

We are grateful to the Weichmann Stiftung for their help with this publication and to our editor Bettina Neuhoff from de Gruyter. Thanks also to friends, colleagues and many former refugees and their family members, who read extracts, corrected and added to our drafts, especially Glenn Cooper, Sophia Kingshill, Joseph O'Connor, Hermann Rasche, Günther Rasche, Luke Drury, Eda Sagarra, Rose Little, Peter Schwarz, Margaret Wynne, Otto Glaser, Hans Reiss, Joachim Fischer, Herbert Karrach, Leo Colgan, Denis Henderson, Peter Melichar, Bernadette Whelan, Mary Rose Curtis, Alison McConnell, Ian Wallace and Stephen Weil. Thanks to Eoin Stephenson, David Lilburn, Pattie Punch, Brendan Bolger and Sinead Keogh for technical support and Maria Rieder for her excellent help with formatting issues. And last but not least we want to thank Annelie and Glenn for their ongoing support and patience.

Gisela Holfter, Horst Dickel, Limerick and Obergeis, July 2016

Introduction

Our narrative begins with Irish emigrants to Germany. In May 1922, William ("Boss") Sinclair, half-Jewish by descent, and his wife Frances ("Cissie", née Beckett) left Dublin and moved to Kassel with their children. As Samuel Beckett recalls, his uncle wished to flee from political entanglements in a critical moment of Irish nation-building.[1] He also hoped to build up an art dealer's trade in the North Hessian town. The Sinclairs remained in Kassel for more than ten years, living precariously on the proceeds of buying and selling modern paintings and the occasional music and English lessons they gave at their flat in Landgrafenstrasse 5, to the west of the town centre. They moved in artistic and Bohemian circles, sometimes accompanied by their nephew who had begun a controversial liaison with their daughter Peggy (born 9 March 1911) and who occasionally sought seclusion at a nearby country house on the Fulda River (Haus Kragenhof). Their German exile ended for a mixture of private, financial and political reasons, all converging in the cataclysmic year 1933: Peggy's death on 3 May 1933, a financial crisis in Boss Sinclair's art trade, the omnipresent anti-Semitism of public life.[2] On 1 November 1933, the family returned to Dublin. Their new Irish life was anything but easy. They came back with "not much more than pyjamas and toothbrushes" (Samuel Beckett).[3] Deirdre, Peggy's younger sister, who had been only two years old when the family went to Germany and was a teenager upon their return, remembers feeling isolated in Mountjoy School and being laughed at because of her unusual clothes and her unpractised English.[4]

Beckett, however, went back to Nazi Germany for another visit. From late September 1936 to 1 April 1937 he toured the country from north to south, attracted by its cultural riches and repelled by the degree of Nazification and anti-Semitism in German society. Traces of anti-Semitism, censorship and other forms

---

[1] "He had some political troubles in Dublin and had to leave." James and Elizabeth Knowlson (eds), *Remembering Beckett. Uncollected Interviews with Samuel Beckett and Memories of Those who Knew Him*. London: Bloomsbury 2006, p. 35. The Sinclair family was registered in Kassel on 27 May 1922. Courtesy Mrs Mennicke, Stadtarchiv Kassel.
[2] James and Elizabeth Knowlson (eds), *Remembering Beckett*, pp. 144–145. See also James Knowlson, Beckett in Kassel. Erste Begegnungen mit dem deutschen Expressionismus. In: Therese Fischer-Seidel and Marion Fries-Dieckmann (eds), *Der unbekannte Beckett: Samuel Beckett und die deutsche Kultur*. Frankfurt/M.: Suhrkamp 2005, pp. 65–66.
[3] Beckett to Thomas MacGreevy, 7 September 1933, quoted in Mark Nixon, *Samuel Beckett's German Diaries 1936–1937*. London: Continuum 2011, p. 6. For the departure date cf. Kassel residential register.
[4] Deirdre Hamilton interview with authors, 27 January 2008.

of intolerance however were also evident in Ireland itself, as Beckett found out in November 1937. He was called back to Dublin to defend the honour of Boss Sinclair, whose Jewishness had been impugned, at least in his own view.⁵ Sinclair died shortly afterwards, and the episode confirmed Beckett's long-standing resolve to exile himself from Ireland.⁶

Part of the reason for the Sinclairs' return from Germany to Ireland was the same that sent many Germans into exile abroad: the rise of Nazism. As foreigners, however, and moving in relatively closed social circles, neither the Sinclairs nor Beckett could have experienced the full destructiveness of Nazi policy. Beckett's determined statement made shortly after his arrival in the country, "I shan't be in Germany again after this trip,"⁷ sheds significant light on the more drastic realities that made native Germans try to leave their *Heimat* – some of them for Beckett's home country.

*We took in no refugees from Europe*⁸

There is still a surprising lack of awareness that any fugitives from the Nazis were admitted to Ireland. In 1945, when Seán O'Faoláin wrote about Ireland's five and a half years of wartime isolation, one of his reflections was on the absence of refugees. In general, the topic of 'Germans in Ireland' has been researched mainly in the context of Irish-German studies: in the 1920s, slightly more than 900 Germans lived in the Irish Free State, its largest non-English speaking minority.⁹ The restrictive policy of the government and issues of Irish anti-Semitism have formed the

---

5 On the Gogarty/Sinclair libel suit see Dermot Keogh, *Jews in Twentieth-Century Ireland: Refugees, Anti-Semitism and the Holocaust*. Cork: Cork University Press 1998, pp. 111–112.
6 Beckett's estrangement from Free State society can be seen from a letter to MacGreevy of 1932 in which he mockingly referred to himself as a "dirty low-church P[rotestant]", quoted in Sinead Mooney, Ghost Writer: Beckett's Irish Gothic. In: Seán Kennedy (ed.), *Beckett and Ireland*. Cambridge: Cambridge University Press 2010, p. 136. His early fiction *Dream of Fair to Middling Women* (1931–1932), the short story collection *More Pricks than Kicks* (1934) and *Murphy* (1938) also reflect their author's estrangement. In the story "A Wet Night" (contained in *More Pricks than Kicks*) his fictitious *alter ego* Belacqua uses the same words as Beckett in the MacGreevy letter. See also Declan Kiberd, *Inventing Ireland*. Cambridge: Harvard University Press 1995, p. 455.
7 Beckett to MacGreevy, 18 January 1937, quoted in Nixon, *Samuel Beckett's German Diaries*, p. 7.
8 Seán O'Faoláin, The Price of Peace. In: *The Bell*. Vol. 10, no. 4 (July 1945), pp. 281–290, 288.
9 Central Statistical Office of Ireland (CSO), Census 1926. Birthplaces. Table 1A. Most were employed by Irish affiliates of German firms, notably by Siemens-Schuckert, which had been contracted to build a hydroelectric power station in Ardnacrusha, Co. Clare. The so-called 'Shannon Scheme' was one of the largest building projects of its kind in the world at this time. Ten years later, in 1936, the number of German residents had fallen to 529 (a handful

subject of a number of articles since the late 1990s,[10] but the question of how Ireland[11] dealt with those victims of Nazi rule who escaped to its shores has been obscured by other concerns, such as the degree to which Ireland's neutrality benefited German interests and the extent of political and military German-Irish interaction.[12] The mistaken belief that hardly any refugees were allowed to enter the State has also played a part.

In 2004, the Centre for Irish-German Studies in Limerick organised the first conference to focus on 'German-speaking Exiles in Ireland 1933–1945', exploring the issue of refugees from Germany, Austria and Czechoslovakia, as well as Irish policy and history of that time. The conference brought together academics active in exile research, Irish history and Irish-German Studies, such as Wolfgang Muchitsch, Wolfgang Benz and Dermot Keogh, as well as former refugees and their family members. The subsequent 2006 publication[13] was intended as a "first step", introducing the experiences of the German-speaking exiles in Ireland, and the structures, policies and groups that both helped and hindered their migration to Ireland. The present volume greatly expands upon that initial research.

We are indebted to the work of others. Dermot Keogh's study *Jews in Twentieth-Century Ireland* has been a key resource.[14] A valuable reference point, allowing us to contrast the immigration experiences of the two largest groups who came to Ireland in the last century, was Cormac O'Grada's monograph on Jewish Ireland

---

of whom were refugees), in comparison with 1757 born in India, 483 born in the USSR/Russia and 351 born in France. Central Statistical Office of Ireland (CSO), Census 1936. Volume 3 - Religion and Birthplaces. Table 16.
10 For example, Katrina Goldstone, 'Benevolent Helpfulness'? Ireland and the International Reaction to Jewish Refugees, 1933–9. In: Michael Kennedy and Joseph M. Skelly (eds), *Irish Foreign Policy 1919–1966*. Dublin: Four Courts Press 2000, pp. 116–136 and Bryan Fanning, *Racism and Social Change in the Republic of Ireland*. Manchester: Manchester University Press 2002.
11 Firstly as the Irish Free State (Saorstát Éireann) and then Ireland (Éire) since 1937 – in this volume the name Ireland is used throughout.
12 See for example Mervyn O'Driscoll, Ireland, Germany and the Nazis. Politics and Diplomacy, 1919–1939. Dublin: Four Courts Press 2004; Mark Hull, *Irish Secrets. German Espionage in Wartime Ireland 1939–1945*. Dublin: Irish Academic Press 2004; David O'Donoghue, *The Devil's Deal. The IRA, Nazi Germany and the Double Life of Jim O'Donovan*. Dublin: New Island 2010 and Mark Hull, Perdition's Guests: Irish in Germany during World War II. In: Claire O'Reilly and Veronica O'Regan (eds), *Ireland and the Irish in Germany: Reception and Perception*. Baden-Baden: Nomos 2014, pp. 45–62.
13 See Gisela Holfter (ed.), *German-speaking Exiles in Ireland 1933–1945*. German Monitor no. 63, Amsterdam, New York: Rodopi 2006.
14 Dermot Keogh, *Jews in Twentieth-Century Ireland: Refugees, Anti-Semitism and the Holocaust*. Cork: Cork University Press 1998.

in the 'Age of Joyce',[15] which focuses on Jewish immigration before and during the 1920s, partly building on literature from members of Jewish immigrant families to Ireland.[16] Diarmaid Ferriter's reassessment of Éamon de Valera presented previously little-known archival sources from that time.[17] Ireland's situation during World War II (or 'the Emergency', as it was called) has been the focus of a number of interesting recent studies, notably those of Clair Wills[18] and Bryce Evans.[19] Specifically concentrating on German-speaking refugees and their reception, Siobhán O'Connor's unpublished 2009 PhD thesis deals chiefly with public and government reactions in Ireland to the applications of German-speaking asylum seekers.[20] Furthermore, a number of personal recollections and historical analyses were presented to a second conference held at the University of Limerick and published in late 2014.[21]

The theme of exile during the war years has been a source of fascination, and not only for historians and scholars. There are numerous literary and biographical

---

[15] Cormac O'Grada, *Jewish Ireland in the Age of Joyce: A Socioeconomic History*. Princeton, Oxford: Princeton University Press 2006.
[16] Among them were Nick Harris, *Dublin's Little Jerusalem*. Dublin: A. & A. Farmar 2002; Stanley Price, *Somewhere to Hang My Hat. An Irish-Jewish Journey*. Dublin: New Island Books 2002; Ray Rivlin, *Shalom Ireland. A Social History of Jews in Modern Ireland*. Dublin: Gill and Macmillan 2003. David Marcus, author of *Who Ever Heard of an Irish Jew? and Other Stories*. London: Bantam 1988, also penned more autobiographical writings such as *Oughtobiography: Leaves from the Diary of a Hyphenated Jew*. Dublin: Gill & Macmillan 2001 and *Buried Memories*. Cork: Mercier Press 2004. Also of interest is Valerie Lapin Ganley's film about the Jewish community, *Shalom Ireland*, Share Productions 2003.
[17] Diarmaid Ferriter, *Judging Dev. A Reassessment of the Life and Legacy of Éamon de Valera*. Dublin: Royal Irish Academy 2007.
[18] Clair Wills, *That Neutral Island*. London: Faber & Faber 2007.
[19] Bryce Evans, *Ireland During the Second World War – Farewell to Plato's Cave*. Manchester/New York: Manchester University Press 2014.
[20] Siobhán O'Connor, Irish Government Policy and Public Perception toward German-speaking Refugees in Ireland, 1933–1945, University of Limerick: Unpublished Ph.D. thesis 2009.
[21] Gisela Holfter (ed.), *The Irish Context of Kristallnacht. Refugees and Helpers*. Irish-German Studies 8, Trier: Wissenschaftlicher Verlag 2014. A number of further explorations of the lives of individual refugees who came to Ireland have been published by Holfter, such as Akademiker im irischen Exil: Professor Ernst Lewy. In: *German Life and Letters*. Vol. 61, no. 3 (July 2008), pp. 361–385; Ein Fallbeispiel zur Rückkehrproblematik aus dem Exil – Ernst Lewy (1881–1966). In: A. Goodbody et al. (eds): *Dislocation and Reorientation*. Amsterdam/New York: Rodopi 2009, pp. 139–151; Ludwig Hopf. In: Ian Wallace (ed.), *Voices from Exile. Essays in Memory of Hamish Ritchie*. Amsterdamer Beiträge zur Germanistik, Amsterdam/New York: Rodopi 2015, pp. 113–140, and most recently by both authors: Horst Dickel and Gisela Holfter, Everyday Life of German-speaking Refugees in Wartime Ireland. In: *The Yearbook of the Research Centre for German and Austrian Studies*. Vol. 14 (2015), pp. 107–130.

(as well as autobiographical) publications in German and English dealing with the topic of refugees and their experiences.[22] Also, the Irish situation has been explored in fiction,[23] together with portrayals in other media, such as Louis Lentin's 1997 documentary *No More Blooms*, which followed Jewish entrepreneurs in the West of Ireland, and Mary Rose Doorly's short film *Blind Eye*, based on her interviews with Sabina Wizniak, with a script by Irish writer Hugo Hamilton.[24]

The present volume is the first attempt to give a comprehensive picture of German-speaking refugees in Ireland from 1933 to 1945 and answer the question to what extent Ireland proved to be a sanctuary for them.[25] Our study seeks not only to close a gap in the research on countries that received refugees from the Third Reich, but to break new ground by narrating the two sides of the exile issue on the basis of hitherto unexplored archival and other material. We are concerned with Irish governmental policies and many different stakeholders – from politicians to Gardaí, as well as the many people and organisations involved in helping the refugees. Our main concern however is with the personal experiences and perspectives of the immigrants. The text aims to map the histories of all refugees who came to Ireland, beginning with their origins in Germany, Austria and Czechoslovakia, and following their paths into exile and their lives in war-time Ireland and afterwards. In principle, this study includes everyone who was trying to escape the Nazis and the war they set in motion on the Continent. It speaks of persons of varying religion, race, social status and political outlook, coming for shorter

---

22 Publications by Anna Funder (*All that I Am*, 2011), Evelyn Juers (*House of Exile*, 2011) and Vikram Seth (*Two Lives*, 2005) demonstrate the ongoing interest in English-speaking countries. Similarly in German literature, the topic continues to attract writers and readers alike, whether following the footsteps of refugee writers, as in, for example, Michael Lentz's *Pazifik Exil* (2007) and Klaus Modick's *Sunset* (2011) or tracing family members, as in Katja Petrowskaja's *Vielleicht Esther* (2014). Renate Ahrens introduces an Irish-German dimension in *Das gerettete Kind* (2016).
23 Such as Neil Belton's *A Game with Sharpened Knives* (2005), concentrating on Erwin Schrödinger in Ireland and the atmosphere of uncertainty where refugees and suspected spies mingled (a theme also explored by Rose Doyle in *Gambling with Darkness*, 2003). Marilyn Taylor focused on child refugees brought to Millisle Farm in Northern Ireland in *Faraway Home* (1999, chosen as 1999/2000 Children's Books Ireland/Bisto Book of the Year), and wrote in 2008 about a refugee girl in Dublin (*17 Martin Street*). Ruth Gilligan explores the theme of Jewish immigration to Ireland (*Nine Folds Make a Paper Swan*, 2016).
24 The script was published by Hugo Hamilton, Blind Eye – Film Script. In: Gisela Holfter (ed.), *The Irish Context of Kristallnacht. Refugees and Helpers*. Irish-German Studies 8, Trier: Wissenschaftlicher Verlag 2014, pp. 121–132.
25 A study on refugees to Ireland after 1945 such as Carl von Metzradt, Agnes Bernelle, Hermann Brück, Gerhard Bersu, Johannes Matthäus Koelz, Tomi Reichental and many others is still outstanding.

or longer periods, some as visitors. There were entrants with and without legal permission, there were those who were given privileged access to their country of exile and others who were admitted only as 'ordinary refugees' or, indeed, were not allowed to stay. There were people who were directly threatened by measures of the Nazi rulers and others who had reasons to suspect that they would potentially be in danger under the new political conditions. Such an inclusive study was feasible only in the case of a country small and distant enough to take no more than a limited number of exiles, but nevertheless demanded a large amount of empirical research. We were, however, unable to fill all the gaps or fully resolve all our questions relating to the passage of migrants or their status in Ireland; indeed it is highly likely that especially the group of visitors has not been recorded completely. We have concentrated on collecting data along a set of socio-biographical determinants such as family background, education, social and economic positions, religious affiliations, generational divisions, etc., leaving scope for general assessments and turning individual stories into 'collective biographies' without being too reductive.[26] From this follows another aspect of our work. In the early days of exile studies, the focus was largely on well known writers and academics, their background in the old country and their impact in the new one. It was only later that research was undertaken into the experiences of 'ordinary refugees' – in the words of the German historian Wolfgang Benz "das Exil der kleinen Leute" (the exile of the little people), a term that comprises many nuances and distinctions.[27] Our inclusive approach tries to cover all social groups.

In Part I we analyse the background of exiles and the circumstances of their flight to Ireland. The subdivisions reflect the territorial expansion of Hitler's *Reich* and the ways it impinged on individuals' lives prior to their passage to Ireland. Chapter 1 deals with those refugees who left the borders of the *Reich* between 1933 and October 1938. At that time Hitler's policies had already compelled increasing numbers of persecuted people in Austria and the Czechoslovakian Republic to flee to Ireland (chapters 2 and 3). The November Pogrom in 1938 and its aftermath led to further emigration which also reached Ireland (chapter 4). 1938 was also a critical year for those refugees who had earlier sought safety elsewhere in Europe. They found themselves in renewed danger as the Nazi state extended its influence in the course of 1938. A special case was Fascist Italy which adopted some of

---

[26] On the term 'collective biography', see Alfons Söllner, 'Exilforschung' as Mirror of the Changing Political Culture in Post-War Germany. In: David Kettler and Zvi Ben-Dor (eds), *The Limits of Exile*. Berlin/Madison: Galda 2010, pp. 65–77, 72.
[27] See also Andrea Hammel and Anthony Grenville, Introduction. In: *Yearbook of the Research Centre for German and Austrian Exile Studies*. Vol. 16 (2015), pp. xi-xv.

Hitler's anti-Jewish policy in late summer of that year, leading to some refugees there moving on to Ireland (chapter 5).

Part II focuses on the question of how these refugees tried to find favour from the Irish government and live in a country that had a long history of emigration and from where people had to leave for religious, economic, cultural and political reasons. Having at long last gained independence, the country itself displayed signs (albeit in comparatively mild form) of intolerance. How many applicants for asylum actually managed to come to Ireland and how they arranged their lives in exile depended on decisions formulated within the Irish political establishment, and the degree of benevolence and practical help offered within Irish civil society (chapter 6). A large number of exiles (workers, industrialists, teachers, students and religious persons) came to live in rural Ireland, in villages and towns, which must have seemed very unfamiliar to people who had grown up mostly in urban settings on the Continent (chapter 7). The majority of German-speaking refugees to Ireland came from two cities and their hinterlands – Berlin and Vienna – and many among them preferred (or were made) to settle in Dublin, where adolescents could attend secondary school, college or university, where adults could find jobs and others could be taken care of by aid societies (chapter 8). Chapter 9 examines specifically the small group of academic exiles whom the Irish government and university boards had brought to Ireland. It is not only because of their prominence and achievements - circumstances which also explain why in their case there is distinctly more empirical material available than in the case of 'normal refugees' - but also because of the special features of an academic life in exile that they are treated more individually and extensively. Even before their emigration, the crossing of national boundaries had formed a common condition of their professional lives. The hope for a second and more rewarding exile outside Ireland had accompanied many refugees from the beginning. Some used the country only as a stepping stone towards other destinations, and left before or during the war years (chapter 10).

Part III views the Irish exile experience from a post-war perspective, taking into account the fact that assessments are bound to change over the course of a full life-span. These biographical vignettes, focusing on the exiles' social and economic experiences after the war, provide an insight into the influence the rupture of their former lives and the ensuing Irish exile had on the future lives of these former refugees and explore the mark they left on Irish society (chapter 11).

The experiences of refugees often included the uncertainty of their legal status and a resulting reluctance to enter into frequent contacts with state authorities. The records of interactions between individuals and the state, retained in national archives such as the Bundesarchiv in Berlin (BA), the National Archives of Ireland (NAI), the Military Archives of Ireland (MAI) in Dublin, and the Archiv der Republik (AdR) in Vienna, provide the main source material for this study.

While shedding light on inter-departmental decisions, the files also record these individuals' status as victims of expulsion, applicants for help, and targets of observation, to name only the three most important areas of interaction. The data flow was not unimpeded. In Germany much of the material, including Gestapo and other Nazi Party files, has been lost or destroyed due to the events of war. In Ireland, we were given access to hitherto closed files of the Department of Justice (DJ), and the files of the Secret Service G2, stored in the Military Archives (MAI). Sifting through the mass of correspondence between departments – the Department of Justice (DJ), the Department of External Affairs (DFA), the Department of Industry and Commerce (DI&C), the Department of Taoiseach (DT) – provided key insights into the mechanisms of Irish refugee policy. The many observational reports of G2 agents provide an understanding of the refugees' ways and whereabouts in wartime Ireland. The single most regrettable gap in the records is that left by the lost files of the Irish Co-ordinating Committee for Refugees (ICCR), although it was possible partly to fill this gap by reference to correspondence between the committee and the departments. A trove of relevant documents is to be found in the files of restitution and compensation suits in post-war West Germany and Austria. To prove their claims, applicants had to provide affidavits and autobiographical texts revealing their plight in Nazi Germany (and sometimes in Ireland). Most of these files are held in the Austrian Archiv der Republik, in the archives of the German *Länder* and in those of the regional *Regierungspräsidien*.

Our hope that we might also be able to document the contribution of the religious aid committees was partly disappointed; evidence on an individual level could only be unearthed in the Archiv der Evangelischen Kirche von Österreich (AEKÖ), Vienna, the Church of Ireland's Representative Body Church Library (RCBL), Dublin, and the Quaker archives in Dublin (Society of Friends House Dublin, SFHD) and London (Society of Friends House London, SFHL). As to Jewish archives, we were granted full access to the personal files of the Emigration Department of the *Israelitische Kultusgemeinde* (IKG), Vienna,[28] but nothing comparable could be found either in Dublin or Berlin.[29] Some insights into the role of Irish-Jewish institutions could be gleaned from the records of the Anglo-Jewish Community deposited in the London Metropolitan Archives. In general, the Catholic archives in Dublin and Vienna proved barren as far as documentation on aid committees was concerned. Material on the main Catholic emigration

---

28 The originals are held by the Central Archives for the History of the Jewish People, Jerusalem.
29 The German central archives were lost during the war. In Ireland there is no central depository for documents on the Irish-Jewish community, and very few documents covering the relevant time are available in the Irish-Jewish Museum in Dublin.

body, the St Raphaelsverein, has been largely destroyed, only fragments relating to the role of the Hilfswerk to the Berlin Ordinariate have being preserved in the Diocesan Archives of Berlin (DAB). The presence of a number of refugees at Irish schools and universities has left traces in the relevant archives, especially those of Newtown School in Waterford, attended by a dozen refugee children. The comprehensive archives of Trinity College Dublin (TCD Manuscripts & Archives Research Library) and University College Dublin (UCDA) store important documents. Of special value were the Hubert Butler Papers in Trinity and in Maidenhall. Further relevant material was available in the archives of the Royal Irish Academy (RIA), of the Dublin Institute of Advanced Studies (DIAS), and particularly in the files of the Society for the Protection of Science and Learning in Oxford (SPSL). The National Archives at College Park, Maryland, provided material on the United States view of the Irish situation, while other university archives in the US were helpful for individual cases. The holdings of papers of Arnold Sommerfeld in the Deutsches Museum in Munich and the Albert Einstein Archive in Jerusalem were also valuable.

We frequently left the confines of library and archive rooms searching for physical and personal traces of refugees and their environments. As untrained 'promenadologists' we took to many streets, boulevards and lanes in Berlin, Vienna and Dublin, in Castlebar, Longford, and such distant places as Chomutov in the Czech Republic, trying to visualise the space and atmosphere these people had at least temporarily inhabited. We were often able to communicate with their relatives, or people who knew them or had at least heard of them, often on the recommendation of local archivists or members of local historical societies in Ireland who were of tremendous help. As to authenticity and impact on our research, no testimony ranks with the memories of the refugees themselves or their closest living relatives. A few have chosen to make their reminiscences public. George Clare's acclaimed *Last Waltz in Vienna: the Destruction of a Family 1842–1942* (1982) was a pioneer text, and others followed.[30] Some wrote private

---

30 George Clare, *Last Waltz in Vienna: the Destruction of a Family 1842–1942*. London: MacMillan 1982. Other memoirs were collected in Mary Rose Doorly, *Hidden Memories. The Personal Recollections of Survivors and Witnesses to the Holocaust living in Ireland*. Dublin: Blackwater Press 1994 (Doris Segal and Sabina Shorts). In: *Ardmore Journal* 1989 (Erwin Strunz and Fritz Hirsch) and in the Holocaust memorial series *Visual History Archive* of the USC Shoah Foundation (Henry Kent=Heinz Krotoschin and John Menkes). The most recent memoirs are in Gisela Holfter (ed.), *The Irish Context of Kristallnacht. Refugees and Helpers*. Irish-German Studies, no. 8. Trier: Wissenschaftlicher Verlag 2014 (Stephen Weil, Klaus Unger, Hans Reiss, Herbert Karrach, Sophia Kingshill, Paul Dubsky, Denis Henderson). See also John Hennig, *Die bleibende Statt*. Bremen: privately published 1987. Annelies Becker, *Tread Softly. Scenes from my Life*. May 1999

memoirs, wishing to make a record for themselves and bear witness to the experience of their families.[31]

Meeting former refugees or their relatives and asking them to share their memories and help us understand critical parts of their lives was a highly rewarding undertaking. Nearly all were ready to respond to our questions and were greatly encouraging. We are most grateful for their help and trust, and hope that this volume contributes to adding their voices and experiences to both exile studies worldwide and the narrative of Irish history.

---

http://homepage.eircom.net/~interfriendpublisher/tread.html [last accessed 2 February 2015]. Ernst von Glasersfeld, *Unverbindliche Erinnerungen. Skizzen aus einem fernen Leben*. Vienna: Folio Verlag 2008 (English: *Partial Memories: Sketches from an Improbable Life*. Exeter: Imprint Academic 2009). Peter Kingshill, *Footnote – A Memoir*. London: privately published, 2007; Konrad Kingshill, *On the Precipice of Prejudice and Persecution*. Bloomington: Authors House 2008. Hans Kohlseisen, *Und ich reise immer noch – Die Geschichte des Hans Kohlseisen zwischen Gmünd, Stadlau und Irland*. Ed. Margarete Affenzeller and Gabriele Anderl. Vienna: Mandelbaum 2015; Hans Reiss, *Erinnerungen aus 85 Jahren*. Göttingen: Petrarca Verlag 2009.

31 For example Fred Hainbach, *1920–1950. A Memoir*. 2002; Walter Heitler, *Lebenserinnerungen*; Esther Moore and George Moore-Lewy, *A Sister and Brother Remember – Wechterswinkel to Dublin and a Little Beyond*; Joy Roger Hammerschlag, *Kurt Roger 1895–1966*. 1997; Erwin Strunz, *My Connection with the Kagran Group 1938*. Butler Papers, Maidenhall, Kilkenny; Erwin Strunz, *Memoir*. June 1989; Peter Schwarz, *An anecdotal biographical note*. March 1996; Robert Weil [Notes, 1940].

Part I **Passages to Ireland**

Chapter 1
The Distant Option – German Refugees to Ireland, 1933–1938

When the terror began in 1933 with a large-scale boycott movement against Jewish shop owners, persecution of political opponents and increasing ostracism of Jews and non-Aryans,[1] only a minority among the victims were prescient enough to assess their future in Germany realistically. Many hoped against all the evidence for an early end to the regime, and did not develop concrete emigration plans as long as they could eke out an existence, however precarious. The first years seemed to give time for adjustments, delays, hopes (however deferred or frustrated) and possibly better emigration options. Moreover, Jews in the larger area of Germany were more widely scattered than in Austria, for example, which allowed for greater possibilities of domestic migration, mainly to the bigger cities. It has been estimated that of the roughly half-million Jews in Germany in 1933, only 143,000 had by June 1938 left the borders of the Old *Reich*.[2] It was only after the November Pogrom in 1938 that the past six years appeared to many who had stayed as lost time.

The discriminatory rules that drove them from their homeland hit them differently depending on location, age, and economic and social position. All these factors influenced their flight options and the ways they proposed to live in exile.

For the vast majority who attempted to flee the Nazi state in this earlier period (as, indeed, from 1938), Ireland was not a preferred option. It was not, indeed, generally considered as a possibility – even by those who eventually came there. From an average German or Austrian perspective, Ireland was very much *terra incognita*: it hardly featured in information provided for would-be emigrants.[3] For German speakers, Ireland had been in the spotlight only between 1830 and 1850,

---

[1] In this volume the use of Nazi expressions such as "Aryan", "non-Aryan" and "Aryanisation" has been unavoidable due to the subject matter and they appear in the conventional usage of their time.
[2] These figures comprise only confessing Jews, and are not based on official statistics. The full and exact number of Nazi-defined Jews is still unknown. The text on which all later estimates rely is Werner Rosenstock, Exodus 1933–1939. A Survey of Jewish Emigration from Germany. In: *Leo Baeck Institute Yearbook* 1956, pp. 373–390.
[3] See Ernst G. Löwenthal (ed.), *Philo-Atlas – Handbuch für die jüdische Auswanderung*. Berlin: Jüdischer Buchverlag 1938 (reprint version, Philo Verlagsgesellschaft: Bodenheim near Mainz 1998) and Gisela Holfter, German-speaking Exiles 1933–1945 in Ireland, an Introduction and Overview. In: Gisela Holfter (ed.), *German-speaking Exiles in Ireland 1933–1945*. Amsterdam/New York: Rodopi 2006, pp. 1–19, 5 and 15.

when romanticism and a Europe-wide fascination with Daniel O'Connell created considerable literary and political interest in and awareness of Ireland.[4] Irish-German links in the 20th century, such as the building of the hydroelectric power station in Ardnacrusha, Co. Clare by Siemens-Schuckert, a project on which several hundred German engineers and labourers worked in Ireland from 1925 to 1929, had far more of an impact in Ireland than in Germany.[5] German and Austrian perceptions of Ireland in the 1930s were not encouraging. It was seen as a "poor and unstable country on the periphery of Europe",[6] and people's reactions, when told that Ireland was being considered as a destination, tended to be incredulous: "Are you crazy? [...] People there have in their right coat pocket the liquor bottle, rosary beads in the left and in the hip pocket the revolver."[7]

For some, however, there were personal connections. Tenuous though they might have been, these connections were significant for many of the émigrés who came to Ireland, whether for longer or shorter periods.

Some early refugees came to Ireland as visitors, often relying on relatives, or other persons or institutions, to support them during their limited stay. Generally the Irish state allowed their entry as long as they could plausibly demonstrate that they came 'only' as visitors and would leave the country after the permitted time (although passport controls were not always enforced strictly in Ireland).[8] Among such visitors were, for example, two Jewish sisters, Emmi and Chana Bulka, from Offenbach/Main, and Ruth Eichmann, daughter of a Jewish shop-owner in Remscheid/Rhineland.[9] Jewish brothers Leo and Kurt Michel

---

[4] See Gisela Holfter, *Erlebnis Irland*. Trier: WVT 1996, pp. 44–132, and James M. Brophy, Rezeption Daniel O'Connells und der irischen Emanzipationsbewegung im vormärzlichen Deutschland. In: *Marx-Engels Jahrbuch 2011*. Berlin: Akademie 2012, pp. 74–93.
[5] See also Joachim Fischer, *Das Deutschlandbild der Iren 1890–1939: Geschichte, Form, Funktion*. Heidelberg: Winter 2000.
[6] Otto Glaser, Personal, Cultural and Academic Links. In: Paul Leifer and Eda Sagarra (eds), *Austrian-Irish Links through the Centuries*. Vienna: Diplomatic Academy of Vienna 2002, pp. 101–142, 116.
[7] John Hennig, *Die bleibende Statt*. Bremen: privately published 1987, p. 117. Translated by authors.
[8] Jewish art historian Erica Tietze-Conrat who came to Ireland in July 1937 noted in her recently published diary that suitcases were checked – passports not. See Erica Tietze-Conrat, *Tagebücher (1937–1938)*. Edited by Alexandra Caruso, Vienna/Cologne/Weimar: Böhlau 2015, p. 115. She and her husband Hans Tietze met George Furlong, the director of the National Gallery of Ireland (who helped Otto Pächt to escape Austria, see chapter 9) and Adolf Mahr, director of the National Museum, who was in charge of Dublin's *NSDAP-Ortsgruppe* at the time, and told them that for him National Socialism had nothing to do with anti-Semitism. The meeting, after dinner at Mahr's house, was uncomfortable for the Tietzes, being held under a photograph of Hitler. Ibid., pp. 115–117.
[9] The Bulkas wished to visit their relatives Abraham and Gitla Bayer in 1934 and 1937 respectively. See NAI, DFA 2/712, DJ to DEA, 15 September 1934; DJ 69/41. Ruth Eichmann had her visitor's

came in January 1934, also from the Rhineland. They had lost their employment due to "present conditions in Cologne" as their aunt Rosa de Lancy, with whom they stayed, explained.[10] While she was living in comfortable circumstances as a medical practitioner in Dublin and tried hard to convince the Department of Justice to extend the initial two month visa to at least twelve months,[11] it was in vain – the Department held it against the two young men that they had indicated upon landing that they would return to their employment after two months. They had to return to Cologne in mid-March 1934.

Among the visitors there were some prominent persons. The earliest case within this category was Paul Kirchhoff, a distinguished ethnologist and a political radical belonging to the Trotskyist camp of opponents to the established Communist parties in the Soviet Union and Germany. Already in exile in the USA before Hitler's party took power, he and his wife Johanna were sent on a scholarship from the Rockefeller Foundation to inspect the results of Irish land reform in January 1933. They stayed in Ireland for more than a year, moving in leftist political circles – Peadar O'Donnell and Hanna Sheehy-Skeffington, for example, were among their acquaintances –watched suspiciously by the Irish police who were aware of Paul's political background. In 1934 they left for Paris.[12]

Another early visitor was Annette Kolb, one of the best known German writers of the 1920s.[13] Born into an artistic and liberal German-French family,[14] she had already spent World War I as an exile in Switzerland. She knew Ireland from many visits (it featured, briefly but importantly, in her first novel *Exemplar*, published

---

permit repeatedly renewed over a period from 1933 to 1936, and stayed with her well-established cousin Maurice Wise at 177 Harold's Cross Road. See DJ 2014/85/2329.
10 DJ 69/24, Garda report to DJ, 25 January 1934.
11 She even got the support of an official from the Department of Agriculture who wrote to his colleagues in Justice to support her application and stressed that her husband had saved his wife's life twice. See ibid., R.J. Purcell to Duff, 19 February 1934.
12 In 1935, the Kirchhoffs went to the USA and finally to Mexico, where they were honoured with Mexican citizenship in 1941. Kirchhoff's reputation as an ethnologist rests on his extensive pioneering work on the indigenous people of America. See http://atlantisforschung.de/index.php?title=Paul_Kirchhof; http://www.iai.spk-berlin.de/fileadmin/dokumentenbibliothek/Indiana/Indiana_2/IND_02_Kirchhoff.pdf [last accessed 12 January 2016]. The Kirchhoffs' Irish year is documented in NAI, DJ 2014/85/1983.
13 Her work was praised by Hermann Hesse, Joseph Roth and Rainer Maria Rilke. She was also well acquainted with Thomas Mann and especially his children Klaus and Erika Mann. She was not the only visiting writer: Austrian writer Joe Lederer also came to Ireland for short periods during her exile in Great Britain, though very little is known about her visits. Thanks to Charmian Brinson for the information.
14 Her father, allegedly an illegitimate son of the royal Wittelsbach family, was Munich's garden architect; her mother was French pianist Sophie Kolb-Danvin.

in 1913, for which she received the prestigious Fontane prize), as in 1908 her older sister Germaine had married William Stockley, professor of English at University College Cork. Kolb's pacifist background meant that she had to go into exile again after Hitler came to power. She went first to Switzerland, then to Luxembourg and Paris, and in late May 1933 she came to Ireland. What she especially hoped to find was peace to write,[15] her project at that time being a novel with strong autobiographical features and critical references to contemporary events in Germany.[16] Kolb was an astute observer of the social and political situation.[17] Her stay in Ireland lasted until the end of August, interrupted only by a trip to visit friends in England in July. She returned to Ireland for some weeks in December 1933. That she lived mainly in Paris rather than in Ireland for the next few years was probably due to financial considerations.[18] She visited Ireland several times before the outbreak of the war, often staying for several weeks. A talented musician, she played the piano more than once on Irish radio. In that context, she is named in Irish newspapers, though her status as a refugee is never explicitly mentioned.[19] Kolb's trips to Ireland in 1933 and later met with no opposition from the Irish

---

15 On 3 May 1933, she wrote to her friend René Schickele that she intended to stay with Germaine in Ireland as long as possible, if she could work there. Kolb to Schickele on 3 May 1933. In: Annette Kolb, René Schickele, *Briefe im Exil 1933–1940*. Edited by Hans Bender, Mainz: v. Hase & Koehler 1987, p. 56.

16 Her novel *Die Schaukel* ('The Swing') about a liberal Catholic German-French family in Munich, clearly modelled on her own family, also included the character of a Jewish friend, generous, supportive and sensitive, and contained a footnote stating that at least a few Christians in Germany were still aware of their debt to Jews and their contributions to the arts – not a common statement for a book published in Germany in 1934.

17 She assessed de Valera's standing and carefully registered the influence of the Catholic Church, noting that the situation in the country seemed once more to be approaching civil war. See especially her letter to Schickele of 18 August 1933. Kolb, Schickele, *Briefe im Exil*, p. 71.

18 Ireland seemed to her "the most expensive country in the world" (Kolb, Schickele, *Briefe im Exil*, p. 65), and she did not want to pose an extra burden on her sister in the cramped and somewhat impoverished living conditions in Cork. Plans to support herself through music did not come to fruition. On 19 December 1933, she was given the opportunity to play for Irish radio, but a hoped-for engagement on British radio did not materialise (she believed the rejection was due to her Irish address). Kolb to Schickele, 20 December 1933. Kolb, Schickele, *Briefe im Exil*, p. 100.

19 See, for example, *Irish Press*, 7 and 25 August 1937; *Nenagh Guardian*, 24 September 1938. She also returned to Ireland in 1939, see Charlotte Marlo Werner, *Annette Kolb*. Königstein: Helmer 2000, p. 222. In 1941, she managed to escape to New York. As soon as travel was possible again after the war, she returned to Ireland, and after some weeks she went on to Switzerland and Paris – as she had done in 1933. See Armin Strohmeyr, *Annette Kolb – Dichterin zwischen den Völkern*. Munich: dtv 2002, pp. 237–238. Annette Kolb returned to Munich in 1961 and died there in 1967, two months before her 98th birthday.

state – in fact, we found no references to her in any files in the National Archives or the Military Archives.[20]

An Austrian who came to Ireland several times for visits of a few weeks, in 1934, 1936 and again in 1938, should also briefly be mentioned here – Ludwig Wittgenstein. As George Hetherington rightly argues, however, despite his name, his three Jewish grandparents, and the dates he visited, Wittgenstein cannot be called a refugee, having already moved to England in the late 1920s.[21]

Max Warburg[22] came to Ireland in spring 1937, apparently to investigate possible places to emigrate for his brother-in-law, a doctor in Hamburg,[23] rather than for himself, as he had already settled in the Netherlands. In a letter from London, Warburg rated the prospects of emigration to Ireland poorly, as the state was pursuing a policy of autarky and unemployment was high. He stressed that on a personal level the Irish were wonderful warm people, more willing than the English to welcome immigrants,[24] and that the country was well worth visiting: "Ireland and the Irish are indescribably enchanting, despite the dirt and all deficiencies."[25] His overall impression, however, was "Irland: Entzückend, aber ziemlich aussichtslos!" (Ireland: delightful, but pretty hopeless!) He gave an interesting description of the transfer qualifications necessary to practice medicine – he understood that a one-year diploma would be sufficient, rather than an entire degree having to be repeated. He mentioned that he had heard of another German doctor currently in the process of finishing the diploma in Ireland, and that he hoped to find out

---

20 It should be noted, however, that according to Georg von Dehn-Schmidt, the first German envoy to Ireland, who invited Annette Kolb for lunch in June 1933, her movements in Ireland were closely observed. Kolb to Schickele, 10 June 1933, Kolb, Schickele, *Briefe im Exil*, p. 64.
21 See George Hetherington, Wittgenstein in Ireland: An Account of His Various Visits from 1934 to 1949. In: *Irish University Review*. Vol. 17, no. 2 (Autumn 1987), pp. 169–186, 170.
22 Max Adolph Warburg (1902–1974), son of renowned art historian Aby Warburg, whose famous library, the 'Kulturwissenschaftliche Bibliothek Warburg', was brought in 1933 from Hamburg to London, where the Warburg Institute became part of the University of London in 1944. Max Warburg had emigrated to the Netherlands in 1934 and survived there in hiding during the war. Afterwards he and his wife went to live in England.
23 This was probably Peter Paul Braden, husband of his sister Marietta. Thanks to Dr Claudia Wedepohl, archivist at the Warburg Institute, London.
24 See Max Adolph Warburg, Irland: Entzückend aber ziemlich aussichtslos. In: Charlotte Ueckert-Hilbert (ed.), *Fremd in der eigenen Stadt: Erinnerungen jüdischer Emigranten aus Hamburg*. Hamburg: Junius 1989, pp. 84–87, 84.
25 Ibid, p. 85. Translation by authors. Warburg was clearly much taken by Ireland and adds that a joint trip there should be considered. He concluded, however, that during his visit he achieved nothing with regard to Ireland – but that he did get good information on potentially promising positions in New Zealand.

more about any requirements. He added, however, that an excellent command of English (which his brother-in-law did not possess) was essential for a practising doctor. In his opinion the diploma would be very worthwhile too for any plans to emigrate to one of the colonies or dominions of the British Empire. He recommended Trinity College Dublin, as it enjoyed a worldwide reputation second only to London. What Warburg had suggested in theory had in fact already been put into practice by a number of students.

The students

In June 1933, 116,961 Jews between six and twenty-five years old lived in Germany; by January 1938 their numbers had fallen to 67,200[26] – a demographic decline that was almost totally due to emigration, which set in when the Nazis began to exclude Jews from the racially defined *Volksgemeinschaft* and, specifically, to segregate Jewish and non-Aryan youngsters from their Aryan peers at schools, universities, *Vereine* (sport associations) and *Jugendbünde* (youth leagues). The so-called *Gesetz zur Wiederherstellung des Berufsbeamtentums* (Law for the Restoration of the Professional Civil Service) of 7 April 1933 and its various by-laws, which blocked professional opportunities in law, medicine, etc., became the blueprint for many prohibitive decrees against Jews and non-Aryans, such as the "Law Against the Overcrowding of German Schools and Universities", signed by the Ministry of the Interior on 25 April. According to this legislation, the ratio of non-Aryans was not to exceed 1.5% among new students in all second- and third-level educational institutions and was not to exceed 5% of all students in any institution, although until 1935, the children of former soldiers who had fought at the front and those born of mixed marriages before 1933 were exempted.[27] Conditions varied locally, but already in 1933 many *Gymnasien* (grammar schools) refused to grant Jewish students entrance qualifications to universities, and Jewish students were not admitted to exams. At least as important as such statutory barriers was the experience of exclusion from numerous school rituals. Jewish pupils were prevented from

---

26 http://www.s-port.de/david/angress.html: Werner T. Angress, *Jüdische Jugend im Umbruch nach 1933 – Schule, Freizeit, Beruf.* MS Bremen 1999 [last accessed 5 October 2015]. On the aging Jewish sector of the population, see also Avraham Barkai, *Vom Boykott zur 'Entjudung'. Der wirtschaftliche Existenzkampf der Juden im Dritten Reich 1933–1943.* Frankfurt/Main: Fischer 1988, p. 168.
27 Reichsgesetzblatt 1933, Part I, no. 43, 26 April 1933. See also Saul Friedländer, *Nazi Germany and the Jews,* Vol. 1: The Years of Persecution, 1933–1939. Phoenix, paperback edition: London 1998 (first published London: Weidenfeld & Nicolson 1997), pp. 30–31.

attending school trips or swimming courses, they were "freed from" taking part in obligatory *Rassenkunde* (racial studies), and stood still when the rest of the class saluted to the Führer, etc., not to mention other unsavoury forms of discrimination. Peter Königsberger, for example, a boy from the Saxon town of Burgstädt, remembers being "teased and nicknamed Samuel at school and sometimes called 'Itzig', which was a less pleasant name for Jews". Even if this was "not ill-meant", as he benevolently recalls, and other students had to withstand worse insults from teachers and classmates, the experience was "painful and hurtful".[28]

The Nuremberg Laws of 1935 sanctioned what many Jewish and non-Aryan pupils had experienced on a daily basis both in their classes and their free time: segregation from the German *Volksgemeinschaft* and *Bildung* both of which had come to be considered by most assimilated Jews over the generations as an ideological substitute for their relinquished Jewish identity, traditions and religion. Although it seems that in early 1937 about 39% of all Jewish pupils still attended German schools,[29] the majority of parents tried to protect their children either by sending them to one of the newly formed Jewish schools – which before 1933 had mostly been attended by children of the minority of *Ostjuden* – or by sending them out of the country. This type of emigration posed its own problems. It meant a separation of family members – though, ironically, it later enabled many young people to reunite with their parents – and it was primarily open only to children of prosperous families with international connections. The case of the thirteen children and adolescents who came to Ireland in this early period between 1933 and mid-1938 confirms this point. There were ten boys and three girls, most of them teenagers – the desperate times of *Kindertransporte* had not yet arrived. The parents had availed themselves of private connections or the mediation of charity societies to get their children out of Germany. In most cases the Irish option only materialised once the children were in the United Kingdom, by which time matters had come to depend on circumstances and British/Irish links outside the parents' sphere of influence.

The Society of Friends (Quakers) had a tradition of helping refugees, and committed themselves to the new challenge immediately after January 1933.[30] Quakers

---

28 Peter Kingshill (formerly Königsberger), *Footnote – A Memoir*. London: Private publication 2007, pp. 31–32. For other examples of social exclusion see Friedländer, *The Years of Persecution*, p. 38. For the Königsberger family see chapter 4.
29 In 1938, however, numbers fell to 25%. Friedländer, *The Years of Persecution*, p. 168.
30 Most relevant for émigrés to Ireland was the foundation of the London-based German Emergency Committee (GEC) in 1933, even if its role is rarely mentioned in the stories of refugees to Ireland (see chapter 6).

in Germany, Great Britain and Ireland enabled a number of young Germans to settle in Ireland up to 1938. Remarkably, some of them were non-Jewish and would not have had to endure racist slurs and other forms of prejudice at their schools, if the political opposition of their families to Nazism had not isolated them from their Aryan peers. The story of their escapes in a nutshell:
- Einhart and Sigurd Kawerau's father Siegfried Kawerau (1886–1936), pacifist, leftist Social Democrat, was politically undesirable in the eyes of the Nazis. His sons had therefore been sent to the Reformist Odenwald School near Darmstadt to conclude their schooling.[31] The Kaweraus had long favoured England as their eldest son's destination. Einhart arrived there in April 1934, a few weeks after his *Abitur* at the Odenwald School, with the intention of studying medicine,[32] but in the UK he found all places filled. Under these circumstances he applied for a place at Trinity College Dublin.[33] He was admitted and began his studies in September 1934, living on a scholarship of £54 per year with support from an Irish Quaker family.[34]
- Annelies Becker and Kurt Brehmer had grown up in Quaker families opposed to the Nazi regime.[35] Both reached Ireland thanks to personal links connecting

---

31 Siegfried Kawerau was dismissed as headmaster of the progressive Köllnisches Gymnasium in Berlin on 1 September 1933, was imprisoned by the SA for several months, and died in 1936 aged 50, suffering from the after-effects of his imprisonment. See Wolfgang Hasberg, Siegfried Kawerau 1886–1936. In: Michael Fröhlich (ed.), *Die Weimarer Republik. Porträt einer Epoche in Biographien*. Darmstadt: Primus 2002, pp. 293–330; also TCD Archives, Mun/Sec/248/ref/16, Einhart Kawerau undated CV; Entschädigungsamt (EA) Berlin, no. 773.831, Einhart Kawerau CV, 19 January 1966 and Sir Richard Stapley Educational Trust to Einhart Kawerau, 7 June 1934 (in the same file).
32 EA Berlin, registration no.773.831, Einhart Kawerau CV, 19 January 1966; Sir Richard Stapley Educational Trust to Einhart Kawerau, 7 June 1934.
33 Kawerau was helped by his English hosts and by the liberal historian G. P. Gooch, an acquaintance of his father. Gooch was chairman of the Sir Richard Stapley Educational Trust, which gave grants to students in financial need. He secured a grant for Kawerau, and also probably had a hand in his TCD application. EA Berlin, no. 773.831, Sir Richard Stapley Educational Trust to Einhart Kawerau, 7 June 1934.
34 TCD Archives, Mun/Sec/248/Ref/16, Einhart Kawerau undated CV. For the role of the Bewley family see chapter 6. They also supported his younger brother Sigurd. After his *Abitur* at the Odenwald School in mid-1935, Sigurd had paid a visit to the USA before entering Ireland on 27 April 1936 to begin his studies at University College Dublin. Information provided by Mrs R. Netzer, Odenwald School; also NAI, DJ 69/80/31, Coffey, UCD President, to Roche, DJ, 9 February 1939.
35 Annelies Becker mentions in her memoir that she had a close friend who ran an underground opposition movement. http://homepage.eircom.net/interfriendpublisher/tread.html: Annelies Becker, *Tread Softly. Scenes from my Life*, Chapter 3, May 1999 [last accessed 2 February 2015].

their families with, respectively, hosts in England and a Quaker family in Ireland.³⁶
- Jürgen Holländer's father, a lawyer and a Protestant of Jewish descent, was targeted mainly for his early political opposition to the Nazis in his hometown Naumburg/Saale. In May or June 1933, Jürgen followed him into exile in France. In Paris they took advantage of an apparently accidental meeting with Lord Buxton (probably Rodan Buxton, Quaker and peace activist) who persuaded the directorate of the Irish Quakers' Newtown School in Co. Waterford to take Jürgen as a boarder.³⁷
- In 1934, Newtown School also received the two Berliners Kurt Böhm and Käte Schulz as boarding students, but nothing is known about their background and passages to Ireland.³⁸

Initiatives of the Catholic and Protestant Churches to bring young people to the United Kingdom and Ireland were fewer and came later. Hans V. Ledermann and Anna Maria Tuchmann entered Ireland with the help of two Catholic orders. In 1935, Hans was admitted to the Jesuits' Clongowes Wood College, in Co. Kildare. Very probably, his father, a renowned throat surgeon in Breslau who was closely linked with Catholic charity work, had mobilised Jesuit acquaintances to direct the College's attention to the case of his (still Jewish) son.³⁹ The Loreto Sisters

---

For Brehmer, see his entries in his University of Limerick German-speaking exiles in Ireland project questionnaire, 1 October 2007.

36 Annelies came to Ireland through a contact between her Quaker mother and an Irish Quaker family which had applied for an *au pair* girl. See Becker, *Tread Softly*, chapter 4. For the Kingston family see chapter 6. Kurt Brehmer was sent by his widowed mother to England after his *Abitur* to study and learn farming at an anthroposophical Rudolf Steiner School near Birmingham. He stayed there more than four years before going to Ireland in 1938 (see chapter 6); questionnaire filled in by Kurt Brehmer, 1 October 2007.

37 Otto Holländer was a member of *Reichsbanner Schwarz Rot Gold* (a political organisation founded in 1924 to protect the democratic substance of the Weimar republic, its name referring to the German flag and its colours) and a known anti-Nazi agitator. The story of his son is based on CVs and letters written by Otto, his wife Hildegard, Jürgen's uncle Christoph Holländer and Christoph's daughter Anja, all in http://www.naumburg-geschichte.de/geschichte/juden.htm#04 [last accessed 12 July 2016]; also Joanna Cahir, Jürgen's daughter, emails to authors, 14 and 15 April 2013.

38 Society of Friends House Dublin (SFHD), Newtown School committee minutes 1925–1952. See also Maurice J. Wigham, *Newtown School Waterford – A History 1798–1998*. Waterford: Newtown School 1998, p. 146.

39 In 1933, the Nazis had dismissed Hans's father as head doctor at the hospital of the *Barmherzigen Brüder* (Merciful Brothers), Breslau. Letters of Fergal McGrath to Reverend Francis X. Talbot, New York, 25 and 26 May 1939. See also "Long time Ruler of Grand Priory of America

(Mary Ward Sisters) were instrumental in bringing Anna Maria Tuchmann to Ireland. In 1933 Hans Sigmund Tuchmann, Catholic convert and part-owner of the hop merchants' company S. Tuchmann and Sons in Nuremberg, and his wife Marianne sent their daughter Anna Maria away to the Mary Ward School in Bamberg, probably to shield her from political disruption in Nuremberg, the *Stadt der NS Reichsparteitage* (City of Nazi Party Rallies).[40] During her time in Bamberg, arrangements were made for her to leave Nuremberg after her return in March 1937. From the available data it appears that she was first taken care of within the institutional network of the Loreto Sisters in England. From there she left for Dublin in early October 1937, and stayed at Loreto Convent Hall, 77 St. Stephen's Green.[41]

In mid-1938, the nascent Protestant refugee network helped Georg and Eva Maria Pick, son and daughter of a part-Jewish politician and member of the *Bekennende Kirche* (Confessing Church), a body critical of the Nazis, to reach Irish shores. In Berlin, Georg had been forced to leave first the Schiller Gymnasium and then a private school that had been meant to be a refuge from Nazi pressures.[42] Georg and Eva Maria owed their escape to their father's friendship with Dr Conrad Hoffmann, a key figure in Protestant refugee operations who had links to leading representatives of the Church of Ireland.[43] Hoffmann organised their passage to

---

Dies on Ash Wednesday" (obituary on Hans von Leden=Hans V. Ledermann). In: *Augustan Omnibus*, issue 126, unpublished. Courtesy Howard Browne, Williamsburg (Virginia). For Clongowes, which features prominently in James Joyce's largely autobiographical *A Portrait of the Artist as a Young Man*, see Peter Costello, *Clongowes Wood: a History of Clongowes Wood College 1814–1989*. Dublin: Gill and Macmillan 1989.

40 See Nuremberg Civil Register. She attended the school until 1935, but it is uncertain whether she left with an *Abitur*. Stadtarchiv Nuremberg to authors, 13 November 2006; also Bamberg City Register and Stadtarchiv Bamberg to authors, 19 October 2006. Anna Maria then attended Mariahilf, a school for domestic workers, until March 1937, possibly a step intended to improve her emigration prospects.

41 MAI, G2/0848; NAI, DJ 69/80/31, Coffey, UCD President, to Roche, DJ, 9 February 1939.

42 Their father Heinrich Pick was a member of the left-liberal German Democratic Party and the elected Mayor of Stettin/Oder from 1920 to 1933. In March 1933 local Nazis ended his tenure, and after that he suffered frequent tribulations because of his Jewish family background and affiliations with the *Bekennende Kirche*. All biographical data are from letters of Georg Pick to Wiedergutmachungsamt Siegen, 14 February 1958, 18 March 1958, 25 July 1958, 27 January 1960; Ingeborg Pick to Entschädigungsamt (EA) Arnsberg, 16 August 1960 – all in EA Arnsberg, no. 55.511; Hessisches Hauptstaatsarchiv (HHSA) Wiesbaden, file group 503, no. 3989–b, Heinrich Pick CV, 15 October 1945.

43 In 1938, Hoffmann visited the Pick family in their Schöneberg flat, wishing to recruit Heinrich Pick as a "co-worker in the USA", at which time he also "arranged an invitation" to Georg and Eva Maria by the "Protestant Bishop of Dublin". HHSA, file group 503, no. 3989–b, Heinrich Pick CV, 15 October 1945.

Ireland with the cooperation of the Swedish Mission in Vienna (see chapter 2), the Berlin Centre of the Quakers and, on the Irish side, the Dublin United Missionary Council.[44] During his time in Berlin, Hoffmann also managed to have Hans Forell, another Protestant-Jewish student, sent to Ireland. Forell arrived in Ireland only in mid-December 1938.[45]

In 1935, Ernst Scheyer, Jewish veteran of World War I, highly respected lawyer and prominent member of the Reform community of Liegnitz, Silesia, and his wife Marie organised their son's educational future in England (whether with the support of a Jewish help network, as might be assumed given Ernst's position, could not be ascertained). At any rate Heinz, then fifteen years old, was given the opportunity of studying at Aryeh House, a Jewish boarding school near Brighton.[46] After his graduation, like Einhart Kawerau three years earlier, he was not admitted to a British university medical school. So instead, he enrolled at the Medical School of Trinity College Dublin, his maintenance guaranteed through a five-year scholarship and further funding from a German-Jewish charity.[47]

Einhart Kawerau and Heinz Scheyer were not the only German-speaking students who went from the United Kingdom to Ireland to study medicine. Since British admission rules for doctors took no account of academic honours gained abroad, but demanded diplomas which under the circumstances were hard to achieve at British universities, at least six other German-Jewish doctors (Paul and Karl Schnitzler, Wilhelm Emanuel, Robert Haas, Otto Nelki and Ernst Sommer) and one dentist (Edeltraut Reinert) came to Dublin from 1933 onwards to qualify for specific degrees as required by British regulations,[48] while another, Viktor

---

44 NAI, DJ 69/80/7, Dublin United Missionary Council to DJ, visa applications on behalf of the Pick children, undated.
45 See chapter 7. Not much could be found about Forell's family background, but it seems possible that the Forell family also belonged to Hoffmann's circle of Protestant friends. Hans was born in 1920 in Pomeranian Züllichau; in 1938 he lived at Reichsstrasse 47 in Wilmersdorf, a typical Jewish quarter in western Berlin (see chapter 4). The delay was due either to transport problems or extended deliberations in the Irish departments. NAI, DFA 102/525, Duff, secretary DJ, to DEA, 4 November 1938; see also correspondence in NAI, DJ 69/80/57.
46 Stephen Weil, 'Children of Goethe': The Scheyer-Weil Family. In: Gisela Holfter (ed.), *Irish Context*, pp. 23–28, 25; Gisela Holfter, Ernst Scheyer. In: Holfter (ed.), *German-speaking Exiles*, pp. 149–169.
47 NAI, DJ 69/2404, Garda Siochana to DJ, 13 October 1937.
48 Paul Schnitzler and his twin brother Karl, sons of a Jewish vet practising in Berlin, had already obtained doctorates in medicine in Germany. They came to England in mid-1933, and in October of that year applied to re-qualify at Apothecaries Hall, Dublin. Both lived in Dublin's Jewish quarter (6 Harrington Street and 18 Westfield Road – for both addresses see chapter 8) and remained there, after Robert Briscoe had intervened to prolong their residence in Ireland by a year, until 29 March 1935. DFA 202/99; DJ 2014/85/2285; also Paul Weindling, email to authors,

Hähnlein, studied in Dublin before going to the USA.[49] Faced with a number of applications, some of which were initially turned down, the Department of Justice took a pragmatic decision:

> All these cases, Nelki, Hahnlein, Haas, Sommer and similar cases may be dealt with in the same way. Given their twelve month residence, for the purpose of their studies, they must not practise or take up any employment or occupation and they must understand that they will be required to leave on the termination of their studies.[50]

Having gained their Irish diplomas, these practitioners, unlike Kawerau and Scheyer, left the country as required, all of them but Hähnlein returning to the UK.

---

9 June 2004; http://sounds.bl.uk/related-content/TRANSCRIPTS/021I-C0410X0011XX-ZZZZA0.pdf: National Life Stories. Living Memory of the Jewish Community: Ilse Sinclair interviewed by Jennifer Wingate. Wilhelm Emanuel, a member of a settled and assimilated Jewish family in Herne (Westphalia), had been an assistant doctor before his passage to Ireland in January 1934, at the age of 26. In December of that year he moved to Glasgow. Courtesy Mrs Wiesniewski and Koch, Stadtarchiv Herne. NAI, DFA 202/207, Garda Siochana to An Ceannphort, Detective Branch, 10 May 1939. Robert Haas (born in 1903), Jewish, had come on 4 November 1933 from London to prepare for a medical examination in order to obtain a British qualification. He had been invited by Dr Tomkin for a year's practical training at Mercer's Hospital. He departed for Glasgow on 29 October 1934. See DJ 2014/85/2300 (formerly 221/2595), Garda to DJ, 7 November 1933. Otto W. Nelki also came to Ireland in 1933–1934. See NAI, DFA 202/172. In the 1920s he had established himself as an ear, nose and throat specialist, practising together with his father and two of his brothers in the so-called *'Nelki-Haus'* in the Bavarian Quarter of Berlin. He came to Dublin on 27 October 1933 and lived near the German Legation at 16 Northumberland Road – the address where Robert Haas also stayed for a while – supporting himself partly by giving private German lessons. On 11 November 1934 he returned to England. See NAI, DFA 202/172. See also Dr O.W. Nelki 70. In: *AJR Information* June 1969, p. 16; In Memoriam Dr O.W. Nelki. In: *AJR Information* July 1972, p. 10. Ernst Sommer also stayed in Ireland until November 1934. It seems that, as in the Schnitzler case, Robert Briscoe played an important role in securing his stay. NAI, DFA 202/242, DJ to DEA, 31 May 1939; also correspondence in DJ 2014/85/2298; Kevin McCarthy, An Introduction to Robert Briscoe's Extraordinary Immigration Initiative, 1933–1938. In: Holfter (ed.), *Irish Context*, p. 82. Edeltraut Reinert, like other Austrians, had left her country years before the *Anschluss*. She came from Edinburgh to Ireland in 1936 to study for a Bachelor's degree in Dental Surgery. In April 1938, she returned to the United Kingdom. See correspondence in NAI, DJ 68/1/640; MAI, G2/2524, G2 report, 23 October 1941.

49 Viktor Hähnlein, who had established a large practice in Dresden and had written several books, came to Dublin on 5 October 1933. See DJ, 2014/85/2248, formerly DJ 221/2536. After a year of study at the Rotunda Hospital, he left from Galway for the USA on 1 September 1934, accompanied by his wife Margarete and probably by their daughters Annelies and Renate. See http://www.stadtwikidd.de/wiki/Viktor_H%C3%A4hnlein [last accessed 4 July 2016]).

50 NAI, DJ 2014/85/2273 (formerly DJ 221/2562), handwritten memo DJ, 17 November [1933].

The businessmen

As we shall see, at a later period from 1938, the immigration of refugee businessmen seeking to establish commercial operations in Ireland became a significant element of Irish rural and urban development. Even in this earlier 1933–1938 period, however, refugees of this class found their way to Ireland.

In November 1921, Abraham Bayer had left behind his life in the new Polish state, migrating to Karlsruhe/Baden, then to Frankfurt/Main and, in 1925, to industrial Offenbach just across the River Main. Though denied naturalisation papers, Abraham had been attracted by the town's prestigious leather industry as well as by its more liberal attitude towards Eastern Jews (compared with Prussian Frankfurt) – and by Gitla Bulka, like himself Polish and Jewish. He married her soon after his arrival in Offenbach.[51] Abraham operated a handbag factory that employed an average of 40 workers in the late 1920s. When the Nazis took over Germany, he originally intended to start a second entrepreneurial career in the UK.[52] That plan had to be abandoned; instead he investigated the Irish option via his London agent and the Irish High Commissioner. On 31 August 1933, he applied to the Department of Industry and Commerce, using the letterhead of his old Offenbach factory, explaining that he wished to operate from Ireland to develop existing links to customers in the lucrative British market, and proposing an initial investment of £800, much of it comprising his "machines and accessories".[53] In December 1933, he and representatives of the Department of Industry and Commerce fixed the details of the projected industrial transfer,[54] his application was granted on 31 January 1934,[55] and the next day the Bayers and their young son Manfred arrived in Ireland.[56]

The story contains elements common to several refugees' experiences. Fearing pogroms, many Jewish families like Bayer's had left Poland during and after World War I and sought provisional refuge in Germany, which many expected to be only a stage on their way to the USA. In their new country, these mostly stateless immigrants found themselves targeted by the political right and

---

51 The biographical data are taken from the Bayer file of the Jewish Register of the City of Offenbach (Haus der Geschichte, archive, Offenbach), and from MAI, G2/0333. In the G2 file Gitla's year of birth is given as 1902.
52 NAI, TID 1207/300, Bayer to DI&C, 31 August 1933.
53 NAI, TID 1207/300, Bayer to DI&C, 31 August 1933; Dulanty to DI&C, 28 July 1933; Bayer to DI&C, 16 September; draft memorandum DI&C, 27 September 1933.
54 See DJ 69/41, landing report Dover, 26 January 1934.
55 NAI, TID 1207/300, minute of a DI&C official, 6 February 1934.
56 MAI, G2/0333.

only half-heartedly accepted by many assimilated German Jews who feared that their own contested integration into German bourgeois society would be compromised by the presence of the *Ostjuden*. Having internalised the experiences of discrimination in Poland, and on the margins of pre-Nazi society, they were more sensitive than assimilated Jews to the dangers lurking in Germany,[57] which became manifest in 1933.[58]

Three other early refugees to Ireland had experiences that resemble the Bayer story, though differing in detail. Serge (originally Szulim) Philipson's parents had left Warsaw two or three years after their son's birth and moved to Berlin, joining the ranks of (mostly) poor Eastern Jews in the German capital. Serge and his fiancée Sophie had already been subjected to right-wing attacks in the late 1920s.[59] As a consequence, they left Berlin in 1930, moving to Paris on the invitation of Sophie's eldest brother, Henri Orbach, who owned Les Modes Modernes, a small hat factory in the Rue du Temple in the centre of the French capital's Jewish quarter. In 1935, Serge went to Ireland (see chapter 7).

In 1895, Leib Margulies' parents had left Galician Tarnobrzeg and moved to Frankfurt/Main. Leib grew up in Rechneigrabenstrasse in the Frankfurt East End, where many *Ostjuden* clustered. After his military service in World War I, Leib and his brother within a few years turned the little business their father had founded into a well-known commercial enterprise in Frankfurt's city centre. The boycotts and other intimidations of 1933 halted their progress. On 20 October, Leib, his wife and their daughters Inge and Paula crossed the still relatively open border to France.[60] Like Philipson, he only came to Ireland in 1935 (see chapter 8).

---

57 On the construction of terms like *Westjuden* and *Ostjuden* see Steven A. Aschheim, *Brothers and Strangers. The East European Jew in German and German-Jewish consciousness, 1800–1923*. Madison: University of Wisconsin Press 1983; Trude Maurer, Die Wahrnehmung der Ostjuden in Deutschland 1910–1933. In: *LBI Information: Nachrichten aus den Leo Baeck Instituten in Jerusalem, London, New York und der Wissenschaftlichen Arbeitsgemeinschaft des LBI in Deutschland*, no. 7, 1997, pp. 67–85. For Offenbach see Klaus Werner, Zur Situation der "Ostjuden" in Offenbach am Main. In: Magistrat der Stadt Offenbach am Main (ed.), *Zur Geschichte der Juden in Offenbach am Main*, Vol. 2, pp. 140–195.
58 One of the first "legal" anti-Semitic measures of the new rulers was a "law" of 14 July 1933 which in principle revoked all naturalisations of *Ostjuden* who had entered the country after November 1918. Reichsgesetzblatt, Vol. I, p. 480.
59 An example can be found in Rachel Philipson Levy's Memoir: "Serge and Sophie [were] strolling through a park when two German 'Brownshirts' walking towards them on the sidewalk push [sic] the young woman aside saying 'Juden hinunter'." See migs.concordia.ca/memoirs/levy/levy.html. Rachel Philipson Levy, Memoir: An Odyssee Revisited [last accessed 22 October 2014].
60 Hessisches Hauptstaatsarchiv Wiesbaden (HHSA), no. 34.962/94A, Lionel V. Lee (= Leib Margulies) CV, 11 July 1955.

Heinz Krotoschin's German background was different. He had grown up in the atmosphere of a wealthy German-Jewish family in the western part of the German capital. Though he too was exposed to anti-Semitic attacks, he seems to have been shielded against their more robust forms by his family background, his position as an architect and his secluded residence in the Rheingau Quarter in Charlottenburg-Wilmersdorf.[61] Nevertheless, his Zionist views alerted him earlier than other Jews to the dangers that lay ahead.[62] "I am a German Jew who left Germany immediately when Herr Hitler came to power," he later claimed.[63] On 1 April 1933, the very day when Jewish shops were beleaguered by SA troopers calling for a boycott all over the *Reich*, Heinz and Alice Krotoschin and their baby departed from Berlin. They had little difficulty in escaping to Amsterdam. As Heinz was not able to find a job in Holland or England, he gladly accepted employment as a dubiously-qualified "ink specialist" for Messrs Haughton Ink Manufacturers in Bray. Thanks to the support of Robert Briscoe he was issued with a work permit by the Department of Industry and Commerce.[64]

The Lisowski story

The story of the Lisowskis' passage to Ireland was unique, if only because no other persons up to 1938 chose Ireland as their primary and ultimate place of exile. On 20 November 1937 Käte [Katharina] Müller-Lisowski and her husband Friedrich were registered as immigrants in Ireland.[65] Days before, at their home

---

61 See Henry Kent (= Heinz Krotoschin): Interview with Bettina Kaufmann (10 May 1996). *Visual History Archive*, USC Shoah Foundation, The Institute for Visual History and Education. The fact that the Krotoschins had engaged a governess for their child hints at their relatively high social and economic status. In the Berlin directory of 1933 Heinz is described as a Fabrikant (manufacturer), obviously in the construction business.
62 His interest in Zionism is evidenced by his membership of the Blau-Weiss, the Zionist youth league. Kent, *Visual History Archive*, 10 May 1996.
63 MAI, G2/0111, Krotoschin to Irish Post, 4 September 1939.
64 MAI, G2/0111, hand-written and undated G2 report. For Briscoe's support see also *Visual History Archive*, 10 May 1996.
65 Biographical details about their life in Germany are from Niedersächsisches Landesarchiv Hannover (NLA), Nds. 110 W, Acc. 8/90, no. 269/11, and from http://www.ucc.ie/celt/muellerlisowski.html, a text on Katharina Lisowski's "Life and Works", compiled by Beatrix Faerber and relying on information from Peter Lisowski [last accessed 20 October 2014]; Christoph Knüppel, Aus der Scholle festem Grunde wächst dereinst die Freiheitsstunde. Gustav Landauer und die Siedlungsbewegung. In: *Von Ancona bis Eden. Alternative Lebensformen*. Lübeck: Erich-Mühsam-Gesellschaft 2006, Vol. 27, pp. 45–63. Primary sources of the Eden Colony Archive were provided by Sabine and Robert Schurmann.

in Oranienburg near Berlin, they had packed their car with furniture and machinery and driven to Hamburg, where they embarked for Cork. For years the family had taken part in a social experiment on the northern fringe of the German capital. The *Gemeinnützige Obstbausiedlung Eden* (Non-profit Orchard Community Eden) near Oranienburg had been founded in 1893 as the first German vegetarian community, a social and ecological alternative to modern industrial-urban life devised and organised by an odd assortment of utopian socialists, anarchists, homesteaders, vegetarians, disciples of body cults, and later even a few followers of Nazi ideology. Friedrich, a plumber and veteran of the Great War, was a member of one branch of Gustav Landauer's anarchist *Sozialistischer Bund* (founded in 1908) that tried to realise its ideals of co-operative living by forming a cell within Eden.[66] He enlisted as a full member of the community in June 1919 in spite of reservations within the administration about his "radical" political ideas.[67] His wife Käte had made herself a name as a scholar in Celtic literature through her translations of Irish folk songs and fairy tales collected and edited by, among others, Douglas Hyde, founder of the Gaelic League and later President of Ireland.[68] Käte joined the community only from a sense of marital obligation.[69] In the 1920s the family lived comfortably from the proceeds of Friedrich's plumbing business which employed nine workers by 1932, while Käte occupied herself with translation and cultural activities in Eden.[70] One special event was an Irish Evening in November 1932 with Irish songs and poems translated by Käte.

---

66 Friedrich Lisowski's political background is explored in Knüppel's essay. Particularly relevant is his speech at the grave of a fellow Eden anarchist in 1928, published in *Edener Mitteilungen* (EM), Vol. 1938, no. 1–2, September 1938, pp. 4–7. His main contribution to the pre-war anarchist movement was bringing out the newspaper *Der Sozialist*.
67 See Lisowski application sheet for membership from 25 June 1921 and hand-written comments by the administration revealing their suspicion of Lisowski's reputed radicalism. Eden Archive, file Lisowski.
68 *Irische Volksmärchen*. Berlin: Ernst Rowohlt 1920 (last edition published by Rowohlt in Reinbek in 1993, see also http://www.ucc.ie/celt/muellerlisowski.html [last accessed 13 July 2016]). Another volume with the same title, but edited by herself (with a preface by Julius Pokorny), which appeared in 1923, was first published with Eugen Diederichs in Jena and has also gone through numerous editions.
69 In a letter to the administration of 19 November 1935 she expressed her estrangement from the ideas of Eden. She had already withdrawn her membership in 1925, but re-entered in 1929. Eden Archive, file Lisowski.
70 She was engaged in running the *Familienschule* (Family School) in Eden in 1928, but left its board after a dispute in the following year. EM, Vol. 1929, no. 1–2, p. 7; Vol. 1930, no. 1–2, pp. 5, 7. Her role in the cultural scene of Eden is also apparent from EM, Vol. 1932, no. 2, p. 32. See also Eden Archive, file Lisowski, Käte Müller-Lisowski to Eden administration, 19 November 1935.

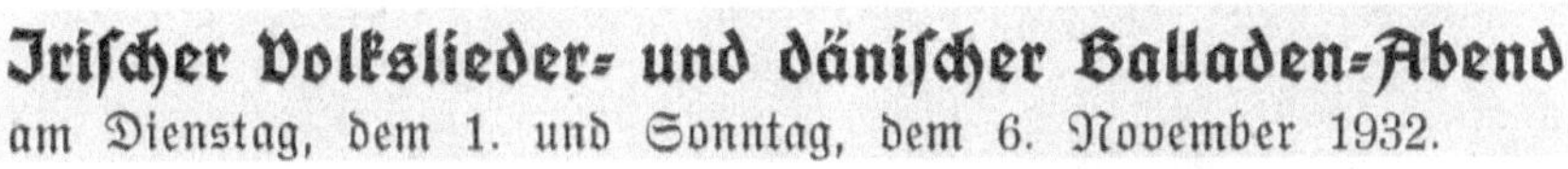

Jrifcher Volkslieder- und dänifcher Balladen-Abend
am Dienstag, dem 1. und Sonntag, dem 6. November 1932.

Image 1: Advertisement for an Irish and Danish folksong evening, organised in 1932 by Käte Müller-Lisowski.

The Lisowskis, however, had begun to feel marginalised,[71] and on 27 November 1933, Käte declared her final withdrawal from the community.[72] They were also suffering Nazi persecution, in the first place because Friedrich, a member of the SPD, had turned their house into a meeting place for anti-Nazis of various parties calling themselves the *"Winkel Group"*.[73] In 1935, Friedrich was briefly sent to Potsdam prison by the Gestapo, and their son Peter's increasingly difficult situation at school made their emigration more urgent. Their decision to leave Germany was also fuelled by their social isolation and the boycott that came near to ruining the business, forcing Friedrich to dismiss almost all his employees.[74] Given Käte's contacts with Douglas Hyde and other Celtic scholars, Ireland seemed a suitable destination. The Lisowskis visited the country in 1936, obviously preparing for emigration, and arranged for their son's registration at the Quakers' Newtown School, Co. Waterford (see above). In June 1936, Peter was sent to Ireland; two months later he was enrolled at Newtown School where Käte was also employed to teach Irish until December 1936.[75] Back in Germany there were some last-minute hurdles to surmount before the official emigration could proceed, but once the flight tax was paid and a tax clearance had been confirmed in April 1937, they were free to leave.[76]

---

71 Apart from political issues, the administration was dissatisfied with Lisowski for allegedly failing to carry out plumbing work, whereas Lisowski felt that he was being systematically excluded from commissions. Eden Archive, file Lisowski, Eden administration to Lisowski, 13 October 1931; Lisowski to administration, 27 November 1931.
72 Eden Archive, file Lisowski, Käte Müller-Lisowski to administration, 27 November 1933.
73 Niedersächsisches Landesarchiv Hannover (NLA), Nds. 110 W, Acc. 8/90, no. 269/11, Bruno Sander to Entschädigungsamt (EA) Hildesheim, 12 August 1958.
74 NLA, Nds. 110 W, Acc. 8/90, no. 269/11, Friedrich Lisowski to EA Hildesheim, 4 June 1957.
75 NLA, Nds. 110 W, Acc. 31/99, no. 232.812, Peter Lisowski undated CV; on Käte Müller-Lisowski in Newtown School see also chapter 7.
76 NLA, Nds. 110 W, Acc. 8/90, no. 269/11, Friedrich Lisowski to EA Hildesheim, 13 September 1958. In 1953 Käte Müller-Lisowski recalled that they had to "suffer much" before they could leave Germany. "We left behind much of our money and property," which is also why they had to "work and struggle much" in Ireland. Eden Archive, Lisowski file, letter Käte Müller-Lisowski, 25 July 1953. Translated by authors.

Image 2: Dr Käte Müller-Lisowski.

Altogether only a small number of refugees came to Ireland between 1933 and October 1938 – we know of 52 (not counting visitors). It is likely that this is not the full total, and that the number of applicants was higher than the number of entrants, but nevertheless the figures confirm the assertion that Ireland and Iceland were the only two European countries that did not host "a large number of refugees" up to 1938.[77] Geographical and cultural distance, and arduous and expensive travel requirements played a role, as did passport and visa regulations that were often unclear, and even more so the limited personal contacts between Ireland and Germany. Ireland was not a stepping stone to a more promising exile destination and, even more importantly, did not offer many prospects for business or sustainable livelihood. In fact, in the mid-1930s there were as many emigrants leaving Ireland as there were leaving Germany, despite Ireland's far smaller population (see chapter 6).

---

77 Claus-Dieter Krohn (ed.), *Handbuch der deutschsprachigen Emigration 1933 – 1945*. Darmstadt: Primus Verlag 1998, p. 130. Translated by authors.

Chapter 2
"Those days in Vienna..."

Georg Klaar/George Clare

Moving on from the early period, we turn first to those refugees who came from Vienna, where the situation rapidly deteriorated for Jews and non-Aryans from March 1938, almost eight months before the November pogroms in Germany. A relatively high proportion of those who sought refuge in Ireland came from Vienna. One of them was Georg Klaar.

The Klaars' flat was in Vienna's 9th district, at the corner of Pichlergasse and Nussdorferstrasse. In his autobiography, George Clare recalls a return visit after 36 years to the house where he had been born and reared as Georg Klaar until 1938: a typical *Gründerzeit* building which, while not quite matching the pomp of palatial residential buildings lining the Ring, recalls the wealth and self-assuredness of Vienna's grand bourgeoisie before the Emperors' demise. Flat 9 had nine rooms. It housed four occupants: Ernst Klaar, well-to-do Vienna banker and World War I officer, his wife Stella, the maid, and Georg. While describing the awkward encounter with the new resident, George Clare also recalls the 12th March 1938, the day the Wehrmacht, SA and SS annexed Austria, and the Nazis' unimpeded penetration of the country's public life began. George interprets the outburst of anti-Semitic mass violence as the emanation of a dominant petty bourgeois mentality.[1] His memory, never to be wholly trusted as his critical mind realises, reconstructs the behaviour of his family and their acquaintances: the women's newfound strength, the men's helplessness and torpor, as well as his own curious mixture of fear and fascination. He especially notes that his once domineering father, who would be dismissed from his influential post just two months later, and who, like many other Jews, had been made to scrub streets to the sadistic cheers of Aryan onlookers, was reduced to an almost infantile condition.[2] In hindsight, what Georg witnessed was the destruction of a Jewish family tradition which had begun in East European *Shtetls* and had, over centuries, climaxed in successful bourgeois assimilation in the old Habsburg capital. Now, however, the assimilatory progress that had survived Vienna's notorious everyday anti-Semitism after the First World War was wiped out "overnight".

---

[1] George Clare, *Last Waltz in Vienna: the Destruction of a Family 1842–1942*. London: MacMillan 1982, pp. 75–78.
[2] Clare, *Last Waltz in Vienna*, pp. 191–192, 194–195, 197–198.

Or so it seemed. Momentous decisions had to be made. George remembers that he immediately wanted to join the British Army and fight the Nazis, but imagined that his application would be rejected by the British Consulate in Wallnerstrasse.³ Emigration seemed imperative and feasible given his father's links to his bank's headquarters in Paris. The family's best friend had already emigrated, but there were the practical obstacles ("How? Where?") and the usual self-deception ("Hitler cannot last long").⁴ Both were overcome in the end. On 12 November 1938 Georg and his mother arrived in Dublin.

Social profiles

It is difficult to make generalised statements about the socio-economic status of Viennese emigrants to Ireland.⁵ "Middle-class" would have suited the self-description of most emigrés, but the term obscures the enormous differences of income and social status within that broad category. Nor does a tableau of professions shed full light on these differences. Among the 58 income earners were four doctors, two lawyers, one journalist, ten managers in leading positions, twenty further employees and workers (especially in two enterprises transferred to Ireland; see below), four military persons, three scientists, four engineers and five entrepreneurs. Wide income disparities existed especially in the private sector. On the one hand, there were men such as Ludwig Heinsheimer, legal consultant and vice chairman of Vienna's international Hemp, Jute and Textile Manufacturing Co., Fritz Wiedmann, senior executive of an insurance company, Ernst Sonnenschein, export manager in Emil Hirsch's ribbon factory, Ferdinand Karrach, representative of two German crystal and ceramic enterprises in Austria and the Balkans, and Ernst Klaar; on the other, many earning considerably less, such as Kurt Billig, an engineer, and Robert Donath, a journalist,⁶ as well as Ignaz Schulz and Josef Kalman,⁷ both book-keepers. Income and status were also vastly disparate within the small group of entrepreneurs. The two factory owners Emil

---

3 Clare, *Last Waltz in Vienna*, pp. 235–236.
4 Clare, *Last Waltz in Vienna*, p. 190.
5 A rough estimate can be based on the data contained in the Property Declarations of 26 April 1938 and on restitution claims after the war.
6 Donath worked as assistant foreign news editor for almost 20 years for the internationally renowned *Neue Freie Presse* (New Free Press), a Viennese newspaper founded in 1864 but closed down following Hitler's takeover of Austria, due to its many Jewish journalists and liberal outlook.
7 Kalman could dispose of a monthly net income of 232 Reichsmark at the end of April 1938. AdR-Vermögensanmeldung (VA), no. 32.311.

Hirsch and Fritz Blaskopf could hardly be compared with a much less prosperous man like Friedrich Hirsch, who financed an average middle-class lifestyle from his one-man dye and chemicals shop in Laudongasse 54. The thorough "middle-to-upper class" background of emigrants to Ireland is also highlighted by the fact that all the 19 pupils among the emigrants had attended higher secondary schools, either a *Gymnasium*, or a *Realgymnasium* or at least a higher commercial school. Ten had already begun (or were about to begin) their university studies.

Most of the 155 Austrian emigrants to Ireland had spent their whole lives in Vienna. Among those whose birthplace is known, roughly 75% were born in the capital. Most others had come to Vienna from the wider reaches of the Austrian Empire. Some had origins in Moravia or Slovakia, with birthplaces like Pressburg (Donath), Prossnitz (Emil Hirsch), Eiwanowitz (Friedrich Hirsch), Diviso/Diwischau (Richard Hitschmann), Tapolcsan (Risa Heinsheimer), and Neudorf (Valerie Menkes). Others were born in places such as Strzelbice, a village six kilometres from the town Stary Sambor (Wolf Zeiler and the brothers Witztum), Lviv, fomerly Lemberg (Lothar Fuchs), Wojnilov (Josef Kalman), Przemysil (Helena Lowy), Stanislau (Theodor Honig) or Plotyeze (Benjamin Kurz) – all localities in far-off Galicia, the East European borderland torn by endless strife between the antagonistic Polish, Ukrainian and Jewish ethnic communities and subject to shifting national boundaries between 1914 and 1920. Before the First World War, thousands of poor Jewish *Galizianer* had already migrated from these "Bloodlands" (Timothy Snyder)[8] to Vienna. Between 1914 and 1920 many found themselves wedged between warring sides and subjected to repeated pogroms. All the post-*Anschluss* emigrants to Ireland who originated from the East were born in the last decades of the nineteenth century or at least before the First World War, and most of them had come to Vienna before 1920–1921. Josef Kalman can be taken as one example. He was born in Wojnilov, an Eastern Galician town of roughly 3,000 inhabitants (one third of them Jews), one of six children of Adolf and Beile Kalman. At the beginning of the First World War he fled from his home town when the military advance of Russian troops and pogroms sent thousands of his co-religionists fleeing westwards, most of them to Vienna. In 1915 he arrived in the Austrian capital, possibly residing in neighbourhoods in Vienna's Leopoldstadt with other *Galizianer*. Josef attended a *Realschule* and then a *Handelshochschule*. In 1928, he was employed as a *Kontorist* (book-keeper) in Max Blaskopf's zip fastener factory (see below), and it was here that he met his Vienna-born wife Lucie, likewise Jewish.[9] After their marriage they resided in Kochgasse 34 in Vienna's well-to-do 8th district (Josefstadt).

---

8 Timothy Snyder, *Bloodlands: Europe between Hitler and Stalin*. New York: Basic 2010.
9 IKG Archives, Emigration Department, no. 36.692, 11 July 1938; no. 52.229, 17 April 1939. Lucie was also employed as a book-keeper in Blaskopf's factory.

Of the 155 Austrian refugees to Ireland, 54 (including children) were Jewish. How many of them were practising Jews is difficult to assess. Some, like Josef Kalman and other *Galizianer*, remained loosely orthodox in spite of the secularising pull of Vienna society;[10] others, like George Clare, were proud German-Austrian Jews and looked down on their Eastern relatives.[11] But to many, religion did not matter at all: "All members of my family were Jewish, we were not religious and until I entered school [in 1923–1924] I had no idea of my being Jewish," recalls Ines Mandl, née Hochmuth.[12] Some rediscovered their Jewish roots only after the *Anschluss*.[13] A small majority of Austrian emigrants to Ireland had already converted in their own or their parents' generation, but those we know of, 47 Catholics and 17 Protestants, also fell foul of racist Nazi norms (as did the men or women in four inter-religious marriages).[14]

---

10 Kalman's orthodoxy probably went back to his mother's family of orthodox rabbis. Rudi Lindner, Kalman's nephew, email to authors, 12 August 2007. The shades of orthodoxy among Jewish immigrants to Ireland may be demonstrated by the three Witztum brothers. According to Anna Adler her father Arnold Witztum was an orthodox Jew though not literally observing the Sabbath rules ("he made his own rules"), whereas Naftali remained a devout Jew, with Marcus standing somewhat in the middle. All three had shed the outward symbols of Galician Jewishness, the beard, the ear locks, the kaftan, in this ostentatiously differing from their parents, Abraham Witztum and Feiga (or Fani) in Galicia. Anna Adler interview with authors, 13 September 2005.
11 As George Clare described it: "I was already second-generation Viennese, and Viennese-born Jews felt resentment towards the less assimilated Jews from the East. We were, or rather thought we were, quite different from that bearded, kaftaned lot. We were not just Austrian, but German-Austrian." Clare, *Last Waltz in Vienna*, p. 37.
12 Ines Mandl to authors, 8 December 2004. Ines was the daughter of an owner of a leather factory who was also elected as the First President of the Viennese International Trade Fair. Her mother came from an Italian-Jewish banker's family. Both were non-observant Jews and educated their daughter in a secular spirit. Ines Mandl reports that in her *Gymnasium* "some of the girls were known to be illegal Nazis" but her main adversaries in 1934 were still the Christian Social *Vaterländische Front* (Patriotic Front) with its specific brand of Austrian anti-Semitism. When "the Gemeindehäuser [community houses], the social-democratic workers buildings, were shot at in 1934 the Jewish students developed a political conscience. Thereafter most of us became at least temporarily ardent Zionists, our teacher of religion offered five classes of modern Hebrew which we attended."
13 Georg Klaar believed in "Austria" and its German cultural values before he discovered his Jewishness as a new basis for his identity in the critical days of 1938. Clare, *Last Waltz in Vienna*, p. 204. Within the Menkes family such a reorientation developed only after they had reached Ireland. "I started to study the Torah," remembered Hans (John) Menkes, "and began to learn Hebrew [...] I felt that it was time to know why I had lost family, home, and language." John Menkes, A Didactic Autobiography. In: *Journal of Child Neurology*. Volume 16, no. 3 (2001), p. 192; see also *Visual History Archive*, interview with Hans (John) Menkes, 18 July 1996.
14 Friedrich Lederer, Richard Wallach, Adolf Adler and Ignaz Schulz went to Ireland without their Aryan partners.

The political orientations of the Austrian refugees who came to Ireland are likewise difficult to categorise. To Austrians such as Stefan Feric, Robert Dubsky and others whose families had abandoned their Jewish roots, "Austria" had reached a zenith in the Catholic, anti-socialist, corporate state of 1934, which in contrast to the Nazi state differentiated, at least to some extent, between confessing and converted Jews.[15] Most confessing Jews felt committed to enlightened traditions of the Dual Monarchy of Austria-Hungary and nostalgically stuck with them in spite of the Republic's growing anti-Jewish tendency in the 1930s. "Our family was proud of being Austrian citizens of the Mosaic persuasion," recalled Hans (John) Menkes,[16] and even an orthodox Jew like Arnold Witztum, who had spent no more than two years in Austria (1928 to 1930), demonstrated his estrangement from his original nationality by defiantly deleting the word "Polish" in his passport and replacing it by "Austrian".[17] These Jews and recently converted Catholics would have considered the corporatist *Ständestaat*, despite its anti-Semitic tendencies, as a barrier against the Nazification of Austria;[18] only leftists such as Kurt Hainbach, Erwin Strunz and Friedrich Lederer already felt politically marginalised before the *Anschluss* and had suffered economic consequences following the Austrian civil war of 1934.

"Those days in Vienna..."

The eruption of anti-Jewish hatred, the countless forms of public humiliation and robberies of valuables, furniture etc. by party members and non-Nazis targeting private apartments, little shops and department stores, reached proportions in

---

[15] Stefan Feric's parents had migrated to Vienna from the Croatian town of Daruvar near Zagreb. Stefan attended a Jesuit school, obtained a Leaving Certificate (*Matura*), and studied Bacteriology at Vienna's University in the 1920s and 1930s. He and his family cut their ties to Judaism at an unknown date, much earlier at any rate than August 1933 when the young doctor was baptised. He became a member of the *Katholische Aktion* (Catholic Action), rounding off his education as a "true Austrian" by joining one of the popular Tyrolean *Heimatvereine* (tradition clubs) and becoming a member of the Vienna branch of the *Ostmärkische Sturmscharen*, which under the leadership of Kurt Schuschnigg committed itself to the Christian-Social ideas of the *Ständestaat*. He also received an officer diploma in the Austrian Army. Nuala Feric interview with authors, 16 November 2004. DAV, Cardinal Innitzer letters, no. 1767, Michael Pfliegler, professor of moral theology at Vienna University, 25 May 1938.
[16] Menkes, A Didactic Autobiography, p. 192.
[17] Anna Adler interview with authors, 23 September 2005. It is likewise significant that Arnold and Marcus, when asked to state their citizenship at the time of their birth, entered "Austria currently occupied by Poland at the end of 1918" into an official document. See NAI, DJ 2013/50/239 and 259.
[18] Sylvia Maderegger, *Die Juden im österreichischen Ständestaat*. Vienna: Geyer 1973, p. 83.

the weeks after the *Anschluss* that distinctly surpassed the brutalities against Jews in the Old *Reich*. All this alarmed even leading National Socialist activists in the "Ostmark".[19] It was only in late April that the Nazis began to supplant the anarchic terror with a system of institutionalised repression. The days of the November Pogrom, one of the most brutal in what was now called Greater Germany, however, led to renewed fervent eruptions of mass hostility.[20] A catalogue of happenings in "those days in Vienna..." (Carl Zuckmayer) involving those who would eventually escape to Ireland:[21] Stefan Feric, the young aspiring officer, had his epaulettes torn from his shoulders by other soldiers and barely managed to escape to a railway station where he hid before finally making it to his parents' house in Währingerstrasse; uniformed National Socialist troopers broke into Emil Hirsch's flat at elegant Schwarzenbergplatz, beat him and his son Robert, arrested both and took them to the central Gestapo prison *Rossauer Lände*;[22] Robert Aberbach was imprisoned in October 1938 and tortured at the same location for so-called *Rassenschande* (racial defilement);[23] Richard Wallach, lecturer

---

19 Saul Friedländer, *Nazi Germany and the Jews. The Years of Persecution 1933–1939*. New York: Harper Collins 1997, pp. 242–243.
20 A description of typical anti-Semitic measures in 1938 and 1939 is contained in Gerhard Botz, The Jews of Vienna from the *Anschluss* to the Holocaust, In: Herbert A. Strauss (ed.), *Hostages of Modernization. Studies on Modern Antisemitism 1870–1933/39. Austria – Hungary – Poland – Russia*. Berlin/New York: de Gruyter 1993, pp. 836–885.
21 Carl Zuckmayer's description of *Kristallnacht* in Vienna in his memoir *A Part of Myself: Portrait of an Epoch* has often been used to evoke the nightmare scenario that unfolded and still remains the most vivid portrayal of the atmosphere: "That night hell broke loose. The underworld opened its gates and vomited forth the lowest, filthiest, most horrible demons it contained. [...] People's faces vanished, were replaced by contorted masks: some of fear, some of cunning, some of wild, hate-filled triumph. In the course of my life I had seen something of untrammelled human instincts, of horror or panic. I had taken part in a dozen battles in the First World War, had experienced barrages, gassing, going over the top. I had witnessed the turmoil of the postwar era, the crushing of uprisings, street battles, meeting-hall brawls. I was present among the bystanders during the Hitler Putsch of 1923 in Munich. I saw the early period of Nazi rule in Berlin. But none of this was comparable to those days in Vienna." Translated by Richard and Clara Winston. New York: Carroll & Graf 1984, p. 50.
22 AdR-06/5.426/3, Ludvika Richter, secretary at the Hirsch factory, affidavit 28 January 1965. Other Gestapo prisoners were Rosa Kobler and Alice Kappeler, both imprisoned during the Pogroms on 10 November 1938 (AdR, Hilfsfonds Alt, no. 28.311, application sheet, 31 May 1957). It is noteworthy that even Ernst Sonnenschein, who had already been listed as a candidate for emigration to Ireland, was briefly imprisoned at *Rossauer Lände* in November 1938. See data in AdR, Neuer Hilfsfonds Grün (NHG), no. 31.940/3.
23 AdR, Hilfsfonds Alt, no. 18.274, application sheet Robert Aberbach, 5 April 1957. NAI, DJ 69/80/93, ICCR list of refugee candidates. Here Robert is described as a "clerk" and his brother as an "artist".

at the *Handelsakademie* (Business Academy) and former front line soldier in the Imperial Army, was badly injured during a raid on Jewish homes in these Pogrom days.[24] From late April 1938 non-Aryan pupils were progressively expelled from inter-religious secondary schools; at the end of the year the approximately 500 remaining non-Aryan secondary school pupils were crammed into a single school.[25] Outside school premises lurked further dangers. Herbert Karrach, then a 13-year-old Protestant pupil who had been removed from his *Gymnasium* in Esterhazygasse, remembers being "boxed and stoned when [he] emerged from [his new] school" in the 2nd district, to which he had to walk for 30 minutes from his flat in Fillgradergasse 15 (6th district).[26] Hans Kohlseisen, the same age as Herbert, also remembers acts of violence at his school in Waidhofen, where he was enrolled before his family's forced departure from Gmünd to Vienna.[27] A number of those who would later become refugees to Ireland were among the roughly 6,000 Viennese males who were confined in Dachau or other concentration camps for shorter or longer periods, to be released only if they could show evidence that they had been granted asylum in another country.[28]

The persecution also affected the victims' residential environments. Altogether, 44,000 of Vienna's 63,000 Jewish or non-Aryan flats were 'Aryanised'

---

24 Wallach was married to an Aryan wife and after his dismissal had to make a living for his wife and two children from a pension of 254 Reichsmark. AdR, Abgeltungsfonds, no. 8244, Gustav Pscholka affidavit, 4 November 1963. See also Gertrude Wallach (Richard's wife) to Reichskommissar Bürckel after the November Pogrom. In: *Niemals Vergessen. November-Pogrom 1938 in Wien*, Reader zum Antifaschistischen Rundgang am 11. November 2009 in Wien-Favoriten, http://rundgang.blogsport.de/images/11November_Broschuere_Einzeln.pdf, p. 31 [last accessed 4 September 2015].
25 See Gerhard Botz, Jews of Vienna. In: Strauss (ed.), *Hostages of Modernization*, p. 842.
26 Herbert Karrach entry in questionnaire, 30 November 2005. It was probably due to harassment such as this that Herbert and his mother temporarily moved to Herbert's grandparents' address in Streichergasse (3rd district). On Herbert's grandparents and his school experiences see also Herbert Karrach, The Karrach Family. In: Gisela Holfter (ed.), *The Irish Context of Kristallnacht. Refugees and Helpers*. Irish-German Studies. Vol. 8. Trier: Wissenschaftlicher Verlag 2014, pp. 44–45. His father may have remained at 15 Fillgradergasse until their emigration to Ireland. WSLA, residential register of Vienna.
27 Hans Kohlseisen, *Und ich reise immer noch - Die Geschichte des Hans Kohlseisen zwischen Gmünd, Stadlau und Irland*. Ed. Margarete Affenzeller and Gabriele Anderl. Vienna: Mandelbaum 2015, pp. 55, 59.
28 Two examples: Walter Storch, a Jewish advertising designer, had been in Dachau and Buchenwald from 27 May 1938 until 20 April 1939. He was then released under the obligation to document a land of exile by 23 July 1939. IKG Archives, Emigration Department, no. 24.882/11.047; NAI, DFA 202/361, ICCR application to DEA, undated. See also Brian Barton, *Northern Ireland in the Second World War*. Belfast: Ulster Historical Foundation 1995, p. 30. The same happened to Siegfried Dziewientnik. See undated DJ statement on him in NAI, DJ 69/80/356.

within one year, their former tenants forced to move to specially assigned 'Jewish houses' or to independently found new residences. Many moved to stay with relatives.[29] Some had to give up their flats due to unemployment, others through violence of local Nazis, or the hostile attitudes of neighbours. Still others saw to it that their children were sent to safe addresses or the houses of aid organisations which could be expected to send them abroad. We cannot be sure about the precise number of people expelled from their flats and houses before their departure to Ireland.[30] "Before I left Vienna we lost our home, our position, business and since October we had been living in the 'Emergency Huts', Wien XI," recalled Else Petersilka.[31] Josefa Stein, a medical student, also had to leave her flat in Vienna, Kegelgasse 14, in which she lived with her mother: "By 31 October 1938 she must have cleared her flat," noted an officer of the Welfare Department of the *Israelitische Kultusgemeinde* (IKG); but she was able to find lodgings with her aunt in nearby Hanselgasse 3, before she managed to emigrate to Ireland.[32] Friedrich and Robert Aberbach moved to Darwingasse in Leopoldstadt on 5 October, where they had to live in confined conditions together with their father, a former conductor of the Vienna *Rathaus* orchestra, for roughly two and a half months before their emigration.[33] In the light of such examples it does not seem accidental that 17 refugees to Ireland reported Leopoldstadt as their last Viennese address. The traditional Jewish quarter with its maze of narrow streets and densely packed house blocks had attracted thousands of Jews from the Eastern parts of the Empire since the last decades of the nineteenth century; parts of it were now turned into 'half-ghettoisised' areas.[34] Other parts of Leopoldstadt however seem to have remained untouched by residential Aryanisation. Richard Kappeler, the former head doctor of Vienna's public health insurance system, his wife Alice and her mother, singer Rosa Kobler, were allowed to remain in their large flat in bourgeois Thugutstrasse until the end of their time in Vienna; so were Karl Menkes, a former dentist living

---

[29] Brigitte Bailer-Galanda, Eva Blimlinger, Susanne Kowarc, "*Arisierung*" *und Rückstellung von Wohnungen in Wien*. In: Publications of Austrian Commission of Historians. Vol. 14. Vienna, Munich: Oldenbourg 2004, pp. 111–113.
[30] Their full number can be roughly gleaned from the incomplete records of the Viennese residential register for 1938–1939. On its evidence 25 emigrants to Ireland moved to a new residence under unknown circumstances after the *Anschluss*.
[31] NAI, DJ 69/80/316, Petersilka to DJ, February 1939.
[32] IKG Archives, Emigration Department, no. 51.205, Josefa Stein application sheet. Translated by authors; also NAI, DJ 69/80/240, application for certificate of identity, 25 July 1942.
[33] AdR, Hilfsfonds Alt, no. 18.274, Robert Aberbach, 5 April 1957; Paul Auerbach, Robert's son, to authors, 21 August 2010.
[34] Christine Klusacek and Kurt Stimmer, *Leopoldstadt*. Vienna: Kurt Mohl 1978, p. 158. See also Botz, Jews of Vienna. In: Strauss (ed.), *Hostages of Modernization*, p. 848.

in a house near the Prater (Venedigerau 3), and Stefan Lendt, former solicitor residing at Lilienbrunngasse 2.

Economics of the dispossessed

What all the 58 income earners among the Viennese emigrants to Ireland had in common was the collapse of their income within weeks of the *Anschluss*. By or around the Pogrom nights in November, most Jewish and non-Aryan employees in Vienna in higher and middle positions, the members of the professions (lawyers, doctors) and public services (teachers, professors, military), had lost their jobs.[35] Officially, all Jewish employment in the private sector was to be terminated by 30 June 1938, but many, like Georg Klaar's father, had already been dismissed before then, or had left Vienna. Already on 15 and 20 March orders had been issued by which "Jews" were not to be tolerated as public servants. Universities were purged of lecturers such as Wilhelm Winkler (see chapter 9) and Richard Wallach, while soldiers (or soldiers-to-be) such as Robert Aberbach, Alfred Schulhof, Ludwig Maria Friedrich (called Fritz) Hirsch and Stefan Feric were ousted from the Wehrmacht.[36] Older civil servants in higher positions were at least accorded small pensions, enabling them to maintain their families to some degree following dismissal.[37] How much money they had at their disposal

---

[35] For a detailed analysis see Alexander Mejstrik, Therese Garstenauer, Peter Melichar, Alexander Prenninger, Christa Putz, Christa Wadauer, *Berufsschädigungen in der nationalsozialistischen Neuordnung der Arbeit. Vom österreichischen Berufsleben 1934 zum völkischen Schaffen 1938–1940*. Publications of Austrian Commission of Historians. Vol. 16. Vienna, Munich: Oldenbourg 2004.

[36] Friedrich and Marie Hirsch's son, Catholic by birth, was removed from an officer's course of the Luftwaffe to which he had been "automatically transferred" after the *Anschluss*. Otto Glaser, Personal, Cultural and Academic Links. In: Paul Leifer and Eda Sagarra (eds), *Austrian-Irish Links through the Centuries*. Vienna: Diplomatic Academy 2002, p. 119. Robert Aberbach had already been dismissed on 1 April 1938. AdR, Hilfsfonds Alt, no. 18.274, 5 April 1957. Schulhof followed in July 1938. Schulhof email to authors, 1 December 2008; MAI, G2/0762. Feric was dismissed shortly before his emigration to Ireland in October 1938. T.W.T. Dillon to Feric, handwritten, 1 October 1938. Courtesy Nuala Feric, Stefan's widow, and her interview with authors, 16 November 2004.

[37] Pensions rarely reached 200 Reichsmark per month. Two of the few examples were Adolf Adler and Gerhard Harant's father Richard. Adler was forced to give up his position as a senior official of the *Reichspost* in March or April 1938 and was granted a pension of 200 Reichsmark. AdR, VA, no. 46.267. It seems that as a consequence he had to move from Paulinengasse, 18th district, to Hüttelberger Straße, 14th district, and in July 1939 very probably to another address shortly before his emigration to Ireland, where his son Kurt had already fled (see below). His Aryan wife and unemployed son back in Vienna received the pension. Richard Harant, his wife Valerie, and their sons Gerhard and Heinz could dispose of a monthly net income

depended on their savings and if there were other sources of income or funds not confiscated by the new Nazi rulers.[38] The relatively well-to-do among the future emigrants may have been able to continue a moderately satisfactory lifestyle, even if they could not freely access their savings in bank accounts. Losing one's job was however a very serious affair for someone such as Erwin Strunz who had family responsibilities, a limited income and no other financial resources: Erwin had been a secretary of the co-operative housing movement in Vienna but was dismissed after the workers' abortive uprising in February 1934.[39] From then on his family had to live on the meagre income Erwin received from a minor job which his father-in-law had provided for him with a Romanian oil company, and his Jewish wife's teaching at a municipal Montessori school. In March 1938, their second child was born, and the new situation after the *Anschluss* meant that his wife could not return to her former employment. Financially, their situation must have become extremely tight as welfare payments were very meagre.[40]

The strategic aim of such planned pauperisation was to urge Jews (as defined by the Nazis) into emigration and to dispossess the relatively well-to-do among them before allowing them to leave.[41] Basically, the freezing in April 1938 of the bank assets of Jewish persons, all of whom were automatically considered as would-be emigrants, meant that any extra expenses for goods, down to minor purchases, had to be sanctioned by the state *Devisenstellen* (Currency Agencies) which were thus given power of disposition over the household finances of all families waiting for a chance to emigrate. In the aftermath of the November Pogrom in Vienna, the dispossession of the expellees was completed. They were subjected to a variety

---

of 216 Reichsmark after Richard's dismissal. AdR, VA, no. 21.697. See also the case of Richard Wallach and his family, above.
38 Mejstrik et al., *Berufsschädigungen*, pp. 10–11. Ludwig Heinsheimer, for example, was dismissed from his position at a textile company with an annual income of sh. 22,750. He received a final compensation of 9,260 Reichsmark. AdR, VA, no. 20.942.
39 MAI, G2/1827; also AdR, NHG, no. 11.411/3, Strunz to E. Mahler, United Restitution Office London, 17 July 1963.
40 Ibid.; MAI, G2/1827, Strunz to International Trade Union Congress Amsterdam, 17 February 1940. See also Erwin Strunz, Memoir, June 1989, unpublished, pp. 17–19. We are grateful to Dr. Freda Mishan and Robert Strunz for providing this source. Strunz wrote three other memoirs: http://www.waterfordmuseum.ie/exhibit/web/Display/article/373/3/Ardmore_Memory_and_Story__Troubled_Times_Austrian_Refugees.html: The Austrian Refugees [last accessed 3 November 2014], first published in Ardmore Journal 1989; Lorna Siggins in *Irish Times*, "An Escape from Hell Remembered", 19 December 1988, which is based on Strunz's recollections; *My Connection with the Kagran Group in 1938*. Butler Papers Maidenhall, Kilkenny (undated, unplaced).
41 Our research in the Viennese Archive of the Republic has brought forth evidence that Emil and Robert Hirsch, Friedrich Wiedmann, Ludwig Heinsheimer, Richard Wallach, Ludwig Kende and Karl Menkes, among others, belonged to this category.

of confiscatory measures, implemented by the *Reichsbank*, the Viennese *Devisenstelle* and the *Finanzamt* (Revenue Office). By December 1938, a comprehensive dispossession system was in place. Would-be emigrants were, first, subjected to the *Reichsfluchtsteuer* (Reich Flight Tax) amounting to 25% of their capital property beyond 50,000 Reichsmark; second, a punitive wealth tax levied on all Jews and comprising 20% to 25% of remaining assets (*Judenvermögensabgabe*, 'Juva' which had to be paid in five instalments); third, a toll levied on all newly purchased goods the applicant was allowed to take abroad (*Dego* toll);[42] fourth, a tax on all capital transfers to the new country (which at the end of 1938 added up to 96% of the capital sum, making transfers virtually pointless). Moreover, wealthy Jews had to pay an *Auswandererabgabe* (Emigration Fee) of 20% of the *Reichsfluchtsteuer* to the residual, Gestapo-controlled Jewish communities. The amount of these payments, which normally ate up a person's whole fortune, was calculated on the basis of the compulsory Property Declarations of 26 April 1938 and its sequels. Jewellery had to be delivered to pawn shops and its value refunded at very low prices. The confiscation was concluded with a tax clearance, issued by the local *Finanzamt*, that allowed police stations to hand over the passport as evidence of the emigrant's citizenship, without which few countries were willing to open their doors.

Ribbons and zip fasteners

Only one person among Viennese refugees to Ireland did not lose his job before December 1938: Ernst Sonnenschein, leading executive of two ribbon enterprises owned by Emil Hirsch – one in Vienna (6th district, Millergasse 9) and the other in Göpfritz, Lower Austria.[43]

According to Nazi estimates, about 25 per cent of 146,000 Viennese businesses were in Jewish hands, and about 26,000 of these had remained Jewish even after the first wave of Aryanisation.[44] Among them were Hirsch's enterprises, which by 31 December 1937 had a capital value of 193,000 Austrian Schilling and employed 159 workers.[45] On the very day of the National Socialist annexation

---

42 The toll had to be paid to the *Deutsche Golddiskontbank (Dego)*.
43 In 1930, the workforce in Göpfritz comprised between 100 and 110 workers. Franz Glanz, *Gedenkbuch Göpfritz a.d.Wild*. Göpfritz: Private publication 1930, p. 27; WSLA, A 72/156, Chamber of Commerce Vienna to Commercial Court, 10 December 1929.
44 Botz, Jews of Vienna. In: Strauss, *Hostages of Modernization*, p. 844.
45 AdR-06/2.247, Hirsch to Vermögensverkehrsstelle (VVSt.), 20 August 1938. In the *Longford Yearbook* of 1940 the workforce was said to consist of 150 and the office staff of 30 persons.

Hirsch was asked for a "donation" of 14,000 Austrian Schilling;[46] he also had to accept that the premises in Göpfritz be leased to the Wehrmacht. The arrest of his son Robert in May was the final straw, and not, as his former rival alleged after the war, the only reason he resolved to emigrate.[47]

Image 1: Emil Hirsch's ribbon factory, Göpfritz.

Economic interest is likely to have come into play as well. Efforts to merge Hirsch's enterprise with the Vereinigte Bandfabriken AG dated back to 1934.[48] In 1938, however, that merger was completed by political diktat although the liquidators couched it in economic terms. Hirsch's enterprise, it was said, was to be fitted into existing structures of the Vereinigte Bandfabriken AG to secure synergistic cost advantages in a dwindling market. The liquidation process officially began on 1 June 1938 when the *Vermögensverkehrstelle* (Property Transfer Office), the controlling institution which had been founded on 18 May to secure a more regular and pseudo-legalistic approach to the 'de-judification' of the Austrian economy, handed over the Hirsch factory to a *kommissarischer Verwalter* (commissioned administrator), giving the Vereinigte Bandfabriken AG ample opportunities to

---

46 Franz Hirnschall, *Beiträge zur Geschichte von Göpfritz a.d.Wild*. Göpfritz: Buschek 1979, p. 64.
47 WSLA, VEAV, no. 387/1, Walther Schwarz, VBAG to Vienna *Bezirksamt* 6th district, 15 November 1946.
48 Ibid.

Image 2: Emil Hirsch and staff in Vienna.

inspect and control the books and production system of Hirsch's business. Talks on financial compensation also began in June. Sham negotiations were concluded at the end of August when Emil Hirsch handed in his formal application for a sale of his enterprise to the *Vermögensverkehrsstelle*. The text of a first agreement between the administrator and the new owners contained an interesting clause: compensation included 20 used looms and one half of the ribbon stocks, which Emil Hirsch could transfer to another country. By that time it was clear that Ireland was meant to be the recipient of the export goods. This accord had to be sanctioned by various institutions: the *Devisenstelle* Vienna, the Export Department of the *Vermögensverkehrsstelle*, the *Reichsbank* and the Gestapo; in addition, an auditing expert was asked to suggest a new sales price. The final text was signed on 13 December. The price of 180,000 Reichsmark, fixed by the *Vermögensverkehrsstelle*, went largely to pay Emil Hirsch's emigration costs.[49]

---

[49] See AdR-06/2.247, text of contract, 13 and 14 December 1938. Hirsch was forced to pay the transport costs to Spedition Eger Co., Vienna (17,203 RM), the *Reichsfluchtsteuer* (56,492 RM), export fees (55,985 RM), other taxes (3,927 RM), and a so-called Aryanisation fee (30,000 RM) from his frozen accounts. He was allowed to use 9,192 RM for necessary expenses in connection with the emigration process. AdR-06/2.247, list Dammer, 14 December 1938; Dammer to VVSt., 5 August 1941.

On 5 July 1938, the administrator pleaded to the Vienna Industrialists Association that the Jewish Ernst Sonnenschein was to be retained as he was deemed indispensable for the export business and the liquidation process.[50] There was opposition inside the National Socialist elite against such "rational" economic arguments, but the position of the *Vermögensverkehrsstelle* prevailed.[51] Thus Ernst Sonnenschein ended his employment only after the new owners had been formally installed in the enterprise, i.e. in December 1938.

George Clare remembers that he owed his rescue partly to his father's friendly relations with Richard Mautner, but also to "Herr Direktor" Walther Schwarz of the Vereinigte Bandfabriken AG, an "anti-Nazi",[52] as well as to Emil Hirsch, Seán Lemass and Marcus Witztum. The central idea of the plan was to enable Emil Hirsch to continue his production of ribbons in Ireland (rather than Australia, as had been the first intention).[53] On the Irish side, the plan was officially sanctioned by the Department of Industry and Commerce in late September 1938.[54] Emil Hirsch secured the cooperation of the Nazi authorities in Vienna by bribery; at the same time he obtained about £1,000 from Ernst Klaar (actually from Klaar's friend Mautner) as "starting capital" in his land of exile. In return, the Klaars and further employees were promised work and Irish visas. Schwarz's part was establishing the contact between Emil Hirsch and Ernst Klaar. The deal was completed in talks between Hirsch and Seán Lemass's envoy Marcus Witztum – who probably knew each other from prior commercial contacts between the Hirsch factory and Witztum's Modes Modernes Ltd in Galway (for Witztum's role in that enterprise see chapter 7).[55] In spite of the hurdles that Charles Bewley, the Irish envoy in Berlin, tried to erect, the visas were stamped into the passports and enabled Mrs Klaar and her son to reach Dublin via London.[56]

---

50 AdR-06/2.247, Dammer to Vienna Industrialists Association, 5 July 1938. On 17 October 1938, Dammer and the new owners reiterated their plea, arguing that Sonnenschein's expertise was an important factor in smoothing the transition to the new factory. Originally, Sonnenschein had been notified on 30 June 1938 that his dismissal would take effect on 30 September 1938. AdR-06/39.753.
51 Mejstrik et al., *Berufsschädigungen*, pp. 393–398.
52 Clare, *Last Waltz in Vienna*, p. 240.
53 Australia was temporarily considered as a destination as the Rosenbergs – Emil's wife Elsa was born a Rosenberg – were pursuing plans to emigrate there. Jennifer Kenny and Desmond Hirsch, granddaughter and grandson of Emil Hirsch, interview with authors, 9 November 2006. One Rosenberg, probably their nephew Paul, did emigrate to Australia. Emil Hirsch to Witztum, 3 May 1939. Courtesy Jenny Kenny.
54 NAI, TID 1207/1340, DI&C minute, 22 August 1939.
55 According to a list in AdR-06/2.247 the ribbon factory claimed 452.92 Reichsmark from Les Modes Modernes.
56 Clare, *Last Waltz in Vienna*, pp. 240–241, 270–280.

There is no reason to doubt the correctness of George Clare's memory, but some aspects need to be clarified. In his narrative the transfer of Hirsch's materials appears as an exceptional if not unique phenomenon. In fact, the Viennese authorities did not allow Emil Hirsch to ship "virtually a whole factory" abroad, as Clare assumes.[57] What Hirsch could take along to Ireland were the looms (valued at 5,200 Reichsmark by the authorities) and a stock of ribbons (32,000 Reichsmark) – negligible concessions from the perspective of Nazi officials and the Vereinigte Bandfabriken AG who explicitly sought to "liberate" the domestic market of ribbons from "superfluous machines and goods".[58] It therefore seems doubtful if from the confiscators' point of view the act, allegedly paid by "a fortune in bribes", was as exceptional a favour as Clare supposes. The liquidators, including Walther Schwarz, must have known that Emil Hirsch could not really profit from the 180,000 Reichsmark purchase price, which also makes clear why Emil Hirsch needed the £1,000 from his friend Mautner as part of the "starting capital" for his new factory in Ireland. He did however somehow manage to smuggle to Ireland a portion of his wealth.[59]

As we saw, the whole package negotiated by Witztum and Hirsch contained provisions for a grant of permits and visas to a group of employees in Hirsch's former factories. They were needed as experts, they belonged to Emil Hirsch's entourage or family, and they were Jewish, except for Catholic Alois Goebl, his wife Pauline and her sister Hedwig Lintner.[60] Ludwig Kende (and his wife Adolphine and their daughter Erika), Ernst Sonnenschein (and his wife Elisabeth), as well as Emil Hirsch himself (and his wife Elsa and son Robert) and Alois Goebl arrived in Ireland within a few days of each other in the second half of December 1938. Pauline Goebl and Hedwig Lintner followed later.[61] The Klaars had never

---

57 Clare, *Last Waltz in Vienna*, p. 241.
58 AdR-06/2.247, Vereinigte Bandfabriken AG to VVSt., 12 September 1938. Translated by authors.
59 It seems that before the *Anschluss* Hirsch had exchanged considerable sums into gold and diamonds which he managed to smuggle to Ireland. Jennifer Kenny and Desmond Hirsch, grandchildren of Emil Hirsch. Interview with authors, 9 November 2006.
60 The Goebls and Lintner voluntarily accompanied Hirsch to Longford. This is at least what the Goebl family asserts. Esther Goebl, Alois Goebl's daughter-in-law, interview with authors, 16 June 2008. All three were baptised Catholics, and very probably their parents too were Catholics. Courtesy Friedel Moll, town archivist of Zwettl.
61 Pauline Goebl repeatedly tried to join her husband in Ireland, but the Irish Legation in Berlin refused a visa (whether under instructions from Dublin could not be ascertained). She managed to come to Ireland only after Alois threatened to return to Austria if his wife was not granted the necessary papers. Emil Hirsch to DJ, 22 June 1939; for Hedwig Lintner see letter Emil Hirsch to Witztum, 3 May 1939. Courtesy Jenny Kenny. Lintner was registered in Ireland on 2 August 1939, one day before Pauline Goebl. NAI, DFA, 10/2/18 (Co. Longford).

considered Ireland as more than a first stage on the way to safety, but as it was, Georg stayed longer in neutral Ireland than originally intended.[62] Emil Hirsch's machinery and goods were transported by rail to a Belgian port and from there to Ireland.

The story of the "Ritsch" Reißverschluss-Fabrik Max Blaskopf, a zip fastener factory in Lindengasse 56, varies to some degree from the Hirsch case. In 1938, "Ritsch", one of Austria's leading enterprises in the trade, employed more than 93 people; its capital value was estimated at 206,000 Reichsmark.[63] Fritz Blaskopf was the only heir to his father's 50% share of "Ritsch" and an affiliated enterprise in Cracow, Poland; he was also a large shareholder of a clothes factory in Graz.[64] He and his wife Grete had left Graz (where both had gained a reputation as patrons of modern art) at the end of May (Grete) and June (Fritz) 1938, moving to his father's luxurious villa in Hietzing, Vienna. We know little about the new regime's interference in their lives in the weeks before Fritz Blaskopf came to Vienna, but the fact that a car was confiscated one day after the *Anschluss* and that Max Blaskopf had to nominate an Aryan general manager on 8 April 1938 indicates the kind of pressure he must have been under.[65] After the *Vermögensverkehrsstelle* had been established it became clear that "Ritsch" was among those Austrian enterprises that were to be 'Aryanised' by the *Österreichische Kontrollbank für Industrie und Handel* (a liquidation was seemingly never contemplated). The *Kontrollbank* had been given extra powers to accelerate the Aryanisation of bigger companies. Its function was to acquire those enterprises and act as a pseudo-neutral trustee before their sale to private applicants, the final decision still resting with the *Vermögensverkehrsstelle*. In August, it was evident that there were a lot of private Aryanisers competing for "Ritsch". At the same time, Fritz Blaskopf and his father were pressured into agreeing to the details of the sale. On 23 August, Max Blaskopf declared his formal willingness to sell his factory, and on 30 August he authorised his son to sign in his name.[66] Then, obviously in the midst of Witztum's negotiations over the Hirsch project, the Blaskopfs were offered an option to establish a new zip fastener factory in Ireland. The story of

---

[62] Stella and Ernst Klaar departed for London soon after their arrival in Ireland, while Georg was made to work as an interpreter in the Longford factory. Clare, *Last Waltz in Vienna*, p. 205, 234. In George Clare's account, this was a voluntary arrangement inside the family. See Clare, *Last Waltz in Vienna*, pp. 234–235. The possibility cannot be excluded however that the Irish refused to grant the elder Klaar a visa. See NAI, DJ 69/80/496, G. Boland to Seán McEntee, 29 February 1940.
[63] AdR-06/7.146, Volume 2, Max Blaskopf to VVSt., 23 August 1938; further data in AdR-06/33.790.
[64] Ibid.
[65] WSLA, A69/157a, Chamber of Industry and Commerce Vienna to Geissler, 31 July 1941.
[66] AdR-06/7.146, Volume II, Max Blaskopf to VVSt., 23 and 30 August 1938.

their emigration played out not only in Vienna, but also in Antwerp, Belgium, and was linked with the family story of the Witztums, earlier migrants to Ireland.

The Witztums had originated from the Galician village of Strzelbice near Stary Sambor.[67] Their parents Abraham and Feiga (or Fani) Witztum wore traditional Jewish clothes and spoke Yiddish, as did their eleven children; even in their later years Marcus, Arnold and Naftali – the three who later made it to Ireland – still conversed among themselves in either Yiddish or German.[68] The dates when they left Galicia cannot be precisely determined, but the fact that in Irish documents they were labelled Polish suggests that they must have emigrated after the inclusion of Galicia into the new Polish state, possibly after their home region had been swamped and looted by Polish troops.[69] Arnold first emigrated to Barcelona, then to Vienna (in 1928) and to Antwerp (in 1930), where Naftali (Nathan), the youngest, had already taken up residence.[70] In 1920, Marcus, seemingly the most adventurous of the three brothers, had gone to Argentina, one overseas destination favoured by emigrant *Galizianer*. Six years later he was even awarded Argentinian citizenship. But he retained his links with Vienna – it was here that he had married in 1923 and had become a father one year later – and with Antwerp, where he turned up in the late 1920s before going once again to Vienna for a few months in 1930.[71] In May 1932, he and Arnold came to Ireland (see chapter 7). Naftali followed in 1936.[72]

---

67 In 1910 Stary Sambor had 20,257 inhabitants, 5,418 of whom were Jews. See Alexander V. Prusin, *Nationalising a Borderland. War, Ethnicity, and Anti-Jewish Violence in East Galicia, 1914–1920*. Tuscaloosa: The University of Alabama Press 2005, p. 120; also www.jewishgen.org/yizkor/sambor/Sam XIX.hmtl.87k. [last accessed 20 September 2014]. The following family portrait is based on interview of Anna Adler with authors on 13 September 2005 in Dublin; cf. also MAI, G2/2631 and NAI, DJ 68/1/605; DEA 202/285, Archer to Walshe, 23 July 1940; Stadsarchief Antwerp email to authors, 12 July 2007 with copied attachments MA-VR, 215.168 and MA-VR, 237.789; WSLA, residential register of Vienna (entries on Witztum brothers).
68 Anna Adler interview with authors, 13 September 2005.
69 Prusin, *Nationalising a Borderland*, p. 102.
70 Arnold arrived in Antwerp on 16 June 1930. Stadsarchief Antwerp email to authors, 12 July 2007. See also DJ 68/1/605. The brothers could have witnessed the forced fusion of their homeland with the new Polish state and its short-lived Communist takeover soon after, which would explain Arnold Witztum's lifelong antipathy against Poland and Soviet Communism. Anna Adler interview with authors, 13 September 2005.
71 Cf. DJ 2013/50/259, Garda report, September 1937. For residential addresses see also WSLA, residential register of Vienna.
72 Naftali tried to come to Ireland in 1934, but in spite of DI&C recommendations the DJ refused a permit as it feared that he could not be repatriated to Belgium. See correspondence in NAI, DFA 2/770. He was given an entrance permit for Ireland only in 1936, very probably through Marcus's help. MAI, G2/2631 and NAI, DJ 68/1/605.

Chapter 2 "Those days in Vienna..."

The crisis over the Blaskopf enterprise must have come to Witztum's attention, possibly through Josef Kalman's links to his brother Saul who lived in the Belgian town. The talks between Blaskopf and Witztum had to take place in a great hurry, given the critical stage of the Aryanisation of "Ritsch" during the summer weeks of 1938.[73] As in the Hirsch case, the Blaskopfs were compensated with materials that helped them to establish a new factory in the new country (see chapter 7). The plan was also to assemble a group of experts for a new zip factory: one was Florian Oberer, the non-Jewish foreman whose services were urgently needed in the new enterprise,[74] the other Josef Kalman, the accountant in the old factory. To include Hans Lowy, an occasional musician and, according to his wife, "one of the leading dental technicians of Vienna",[75] was plainly a subterfuge. Lowy was married to Helena, a sister of Marcus Witztum's wife Deborah, both born in Galician Przemysl.[76] In other words, Witztum linked the Blaskopf project with a rescue operation for related members of the Galician exile communities in Vienna and Antwerp, a plan which the Blaskopfs were ready to accept under the circumstances and to which government officials, as in the Klaar case, awoke only later.[77] Hans and Helena Lowy had managed to reach Antwerp, where they were probably equipped with visas by the Irish Legation in Paris. The others, Fritz and Grete Blaskopf, Josef Kalman and Florian Oberer, went to Berlin to have visas stamped into their passports by the Irish Legation. They arrived in Ireland on 19 November 1938, leaving the Aryanisation process in Vienna incomplete.[78]

---

[73] See MAI, G2/0348, Grete Blaskopf to parents, undated, probably winter 1939.
[74] MAI, G2/2631, Helena Lowy to her father David Künstler, 3 January 1940.
[75] NAI, TID 1207/2165, Ellis to DI&C, 23 November 1946.
[76] See NAI, DFA 202/285, Archer to Walshe, 23 July 1940. Anna Adler interview with authors, 13 September 2005. Anna is adamant that Helena and Deborah were daughters of David Künstler. Cf. also data in MAI, G2/2631. In DJ 2013/50/318 it is stated however that Deborah was a daughter of one David Horowitz. The discrepancy could not be resolved.
[77] NAI, TID 1207/2165, minutes Bourke, 30 November 1946; DJ 69/80/496, G. Boland to MacEntee, 29 February 1940.
[78] On 17 November 1938, an administrator was appointed and commissioned to act in the name of Max Blaskopf. WSLA, Handelsgericht, A 69/157a. Formally, he sold Max Blaskopf's factory to the *Kontrollbank* which resold it to the new partners of a *Kommanditgesellschaft* (limited partnership) calling itself "Ritsch" Reissverschlussfabrik, Geissler, Höfermayer und Co. Both transactions were realised on the same day, 6 April 1939. The price for the first transaction was 140,550 Reichsmark, and for the second 222,000 Reichsmark. WSLA, A69/157a, Finanzlandesdirektion für Wien, Niederösterreich und Burgenland, 8 July 1948.

Getting out

The Hainbachs were a highly educated family, counting Alfred Adler, head of the opposition against Sigmund Freud's school of psychotherapy, among the guests in their flat in Vienna's 1st district.[79] From 1921 on, Heinrich Hainbach owned a small textile factory in Fockygasse 27 in the midst of a typical working-class part of Meidling (12th district). It barely supported the family during the economic crisis of the early 1930s until it stopped production in April 1937.[80] On 1 July 1938, Heinrich Hainbach was put into a concentration camp for four months. A few weeks later his sons Kurt, member of a Socialist youth organisation, and Fritz left Vienna: "Someone in the Zionist club had given me the name of a young farmer in an Austrian village at the Swiss border, who for money and jewellery helped people cross the Rhine over into Switzerland. A few weeks later my brother, Kurt, and I were on a train to Vorarlberg, Austria's westernmost province."[81] In Switzerland Kurt got transit visas to France and England through the support of a League of Nations Committee. Once in London, the British German Jewish Aid Committee provided a contact to the directors of a knitwear plant in Miltown Malbay, Co. Clare, who were looking for a suitable production manager from among the refugees. Upon the application of the company, the Irish Department of Industry and Commerce approved a visa, and on 19 January 1939 Kurt crossed over to Ireland.[82]

The Hainbach story, as remembered by Kurt's brother, exhibits some features that recur in other stories of passages from Vienna to Ireland. The Hainbachs' Irish option only crystallised in England. Moreover, seeking immediate rescue in Switzerland was not an accidental choice, given the country's geographical proximity, its humanitarian traditions and the many diplomatic and non-government societies which its neutral status had attracted. From October 1938, entering Switzerland became more difficult as passports were stamped with a "J" allowing Swiss border authorities to curb the immigration of unwanted Austrian and German Jews and non-Aryans.[83] Nevertheless, the country housed institutions that continued to be important for a number of refugees on their way to Ireland, as we will see.

---

79 Colin Hainbach, Kurt's son, interview with authors, 19 February 2009.
80 WSLA, A14/78, Commercial Court Vienna to Heinrich Hainbach, 16 May 1938; also Fred Hainbach, *1920 – 1950, A Memoir*. Unpublished, 2002, pp 5, 9. Courtesy Mark Hainbach.
81 Fred Hainbach, *1920 – 1950, A Memoir*, p. 9; also NAI, DJ 69/80/275, Kurt Hainbach to Miltown Malbay Gardai, 26 April 1939.
82 MAI, G2/0441; also DJ 69/80/275, Kurt Hainbach to Miltown Malbay Gardai, 26 April 1939.
83 See Simon Erlanger, *"Nur ein Durchgangsland". Arbeitslager und Interniertenheime für Flüchtlinge und Emigranten in der Schweiz 1940–1949*. Zurich: Chronos 2006, pp. 49–52.

The Hainbach brothers were not the only persons fleeing on their own initiative to neighbouring countries like Switzerland, Italy (see chapter 5) or Yugoslavia[84] in the weeks and months after the *Anschluss*. However, the difficulties of finding a receiving country, the arbitrariness of Nazi authorities, time pressure and the organisation and funding of passages were obstacles that many would have found insurmountable if they had not been supported by the various philanthropic societies, most of which had offices in the centre of Vienna. The assistance they offered must not be understood as a uniform process. By necessity, the helpers were to be found in religious societies, since, as in the Old *Reich*, all other political and social groups, parties and unions had been dissolved. As in the Klaar case, however, the refugees did not necessarily seek support from their own religious fraternity, but tended instead to look to a variety of cooperating agencies for assistance to bring them abroad. Sometimes they needed intermediary organisations to channel them to a country that lay on the periphery of European networks. The help they received was also different in kind, as we will see.

The Kagran Group

The organisation most engaged in refugee welfare was the Vienna branch of the Society of Friends (Quakers),[85] and it was to them the Klaar family immediately turned once their emigration had been approved – although they must have known that the *Israelitische Kultusgemeinde Wien* (IKG, Vienna Israelite Community) had its own emigration apparatus. Between 15 March 1938 and 28 August 1939, the Friends' Vienna staff, headed by the American activist Emma Cadbury, helped 2,408 persons to leave Austria, almost half of them emigrating to the United Kingdom.[86] The few who came to Ireland benefited considerably from the

---

84 One refugee to Yugoslavia, possibly the only one among later emigrants to Ireland, was Ignaz Schulz, a Jew who was married to a Catholic-Aryan wife. He had been dismissed from his job as a book-keeper in the 1st district and left Vienna on 10 September 1938 on his own initiative. He fled to Zagreb, where he stayed with a Catholic priest, and it was from there and through the offices of the local German and British Consulates and the Irish High Commissioner in London that he organised his flight to Ireland. His listing as an ICCR-approved candidate was made possible by two Irish Vincentian priests who assumed responsibility for his maintenance in Ireland. See diplomatic correspondence in NAI, DFA 202/281; also DJ 69/80/414, Mulcahy, Garda, to DJ, 28 August 1939.
85 Clare, *Last Waltz in Vienna*, pp. 203–204.
86 Hans A. Schmitt, *Quakers and Nazis. Inner Light in Outer Darkness*. Columbia and London: University of Missouri Press 1997, pp. 139–140.

mediation of Hubert Butler, a Southern Irish Protestant who happened to be a volunteer at the Vienna Centre in Singerstrasse in the critical months of 1938. His initiatives fortuitously coincided with a change in Irish refugee policy in November 1938 (see chapter 6).

The Quaker project that has drawn most attention took place at Kagran, a village at the northern rim of the Austrian capital. In May or June 1938 it had been selected as the site of an agricultural training camp in which 189 refugee candidates, among them 100 women and twelve children, were to be trained for an uncertain future in rural environments overseas, especially in South America.[87] Originally, the camp had been founded by the Vienna IKG as a Gestapo-supported parallel to a similar camp at nearby Stadlau.[88] At the request of the leaders of the group and "with the consent of the Jews", the Quakers applied to the Vienna SS to allow non-Aryans to take part in their project. "After a rather trying interview permission was granted."[89] The camp management lay jointly in the hands of the overseeing SA and Hubert Butler and Mary Campbell of the Quaker Centre. The group was composed of members from all walks of life:

> Seven academics, 98 artisans, nurses, teachers, merchants and clerks, plus housewives or people without training. There was one air pilot from the Austrian army, a goldsmith and a blacksmith, a cobbler, a hairdresser and a glove and umbrella maker. Apart from 13 pupils and 12 students they were all middle aged.[90]

They were now engaged in new activities such as "cutting trees, digging irritation trenches, making a road" under armed supervision.[91]

Group dynamics at Kagran had been tense from the beginning, but there was a crisis in September 1938 when a few persons, among them Erwin Strunz and his family, were offered a chance to go to England. Whether because this small group had been asked to embark on a political mission to London (in order to

---

[87] The number is recorded in Strunz's memorial text *My Connection with the Kagran Group in 1938*. Butler Papers Maidenhall, Kilkenny (undated, unplaced). Butler speaks of 200 persons. Hubert Butler, *The Children of Drancy*. Dublin: The Lilliput Press 1988, p. 204. Darton knows of 150 persons. Lawrence Darton, *An Account of the Friends' Committee for Refugees and Aliens, first known as the German Emergency Committee of the Society of Friends 1933–1950*. Friends Committee for Refugees and Aliens (ed.), typescript 1954, p. 48.
[88] Conditions at Stadlau are described in Kohlseisen, *Und ich reise immer noch*, pp. 62–66. Not only Hans Kohlseisen but also Herbert Karrach was made to spend some time at Stadlau. Herbert's name appears on a list of camp participants drafted by the Vienna branch of the Protestant Swedish Mission (see below). SIM to Dr Kauer, 27 September 1938. AEKÖ, SIM files.
[89] Mary Campbell, quoted in Darton, *An Account*, p. 48.
[90] Strunz, *My Connection*.
[91] Butler, *Children of Drancy*, p. 204.

"heighten public concern and persuade the Foreign Office to act", it was said[92]) or because "about 20 people" had autonomously planned to secede (Butler),[93] the London scheme led to an internal crisis and eventually to a split.[94] In late September 1938 Strunz and some other Kagraners, Friedrich, Marie and Ernst Hirsch, Kurt Adler, and possibly Kurt Stiegwardt among them, arrived in London.[95] Here, in consultations between the Quakers' German Emergency Committee, Butler and members of the small group, it was decided to transfer the Strunz family to Ireland, where Erwin was to recover from a "nervous breakdown" at Annagh-makerrig, the family estate of Butler's wife Peggy in Newbliss, Co. Monaghan.[96] The others continued their agricultural training at the *Bruderhof*, a pacifist, Christian-utopian and German-speaking community in Wiltshire.[97] The German Emergency Committee and Butler also had a hand in bringing another group of 15 persons to Ireland in December 1938. Most of them seem to have sought the help of the Quaker Centre in Singerstrasse, but it is unclear how many had taken part in the preparatory Kagran project.[98]

Protestant helpers

Some of the links established between Austrian refugees and Protestant aid organisations in Ireland went through Switzerland and Sweden. Already in August 1938, and, it seems, independently, Hans Morgenstern, a 22-year-old electrician,

---

92 Strunz, *My Connection*.
93 TCD Archives, Butler Papers, 10304/625/198/1, Butler to his wife Peggy, 2 August 1938.
94 Strunz (in *My Connection*) even speaks of a plot to have him murdered.
95 Strunz's passage was at least partially financed by the Hilfsbüro Gildemeester (see below). Butler, *Children of Drancy*, p. 205.
96 Strunz, *My Connection*. The estate belonged to the Guthrie family. Tony Guthrie, Director of the Old Vic in London, had become Hubert Butler's friend in the 1920s when both were studying at Oxford. In 1930, Butler had married Tony's sister Peggy.
97 At least Kurt Adler's and the Hirsch family's presence at the community farm at Ashton Keynes in Wiltshire can be documented. See NAI, DJ 68/1/624; TCD Archives, Butler Papers, 10304/625/130, Butler to his wife, undated (probably late September 1938); NAI, DJ 69/80/23, list of candidates, 1938. For the *Bruderhof* see http://www.ocotilloroad.com/geneal/background/UK_WIL_Ashton_Fields_Farm.html [last accessed 23 August 2015].
98 Their names: Gustav Beisser, Fritz Hirsch, Ernst Einäugler, Friedrich and Robert Aberbach, Peter and Hilda Gahr, Hilda's mother Friederike Goldstein, Richard and Alice Kappeler, Alice's mother Rosa Kobler, Paul Wessely and Ferdinand, Emilie and Herbert Karrach. For Herbert Karrach see footnote 88. Their names appear on various lists that were circulated in November and December 1938 between the DJ and the ICCR and its secretary, T.W.T. Dillon. See NAI, DJ 69/80/93.

had crossed the border to Switzerland. He was given provisional refuge in 'Haus Sonneblick' at Walzenhausen near Lake Constance, a home that had been founded by the Swiss "refugee pastor" Paul Vogt. Morgenstern's permit expired in 1939, and it was through the mediation of the Zurich-based Hebrew Christian Alliance for Switzerland that his case came to be taken up by the Irish Hebrew Christian Refugee Committee (see below).[99] Probably, the same partners helped Konrad Topper, described as a merchant, to come to Ireland in early 1939. He, too, had been housed at 'Haus Sonneblick'.[100] Alfred Schulhof relied on another Swiss help committee. Faced with a Gestapo ultimatum either to emigrate or to be deported to imprisonment in Vienna, he turned to a Lutheran pastor in his home town of Innsbruck, who liaised with the Zurich Subcommittee for Helping Non-Aryan Refugees under Pastor Gelpke. Its mediation led to a guarantee from the small Irish Presbyterian Refugee Committee.[101]

It seems however that Schulhof had also contacted the Vienna station of the Protestant Svenska Israelsmission (SIM), founded in 1920 to proselytise Viennese Jews.[102] Between 1933 and 1938, the station was headed by the emigrant German Pastor Friedrich Forell; after the *Anschluss* he was succeeded by Pastor Göde Hedenquist. Conrad Hoffmann (see chapter 1) became Hedenquist's most active partner outside the Swedish Mission. Rooted in the broad tradition of American Evangelism, Hoffmann was the second director of the Department of Jewish Evangelisation of the US Presbyterian Church, whose charity work had enabled many Jewish immigrants to reach the USA. In the 1930s, the Presbyterian evangelists shifted their attention to the harassed Jews in Europe, the refugee question becoming Hoffmann's domain.[103] He was appointed first Director of the International Missionary Committee on the Christian Approach to the Jews (IMCCAJ), based in New York and London under the umbrella of the International Missionary Council (IMC), a partner institution of the developing ecumenical World Council of Churches and its own refugee organisation.[104] The ultimate purpose

---

99 See DJ statement on Morgenstern in NAI, DJ 69/80/417.
100 RCBL, JC, 2 February 1939 (the first reference to his case); see also NAI, DFA 102/643.
101 Entries of Schulhof in questionnaire, 1 December 2008; also correspondence in NAI, DFA 202/184. On Gelpke see Eberhard Roehm and Jörg Thierfeder, *Juden, Christen, Deutsche*. 7 Volumes. Stuttgart: Calwer 1992–2007. Vol. 4, no. 1, p. 234.
102 See a note in NAI, DFA 202/184.
103 Hoffmann's reputation reached beyond Protestant churches. In 1935 while in Germany he tried to form an inter-denominational forum on the refugee question but without success. See P. L. Ludlow, The Refugee Problem in the 1930's. The Failures and Successes of Protestant Relief Programmes. In: *English Historical Review*. Vol. 90, no. 356 (1975), pp. 575–576.
104 The ecumenical World Council of Churches (WCC) was established only in 1948. In its infancy before the World War there existed only a rudimentary Provisional Committee (PC). At that time

of his transatlantic activities was still to convert Jews by methods officially to be based on "understanding, appreciation and good will".[105]

On his annual tours to European mission centres, Hoffmann, a fluent speaker of German, alerted various Protestant denominations in Europe to the predicament of Jews. When the refugee situation grew tense in 1938, Hoffmann spent some weeks in Vienna at the Swedish Mission House at Seegasse 16 in the 9th district. Failing to persuade Nazi authorities in Vienna to accept schemes for Protestant non-Aryans analogous to the Stadlau and Kagran projects,[106] Hedenquist's and Hoffmann's main concern in these August days was to organise emigration routes for the persecuted outside such collective emigration programmes. One result of these efforts is described in a SIM letter to Adolf Eichmann's Agency for Jewish Emigration of 30 May 1939: "Our links with Ireland have become increasingly cordial, which is why we are able to send more and more people there."[107] It was specifically due to Hoffmann that the race for safe places outside the *Reich* borders did not bypass Ireland. Each year he spent some weeks in Great Britain, during which he also visited the Church of Ireland's Jews Society (JS) and the Church Missionary Society (CMS), whose aims ran parallel to his own efforts.[108] Following his summer visit in Vienna

---

the IMC, focusing more on missionary work in non-European countries, was organisationally independent though working closely together with the PC. See Ökumenischer Rat der Kirchen, *Die zehn Aufbaujahre 1938–1948. Arbeitsbericht des Ökumenischen Rats der Kirchen über seine Aufbauzeit*. Amsterdam 1948, p. 12. Both the ICM and the PC had had their own international committees since the *Anschluss*. The PC's committee, based in London, was headed by the German pastor A. Freudenberg from Berlin; it collaborated closely with Hoffmann's IMCCAJ. His later successor as IMCCAJ director was his co-worker from their Vienna days at SIM, Göte Hedenquist.
105 Ariel Yaakov, *Evangelizing the Chosen People. Missions to the Jews in America, 1880–2000*. Chapel Hill and London: The University of North Carolina Press 2000, pp. 123–124; also Jonathan Kaplan: http://www.theologymatters.com/TMIssues/Kaplan01.pdf [last accessed 20 August 2014].
106 See AdR, Bürckel Material, no. 2.509.
107 AEKÖ, SIM files, SIM report to the Central Agency for Jewish Emigration, 30 May 1939. Translated by authors.
108 For Hoffmann's role in England and Ireland in the 1930s see RCBL, JS, 1 March 1934, 2 March 1937; *Church of Ireland Gazette*, 16 September 1938; IMC Archives, Geneva, minutes on the meeting of British members of IMCCAJ, 3 August 1939. A good example of the cooperation between Hoffmann's Presbyterian mission and the Church of Ireland missionary activities on the Continent is the friendly meeting between Martin Parsons and his wife Emily, at that time CMS representatives in Warsaw, and Hoffmann a few weeks before in the Polish capital. A text on the meeting from Parsons' point of view is in the latter's online autobiography http://www.parsonsfamily.co.uk/martin_autobiography/poland.php in chapter 7 ("To the Jews of Poland") [last accessed 1 December 2014]. During the war Parsons, then a Rector of St. Kevin's Church in Dublin, temporarily housed the two girls Ottilie Schwarz and Erica Fischer (see below). See chapter 8 of the above online text ("Settled in Ireland").

Hoffmann travelled to the United Kingdom for conferences with representatives of the Anglican Church to discuss the possibilities of assisting refugees. In that connection a visit to Dublin had been planned since May 1938[109] and took place between 23 and 27 September.[110] One success was the formation of the Church of Ireland's Hebrew Christian Refugee Committee (HCRC), to which Hedenquist's Swedish Mission station could frequently turn for help (see chapter 6).[111] Hoffmann also brought the names of Swedish Mission applicants to the committee's attention, which raised hopes that after a temporary stay in Ireland they could expect him to arrange access to America.[112] Out of a total of 1,256, 22 persons had emigrated to Ireland by the beginning of November 1939, a figure that ranks with Belgium's 23 or Sweden's 24 SIM-supported refugees.[113] Seegasse 16 was their common *point de depart*; it was here that Hedenquist and his staff, often in Hoffmann's presence, provided visas from the Irish Legation in Berlin, corresponded with the Dublin committee or intermediate Protestant agencies in Zurich, the offices of Hoffmann's IMCCAJ and the Hebrew Christian Alliance in London, or cooperated with other aid agencies such as the Quakers, the Catholics or the Aktion Gildemeester (see below).[114]

"We have placed individually twelve children in Christian host families in Ireland," the Swedish Mission announced on 13 February 1939.[115] Of these twelve

---

109 RCBL, JS, 5 May 1938.
110 *Church of Ireland Gazette*, 16 September 1938, announced his visit to his "many friends" for the days between 23 and 27 September. A speech was planned in Metropolitan Hall on 23 September. The minutes of his talks with members of the Jews Society could not be found. The visit is referred to in RCBL, JS, 15 September and 3 November 1938.
111 Ireland played a role in another of Hoffmann's projects. On 15 October 1938, he suggested the erection of fugitive camps in a number of countries, among them Ireland. Quoted in Eberhard Roehm and Jörg Thierfelder, *Juden, Christen, Deutsche*. Vol. 3, no. 1. Stuttgart: Calwer Verlag 1995, p. 260.
112 AEKÖ, SIM files. On 10 November 1939 SIM reported to the Central Agency for Jewish Emigration that Hoffmann "often visited the mission station to discuss affidavits and job opportunities" in the USA with emigration candidates. Translated by authors.
113 AEKÖ, SIM files.
114 How important the cooperation between all aid agencies in rescue operations had become is clearly expressed in a letter from SIM to the President of the Superior Church Council, Dr Kauer, on 13 February 1939. AEKÖ, SIM files. The involvement of the IMCCAJ office becomes evident from a remark of its secretary S. Barker when speaking about an expected Viennese refugee to Ireland, referring to the "good deal of the work which Dr Hoffmann left me to carry on", letter to Hedenquist 7 November 1938, AEKÖ, SIM files, file Austerlitz. The same letter also hints at the close links between the IMCCAJ office and the Hebrew Christian Alliance in London.
115 AEKÖ, SIM files, SIM to Dr. Kauer, 13 February 1939. Translated by authors.

we know the names of Georg and Eva Maria Pick (see chapter 1), Ottilie Schwarz,[116] Helene Deutsch,[117] Doris Brünn,[118] Karola Schönberg,[119] Kurt Schwarz,[120] and the half-sisters Erika and Lisa Fischer.[121] The intention was for these children to complete their education in Ireland and stay there until they could be reunited with their families in another country. In the case of Erika and Lisa Fischer, Erika had attended a secondary school for four years and then tried to qualify as a domestic and cook at a technical school in Vienna, while Lisa studied at a classical *Gymnasium,* until the new Nazi authorities put an end to both their school careers.[122] In the months after the *Anschluss* the family turned to the office at Seegasse 16, which placed the girls within its Girls' Club for further schooling. Their plan to emigrate as a family to Sweden failed for unknown reasons, but then a letter to Kathleen Huggard seemed to open up possibilities in Ireland.[123] On 21 November 1938, Lisa's father Georg Fischer was told by Swedish Mission officials that the two teenagers had been accepted by a school in Dublin, their maintenance guaranteed by the Hebrew Christian Refugee Committee.[124] The visa stamp of the Irish

---

116 Ottilie, a merchant's daughter, had attended a *Reformgymnasium* in Vienna. Her passage to Ireland was implemented through a guarantee of the Dublin Missionary Society, which was closely affiliated with the Church of Ireland, at 28 Molesworth Street, Dublin. See correspondence in NAI, DJ 69/80/103.
117 The daughter of a director of a printing firm who was to join her family in Stockholm after her time in Ireland. Her schooling finished, she had taken some technical courses in ladies' dressmaking before she appeared at the SIM station in Seegasse. Her passage to Ireland was also made possible through the promotion of the Missionary Society. NAI, DJ 69/80/102, Canon Cross to DJ, 26 October 1938.
118 Doris came from a once-wealthy family (her father was a former director of an insurance company who had died under unknown circumstances). The Irish Methodists and the ICCR secured her entry to Ireland until a hoped-for reunion with her mother in the USA. See NAI, DJ 69/80/362.
119 She had grown up in a "very respectable family", her father a former manager of a large factory who was now "reduced to extreme poverty". The parents and the Swedish Mission, whose Girls' Club she joined, saw to it that her name was put on a list of *Kindertransport* children to the UK. NAI, DJ 69/80/432.
120 The son of a dismissed and now impoverished worker, he also came to Ireland on a *Kindertransport*. NAI, DJ 69/80/413.
121 It is probable that the list also included children who were permitted entry to Ireland but did not actually come to the country. An example: Peter Friedländer, 16 years old and under the care of the Swedish Mission, was to learn English in Ireland before joining his father in the USA. He was granted a visa but his passage was cancelled for unknown reasons. See NAI, DJ 69/80/280.
122 See correspondence in AEKÖ, SIM files, Fischer file, no. 1277a.
123 See a reference to a letter of 26 October 1938 in the same file.
124 See NAI, DJ 69/80/99; AEKÖ, SIM files, no. 1277a, Hedenquist to Georg Fischer, 21 November 1938.

Legation in Berlin of 17 January 1939 sealed formalities, after which the two girls reached Ireland via England.[125]

Catholic attempts

On 29 July 1938, Wilhelm Winkler, dismissed Catholic professor at the University of Vienna, complained that "while different Jewish Organisations take care of their displaced people, there is nothing of the kind on our side".[126] Winkler was speaking of the slim chances Austrians had of fleeing to Ireland. Given the role of Catholicism in both countries, the number of Church-supported non-Aryan refugees to Ireland was low indeed. This is doubly surprising as Cardinal Innitzer, head of Austria's largest diocese by far, not only furthered initiatives to bring as many Catholic non-Aryans abroad as possible,[127] but also sent petitions to various cardinals in the USA and England and also to the Cardinal Primas of Ireland, Joseph MacRory, asking them to form refugee committees and urge their governments to issue permits for persecuted Austrians (see chapter 7). The Cardinal wished to "recommend for immigration only those of the Austrian converted Jews who offer sufficient security as to character and abilities",[128] a proviso which anticipated possible reservations about the rapid rise in the number of new converts in the weeks following the *Anschluss*.[129] Innitzer's plea seems to have met with no official response from Ireland. Apart from these initiatives, Cardinal Innitzer also intervened on behalf of individual candidates, including Stefan Feric. Originally Feric wanted Innitzer to help him emigrate to the USA.[130] After an appeal to

---

125 MAI, G2/0414.
126 NAI, DJ 69/80/274, Winkler to Lyon, UCD, 29 July 1938 (see also chapter 9).
127 Father Georg Bichlmaier was a central figure in these efforts. In 1936, he had presided over the Pauluswerk, which officially aimed to reconcile Christianity and Judaism but primarily tried to proselytise Austrian Jews. In 1938, he played a pivotal role in Innitzer's plans to rescue non-Aryan Catholics, until he was arrested by the Gestapo on 10 November 1938. See Bruce Pauley, Political Antisemitism in Interwar Vienna. In: Herbert A. Strauss (ed.), *Hostages of Modernization*. Vol. 3, no. 2. Berlin/New York: de Gruyter 1993, p. 820; also Erika Weinzierl, *Zu wenig Gerechte. Österreicher und Judenverfolgung 1938–1945*. Vienna: Styria 1997, pp. 103–105. Bichlmaier also considered Ireland as a destination for Austrian Catholics. His links to Dillon's UCD Committee for Refugees (see chapter 6) are evident, for example, from the case of Greta Praeger (NAI, DFA 202/48) – though for unknown reasons she did not come to Ireland.
128 DAV, Innitzer Material, box 17.
129 Between March and September 1938, 1,972 Jews converted to Christianity. Weinzierl, *Zu wenig Gerechte*, p. 103.
130 DAV, Innitzer's letters and recommendations, no. 1767, Innitzer to Cardinal Mundelen, Chicago, 17 June 1938 (in Latin).

his colleague in Chicago had failed, the Cardinal engaged the support of Professor T.W.T. Dillon, of the Medical and Pharmacological Department of University College Dublin, whom he probably knew from the latter's studies in Vienna in 1928 and 1929.[131] Due to Dillon's backing, Feric and Robert Steiner, another medical student, were provided with entry permits (see chapter 9).[132] In general, however, Dillon was painfully aware that Austrian Catholics had to look mainly to non-Catholic charity organisations at both the Austrian and Irish ends (see chapter 6), particularly the Quakers, whose inter-denominational approach had already made Kagran possible. The Friends were also involved in bringing Catholic children to Ireland – Hans Kohlseisen, Gerhard P. Friedjung and Otto Glaser[133] – and

---

[131] Theobald W.T. Dillon (1898–1946) was a member of a famous Irish political dynasty. He was the second son of Irish politician John Dillon. His younger brother was James Matthew Dillon, the only TD who urged the government to abandon neutrality and side with the Allies during the Second World War; later he became the leader of Fine Gael (1959–1965). In the 1930s another brother, Fr Matthew (Brian) Dillon, was Headmaster of Glenstal Abbey. For both see chapter 7. Due to health problems Theo Dillon spent several years in Switzerland after graduating in medicine in UCD in 1921. During his time in Vienna in 1928–1929 he studied modern methods of medicine, including psychotherapy. After returning to Dublin in 1929 he was appointed Professor of Therapeutics and Pharmacology in UCD. See Gerard Murphy, Theobald Wolfe Tone Dillon 1898–1946. In: *Studies: An Irish Quarterly Review*. Vol. 35, no. 138 (June 1946), pp. 145–152. While Dillon's work as a member of the Society of St Vincent de Paul is mentioned here, his work for the refugees is not.

[132] An Innitzer-Dillon communication in the Feric case could not be found. G2 officials however were sure that the Cardinal's recommendation had played a role in enabling Feric's passage to Ireland. MAI, G2/0409. A hand-written note by Dillon to Feric, 18 September 1938, shows that he had provided Feric with a practical suggestion about how to behave after landing in Cobh. In his possible absence he advised him on 1 October 1938 to contact Erich Serff whom he had previously helped (Dillon: "another non-Aryan German"; see chapter 4). Courtesy Nuala Feric. The correspondence highlights again Dillon's help for refugees, but no further evidence of his support in that case could be found. Robert Steiner arrived in Ireland in early September 1938 and then began studying at UCD. See NAI, DJ 69/80/182.

[133] Hans Kohlseisen: "On 10 December 1938, I was at the Westbahnhof together with hundreds of other children and said farewell to my family." Translated by authors. The *Kindertransport* reached England, from where a British Catholic organisation sent him to Ireland. Kohlseisen, Hans, *Und ich reise immer noch-Die Geschichte des Hans Kohlseisen zwischen Gmünd, Stadlau und Irland*, pp. 68, 70–74. NAI, DJ 69/80/449, ICCR to DJ, 30 June 1939. For the transport which enabled eleven-year-old Gerhard P. Friedjung to reach Ireland see NAI, DJ 69/80/559. 13-year-old Otto Glaser also had to leave behind his mother and his father, a high-ranking official in the Austrian Department of Finance who had been put into a concentration camp but was then able to find refuge in a convent in the Netherlands. In contrast to Kohlseisen and Friedjung he knew at least his destination in Ireland: Blackrock College, Co. Dublin, which had become known to the better-connected Glaser family through an Irish acquaintance in Vienna and her contacts to John Charles McQuaid, then President of Blackrock College and soon to become Archbishop of Dublin. McQuaid and the Catholic Council for Refugees (CCR), which had been founded in late May 1939

a young woman, Annemarie (called Mimi) Höfer. She had grown up in a family of former migrants from Moravia who had completely relinquished their Jewish heritage.[134] In 1938, however, no outward demonstration of 'Austrian-ness' and Catholicism could keep her father from being ousted as a senior railway official or herself, a law student, from being ejected from the University of Vienna.[135] The institutions she appealed to were the Swedish Mission station and the Quaker Centre. The Quakers first offered her a job in 1938 as a domestic in the south of England, but she thought that a "chambermaid's job would offer her no chance for the future",[136] so she remained at Seegasse 16, where she had come because of a long-time friendship between her family and one of the officials.[137] It was here that she tried to obtain qualifications for the kind of commercial and domestic jobs that were believed to be available to exiles in countries like Sweden.[138] Contact with a Catholic-Irish woman, Vida Lentaigne, who was looking for a governess for her 17-year-old daughter, was established through existing SIM links with Kathleen Huggard and Theo Dillon.[139] The Swedish Mission secured Höfer's visa in late April or early May 1939, and the Aktion Gildemeester seems to have covered the costs of her passage.[140] The Aktion was named after its founder, Dutchman Frank van Gheel Gildemeester, a philanthropist who was in favour with Austrian Hitlerites, due to his interventions on behalf of National Socialists when the movement was still illegal.[141] Operating through its Hilfsbüro in Vienna's Wollzeile 7, the Aktion became an important partner of all religious aid agencies. It was based on the idea of forcing wealthy Jews and non-Aryans to pay 10% of their capital

---

largely through Dillon's influence (see chapter 6), guaranteed Otto's board and schooling at the College, and this secured the consent of the ICCR. Otto Glaser entry in questionnaire, 15 June 2004 and email 10 June 2016. See also correspondence between Garda, DJ and ICCR in NAI, DJ 69/80/585.
134 Mimi Höfer was baptised in 1922. In 1930 her parents "Austrianised" the family's surname from the easily targetable Löw to the very common Höfer. Mimi Höfer's daughter Gloria Dobbin to Philip Jacob, 26 November 2004 (forwarded to authors).
135 AEKÖ, SIM files, no. 1500, Mimi Höfer CV, 28 November 1938; Liechtenstein note, 18 November 1938.
136 Gloria Dobbin to Philip Jacob (see footnote 134).
137 AEKÖ, SIM files, no. 1500, Göte Kronvall note, 6 June 1939.
138 AEKÖ, SIM files, no. 1500, Liechtenstein note, 18 November 1938.
139 AEKÖ, SIM files, no. 1500, Kronvall to Dillon, 14 February 1939; Hedenquist to Huggard, 16 March 1939.
140 AEKÖ, SIM files, no. 1500, Hedenquist to Aktion Gildemeester, 16 April 1939.
141 Jonny Moser, *Demographie der jüdischen Bevölkerung Österreichs 1938–1945*. Schriftenreihe des Dokumentationsarchivs des Österreichischen Widerstands (DÖW), Vol. 5. Vienna 1999, p. 115.

property into a fund to finance their own emigration and that of poorer Jews and non-Aryans. In most cases, Gildemeester officials helped to pay for tickets.[142]

It still took weeks until Annemarie Höfer arrived at Lentaigne's estate, Newtown House in Termonfeckin near Drogheda. Here, to her surprise, she met a number of other Catholic exiles from Austria who had been supported by Viennese Quakers (see chapter 7).[143]

... and the Jews?

Fifty-four Viennese Jews (including children) emigrated to Ireland in 1938 and 1939. Some were hired by Marcus Witztum's 'refugee factories' (see chapter 7), others left on their own or relied on non-Jewish helpers (like Walter Simon and Friedrich Lederer, who were able to use contacts between representatives of the Irish and European Labour movements to provide escape routes to Ireland).[144] Not even half of them turned for help to the *Israelitische Kultusgemeinde* (IKG) of Vienna. Between May 1938 and November 1939, the Emigration Agency of the IKG advised 18 would-be emigrants who had named Ireland as a destination.[145] What "counselling" meant in practice is hard to know. On the basis of available evidence it seems that the most valuable service of the IKG consisted of funding passages to Ireland. Among the petitioners were impoverished Josefa Stein[146] and

---

142 Other examples among emigrants to Ireland were Erwin Strunz, Anselm Horwitz and Richard Wallach (on Wallach, see correspondence in AdR, Abgeltungsfonds, nos. 8.244 and 11.032).
143 In the G2 list Germans in Ireland, Co. Dublin, in NAI, DFA 10/2/18, her registration date is recorded as 5 June 1939 (28 July 1939 in MAI, G2/0485).
144 Walter, son of a Jewish maths and physics professor at the University of Vienna, reached Ireland in summer 1938. Here he met Senator Patrick Hogan and other members of the Labour Party – whether by accident or prior arrangement with the leftist Simon family could not be ascertained. Hogan guaranteed Walter's subsistence and also provided a work permit, which allowed him to stay in Ireland. See correspondence in NAI, DJ 69/80/12; see also Claims Resolution Tribunal, case no. CV96-4849, re: Accounts of Otto Simon and Josef Simon. Friedrich Lederer had been dismissed by the former Austrian Post. In 1938, he fled to Switzerland, probably seeking the support of the Post & Telegraphs International in Bern. See MAI, G2/0567, G2 note of 6 January 1940. He owed his passage to Ireland to his acquaintance with Labour TD William Norton who guaranteed his maintenance and persuaded the ICCR to adopt his case, very probably with the support of the Dublin Jewish refugee committee. NAI, DJ minutes of 4 July 1939 and other correspondence in DJ 69/80/309; also NAI, DFA 202/358, hand-written undated note.
145 Moser, *Demographie*, pp. 56, 66.
146 The IKG paid for her flight to Dublin, where her cause had been adopted by Professor Ditchburn (see chapter 9) and a private helper (Mrs Mary Hanaghan). How Mrs Hanaghan's interest

Walter Storch.¹⁴⁷ The once-wealthy Menkes family,¹⁴⁸ and, surprisingly, Katharina Hein¹⁴⁹ and Lucie Kalman,¹⁵⁰ both belonging to the Witztum clientele, may also have applied for financial support. In all of the documented cases, the Irish government had provided visas following various contacts between persons in Vienna and Dublin, before applicants asked the IKG to contribute to travel costs.

Another Jewish emigrant to Ireland was Anselm Horwitz, the 17-year-old son of Hugo Th. Horwitz, renowned academic and author of various works on the history of technology.¹⁵¹ Debarred from continuing his school career, Anselm had improved his emigration chances by attending a training course for Jews in

---

had been attracted to Stein's case is unknown. See also IKG Archives, Emigration Department, no. 51.205.

147 IKG Archives, Emigration Department, no. 24.882/11.047. Walter had lived through unemployment, residential Aryanisation, and months of suffering in Dachau and Buchenwald before he reached Ireland through the initiative of the Chief Rabbi of Vienna and ensuing links to the Jewish refugee committee in Dublin. See correspondence in NAI, DJ 69/80/439; DFA 202/361.

148 Karl Menkes and his family had been recommended to the Jewish refugee committee in Dublin by the Chief Rabbi of Vienna and an Irish woman living in Vienna at the time. NAI, DJ 69/80/416, undated DJ statement on the Menkes family; *Visual History Archive*, John Menkes, 18 July 1996. The RFT of 11,063 Reichsmark indicates the family's relative wealth before the confiscation of their assets. AdR, VA 1.986; IKG Archives, Emigration Department, no. 28.500/0, only contains an index card, documenting at least that the Menkes had applied to the IKG.

149 Katharina had been dismissed as a model hat-maker in the early weeks after the *Anschluss*. She, too, had to give up her accommodation in the 1ˢᵗ district, Bäckerstrasse 14, and move to Leopoldstadt. Originally, she had sought to emigrate to Latin America, but when these plans failed she accepted Witztum's offer to work for the Galway factory. On 27 October 1938, she asked the IKG and the Hilfsbüro Gildemeester to fund her passage to Ireland, but it is unclear if either granted her petition. IKG Archives, Emigration Department, no. 15.939.

150 Josef Kalman first asked the IKG to finance and organise his emigration to an unspecified country. Then Witztum and Blaskopf offered an exit option, as we saw above. His wife however had to stay behind. Her financial means depleted and her emigration prospects hazy, she was forced to move to her parents' one-room flat in Brigittenaue and live off the "*Ausspeisungen*" (public meals) financed by the IKG. Marcus Witztum secured the Irish permit, but she asked the IKG to take over part of the cost of her passage. IKG Archives, Emigration Department, no. 36.692, 11 July 1938; no. 52.229/5122.

151 Hugo Theodor Horwitz (born in Vienna in 1882) had spent most of his professional life in Berlin and Vienna. In 1938, the family lived at Schönburgstrasse 48, 4ᵗʰ district. Lehmann Vienna directory 1938. Since 1939 the Gestapo had forced him and his wife Marianne (born in 1893) to move more than once to "Jew houses" (their last resort was 15 Ungargasse in the 3ʳᵈ district). Vienna City Library, Collection Hugo Theodor Horwitz. On his life see Thomas Brandstetter and Ulrich Troitzsch (eds), *Das Relais-Prinzip: Schriften zur Technikgeschichte*. Vienna: Löcker 2007.

tool-making ("it was said that there was great demand for mechanics and certain other trades").[152] This is how Anselm remembers his passage to Ireland:

> Mother had [...] received from her cousin most documents for my admission to the States, but the most vital – the "Affidavit" – was delayed. This made us – especially mother – worried because she felt that travel would become impossible for Jews once the fighting started. Then out of the blue I received a letter notifying me that a visa for Eire was waiting for me at the Irish Legation in Berlin, but it was only for me! Both my parents did not seem to care as long as I got out. As the visa was only valid for one month all three of us worked as frantically as we could. Then just before this document expired I made it to Hamburg and boarded the American Liner "President Harding" for Ireland. The American Consulate in Wien had agreed to send all the papers for my immigration to the USA to their Legation in Dublin where I could safely await its arrival. So I expected to be only a short time in Ireland. The ship left during the night and we were in Le Havre the following morning, but still in continental waters. I really did not feel safe and free until the next day when we anchored in Southampton. The third day we slowly approached the green hills surrounding Cobh in Ireland.[153]

His parents stayed behind in ever-worsening circumstances.[154]

---

152 Anselm's school life: After completing the *Mittelschule* he intended to join the Austrian Military as an officer cadet, which would pay his studies at a *Technische Hochschule* and help him to get an engineer's degree. Then he planned to join a tank regiment in the military. All this ended in March 1938. Anselm Horwitz email to authors, 15 January 2008. His Property Declaration of 27 June 1938 reveals that the adolescent minor – his father had to sign the document – owned substantial assets. AdR, VA 3.251. Whether this was due to a tactical transfer of family property cannot be safely said.
153 Anselm Horwitz email to authors, 15 January 2008. Horwitz does not remember who had directed the ICCR's attention to his case. Nor would he have known that his parents had engaged the Aktion Gildemeester to fund his passage to Ireland. This is indicated by a Gildemeester signature on document AdR-06, VA 3251.
154 On 28 November 1941, Hugo Theodor and Marianne Horwitz were deported to Minsk and murdered.

Chapter 3
The Jews of Komotau

Sprawling down the southern slopes of the *Erzgebirge* and spreading into the Northern Bohemian plain, Chomutov today is a thoroughly Czech town of about 50,000 inhabitants. Among them is a tiny German-speaking minority, whose forefathers, a German-speaking majority, had lived here since the Middle Ages. The Sudeten town had been part of the Austrian Empire – one reason why most of its inhabitants felt marooned and marginalised in Tomas Masaryk's Czechoslovakian state of the 1920s and 1930s.[1] The "urbicide" of German-Austrian Komotau did not begin in 1945, though; it began in 1938 with the exodus of 444 Jewish people from a town of a little more than 33,000 inhabitants in 1938, an event which in German, specifically Sudeten-German, historiography is rarely mentioned.

The founding of the synagogue in 1876, at the intersection of Weingasse and Hutergasse, reflected the growth and wealth of the Jewish community in Komotau.[2] Here the Jews of Komotau celebrated their religion, which most of them considered a private affair and the only thing that distinguished them from their non-Jewish German surroundings. Some descriptions of the period hint at the assimilationist and liberal bent of the community in which, as in other Sudeten towns, doctors, lawyers, employers, merchants, and office workers seem to have dominated.[3] In the minds of average Komotavians, Jews featured mostly as "shop owners".[4] But the building that most visibly represented the Jewish presence in the town was the hat factory of Reiniger and Co. on Hammerweg, at the southern periphery of the town.

---

1 Volker Zimmermann, *Die Sudetendeutschen im NS-Staat. Politik und Stimmung der Bevölkerung im Reichsgau Sudetenland (1938–1945)*. Essen: Klartext 1999, pp. 57–66.
2 Rudolf Wenisch and Emil Krakauer, Geschichte der Juden in Komotau. In: Hugo Gold (ed.), *Die Juden und Judengemeinden Böhmens in Vergangenheit und Gegenwart*. Brno/Prague: Jüdischer Buch und Kunstverlag 1934, pp. 302–304; Heimatkreis Komotau (ed.), *Komotau Yearbook*, no. 4, 1997, p. 82.
3 Jörg Osterloh, Judenverfolgung und "Arisierung" im Reichsgau Sudetenland. In: Monika Glettler, Lubomir Liptak and Alena Miskova (eds), *Geteilt, besetzt, beherrscht. Die Tschechoslowakei 1938–1945, Reichsgau Sudetenland, Protektorat Böhmen und Mähren, Slowakei*. Essen: Klartext 2004, p. 214; also Dorothea Rein (ed.), *Milena Jesenska, Alles ist Leben. Feuilletons und Reportagen 1919–1939*. Munich: btb Verlag 1999, p. 195. Milena Jesenska, Franz Kafka's love, had been writing for the Czech liberal weekly *Pritomnost* ("Present") since 1937.
4 An impressionistic testimony, which surely exaggerates the extent of Jewish property in Komotau: "Every second shop owner was a Jew and many people were in debt to them." Mrs S., interview with authors in Chomutov, 7 September 2005. Translated by authors.

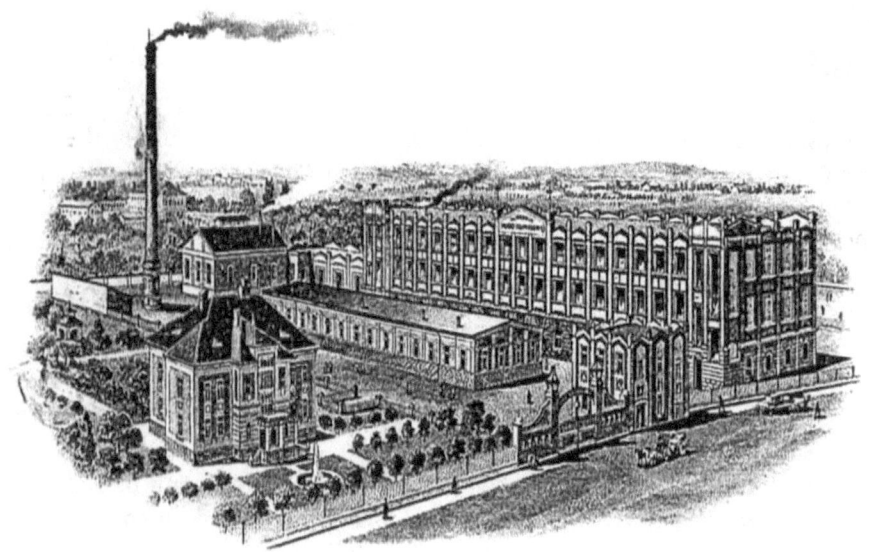

Image 1: Reiniger & Co. factory, Komotau.

The factory nowadays: two brick edifices, geometrical structures, large windows and typical architecture of the industrial age. There is no name or other symbolic reference to its industrial history from 1906 to 1938, nor any allusion to what happened to its former owners. Reiniger and Co. was a key enterprise in Sudetenland's traditional textile industry, sharing its strong export orientation and suffering when European textile markets slid into the depression at the end of the 1920s.[5] In the 1930s, its net profits still oscillated between 1,000,000 and 3,000,000 Czechoslovakian Crowns (CSK) p.a.[6] In 1937, Franz Schmolka was a personally liable partner in the firm, along with other members of the Schmolka and Reiniger families.[7] Reiniger and Co. gave work to roughly 400 people, among them many women and girls.[8] One side building housed Schmolka, Fischer and Co., an enterprise specialising in ladies' hats and employing a workforce of

---

[5] Gustav Otruba, Der Anteil der Juden am Wirtschaftsleben der böhmischen Länder seit dem Beginn der Industrialisierung. In: Ferdinand Seibt (ed.), *Die Juden in den böhmischen Ländern. Lectures to the Collegium Carolinum in Bad Wiessee from 27 to 29 November 1981*. Munich: Oldenbourg 1983, p. 257.
[6] Bundesarchiv (BA) Bayreuth, file Reiniger, no. 15.000.234, p. 32.
[7] Litomerice District archive, branch Most (Lit-Most), file group 149, box 1, list of partners in hat factory Chomutov.
[8] BA Bayreuth, no. 15.000.234, p. 36; file Grete Hansel, no. 12.215.726.

roughly 60 people. From 1934 onwards, Franz Schmolka was its sole owner.[9] The two factories were publicly labelled "Jewish" not only because the owners were Jews: Walter Porges had been a director of Reiniger and Co. from 1918 onwards and later an authorised signatory in the smaller enterprise,[10] Siegfried Klepper was a leading production manager in the main enterprise,[11] Fritz Konirsch, son of an established Jewish family that played an important role in the Jewish community, headed another of its production branches[12] and Ernst Glass ran the important export departments of both enterprises from the mid-1920s.[13]

The key figure, however, was Franz Schmolka. Son of a patent solicitor, Schmolka had grown up in Franz Kafka's well-to-do German-Jewish milieu of Prague. He attended the German *Volksschule*, the *Realschule*, the Prague *Handelsakademie* (Trade Academy), and the *Textilschule* (School of Textiles) in Brno before beginning an apprenticeship at Reiniger and Co. After his military service in World War I, he acquired one sixth of the company shares. In 1922, he co-founded the other factory together with four Jewish partners from Vienna.[14] He was the main executive in the enterprises, which profited from his numerous technological inventions.[15] Moreover, he owned a substantial shareholding in Jureifi, Yugoslavia's most important hat factory (see below), in Sisak/Croatia.[16] Schmolka's career was embedded in a family project. His two brothers Paul and Hans and his sisters Friederike and Grete were also partners of Reiniger and Co., his cousin Fred Schmolka (son of Franz's uncle Moritz) was a Jureifi director.[17] Friederike had married Josef Drechsler, co-owner of an important ceramic enterprise in Pilsen and factories in other towns.[18] In Komotau Schmolka was the "Jew who owned the hat factory", and the workers in it seem to have considered him

---

9 Compass, *Industrie und Handel, CSR*. 1925. Vienna: Compass Verlag 1925.
10 BA Bayreuth, file Erika Smolka, no. 15.006.823, p. 108; also file Walter Porges, no. 16.009.639, pp. 120–121.
11 Doorly, *Hidden Memories*, p. 77; also BA Bayreuth, files Klepper, nos. 16.009.633 and 16.009.634.
12 BA Bayreuth, file Gertrude Steiner (née Konirsch), no. 15.000.813.
13 BA Bayreuth, file Ernst Glass, no. 16.011.012, p. 23.
14 See data in Bezirksvertriebenenamt (BVA) Cologne, file Erika Smolka, no. 5683/53.
15 Litomerice District archive, branch Most (Lit-Most), file group 149, boxes 13, 15.
16 BA Bayreuth, file Fred and Steffka Schmolka, no. 16.009.899.
17 BA Bayreuth, no. 16.009.899, p. 5.
18 On the factory of the Brothers Drechsler in 14 Tylova see State archive Plzen, no. A 193: Firma Drechsler, Krajsky soud v Plzi A III, Oddeleni c. VI; see also an entry in the autobiography of Frantisek Basik, former accountant in the household of Franz Kafka's father in Prague. Frantisek Xaver Basik, *Padestat let, slozka 7d*. Unpublished 1940. Courtesy Jiri Nebesky.

and the other managers very social-minded "capitalists" who "cared for their workers".[19]

Now, in post-Communist times, with the facades of houses in midtown Chomutov restored to their historical charm, it can be gauged again how much their former Jewish tenants imagined they lived in the cultural centre of German Komotau. These houses were in streets with names like Kant-Straße, Schiller-Straße, Richard Wagner-Straße, all close to the two focal squares in the town's old quarter, the Marktplatz and the Deutschherrenplatz. Their occupants lived within walking distance of each other and the synagogue in Weingasse. Their German-ness was most clearly expressed by a bureaucratic act. In 1930, all citizens of Czechoslovakia were required to declare their ethnic loyalty, and all the Jewish Reiniger and Co. men and their wives entered "German" – which is remarkable as they could have entered "Jewish".[20] This need not necessarily have expressed a full integration into German-Komotau society. Politically at least, and unlike most other German Komotavians, they did not question their loyalties to the new successor state of the Habsburg monarchy. Membership in German *Vereine* (societies) would have been a safer indication of their integration into German-Komotau society, but little documentation has survived.[21] Nor can childhood memories of German people at present living in Chomutov or Ireland be

---

19 H. Platz, former Komotavian, interview with authors, 7 June 2005; Edelhard Kozarova, Chomutov, to authors, 1 October 2005. The mothers of both worked in the hat factory.
20 BVA Cologne, files Porges, Glass, Erika Smolka, Polesie, Konirsch, Klepper; also BA Bayreuth, no. 16.009.899. For the role of Zionists see Rudolf M. Wlaschek, *Juden in Böhmen. Beiträge zur Geschichte des europäischen Judentums im 19. und 20. Jahrhundert*. Munich: Oldenbourg 1997, p. 75; Wenisch and Krakauer, Geschichte der Juden in Komotau, p. 304.
21 Fritz Konirsch had joined the *Deutscher Turnverein* (gymnastics club) Komotau. BA Bayreuth, no. 15.000.813. Ernst Glass was a member of the German tennis club and of a separate German-Jewish, anti-Zionist *Turnverein*. BVA Cologne, nos. 6820 and 6821/53, Glass to BVA Cologne, 6 April 1959. Siegfried Klepper specified that he had joined the *Deutsche Heimatsöhne* (Sons of German Heimat). See BVA Cologne, no. 235/59. On the other hand we have Doris Segal as a witness that her father, born a Polish Jew, had been a member of the nationalist Czech sports movement Sokol. Doorly, *Hidden Memories*, p. 77. It is possible that her father's Polish background gave him a different perspective to the other native Komotavian Jews (possibly this remained so even in their Irish exile; see chapter 7). See also a letter written by him while in Ireland which touches on intra-Jewish tensions resulting from arrogant attitudes among assimilated Jews towards their Polish co-religionists. MAI, G2/1117, letter Klepper, undated (probably 1939). Any assessment of these statements should take into account, firstly, that these applicants for compensation in post-war West Germany would have strongly stressed their former German-ness, and, secondly, that some German *Vereine* in the Sudetenland excluded Jews. See Barbara Esser, *Sag beim Abschied leise Servus. Eine Liebe im Exil*. Vienna: Kremayr & Scheriau 2002, pp. 27–28.

fully trusted (such as the assurance that "before the Nazis came we did not know any difference between Jews and us").[22]

The year 1938 exposed the vulnerability of the Jews' status in the Sudetenland. The agitation of Konrad Henlein's Sudeten German Party, the Austrian *Anschluss*, the dispossession of Jews and their treatment in Vienna's streets were events alerting them as well as other threatened groups – Social Democrats, Communists, Czechs – to what would await them if Hitler tried to bring the German parts of Czechoslovakia "heim ins Reich" ("back to the *Reich*"). A military clash between the *Reich* and Czechoslovakia which seemed imminent in the May Crisis of 1938, the daily violence Konrad Henlein and his troopers perpetrated against their domestic opponents, seemingly supported by many German-speaking citizens, prompted them to look for means of escape.[23] In the spring and increasingly in the summer of 1938, Jews began to leave the Sudeten area.[24] Hitler's speech of 12 September on Greater Germany fanned the crisis, giving rise to further aggression against Jews and members of left-wing opposition parties. There was an easy exit option. They did not even have to cross frontiers to escape – they could just move to a different part of Czechoslovakia.

The children of former Reiniger and Co. workers relate that their parents did not know much about the flight of their factory bosses. "They disappeared overnight" is how they described the departure[25] – the fact itself could not really have astounded them as it tied in with their daily experience of anti-Semitic practice all over the Sudeten area. Franz Schmolka and Walter Porges as well as the Glass, Klepper and Konirsch families left on different days, depending probably on how severely they were harassed by the Henlein activists in the factory and on the availability of an escape route: Siegfried Klepper and his family departed on 11 September, Ernst Glass on 17 September; Fritz, Margarete and Gertrud Konirsch followed before the Munich Agreement. Franz Schmolka also left in September, as did Walter Porges.[26] However, the triumphant claim in the Nazi press that Komotau

---

22 Statement of a participant at a meeting of the authors with elderly Germans in Chomutov, 7 September 2005. See also Doris Segal's childhood memoir, similar in tone, in Doorly, *Hidden Memories*, p. 74.
23 Zimmermann, *Die Sudetendeutschen*, pp. 79–80; Rein (ed.), *Jesenska*, pp. 188–198.
24 Osterloh, *Judenverfolgung*, pp. 215–217; Wlaschek, *Juden in Böhmen*, p. 68; Zimmermann, *Die Sudetendeutschen*, pp. 388–389.
25 H. Platz interview with authors, 7 June 2005.
26 The dates have been drawn from their files at BA Bayreuth. On 6 November, 1958 Ernst Glass wrote a special report *"Über die Umstände meiner Flucht aus dem Sudetengebiet"* ("On the circumstances of my flight from the Sudeten area") in which he described how the followers of Henlein in the factory and Glass's co-tenants urged him to leave Komotau. BA Bayreuth,

was "Jew-free" before the Munich Agreement was not true.²⁷ Karl Polesie, co-owner of the law firm Fried and Polesie, Schmolka's legal adviser and president of the local Synagogue community, did not leave until 6 October, after Jews had been forbidden to practise law.²⁸ All of the above named were spared the ordeal of Komotau's Pogrom nights on 9 and 10 November, in the course of which the synagogue was pillaged and set on fire, and the remaining 21 Jews were driven across the border to the *"Rest-Tschechei"* by the Gestapo.²⁹ After the occupation of the Sudeten areas Franz Schmolka's factories were administered by a trustee and then handed over to provisional managers.³⁰

Among the refugees were also many members of the German Social Democratic Workers' Party (DSAP) and other Social Democrats exiled from the *Reich*. One was Franz Dielenz, technical master and *Betriebsrat* (shop steward) in Schmolka's hat factory, the last Social Democrat mayor of Eidlitz (today Údlice), a village near Komotau. He and his wife had grown up in classic Social Democrat settings: the trade union, the party and its many affiliated organisations. "We were like a big family," remembers one elderly lady who knew him very well.³¹ He fled on 8 October together with his wife and some other endangered party members, two days before the Wehrmacht occupied Komotau amid cheering crowds.³²

---

no. 16.011.012, p. 23. On Walter Porges see NAI, DJ 68/1/615. The exact date of Franz Schmolka's flight in September 1938 could not be found. It is even possible that he returned once or twice to Komotau after the Nazi takeover to try to clarify what would happen to the factory.

27 *Jewish Chronicle*, 23 September 1938.

28 BA Bayreuth, file Polesie, no. 16.009.790. The measure of despair among Komotau Jews is indicated by the fact that Polesie's law partner, Alois Fried (his wife's uncle), committed suicide on 26 October 1938. BA Bayreuth, no. 16.009.790.

29 On the Pogrom see Zimmermann, *Die Sudetendeutschen*, pp. 103, 107; *Komotau Yearbook* 1997, p. 82. In the emigrant press the events in Komotau were presented as the isolated work of SA troopers. See *Neue Weltbühne*, 23 February 1939. An eyewitness to the burning of the synagogue, however, reported that ordinary Komotavians had also taken part. Mrs S., interview with authors, 7 September 2005.

30 A provisional management was in place until Aryanisation was ordered by the regional authorities in Karlsbad. Franz Schmolka and his partners did not receive any compensation. Litomerice District archive, branch Most (Lit-Most), file group 149, box 6; BA Bayreuth, no. 15.000.234, pp. 101, 144.

31 Mrs A. Zakon, former neighbour of the Dielenzes in Eidlitz, interview with authors, 23 September 2005.

32 See especially his two CVs in BVA Cologne, file Dielenz, no. 53/2935, and BA Bayreuth, no. 15.006.426; also BA Bayreuth, Ost-Dokumentation, Group 11, I/13, J. Kölbl affidavit; also interview with Mrs A. Zakon, 23 September 2005.

It is questionable whether at the moment of leaving these Komotau citizens knew that in the near future they would find refuge at the Western periphery of Europe's most peripheral country.[33] However, it was not a novel idea to engage citizens from Bohemia and Moravia, two of the most developed regions of the Continent, for Irish industrialisation projects (and these Komotavians may have been aware of that). The expertise of individual specialists from both regions had been coveted on many occasions by various Irish semi-public industrial enterprises.[34] In this way, a total of 43 persons had come to Ireland between 1933 and 1938 (see chapter 6).[35] The most successful of the state companies, Irish Sugar Ltd, engaged a number of Czech specialists in its four factories.[36] A typical case was Vaclav Litera, a Czech Jewish expert from the Bohemian town of Podebrady. In 1937, the Department of Industry and Commerce permitted his employment as a master designer in an alcohol factory near Carrickmacross, Co. Monaghan. Litera, born in 1910, came to Ireland with his Jewish wife, Julia, looking for work.[37] Vaclav had been recommended to the Department of Industry and Commerce by a firm of contractors who had built the Skoda Works in Pilsen and sent experts for the construction of alcohol factories to Ireland.[38] The Department of Industry and Commerce gave Litera a three-year permit stipulating that after that time he should be replaced by an Irish national.[39]

The Czechoslovakian Republic (CSR) did not only export specialists to Ireland. Leitmeritz (today: Litomerice), a middle-sized town at the confluence

---

[33] Doris Segal, however, mentions in her memoir that her father had "heard about these factories [in Ireland] in Komotau". Doorly, *Hidden Memories*, p. 75.
[34] John Horgan, *Seán Lemass.The Enigmatic Patriot*. Dublin: Gill & Macmillan 1997, pp. 87–96. A comparison between the numbers of persons of Czechoslovakian descent in Ireland in 1926 (26) and 1936 (134) is also revealing. CSO data for the two years. Birthplaces. Tables 1A. For a personal recollection of the Czech presence in an Irish town see Norman Freeman, *Irish Times*, 2 June 2010.
[35] The number includes dependent family members. It is based on a G2 list of Czechoslovakians in Ireland. MAI, G2/x/0789.
[36] NAI, DFA 10/2/18: The 1943 G2 list of Germans in Ireland names at least four specialists from Czechoslovakia who were employed by the company in 1934; others followed in the pre-war years. Among them was Leo Cernik, resident in Ireland since 1935 and employed in the Tuam sugar factory. Given his later links to the Castlebar factory and Schmolka (see chapter 7), it is tempting to speculate whether he had directed the latter's attention to Ireland.
[37] Viktor Litera, their son, interview with authors, 17 November 2004.
[38] There were other former Skoda workers from Pilsen who found employment in Ireland. One of them was Fridolin Schrötter. See chapter 7.
[39] MAI, G2/1129, DI&C to Liam Archer, 16 May 1940.

of the Eger and Elbe, was the site of Plunder & Pollack Ltd – a "very important enterprise",[40] in fact the second largest producer of calf leather in Europe. It was situated off the town centre on the opposite side of the Elbe in the suburb of Mlekojody.[41] Its workforce, consisting normally of 250–300 men and women, had produced leather products including drive belts from the 1890s onwards.[42] In 1912, it was organised as a shareholder company, its capital value amounting to an average 6,000,000 CSK; 18,000 of the 30,000 shares were held by members of the Jewish Viennese Hitschmann family.[43] Karl and Irma Hitschmann, respectively from the Bohemian towns Ledeč and Divišov, had like many other Jewish families migrated to the metropolis in the early twentieth century. It was here that the family became prosperous as exporters of leather throughout Europe. Their three sons, Fritz, Paul and Albert, grew up in a roomy Leopoldstadt flat (Kleine Sperlgasse 1/33) and were raised on the classic fundamentals of German *Bildung*.[44] Though possessing a *Heimatschein* authenticating their Viennese citizenship, the Hitschmanns continued to cultivate links to their home region.[45] Their wealth enabled them to buy the majority of shares in the Leitmeritz enterprise. Until the mid-1930s, Plunder & Pollack Ltd was managed largely by Karl's brother Richard Hitschmann, who rented a huge flat in Lippertgasse in the centre of Leitmeritz, while Fritz and Albert Hitschmann used to spend their academic holidays doing practical work at Plunder & Pollack Ltd.[46] Moreover, their mother owned a luxurious flat in Kartäusergasse (Kartouska), Prague-Smichov.[47] In December 1935, after his university years, Fritz Hitschmann also moved to Leitmeritz (Grillparzerstraße 14) to take up management functions at the tannery.[48]

---

[40] The quotation is from BA Bayreuth, file Richard Hitschmann, no. 15.002.620, Gertrude Harriman affidavit, 1ˢᵗ May 1967. Translated by authors.
[41] NAI, DFA 202/27, British Consulate Prague to Foreign Office, 25 July 1939; Carlos Hitschman [sic], Albert Hitschmann's son, email to Richard Denny, 9 June 2008 (forwarded to authors).
[42] Compass, *CSR*, 1938. Vienna: Compass Verlag.
[43] The rest were split between three shareholder groups, one of them the Anglo-Czechoslovakian Bank. BA Bayreuth, 15.002.620, Paul Hitchman affidavit, 5 October 1965.
[44] BA Bayreuth, no. 15.007.030, questionnaire filled in by Hana Hitchman. They attended a *Volksschule* and a *Realgymnasium*, which was followed by an academic education at a practice-oriented university.
[45] The *Heimatschein* was issued by the district magistrate of Leopoldstadt on 31 January 1921. BA Bayreuth, no. 15.007.030.
[46] NAI, DFA 202/27, DI&C to DEA, 9 December 1938.
[47] The itemised account of the interiors betrays her grand-bourgeois living style. BA Bayreuth, 15.007.030.
[48] WSLA, residential register of Vienna.

In September 1937, he visited Ireland.⁴⁹ On the evidence of a family document it appears that the visit was the outcome of prior negotiations with representatives of the Department of Industry and Commerce, either Marcus Witztum or Seán Lemass.⁵⁰ The purpose of Fritz Hitschmann's visit to Carrick-on-Suir was to explore export opportunities for the English market. The final decision to settle in Ireland, however, was made under the shadow of the growing strength of Konrad Henlein's Sudeten German Party and the worsening situation in East Central Europe after November 1937.⁵¹ Plunder & Pollack Ltd sold parts of their leather stock to a Swiss shoe enterprise, which enabled them to fund the new Irish investment. Moreover, some machinery from the Leitmeritz factory was shipped to Ireland via Italy.⁵² On 14 April 1938, Pollack & Plunder Ireland Ltd was incorporated (see chapter 7).⁵³

The Hitschmann case demonstrated to the Irish side the opportunities which the European crisis in 1938 presented for Irish economic policy. By that time, Witztum and his committee had amassed detailed knowledge of the economic landscape of Bohemia and Moravia, especially of places like Pilsen, Leitmeritz, Prague, Brno – and Komotau. In October 1938, Edmond Claessens, co-owner of a Belgian textile firm, Mayo Senator John McEllin and Witztum toured the West of Ireland to inspect possible sites for another hat factory. In the same month they formally proposed a plan to construct a factory in Castlebar, County Mayo, with an investment of £100,000, to which Claessens contributed £25,000 to be spent on imported machines. It was also planned to engage about 30 "alien" experts as a start. After completion, the factory was to provide work to 400

---

49 G2 recorded 26 September 1937 as his date of arrival. See MAI G2/0484.
50 Carlos Hitschman, email to Richard Denny (forwarded to authors), 9 June 2008. Hitschman claims that Lemass had negotiated with the Hitschmanns; the term "representative", however, seems to point to Witztum, whose network must at least have laid the groundwork for the negotiations. It is not known how the link between the Hitschmanns and the Witztum network had developed, but it was possibly through the contacts the latter had already established with parts of the Czechoslovakian economy in 1934 (see above).
51 Carlos Hitschman, email to Richard Denny (forwarded to authors), 9 June 2008. Fears of an imminent crisis over the uneasy proximity between the German Sudetenland and the Nazi state had been strong within the Jewish-Sudeten population from 1933. Fritz Lönhardt, for example, owner of a tar factory in Türmitz (Czech: Trmice) near Aussig (see Esser, *Sag beim Abschied leise Servus*, pp. 32–35), in August 1938, shortly before the height of the Sudeten Crisis, sent his stepdaughter Ilse to Ireland, where she was employed as a governess by Sally Citron, a well-to-do proprietor of a textile shop in Dublin. Ibid., pp. 53–57.
52 Carlos Hitschman to Richard Denny (forwarded to authors), 9 June 2008; also Richard Denny to Michael Coady (forwarded to authors), 18 June 2008.
53 *Irish Times*, 21 January 1939.

people. On 22 October 1938, the Department of Industry and Commerce approved the plan, ignoring anti-Semitic objections and warnings from the Department of Justice and the Irish Plenipotentiary in Berlin.[54] At that time, Claessens and Witztum must have been aware of the critical status of the Komotau factory (one of Claessens' main rivals in the European textile market) and the predicament of its former managers. They were fully informed about the situation by Franz Schmolka himself, who went to Belgium after his stay in Prague.[55] The first details about the role the Komotau experts could play in the new factory were negotiated at three meetings between Schmolka and Claessens in Verviers and Dublin in January 1939.[56]

By that time, the other Komotavians, apart from Ernst Glass and Franz Dielenz and their families, had fled to Prague. In the capital they also met Hanus and Frantisek Drechsler, the two sons of Josef and Friederike Drechsler from Pilsen who decided to throw in their lot with their uncle and establish a new existence abroad.[57] They were admitted to Ireland as "dependants" of their father, whom Schmolka and Witztum wanted to present as "one of our experts" to the Department of Industry and Commerce and the Department of Justice. Josef Drechsler and his wife, however, were arrested at the German-Dutch border while their "dependent" sons safely reached Ireland via England.[58]

The negotiations and departmental discourse on the implementation of the Castlebar project took months. On 13 April 1939, the Department of Industry and Commerce issued work permits which, as in other cases, were based partly on lies born of necessity. As Doris Segal remembers, her father Siegfried Klepper was granted a visa after he "had to say that he was skilled in hat-making",[59] and others will also have posed as technical experts in order to be given a work permit. Meanwhile, Hitler's troops had occupied Prague and the Czech rump state. After that, Jewish emigration from the newly formed Protectorate hinged on a letter of permission from the Gestapo; a visa-free entry to Ireland was no longer possible,

---

54 NAI, DFA 202/285, Ferguson, DI&C to DJ, 21 June 1940. For Charles Bewley's position and the DJ's warnings see Keogh, *Jews in Twentieth-Century Ireland*, pp. 129–132.
55 BA Bayreuth, file Konirsch, no. 15.000.813, Landesausgleichsamt Bavaria to Ausgleichsamt Frankfurt/M., 12 February 1963. In Prague, Schmolka married Erika de Leon (née Wilka, of Marienbad). See NAI, DJ 68/1/748.
56 MAI, G2/1173.
57 MAI, G2/1082.
58 The Drechsler parents were sent to a concentration camp. See NAI, DJ 69/80/678, Witztum to DJ, 4 May 1939; also solicitors Little, O'hUadhaigh & Proud to DJ, 18 May 1940.
59 Doorly, *Hidden Memories*, p. 75.

either.⁶⁰ Applicants either had to contact the Irish Legation in Berlin or, in most cases, the British Passport Office in Prague to be given the transit visa to Britain and the visa to Ireland. The new situation also meant that the would-be refugees had to pay the various emigration fees and taxes from their frozen bank accounts as well as from the money they had managed to save since leaving Komotau. All of them reached Dublin after a train and boat passage across the Continent and through England between May and July 1939.⁶¹

Franz and Marie Dielenz's flight route was different. Their first stage was a little village near Rakonitz in inner Bohemia, where they were threatened with expulsion by the local police. As a witness reports, many fleeing Social Democrats were driven back to the Sudetenland across the new border but the two Dielenzes managed to continue their flight.⁶² They first went to Prague. Then they were moved to a refugee camp, Svetla near Sasava, between Prague and Brno, staying there from the beginning of November until the end of February 1939. On 28 February, Marie and Franz found themselves listed for an organised refugee transport that brought them first across Poland to Gdynia/ Gdingen on the Baltic Sea. They were then shipped to Oslo for temporary residence.⁶³ Dielenz profited from a selection system that lay in the hands of exiled Social Democrat leaders, who also provided the necessary Polish and Norwegian visas for loyal members of the party.⁶⁴ In Oslo, Dielenz was informed that the initiators of the Castlebar project wished to bring them to Ireland. He and his wife, as well as the other

---

60 Peter Heumos, *Die Emigration aus der Tschechoslowakei nach Westeuropa und den Nahen Osten 1938–1945. Politisch-soziale Struktur, Organisation und Asylbedingungen der tschechischen, jüdischen, deutschen und slowakischen Flüchtlinge während des Nationalsozialismus. Darstellung und Dokumentation*. Munich: Oldenbourg 1989, pp. 58, 69.
61 The Konirsch family arrived on 1 May, Walter Porges, the Polesie and Klepper families on 11 June 1939. See dates on their registration cards in their MAI, G2 files. Porges had already tried to flee on his own in April. He was arrested on the train at Mies, where he was detained in a local prison for one week and then in Gestapo custody in Prague. His passport was only returned to him after he had handed over his bank account. His exit from Prague was possibly arranged by the Czech Refugee Trust Fund, as far as this can be inferred from his later membership of the organisation. After his release he joined the Polesie and Klepper families on their passage to Ireland. BVA Cologne, no. 4296/53. Ernst Glass had already reached Dublin via Dover in February 1939. See MAI, G2/1101.
62 Mrs A. Zakon interview with authors, 23 September 2005.
63 For the story of Marie and Franz Dielenz's flight see Dielenz's two CVs in BA Bayreuth, no. 15.006.426 and BVA Cologne, no. 53/2935.
64 The Social Democrat responsible for listing the two Dielenzes on the refugee transport was Ernst Paul. See BVA Cologne, 53/2935, Franz Dielenz CV. On Paul's role see his *Aufzeichnungen und Erinnerungen*, Vol. 2. Boldt: Boppard am Rhein 1983. pp. 141, 151. See also NAI, DJ 68/1/623.

Komotau refugees still in Prague, were given Irish permits on 13 April 1939.[65] Franz and Marie Dielenz landed in Newcastle on 22 May. On the following day they were in Ireland.[66] The transfer of the Schmolka clan to Ireland was completed on 17 June 1939, when Fred Schmolka and his wife Steffka arrived from Sisak/Croatia. They, too, had been given permits on 13 April 1939 by the Irish government,[67] their passage to Ireland linked with expectations that parts of the machinery of Jureifi could be shipped to Castlebar.[68]

As indicated above, after the Munich Agreement the remaining territory of Czechoslovakia was by no means a safe place for Jews and anti-Nazis.[69] Moreover, a German takeover of the rump state looked imminent in the weeks and months after 30 September 1938. German-speaking inhabitants from Bohemia and Moravia had already applied for entry into Ireland before that date, and more applications followed as long as there was still enough time for preparing an emigration or realising capital transfers. Dublin was ready to authorise permits to some of them, if the Department of Industry and Commerce and the Department of Justice could be convinced that they served Irish purposes – whether as reputed academics such as Leo Pollak (see chapter 9), industrial managers and specialists like the Komotavians, or entrepreneurs such as the Kröner family from Brno.[70]

Albert Kröner and his parents, Leo and Beate Kröner, were 50% shareholders of a textile enterprise employing 900 workers, and part-owners of an electrical company with a workforce of 1,000.[71] Albert had already left Brno before the Munich Agreement. In September he arrived in Ireland, from where he seems to have arranged the safe passage of his parents and the family of their close rela-

---

[65] The DEA used the British diplomatic channel to reach the Dielenzes in Oslo. NAI, DFA 202/285, DEA telegram to London, 17 May 1939.
[66] MAI, G2/1081.
[67] MAI, G2/1170 and 1172.
[68] MAI, G2/1173, Schmolka to Ossias Teicher, 6 December 1939; Schmolka to Prodaska (Jureifi manager), 2 January 1940.
[69] In compliance, the Czechoslovakian government decided that the German-Jewish refugees had to leave by 15 January 1939. Frank Caestecker and Bob Moore, Comparative analysis. In: F. Caestecker and B. Moore (eds), *Refugees from Nazi Germany and the Liberal European States*. New York/Oxford: Berghahn Books 2010, p. 246.
[70] Other Moravian entrepreneurs invited to the country were Leopold Schenk, who was expected to help initiate the production of bicycle dynamos in Ireland (see MAI, G2/1163 and 1164), and Richard Jeric, who came in early June 1939 to help establish a glass factory. NAI, DJ 69/80/351 and DFA 202/166.
[71] Compass, *Industrielles Jahrbuch Protektorat*, 1939. Vienna: Compass Verlag 1939. In an Irish document the wife's first name is given as "Berta". MAI, G2/x/0789.

tives Paul and Katharina Ney to Ireland in October 1938 after riots had made their lives difficult in post-Munich Brno.[72] All of them were assigned to set up a textile enterprise in Ballina, Co. Mayo. The Kröners also persuaded Rudolf Schwarz, Albert's cousin and a leading manager of the Brno factory, and his wife Eva to follow them to Ireland by offering him a directorship at the new enterprise, a guaranteed annual income of £450 and the payment of passage costs.[73] Again, these contacts had been arranged within the Witztum network (see chapter 7).

---

[72] BA Bayreuth, no. 12.008.367, Katharina Ney affidavit, 29 December 1966. MAI, G2/1123, Albert Kröner CV, undated.
[73] MAI, G2/0771, Rudolf Schwarz letter, 21 March 1940.

Chapter 4
The German Pogrom and After

Georg Klaar and his mother were staying at Pension Lurie, a Jewish boarding house on Kurfürstendamm, impatiently waiting for the Irish visa that they had been told to collect at the Irish Embassy almost three months earlier. On 9 November 1938, they sat "in the small lounge, saw other Jewish guests pale-faced, whispering to each other, heard the crash and tinkle of breaking glass, muted by distance, from the streets ..." – *Kristallnacht* had "erupted".[1] Georg was only moderately shaken – after all it was only now that Old *Reich* Nazis had caught up with the level of brutality he had witnessed in Vienna in the past months.[2] To the other "pale-faced" guests, and to most other German Jews and non-Aryans, the events of that night still came as a shock despite what they had already been through in previous years. As in Vienna, *Kristallnacht* forced the issue and finally removed all justifications and prevarications that had kept them in their homeland. More damage was to come in the following days and weeks. All over the *Reich* 30,000 male and mostly wealthy Jews were deported to three concentration camps. About 6,000 of them were incarcerated in Sachsenhausen near Berlin, and only released if they could show an emigration address outside the German border; at the same time the financial agencies of the state were busy confiscating their remaining material assets (see chapter 2). The German Pogrom and its aftermath made emigration from the Old *Reich* spiral upwards, even towards a country such as Ireland that until then had seemed off the beaten emigrant track.[3] But now, in dire necessity and lacking alternatives, a number of would-be refugees from the Old *Reich* came to consider Ireland as a target country, if only a temporary one. At the same time, their opportunities improved when at the end of 1938 a new Irish refugee policy opened doors, at least in principle, to all shades of the persecuted.

---

1 George Clare, *Last Waltz in Vienna*, p. 269.
2 Dokumentationsarchiv des Österreichischen Widerstands (DÖW), George Clare, manuscript of a lecture on British views of Austria, unpublished 1988, p. 17.
3 General population figures document the trend. In November 1938, slightly fewer than 300,000 Jews lived in the Old *Reich*. The census of May 1939 recorded only 214,000, and by September 1939 the figure had sunk to 185,000. See Avraham Barkai, Vom Boykott zur 'Entjudung', p. 168. See also Friedländer, The Years of Persecution, pp. 316–317.

The capital and the concentration camp

Peter Wilhelm Brandenburg and his family owed their arrival in Ireland in 1939 to an Irish entrepreneur: Keith Eason, the owner of Eason & Son Ltd on Dublin's O'Connell Street.[4] Brandenburg had invented the first German filing system to bear economic fruit in the 1920s when mass-produced by Ferd. Ashelm, Berlin-Reinickendorf, with Brandenburg as a freelance company consultant. The opportunity to escape the persecution in Germany – his wife Else was Jewish,[5] and their son Rolf, who had joined a resistance group, was arrested and executed in 1938[6] – came in early 1939, when Peter met an agent of the Dublin enterprise at the Leipzig Fair. Eason & Son provided a work permit from the Department of Industry and Commerce. As it turned out, Brandenburg's position with his new firm provided leverage which led to a family reunion. In November 1939, his daughter Ruth was able to join them from Rotterdam.[7]

Altogether, at least 19 of the 49 Berliners who found exile in Ireland during the Nazi years had roots in the assimilationist Jewish milieux of Wilmersdorf, Charlottenburg or the western parts of Schöneberg. It was in these districts that relative wealth, mostly of a middle-class type, was concentrated, whereas Jewish shop owners, small businessmen, employees, workers and unemployed people tended to reside in the more central and eastern districts of the capital.[8] Six of these West Berliners lived through the horrors of the Pogrom:

---

4 MAI, G2/0014, G2 report, 30 July 1940. NAI, DJ 69/80/345, O'Catháin, DI&C, to DEA and DJ, 1 May 1939. The landing protocol at Harwich in the same file suggests that Brandenburg had seen Keith Eason on a short scouting visit to Dublin in the first week of April 1939. For the Brandenburgs' German background and their passage to Ireland see also the memoir of their grandson: Denis Henderson, On Ruth Henderson and her Parents, Peter and Else Brandenburg. In: Holfter (ed.), *Irish Context*, pp. 65–66.
5 The Brandenburgs had lived in the so-called Weiße Stadt ("White Town"), an avant-gardist settlement which was frequently targeted by Brownshirts in the late Weimar Republic. Under these circumstances they decided to buy a house in still-rural Rudow in 1932. Entschädigungsamt (EA) Berlin, no. 252.909, Brandenburg CV, 4 October 1954. Peter was repeatedly pressed by the Gestapo to divorce his wife ("...if I did not do so I would be responsible for the inescapable consequences"). Ibid. Translated by authors. See also data in DJ 68/1/808.
6 See Henderson, On Ruth Henderson and her Parents, p. 66.
7 MAI, G2/0358.
8 Gabriel Alexander, Die jüdische Bevölkerung Berlins in den ersten Jahrzehnten des 20. Jahrhunderts: Demographische und wirtschaftliche Entwicklungen. In: Reinhard Rürup (ed.), *Jüdische Geschichte in Berlin*. Berlin: Edition Hentrich 1995, pp. 121–122.

Image 1: Passport Else Brandenburg.

- the two adolescents Hans Forell (see chapter 1) and Robert Weil, youngest son of a pharmacist and his wife who had already sent three of their four children abroad,[9]

---

[9] For Robert Weil's life story following his departure from Berlin see Colin Walker, Robert Weil. In: Holfter (ed.), *German-speaking Exiles*, p. 133; Stephen Weil, "Children of Goethe": The Scheyer-Weil Family. In: Holfter (ed.), *Irish Context*, pp. 23–28.

- Curt Heilfron, who had been dismissed from his post as director at the German *Reichsbahn* in accordance with the Law of 7 April 1933 and could still live fairly well on his pension and proceeds from his rental properties,[10]
- David Nachmann, a resident of Meineckestrasse who had become Heinz and Alice Krotoschin's brother-in-law through his marriage into Alice's wealthy and established Jewish family (see chapter 1),[11]
- Else Samter, a widow who resided with her daughter in the Bavarian Quarter of western Schöneberg, a favourite milieu of Jewish artists, lawyers, doctors, etc., and then in her parents' house in Lichterfelde-Ost.[12]

It is difficult to assess precisely how much the boycotts and other abuses of the Nazi years had already eroded the upper-middle-class living standards of these families, but the decline may have been tolerable at least until 1938,[13] compared

---

10 Landesverwaltungsamt Berlin, Heilfron CV, 7 January 1957. The extent of their real estate holdings can be gauged from their post-war restitution claims. See Landesarchiv (LA) Berlin, nos. 203, 204/49, 302/49 and 303/49. The Heilfrons had been prescient enough to send their son and daughter to Britain in the mid-1930s. In London their daughter Marianne, who had been forbidden to continue her medical studies in Germany, married a former countryman, Rudi Neumann, son of an Irish-born mother, in August 1936. Rudi had to leave his position at the Berlin Charité hospital and qualified again in Scotland in early 1936. According to her recollections, Rudi and Marianne arrived in Dublin in early 1937, thanks also to the help of Cearbhall Ó Dálaigh, the later Irish president. Interviews Marianne Neuman with authors, 22 November 2002 and 12 July 2004. According to their G2 file, the Neumans arrived only in 1939 (MAI, G2/0650), though this is clearly wrong as Marianne applied in September 1938 for naturalisation, which was granted in February 1939 (see DJ68/1/363). See also her obituary in *Irish Times*, 5 April 2008. The application of Rudi's brother Kurt Neumann to visit his brother in 1939 was refused due to his involvement in "foreign political propaganda", NAI, DFA 202/152.
11 At an unknown time during or after the First World War David and his parents had left Podgorze, a settlement near Cracow on the right bank of the Vistula, and moved to Berlin. About their time in the capital we know nothing apart from his marriage into the Hettmann family. Brandenburgisches Landeshauptarchiv (BLHA), file Nachmann, A Rep. 092/27777; see also MAI, G2/0645.
12 Entries in Jewish directory Berlin 1931, 1933 and 1934. Wilhelmstrasse 13 was her last address in Germany. EA Berlin, no. 75.780; on her pre-emigration life see John Cooke, Charlotte and Hans Sachs. In: Holfter (ed.), *German-speaking Exiles*, p. 243, footnote 44.
13 This may be inferred from the sums the Nazis exacted from their frozen accounts before emigration. Curt Heilfron had to pay RFS 89,140 Reichsmark plus 17,863 Reichsmark for Charlotte Heilfron, *Juva* 106,209 Reichsmark (26,907 Reichsmark for her), *Dego* toll for both 1,300 Reichsmark, Jewish Community contribution 21,777 Reichsmark. Transfer losses were estimated after the war at 103,241 Deutsche Mark (DM). The figures have been calculated on the basis of sums recorded in LA Berlin, Wiedergutmachungsamt (WGA), no. 3245/50. Else Samter paid *Juva* 52,000 Reichsmark, RFS about 63,000 Reichsmark, *Dego* toll 815 Reichsmark, Jewish Community contribution 125,000 Reichsmark. See also Else Samter affidavit, 8 January 1954 and the correspondence between her and the US General Consulate, all in EA Berlin, no. 75.780; also data in MAI, G2/0720.

with the drop of income and status that men like Max Rund[14] or Bernhard Frankl,[15] both residing in Kreuzberg, suffered after 1933.

As before 1938, the combined effects of personal connections and the aid of charity societies brought these Berliners to Ireland. Relatively few turned to the societies at the start of their passage to Ireland. The majority had recourse to the support of daughters and sons, siblings, or other relatives who had gone into exile in the previous six years – an opportunity denied to the Viennese refugees, who found themselves in much more oppressive circumstances in the few months after the *Anschluss* (see chapter 2). In some cases, too, personal friends in England or Ireland approached aid organisations in those countries, as the following examples of emigrants to Ireland show.

Herbert Unger's passage to Ireland was influenced by his sister Ursula – she had gone to England as an au pair in 1936 and may even have "put him in touch with the Co-ordinating Committee in Ireland"[16] – but in his case, and that of his step uncle, Wolfgang Eisenstaedt, the necessary chain of assistance had already been formed by Catholic aid committees in Germany. At the beginning of 1939 would-be refugees could turn to two institutions within the Catholic Church of the Old *Reich:* the established St Raphaelsverein (RV) with offices in Hamburg and Berlin, and the Hilfswerk of the Berlin Episcopal Ordinariate, which had been established expressly to help Catholic non-Aryans flee the Nazi State. In total, however, the St Raphaelsverein enabled only two emigrants to reach Ireland up

---

[14] Max Rund had moved to Berlin from his birthplace Sandowitz, Upper Silesia, at an unknown date before the First World War. In 1933–1934 Max was still registered as an independent merchant living at Kaiserstrasse 11/12. See Berlin directory 1934. On 15 April 1934, he was even decorated with the Cross of Honour, an honorary medal that had been instigated by Hindenburg and was given in the name of another former soldier at the front – Adolf Hitler. The protection of the 'Hindenburg factor' ended in 1935, as we have seen earlier. In the following years Max and his wife Hedwig, then living at Neue Grünstrasse 31, could have made only a very modest living from his employment as a "commercial agent" for Rund und Sohn, a small family business run by his brother Rudolf. The biographical data are from EA Berlin, no. 310.868.

[15] In the 1920s, Bernhard had been well off, employed as an itinerant representative of various textile businesses in North East Germany. He was dismissed in May 1932 by his last employer who feared that in the Prussian province potential customers might look askance at any visible contact with a "Jew". EA Berlin, no. 301.262, Docter, solicitor, to EA Berlin, undated; also Docter to EA Berlin, 24 June 1957. After 1933 he, his wife and their two sons lived precariously on his irregular and short-term employments as chauffeur, mason, electrician and mechanic. NAI, DJ 69/80/472, undated statement on Bernhard Frankl.

[16] This at least is Klaus Unger's recollection. See Klaus Unger, On Herbert Unger. In: Holfter (ed.), *Irish Context*, p. 30. For Ursula's emigration to England see her statements in NAI, DFA 202/814.

Image 2: Herbert Unger in Berlin 1938.

to the beginning of April 1939 and the Hilfswerk another two up to 1941.[17] Herbert Unger had been educated at Siegfried Kawerau's progressive Köllnisches Gymnasium in Berlin-Neukölln. After his *Abitur* he looked for practical opportunities to develop his talent as a graphic designer. In constant danger due to his non-Aryan status and his leftist convictions and encouraged by the example of siblings, he decided to emigrate in view of the social and political conditions in Berlin before and especially after the Pogrom, hoping that Ireland would be only a transit stage to some yet undecided destination in the Americas.[18] Very probably, he was one of

---

[17] Diözesanarchiv Berlin (DAB), I/1–94, Annual report of Hilfswerk, 1 April 1939 to 30 March 1940. See also Jana Leichsenring, *Die katholische Kirche und "ihre Juden". Das Hilfswerk beim bischöflichen Ordinariat Berlin 1938–1945*. Berlin: Metropol 2007, p. 124. Jana Leichsenring, Die Auswanderungsunterstützung für katholische 'Nichtarier' und die Grenzen der Hilfe. Der St. Raphaelsverein in den Jahren 1938–1941. In: Susanne Heim, Beate Meyer and Francis Nicosia (eds), *"Wer bleibt opfert seine Jahre, vielleicht sein Leben". Deutsche Juden 1938–1941*. Hamburger Beiträge zur Geschichte der deutschen Juden, Vol. XXXVII. Göttingen: Wallstein, p. 101.

[18] Herbert's family history: After his father's death in 1920 his mother Elisabeth had returned from Pomerania to her native Berlin and later married Rudolf Eisenstaedt. In 1930, they moved from their Lichtenberg home to 56 Frankfurter Allee in Friedrichshain, a densely populated workers' district in pre-war Berlin. Klaus Unger interview with authors, 15 November 2006; also data in NAI, DJ 68/1/630. The *Abitur* certificate of 1935 records his talent as a "Reklamezeichner" (graphic designer). LA Berlin, A Rep. 020-09, no. 75. In the following years he was temporarily employed as an industrial designer in a steel factory. Klaus Unger, On Herbert Unger. In: Holfter (ed.), *Irish Context*, p. 30. In 1938 Herbert moved to a separate address in Friedrichshain (Boxhagener Strasse 93).

the two German Catholics whom the Berlin office of the St Raphaelsverein helped to emigrate through links reaching via London to Theo Dillon's UCD refugee committee.[19]

Throughout the 1920s, Wolfgang Eisenstaedt had been entrusted with the maintenance of residences in the capital; he also ran a small poultry farm in rural Schönschornstein outside the Brandenburg town of Erkner. In 1938, he was forced to sell it at a heavy loss.[20] After a failed attempt to flee to Holland, Eisenstaedt was arrested and deported to Dachau concentration camp, from which he was released in mid-February 1939 on a binding assurance that he would leave the country.[21] His exit was achieved through cooperation between the Hilfswerk, the Utrecht-based Catholic Refugee Committee (Katholiek Comite voor Vluchteline), the Catholic Committee for Refugees in Bloomsbury House, London, the newly established Irish Catholic Council for Refugees (CCR) and two Vincentian Irish priests.[22]

On the Protestant side, Conrad Hoffmann's personal initiatives had allowed three Berliners to reach Ireland before the Pogrom (see chapter 1). On 3 November 1938, the names of Georg and Eva Maria Pick and of Hans Forell appeared on the list of persons under the current or future tutelage of the Irish Hebrew Christian Refugee Committee (see chapter 6).[23] The case of the Protestant-Jewish family of Bernhard and Margarete Frankl, however, shows that, as in Vienna, help was sought outside the established Churches. "German Quakers in Berlin helped us to London," remembered Heinz Frankl, the elder son. They left on 22 June 1939, staying for roughly one month in London under the care of the Quakers' German Emergency Committee. Subsequently Irish Quakers persuaded the Irish

---

[19] Klaus Unger thinks it likely that in Germany his father was helped by a German Catholic organisation. Whether this was the Berlin branch of the St. Raphaelsverein, as we suppose, could not be confirmed. Klaus Unger interview, 15 November 2006. The role of Dillon's UCD committee in Unger's emigration is indicated in a list of ICCR candidates under the care of that committee. NAI, DJ 69/80/93 (17 December 1928).
[20] EA Berlin, no. 56.376, Eisenstaedt CV and affidavit, 7 December 1953.
[21] Eisenstaedt later noted that in Dachau he "was beaten by an SS man with plates and dishes. He beat at my right temple, and since that time my hearing has rapidly deteriorated; my hearing is severely impaired." Translated by authors. EA Berlin, no. 56.376, Eisenstaedt affidavit of 21 May 1952; DAB I/1–6, Hilfswerk to Father Quinn, Catholic Committee for Refugees from Germany, London, 23 May 1939.
[22] See correspondence in DAB I/1–6. The two Vincentians Father Patrick O'Gorman and Fra Henry O'Connor guaranteed Eisenstaedt's maintenance in the country. NAI, DJ 69/80/468, undated statement on Eisenstaedt; O'Gorman to de Valera, 12 December 1940. Both had already helped Ignaz Schulz to come to Ireland (see chapter 2).
[23] RCBL, JS, 3 November 1938.

Co-ordinating Committee for Refugees to adopt their case.[24] The London committee of the Quakers was also a vital link in Robert Weil's passage to Ireland. After it had been alerted to his case by his exiled elder sister, it successfully approached Newtown School in Co. Waterford to accept him as a boarder.[25]

Jewish aid societies came to help in later stages of the emigration process. Curt and Charlotte Heilfron first relied on their exiled son to realise a passage to London in mid-August 1939; for their trip to Dublin they called on their daughter Marianne and her husband to bring their case to the attention of the newly established Central Jewish Refugee Aid Committee and the Irish Co-ordinating Committee for Refugees.[26] Else Samter's transit to Ireland followed a similar pattern of relatives' and institutional help.[27] In the case of Max and Hedwig Rund it is unknown how their appeal came to the attention of the Jewish refugee committee and the Irish Co-ordinating Committee for Refugees.[28]

The only refugee to Ireland from Berlin who was imprisoned in Sachsenhausen in the days of the Pogrom was David L. Nachmann. In the concentra-

---

24 Society of Friends House Dublin (SFHD), MS Box 70/10, shelf 32c, Heinz Frankl to Society of Friends Ireland, 8 April 1998. See also NAI, DJ 69/80/472, undated statement on Bernhard Frankl.
25 NAI, DFA 202/44 and DJ 69/80/260, correspondence between Arnold Marsh, headmaster of Newtown School, the DJ and DEA. On 20 January 1939, Robert arrived in Waterford after he had been granted a visa by the British Consul in Berlin and spent a few days with his sister in London. His parents stayed behind. It was several days after his arrival that the ICCR and the DJ officially sanctioned his status in Eire. NAI, DJ 69/80/260, Duff to ICCR, 10 February 1939.
26 Charlotte Heilfron: "I had to ask our son-in-law to come to London to fetch us, because I was not able alone to bring him [Curt] over here. He had to stay in bed for months, was not nearly able to eat anything and lost more than forty pounds of his weight which had already decreased the last months at home." MAI, G2/0453, Charlotte Heilfron to Käte Honig, 20 September 1941. Once on Irish soil they received a guarantee from the Jewish refugee committee which enabled the ICCR to legalise their presence. See correspondence in NAI, DJ 69/80/538, especially Central Jewish Refugee Aid Committee (CJRAC) to ICCR, 7 September 1939; Duff, DJ, to Garda Siochana, 12 October 1939.
27 Else Samter first reached England with the assistance and hospitality of relatives living in London and Oxford. Then she crossed to Ireland, where her exiled sister and her husband, Professor Hans Sachs, had alerted the Dublin Jewish community to her case and guaranteed her maintenance in the country pending her hoped-for exit to the USA. For Hans Sachs and his wife see chapter 9. The role of the Jewish community in the Samter case is explicitly stated in NAI, DJ 69/80/573, Edwin Solomons to DJ, 25 October 1939; Duff to Solomons, 11 November 1939.
28 On 20 February 1939, they were sent a letter by ICCR Secretary Maud S. Slattery who told them that permission had been obtained to come to Ireland "for temporary refuge while you are finding a home in another country". EA Berlin, no. 310.868, Slattery to Max Rund, 20 February 1939. See also NAI, DJ 69/80/302, Duff to ICCR, 17 February 1939, Garda to DJ, 1 May 1939; DJ 69/80/93, minute from within DJ, 16 February 1939.

tion camp he may have become acquainted with Ernst W. Königsberger and Siegmund Liffmann (see below), and with two Silesians, Ernst Scheyer, from Liegnitz, and Erich J. Priebatsch, from Hirschberg. The initiative for the rescue of Ernst Scheyer and his wife came from their son, whom they had sent to England in 1935 and who by 1938 was studying medicine at Trinity College Dublin (see chapter 1).[29] In David Nachmann's case it came from his sister-in-law Alice and her husband Heinz Krotoschin (see chapter 1).[30] In November 1938, they asked a prominent member of the Dublin Jewish community to help Nachmann to safety in Ireland. Through his mediation the Jewish refugee committee took up Nachmann's case, and the Irish-Co-ordinating Committee for Refugees then became involved.[31] Erich Priebatsch, owner of a large textile shop in Hirschberg, a middle-sized town at the foot of the Silesian Riesengebirge, was saved through a private contact to an Irish family whose initiative led to the intervention of the two aid committees.[32] The effects of emigration to Ireland on the three families were quite different. The Scheyers had managed to send their daughter Renate to the same English school their son Heinz had attended between 1935 and 1937 and were finally reunited with her on Irish soil in 1940.[33] David Nachmann saw his two sons again, one in Ireland, the other in Canada (though him only after the war). His wife, however, perished in the *Shoa*.[34] The Priebatsch family also

---

[29] He had contacted Harris Tomkin, vice-chairman of the CJRAC, and Robert Ditchburn, leading representative of the ICCR (see chapters 6 and 9). See correspondence in NAI, 69/80/121. See Gisela Holfter, Ernst Scheyer. In: Holfter (ed.), *German-speaking Exiles*, p. 151.

[30] For their Irish life until 1938 see chapter 7.

[31] It was through links with Michael Noyk (see chapter 6) and the CJRAC that Nachmann's name was entered on a list of candidates approved by the ICCR. NAI, DJ 69/80/128, Noyk to DJ, 16 and 18 November 1938.

[32] On the night of 9th November, Priebatsch's shop in Hirschberg was ransacked; on the following day he was taken to Sachsenhausen. EA Berlin, no. 431.019, Priebatsch CV, 22 February 1954; copied document of his discharge from Sachsenhausen, 13 December 1938. In Dublin Mrs Eileen Davitt, whom the Priebatsch family had got to know on holidays, communicated with the Jewish refugee committee and its liaison officer to the ICCR, Professor Joshua Baker. NAI, DJ 69/80/191, Eileen Davitt to "John" (inside the DJ), 11 December 1938. MAI, G2/1680, G2 report 11 September 1940. See also correspondence in NAI, DFA 202/273. It was only in August 1939, however, that he was allowed to set foot on Irish soil for a supposedly short-term visit, his ultimate destination being Uruguay (squabbles with the finance authorities and the application for an extension of his permit, which was granted, may have caused the delay). NAI, DFA 202/273, Boland to Irish Legation, 27 May 1939, and further correspondence. See also correspondence in MAI, G2/1680.

[33] See Holfter, Ernst Scheyer. In: Holfter (ed.), *German-speaking Exiles*, p. 152.

[34] NAI, DJ 69/80/128, Robert Kahan, Secretary of the CJRAC, 18 July 1939, and other correspondence.

met disaster. Erich's wife Johanna and his daughter Eva-Agnes were murdered in 1944.[35]

Out of Saxony

Most German refugees to Ireland came, as one would expect, from industrial regions and urban centres with a relatively strong Jewish population, such as Saxony (administratively divided into the Free State Saxony and the Prussian province Saxony) and the northern Rhineland.[36] Altogether eight Saxon refugees ended up in Ireland after the November Pogrom – Siegmund and Rosa Liffmann, Julius Silber (Rosa's brother), Maria and Fritz Marckwald, all from Dresden; Ernst Wilhelm and Gertrud A. Königsberger from Burgstädt, a small town near Chemnitz; and Adolf Mündheim from Halle. All the men had occupied leading positions within important enterprises in this heavily industrial landscape between the large cities of Leipzig, Halle, Chemnitz and Dresden, and it was mostly through business and personal contacts, rather than through support from philanthropic societies, that they came to Ireland.

Victor Klemperer's diaries of the time reveal that Dresden, otherwise celebrated for its rich cultural heritage, had been at the forefront of the Nazification of Saxony. One of the SA's early targets in the city was the imposing department store of the Brothers Alsberg in the old town centre at the corner of Wilsdruffer Strasse and Schloss-Strasse.[37] The building was intimately connected with the emigration stories of Julius Silber and the two Liffmanns. They had a provincial background. Julius and Rosa were the children of a Jewish wine wholesaler in the Main River town of Kitzingen. Siegmund came from Odenkirchen, Lower

---

35 Later, Priebatsch was adamant that responsibility rested with the Irish government who had refused a permit for the family. EA Berlin, no. 431.019, Priebatsch CV, 22 February 1954. The ICCR argued that they had advocated Priebatsch's solitary passage to Ireland merely as a preliminary step to the emigration of the whole family. NAI, DJ 69/80/191, Ditchburn to Costigan, DJ, 14 December 1938. See also a G2 report of 11 September 1940, which suggests that the Irish officials had expected the whole family to come to Ireland. MAI, G2/1680.
36 The German background of refugees from outside these areas will be contextualised in other chapters.
37 It belonged to the Alsberg conglomerate of department stores that had been founded in the Rhineland in 1917 and rivalled two other Jewish concerns, Hermann Tietz and Karstadt, for sales and economic importance. In 1933, however sales figures sharply dropped. See www.das-neue-dresden.de/kaufhaus-alsberg.html [last accessed 15 November 2014]. For Alsberg see also an entry of 31 March 1933 in Victor Klemperer's diaries. Victor Klemperer, *I Shall Bear Witness: The Diaries of Victor Klemperer 1933–41*. London: Phoenix 1998, p. 12.

Rhineland, and moved to Dresden some time during the First World War, looking for social and economic advancement in the Saxon capital. The two men were linked through Rosa and Siegmund's marriage in 1919 and rose steadily in the Alsberg company hierarchy until 1933.[38] Julius emigrated to England at the beginning of 1934 and from there regularly came to Ireland (see chapter 8).[39] Siegmund, a father of two girls, stayed in Germany. An elected member of the Board of the Dresden Jewish Community from 1929 and a prominent Social Democrat – he was known as the "Red Boss"[40] – he had to endure various forms of persecution, beginning only a few weeks after 30 January 1933 and lasting until the end of 1938.[41] On 10 November 1938, Liffmann was deported to Sachsenhausen and released only on 18 December "on the explicit instruction" that he "had to leave Germany in the immediate future" and present himself to the Gestapo twice a week.[42] It was Julius Silber who initiated his sister's and brother-in-law's flight first to England and then to Ireland.[43] On 6 May 1939, Siegmund and Rosa Liff-

---

[38] By 1933, Siegmund Liffmann had attained the position of a liable partner and managing director at the Dresden branch. NLA, Nds. 110 W, Acc. 8/90, no. 267/21, ruling Entschädigungsamt (EA) Hildesheim (copied), undated. Silber had become sales director of the women's clothing sector and in the view of the Alsberg owners was the "strongest pillar in the enterprise". NLA, Nds. 110 W, Acc. 8/90, no. 339/6, Brothers Alsberg affidavit, 12 September 1933.

[39] NLA, Nds. 110 W, Acc. 8/90, no. 339/6, Julius Silber application sheet, 5 November 1956.

[40] Liffmann also belonged to the socially-engaged Fraternitas Lodge and had founded a holiday home for Alsberg employees and a soup kitchen for the poor. Lilli Ulbrich (Arbeitskreis Gedenkbuch der Gesellschaft für christlich-jüdische Zusammenarbeit) email to authors, 3 December 2006. NLA, Nds. 110 W, Acc. 8/90, no. 267/21, Wilhelm Sander, SPD member of the West German Parliament, affidavit, 5 November 1956.

[41] In the night of 21 March 1933, his house was ransacked by 50 SA and SS men. He was put into a police prison for one week after which he had to watch the siege of the Alsberg building by the SA on 1st April. He was then deported to a concentration camp near Forst/Lausitz which he could leave only to take part in "negotiations" on the Aryanisation of the department store (in August 1933 Alsberg passed into Aryan hands). These traumatic events caused a nervous breakdown and led the Liffmanns to decide to move to Leipzig, whose larger Jewish community promised a safer existence than in Dresden. But Liffmann's attempts to launch and develop a clothes shop failed ("due to the increasing agitation I could not earn a livelihood"). NLA, Nds. 110 W, Acc. 8/90, no. 267/21, Dr A. Strauss affidavit, 24 November 1957. All quotations translated by authors. In 1935, they were forced to send their two daughters to the local Jewish school to escape their difficulties at the Max Klinger School, Leipzig. See http://geschichte.max-klinger-schule.de/ursula-liffmann/ [last accessed 18 November 2015].

[42] The quotation is Siegmund Liffmann's. Translated by authors. It is contained in NLA, Nds. 110 W, Acc. 8/90, no. 267/21, Dr A. Strauss affidavit, 24 November 1957.

[43] "My father was well connected with influential people in Dublin who would have helped him to achieve this." Sir Stephen Silver, Silber's 1944-born son, email to authors, 10 January 2010. The "influential people" Sir Stephen referred to were very probably Robert Briscoe, Kurt Ticher

mann landed at Croydon with an English transit visa; when this visa expired he, but not his wife, boarded a ship to Dublin.⁴⁴ The Liffmanns, at Dresden's Liebigstrasse 30, lived only a few houses away from Fritz and Maria Marckwald in this upper middle-class part of old Dresden. Fritz, second son of a grand bourgeois Lutheran family, had risen to the position of regional sales manager of Villeroy & Boch, one of Germany's leading ceramics companies.⁴⁵ He was dismissed on 19 October 1937.⁴⁶ It is not clear when the Marckwalds began to plan their emigration nor how they organised it from their Dresden home in the following year. In Ireland, Quakers took care of them. The Quakers' influence may also have promoted their acceptance by the Irish Co-ordinating Committee for Refugees and the implementation of Fritz Marckwald's plan to train "for an agricultural career in a non-European country".⁴⁷ They came to the country robbed of nearly all their material possessions.⁴⁸

Burgstädt was the site of Wünsch and Co., where several hundred factory and home workers produced gloves and other textiles. One of the two partners and a senior executive in the enterprise was Ernst Königsberger.⁴⁹ Ernst and his wife Gertrud had been raised as Protestants and German patriots by their still

---

and members of the Jewish refugee committee (see chapter 8). The ICCR put him on its list of accepted asylum seekers, and on 19 January 1939 the DJ issued a temporary permit. MAI, G2/0582, hand-written summary of Liffmann's emigration, probably of 21 July 1942.

44 MAI, G2/0582.

45 NLA, Nds. 110 W, Acc. 31/99, Villeroy & Boch affidavit, 23 November 1937.

46 NLA, Nds. 110 W, Acc. 31/99, Fritz Marckwald CV, 10 October 1956. Marckwald may have been shielded against prior harassments by his membership of the right-wing, and partly anti-Semitic, Deutschnationaler Handlungsgehilfen-Verband (German National Union of Employees). He was accepted in the ranks of the Deutsche Arbeitsfront (DAF), the Nazi agency controlling Germany's economic and social life, until it was discovered that he could not provide his *Ariernachweis* (certificate of Aryan status), leading to his automatic exclusion from the DAF and dismissal from his job.

47 NLA, Nds. 110 W, Acc. 31/99, Marckwald CV, 10 October 1956. Translated by authors. For the role of Quakers in the Marckwalds' Irish life see chapter 7.

48 They managed to keep a remnant of their savings. The figures of their losses: jewellery (estimated at about 5,000 RM), sale of antique furniture at prices that did not cover the freight costs of their remaining furniture, *Dego* toll 270 Reichsmark, tickets 250 Reichsmark, transport costs 450 Reichsmark; the considerable RFS and *Juva* sums are unknown. The value of their transfer losses was fixed at more than 31,000 DM after the war. NLA, Nds. 110 W, Acc. 31/99, Marckwald CV, 10 October 1956; Devisenstelle Dresden to Fritz Marckwald, 25 March 1939; Fritz and Maria Marckwald affidavit, 3 January 1961 and Louise Gurazde, affidavit, 30 May 1958.

49 NLA, Nds. 110 W, Acc. 8/9, no. 241/22, Schade, solicitor, to Entschädigungsamt (EA) Cologne, 20 May 1957 and 8 July 1958.

practising Jewish parents.[50] Though realising that under the new regime they were turned into "Jews" of sorts, they entertained hopes that by making minor concessions they would be able somehow to survive.[51] In spite of all tribulations – in 1936 they had to send their son Peter to a grammar school in Newport, England[52] – Königsberger managed to secure his position in the company and his family's livelihood until 1938. On 4 April 1938, however, he was ousted as an executive, a few weeks later he lost his position as a silent partner in the enterprise, and on 11 November he was arrested and transported to Sachsenhausen.[53] Gertrud Königsberger enlisted the support of British business friends, and it was through their intervention that she managed to convince the Gestapo that the Board of the Tipperary Glove Factory Ltd wished to engage her husband as a General Manager. She also succeeded in dispatching their younger son Konrad to join his elder brother Peter in Newport.[54] After the regional finance agencies had concluded their customary round of confiscations, the Königsbergers were allowed to leave.[55]

In 1921, Adolf Mündheim and his brother Siegfried were recorded as co-owners and managers of Berbet Maschinenbau GmbH in Halle, which specialised

---

[50] In World War I Königsberger served as a staff officer on the French front while his wife and her cousins "sewed the German flag on their knickers to spite the French-speaking part of the population" in her native German-Alsatian town Mühlhausen (Mulhouse). Peter Kingshill, *Footnote – A Memoir*. London: Self-published 2007, pp. 4 and 7.

[51] One such concession was their attempt to have their sons enrolled in the Hitler Youth. When this was refused, they had them join the Scharnhorst Youth, a branch of the conservative-militarist Stahlhelm organisation. See Sophia Kingshill, Willi and Trudi Königsberger in Tipperary. In: Holfter (ed.), *Irish Context*, p. 51.

[52] Sophia Kingshill, Willi and Trudi Königsberger (see above), pp. 52–53; also Kingshill, *Footnote*, pp. 37–48.

[53] Kingshill, *Footnote*, p. 55; NLA, Nds. 110 W, Acc. 8/9, 241/22, Schade to EA Hildesheim, 8 July 1958; E. W. Kingshill to German Legation Dublin, 16 November 1953; Kurt Wünsch to Schade, 26 June 1958.

[54] Sophia Kingshill, Willi and Trudi Königsberger (see above), pp. 52–53; also Kingshill, *Footnote*, pp. 48–49.

[55] The figures of confiscation: *Juva* 35,500 Reichsmark (plus 1,000 Reichsmark each for Peter and Konrad), RFS 25,597 Reichsmark, *Dego* toll 2,000 Reichsmark. An emigration toll of 5,315 Reichsmark had to be paid to the Dresden Israelite Community (of which they were not members), and their remaining family gold and silver had to be delivered to the Chemnitz pawnshop, its value refunded at the ridiculously low figure of 472.50 Reichsmark. The capital shares in Wünsch and Co. were transformed into a compulsory loan on 1 January 1939 and confiscated by the Oberfinanzpräsidium (Higher Finance Authority) Dresden in 1944. See NLA, Nds. 110 W, Acc.8/9, no. 241/22, ruling of EA Hildesheim, September 1962.

in machinery for stone artefacts.[56] One of their customers in the 1920s was James Boylan of Tiravera, Glasslough, Co. Monaghan.[57] The Mündheims' villa and the factory were 'Aryanised' in late 1938, after which Adolf was taken to a concentration camp, either Buchenwald or Sachsenhausen, and faced with the customary Gestapo demand to find asylum abroad. It was then that he turned to James Boylan for help.[58] Boylan appealed to Theo Dillon and probably also to the Jewish refugee committee – obviously with success, as the ICCR put Adolf on the list of recommended refugees after his maintenance had been guaranteed by Boylan and the committee. This secured his visa and his passage to Ireland.[59]

Out of the Rhineland

By 1939, a number of emigrés from the Rhineland had assembled in Dublin. The first exiled Rhinelander in Ireland was Erich Serff from Cologne – a half-Jewish police officer who had been dismissed following the Law for the Restoration of the Professional Civil Service of 7 April 1933. He came to Ireland in early 1937 when he was employed by a radio assembly company in Dublin.[60] In 1939 he could have encountered in the Irish capital: Ludwig Hopf and his family (see chapter 9), Ludwig and Gisela Karrenberg (chapter 6), or Richard Marx (chapter 5). He may have also visited Donamon Castle, Co. Roscommon, where he would have had an opportunity of talking to some missionary brothers who had spent years in St

---

56 The Mündheims, too, had a provincial background. They came from the small town of Dransfeld, South Lower Saxony. Their father, a salesman, moved from there to Halle with its 210,000 inhabitants, hoping for a better economic and social life in a bigger city. In its public directory the name Mündheim first appeared in 1909. Information provided by town archive Dransfeld, 8 March 2010, and Ronald Kohne, city archivist of Halle.
57 James Boylan's son recalls family talks: "(My father) bought concrete tile making machinery from Adolf's Company and they remained friends." Sean Boylan email to authors, 17 November 2009.
58 Initially, Adolf hoped to bring some of their machinery to Ireland, but in Dublin this was seen as unwelcome competition. In the end he was accepted as a regular ICCR refugee. NAI, DJ 69/80/196, Mündheim to J.H. Niblock, mid-December 1938; further correspondence in NAI, DJ 69/80/251; also Jewish Community Halle (ed.), *300 Jahre Juden in Halle. Leben, Leistung, Leiden, Lohn*. Halle: Mitteldeutscher Verlag 1992, p. 92. See also various entries in the notebook of Maggie Boylan, James's sister, in the critical weeks after December 1938. Her detailed notes record important events, personalities and addresses around the Boylan household. We are grateful to Grace Moloney of the Clogher Historical Society for forwarding the document.
59 Entries of December 1938 and January 1939 in Maggie Boylan's notebook.
60 See Wiedergutmachungsamt Cologne, no. 295.472, Serff undated CV.

Augustin near Bonn at a House of the Society of the Divine Word Missionaries (see chapter 7). Or he might by chance have met Philip Moddel and Paul and Johanna Boas, three Jews from his hometown Cologne.

Paul and Johanna Boas may be taken as representing the Reform majority of the Jewish Community of Cologne, one of the oldest and largest in Germany. During the depression years, Paul had to sell his wholesale business in Cologne, Zeppelinstrasse 7 and was lucky to be employed as a secretary ("chancellor") at the Turkish Consulate in Cologne.[61] Johanna was a bridge teacher, but after 1933 the number of her non-Jewish students dropped.[62] In October-November 1938 the imminent closure of the Turkish Consulate further darkened their economic future; it also removed a protection against anti-Semitic attacks.[63] At the end of confiscations they were given a tax clearance certificate by the *Finanzamt* Cologne South and received permission to have their belongings transported to Ireland (although these never arrived).[64] It can be assumed that as in many other cases their passage to Ireland followed initiatives of relatives, in their case those of their son Hans and daughter Mathilde who had already emigrated to England in 1938.[65]

Though the Jewish community of Cologne had passed through long processes of assimilation, an orthodox community still existed in the old city. Philip Moddel was an orthodox Jew, though "on the liberal side", as his son remembers.[66] The Moddels had come from Pozna at the end of World War I and settled in eastern Frankfurt/Main, where they resided in Rechneigrabenstrasse near the Margulies family (see chapter 1). Here Moddel attended the local Kaiser-Friedrich-Gymnasium.[67] His further career in a nutshell: teacher student in Cologne,

---

[61] District government Düsseldorf, no. 615.124, Turkish Embassy to Land Court Cologne, 27 July 1959.

[62] District government Düsseldorf, no. 86.935, Johanna Boas affidavit, 6 November 1957; further texts on the Cologne Bridge Club and her career as a bridge teacher in the same file.

[63] On 13 November 1938, shortly after the Pogrom in Cologne, Paul Boas wrote to the Turkish Ambassador expressing his fears of imminent dismissal from his diplomatic position. District government Düsseldorf, no. 615.124, Turkish Embassy Berlin to Paul Boas, 15 November 1938.

[64] The tax clearance of 27 July 1939 confirmed that they had paid the *Juva* (3,600 Reichsmark). MAI, G2/2049. Johanna's affidavit of 27 March 1961 contains a list of furniture they were forced to sell in 1938 and 1939 to finance their emigration. District government Düsseldorf, no. 86.935.

[65] Paul was employed as a representative of a British firm which had already given Hans a job – a factor which may have influenced the DI&C's decision to grant a work permit to his father and eased his and his mother's Irish entry (see chapter 8).

[66] Garret Moddel, Philip's son (Boulder, Colorado), email to authors, 8 August 2005. In Garret's view his father's liberality was "at least partially due to his strong interests in athletics and music".

[67] Entschädigungsamt (EA) Cologne, no. 420.613, Philip Moddel CV, 20 March 1953.

academic years in Frankfurt and Hamburg until 1937, simultaneously teaching at the Talmud Tora School of the Israelite Community in Altona near Hamburg, then at the Jawne in Cologne, a bi-educational grammar school closely associated with the orthodox Adass Jeruschun congregation, whose synagogue choir he also directed.[68] In the November terror nights the orthodox synagogue was devastated, and Moddel escaped an imminent arrest.[69] He was engaged by the large Jewish community in Leeds to teach *Kindertransport* children, but soon "our Mr. Model [sic] left us to pick up a better position in Dublin", a pupil remembers.[70] In the Irish capital members of the Jewish community had strongly advocated his entry.[71]

---

[68] Ibid. See also Bundesstelle zur Entschädigung ehemaliger Bediensteter jüdischer Gemeinden, Cologne (BEBJG, Cologne), file II 6 – 10/91, Vol. 1, Neuberger affidavit, 23 May 1954.
[69] The details of his passage from Cologne to Leeds and then to Ireland are somewhat obscure. Maybe this resulted from what Moddel later called his "Irrfahrten" ("vagaries") which obviously included a short previous trip to Ireland in July 1938 and a temporary return to Germany. Translated by authors. His second departure was a flight from danger. EA Cologne, no. 420.613, Moddel CV, 20 March 1953. How his links to Leeds had come about is unclear.
[70] The quotation is from one of his former pupils: "We all loved and respected him." Translated by authors. Gideo Behrendt, *Mit dem Kindertransport in die Freiheit. Vom jüdischen Flüchtling zum Corporal O'Brian*. Frankfurt/M.: Fischer 2001, p. 225.
[71] See correspondence in NAI, DJ 69/80/496.

Chapter 5
The Routes of the Refugees: Italian Passages to Ireland

Between 1933 and 1938, Italy was host to more than 4,000 refugees from the German *Reich* (including Austria). Refugees could enter the country without a visa, and stay there if they abstained from any visible anti-Fascist activity and were ready to accept jobs other than those they had practised in Germany.[1] The situation became precarious, however, when on 7 September 1938 the Fascist state decreed that all Jewish immigrants who had arrived after 1919 were to leave the country by 12 March 1939.[2] Though the decree was not executed to the letter, there was a constant threat of expulsion from that date. In this situation, some applied for an Irish visa via the Legation in Rome. Eleven finally came to Ireland, but many more were denied access by the Irish authorities (see below).[3]

Among the emigrants to Ireland who came via Italy were Gerhard Hirschberg, a lawyer, and Werner Schwarz, a doctor, both belonging to groups of professionals affected by the employment ban of 7 April 1933. Hirschberg was a baptised Protestant from Lyck, a middle-sized town in the eastern corner of East Prussia. He decided to emigrate only a few days after 4 September 1933, when his name was deleted from the list of members admitted to the bar. Not being able to provide an affidavit for immigration to the USA, he resolved to go to Italy.[4] Until 1938, Hirschberg managed to eke out an existence on the money he had been allowed to take with him and earned in occasional jobs as translator, private teacher, etc.[5] He managed to escape to Ireland through a helper network that involved the pastor of his Evangelical Church in Milan, the President of the Hebrew Christian Alliance for Switzerland in Zurich (see chapter 2) and the Church of Ireland's Hebrew Christian Refugee Committee. The latter guaranteed his maintenance in Ireland and thereby won him a place on the ICCR list of immigrant candidates.[6]

---

1 Klaus Voigt, *Zuflucht auf Widerruf. Exil in Italien 1933–1945*. 2 volumes. Stuttgart: Klett-Cotta 1989 and 1993, pp. 19–54, 147–148, 169–170, 189–190.
2 Voigt, *Zuflucht*, pp. 275–276.
3 Among the eleven successful applicants were the three members of the Baumgarten family. For their background and Irish situation see chapter 9.
4 See Wiedergutmachungsamt (WGA) Saarburg, no. 41.050, appendix 1. Memory of Gerhard Hirschberg's wife Alison Nugent; also entry in Benita Stoney's unpublished diary, 1 March 1994. Stoney email to authors, 23 March 2010.
5 WGA Saarburg, no. 41.050, appendix 1.
6 NAI, DJ 69/80/466, undated certificate on Hirschberg; Slattery to DJ, 12 July 1939.

DOI 10.1515/9783110351453-006

It is unclear exactly when in 1933 or 1934 Werner Schwarz left his Wilmersdorf residence in Berlin and emigrated to Verona, where he supported himself by giving lessons in English and fencing besides doing voluntary work at a hospital and helping in the religious youth movement of a Waldensian (Protestant) pastor. He probably availed himself of the same Protestant support line between Switzerland and Ireland as Hirschberg.[7]

The Nazi ban affected not only practising doctors and lawyers but also medical and legal students. Two who emigrated to Ireland via Italy were Georg Liss and Richard Marx. In 1934, Marx, the baptised son of a Jewish father and a Catholic mother, found that no medical school in a German university was ready to accept a "half-Jew". On 14 December 1934, the 20 year-old left his native Remscheid/Rhineland and emigrated to Rome, where he studied medicine with the financial support of his father.[8] Then came September 1938. "I could no longer stay at the University of Rome. With the help of my Catholic friends I succeeded in getting a permit to Ireland."[9] His Catholic "friends" included helpers in the Vatican and, on the Irish side, members of Theo Dillon's University College Dublin (UCD) committee.[10] Marx entered Ireland and was registered as a student of the UCD Medical Department on 10 April 1939.[11] In early August 1938, Georg Liss, a Viennese law student, had reacted to his hopeless situation in post-*Anschluss* Austria and fled to Italy.[12] Only four weeks later, having settled in Torino, he found himself caught in the net of the new Italian exile policy. How he managed to arrive in Ireland in mid-March 1939 cannot be established with certainty, but it seems that, as in

---

7 In Ireland, Schwarz's case was promoted by John Doyle, lecturer at UCD, and Arnold Marsh, Headmaster of the Quakers' Newtown School (see chapters 1 and 7). NAI, DJ 69/80/340, Slattery to DJ, 20 March 1939, and further correspondence.
8 District government Düsseldorf, no. 235.139, Università degli Studi di Roma, Facoltà di Medicina e Chirurgia, copied affidavit, 29 March 1939; Karl Rudolf Marx, Richard's brother, affidavit, 4 May 1959.
9 District government Düsseldorf, no. 235.139, Richard Marx CV, 1 March 1959. Translated by authors.
10 See Dillon's correspondence with Marx, the DJ and the Irish High Commissioner in NAI, DJ 69/80/324; also correspondence between DJ, DEA and the British Foreign Office in NAI, DFA 202/566 and data in MAI, G2/2097.
11 In July 1939, Marx visited relatives in Southampton. British war measures prevented a return to Ireland ("I had to sit before the Enemy Aliens Tribunal in Southampton") and it took the concerted efforts of Dillon, the Irish government and the High Commissioner in London to enable him to continue his studies at UCD in January 1940. See correspondence between Marx, Dillon and the High Commissioner, NAI, DJ 69/80/324; see also correspondence in DFA 202/566; also data in G2/2097.
12 WSLA, residential register of Vienna.

other cases, the guarantee of the Church of Ireland refugee committee had been an important leverage in legalising his entry.[13]

The cases of Liss, Schwarz and Hirschberg suggest that many German-speaking refugees favoured Northern Italy as their region of exile. Especially, the South Tyrolean parts of the Alto Adige with their Austrian revisionist population strongly attracted German-speaking refugees – in 1938 more than 900 Jews, most of them foreigners, were counted in the famous wintersport spa Meran. They, and all other Jews who had lived there before 1933, were hit by the new Italian policy of 1938 which was particularly strictly implemented in the region north of Bolzano.[14]

Leopold von Glasersfeld came from a wealthy German-Bohemian family.[15] The son of a converted Catholic, he served as Vienna's cultural attaché in Munich between 1913 and the end of World War I. At the beginning of the 1920s, Leopold, Helena and their son Ernst moved to Meran in South Tyrol where they had a house built on the outskirts of the town. Here Leopold continued his work as a photographer, a profession in which he had gained international repute. His son, a student of mathematics at Vienna University, experienced the incipient Nazification of Austria in 1936, and in March 1938 met refugees arriving from the newly-annexed Austria at the railway station in Zurich.[16] As supporters of Count Coudenhove-Kalergi's Pan-European ideas, the von Glasersfelds were repelled by the excesses just across the Brenner border and the radicalisation of Italian policy in 1938.[17] Ernst von Glasersfeld wrote: "In Meran we were known as enemies of any form of nationalism. Moreover the Nazis surely knew that grandfather Glasersfeld was born a Jew and then converted to Catholicism."[18] Leopold and Helena stayed on

---

13 Liss was under the tutelage of the HCRC until 1941. See RCBL, JS, 3 June, 9 September, 2 December 1941.

14 Meran had attracted Jews long before 1933. A synagogue had been erected in 1901, and the town had a branch of the Zionist *Blau-Weiss* movement and an Alpine School resort for Jewish students at the Virgiljoch (which, significantly, was closed in December 1938). Cinzia Villani, Fra tolleranza e persecuzione: ebrei in Alto Adige, Trentino e Bellunese. In: *Geschichte und Region/ Storia e regione*. Vol. 6 (1997), pp. 295–300.

15 The text on the Glasersfeld family is based on emails from Ernst von Glasersfeld to authors of 12 May 2006 and 2 August 2006, a questionnaire filled in by him on 13 March 2008 (courtesy Birte Schultz); also autobiographical passages in Heinz von Förster and Ernst von Glasersfeld, *Wie wir uns selbst erfinden. Eine Autobiographie des radikalen Konstruktivismus*. Heidelberg: Carl Auer 1999, especially pp. 14–17, 82–83, 148–155; further Ernst von Glasersfeld, *Partial Memories. Sketches from an Improbable Life*. Exeter: Imprint Academic 2009.

16 von Förster/von Glasersfeld, *Wie wir uns selbst erfinde*n, pp. 25, 151.

17 Ibid., pp. 14–15.

18 von Glasersfeld email to authors, 12 May 2006. Translated by authors.

in Italy, while their son, then living in Paris with Isabel Yves, a British national, found it difficult to obtain a French permit as a citizen of Czechoslovakia, a state that faced imminent dissolution. A chance encounter led to Ireland being considered as a destination. Ernst von Glasersfeld recalled:

> At the beginning of the 1920s Herbert Briscoe, the brother of T.D. Robert Briscoe, owned a house in Meran and became acquainted with my father. When my wife and I were in Paris in autumn 1938 we accidentally met Herbert Briscoe. I told him that we wished to leave Europe and were thinking of Mexico. He said: Why not Ireland? – and this immediately sounded convincing. Isabel's mother had been a friend of Sylvia Beach, the editor of Joyce's "Ulysses", and the idea of staying in Dublin was irresistible.[19]

Apart from literary interests, Ernst and Isabel were persuaded to accept the Irish offer out of considerations of personal safety, as a Central European war seemed possible at the time, and an Irish visa would protect Ernst from being enlisted in the Czechoslovakian Army. It remains unclear how their access to Ireland was practically and diplomatically organised, as it did not comply with the general rules of Irish immigration at the time – in other cases the Irish authorities were hesitant in offering visas to Czechoslovakian citizens (see chapter 6).

Another applicant from Meran was among 29 other applicants and their families denied entry to Ireland between September 1938 and late April 1939.[20] In the case of the von Glasersfelds, there is no evidence that either Robert Briscoe or J.P. Colbert, an important figure in Irish financial circles and husband of Ernst's cousin, played a role in giving them privileged access.[21] Two factors are more likely to have been instrumental in facilitating an extension of Ernst's stay beyond the time limits initially imposed (at first two weeks and then three months) towards permanent status: the British passport of his fiancée Isabel, and his financial independence, which allowed the von Glasersfelds to invest money in a farming

---

19 Ibid.
20 The figure is based on the cases listed by the DJ under file group DJ 69/80. The man from Meran was Erich Spitz, a non-Aryan Catholic, who was threatened with expulsion from Italy in January-February 1939. He had the support of a Catholic clergyman in Ireland who attempted to utilise his acquaintance with Joseph Walshe at the DEA in order to support Spitz's case, but failed to overcome the opposition of the DJ. On the case see O'Connor, *Irish Government Policy*, pp. 110–112.
21 P.J. Colbert was chairman of the Industrial Trust Company and a member of the prestigious Social and Inquiry Society. A G2 observer was certain that Colbert's views had considerable weight in the highest echelons of the government (MAI, G2/0304, G2 report 19 August 1940), but in Glasersfeld's memoirs nothing is said about any role played by his relative in his immigration transactions.

enterprise.²² Leopold and Helena von Glasersfeld followed their son and daughter-in-law from Meran to Ireland in late June 1939,²³ their decision clearly influenced by awareness of the coming war.²⁴

---

22 They also had the support of Irish politician Erskine Childers, who, following another chance encounter, became a good friend and helped to integrate them into Dublin society. See von Glasersfeld, *Partial Memories*, pp. 66–74. For the farm project, see chapter 8.
23 MAI, G2/0304.
24 Ernst von Glasersfeld and his wife were "glad that my parents were in Ireland, too", which implies at least an inkling of the potential dangers on the Continent. Glasersfeld email to authors, 12 May 2006. Translated by authors. Helena von Glasersfeld had also urged her husband to abandon his photographic studio in Meran. In a letter of 5 October 1939, she says that it was only "from the first of September" that her husband finally realised that it was good for them to have made their summer trip to Ireland. Translated by authors. To G2 Leopold described himself as a "Czechoslovakian refugee". MAI, G2/0304, G2 report, probably June 1940.

Part II **Exiled in Wartime Ireland**

Chapter 6
The State, the Helpers and the Refugees

Separated by a broad geographic and cultural gulf from the *Reich*, Irish governments could observe refugee currents on the Continent with relative detachment, at least until 1938. Up to this time, very few endangered persons applied for entry to Ireland, a state of affairs that meant the government did not have to formulate a positive and systematic response to the German situation.

Although the Irish Free State was a member of the League of Nations, and had participated in a High Commission on the German refugee crisis,[1] the League had not succeeded in creating any binding international mechanism to direct the movement of refugees in a purposeful and effective manner. Irish indifference was perhaps understandable in view of the less than enthusiastic support for Geneva's projected policy by larger and wealthier states. Germany itself made no attempt to influence Dublin's attitude. In principle, it regarded foreign immigration rules as internal affairs of state as long as the countries concerned did not allow immigrants they had admitted to protest against its own regime.[2] Equally, Dublin also practised a policy of restraint towards the internal affairs of Germany, including its programme of expulsion.[3]

When considering "external" influences on Ireland, it should be borne in mind that even by 1934, almost half its politicians and civil servants had trained in the British civil service. The United Kingdom had practised a restrictive immigration policy since 1905, and notwithstanding independent Ireland's desire to assert a separate identity, British tradition shaped its policy on aliens in the 1920s and 1930s.[4] Even after the change of government in 1932, Irish legislation

---

1 See Michael Kennedy, *Ireland and the League of Nations, 1919–1946. International Relations, Diplomacy and Politics*. Dublin: Irish Academic Press 1996.
2 In January 1935, to take one notable example, the exiled German-Jewish Socialist Ernst Toller planned to address a meeting in Dublin of the Irish Labour League against Fascism, but because of the political character of the event, the German government intervened. Joachim Fischer, Ernst Toller and Ireland. In: Richard Dove and Stephen Lamb (eds), *German Writers and Politics, 1918–39*. Warwick Studies in the European Humanities. Basingstoke/London: MacMillan 1992, pp. 192–206; O'Driscoll, *Ireland*, pp. 155–156.
3 See O'Driscoll, *Ireland*, pp. 98–101, 175–176.
4 Louise London, *Whitehall and the Jews, 1933–1948. British Immigration Policy, Jewish Refugees and the Holocaust*. Cambridge: Cambridge University Press 2000, pp. 16–24. The file DJ 2014/85/2372 (Visa regulations for the territories of the Soviet Union, 1927) contains a typical example of the trust that Irish policy makers continued to place in British decisions on immigration. In a memo of 9 November 1927 addressed to the DEA, a DJ official argued that the British government had sources of information "not available here and it is highly improbable that any

on citizenship continued to be informed by the British model: the Aliens Act 1935, for example, made no reference to the refugee problem.[5] In it, the history of refugees such as Jews or other victims of Nazi Germany was ignored: all such persons were categorised as "aliens" to Ireland. Policy on dealing with these aliens was the responsibility of the Departments of Industry and Commerce and External Affairs, with the Department of Justice having the final word. The Act and subsequent executive orders did not specify any material principles on which departmental decisions were to rest, except to demand that if aliens were accepted they should be able to support themselves and to do so in ways that did not jeopardise native Irish employment.[6] Otherwise they focused on how to keep aliens away from Irish shores, how they were to be controlled once in the country, and how subsequently expelled, if necessary.

There was no lack of information on the German situation after 30 January 1933, either in political circles or amongst the Irish public. While the latter was kept informed through critical if somewhat watered-down articles in the Irish newspapers,[7] policy-makers in Dublin were sufficiently equipped with reliable information through the two Chargés d'Affaires in Berlin, Leo T. McCauley and Charles Bewley, who took office in July 1933.[8] Possibly de Valera, then President of the Executive Council of the Irish Free State (the office of Taoiseach would only be introduced in 1937) and Minister of External Affairs, was the most knowledgeable Irish politician about the German situation, if only through his frequent conversations with leading Jewish representatives (Isaac Herzog, the Chief Rabbi of Ireland, Robert Briscoe and Nahum Sokolov, President of the World Zionist Organisation, for example).[9]

Soviet citizens who are considered unsuitable for admission to Great Britain would be desirable acquisitions to the population of the Saorstat. The converse case, that of the alien who would be allowed to enter Great Britain but who is not wanted here is also unlikely to arise."

5 For a detailed analysis, see Keogh, *Jews in Twentieth-Century Ireland*, pp. 116–117; O'Connor, *Irish Government Policy*, pp. 75–100.
6 O'Connor, *Irish Government Policy*, pp. 83–84; also NA Washington, box 6163. 841 D.55/7, Belovsky, US Vice Consul to State Department, 9 November 1934.
7 The *Irish Press* was most outspokenly critical of developments in Germany, while the *Cork Examiner* published justifications of Nazi policy. O'Driscoll, *Ireland*, pp. 95–96.
8 O'Driscoll, *Ireland*, pp. 125–133, 135–39.
9 Reports of these meetings were published in *The Jewish Chronicle*, 12 and 19 May 1933. The meetings were also chronicled in the Irish dailies. O'Driscoll, *Ireland*, pp. 98–99. On Sokolov's visit, see also Keogh, *Jews in Twentieth-Century Ireland*, p. 91. The DEA and de Valera were also kept informed of events in Germany by the Irish delegation with the League of Nations. See reports in NAI, DFA 243/67.

What some government departments in Dublin might not have known in the first weeks of the new German regime in 1933 was that the Irish representative in Berlin, Leo McCauley, had already "discouraged" applications from refugees seeking to enter Ireland. On 7 April 1933 – the very day when the Law for the Restoration of the Professional Civil Service was passed, and after glaring examples of human rights violations – he informed his Department in Dublin that

> many inquiries and applications for visas have been received by the Legation within the past week from Jews desiring to leave Germany and take up their residence in the Irish Free State. Jews of German nationality, of course, require no visa, but the inquiries have included Jews resident in Germany who are of Polish or other nationality. As far as possible the Legation has discouraged such persons from going to Ireland, as they are really only refugees; and it assumes that this line of action would be in accordance with the Department's policy.[10]

The negative attitude to Eastern-Jewish immigrants entering Ireland expressed in the last sentence was established policy in the Department, and dated back to the founding days of the Irish Free State.[11] The Department of External Affairs confirmed McCauley's decision ("such persons should be discouraged from coming here"),[12] thereby equipping the Legation with a *carte blanche* to reject all further applicants of that status.

McCauley's differentiation between German and Polish Jews did not mean that the former had a better chance of coming to Ireland than Jews with an Eastern background, if they appeared to be "only refugees" (rather than visitors, for example). Walter Nathan, a teacher from Magdeburg seeking refuge in Ireland, told the Irish Minister that his preference for an Irish exile expressed his personal interest in Irish literature; he also declared that locally he had already made himself a name as a director of Irish plays.[13] McCauley's report signalled cautious support for the appeal,[14] which is remarkable as in general he believed that "to some extent" German Jews had "brought the trouble on themselves" through their omnipresence at restaurants and theatres ("to the exclusion of the ordinary German citizens") and their conspicuous wealth, both conventional tropes in anti-Semitic rhetoric.[15] The Department of Justice, however, expected that

---

10 NAI, DFA 102/9, McCauley to Walshe, 7 April 1933.
11 See O'Driscoll, *Ireland*, p. 101.
12 NAI, DFA 102/9, Fahy to McCauley, 19 April 1933.
13 Nathan, born on 3 March 1905, taught at a secondary school ("Aufbauschule") in Heiligenstadt in the then Prussian province of Saxony. Landesarchiv Sachsen-Anhalt (LASA) to authors, 26 January 2007.
14 NAI, DFA, 2/390, McCauley to DEA, 26 April 1933.
15 O'Driscoll, *Ireland*, p. 98.

numerous applications of this type will be received from Jews in Germany who are likely to lose their employment and the Minister is of the opinion that it would be undesirable to grant permission to these aliens to enter this country. In the present case, Doctor Nathan does not give an indication of the manner in which he proposes to make a livelihood.[16]

Again, the language intimated that masses of unemployed refugees were about to descend on the Free State. On 16 May, the Department instructed McCauley to refuse Nathan's application and, more significantly, not to pursue the query about how he planned to support himself in Ireland.[17] Obviously, his case had elicited scant attention in the relevant departments. Other candidates seemed to promise the country more tangible benefits. In May 1933, Julius Fabian, a Jew living at 1 Blockdammweg in Berlin-Lichtenberg, approached McCauley asking for a visa to Ireland as he wanted "to leave Germany because of the present unfavourable conditions". He offered to "transfer" his business, a plant producing alabaster, to Dublin, arguing that the country was said to be rich in raw materials for this type of production.[18] For unknown reasons Fabian did not come to Ireland but Dublin's positive reaction to his application seemed to indicate that the Irish government, especially the Department of Industry and Commerce, was alive to economic arguments. The story of Abraham Bayer (see chapter 1) is particularly telling in this context. Since his first approaches in June 1933, the Department of Industry and Commerce realised that "owing to the present situation in Germany [...] it is quite possible that we could have [...] industries started here by Jews," and that "this particular one may be a case in point".[19] Bayer's factory, the first in the country to produce ladies' handbags, would eliminate the Free State's dependence on imported bags, hence fitting well into the policy of creating new jobs by import substitution. Bayer could point to eleven years' practice in the trade and sound finances safely stored at London banks, and offered an initial £800 investment including his "own machines and accessories" as well as jobs for 20 persons initially. He also gave assurances that once Irish Leather Goods had passed an initial critical phase, he would accept Irish capital in a future company.[20] The offer was so appealing that the Department even accepted the entry of two Polish-Jewish experts from Bayer's former Offenbach factory and

---

16 NAI, DFA 2/390, de Brun, DJ, to DEA, 11 May 1933.
17 NAI, DFA 2/390, DEA to Irish Legation, 16 May 1933. Nathan was formally dismissed from the Civil Service on 25 August 1933. LASA to authors, 26 January 2007. Nothing could be ascertained about his further life.
18 NAI, DFA 2/406, McCauley to DEA, 24 May 1933; Fahy, DEA, to McCauley, 28 June 1933.
19 NAI, TID 1207/300, minutes of a DI&C official, 13 July 1933.
20 NAI, TID 1207/300, Bayer to DI&C, 31 August 1933; draft of a memorandum by a DI&C official to Lemass, 27 September 1933.

withdrew its preference for a location in the provinces, since Bayer insisted on Dublin.[21] By this time the Department of Justice had long shelved its concerns about Bayer's immigration and even accepted the visit of his Jewish sister-in-law, as noted above (see chapter 1).[22]

The Department of Industry and Commerce under Seán Lemass fully understood the potential for Irish industry of investors like Bayer or skilled experts coveted by individual firms. In 1934, that approach was put on a more systematic basis (possibly inspired by similar developments in the United Kingdom).[23] A group was formed, headed by Marcus Witztum and Mayo Senator John McEllin, whose members were to scout for investors and experts from countries like Austria, Czechoslovakia, France, Belgium, and also Germany.[24] The Department expected foreign capitalists, managers and experts dissatisfied with conditions in Germany and other Continental economies to infuse non-industrialised regions, especially in western Ireland, with new opportunities for a chronically underemployed population.

Lemass's pragmatic approach was by no means uncontested within the government. The Nuremberg Laws of 1935, which stripped "Jews" as defined by the Nazis of their German citizenship, reawakened fears within the Departments of Justice and External Affairs that Jewish-German industrialists might visualise new opportunities in the Irish economy. One such opportunity had been sought by the Jewish owners of Simson and Co. Ltd, an important armament enterprise in the southern Thuringian town of Suhl. The proprietors, who had lost their property due to Aryanisation in late November 1935, and were now residing in Switzerland, had obviously heard of the industrialisation drive in Ireland and applied to launch

---

[21] The experts were Gustav Amsterdam – he stayed for only three months from November 1934 – and Elias Stiel, who collaborated closely with Bayer throughout the history of the factory. On Amsterdam, see DJ 69/41. For Stiel's passage to Ireland, see NAI, TID 1207/300, Bayer to DI&C, 22 February 1934. On 17 March 1934, his name was officially deleted from the Jewish Register of the City of Offenbach. For the location issue, see NAI, TID 1207/300, DI&C to Bayer, 23 October 1933; Bayer to DI&C, 28 October 1933.
[22] NAI, TID 1207/300, minute of a DI&C official, 1 July 1934. NAI, DFA 2/712, DJ official to DI&C, 15 September 1934.
[23] Roughly at the same time, Britain began to stimulate foreign investment in its "depressed areas", which also included parts of Northern Ireland. See Herbert Loebl, Refugees from the Third Reich and Industry in the Depressed Areas of Britain. In: Werner Mosse (ed.), *Second Chance. Two Centuries of German-speaking Jews in the United Kingdom*. Tübingen: Mohr Paul Siebeck 1991, pp. 379–404.
[24] Unfortunately, documentary evidence on this group is extremely scarce. Apart from other sources cited in chapter 7, some helpful anecdotal evidence was provided by John C. McEllin, nephew of Senator McEllin. Interview with authors, Castlebar, 14 June 2008.

a project in the country, but the Department of Justice flatly rejected the offer.[25] In the same year, Department officials also felt threatened by an initiative of the British Council of German Jewry who recommended opening the Irish economy to German-Jewish investors, contending that such a policy had created an additional 6,000–7,000 jobs in the United Kingdom and 4,500 in Holland. Stephen A. Roche, secretary at the Department of Justice, issued a dire warning against copying the British model: "There have of recent years been numerous protests regarding the number of alien Jews who have established themselves in this country and the Minister would not look with favour on any policy which might tend to increase that number."[26] Such fears were also common in the Department of External Affairs, whose secretary Joseph Walshe dreaded a "surplus" of Jews in Ireland through new entrants from Germany.[27] In practice, however, these voices did not obstruct Department of Industry and Commerce policy.[28] Roche himself made it clear that in principle his department did not exclude candidates with significant means, and was routinely prepared to look at each case on its own merits. Even German-Jewish doctors could be accepted as students or visitors, since they did not jeopardise the strict 'Irish-first' employment policy, as long as they were privately maintained during their residence in Ireland and could be sent back within fixed time limits (see chapter 1). The case of Leib Margulies tested this policy to its limits. After the British Home Office had refused to grant

---

25 On the negotiations between a member of the owners' family, their London representative and the DJ, see correspondence in DJ 2013/50/166. For the history of the enterprise, see Ulrike Schulz, *Simson. Vom unwahrscheinlichen Überleben eines Unternehmens 1856–1993*. Göttingen: Wallstein 2013.
26 NAI, DFA 2/994, Roche to DEA, 14 August 1936, regarding memorandum of Council of German Jewry, 23 June 1936.
27 Anxious about the "surplus trauma", Walshe had the number of Irish Jews checked in 1936. His and the DJ's recommendation was to keep existing ratios (0.13 per cent of the Irish population) unchanged. O'Driscoll, *Ireland*, p. 237. Walshe's politically motivated opposition to the immigration of further Jews could however be overridden when his personal sympathies were invoked in particular cases. In November 1937, he intervened on behalf of Dr Bernhard Laske, a renowned gynaecologist from Berlin who was a personal acquaintance of his. According to Walshe, he appeared to "be the first refugee from the German religious persecution to have made such an application, and would be the first, if his application is granted, to receive asylum in this country". NAI, DFA 131/80, Walshe to DJ, 25 November 1937. Laske was not, however, admitted (see correspondence in NAI, DFA 131/80), despite prominent support not only from Walshe but from Briscoe and other Jewish leaders, and also from the Irish Registration Council. This had been founded in 1927 and consisted of eleven members, among them representatives of the universities, Apothecaries Hall and the College of Surgeons. See John Fleetwood, *History of Medicine in Ireland*. Dublin: The Richview Press 1951, pp. 317–318.
28 The DI&C expressed a guarded consent to the British Council's recommendation. See NAI, DFA 2/994, Leydon to DEA, 28 July 1936.

him a permit, he came to Dublin in mid-October 1935, wishing to "investigate" the chances of setting up a "business in manufacture of fancy leather".[29] Although this was refused, Margulies remained in Ireland – not, ultimately, because a number of prominent Jews, including Chief Rabbi Herzog, intervened on his behalf, but because Berlin had meanwhile revoked Margulies's citizenship in accordance with the provisions of the Nuremberg Laws and would not allow him to return if he were deported.[30] In this situation, the Irish government could not but provisionally accept Margulies' continued residence in Ireland.[31] The officials' frustration over their inability to expel him was allayed by the fact that his presence turned out to be an asset for the Irish economy (see chapter 8). The real menace in their view was posed by the "penniless" foreigners who could not support themselves – a largely imaginary category, as hardly any applicant of that status knocked at Ireland's doors in these early years of the crisis.

In Ireland, as elsewhere, anti-Jewish positions tended to come to the fore during phases of domestic and foreign crisis. In 1933, such a crisis was provoked by the main opposition party. Cumann na nGaedheal transformed itself from a conservative-liberal pro-Treaty party to a rightist opposition movement integrating the extra-parliamentary Blueshirts (United Ireland Party/Fine Gael). In November, UIP leaders Mulcahy and Dillon, probably not speaking for the whole party, indirectly alleged an over-representation of Jews in the Irish business world.[32] Some months later, the idea that the new factories were "largely under the influence of Jews" was openly expressed at a UIP meeting.[33] By November 1934, there was a widespread view inside the Irish Jewish community that the party had "developed an anti-Semitic stand" since its fall from power in spite of the reassuring rhetoric of its leaders.[34] More explicit anti-Semitic tendencies developed from among the ruins of the Blueshirts. Although they failed

---

29 DJ 69/1145, Garda to DJ, 18 October 1935.
30 DJ 69/1145, von Kuhlmann, German Legation, to de Valera, 2 March 1936.
31 DJ 69/1145, DJ to Garda, 11 March 1936. For Herzog's intervention, see his letter to DJ, 14 January 1936 in the same file.
32 In 1933, Mulcahy and Dillon "quizzed" Lemass on the question whether certain persons, the likes of Matz, Gaw, Lucks and Silverstein, could be called nationals within the terms of the Control of Manufactures Act. Lemass's combative defence: "Amongst the names read out by the Deputy are names associated with industry in this country for a long number of years, some of whom are a lot better Irishmen than the Deputy." DD, Vol. 50, 22 November 1933.
33 *Jewish Chronicle*, 23 March 1934.
34 *Jewish Chronicle*, 23 November 1934. The paper's Dublin correspondent cited excuses from UIP leaders for anti-Semitic expressions used by their followers. *Jewish Chronicle*, 4 August 1933 (interview with O'Duffy), 23 March 1934 (O'Duffy), 23 November 1934 (Senator E. Blythe). On Blythe, see also Keogh, *Jews in Twentieth-Century Ireland*, p. 96.

to draw any mass support,[35] the aftermath of the Nuremberg Laws and international crises, especially the Spanish Civil War, refuelled the antagonisms of the Irish Civil War and the turbulence of 1933, and again led to confrontations fomenting xenophobic and anti-Semitic reactions such as the views expressed by Roche and Walshe. In 1936, Patrick Belton, ex-Blueshirt and TD for north Dublin between 1933 and 1943, formed the Irish Christian Front, whose position – anti-Communist, anti-capitalist and pro-Franco – was given qualified backing by the bishops and also temporarily stirred up some mass support in spite of the Free State's official neutrality.[36] At the same time, Mulcahy and others attacked the "alien penetration" of Irish industries, thereby indirectly buttressing the Christian Front's anti-Semitic rhetoric.[37] On 7 January 1937, the *Irish Catholic* observed that "Hitler has many admirers among Irish Catholics."[38] It is hard to qualify (and quantify) such sweeping estimates as "many admirers", though its appearance in a widely read Catholic paper tells its own story. Moreover, the *Irish Catholic* was not alone in encouraging the mixed anti-alien and anti-Jewish chorus.[39]

---

[35] In March 1935, an Ireland for the Irish Association was founded, whose aims were to "promote the industrial development of the country by Irishmen against development by foreigners" and to "clear all Jews out of the country". *Jewish Chronicle*, 15 March 1935. A few weeks later, an anti-Semitic weekly, the *Aontas Gaedeal Weekly Post*, wished to establish a forum of protest against the government's industrial policy and the part allegedly played in it by Jews. *Jewish Chronicle*, 14 June 1935. In July, the journal ceased publication. *Jewish Chronicle*, 26 July 1935. The parallel founding of the anti-Semitic National Corporate Party by O'Duffy likewise "ended in farce". Keogh, *Jews in Twentieth-Century Ireland*, p. 96; O'Driscoll, *Ireland*, pp. 115–118.

[36] Keogh, *Jews in Twentieth-Century Ireland*, pp. 107–110. In the Dáil, Belton repeatedly agitated against the alleged role of international Jewry within the Irish industrialisation process. On 4 March 1937, for example, he charged the government with having handed over Irish industries to "a gang of international Jews" and "undesirable aliens" who were "reaping the harvest out of the sweat of the Irish people". MacEntee and Lemass dismissed these positions as irrational. DD, Vol. 65, 4 March 1937; see also Vol. 62, 12 May 1936.

[37] As in 1933, Mulcahy attacked Lemass on the "alien penetration" of Irish industries. DD, Vol. 64, 18 November 1936. A few months later, the *Irish Independent* ran an article ("Aliens in Ireland", 5 April 1937) that described the "process of penetration" as "somewhat alarming". A racist undertone can also be seen in Patrick McGilligan relating Lemass's policy to his "Huguenot blood". Daly, *Industrial Development*, p. 106. A mistaken imputation of philo-Semitism accompanied Lemass throughout his career. On 9 March 1950, Deputy O'Leary: "You let in all the Jews." DD, Vol. 119, 9 March 1950. Horgan, *Seán Lemass*, pp. 26, 244–245.

[38] Quoted in Ferriter, *Judging Dev*, p. 260.

[39] For an overview, see Keogh, *Jews in Twentieth-Century Ireland*, pp. 92–96. In the weeks before the Austrian *Anschluss* in 1938, the anti-Semitic note was sounded again in the popular Catholic press, provoking hostile reactions. On 18 February 1938, the *Jewish Chronicle* complained that the "old charges again" – Jews were without a nationality, did not work in agriculture but only in

Though these voices did not go unnoticed in the Jewish community, they obviously did not shake the trust of its leaders in the Fianna Fáil government.[40] Most historians endorse that assessment, pointing especially to de Valera's personal record.[41] His public statements on the Jewish presence in Ireland, the calculated interviews he conducted with leaders of national and international Jewry, and his occasional later interventions on behalf of Jewish refugees leave no doubt about his sympathies with and solicitude for the Jewish community in Ireland, the lot of refugees from Germany and the aims of the Zionist movement.[42] In an early phase of his life, he had himself been an immigrant of sorts, and in 1933, sections of the opposition sought to disparage him as non-Irish and a "Jew", in order to bolster their campaign against the imagined danger of a Jewish-instigated Communist takeover in Ireland. This sort of vacuous rhetoric may perhaps have immunised him against xenophobia– he flatly refuted the rumours, adding that he was "not one of those who try to attack the Jews or want to make any use of the popular dislike of them".[43] He did not, however, consistently throw his national and international weight behind a more receptive Irish refugee policy, and in 1936 he refused to commit himself to "any definite lines of action in anticipation of any discussion on the whole Jewish case which might take place at Geneva".[44]

The question was whether Ireland could remain unscathed by developments on the Continent, and whether its government would be able to maintain its aloof

---

exchange, got rich too quickly – were being propounded by Father Fahy and disseminated in the *Irish Rosary* and the *Irish Catholic*. The Church of Ireland's Jews Society appealed to the Catholic hierarchy to refute these attacks. RCBL, JS, 1 February 1938. It should however be noted that anti-Semitic diatribes were criticised not only in the Jewish press, but in the Catholic Church itself. See Keogh, *Jews in Twentieth-Century Ireland*, pp. 96–97.

40 For example, the *Jewish Chronicle*'s reassuring comment on *Aontas Gaedeal Weekly Post* of 14 June 1935; see also the article in the *Jewish Chronicle*, 18 February 1938, cited above. With reference to the Jewish community's alignment behind Fianna Fáil politics, we may note Robert Briscoe's efforts to encourage subscriptions by Jewish leaders for the ruling party. See especially the materials in NLI, Robert Briscoe Papers, MS 26, 447–451.

41 For a more critical view of de Valera's role, see Rivlin, *Shalom Ireland*, pp. 36–37; Goldstone, 'Benevolent Helpfulness'? In: Kennedy and Skelly (eds), *Irish Foreign Policy*, p. 122.

42 See footnote 9, and further, *Jewish Chronicle*, 4 December 1936, on a talk with the President of the British Board of Deputies, Neville Laski; also *Jewish Chronicle*, 31 December 1937, on his meeting Professor Selig Brodetsky of the World Zionist Organization, accompanied by Robert Briscoe and Arthur Newman. See also Price, *Somewhere to Hang My Hat*, p. 119.

43 DD, Vol. 50, 2 March 1934.

44 NAI, DFA 243/67, D/T note, 31 August 1936. De Valera also declined to receive a member of the American Jewish Congress who had demanded stronger Irish government support for German Jews. NAI, DFA 243/67, Fagen to de Valera, 20 July and 7 August 1936. Goldstone, 'Benevolent Helpfulness'? In: Kennedy and Skelly (eds), *Irish Foreign Policy*, p. 122.

posture if and when one defining condition, the low number hoping to enter the country, no longer applied. In that case, Ireland might no longer be able to deflect refugee currents from its shores.

"A certain degree of confusion ..." – New challenges in 1938

The *Anschluss* of Austria and the subsequent crisis over the dismemberment of Czechoslovakia between March 1938 and March 1939 created a new interest, among the Irish public and in government circles, in Hitler's policy and the situation of persecuted persons in the enlarged *Reich*. Stories of the victimisation of Jews and Catholics in former Austria, Sudetenland and Germany circulated in the dailies and other papers,[45] spawning fears that its effects might in one way or another spill over into distant Ireland. Indications of a changed perception began with controversies over the legitimacy of German policy after the *Anschluss*. The combination of administrative-economic strangulation and physical violence against Jews led to rising emigration. Ireland, however, still remained largely immune. By our calculations, roughly 90 refugees had entered Ireland up to October 1938 (of whom 14 had already left, and others had been only visiting), too few to become a topic of general debate, in spite of the heightened awareness in Ireland of the situation in the *Reich*.[46] There were neither domestic nor foreign policy issues that might have led to a change in official policy. In Geneva, the government preserved its passivity, unperturbed by the criticism of two Irish internationalist pressure groups, the League of Nations Society of Ireland (founded in 1918 and temporarily presided over by Senator James G. Douglas) and the Irish Women Citizens and Local Government Association.[47] Neither the Evian Conference in July nor the League of Nations High Commission for Refugees seemed able to make the government deviate from a strict policy of national interest.[48] As before, Irish internal deliberations were ruled by general principles

---

[45] On press reactions to the Austrian annexation, the takeover of the Sudetenland and the November Pogrom, see O'Driscoll, *Ireland*, pp. 221–222.
[46] Keogh's statement that numbers of entrants had "increased dramatically" in the course of 1938 is only valid for the situation after the November Pogrom. Dermot Keogh, Irish Refugee Policy, Anti-Semitism and Nazism at the Approach of World War Two. In: Holfter (ed.), *German-speaking Exiles*, p. 47.
[47] Both organisations demanded a more concerted Irish effort on refugee policy within the League of Nations. See the correspondence between them and the DEA, especially NAI, DFA 243/67, Doreen M. Ditchburn to DEA, 31 March 1937.
[48] For the Irish attitude to Evian, see Dermot Keogh, Irish Refugee Policy, Anti-Semitism and Nazism at the Approach of World War Two. In: Holfter (ed.), *German-speaking Exiles*, pp. 39–40.

of restrictiveness, exceptions being made for carefully selected candidates who, at a minimum, were "financially independent" and did not "require to take up employment",[49] or others specifically invited by the Department of Industry and Commerce.

Nevertheless, by mid-1938 new tendencies were emerging in response to the swelling numbers of refugees in Europe. One factor was the growing impact of Irish aid organisations and private citizens wishing to help the Nazis' victims. The established Christian churches had come late to the refugee problem. The Protestant churches focused mainly on missionary activity, a hopelessly inadequate approach to dealing with the German situation after 1933. The Church of Ireland's Jews Society (officially the 'Irish Auxiliary to the London Society for Promoting Christianity among the Jews', founded in 1810) had maintained a missionary base in Hamburg-Wandsbek that took care of and proselytised among "transmigrant Jews from the East passing through Germany",[50] some of whom, it was thought, aimed to settle in Ireland. The Belfast-based Presbyterians had a separate missionary station for the same clientele. They assembled in the church and a social welfare house of the large Jerusalem Community in working-class Hamburg-Eimsbüttel.[51] Theoretically, after 1933 the two houses could have turned to dealing with the Eastern Jews passing through Nazi Germany, but this proved difficult under prevailing conditions.[52] The Jews Society's Home was closed in 1934.[53] It was only in 1937, probably inspired by a visit of the ever-active Conrad Hoffmann (see chapter 2), that the Church of Ireland's refugee work began to focus more specifically on the situation of non-Aryan Protestants. As for practical help, church members could make donations to the Jews Society's Hebrew Christian Refugees from Germany Fund,[54] or to the Irish Committee for Austrian Relief (ICAR) which was established in mid-May 1938, with the stated purpose of raising funds on behalf of Austrian victims of Nazi aggression "irrespective of race, creed or political affiliations". Its trans-denominational character was reflected in its founding members – Jewish Leonard Abrahamson, Quaker James G. Douglas, Catholic Walter Starkie, among others – as well as the broad range

---

49 NAI DJ 2013/50/2640, note by Seàn Murphy, DEA, 10 May 1938.
50 RCBL, JS, 4 September 1934.
51 Collection of press articles in Hamburg State archive, A 640.
52 According to *Die Welt*, 22 March 1965, the Jerusalem Community succeeded in helping many Eastern Jews reach the USA before 1938. The Church of Ireland's Hamburg Home, however, was not involved in such rescue operations.
53 It was threatened with prohibition by the Gestapo. RCBL, JS, 1 March 1934. Moreover, since the flow of Jewish immigrants from Eastern Europe had dried up the Home's working basis had collapsed. RCBL, JS, 3 July 1934.
54 RCBL, JS, 2 November 1937.

of the English recipients and distributors of the collected money (for example, the Children's Inter-Aid Committee, the English Catholic Relief Committee, the Friends' Service Council).[55]

Until 1938, the Irish Catholic Church had remained inactive. In May 1938, Cardinal Innitzer sent a plea to Ireland's highest ecclesiastical authority Cardinal MacRory (see chapter 2), proposing a committee to raise funds for Catholic non-Aryans, as well as more entry permits for refugees and, specifically, Mary Ward sisters wishing to continue their religious studies in Ireland.[56] It seems that the Cardinal ignored these entreaties. When immigration policy did change, however, it was due partly to an initiative with a Catholic dimension. The key role was de Valera's.

A proposal to offer free attendance to refugee students was made at a Standing Committee meeting of UCD on 6 July 1938, in reaction to pleas for help from Austria, and was adopted by the Senate meeting on 7 July (see also chapter 9).[57] When in mid-August the Department of Justice was informed by Denis Coffey, the President of UCD, about the decision, the officials were not impressed.[58] As Stephen A. Roche, Department of Justice, wrote to his colleague in the Department of External Affairs, Joseph Walshe, the "strictly official response would probably have been a refusal based on the ground that the German Government would cancel the students' passports" – but that reaction was undermined "as it appeared that the scheme was decided on at a meeting of the Senate at which the Taoiseach was present and he personally wished that the attitude of the Department would be sympathetic".[59] This was good news not only for Austrian students but also for two German Protestant adolescents, Georg and Eva Pick (see chapter 1), as Roche argued that if Austrian Catholics attending University College were accepted as residents, it would become difficult for the Department to refuse the Lutheran Germans.[60] After referring to the Evian Conference he addressed his main problem – the fear of establishing precedents. Walshe agreed with his concerns, and proposed that Bewley should report "very fully on all cases".[61] On 7 September 1938, however, the day of Walshe's reply, he met with Roche and

---

55 *Irish Times*, letter to the editor, 14 May 1938. Keogh describes it as a Catholic-only committee. *Jews in Twentieth-Century Ireland*, p. 140.
56 DAV, BA Innitzer, box 17.
57 See NUI, Minutes of Senate, Vol. XVII, May 19, 1938 – October 26, 1939, Senate Meeting 7 July 1938 "Provision of Assistance for Austrian Professors and Students".
58 NAI, DJ 69/80/31, DJ to Coffey, 20 August 1938.
59 NAI, DJ 69/80/7, Roche to Walshe, 29 August 1938.
60 Ibid.
61 NAI, DJ 69/80/7, Walshe to Roche, 7 September 1938.

de Valera. The memo which Roche put together two days later on this meeting for Daniel Costigan, his colleague at the Department of Justice, makes plain their view of de Valera's role and their own.

> In all this I am acting in accordance with the Taoiseach's expressed desire, and generally I feel that, for the present at least, nothing but unprofitable friction can result from our attempting to enforce with any rigidity the policy which we enunciated officially at the Evian Conference. In any case where the people who want to come here possess high educational qualifications or where the claims of humanity are strong, we must adopt a sympathetic attitude. If we find in the course of the next few months or so that the number actually admitted under this sympathetic policy is alarmingly large or if there are protests (e.g. by the representatives of Labour or by professional bodies) we may have to put the question up again for fresh consideration and possibly new instructions, but until then I am clear that what the Taoiseach wants is a policy distinctly on the sympathetic side. We are in the position of sentries whose orders are not to interfere with occasional individuals crossing the lines, because the general does not think they can do much harm and may even be useful to us and he wants to show patience and humanity, but if they begin to come in troops we must ask for fresh orders. We must just do our best to carry out these instructions, remembering, if we find it difficult, that if official work were free from such difficulties there would be no Higher Civil Service![62]

The orders of "the general" were clear, as was the feeling that the departments had no choice but to follow "this sympathetic policy". As a result, the Austrian students and the Pick children, as well as Esther Britz, daughter of Jewish linguist Ernst Lewy – all the cases that had been under negotiation – were to be admitted, even if there was a grave danger that they would never go back. Fears of an "alarmingly large" number coming were to be kept in check by the old formula that "all the cases" should be examined "on their own merits".[63] What the officials would really have liked was a prohibitive visa policy in line with the negativism of Charles Bewley, Dublin's representative in Berlin.[64]

Walshe and Roche's preoccupation with precedents and numbers receded in importance as rising Continental tensions and concomitant internal Irish developments before and after the seizure of the Sudetenland created a new

---

62 Ibid., Roche to Costigan, 9 September 1938.
63 NAI, DFA 102/438, Walshe to Roche, 7 September 1938.
64 Walshe wished to grant Bewley a right to withhold DI&C work permits if he was not convinced that the applicants would be allowed to return to Germany. He recommended that "every possible precaution shall be taken to prevent the influx of persons who could not be subsequently removed from this country." NAI, DFA 102/437, Walshe to Bewley, 12 September 1938. Just one week later, External Affairs and Justice prevailed against de Valera's "sympathetic" approach in the case of Dr Otto Weiss from Vienna, arguing that Weiss was not particularly prominent and was a potential threat to Irish medical professionals in need. See NAI, DJ 69/80/37, Bury to Private Secretary of Taoiseach, 19 October 1938.

situation. In Geneva, de Valera claimed a more active role for the League in refugee matters and criticised narrow nationalist aims.[65] It seemed that for the first time the Irish government was ready to take a positive stance in the formulation of a coherent League of Nations refugee programme, instead of using Geneva's impasse as an excuse for its own inaction.

At the same time, Irish policy had to reflect the fact that the country now had to deal with more than the limited overspill from England. A rising number of refugees were considering Ireland as a first-choice destination. On the domestic front, certain politicians voiced their opinions, and a rising number of charitable individuals and groups were inspired to help not only by collecting funds but also by supporting refugees on Irish soil. On the Catholic side several professors at University College Dublin founded a Catholic Committee for Refugees in early November, around the time when Stefan Feric, the first of the twelve Austrian students to be admitted, arrived in Dublin, thanks to the action of the Committee's secretary Theo W. T. Dillon (see chapters 2 and 9).[66] The case of the two Picks and the initiatives of Conrad Hoffmann and his affiliated organisations prompted the formation of a body to settle Protestant non-Aryans in Ireland.[67] On 6 October 1938, the Church of Ireland's Jews Society formed a Hebrew Christian Refugee Committee, headed by Ernest Lewis-Crosby,[68] former Head of the Society and long familiar with German Protestantism, and Kathleen Huggard, among others.[69]

---

[65] The positive Jewish reaction to de Valera's speech at the League of Nations is reflected in the *Jewish Chronicle*, 7 October 1938.

[66] The exact date of its foundation could not be ascertained, nor can we be sure who else served on the committee at this time, though it seems probable that Mary Macken and Canon Patrick Boylan (for both see below) played an important role from the beginning.

[67] The Picks' case was the first to be presented to the Department of Justice in late August 1938, the visa application made by the Dublin United Missionary Council. Undated application Missionary Council; Heinrich Pick to the Council, 28 August 1938 (both in NAI, DJ 69/80/7); also RCBL, JS, 15 September 1938.

[68] Ernest Lewis-Crosby had studied at Trinity College Dublin and became Dean of Christ Church Cathedral Dublin in 1938, a position he kept until his death in 1961, aged 96, "the oldest active minister of the Church of Ireland and one of its best-known and best-loved figures." See obituary *Irish Times*, 19 May 1961.

[69] Kathleen Huggard had been among the second cohort of women students at Trinity, winning a scholarship for Modern Languages in 1909. Susan M. Parkes (ed.), *A Danger to the Men? A History of Women in Trinity College 1904–2004*. Dublin: Lilliput 2004, p. 69; also "Miss Kathleen Huggard – An Appreciation", *Irish Times*, 25 January 1971. Huggard worked tirelessly in the Church Missionary Society and the Irish Council of Churches. She had a special bond with the refugee children, "more or less adopting" them, as Herbert Karrach remembers. Interview with authors, 4 October 2006. Other members of the committee were W. Smyth, J. W. Johnston, Miss Ormsby. RCBL, JS, 6 October 1938.

At its first working session on 19 October, it discussed 18 cases of Protestant applicants for whom visas and accommodation had to be sought.[70]

E. M. Wigham, a member of a prominent Quaker family, also took part in the Hebrew Christian Refugee Committee meeting on 19 October, thus launching a new form of co-operation between the Church of Ireland and the Society of Friends.[71] While the established Churches were still experimenting with new organisational approaches to helping refugees, the Quakers could already look back on practical results by mid-1938. Altogether, it is believed there were about 2,000 Quakers in Ireland, north and south, in the 1930s.[72] In the Free State, as already noted, their aid to refugees had taken two forms between 1933 and 1938:[73] Newtown School provided education and board for refugee children, while individual Quakers such as Lucy and Samuel Kingston, Ernest and Susan Bewley and Senator James G. Douglas offered hospitality and protected the social interests of the newcomers. From 1936, the Kawerau brothers were invited to lodge at Danum House, the family estate of the Bewleys on Zion Road in Rathgar, first free of charge and then for "little money".[74] Until 1938, Annelies Becker (see chapter 1) was permitted to stay in Ireland thanks to support from friends of the Kingstons in "suitable positions", who defended her against suspicions that she was a Communist and an IRA sympathiser.[75] Kurt Brehmer, like Becker, had grown up in a family strictly

---

70 RCBL, JS, 3 November 1938.
71 An earlier association can be traced to 1932 when Charles E. Jacob (of Dublin's biscuit factory W. & R. Jacob) had been a vice-chairman of the trans-denominational Dublin United Missionary Council, with Kathleen Huggard as one of its secretaries. RCBL, Missionary Council, no. 49/5, Huggard to Women's Organisations and Missionary Committees, 8 September 1932. In October 1938, Jacob made a donation via Conrad Hoffmann to the Jews Society Refugee Fund. RCBL, JS, 3 November 1938.
72 Philip Jacob, The Religious Society of Friends and the "Helpers" Side. In: Holfter (ed.), *Irish Context*, p. 77.
73 Irish Quakers were familiarised with the situation in Austria through Mary Ormerod, member of the newly founded British Co-ordinating Committee for Refugees and former Quaker relief administrator in Vienna. In May 1938, she spoke at a Quaker meeting and also addressed members of the internationalist League of Nations Society. *Irish Times*, 16, 17 and 18 May 1938; *Irish Independent*, 18 May 1938. In her subsequent report to the International Christian Churches Committee for German Refugees in London, chaired by the Bishop of Chichester, she stressed that both Catholic and Protestant clergy had been present at one of her talks and that there was every reason to hope that free places for refugee children would become available in both Catholic- and Protestant-endowed schools. See SFHL, FCRA/25/7, International Christian Churches Committee for German Refugees May-September 1938.
74 Odenwald School archive, Einhart Kawerau to Geheeb, 23 August, 9 September and 21 December 1936, 14 June 1937. See also EA Berlin, no. 77383, Einhart Kawerau CV, 19 January 1966.
75 Becker, *Tread Softly*, chapter 5. See also NAI, DJ 69/80/396, letters from the secretary of the Civics Institute of Ireland to DJ, 27 March 1936; Boyle, Garda, to DJ, 15 April 1936.

opposed to Nazi ideology. In 1934 he was sent to England, where he was introduced to agricultural work at two anthroposophical farms. After vain attempts to obtain British citizenship, he went to Ireland in 1938 and was received in the Kingston household. When the Irish government too declined his application for agricultural employment, he emigrated to New Zealand.[76] Another of the charitable Quakers was Senator James Douglas, descendant of a business family in Northern Ireland. Convinced that Ireland could not withdraw into isolation from world affairs, he took a practical interest in the refugee issue among other internationalist concerns.[77] In late summer 1938, he assisted Robert Donath and his Irish-born wife to come to Ireland, after Donath was dismissed from his post as foreign policy editor of the liberal *Neue Freie Presse* (see chapter 2); in the first phase of their Irish exile, the couple shared his home.[78] The events on the Continent in late 1938 also led to new directions in the work of the Quakers on behalf of the refugees. In late November and early December, Lucy Kingston made it known that urgent calls for further activity had come from the German Emergency Committee in London and from Vienna Quakers in September 1938 – a clear reference to Hubert Butler's and Erwin Strunz's co-ordinated attempts since that month to form Irish pressure groups for a more generous admission policy (see chapter 2).[79]

The political momentum of the Irish Jewish community was almost identical with the influence of the "only Jew in Free State public life" – Robert Briscoe,

---

[76] Daisy L. Swanton, *The Lives of Sarah Anne Lawrenson and Lucy O. Kingston – Emerging from the Shadows (Based on Personal Diaries, 1883–1969)*. Dublin: Attic 1994, pp. 132–133. Questionnaire filled in by Kurt Brehmer, 1 October 2007; Elsa Peile interview with authors, 11 November 2004. See also data in MAI, G2/x/0028.

[77] Apart from his role as chairman of the League of Nations Society of Ireland (see above), he was also a member of the Irish Institute of International Affairs, a body critical of Ireland's neutrality. NAI, DFA 202/1654, DEA official to de Valera, 27 April 1942.

[78] Douglas had been alerted to the Donath case by Mary Campbell and the Quakers' Service Committees of Philadelphia and London in July 1938. NAI, DJ 69/80/29, Mary Campbell to Friends, 8 July 1938; Douglas to DJ, 22 September 1938, and other correspondence. As early as 1936, Donath's wife (née Fitzsimon) had registered as a natural-born citizen and requested a certificate of nationality. This helped the success of her and her husband's application to take up permanent residence in Ireland in 1938. NAI, DFA 102/393. See O'Connor, *Irish Government Policy*, especially pp. 86–87 and 263, on the effects of the Aliens Order, 1935, on Irish women marrying German nationals.

[79] Strunz approached public figures such as Terry Trench, founder of the Irish youth hostel organisation An Óige, politicians like Erskine Childers, James Dillon, and William Norton, other Trade Union leaders and representatives of the two Dublin universities. Siggins, "An Escape from Hell", *Irish Times*, 19 December 1988. In his autobiographical text *My Connection with the Kagran Group* (see chapter 2), he indirectly claimed responsibility for the entry of 300 refugees to Ireland, a rather inflated assessment.

Fianna Fáil TD.[80] His mother's family had come from near Frankfurt/Main; he also spoke German and seems to have frequently visited the country in the 1930s, and received many appeals from would-be immigrants.[81] Aware of the anti-Semitic tendencies within the departments – and knowing how to circumnavigate them – he made frequent applications on behalf of persecuted Jews for entry to Ireland, but his initiatives remained essentially within the bounds of Irish refugee policy. His pragmatism can be seen on the one hand in his lukewarm response to the idea of admitting German refugees other than industrialists or experts in niche sectors of the Irish economy ("toy making, leather goods, chemicals, etc."),[82] and on the other, in his determined and successful interventions on behalf of medical students such as Ernst Sommer and others in 1933–1934 (see chapter 1), or of German-speaking officials to serve in Dublin congregations. One case was Briscoe's successful support for Bernhard Holländer. Holländer's religious education as a future rabbi and his political development as a Zionist had taken place in his hometown Bobowa, a stronghold of Hassidism in Austrian Galicia.[83] In 1920, he left Galicia amidst anti-Jewish agitation, moving to Breslau, where he completed his education, and then to Gladbeck and Berlin to be employed by the local

---

80 *Jewish Chronicle*, 14 July 1933.
81 Kevin McCarthy, An Introduction to Robert Briscoe's Extraordinary Immigration Initiative, 1933–1938. In: Holfter (ed.), *Irish Context*, p. 84, footnote 17. Briscoe's most dramatic failure was his futile campaign to rescue his aunt in 1938. McCarthy, An Introduction. In: Holfter (ed.), *Irish Context*, pp. 84–86. Kevin McCarthy argues that this was probably a factor in "his apparent reluctance or inability to process an application from members of the Dublin Jewish community for him to request visas for 132 children who were fleeing the Nazis on the *Kindertransport*" (p. 86). For an interpretation of Briscoe's refusal, see below, footnote 116.
82 London Metropolitan Archives (LMA), Central British Fund for World Jewish Relief, ACC/2794/01/09/023–6/1, notes on talk with Briscoe by Norman Bentwich, 16 February 1937. The entry to Ireland of the Krotoschin family fitted this pattern (see chapter 1). Bentwich mentions in his memo that he also spoke with Edwin Solomons, President of the Dublin Jewish community, and Mr A. P. Neuman, "who has a large business, and is one of the heads of the community", among others, and reports: "They were all agreed that there was no chance whatsoever for artisans or young workers from Germany. There is considerable unemployment; and it is the policy of the Government not to admit any foreigners for work which can be done by the Irish. Nor does there seem to be any hope for persons in the liberal professions. An attempt is being made to get a place for a German doctor of the highest qualifications; but great difficulty is experienced. The only class, therefore, for which consideration can be given is that of persons who are able to start industries which will be of use in the country. It is the policy of the Government to make Ireland as self-sufficient as possible; and therefore German Jews bringing new industries might be welcome even if they had small capital, or even no capital, provided they had managing experience and technical knowledge."
83 The following biographical details are based on the Holländers' restitution files in EA Berlin, no. 69.533, and BEBJG, Cologne, no. 921/53.

communities as a chazan (cantor). From 1935 to 1936 he occupied the same position in Schneidemühl, a Pomeranian bordertown to Poland of about 40,000 inhabitants. He had to give up his position as the community was no longer able to pay his salary, following a decline in the number of members, many of whom had fled to the relative safety of the German capital.[84] On 24 September 1936, Holländer also went to Berlin, and it was from there that he managed to organise his emigration to London.[85] He applied for the position as First Reader and chazan at the small Lennox Street Synagogue in Dublin as he may have found it difficult, like others, to find an adequate position in London. In autumn 1937, he officiated in Dublin during the High Festivals, but the Irish immigration laws forced him back to London.[86] The story has already been told of how Robert Briscoe and other members of the Jewish community achieved the re-entry of the Holländers – in December 1937 he had married Gertrud Croner, another refugee from Berlin – against opposition in the Department of Justice.[87] The Holländers were registered in Ireland on 2 June 1938.[88] Their story repeated itself in the cases of German-speaking officials Israel Frankel and Emanuel Fischer, both born and raised outside the *Reich* borders. Like Holländer, they first went to the UK and were then accepted in Ireland against the opposition of the Department of Justice, months before their homelands, Poland and Czechoslovakia, were incorporated into Hitler's *Reich*.[89]

Otherwise the community leadership confined itself to lobbying Irish political leaders to protest publicly about discrimination against Jews in Germany,[90]

---

84 BEBJG, no. 921/53, Alfred Jospe, former rabbi in Schneidemühl, affidavit, 2 February 1954.
85 Bernhard and Gertrud came to London on 28 May 1937. MAI, G2/0489 and NAI, DJ 68/1/634.
86 EA Berlin, no. 69.533, Woolfson, President of Lennox Street Hebrew Congregation, to Wiedergutmachungsamt Berlin, 4 July 1960.
87 Keogh, *Jews in Twentieth-Century Ireland*, pp. 123-124; also Keogh, Irish Refugee Policy, Anti-Semitism and Nazism at the Approach of World War Two, in: Holfter (ed.), *German-speaking Exiles*, pp. 41-42. See also data in NAI, DJ 68/1/634
88 NAI, DFA 10/2/18, list of Germans in Ireland, Co. Dublin.
89 On Frankel see Keogh, *Jews in Twentieth-Century Ireland*, pp. 124–127. It seems that Fischer had already spent some time in the UK in 1935 and 1936, intermittently returning to Czechoslovakia, before his final passage to Ireland in May 1938. In February 1939 he married his Irish wife. See NAI, DJ 68/1/709.
90 For Briscoe's, Herzog's and Sokolov's attempts to encourage de Valera to demonstrate his solidarity with German Jews in 1933, see above. On 1 May 1933, Chief Rabbi Herzog also considered trying to inspire a public demonstration against German policy by assembling 28 Irish dignitaries from religious, political and cultural fields – the list was headed by Cardinal MacRory and included other famous names such as W. B. Yeats and A. E. – but clearly the idea was not pursued. Herzog to Chief Justice Kennedy, 1 May 1933. We are grateful to Yvonne Altmann-O'Connor, Curator Irish Jewish Museum, for a copy of the letter. Another initiative originated in Cork where Gerald Goldberg and Dr Eric Scher prepared a petition for the professorial staff at

raising funds for a British aid committee,[91] and supporting those exiles who had already been accepted in Ireland, such as Bayer and Margulies.[92] They discouraged attempts by German-Jewish organisations to investigate emigration possibilities in Ireland, and impeded attempts to bring more German Jews to Ireland made by leaders of British Jewry such as Norman Bentwich,[93] who, like his Protestant counterpart Conrad Hoffmann, visited his Irish co-religionists from 1937 onwards, urging the needs of Continental refugees.[94] Overall, this self-imposed restrictive

---

University College Cork, protesting against the discrimination against and persecution of Jewish professors and students in European universities. Aloys Fleischmann was the first to sign, and his support was still gratefully remembered by the Jewish community decades later. See Cork Jewish Community Tribute to Conductor, *Irish Examiner*, 24 April 1956 and *Irish Press*, 27 April 1956, 'Adoption' plan to help orchestra. Ruth Fleischmann, Aloys's daughter, recalls from conversations with her father and Gerald Goldberg that the petition was given to the German Legation in Dublin in late 1934. Email to authors, 10 July 2016.

91 In 1934, a canvassing committee had been founded to raise funds for the Central British Fund for German Jewry. *Jewish Chronicle*, 13 April 1934.

92 There is however a reference in a letter from H. Weiner to Stephany, 5 August 1937, to an early Jewish Committee for the Relief of German Refugee Women and Children in Dublin in which Mrs E. W. Harris was involved, stating that there was no other committee in Dublin: "If anything can be done she is the most suitable person to get it done." LMA, ACC/2794/01/09/023-69/6. Little is known about Mrs Harris's relief work. Born Maud Jeanette Boas, daughter of Herman Boas of the Belfast community (originally from Lübeck) and Caroline (née Spiers, born in Rotterdam), she married Ernest Wormser Harris, a prominent member of the Dublin congregation. Thanks to Yvonne Altmann-O'Connor.

93 Norman Bentwich (1883–1971) was a barrister and former Attorney-General under the British military administration of Palestine until 1931. He became an important figure in Anglo-Jewish refugee work from early on. To raise awareness he published in 1936 an account of the first wave of emigrants: *The Refugees from Germany, April 1933 to December 1935*. London: Allen & Unwin. In a later publication, *They Found Refuge* (London: Cresset Press 1956), he described the efforts of British Jewry to rescue victims of Nazi persecution.

94 LMA, ACC/2794/01/09/023–69/4 to 69/29 (1937–38), correspondence of Bentwich and Myer Stephany (Joint Secretary of the Centre British Fund for World Jewish Relief) with Edwin and Bethel Solomons, Reverend Abraham Gudansky (honorary president of the Central Jewish Refugee Aid Committee) and Leonard Abrahamson (chair of the Committee) and others, 1937–1938. See, for example, Bethel Solomons to Bentwich, 14 January 1938: "I have been speaking with several important people about your letter, amongst them my brother and Dr Leonard Abrahamson. There has been an absolute glut of people coming over to Dublin lately to interest the people here in various projects, and those I have spoken to are of the strong opinion that the time is most inopportune, and that you would get no support for anything at present. I am in entire agreement with them, but I would advise you, if you think it worthwhile, to write to Mr Leventhal, Trinity College, Dublin, and send him a copy of my letter if you think it desirable. My brother says there are all sorts of things against the suggestion of a few German Jews establishing themselves in Ireland. This letter feels like very cold water, but sometimes the truth is such that it has to sound like cold water. In the meantime if you still decide that you should come, you will be very welcome." LMA, ACC/2794/01/09/023-69/18.

policy stemmed from the community's reluctance to pursue politics inconsistent with majority opinion and government policy, and, arguably, from a fear, rarely admitted and hard to document, that more Jewish immigration would stimulate latent anti-Semitism.[95] It can only be speculated whether the predominantly orthodox and Zionist outlook of the Irish Jewish community also dampened interest in promoting Ireland as a land of exile for German-assimilated Jews.[96]

As elsewhere, 1938 signalled a shift to a more active engagement. The Dublin and Cork Jewish communities formed support committees in April and May aiming to raise public awareness and mobilise funds for the refugees.[97] In autumn there followed further initiatives. In late October (or early November) 1938, a Polish relief committee, chaired by Bernard Shillman, tried to organise support for thousands of Jews originally from Poland, whom the Nazis had driven out of Germany, leaving them in utter destitution.[98] Isaac Herzog, the former Chief Rabbi, appealed to the Taoiseach to follow the British example and set up a quota system for Jewish refugee doctors in Ireland,[99] but it seems that the scheme was never seriously pursued. The atrocities of *Kristallnacht* in November, their dramatic aftermath and the critical response from the Irish public[100] heightened the opportunities for a policy change which the Irish leader had cautiously promoted since late summer 1938. It seemed that, through a combination of external and internal factors, established patterns no longer held good, although new paths were not yet discernible. Goldstone has aptly termed it a phase governed by a "certain degree of confusion".[101]

The new development did not go unnoticed by the German government. Analysing the Irish attitude towards refugees, the German Minister to Ireland, Eduard Hempel, reported to Berlin that the Irish government overall continued to maintain its negative stance towards Jewish applicants, but he had seen signs of readiness to issue temporary permits to refugees in transit to other countries.[102]

---

95 Assessment of Raphael Siev, late curator of the Jewish Museum. See O'Connor, *Irish Government Policy*, p. 195.
96 Practical early Zionism is described in Price, *Somewhere to Hang My Hat*, p. 145: "As in many such homes, my parents supported the Zionist movement without sharing the dream of settling in the Promised Land." They habitually donated into the ubiquitous blue and white collection boxes or bought land certificates from the Jewish National Fund.
97 *Jewish Chronicle*, 29 April, 20 May 1938.
98 The exact foundation date of this committee could not be established. A report of the *Jewish Chronicle* of 9 December 1938 suggests that an earlier committee had existed and been reorganised after German assaults on Polish Jews.
99 NAI, DFA 3/131/143, Herzog to de Valera, 9 October 1938. See also Price, *Somewhere to Hang My Hat*, p. 116.
100 See O'Driscoll, *Ireland*, p. 239.
101 Goldstone, 'Benevolent Helpfulness'? In: Kennedy and Skelly (eds), *Irish Foreign Policy*, p. 128.
102 See O'Driscoll, *Ireland*, p. 240.

The Irish Co-ordinating Committee for Refugees

The establishment of the Irish Co-ordinating Committee for Refugees (ICCR) aimed to resolve the contradictions of Irish refugee policy by instituting a regulatory framework to bind the government, charity groups and the applicants themselves. By a carefully calculated system of extension and restriction of grants, it seemed possible to allay the discord over admissions that had arisen in the course of 1938. The story of the Committee's foundation has been told in previous studies,[103] but a number of questions remain that could only be clarified by reference to the Committee's own files, which appear to have been lost.[104] However, it is clear that on 1 November 1938, the existing aid committees, apparently on their own initiative, established an umbrella committee, whose task was to "unite the work of all smaller organisations which were working for refugees to present their cases to the Government and to prevent overlapping and wastage in administration".[105] Frank Fahy, Ceann Comhairle (speaker) of Dáil Éireann, the Irish parliament, took the role of chair, and Theo Dillon became the vice-chairman and secretary. To begin with, this 'Austrian and German Refugees Co-ordinating Committee' was conceived as a "working committee" for a newly founded Appeal Committee which was to raise money through an appeal to the Irish people.[106] In the following days, negotiations took place between representatives of the Appeal Committee and the departments. One issue concerned sectarianism in the Christian groups.[107] The results were set out in an authoritative Department of

---

[103] Keogh, *Jews in Twentieth-Century Ireland*, pp. 138–140; Keogh, Irish Refugee Policy, Anti-Semitism and Nazism at the Approach of World War Two. In: Holfter (ed.), *German-speaking Exiles*, pp. 37–74, 53–56; Goldstone, 'Benevolent Helpfulness'? In: Kennedy and Skelly (eds), *Irish Foreign Policy*, pp. 128–32; O'Connor, *Irish Government Policy*, pp. 203–218.
[104] It seems that as early as 1965, Lisl and Erwin Strunz and Hubert Butler tried to find out where the files of the ICCR had gone, and contacted Kathleen Huggard, Stella Webb and others formerly involved, but in vain. See TCD Archives, Butler Papers, 10304/597/1432 (1965).
[105] *Irish Times*, 24 March 1939, letter to the editor by R. W. Ditchburn.
[106] NAI, DFA 243/9, Ditchburn memorandum, 7 March 1939.
[107] Keogh and Goldstone emphasise the crucial role of Theo Dillon, and the indirect one of de Valera, in these negotiations. Keogh, *Jews in Twentieth-Century Ireland*, pp. 138–139; Goldstone, 'Benevolent Helpfulness'? In: Kennedy and Skelly (eds), *Irish Foreign Policy*, p. 129. On 8 November, a set of immigration rules was defined in talks between Dillon and the DJ. A letter from Dillon to de Valera of 10 November "gratefully" acknowledged the part the Taoiseach and the Ceann Comhairle had recently played in securing "friendly working relations" with the departments. Quoted in Keogh, *Jews in Twentieth-Century Ireland*, p. 139. There is little evidence concerning interdepartmental exchanges and the composition of the ICCR. The question of which religious societies should be accepted and what functions they should have within the new umbrella organisation was a vital one, as can be gauged from Canon Lewis-Crosby's public statement that

Justice memorandum of 14 November,[108] in which the new committee was granted powers to receive all applications from would-be refugees and sift their merits before consultation with the government. There were two initial restrictions. First, the committee was to select only "Christians with Jewish blood" – as it was believed that professing Jews were able to access "adequate funds subscribed by the Jewish Communities in other countries". Secondly, the Department of Justice favoured a quota system: no more than 20 children, 20 adults and a further 50 agricultural trainees of the Kagran Group (see chapter 2) were to be accepted for a temporary sojourn in Ireland. It was only within the limits for each category that the ICCR was allowed to select candidates.[109] These categories were confirmed by 24 November and provided the basis for the work of the ICCR.[110] The argument justifying the exclusion of practising Jews from a central instrument of admission policy was one that had often been repeated.[111] It may be surmised that in reality the committee members feared the effects of anti-Jewish sentiments both amongst the Irish public and within the departments. The strength of such sentiments can be judged from the fact that at the time when the new policy was framed, the main concern of the anti-Jewish stalwarts in Justice and External Affairs, and of Charles Bewley, was how to prevent a "further" influx of non-profitable Jews from countries in imminent danger from German arms or ideology.[112]

---

the Church of Ireland's Hebrew Christian Refugee Committee had been conceded its part in the ICCR only after "much agitation and interviews with officials" and thanks to de Valera's and the Ceann Comhairle's support. *Irish Independent*, 11 May 1939.

108 Keogh asserts that the memorandum was produced by an undefined "working group". Keogh, *Jews in Twentieth-Century Ireland*, p. 139. This could have been the "working committee" mentioned above, but it seems clear from the text that it was written inside the DJ. Its main purpose was to set the limits of what the Department was ready to concede to the new body.

109 NAI, DFA 243/9, Memorandum, Forming of an 'Irish Co-ordinating Committee for Refugees'. Also quoted in Goldstone, 'Benevolent Helpfulness'? In: Kennedy and Skelly (eds), *Irish Foreign Policy*, p. 129.

110 This is at least the date that Goldstone suggests. See 'Benevolent Helpfulness'? In: Kennedy and Skelly (eds), *Irish Foreign Policy*, p. 129.

111 That Jewish refugees could rely on the international support of Jewish communities was a defensive argument frequently used in Catholic circles in other European countries. See F. Caestecker and B. Moore, Comparative Analysis. In: Caestecker and Moore (eds), *Refugees from Nazi Germany*, p. 283. It also appeared in Dillon's later article on the refugee question in *Studies*, Vol. XXVIII (September 1939), p. 407.

112 See Keogh, Irish Refugee Policy. In: Holfter (ed.), *German-speaking Exiles*, pp. 48–50; Keogh, *Jews in Twentieth-Century Ireland*, pp. 129–132. The departments were indeed successful in shutting doors to applicants from Czechoslovakia. See, for example, cases referred to in NAI, DFA 202/155, 210, 706. As before, the ban exempted profitable candidates like the Bohemian and Moravian applicants mentioned in chapter 3.

> THE IRISH PRESS, WEDNESDAY, NOVEMBER 23, 1938.
> # IRISH SANCTUARY FOR REFUGEES
> ### Government Grants Visas To Party
> (IRISH PRESS Special.)

Image 1: Newspaper article 'Irish Sanctuary for Refugees', *Irish Press* report about the planned intake of refugees, 23 November 1938.

The Jewish leadership in Dublin and Cork was in a difficult situation. Until this time only Robert Briscoe and Michael Noyk, Jewish solicitor and long-standing Republican, had made personal efforts to offer a safe haven in Ireland to persecuted Jews.[113] The community leadership did not think it "practicable at the moment to have Jewish children admitted to Eire", as the *Jewish Chronicle* reported in November 1938.[114] The only measure they imagined feasible was to form another fund-raising committee, under the chairmanship of Reverend Abraham Gudansky. New challenges were posed by the German Pogrom, and by the formation and Christians-only policy of the new committee, which appeared to claim a monopoly on admissions. On 19 November, members of the Dublin Jewish community implored Robert Briscoe to start a campaign for visas to be granted to 132 children, the first time the community leadership took determined steps to organise flight to Ireland.[115] It seems, however, that Briscoe refused to act on this occasion.[116] Some time in late November a preparatory standing committee was

---

113 For Michael Noyk's Republican background see Keogh, *Jews in Twentieth-Century Ireland*, pp. 72–73; Rivlin, *Shalom Ireland*, pp. 193–194. Between September and November 1938, obviously acting independently from the community, he urged the DJ to grant visas to Stefan Lendt, David Nachmann and Emil Raumann. See correspondence in NAI, DJ files 69/80/38, 69/80/128 and 69/80/572.
114 The Jewish leadership in Dublin rejected as "unpractical" the measures a delegate from the Riga community had described to them as having been taken by Latvian Jews to save Jewish children in Germany. *Jewish Chronicle*, 11 November 1938.
115 McCarthy, An Introduction. In: Holfter (ed.), *Irish Context*, pp. 86–87.
116 McCarthy interprets Briscoe's lack of response as a result of his failure, six months earlier, to mitigate the harshness of official policy, and suggests that this led him to prioritise his Zionist commitments over his immigration initiatives. McCarthy, An Introduction. In: Holfter (ed.), *Irish Context*, p. 87. The events of *Kristallnacht*, however, had created a completely new situation that led Great Britain – until then also very reluctant to admit large numbers of refugees – to receive

founded to represent Jewish interests in the developing aid structures. Another impulse for change came from a faction inside British Jewry. In early November 1938, Solomon Schonfeld, anti-Zionist and President of the British Union of Orthodox Hebrew Organisations, arrived in Ireland.[117] He was introduced to the framework of Irish refugee policy through talks with leaders of the Dublin community, and also had a meeting with de Valera, who did not step outside the paths of established policy. He "expressed his sympathy and promised to do all that was possible" for Eastern European (i.e. Polish) Jews, but did not commit the Irish government to giving any assistance, although he expressed support, in vague terms, for settling Jewish industrialists in Ireland.[118] The Taoiseach's evasive position must have disappointed Schonfeld.[119] His lukewarm response resembled Briscoe's reaction to the *Kindertransport* idea. Both men would have been well aware that a revision of policy was under way which promised a fresh institutional approach to the refugee question.

By the beginning of December, the inclusion of a Jewish committee in the new body still hung in the balance. On 9 December, the new executive committee introduced itself to the Irish public as the Irish Co-ordinating Committee for the Relief of Christian Refugees from Central Europe and issued a public appeal for funds. Remarkably, the new 'Jewish Standing Committee for Refugees'

10,000 children via the *Kindertransport*. In Ireland, the German events added an extra urgency to the development of the ICCR. It is likely that Briscoe was aware of the negotiations concerning the creation of the ICCR and its role of presenting all refugee cases to the government, as well as the plan to allow 20 refugee children into Ireland. He might have felt that the considerably higher number of permits for children sought by the Dublin Jewish community made their proposal less likely to succeed. He continued to support applications from individuals. See, for example, the memoir of Otto Michael Falk in *Holocaust Memorial Day 2009 booklet*. Dublin: Holocaust Educational Trust of Ireland 2009, p. 18. Falk's case had been brought forward in late November 1938 by a teacher at the Zion School in Bloomfield Avenue, Dr Teller, and his wife, who urged the DJ to allow the entry of nine-year-old Falk from Frankfurt/Main. The Tellers had been alerted to the case by Bernhard and Gertrude Holländer, who probably knew the Falk family from their time in Schneidemühl. NAI, DJ 69/80/129, Bessie Teller to DJ, 25 November 1938, and further correspondence. Falk came to Ireland in April 1939, following the efforts of the ICCR and, as he remembers, of Robert Briscoe.

117 Schonfeld to HC Ireland, 16 October 1938. Document exhibited in Jewish Museum Dublin. *Jewish Chronicle*, 4 and 11 November 1938. Goldstone, 'Benevolent Helpfulness'? In: Kennedy and Skelly (eds), *Irish Foreign Policy*, p. 126.

118 *Jewish Chronicle*, 11 November 1938; also NAI, DFA 202/157, Schonfeld to Walshe, 29 June 1939.

119 Schonfeld's disappointment must have been shared by would-be emigrants on the Continent whose hopes were raised by the apparently encouraging new signals from Dublin. See a number of files in the DJ series 69/80. Many pleas, usually connected with an offer to establish new industries in Ireland, were sent to de Valera's department in November 1938 and the subsequent weeks. They were channelled into the departmental process with the DJ as the final and generally negative authority.

participated in the meeting, but the title of the Co-ordinating Committee and the fact that no Jewish name appeared in the list of signatories for the Appeal still betrayed the Christians-only bias of the new forum. The use of a formula stating that "a Jewish member of a Christian family will be eligible to receive help as part of a family unit" (and thereby establishing that lone Jewish individuals or Jewish families were not eligible) highlights how controversial the representation of Jewish interests remained.[120] How the new Jewish committee secured its full representation on the ICCR in the following days and weeks is not known. Retitled the Central Jewish Refugee Aid Committee (CJRAC), and chaired by Leonard Abrahamson, it had offices on the premises of the Board of Guardians at Bloomfield House in Bloomfield Avenue, Dublin. Although the CJRAC claimed a competence to "direct all activities in Eire" and required to be recognised within the new admission policy,[121] the government wanted to deal only with the ICCR, so its members experienced the "unexpected necessity of providing visas for the Jewish Committee", as Robert Ditchburn recalled some months later. The ICCR first pleaded for a "separate quota for Jewish cases", i.e. in addition to its own quotas, but the government refused such a proposal.[122] The ICCR then requested a change to the distribution of permits originally agreed and the addition of a "Jewish Section", which was granted. The situation met with mixed responses in Jewish circles, as can be seen from a letter which Maurice Cohen, the representative of the Cork committee, published in the *Cork Examiner*, 17 December 1938.

> My committee desire to make it clear that they are not members of the Co-ordinating Committee [...] we understand that some members of the Dublin branch of our committee attend meetings of this committee so as to avoid overlapping but are not members of it. The Co-ordinating Committee are dealing only with Germans and Austrians who are Catholic and Protestant but who by reason of their Jewish ancestry are classed by Nazi law as Jews. These unfortunate people who in spite of their religion suffer as much as our co-religionists are being catered for in a certain way by the Co-ordinating Committee. In so far as refugees of the Jewish religion are concerned my committee and our colleagues in Dublin will be solely responsible for their care, maintenance and housing.[123]

Although the last sentence stresses the singularity and independence of the Abrahamson committee, in fact a member of that committee, Professor Joshua Baker, TCD, had become an equal partner in the new committee as representative of the "Jewish Section". The new partnership was the reason why the members of the

---

120 *Irish Times*, 9 December 1938.
121 *Jewish Chronicle*, 30 December 1938.
122 NAI, DFA 243/9, Ditchburn memorandum, 7 March 1939.
123 See also *Jewish Chronicle*, 30 December 1938, on the reactions of the Cork community.

umbrella organisation chose to return to the original label – the Irish Co-ordinating Committee for Refugees.

The functions of the ICCR can be inferred from its subcommittees. One supervised a scheme of agricultural training, another a residential ("hospitality") register, a third the implementation of emigration projects and a fourth a Social Refugee Club in Dublin.[124] Day-to-day administrative work took place in the ICCR committee rooms at offices at 6 Eustace Street, carried out by the committee's permanent secretary, Maud Slattery, an experienced relief worker with a Quaker background.[125] The ICCR was not merely a clearing house where the applications of candidates were balanced against each other; it became a core player in official decision-making. Deliberations on the admission and treatment of individual applicants took place at full sessions with the representatives of the various aid organisations, with Frank Fahy the chairman or Theo Dillon the secretary normally presiding.[126] The new structure meant that in principle the Department of Justice had given up its prerogative on admission policy.[127] It also meant a shift of power at the expense of the State's diplomatic representatives in the most important Continental capitals. Until that time, the issue of visas, made obligatory for Germany and Austria again since 1935, had largely hinged on the questionable information provided by Charles Bewley.[128] The net effect of his interventions until his recall in early August 1939 should not be overrated. His opposition was usually based on the argument

---

124 Documentation on the changing composition of these sub-committees is fragmentary. In *Irish Times*, 7 December 1938, Ditchburn names himself as head of the hospitality section and Huggard as its secretary. In December 1941, Huggard also described her ICCR function as "hospitality secretary". NAI, DJ 69/80/16, Huggard to Abrahamson, 5 December 1941. Donal Sullivan chaired the emigration sub-committee with Oscar Singer, former manager of the Carlow sugar factory, as secretary. See Ditchburn's reference in *Bray Tribune and East Coast Express*, 7 January 1939, 22 July 1939; NAI, DFA 243/9, Ditchburn memorandum, 7 March 1939. For Singer see chapter 10. Another member of the emigration sub-committee seems to have been Edwin Solomons. NAI, DJ 69/80/573, Solomons to DJ, 25 October 1939. The agricultural sub-committee and its functions are mentioned in *Bray Tribune and East Coast Express*, 11 March 1939. For the Social Club see references in SFHD, MM II D19, 7 February and 7 March 1941.

125 The office had been leased from the Quakers. SFHD, MM II D19, 6 January 1939. Slattery had taken part in Quaker relief work in Vienna in the 1920s. Katherine Storr, *Excluded from the Record: Women, Refugees and Relief, 1914–1929*. Bern: Peter Lang 2010, p. 288. Another office was at 12 College Green, where under Ditchburn's direction the Executive Committee of the Appeal Fund tried to square the recommendations of the ICCR with the means of the Central Fund. 12 College Green and 3 Fitzwilliams Square, another address frequently used, were probably the offices of individual representatives of the ICCR.

126 Lewis-Crosby in *Irish Independent*, 10 May 1939.

127 O'Connor, *Irish Government Policy*, pp. 203–204.

128 O'Connor, *Irish Government Policy*, pp. 152–156, 206; O'Driscoll, *Ireland*, pp. 256–59.

that an applicant was "debarred from" leaving Ireland and returning to his homeland because Nazi Germany refused to re-admit its former citizens.[129] He was not the only Irish official who feared Ireland would be burdened in this way. Under the new conditions Bewley's role became less important: the victims of Germany's racist policy and their helpers could now officially apply to the Irish Co-ordinating Committee. Formalities were concluded with a message from the ICCR telling the applicant that he or she could send his/her valid passport to the Irish Legation and have a visa stamped in it; at the same time, the Legation was instructed by the Department of External Affairs to issue the visa. Bewley could delay this last step in a few cases, but not finally prevent it. His obstructionism could have been more significant in cases processed through normal departmental channels. If the Department of Industry and Commerce wished a candidate to come to Ireland, Bewley tended to deprecate the candidate's economic competence, thus forcing the departments in Dublin to consult other sources, a time-consuming process that, however, only stopped one applicant from entering Ireland, as far as we have been able to ascertain.[130] His opposition was futile in cases where the Department of Industry and Commerce categorically stated that the "need for the services" of a candidate was so high as "to warrant his acceptance as a permanent resident in this country should it transpire that he could not be deported".[131]

The ICCR's decisions, like Bewley's, were on occasion pre-empted by departmental directives. In a number of cases, the Department of Justice tried to keep control, especially when applicants had been defined as profitable by Industry and Commerce,[132] or when vested interests such as those of the legal and medical professions were to be protected, because the potential refugees would "either have to live on charity or compete with our nationals in already over-crowded employment".[133]

---

129 See, for example, cases filed in NAI, DFA 202/56, 202/366, 202/667, 102/461.
130 This was Albert Hitschmann, whom his elder brother Fritz wanted to bring to Plunder & Pollack, Carrick-on-Suir, in 1939. Bewley's repeated efforts to prevent his immigration, and the resulting delay, finally caused Albert to emigrate to South America. NAI, DFA 202/27, Boland to Irish High Commission London, 24 February 1939, and further correspondence.
131 A stock formula used for example in files NAI, DFA 202/86, 202/226, 202/456.
132 The DJ seems to have drawn up a full list of what it called "non-Coordinating Committee refugees". Hand-written and undated remark in NAI, DJ 69/80/452. In at least one case, the DJ thought it inadvisable to refer an application to the ICCR as "they might have the feeling that we wanted them to treat the case sympathetically". NAI, DJ 69/80/261, Duff to Rynne, DEA, 28 January 1939. The DJ's discretionary powers are exemplified by several cases. See among others NAI, DFA 202/42 (Bickhart), 202/182 (Böhner), 202/317 (Brand), 202/154 (Braun), 202/25 (Markus), 202/385 (Mauthner).
133 NAI, DJ 69/80/104, Ruttledge to Father Browne, 28 November 1938.

The rules for medical practitioners formed a special case in this context. At the very outset of the new system, the Department of Industry and Commerce made it clear that under no circumstances would "doctors, dentists and other professional men" be admitted.[134] Even de Valera refused to encroach upon the rights and interests of the medical bodies.[135]

As far as medical students were concerned, a relatively easy solution could be found in the case of those who had come from Britain to continue their studies at an Irish university or the Royal College of Surgeons. They were accepted as long as the London authorities guaranteed that they could return at the end of their study period. Such a case was Gerhard Rosenberg, a doctor from Berlin.

Image 2: Gerhard Rosenberg.

Rosenberg had tried to maintain his successful practice in Mariendorf in spite of the discriminatory legislation against Jewish doctors since 1933, but after 1935, when his private clientele was reduced to a few Jewish patients, he and his family (wife and two children) decided to emigrate. In late 1937, they came to Britain. Rosenberg

---

134 NAI, DFA, 203/27, internal minute in DI&C, 14 November 1938, quoted in O'Connor, *Irish Government Policy*, p. 62.
135 See a hand-written note from within the DJ expressing de Valera's view that in Ireland the question of admission lay in the hands of a "council" which "would object strongly to the admission of these doctors [...] and would not allow them to practise". NAI, DJ 69/80/364, minutes in DJ, 8 April 1939. Specific cases demonstrate de Valera's reluctance to oppose the strong faction in the DJ, DI&C and the DEA which wished to protect the Irish medical profession from "alien" competitors. See, for example, the case of Dr Oscar Olbrich, a Czech doctor recommended in late 1938 by Robert Briscoe. Even though de Valera expressed his personal sympathy, Olbrich's application to enter Ireland as a doctor failed due to resistance from the organised medical interests. See correspondence in NAI, DJ 69/80/156.

tried to qualify in new specialities, such as insulin shock therapy, but was told in Edinburgh that there was no place available. The Irish College of Surgeons accepted his application for a place on a post-graduate course, and after concerted efforts of the Jewish refugee committee and its representatives on the ICCR, the Department of Justice sanctioned his and his family's residence, on the proviso, based on an understanding between Dublin and the Home Office in London, that at the end of his studies Rosenberg would have to practise "in some other country".[136]

A more difficult problem was how to deal with those who had done the "full course" in Ireland: in these circumstances, a Justice official warned in April 1939, a student "has a right to get a degree and having got a degree he can register".[137] As it transpired, only two registered candidates – Ludwig Karrenberg and Edeltraut Reinert – made actual use of their right to practise in Ireland (see chapter 8; and for Einhart Kawerau, also registered, see chapter 9).

The autonomy of the Irish Co-ordinating Committee for Refugees was most heavily infringed by the quota rules. As mentioned above, the inclusion of the "Jewish Section" had led to a modification of the original distribution. The 90 visas were now allotted to 40 persons (rather than 50) under the Agricultural Scheme, 34 other adults and 16 children.[138] The concept of a monthly quota was then introduced, numbers to be agreed between the departments and the ICCR, with the Department of Justice having to sanction their decision.[139] In early March 1939, ICCR secretary Robert Ditchburn recommended the introduction of an extended and more flexible system.[140] His suggestions rested on the structure of committee resources. According to Ditchburn, the December Appeal had added £3,000 to the ICCR's Central Fund, plus private donations, the newly formed Methodist Committee had contributed £600 and Pope Pius XI £1,000. Given these figures, Ditchburn suggested, firstly, an extra 'English quota' for applicants from England ("ten per month or sixty in all") if their return after one year was guaranteed by the Home Office; secondly, another quota of "six per month or fifty in all" for candidates to be guaranteed by wealthy individuals or the new charity funds; and thirdly,

---

136 The story of the Rosenbergs is based on various personal documents in EA Berlin, no. 170.383 (especially a CV written by Rosenberg, 30 April 1953, and a ruling of the Entschädigungsamt Berlin, 28 April 1964), and NAI, DJ 69/80/327, which also contains the exchange between the refugee committee and the DJ. The quotation is from the same file (Duff, DJ, to Edwin Solomons, 6 April 1939).
137 NAI, DJ 69/80/364, minute in DJ, 8 April 1939.
138 NAI, DFA 243/9, Ditchburn memorandum, 7 March 1939.
139 See, for example, a statement by Joseph Walshe that the "present quota of the Committee [for February 1939] has been exhausted, and [...] a fresh application is now being made to the Department of Justice". NAI, DFA 202/106, Walshe to P. T. O'Connell, 17 February 1939.
140 NAI, DFA 243/9, Ditchburn memorandum, 7 March 1939.

an 'Employment quota' under which up to 20 applicants with "special ability" were to be accepted. Further, successful transmigrants to other countries were to be substituted by fresh applicants on the admission lists. It was hoped that in this way an average of 16 visas per month could be allotted. The number was, however, to be halved once the cumulative number of ICCR refugees in Ireland reached 150, and was to cease altogether if the number reached 170.[141] The result of this revised quota mechanism could be observed in October 1939 when the ICCR reported an overall number of 123 people under its care.[142] Detailed analysis reveals that nine persons had emigrated and 35 had been trained within the Agricultural Scheme. 54 were dependants (29 children, 10 older people, 15 married women living with husbands). The remaining 25 had entered the country under the combined 'English' and 'Employment' quotas.[143] The government's continuing fixation on numerical limits necessarily implied that any excess entrants were not allowed to stay (for these "Illegals" see chapter 10).

Goldstone suggests that the failure of the ICCR to bring more refugees to Ireland was due to the government's stiff resistance.[144] Lack of finances also played a role. The State had privatised the refugee issue by delegating financial and logistical responsibility to the voluntary organisations, but the finances of the ICCR and its constituent committees hardly sufficed to look after the refugees already in Ireland and fund their further migration. This was not for want of trying. The committees organised a full-blown fund-raising campaign, making use of all the media, which was to continue until the beginning of the war. The Appeal of 9 December 1938, led prominently by leaders of the Christian churches and other pillars of society, resulted in the periodic publication of subscribers' names and their donations between December 1938 and March 1939 in the newspapers.[145] Its outcome however was disappointing.[146]

---

141 DFA 243/9, Ditchburn memorandum, 7 March 1939. The 'Employment quota' of 20 was arranged in talks between Lemass and the ICCR. NAI, DFA 243/72, ICCR memorandum, undated (probably October 1939); NAI, DJ 69/80/340, Ditchburn to Costigan, 25 May 1939.
142 *Irish Independent*, 19 October 1939.
143 The figures have been calculated from the numbers recorded in NAI, DFA 243/72, ICCR memorandum, undated (probably October 1939).
144 Goldstone, 'Benevolent Helpfulness'? In: Kennedy and Skelly (eds), *Irish Foreign Policy*, p.130.
145 The lists were published on 22 December 1938, 14 January 1939, 2 March 1939 and 23 May 1939. There were also audit reports by R.J. Kidney, leading member of the Appeal Fund executive. Among the subscribers were many who were active in refugee aid, members of religious orders and from all other religious backgrounds, academics and politicians, including de Valera.
146 O'Connor, *Irish Government Policy*, pp. 200f., Frank Fahy to Dublin Archbishop Edward J. Byrne, 21 February 1939. The committee had high aims. Capt. J. F. Luce stated in a public lecture that a "minimum sum of £9,000" needed to be raised. *Irish Press*, 9 February 1939. However, a little less

LIST OF SUBSCRIPTIONS
AS AT 20th DECEMBER, 1958.

	£	s.	d.
Miss Sharpe, 21 Trafalgar Tce., Monkstown	100	0	0
His Grace The Most Rev. Dr. Byrne Archbishop of Dublin	50	0	0
A. Guinness, Son and Co., Ltd., Dublin	50	0	0
J. and M. Mirrelson, Burgh Quay	26	5	0
Anon	25	0	0
Right Rev. Hon. Bishop Plunkett, D.D., St. Anne's, Clontarf	25	0	0
Chas. E. Jacob, Enderly, Dalkey	20	0	0
"Sympathiser"	20	0	0
Rev. W. E. Cullen, Methodist Church and Union Hall, Skibbereen	12	0	0
David Vard, Grafton Street	10	10	0
Hugo Flinn, T.D., Leinster House	10	10	0
Thomas S. Martin, D'Olier House, D'Olier Street	10	10	0
T. and C. Martin, Ltd., D'Olier House, D'Olier Street	10	10	0
Capt. Spencer Freeman, 13 Earlsfort Tce.	10	10	0
Frank Fahy, Ceann Comhairle, Leinster House	10	0	0
Professor Binchy	10	0	0
Mrs. Edith Leech, 5 Mespil Road	10	0	0
Miss Eleanor Leech, 5 Mespil Road	10	0	0
Senator Frank McDermott, Leinster House	10	0	0
The Misses Dunne, 6 Ashdale Road, Terenure	10	0	0
The Misses Leslie, Corarahn.			

AUSTRIAN AND GERMAN
CHRISTIAN REFUGEES'
FUND

	£	s.	d.
Jewish Refugee Aid Committee of Eire	100	0	0
Limerick Refugee Aid Committee, per Rev. W. M. Cargin, M.A.	54	11	2
Proceeds of Sale held by Pupils, Rathgar Junior School	31	10	0
J. and L. F. Goodbody, Clara, Offaly	25	0	0
Executors Lydia Rebecca Goodbody, deceased	20	8	1
Anonymous	20	0	0
Proceeds of Concert in Diocesan Hall, per Miss Huggard	19	17	7
J. Harold Douglas, Donnybrook	12	16	0
Alexandra School Branch, Junior League of Nations Society	10	16	6
Ethel Rhodes, Rostrevor Road, Rathgar	10	0	0
Mrs. Reynolds, Cirencester, Glos.	10	0	0
Proceeds of Concert, Carrickmines, per Miss Johnston	7	0	0
Miss Moore, Moorefield, Ballybrack	5	5	0
J. J. McElligott, Secty., Dept. of Finance, Dublin	5	5	0
Walter J. Carroll, Redfarns, Dundalk	5	5	0
Ever-Ready (Ireland), Ltd., Dublin	5	5	0
Arthur Newman, Shrewsbury Road	5	5	0
F. C. McCormack, Thornfield, Blackrock	5	0	0

Image 3: Lists of refugee appeal (in different Irish newspapers, here from *Irish Times*).

The campaign was continued with a series of other events, which often competed with similar activities of the religious societies and took place in an atmosphere of rising xenophobia.[147] The ICCR organised a well-publicised meeting with the Dublin Rotarians on 2 January 1939.[148] Some weeks later, six leading ICCR representatives spoke on radio in daily staged programmes: on Monday, 27 February 1939, Theo Dillon came on at 8.10pm to explain how other European countries were dealing with refugees; on Tuesday, 28 February, Donal O'Sullivan examined the legal and political background of German and Austrian refugees; on Wednesday, 1 March, Canon Boylan discussed the issues from a Christian standpoint; on Thursday, 2 March, Ditchburn talked about the Irish efforts to help; and the

---

than £4,000 had been received in response to the Appeal. *Irish Times*, 24 June 1939. See also Dillon's assessment in *Studies*, September 1939: "Unfortunately the sum collected was only sufficient to provide for about 70 refugees" (p. 412). In anticipation of these difficulties, Dillon had suggested that guarantees by the religious committees should be signed by individual members, who would be liable if committee means should not suffice. NAI, DJ 69/80/93, Dillon to DJ, 28 December 1938.
147 In the first months of 1939, there was a general upsurge of xenophobia and anti-Semitism in Ireland, possibly touched off by the publicity given to the refugee issue. O'Driscoll, *Ireland*, pp. 253–256; *Jewish Chronicle*, 17 February, 3 and 17 March 1939.
148 *Irish Independent*, 3 January 1939; *Bray Tribune and East Coast Express*, 7 January 1939.

final instalment on Friday, 3 March 1939, presented the 'human side', with Maud Slattery and Kathleen Huggard talking about their work, personal experiences and encounters with "the men, women and children they help to rescue".[149] All radio talks were prominently announced in the broadsheets.[150] A "Concert to Aid the Refugees" was staged on 17 March,[151] and the refugees themselves contributed glowing public acknowledgements of their friendly reception in Ireland, and performed Austrian folk dancing at fundraising events.[152]

Image 4: Newspaper article 'Dancing in the Austrian Way', *Irish Independent*, 7 August 1939.

The fundraising operation contained a threefold promise to the public: refugees would not compete with nationals on the labour market; their numbers would

---

149 *Irish Times*, 25 February 1939.
150 See, for example, *Irish Independent*, 27 February to 3 March 1939.
151 *Irish Times*, 28 March 1939.
152 Peter Gahr, "A Refugee's Thanks". *Irish Independent*, 3 January 1939. See also articles by Erwin Strunz in *Irish Times*, 12 April 1939, and *Waterford Standard*, 15 April 1939.

be limited; and they would stay only temporarily in Ireland while being trained, preferably in groups, for a permanent life outside Europe.[153] The arguments interlocked and had a tactical dimension. The work ban was not only to shield the national labour market against possible foreign competitors, but also to "induce [refugees] to leave the country".[154] The preference for collective training was to ensure that the candidates would stay among themselves, and would not settle in the country for good.[155]

On 24 June 1939, R. J. Kidney made it known that the committees had received almost 100 refugees.[156] The ICCR had taken responsibility for 42, while the others were being supported by the religious organisations. It may be doubted if expenses were split as neatly between the ICCR and its member societies as the statement suggests. For example, costs for the trainees at Ardmore and Cappagh within the Agricultural Scheme were primarily borne by the Society of St Vincent de Paul (SVP), but also by the ICCR Central Fund, due to its overall and subsidiary responsibility for the newcomers.[157] Altogether, the expenditure of the ICCR on these 42 persons and the Agricultural Scheme (Kidney: the "heaviest charge upon our fund")[158] and other shared costs was calculated at £6,000, considerably more than had been received from the December Appeal (see above). This kind of burden-sharing inevitably led to squabbles among the constituent committees, and between them and the Central Fund.[159]

---

[153] Fahy to Edward Byrne, Archbishop of Dublin, 17 November 1938, 3 December 1938, 21 February 1939, all quoted in O'Connor, *Irish Government Policy*, pp. 198–200.
[154] NAI, DJ 69/80/93, Duff, DJ, to DI&C, 15 May 1939.
[155] This was also practised in other countries. Caestecker and Moore, Comparative Analysis. In: Caestecker and Moore (eds), Refugees from Nazi Germany, p. 291.
[156] *Irish Times*, 24 June 1939.
[157] The St Vincent de Paul Society was able to channel parts of the £1,000 donation from the Pope into the Scheme. Yearbook SVP 1938, p. 13, 1939, p. 9. Subsequent yearbooks do not contain any reference to support of the Agricultural Scheme, or for refugee aid in general. All in all, the SVP took over costs for 25 agricultural trainees, the ICCR for ten. See NAI, DFA 243/72, ICCR memorandum, undated (probably October 1939). In 1941, the Quakers' German Emergency Committee in London also accepted "financial responsibility to some extent for those they sent to Ireland". TCD Archives, Butler Papers, 10304/597/774, Huggard to Butler, 6 August 1941. See also RCBL, JS, 6 May 1941. The help came at a time when most of the former GEC clientele had given up their agricultural training.
[158] *Irish Times*, 2 March 1939.
[159] Huggard, for example, charged the ICCR and the Catholic Council for Refugees with intentionally disadvantaging Protestant candidates. On 30 August 1941, speaking from an ICCR perspective, she told Butler that the Catholic Council of Refugees, to which "I have the honour to act as a kind of gadfly", had refused to pay an allowance for Gustav Beisser. TCD Archives, Butler Papers, 10304/597/778. In a letter of 9 April 1942, she sternly criticised Ditchburn's parsimonious

In principle, the ICCR mechanism did not exclude any socio-economic or religious group from entry to Ireland, thus opening doors to all victims of racist policy in Germany, most of whom had been deprived of their principal economic means and of any chance of returning to Germany. Quantitative analysis shows that more than half of applicants came as individuals, among them a majority of adolescents and middle-aged persons, the rest in different family constellations, in a few cases with elderly parents.[160] The situation was especially difficult for those parents or other family members who had remained behind and had set hopes on their exiled relatives' ability to arrange their admittance to Ireland. The minimum requirement of the Department of Justice was that the receiving families were able to maintain their parents, which meant that in most cases only employees in the factories, academics or the wealthy stood a chance of successful application. The Department of Justice would acquiesce in these cases but with reservations and ensuing delays, which in some cases impeded an entry before the war. Even in cases concerning ordinary ICCR refugees, it is difficult to determine who was responsible for some belated or failed rescue operations. Disaster could result from a refugee's own misjudgement, or just bad timing. For example, David Nachmann had come to Ireland to establish himself before attempting to bring his wife to join him.[161] In other cases, the monthly quota restrictions could indeed have contributed to failure. Maud Slattery once remarked that in some cases a married couple could remain separated if it was found that "there were more urgent cases at the time".[162]

The aid organisations and the new policy

Aid organisations played a core role in refugee policy, as they mobilised support from private individuals and families, in some cases responding to

---

rule over the Central Fund, complaining that "none of our candidates were taken on to" it. She also alleged that of the nearly £4,000 that had been received from the original Appeal, only £240 was allocated to the Hebrew Christian Refugee Committee. Moreover, of the Protestant participants in the Scheme (Hirschberg, Morgenstern, Liss, the Frankls), only Liss had received small allowances from the Central Fund. TCD Archives, Butler Papers, 10304/59/781, Huggard to Butler, 9 April 1942. See also RCBL, JS, 4 November 1941. Her views are echoed in Butler, *Children of Drancy*, pp. 205–206.

160 For example, the two-generation families of Gahr and Kappeler.
161 See MAI, G2/0654, Nachmann to Ellen Bromet, 4 October 1939. For his vain attempts to save his wife after the beginning of the war, see correspondence in NAI, DJ/69/80/128.
162 NAI, DJ 69/80/424, Slattery to DJ, 4 July 1939.

personal initiatives and channelling new applications into the official channels. Significantly, at the beginning of the new policy incoming refugees were denominationally divided among the societies, at least in principle.[163] Hence, the transdenominational Irish Committee for Austrian Relief (ICAR) lost its impact on policy, although it seems that in November 1938 it began to exceed its original fund-raising brief by having members guarantee the maintenance of individual refugees in Ireland (Gerhard Harant, a Protestant, and Else Petersilka, a Jew).[164]

The Quakers' commitment reached new levels within the new ICCR policy. They had, as we have seen, assisted in its foundation, and were represented on its panel.[165] The focus, however, was still on individual help. Individuals such as Emma Howard, Charles and Stella Jacob, Bernard Lamb, Joseph Wicklow, Lucy Kingston and others were prominent in welcoming, receiving, hosting and employing refugees. A good example was Vallombrosa, a country house on the Bray Road which Philip Somerville-Large, a wealthy eye-surgeon, handed over to the aid committees to enable them to house refugees in need.[166] It provided safe

---

163 TCD Archives, Butler Papers, 10304/597/781, Huggard to Butler, 9 April 1942.
164 NAI, DJ 69/80/144 (Harant) and 316 (Petersilka). The ICAR secretary, Miss J. Power-Steele, and her family even hosted Gerhard Harant at their house at 75 Highfield Road, Rathgar. NAI, DJ 69/80/144, William Power-Steele to Hedenquist, 25 November 1938 and J. Power-Steele to DJ, 2 January 1939. The new dimension of ICAR policy in November 1938 was also indicated by an appeal of John A. F. Gregg, Church of Ireland Archbishop of Dublin, to support its work, which in his words aimed to "assist the children of Jews from Austria by giving them a temporary asylum until their parents could find a way of taking them to settle in other parts of the globe". *Jewish Chronicle*, 11 November 1938.
165 It seems that E. M. Wigham was temporarily considered the chairwoman of the new umbrella committee in its formative days. She was described as such in the *Irish Independent*, 24 November 1938. For her role as counsellor in the early Hebrew Christian Refugee Committee phase, see above. Dublin Monthly Meeting was given representation on the ICCR, and "a committee" had been set up by Dublin Friends which was able to "give much information and to provide temporary hospitality for individual refugees and other help". SFHD, Yearly Meeting minutes, 5 May 1939, p. 11. In some publications this committee has been referred to as the Quakers' German Emergency Committee. See, for example, Keogh, *Jews in Twentieth-Century Ireland*, p. 140. Lucy Kingston herself generally called it the "New Emergency Committee" (*Irish Independent*, 24 and 25 November 1938), thereby stressing the continuity with her own activities in refugee aid since 1933 (see above).
166 Vallombrosa "was large, though not huge, set in its own grounds, as country-houses are. Ivy adorned its walls. It was crowded, overcrowded. A bed was put up for me in the entrance hall, where I spent the night. Although it was late August, I did not feel warm in the house; for it was very damp. That was my first experience of the heating of Irish houses..." Hans Reiss, My Coming to Ireland. In: Holfter (ed.), *Irish Context*, p. 36. See also Herbert Karrach, The Karrach Family. In: Holfter (ed.), *Irish Context*, p. 47.

lodging to a number of refugees in the critical early days of their lives in exile, before they were able to settle into a more regular and independent existence. The Quakers continued to offer education and boarding to young refugees at Newtown School. Beyond individual efforts, various representatives of Monthly Meetings in Dublin and Waterford tended to the social needs of newcomers.[167] Their financial contributions to the maintenance of individuals are hard to quantify, but their Meetings, though sometimes short of money, gave generously.[168] In 1941, the London committee also took over responsibility for the living costs of those refugees it had sent to Ireland in late 1938 (see above and chapter 7).[169] A number of refugees (Annelies Becker, Einhard Kawerau, Peter Lisowski and the Strunzes, for example) continued to be actively engaged in the Irish Quakers' networks, a tribute to the Friends' role as catalyst in refugee aid.

"Here in Ireland we have as yet done very little," said Theo Dillon in September 1939, reviewing what help Irish Catholicism had given refugees since the beginning of the new policy in November 1938.[170] The statement, published in the liberal Jesuit quarterly *Studies*, unequivocally expressed the author's bitter though politely worded disappointment with the progress of that policy. He indicted Catholic society as a whole for ignorance of Continental realities, emphasising that Catholics themselves were seeking help, even if they were categorised by the Nazis as non-Aryans (obviously he believed that the racial distinction between Jews and non-Aryans had escaped the attention of the Irish public). Only 40 Catholic non-Aryans had come to Catholic Ireland, most of them with the help of Quakers.[171] Illogically, Dillon's critique spared the state, which had originated the policy, and the church hierarchy. The main public act of a prominent Irish

---

167 SFHD, Yearly Meeting minutes 1939, p. 11, 1940, pp. 12–13, 1941, p. 8; Yearly Meetings Committee, Executive (13 June 1940), p. 162; also anonymous report on "Friends' work with Jewish refugees brought to Ireland before second world war".

168 "Much more could be done but for the lack of funds", it was noted at a Yearly Meeting on 5 May 1939, SFHD, Yearly Meetings, p. 11. It seems that the Irish Friends provided money in specific emergencies rather than regular payments. Two examples were a grant to the Strunz family before the opening of the Unicorn in late 1940, and another to the Frankl family. SFHD, Monthly Meeting II D19, 6 September and 11 October 1940.

169 See footnote 157. According to a statistical survey, the GEC London helped support 13 men and five women in Ireland in the early 1940s. SFHL, FCRA/25/41–45.

170 *Studies*, 1939, p. 412.

171 A perception that Catholics did not do enough for their co-religionists was expressed in a letter in the *Irish Independent* of 16 December 1938. The perception seems to have been shared by the exiles themselves. Wolfgang Eisenstaedt's personal opinion was that of the 150 refugees he estimated were in Ireland, only 25 to 28 were Catholics. NAI, DJ 69/80/468, Eisenstaedt to Father O'Gorman, December 1940.

Catholic for the benefit of refugees was Cardinal MacRory's leading of the ICCR Appeal of 9 December 1938 on behalf of non-Aryan Christians. Edward Byrne, Archbishop of Dublin, was kept informed about the status and activities of the ICCR through Frank Fahy and was generally supportive, but despite his endorsement a church collection throughout the dioceses requested by the committee did not materialise, as it was not supported by the Catholic clergy.[172] Within the new ICCR policy, which Dillon himself had done more to shape than any other non-governmental figure, only the UCD Catholic Committee for Refugees and the Society of St Vincent de Paul could be called upon to guarantee or maintain non-Aryan Catholic refugees in Ireland.[173] In early summer 1939, the unsatisfactory state of that policy had led to new initiatives from members of the UCD Committee, renamed the UCD Committee for German and Austrian Refugees. Their work, as redefined, would relate not only to UCD students and scholars but also schoolchildren. It could also assist students to find lodging with the help of a hospitality register. In Dillon's view this committee's efficacy was hampered because of the lack of a general Catholic aid committee and it had had to take over responsibility for "all the Catholic refugees admitted to this country".[174]

On 30 May 1939, members of the UCD Committee proposed the foundation of a new Catholic aid committee. At the meeting Dillon demanded a comprehensive effort outside the university and school sector to mobilise funds through a central Catholic organisation with affiliations in all parts of Ireland.[175] He envisaged that each local committee and parish in Ireland would take charge of one refugee and predicted that "the burden would not be a heavy one".[176] The new committee was also to reform the disjointed links to the *Reich*, the defects of which the Catholic aid organisations in Germany were well aware of. On 11 April 1939, the St Raphaelsverein had observed: "We have tried to spur Cardinal MacRory to activity in Rome, we have written to the Apostolic Delegate, the Jesuits and the Great Priest Seminary in Ireland but so far everything without success."[177] In the eyes of the

---

172 See O'Connor, *Irish Government Policy*, p. 202. A later proposal by Professor Schmutzer at the founding session of the Catholic Council for Refugees for an all-Ireland collection at church doors (see *Irish Independent*, 31 May 1939) did not gain traction either.
173 For the Society of St Vincent de Paul see below and chapter 7. Traces of the UCD Committee's support for refugees who came to Ireland, and others who did not, can be found (see NAI, DJ 69/80/93, list of 17 December 1938). For the latter group see NAI, DFA 202/48 (Gisela Praeger), DFA 202/278 (Peter and Heinz Hoffenreich) and NAI, DJ 69/80/93 (Karl Freud).
174 *Studies*, September 1939, p. 413.
175 *Irish Independent*, 31 May 1939.
176 *Studies*, 1939, p. 414.
177 Diözesanarchiv Berlin (DAB), I/1–89, Grösser, St Raphaelsverein Hamburg, to Erich Püschel, Hilfswerk of the Episcopal Ordinariate Berlin, 11 April 1939. Translated by authors.

St Raphaelsverein, the reason for Irish restraint was the poverty of the country.[178] Whatever the reasons for the lack of communication between Irish and German aid organisations, there was felt to be a pressing need to coordinate the organisations in Ireland and the Continent. To this end, Professor Josef Schmutzer, geology professor and chairman of the Utrecht-based International Catholic Office for Refugee Affairs, and his general secretary E. Baumgarten, had been invited to the meeting of 30 May 1939. As a result of the discussions, a central committee was to be appointed at a session on 7 June.[179] The resulting new aid committee, the Irish Catholic Council for Refugees, operated from offices at 36 St Stephen's Green, with Colum Gavan Duffy as its honorary secretary.[180] Whether the Council, like its partner institutions, suffered from limited financial resources is not known, but it does not seem to have undertaken many fund-raising initiatives in the few weeks before the beginning of the war.[181]

It is significant that the two Catholic initiatives to organise refugee committees were initiated by members of the laity with an academic and international background, such as Theo Dillon and his colleagues at UCD, or English-born Vida Lentaigne. Traditionally, Irish-Catholic welfare activities had always been a prerogative of the orders and, especially, of the Society of St Vincent de Paul. It is worth noting that some refugees were offered hospitality and schooling by the Loreto Sisters and Jesuits, and others were provided with guarantees, jobs and education by the Benedictines and Vincentians.[182] The core of the SVP's contribution, however, did not come from indigenous sources. Dillon himself pointed to Pope Pius XI's gift of £1,000 for refugee work and Pope Pius XII's explicit call for a generous response from Irish Catholics: "The Catholics of Ireland cannot refuse

---

178 DAB I/1–89, St Raphaelsverein Hamburg to Püschel, 18 August 1939.
179 *Irish Independent*, 31 May 1939.
180 Dillon, *Studies*, p. 413.
181 One public fund-raising activity by the Catholic Council for Refugees which has come to our notice was a garden party at Blackrock College on 6 August 1939. The Council was also supported by a number of Catholic dignitaries. *Irish Independent*, 7 August 1939; *Irish Times*, 7 August 1939.
182 Indirectly, short-lived groupings such as the Pillar of Fire Society and the Mercier Society, both founded by Frank Duff's Legion of Mary and aiming to bridge the gaps between Catholics, Jews and Protestants in Ireland, contributed to a more sympathetic reception of refugees. Both were closed down within two years (1941–1942) by Archbishop McQuaid. See Finola Kennedy, *Frank Duff. A Life Story*. London: Burns & Oates 2011, pp. 159–167. It seems that the Legion of Mary was not directly involved in aid for German-speaking refugees. In April 1939, the Hilfswerk of the Episcopal Ordinariate Berlin had tried to approach Duff about settling Catholic non-Aryans in Ireland, but evidently received no response. See DAB I/1–89, Grösser, St Raphaelsverein Hamburg, to Püschel, Hilfswerk, 5 April 1939; Püschel to Grösser, 11 April 1939.

to listen to so clear a direction and so solemn an appeal from the Holy See."[183] That the Pope's Fund still amounted to "several hundred pounds" in the war years invites the question whether the Catholic organisations were as engaged with refugee matters as their Protestant counterparts.[184]

As indicated, one aspect in which Protestant aid differed from Catholic endeavours was that Irish Protestants were well connected with Continental partner institutions, mainly through Conrad Hoffmann and his links to the Swedish Mission. Socio-economic conditions played a part also. A disproportionately high percentage of Irish Protestants were owners of large farms or members of the professions, but the motives for their engagement in refugee affairs were primarily political. It seems that the commitment shown especially within Anglo-Irish circles had to do with a general detachment of that minority from mainstream trends in Irish politics. Many of the Anglo-Irish had a Church of Ireland background. The records of the Jews Society's refugee committee clearly document the names and helpful roles of Protestant landowners and Church of Ireland families in the Dublin area. The Society gave "school fees, pocket money, dock and railway charges, expenses en route, and [...] extras to make life liveable" to the refugees,[185] as well as contributing to the expenditure of their hosts. The committee had at its disposal a special Refugee Fund, into which came donations and funds from appeals, church gate collections and fêtes, and which seems to have been better supported by the community than its Catholic counterparts, although it shrank considerably after the beginning of the war. Maintenance expenses for students, schoolchildren and other non-employable persons were a constant drain, and a special appeal in 1942 did little to alleviate the situation, indicating that the refugee question had lost some of its lustre among Protestants during the war years.[186]

---

183 Dillon, *Studies*, September 1939, p. 414. Six months earlier, the St Vincent de Paul Society had already been reminding critics of their support for refugees that they were acting on an appeal by the late Pope. Defending their work at the quarterly general meeting of the Society in March, the president argued that their reply should be: "We are doing what we always did: we are obeying the Pope, and that is enough." Society's Aid for Refugees – Reply to Criticism. *Irish Independent*, 3 March 1939.
184 TCD Archives, Butler Papers, 10304/597/781, Huggard to Butler, 9 April (probably 1942).
185 RCBL, JS Committee Report 1938–1939.
186 In September 1938, the Fund had amounted to £31, which climbed to an average of about £600 in 1939 and 1940. In 1939, money was moreover raised through two public fêtes on 4 June and 13 September 1939. *Irish Independent*, 14 September 1939; *Irish Times*, 10 June 1939; also RCBL, JS, 6 July 1939. In 1942, the Fund sank to less than £400. A "£1000 Appeal for our Hebrew Christians" in that year did not fetch the expected sums. In 1944, the fund sank again to a critical level: "The expenditures [...] reached one third more than our income." RCBL, JS Committee

Officially, help was only given to Protestants, but a number of Protestant landowners, either acting on their own or possibly on Hubert Butler's initiative, also hosted non-Aryan Catholics. Butler's contribution reached beyond a basic humanitarian impulse and must be seen in a wider political context. From a Protestant family of "minor gentry" in the South, he defined himself as an Irish nationalist who aimed to act as a mediator between Protestants and the Catholic majority, and wished his country to occupy a new international position, transcending anti-British bias. In principle, he was reconciled to de Valera's policy of neutrality, knowing the conditions under which it was formulated,[187] but he tried to convert Ireland's isolation from war into a 'positive', and by implication anti-Nazi and pro-British, neutrality. The refugee issue played an important part within Butler's position. He was "determined that Jewish refugees should come to Ireland"[188] and sought to achieve that aim by persuading landowners to open their houses to refugees, by forming pro-refugee coalitions, and by committee work – he described himself as a member of the ICCR.[189]

A further aspect that contributed to the relatively large proportion of refugees under Protestant patronage – and one showing the fissures inside Irish Protestantism – was that Methodists and Presbyterians formed their own refugee committees, which however could dispose of distinctly smaller funds than the Church of Ireland committee. The Methodists' committee was headed by Edith W. Booth and accepted responsibility for eight candidates, some under the care of the Swedish Mission in Vienna.[190] The smaller Presbyterian Refugee Committee, led by William A. Warnock, had guaranteed the Frankl family and

---

Report 1943–1944. All other figures are from RCBL, JS, minutes 1938–1945; also *Church of Ireland Gazette*, 29 May 1942, p. 205. There is only one figure available for the two smaller Protestant refugee committees. The Methodist committee collected more than £600 from an appeal on behalf of refugee children within a few days of its formation at the beginning of 1939. The Presbyterians also organised such an appeal but its outcome is unclear. NAI, DFA 243/9, Ditchburn memorandum, 7 March 1939.

187 For a broader defence of neutrality see Butler's essay of 1943 "The two Languages", published in Hubert Butler, *Grandmother and Wolfe Tone*. Dublin: The Lilliput Press 1990, pp. 43–49. Robert Tobin, *The Minority Voice. Hubert Butler and Southern Protestantism, 1900–1991*. Oxford et al.: Oxford University Press 2012, pp. 78–80. In hindsight, he regarded the "pedestrian" (Joseph Lee) quality of Irish neutrality as undignified. See Butler, *Children of Drancy*, p. 220. Tobin, *Minority Voice*, pp. 69, footnote 79; 74; 81–82.

188 Butler, *Children of Drancy*, pp. 197–198.

189 Butler to Dulanty, 26 August 1939. Quoted in Wills, *Neutral Island*, p. 59.

190 Five of them (Georg and Eva Maria Pick, Doris Brünn, Hans Reiss and Karola Schönberg) actually came to Ireland. The other three (Anna and Karl Platz, Peter Friedländer) found alternative ways out of Vienna.

Alfred Schulhof, as we have seen, and also directed their movements in the war years.

Besides supporting Protestant refugees, the Jews Society considered it a prime task to proselytise confessing Jews who had come to Ireland. This campaign, though largely unsuccessful, provoked criticism in Jewish quarters.[191] A central figure in the mission was Else Leszynski, daughter of a German rabbi and herself a refugee from Nazi Germany.[192]

The Jews' own society, the Central Jewish Refugee Aid Committee, drew its strength from the developed mutual welfare culture of a small and tightly knit minority in Irish society. Its work focused on maintaining and lodging the newcomers, and organising their transmigration, with Leonard Abrahamson making his canvassing rounds in the community every Sunday.[193] On 13 September 1939, a Garda Commissioner expressed a conviction that "practically every Jewish house on the S.C. Road has additional tenants" (i.e. refugees).[194] Facts belied his view – in a statement of accounts in December 1941, Leonard Abrahamson informed the public that overall "sixty-odd refugees" had been helped since the foundation of the Central Jewish Refugee Aid Committee[195] – but the Commissioner's position seems to have reflected a widespread belief. The participation of the Jewish Committee in the ICCR at least meant that a number of professing Jews were admitted to Ireland. Apart from that, Robert Briscoe continued to lobby Department of Justice officials with appeals and protests.[196] Additionally, the combined pressure of Jewish leaders again succeeded in overcoming government opposition to the employment of community officials. As before, the Department of Justice suspected that Jewish community leaders fabricated an artificial scarcity, to justify

---

191 On the dispute, see an exchange of letters between Rabbi Shachter, Belfast, and Conrad Hoffmann in *Jewish Chronicle*, 28 July and 11 August 1939; also IMC Archives Geneva, minutes of the International Committee on the Christian Approach to the Jews, 3 August 1939.
192 RCBL, JS, Committee Report for 1943–1944. A missionary had reported that "work among local Jews is hard [...] Some refugees with whom I am in contact are earnestly seeking the truth." In the Committee report for 1944–1945, a missionary is quoted as saying: "The two refugees who had previously accepted the Lord Jesus as their Saviour are getting on well spiritually." Else Leszynski had applied for a missionary job in November 1938 and was directed by the Jews Society to work among refugees living in Belfast. RCBL, Committee Report 1938–1939; also RCBL, JS, 1 December 1938; further, a note in the *Irish Times*, 20 January 1939.
193 Maurice Abrahamson, interview with authors, 28 March 2012. The money collected also supported the Jewish refugees in Millisle Farm in Northern Ireland (see chapter 10).
194 NAI, DJ 69/4855, Garda memo to DJ, 13 September 1939.
195 *Jewish Chronicle*, 19 December 1941.
196 See for example the cases of Oscar Olbrich (DJ 69/80/156), and Hans Mandl (see chapter 7).

bringing more Jews to Ireland: "The Jews always import their Rabbis although there seems to be no reason why Irish-born Jews should not qualify for the position of Rabbi. Furthermore, they are always trying to get refugees admitted here on one pretext or another," one senior official in the Department of Justice asserted.[197] Department officials tried to prevent the employment of Nandor and David Freilich and Philip Moddel, but failed, partly because, as in other cases, Seán MacEntee defended their case at cabinet level.[198]

Doors shut tight

The German seizure of Poland with the complicity of the Soviet Union started the World War, creating new waves of refugees from regions populated by large numbers of Jews, many of them German speakers. The situation of refugees was also aggravated in primary exile countries, as a German military offensive in the west was in the offing for spring 1940. Neutral Ireland's location in the vicinity of the United Kingdom, a major belligerent, posed new and peculiar challenges. Irish politicians saw their country doubly threatened. In the days before and shortly after the beginning of the war, thousands of people fearing German raids and British war measures fled from Britain to Ireland, among them various

---

[197] NAI, DJ 69/80/518, Berry, DJ, minutes of 28 September 1939. Berry's suspicions were not without substance. Leonard Abrahamson admitted this practice (or rather, his DJ interlocutor thought he had admitted it) but asserted it had only happened in the past. Minutes of the DJ on a visit of Abrahamson in the same file, undated. Later, the President of the Lennox Street Hebrew Congregation declared that Bernhard Holländer's "position which the Synagogue could really not afford was specially created for the Rev. Hollander as he was a German refugee". EA Berlin, no. 6953, Woolfson, handwritten, to EA Berlin, 4 July 1960. See also NAI, DJ 68/1/634, DJ memo, 26 November 1945.

[198] MacEntee (Minister for Finance until 16 September 1939 and then Minister for Industry and Commerce until August 1941) frequently put his personal and political weight behind applications endorsed by Edwin Solomons against restrictionists like Gerald Boland. For his intervention in favour of Philip Moddel, see NAI, DJ 69/80/496; for David Freilich and his brother Nandor, see NAI, DJ 69/80/518. See also a case in NAI, DJ 69/80/391. He also defended Solomons' applications for some exiled doctors in Italy (NAI, DJ 69/80/364), and helped his relatives, Boris and Anna Elkin, come to Ireland (NAI, DJ 69/80/452). The Elkins had left Russia after the Revolution and moved to Germany. In 1933, they had to flee a second time. They were holders of a Nansen Certificate and came to Ireland shortly after the beginning of the war following appeals by both Solomons and MacEntee. See correspondence in NAI, DJ 69/80/452. MacEntee shared a Republican background with members of the Solomons family. In a letter to Ruttledge he pointedly called Estella Solomons, Edwin's sister, a "great friend" of Pearse and other leaders of 1916. NAI, DJ 69/80/452, MacEntee to Ruttledge, 4 September 1939.

"undesirable aliens", as was reported in the Dáil.[199] Another danger appeared to arise from British policy which, defining incoming refugees as a security risk, allowed applications only from persons resident in neutral countries, thus, it was feared, making Ireland an attractive stepping stone to the UK.[200] Irish diplomatic representatives, it was said, would be swamped by applications, while at the same time war conditions seemed to impede the onward migration of refugees from Ireland.[201] It was in reaction to such apprehensions that Dublin abandoned its pre-war policy and devised a strategy that seemed to satisfy both British and Irish interests. Despite Ireland's official neutrality, a security partnership came to be framed between London and Dublin, leading to a mutual understanding that "in the interests of the two countries" it was necessary to reduce "the numbers of Germans at large here" (including refugees).[202] Not all refugees from Britain, however, were excluded. An accord between London and Dublin allowed over 1,200 British families to find refuge from the Blitz in Ireland, their maintenance guaranteed by Westminster.[203]

The new closed door policy was apparently accepted by the ICCR and the aid organisations without serious opposition.[204] In September all the permits that had been granted in pre-war months were annulled.[205] The change seriously affected all those parents or wives of exiles who were in possession of visas but could not reach Ireland before the war started.[206] On 23 October, the immigra-

---

199 Wills, *Neutral Island*, pp. 49–51.
200 O'Connor, *Irish Government Policy*, pp. 53–54.
201 NAI, DJ 69/80/659, Gerald Boland to Briscoe, 7 May 1940.
202 NAI, DFA 202/537, note Belton, 3 October 1939.
203 See data in NAI, D/T, S12125.
204 For the acquiescence of the ICCR, see NAI, DJ 69/80/545, Berry, DJ, minutes 6 October 1939; Gerald Boland to Seán McEoin, 10 October 1939. See also a remark of Frank Fahy in *Irish Independent*, 19 October 1939 ("it was decided that it would not be practicable to bring here any more refugees from Germany or other countries"). The charity organisations also accepted the new policy. The Catholic Council for Refugees gave an assurance that it would "not present any further cases [to the ICCR] until such time as the present restrictions are relaxed". NAI, DJ 69/80/559, Colum Gavan Duffy to Ditchburn, 13 September 1939.
205 MAI, G2/1083, letter to Hanus Drechsler, 7 April 1940. In the very first days of the war, before the ban took full effect, entry seems to have been still possible. See the data on the Heilfron case in MAI, G2/0453.
206 This included those exiles who would clearly have been able to finance their parents' or wives' maintenance in Ireland. For the Blaskopfs' and Lowys' attempts to save their parents, see MAI, G2/0348, Grete Blaskopf to parents, 14 December 1939, and another letter in winter 1939; Hans Lowy to parents, January 1930; Helena Lowy to parents, undated, both in MAI, G2/2631. The applications of Else Storm-Petersilka and Kurt Hainbach on behalf of their parents were accepted, but the grant came too late – travel conditions after September 1939 prevented their

tion ban was made official, complementing the tightening of internal security under the Emergency Powers Order of the same month. There was an extra anti-Semitic bite among some Republicans who wished to extend the new restrictions to refugees already in the country. For example, in October 1939 a Convention of Old Cumann na mBan protested against the "influx of foreign males (mainly Jews)" and called on the government to "have them deported to where they come from" (without specifying to which country).[207] Once the war had started, Ireland could only be reached on regular passenger ships, with a British transit visa.[208] Most applications came from the office of the Irish High Commissioner in London, whom a number of Jewish refugees in Great Britain addressed on behalf of desperate relatives or friends trapped in German-controlled territories on the Continent. The Department of Justice remained unmoved, even by humanitarian appeals from church leaders and prominent citizens.[209] The only avenue to admission was the "very special circumstances" clause which exempted children,[210]

---

progress to Ireland. For Else Storm-Petersilka see especially NAI, DJ 69/80/316, minutes in DJ of 25 August 1939; for Kurt Hainbach see Hainbach, *A Memoir. 1920–1950*, p. 11. Josef and Friederike Drechsler's permits for Ireland had also been annulled with the start of the war. Attempts by Hanus Drechsler to accomplish their exit to Ireland in 1940 and 1941 came to nothing. See especially MAI, G2/1083, letter to Hanus Drechsler, 7 April 1940 and A. Solomons to Hanus Drechsler, 22 June 1941. The Karrach family's hopes to bring Emilie's parents, Otto and Mathilde Nathan, from Vienna to Ireland also had to be abandoned.

207 NAI, DJ 69/4785, Association of Old Cumann na mBan to Secretary DEA, 14 October 1939. Two weeks later the DEA forwarded the statement to the Department of Justice.

208 MAI, G2/1173, DJ to D/T, 27 October 1939 ("no direct passenger travelling possible" to Ireland) and likewise Franz Schmolka to Hilda Kursa, undated.

209 NAI, DFA 202/703 contains submissions by Cardinal Joseph MacRory and Church of Ireland Archbishop of Dublin Arthur Barton, among others. See also DFA 202/706 on an intervention by Theo Dillon and the Bishop of Cavan. The Briscoe family also failed to secure admissions. See the cases of Johanna Pressburger and Friederike Burger, NAI, DJ 69/80/640, or of the Polish couple Kaminski, NAI, DJ 69/80/659. Only Paula Cermak was admitted as she, a lifelong companion and governess of Herbert Briscoe's wife, was received within the Briscoe family itself. See correspondence in NAI, DFA 202/617.

210 The entry of Sabina and Mojzesz Szparak, daughter and son of a Polish Les Modes Modernes worker in Galway, was granted, but they were not able to come to Ireland. See correspondence in NAI, DJ 69/80/623 and DFA 202/770. A special case was that of the Hengstenberg brothers Jochen and Reiner. The two had been in the household of their uncle Kurt Ticher since July 1939, and the DJ decided not to issue "an order for the deportation of the children in view of their age". NAI, DJ 69/80/395, memorandum to Boland, 20 October 1939. For another successful application in October 1939, see NAI, DFA 202/476. Unaccompanied children without relatives in Ireland were refused as a rule. See for example NAI, DFA 202/627 and DJ 69/80/576 (rejection of Walter and Lucy Rojkov in spite of Senator Douglas's advocacy and an offer of free hospitality by an Irish

"famous scholars",²¹¹ members of Catholic religious bodies,²¹² and a few experts in particularly important fields.²¹³ Under the new circumstances, the ICCR had lost its core function.²¹⁴ The bulk of its work concentrated on those who "will [...] be on our hands for some time".²¹⁵ With the assistance of the religious aid bodies it continued to help its charges find jobs, organise their accommodation in Dublin through its hospitality register, and run the Refugee Social Club (see chapter 8).

In the period between the end of the German western offensive in mid-June 1940 until the momentous shift of Hitler's strategy to the East in June 1941, Ireland was a relatively peaceful enclave in the midst of a war surrounding its coasts. Before and immediately following the fall of France, a German invasion of the British Isles looked imminent, further stimulating a defence frenzy that increased restrictions even on those few admission options that had existed during the Phoney War. Ireland's geographical position, its neutral status, and the scarcity of non-military shipping between continental and Irish harbours almost completely eliminated the trickle of refugees to Ireland, and security-fixated Irish politicians made no efforts to help. After the German military advance

---

citizen); NAI, DJ 69/80/488 and DFA 202/419 (the two Platz children). In July 1940, however, the DJ showed some clemency: a five-year-old refugee child without relatives in Ireland was to be let in, but this was not to be "regarded as a precedent", and the sponsor of the application, Senator Douglas, was warned against making it public. NAI, DJ 69/80/686.

211 Such as Ludwig Bieler and Walter Heitler (see chapter 9). Benevolence was also shown to a potential immigrant, Julius Pokorny (see chapters 4 and 9). The widow of Max Zondek, who had been a renowned Red Cross doctor in the First World War, was given permission to come to Ireland, but was unable to leave Germany before November 1941, when the Nazi leadership prohibited further exits. See correspondence in NAI, DJ 69/80/650 and DFA 202/810. Mrs Zondek was deported to Theresienstadt, where she perished in 1943.

212 See cases under NAI, DFA 202/672; also DJ 69/80/559 (Peter Friedjung) and DJ 69/80/580 (Elisabeth Bolten).

213 See the cases of Brandenburg, Hennig and Schloss, all of whom came after the beginning of the war (see chapters 4, 7 and 8).

214 In October 1939, a committee was set up under Senator Douglas to consider ways of using the remaining money and to "budget for further expenditures". *Irish Independent*, 19 October 1939. Fahy predicted a situation where refugees "may become a State liability as soon as our meagre funds are exhausted". He also feared that there existed "even in very exalted circles, a growing resentment against the admission of aliens". NAI, DJ 69/80/580, Fahy to Colum Gavan Duffy, 10 January 1940. It seems that in May 1940 the ICCR got worried that possibly not all of the refugees under their auspices were "reliable". Dillon and Ditchburn went to see Costigan. They found it suspicious that many of the refugees were very anxious to get to Dublin (though it was acknowledged that they were mainly "townspeople") and that not all details that the refugees had given about their backgrounds were correct. See MAI, G2/0202.

215 RCBL, JS, Annual Reports 1939–1940.

in spring-summer 1940, thousands of displaced people fled to the south of France, desperately hoping that they could survive in the unoccupied part of the country or escape through neutral Portugal, where refugees accumulated by the thousands waiting for transport to the USA or South America (see below). Among them were Edmond Claessens, Henri Orbach and members of his family, and Serge Philipson's wife and daughter, as well as some of Marcus Witztum's Belgian relatives; all were granted potentially life-saving visas to Ireland, issued through the Irish Legation at Vichy. The applications by Witztum and Philipson were endorsed by the departments, overriding the security concerns of the Department of Defence.[216] Apart from the few other successful applications throughout the war years mentioned above, only a small number of refugee visitors, mainly from Northern Ireland, were allowed to enter neutral Eire for more or less private reasons (see chapter 10).

From mid-1942, the government received information about the Holocaust and requests to help save small numbers of victims in the death camps. These requests came from prominent Jewish representatives, among them the former Chief Rabbi of Ireland Herzog, from London-based Jewish organisations and from leaders of the Irish Jewish community. The government – most notably de Valera and Joseph Walshe – reacted with diplomatic overtures, which included a cautious offer to receive 500 Jewish children and 200 Polish Jewish families in Ireland.[217] Irish goodwill, however, remained untested, as the Nazis refused to accept Irish visas for non-Aryans in the concentration camps apart from those who could demonstrate concrete connections to Ireland.

Care and control

On 21 November 1942, addressing Bertha Teichmann at her 70th birthday party at Jammet's restaurant in Dublin, Professor Hans Sachs made a reference to his 'Secret Intelligence Service Officer' whose omniscience regarding all rumours in Dublin he thought could be safely trusted. "This is my wife," the professor explained (see also chapter 9). The joke played on the speaker's and his listeners' certain knowledge that all of them were being monitored. Care and control were indeed the twin experiences dictating the lives of exiles throughout their years as

---

[216] NAI, DFA 202/285, Roche, DJ, to DEA, 12 July 1940; Liam Archer to Walshe, 23 July 1940, and extensive correspondence between Philipson and his family in the same file.
[217] Keogh, *Jews in Twentieth-Century Ireland*, pp. 173–192; Niall Keogh, *Con Cremin: Ireland's Wartime Diplomat*. Cork: Mercier Press 2006, pp. 74–78; Wills, *Neutral Island*, pp. 395–396.

"aliens" in Ireland. Their status as refugees, sometimes rendered as "Refujews" in G2 reports,[218] spared them neither surveillance nor suspicion (see in chapter 8 the case of John Hennig). Once registered by the police, they had to report to the local Garda station at regular intervals.[219] Any change of residence had to be officially notified. They were subjected to postal, electronic and visual surveillance, including room searches carried out by the Gardai (Aliens and Special Branch section) and Military Intelligence (G2).[220] The censors at the Postal and Telegraph Office – and their translators – scrutinised letters and telegrams and sent copies of those they thought relevant to G2 Headquarters in the Department of Defence.[221] This material, together with reports of G2 and Garda officers, filled the files that G2 kept on individuals as well as on businesses employing aliens.

Assessment and comparison

In many respects, the motives and methods of Irish refugee policy did not differ from those practised elsewhere in Europe. Attempts to keep refugee figures as low as possible, adoption of formulas like "judging each case on its own merits", insistence on a return option, freeing the state from its obligations by delegating the duty of care to charitable and religious bodies and trying to ensure the speedy exit of any refugees who had gained entry were common to many countries, though not executed everywhere in the same manner. The most remarkable aspect in the Irish case between 1933 and the end of 1938 was that these tactics were employed despite the comparatively small number of refugees seeking asylum.

---

218 See, for example, reports on Ernst Scheyer (MAI, G2/0733), Priebatsch, the "Refujew from Hirschberg" (MAI, G2/1680) and Schwenk (MAI, G2/0775). The term was, however, an international colloquialism that was commonly used, for example in faraway Australia, to denote unwanted aliens of unclear "Jewish" connection. See Claus-Dieter Krohn (ed.), *Handbuch der deutschsprachigen Emigration 1933 – 1945*. Darmstadt: Primus Verlag 1998, p. 165. Derogatory correlations between "Jews" and aliens/refugees were also common at the top of G2, made for example by Liam Archer, Assistant Chief of Staff and head of G2 until 1941, and his successor Dan Bryan. See O'Connor, *Irish Government Policy*, pp. 142–143.
219 Elsa Peile remembers that the Germans staying at their house, 8 Sorrento Terrace, had to report to the local Garda every month. Interview with authors, 11 November 2004.
220 For example, on 24 May 1940 a "search was made of the room occupied by Robert Dubsky German national 26 Northbrook Rd. but nothing liable to seizure was discovered". MAI, G2/0008, Weekly Miscellaneous Reports, 27 May 1940.
221 On censorship, see Wills, *Neutral Island*, pp. 163–173, 265–277 and Donal Ó Drisceoil, *Censorship in Ireland 1939–1945*. Cork: CUP 1996.

The key element in the Irish reaction to refugees was an almost desperate desire to keep anybody out who could be an added burden on a comparatively impoverished society, one that suffered the ongoing trauma of emigration and was not willing or able to respond to the persecution in Germany with particular generosity on a national scale (though many individuals did respond generously). A political and to a large extent cultural self-absorption that was at times tainted with xenophobia and anti-Semitism also came into play (but in this context it is important to note that the Irish Constitution of 1937 was for its time an enlightened document in terms of religious tolerance). Furthermore there was a lack of established personal links between Ireland and Germany.

Ireland's road to statehood had been long and tortuous. It had only relatively recently attained limited independence, and the question of partition was still unresolved. A contemporary explanation of its attitude was that "[if] Ireland was late to think internationally it was because she was for so long repressed nationally."[222] In 1941, Hubert Butler diagnosed such an inward-looking mentality as a typical feature of late-nation-state societies, which had its effect in other fields of the Irish polity, too (censorship, for example).[223] For a new state, finding a number of would-be immigrants at the door arguably constituted a novel experience that gave rise to fears which could not be allayed by the fact that these people came as victims of others' persecution.

As indicated, the anti-refugee agenda also sprang from xenophobic and anti-Semitic sentiments. The popular 'dislike' of Jews, which de Valera found prevalent among his fellow citizens in 1933, had developed with 19th century nationalist thinking in Europe. Anti-Semitic stereotyping had also found its way to some extent into the teaching of the Catholic Church, and was occasionally articulated in Ireland by individual members of the Redemptorists and Jesuits.[224] George Gavan Duffy (father of ICCR member Colum Gavan Duffy), icon of Irish legal history and from 1946 President of the Irish High Court, held in a wartime judgement (*Schlegel v. Corcoran and Gross* [1942] I.R. 19) that a Catholic woman could cancel a contract with a tenant because he was Jewish, arguing that "the antagonism between Christian and Jew has its roots in nearly 2000 years of history" and was a "habit of mind" shared by "a large number of people" in a "country where religion matters". The argument was that co-habitation with a

---

222 A journalist's assessment in 1937. Quoted in Tobin, *Minority Voice*, p. 49.
223 Tobin, *Minority Voice*, p. 207.
224 See summaries in Steve Garner, *Racism in the Irish Experience*. London: Pluto Press 2004, pp. 142–144; Keogh, *Jews in Twentieth-Century Ireland*, pp. 92–97.

Jew would impair the "amenities of her residence".²²⁵ This without doubt contradicted the spirit of the Constitution, especially its commitment to the freedom of religious belief, which Duffy himself had helped to shape. Irish nationalism was not *a priori* anti-Semitic, but some of its leading representatives were, as Steve Garner asserts, citing Arthur Griffith's polemics against cosmopolitan Jewry in his *United Irishman* as seminal texts in that connection.²²⁶ From this melange of different motives, sectors of Irish society were prone to perceive Jews and non-Aryans as non-Irish, non-national, non-territorialised, non-integratable, non-rooted, non-agriculturalist.²²⁷ Anti-Semitic sentiments were also invoked by government officials to claim they were anticipating social trends – which may be "uninformed" but "we cannot ignore" them, it was said – or even to appear as defenders of the established Irish Jewish community, whose position might suffer from a further influx.²²⁸ Such views resonated with widespread anti-alien sentiments and were also deployed in other countries. The Jewish World Congress official Gerhart Riegner termed them acts of "preventive anti-Semitism".²²⁹

---

225 Quoted in G. M. Golding, *George Gavan Duffy 1882–1951 – A Legal Biography*. Dublin: Irish Academic Press 1982, p. 129. See also *Jewish Chronicle*, 23 January 1942. For Duffy's other anti-Semitic views, see pp. 132–133 in Golding's book. See also, however, Colum Gavan Duffy's defense of his father: George Gavan Duffy, in *Judicial Studies Institute Journal*. Vol. 2, no. 2 (2002), pp. 22–23 [reprint from *Dublin Historical Record*, XXXVI, no 3 (June 1983)].
226 Garner, *Racism in the Irish Experience*, p. 151.
227 We should be careful not to attribute restrictive policy and a closed mindset only to anti-Semitism and Catholic traditions. Contemporary discussions in post-Catholic Ireland do not necessarily demonstrate a greater general willingness to provide a home for significant numbers of refugees. See for example the reaction when in November 2015, Tomi Reichental, speaking as a Holocaust survivor and referring to Ireland having closed its doors during the Holocaust, proposed in a newspaper interview with the *Irish Independent* and in a radio interview on *98fm* that Ireland should take in 10,000 Syrian refugees. In a subsequent listener poll, 73 per cent voted no to Ireland taking Syrian refugees. *Irish Times*, 9 January 2016. See also http://www.98fm.com/I-Am-Calling-For-Ireland-To-Take-In-10000-Refugees [last accessed 15 June 2016]. Such a response is not, of course, particular to Ireland.
228 The quotations are from a DJ official's note to Ferguson, DI&C, 9 February 1943. NAI, DJ 69/80/496. The pseudo-protective tone was clearest in a letter of 11 April 1938 from Ruttledge, the Minister of Justice, to Robert Briscoe, in which he argued that restricting immigration was in the interest of the Jewish community, as otherwise, he thought, "anti-Jewish groups [...] would only be too glad to get an excuse to start an anti-Jewish campaign." Quoted in Kevin McCarthy, An Introduction to Robert Briscoe's Extraordinary Immigration Initiative, 1933–1938. In: Holfter (ed.), *Irish Context*, p. 85.
229 Goldstone, 'Benevolent Helpfulness'? In: Kennedy and Skelly (eds), *Irish Foreign Policy*, pp. 117–178; Keogh, *Jews in Twentieth-Century Ireland*, pp. 124–125.

Large-scale emigration and poverty were an ongoing and often traumatic experience for many Irish families.[230] These conditions contributed to a belief that the country could "feed no more mouths". This affected not only desperate refugees trying to escape Hitler's Germany, but even former Irish emigrants who wished to return from the United States to their native country. In the course of our research we have found a number of applications from the latter, who were only granted permission to return if they could prove sufficient means or that their relatives in Ireland could support them.[231] Emigration had become such a feature of Irish life that in some quarters it was considered a panacea for social malaise, and one that removed any need for Ireland to examine or criticise itself, though officially emigration was discouraged and there were attempts to curtail it, especially from rural areas during the war years.[232]

On the evidence of departmental records, roughly 1,500 people altogether, including children, applied for permission to come to Ireland between 1933 and 1945, the overwhelming majority between November 1938 and September 1939.[233] At least 449 applications were granted (possibly slightly more: reliable evidence of Irish responses to applications is not always available)[234]. 426 of these (plus a number of visitors who often did not apply for a visa and who are not included in these estimates) actually came to Ireland. How much they "burdened" Irish society can

---

[230] A review of the numbers emphasises this point – with emigration from Ireland actually exceeding that from Germany in 1937. According to the Department of Local Government and Public Health's *Annual Report of the Registrar-General 1940* (Dublin: Stationery Office 1941, p. ix, table 2, http://www.cso.ie/en/media/csoie/releasespublications/documents/birthsdm/archivedreports/P-VS,1940.pdf [last accessed 8 July 2016]) the negative balance of migration movement between 1933–1938 was 100,552 (1933: 2,615, 1934: 11,002, 1935: 14,345, 1936: 21,539, 1937: 29,716, 1938: 21,335). To compare the situation with Germany, see Wolfgang Benz, *Flucht aus Deutschland – Zum Exil im 20. Jahrhundert*. Munich: dtv 2001, p. 64: 1933: 37,000–38,000, 1934: 22,000–23,000, 1935: 20,000–21,000, 1936: 24,000–25,000, 1937: 23,000, 1938: 33,000–40,000 and 1939: 75,000–80,000. There is of course a fundamental distinction between emigrants moving for predominantly economic reasons and those fleeing from persecution. On Irish emigration in the 1930s see also Mary E. Daly, The economic ideals of Irish nationalism: Frugal comfort or lavish austerity? In: *Eire-Ireland*, Vol. 4 (1994), pp. 77–100, 96–97.

[231] See for example NAI, DFA 202/29 and 202/47; also DJ 2014/85/2267 and 2014/85/2271.

[232] See Mary E. Daly, *The Slow Failure: Population Decline and Independent Ireland, 1922–1973*. Madison, Wisconsin: University of Wisconsin Press 2006, pp. 144–150.

[233] The figures are based on the cases dealt with in the NAI file groups DJ 69/80 and 68/1 and relevant DFA files. Not all files were available. Cf. also Goldstone, 'Benevolent Helpfulness'? In: Kennedy and Skelly (eds), *Irish Foreign Policy*, p. 135.

[234] We have counted about 100 "open cases" (not including family members), in some of them though it is debatable whether these were actually refugees or German speakers. None of them seems to have come to Ireland.

be gleaned from the following figures. Employment records reveal that by the end of the war, 72 specialists, entrepreneurs, employees of the Jewish community and academics received salaries that supported 145 persons. Those who were intended to contribute to Lemass's industrial project and help create jobs for Irish nationals did indeed do so, if only on a relatively small scale. Some other refugees (eleven, by our estimate) were able to maintain themselves or were maintained by relatives. A further 69 who came via the Irish Co-ordinating Committee were employed in positions that made at least some contribution towards sustaining approximately 111 persons altogether. The total figure of 426 also included 73 pupils and students, about 20 of whom relied on their parents' support, while the rest needed funds from charitable societies or other sources. Altogether we estimate that about 50 students and a further 40 persons fully depended on subsidies from Irish help organisations. This burden however was distinctly lessened by the fact that many of these persons managed to migrate to other countries within a few years (see chapter 10).

Systematic comparative analyses of exile countries have yet to be made.[235] Geographical proximity and historical links prompt a comparison of Irish policy with its British counterpart, whose more liberal response after 1938 also brought a greater number of refugees into Northern Ireland.[236]

As part of the United Kingdom, Northern Ireland had very limited independence in terms of policy, as immigration and refugee matters remained the responsibility of the London Home Office, but there were specific regional initiatives, particularly in terms of manufacturing facilities. The New Industries (Development) Act (NI) 1937 and a subsequent notice in the *Zionistische Rundschau* led to numerous applications from Jewish businessmen, a few of which were granted and supported by the Ministry of Commerce.[237] A central gathering point

---

235 The essays in Caestecker and Moore, *Refugees from Nazi Germany*, provide a first systematic overview of refugee policies in the European "liberal" countries (not including Ireland). See especially the editors' long essay in Part II (pp. 193–311), although it largely restricts itself to institutional players in refugee policy.

236 So far, in-depth studies are still outstanding. Preliminary research by Martti Steinke indicates that a study on the refugees in Northern Ireland promises to be an important contribution to exile research and Northern Irish history. A small number of autobiographical accounts exist (for example Eva Gross, *A Kinder Story*. Belfast: privately published 2003), and insights into the work of the aid committees can be gained from Moya Woodside's and Glynn Douglas's account of Douglas's mother's work: Norah Douglas and the Belfast Committee for German Refugees. In: Holfter (ed.), *Irish Context*, pp. 89–101.

237 See PRONI, COM/17/3/1–5, where over 350 letters from prospective immigrants can be found. "Jüdische Kunstgewerbler für Nord-Irland". In: *Zionistische Rundschau*, no. 15 (26 August 1938). Londonderry and Newtownards in particular became centres of refugee enterprises with significant impact on local economies. See also PRONI, HA 8/69.

for refugees was Millisle Farm, where, among others, several dozen *Kindertransport* children were accommodated throughout the war (see chapter 10). Arguably, refugees in Northern Ireland were more visible on several levels. Their number was slightly higher than in the South – estimates indicate that Northern Ireland harboured 400 to 500 refugees during the war[238] – and they concentrated in a much smaller area and among a considerably smaller population. Their impact in local industries was higher. Millisle Farm presented a constant focal point, and the cultural contribution of refugees was more noticeable. Guy Woodward argues that due to the influx and stimulus of foreign troops and refugees, "the Second World War created conditions in which visual artists in Northern Ireland could flourish," and names Alice Berger Hammerschlag as a prime example.[239]

Any comparison with Great Britain must take into account the distinctly better economic conditions there. Moreover, the situations of the respective Jewish communities are hardly comparable, the British community being far larger, with a longer history, higher standing, and greater financial resources than its Irish counterpart. Taking funding as an example, on 8 December 1938, the former Prime Minister Stanley Baldwin launched the Lord Baldwin Fund for Refugees in a special 15-minute national radio appeal broadcast on the BBC. Irish appeals had also been made on radio, and donors' names had been listed in the main Irish newspapers: these fund-raising efforts, however, although promoted, like the British initiative, by church leaders, had raised less than £4,000, as we have seen, whereas the result from the Baldwin appeal was £500,000.[240] In April

---

238 Brian Barton, *Northern Ireland in the Second World War*. Belfast: Ulster Historical Foundation 1995, p. 30. About 300 were at some stage in Millisle Farm. In November 1939, the Belfast Aliens Tribunal recorded that within its area of responsibility 250 male aliens had been examined, 200 of them from Austria and Germany. See *Jewish Chronicle*, 24 November 1939.

239 Guy Woodward, *Culture, Northern Ireland & the Second World War*. Oxford: Oxford University Press 2015, p. 132. Clara Ewald, the mother of mathematical physicist Paul Ewald (see chapter 9) would be another example. Heinz Hammerschlag, Alice's husband, was prominent in Belfast's music scene.

240 Funds raised from a number of activities greatly exceeded the results of the rather small-scale efforts in Ireland. For example, the 'Charity Sale in Aid of the Lord Baldwin Fund for Refugees' by Christie's auction house took place on 24 and 25 May 1939 with lots ranging from valuable paintings donated by Lord Rothschild (see *The Burlington Magazine for Connoisseurs*, Vol. 74, no. 434 (May 1939), p. xv) to wooden dolls given by recently arrived German Jewish children (see Judith Tydor Baumel-Schwartz, *Never Look Back: The Jewish Refugee Children in Great Britain 1938–1945*. West Lafayette: Purdue University Press 2012, p. 92). Over £15,000 was raised from this one auction. Another successful venture was the 'Stage and Screen Day' organised across Britain on 14 January 1939 at all cinemas and theatres, from which 10% of earnings were donated to the Fund. Over £31,000 was collected.

1940, Anthony de Rothschild, chairman of the Central Council for Jewish Refugees in London, noted this figure in his report for 1939, and further recorded that the appeal of the Council to the Jewish community had raised nearly £750,000 by spring 1939,[241] estimating that the total amount contributed to Central Funds for German Jewry since 1933 was about £2,500,000.[242]

Portugal is another instructive comparison. The parallels are striking: both Ireland and Portugal were predominantly rural societies before state-imposed industrialisation in the 1930s; emigration figures were chronically high from both countries, and their societies were ideologically and institutionally dominated by Catholicism. In Portugal, a historically stronger element of anti-Semitism had led to acts of systematic violence, but after the Enlightenment this had given way to a rather philo-Semitic and refugee-friendly mentality. Both Ireland and Portugal, one on the north-western, the other on the south-western periphery of Europe, were geographically removed from military events on the continental mainland and remained officially neutral in the war. Both were perceived within Germany as remote and undeveloped: this, and the poor socio-economic conditions prevailing in the two countries, meant that neither had been a magnet for refugees from Nazi Germany before the 1938 crisis. In addition there is the interesting phenomenon that many Irish politicians and sectors of public opinion regarded Salazarist Portugal as a role model for Ireland,[243] although it is extremely unlikely that they would have wished to imitate the Portuguese attitude towards refugees.

The difference was notable during the war and its prelude. Between 1933 and 1945, Portugal received between 13,000 and 15,000 refugees from Nazi Germany, most of them in 1940–1941.[244] Its diplomatic representatives abroad enabled thousands of applicants to enter the country in 1940: a decisive role was played by just one man, Portuguese consul Aristides de Sousa Mendes in Bordeaux, who,

---

241 This fund contributed a considerable amount to the *Kindertransport*, started by the Central British Fund for German Jewry (now World Jewish Relief).
242 LMA, ACC/2793/01/13/01/34/88.
243 See also Bryce, *Ireland during the Second World War*, pp. 48, 127. Certain intellectuals and newspapers, and Catholic groups like Muintir na Tíre, advocated a corporatist society and state on the Portuguese model. In 1943, the Commission on Vocational Representation, established in 1938 to assess the potential of a corporatist alternative to the Constitution of 1937, handed in its recommendations, but these never came near realisation. For a summary of these initiatives see Wills, *Neutral Island*, pp. 351–358, 362–369. By 1944, most of their support and significance had been lost.
244 Avraham Milgram, *Portugal, Salazar and the Jews*. Jerusalem: Yad Vashem 2011, p. 295. Comparative figures on the ratio of size and population for both countries in 1940: Ireland about 3 million people/70,273 km^2, Portugal (mainland) 7.8 million/88,500 km^2. For the numbers of refugees accepted in Ireland and Portugal see also Bryce, *Ireland during the Second World War*, p. 124.

in striking contrast to Ireland's representatives in Berlin and other European capitals, ignored Salazar's orders and provided thousands of refugees with visas between 1939 and late June 1940.[245] Generally, there was no insistence on guarantees that they would be able to re-emigrate,[246] although, as with Ireland, the majority wished to leave the country as soon as possible for further destinations. In fact, Portugal's geographical position, which meant that refugees could still find sanctuary there after the war began, and its shipping routes, less perilous than those in the North Atlantic, made Lisbon the only important neutral port for overseas emigration, so that a majority of those who entered the country had left it again by 1942.[247] While they remained, Jewish refugees in Portugal were maintained and cared for mainly by international organisations, better equipped and funded than the individuals and committees that had this responsibility in Ireland.

Near the end of the war, a plea reached the Irish Co-ordinating Committee for Refugees on behalf of Hermann and Wetti Loewenkopf. Both had just been freed from a concentration camp and wished to reside at the Hirsch family's Old Vienna Club. The ICCR supported the application. On 15 March 1945, the Department of Justice told Maud Slattery that the application had been refused.[248] The restrictive policy was to continue.[249]

---

[245] José-Alain Fralon, *Der Gerechte von Bordeaux – Wie Aristides de Sousa Mendes 30 000 Menschen vor dem Holocaust bewahrte*. Stuttgart: Urachhaus 2011.
[246] Milgram, *Portugal*, pp. 59–126.
[247] Ibid., pp. 127–153.
[248] NAI, DJ 69/80/750.
[249] There were initial proposals after the war to increase immigration, along the lines established earlier, with a quota of 20 refugees per month and a voluntary committee to select and maintain them (NAI, DT, S11007/B1, memo 24 September 1945). The memo contains clear anti-Jewish bias, arguing that "Jews do not become assimilated with the native population". De Valera stressed the continuing necessity for a "positive and liberal policy" in December 1945, contemplating the admission "of at least 10,000 aliens" (ibid., meeting 15 December 1945), but in the end it needed considerable perseverance even to get permission for 100 Jewish children to come to Ireland temporarily in 1948. Operation Shamrock, which aimed to provide for German children suffering from post-war conditions in their homeland, was more successful (see chapter 11).

Chapter 7
Uncharted Terrain – German-speaking Refugees in the Irish Provinces

And then they were in Ireland, finding themselves in places and circumstances that could hardly be further removed from anything they had experienced before emigration. Most had anticipated the country as being a temporary ante-room to more favoured destinations, which is why some younger and a few middle-aged males among them contented themselves with taking part in agricultural training projects designed to prepare them for a life as manual workers overseas. In rural (or semi-rural) Ireland not only their foreignness and language set them identifiably apart among the Irish, but also their roles as more or less untrained agricultural workers.

Continental urbanites in Irish fields

On 11 February 1939, the ICCR felt obliged to inform the Irish public about the total number of refugees accepted in Ireland: by that date a mere 80 had been granted refuge and half of them were to fall under the provision of an agricultural training programme.[1]

An agricultural commune in Ardmore, Co. Waterford, piloted the Agricultural Training Project, as it was officially termed. It was here that the Anglo-Irish aristocrat Senator Sir John Keane had provided his summer residence, Quarry House, as a temporary lodging for a number of refugees. In September 1938, Quarry House had been earmarked for a group of ten Viennese Old Catholics until April 1939.[2] The plan was dropped when in early November 1938, the newly founded ICCR decided to "select a number of persons from the refugees already in Great Britain", plus the Strunz family, Fritz Hirsch and Ernst Einäugler[3] to be settled

---
1 *Connacht Tribune*, 11 February 1939.
2 See correspondence between Hubert Butler, Keane, Walshe and the DJ in NAI, DJ 69/80/23 and DFA 243/5. TCD Archives, Butler Papers, 10304/625/130, Butler to his wife, undated (probably late September 1938).
3 In September 1938, Einäugler, a former clerk, had emigrated to Antwerp where he signed on as a deck boy on a ship. He came to London via Algiers in late December 1938. Here the Quakers channelled him into the Irish agricultural programme. NAI, DJ 69/80/190, Ditchburn to Costigan, 15 December 1938. In late December, he arrived at Vallombrosa and from there he went to Ardmore. MAI, G2/0397.

DOI 10.1515/9783110351453-008

at Quarry House after the German Emergency Committee in London had found that its own houses in Britain were "full".[4] In line with the general policy of a stricter denominational orientation of refugee care (see chapter 6), only Catholic male candidates, all from Vienna, were required to assemble in Ardmore.[5] In contrast, the Hebrew Christian Refugee Committee accommodated six of the original Viennese Old Catholics (Peter and Hilda Gahr, her mother Friederike Goldstein, Alice and Richard Kappeler, Rosa Kobler) – all of whom had arrived in Cork on 16 December 1938[6] – at Church of Ireland homes: first at the Convalescent Home, Stillorgan, then at the Country Air Home and from mid-January 1939 at Roseville Home, Little Bray.[7] Another factor taken into account when selecting the Ardmore contingent was that these new, and younger, emigrants appeared more capable of adjusting to the physical conditions of agricultural life.[8]

"I still remember vividly arriving in Ardmore [...] with the morning bus from Waterford, where I had arrived early that morning from Fishguard after a rather bad crossing," wrote Fritz Hirsch, recalling the day when "my life in Ireland

---

4 NAI, DJ 69/80/93, Dillon's list of names, 8 November 1938, and minutes of a DJ official. See also Hubert Butler, *Ireland and the Refugees*, MS undated (probably October 1938), p. 3 on the small and overcrowded English training camps. Butler Papers, Maidenhall.

5 On the helpers' side, denominational categories may have been of less relevance, at least on a local level. On 5 May 1939, the Quakers' Yearly Meeting stated that the project had brought forth "the co-operation of all shades of religious thought in the locality [Waterford]". Society of Friends House Dublin (SFHD), minutes Yearly Meeting, 5 May 1939.

6 *Irish Independent*, 17 December 1938. The other refugees disembarking from SS Manhattan on 16 December 1938 were Paul Wessely (see below), the Karrach family, and Hans Forell. In September 1938, the Karrachs had already tried to get a visa to Ireland through the private intervention of their Irish acquaintance Colonel G.E. Briggs, a former officer of the British Army stationed in India, and his wife, but the Irish government refused the application. See correspondence between the departments, Bewley and Mrs Briggs in NAI, DFA 102/453. Obviously, the intervention of Butler and the new direction of Irish refugee policy secured their passage to Ireland at the end of the year. On this and their life with the Briggs family see Herbert Karrach, The Karrach Family. In: Holfter (ed.), *Irish Context*, p. 46. For Forell's life in Ireland see below and chapter 10.

7 RCBL, JS, 1 December 1938: the ICCR had accepted that the Quakers "should manage Cappagh House", while the Hebrew Christian Refugee Committee (HCRC) "should manage another house for Evangelical Hebrew Christian refugees and members of the Old Catholic Church". For the placement of the HCRC affiliates see also NAI, DJ 69/80/93, 3 January 1939.

8 The Aberbach brothers, for example, had been recommended by the ICCR because both were "strong and healthy and capable of hard work". NAI, DJ 69/80/93, undated ICCR list of candidates to the DJ.

began".⁹ In Waterford a few refugee helpers would have welcomed him,¹⁰ and then the bus took him to Ardmore, where he was reunited with his family. On 2 December 1938, Erwin Strunz and his family, coming from Annagh-ma-kerrig (see chapter 2), had already moved in at Quarry House.¹¹ Friedrich and Marie Hirsch, their younger son Ernst and Kurt Adler, all of whom had managed to leave Austria in September 1938 and had spent some weeks at the *Bruderhof* (see chapter 2), arrived on 6 December.¹² At the end of the month, two other Viennese, Paul Wessely and Gustav Beisser, followed.¹³ The group was complete when Ernst Einäugler arrived on 19 January 1939.¹⁴ "We were supposed to learn about agriculture," Fritz Hirsch says of the project, which relied on the fact that some Ardmore families "took it upon themselves" to let them work on their fields as farmhands.¹⁵

The tale of the "Ardmore Refugees" made the regional and national papers, alerting the public to the novel and exotic presence of refugees in their country. The publicity also advertised the government's new refugee policy, taking its tone from the propitious atmosphere of the Holy Season. On 16 January 1939, a photo

---

9 http://www.waterfordmuseum.ie/exhibit/web/Display/article/373/3/Ardmore_Memory_and_ Story__Troubled_Times_Austrian_Refugees.html. "Memories of Fritz Hirsch" (first published in *Ardmore Journal* 1989) [last accessed 14 July 2016].
10 Local helpers had formed such welcome committees. The Church of Ireland Welcome Welfare Committee was established at the end of November. RCBL, JS, 1 December 1938. Edwin B. Jacob was another "welcomer". He "went regularly to Rosslare and Cobh to meet refugees off the boat". SFHD, "Friends' work with Jewish refugees brought to Ireland before second world war" and Jacob, The Religious Society of Friends. In: Holfter (ed.), *Irish Context*, p. 78.
11 MAI, G2/1827.
12 Friedrich and Marie Hirsch were registered in Britain on 24 September 1938, Ernst on the following day. MAI, G2/0480. Kurt Adler reached London on 25 September 1938 via Switzerland and Paris. NAI, DJ 68/1/624. He was registered on 29 September 1938 in Swindon. MAI, G2/3190. Kurt Adler: "From September 1938 to December 1938 I worked in England as a farm-hand" (at the *Bruderhof*). Translated by authors. AdR, Neuer Hilfsfonds Grün, no. 5957, 19 June 1963. The entry in the Irish Aliens register was made on 4 December 1938. NAI, DJ 69/80/93, Waterford-Kilkenny Garda to DJ, 9 December 1938.
13 Wessely was a trainee librarian. Gustav Beisser, described as a "gifted linguist", had also been trained in Kagran and appeared to an Ardmore girl to be the unofficial leader of the group. http://www.waterfordmuseum.ie/exhibit/web/Display/article/373/3/Ardmore_Memory_and_Story__Troubled_Times_Austrian_Refugees.html. "Memories of Siobhan Lincoln" (first published in *Ardmore Journal* 1989); Siobhan Lincoln interview with authors, 11 June 2008. NAI, DJ 69/80/93, list of Kagran Group, landing card Harwich.
14 MAI, G2/0397.
15 http://www.waterfordmuseum.ie/exhibit/web/Display/article/373/3/Ardmore_Memory_and_Story__Troubled_Times_Austrian_Refugees.html "Memories of Fritz Hirsch" [last accessed 21 June 2016].

story in the *Irish Times* showed the twelve unnamed "Ardmore Refugees" around a table and detailed their day-to-day life. On 21 January, the refugees featured with members of the ICCR. The campaign explicitly capitalised on the newcomers' Catholicism (and implicitly on their non-Jewishness).[16] Nevertheless, the project provoked a political debate, with criticism coming from purist Republicans as well as from some representatives of Fine Gael.[17]

Ardmore has stayed longer than other refugee initiatives in the collective memory of the region although the experiment lasted only from early December 1938 to the end of March 1939. 50 years later, Erwin Strunz, Fritz Hirsch and one Ardmore citizen, Siobhan Lincoln, still rhapsodised over the experience in memorial articles in the *Ardmore Journal* of 1989,[18] their reports of the physically demanding everyday work typically varnished with stories of the hospitality they were showered with: the Christmas ceremonies of 1938, the parties, the dances and the English language courses by Mary Odell, painter and regional representative of the Irish Red Cross, figured large in these tales.[19] Strunz and Hirsch, moreover, link

---

16 The "Catholics-like-us" tone was particularly noticeable in *The Standard*, for example in its campaign on behalf of two Catholic refugees, Jean Repanas, a former teacher and member of the German Centre Party, and his Canadian wife, who had escaped the Nazis by flight to the UK in January 1939 and then to Ireland (17 March and 14 April 1939). The writers took pains to impress on their roughly 50,000 readers that Repanas and his wife were not Jews and that the sole purpose of their stay in Ireland was to finance the couple's quick passage to Canada. On the case see also NAI, DJ 69/80/346, note Garda Dublin, 5 April 1939. The campaign, which was strongly supported by members of the conservative Catholic Truth Society, drew subscriptions of £90 within weeks (£10 more than was originally asked for). On the general editorial policy of *The Standard* see Wills, *Neutral Island*, p. 275.

17 At a Fine Gael Ard-Fheis (annual party conference) a delegate thought it a "dangerous thing to take the offal of other countries" and to "welcome" Hitler's victims in Ireland. At the same Ard Fheis a resolution was passed that the government should be forced to publish yearly the number of aliens in Ireland. *Dundalk Examiner*, 18 March, 1939. On the Republican side, Annie MacSwiney, sister of the legendary hunger striker, and Francis Stuart, soon to be an instrument of Nazi propaganda and espionage, attacked Irish refugee policy by resorting to the stock argument that "charity begins at home". *Cork Examiner*, 16 December 1938. Stuart, husband to Maud Gonne MacBride's daughter, also criticised the Pope's biased position in favour of democracies. *Irish Press*, 20 December 1938. Stuart's and MacSwiney's views were publicly refuted by William Glynn and Maurice Cohen of the Cork Jewish community. *Irish Press*, 20 December 1938; *Cork Examiner*, 17 December 1938.

18 See a reference in http://www.waterfordmuseum.ie/exhibit/web/Display/article/373/3/Ardmore_Memory_and_Story__Troubled_Times_Austrian_Refugees.html [last accessed 14 July 2016].

19 http://www.waterfordmuseum.ie/exhibit/web/Display/article/373/3/Ardmore_Memory_and_Story__Troubled_Times_Austrian_Refugees.html. "Memories of Siobhan Lincoln" [last accessed 14 July 2016]; also *Waterford Standard*, 19 January 1939, 15 April 1939.

MR. FRANK FAHY, T.D., Speaker of Dail Eireann, with Miss Slattery and other visitors, talking to a party of refugees from Austria at the residence of Sir John Keane, Bart., at Ardmore, Co. Waterford, on Saturday.

Image 1: Refugees and helpers in Ardmore, *Irish Times*, 21 January 1939.

their memories of the short episode with the success of the "Ardmore Refugees" in their later lives.[20] In essence, these stories still capture the refugees' relief in 1939 at being spared the dangers they would have encountered in their homeland.[21]

After four months the Ardmore episode ended, in compliance with the contractual commitment between Keane and his partners. One visitor at Quarry House had been Arland (= Percy Arnold) Ussher, Anglo-Irish writer and philosopher who was well aware of political conditions in Germany, if only by report, from discussions and correspondence with Samuel Beckett or (more probably) Hubert Butler.[22] Ussher owned an ancestral demesne in Cappagh, about 500 acres of largely

---

20 http://www.waterfordmuseum.ie/exhibit/web/Display/article/373/3/Ardmore_Memory_and_Story__Troubled_Times_Austrian_Refugees.html [last accessed 14 July 2016].
21 Constructing Ireland as the very antithesis to their past life was from the beginning an important strategy to bridge the rupture in the refugees' lives and find a new identity. These later texts do not substantially differ from similar texts of 1939. See, for example, a letter of an anonymous refugee to the ICCR, quoted in *Waterford Standard*, 18 March 1939.
22 Beckett was at least twice in Cappagh on Ussher's invitation, the last time in September 1936 shortly before his German tour. James Knowlson, *Damned to Fame: The Life of Samuel Beckett*. New York: Grove Press 1996, pp. 164, 225.

wooded land with a big lake.²³ There were two houses on the Cappagh estate, and it was the new one (Giant's Rock, built in 1875) that Ussher offered as a provisional residence to be run by the Waterford Quakers.²⁴ This is how 17-year-old Anselm Horwitz experienced the day of his arrival:

> I got off the train by mistake two stations ahead and had to make a 10 minute taxi ride which took me up a long drive to a large, somewhat unusual house. A maid ushered me into a well-furnished living room. Then a lady entered and introduced herself as Mrs. Ussher. I thought "It will be quite nice to live here". At that moment two men entered. They did not seem to fit into these surroundings. Both wore coarse brown overalls over rough clothes, heavy boots and spoke to Mrs. Ussher a few words that I could not understand. Then they turned to me and said in German: "Komm mit uns." [Come with us]. Wordless we started up a steep hill behind the house and after a good climb another smaller house came into view on top of the hill. One of the men said: "This is Giants Rock where we live." Inside all the residents (refugees) were waiting.²⁵

Image 2: Fritz Hirsch in Ardmore.

At the time of Horwitz's arrival, Giant's Rock housed eight refugees: Herbert Unger,²⁶ Kurt Staudt,²⁷ Kurt Stiegwardt (lawyer from Vienna whom Horwitz remembers

---

23 onlineresourcesarticle117/ita_word_modeligo_parish_opt [last accessed 13 December 2013].
24 "The new Emergency Committee in Dublin has acquired a house in Cappagh, Co. Waterford, to house some of the German refugees" (Lucy Kingston in *Irish Independent*, 23 and 24 November 1938).
25 Anselm Horwitz, email to authors, 20 January 2008.
26 This list of residents follows Anselm Horwitz's memory; also Hetty Staples, the Usshers' daughter, email to authors, 10 August 2008; TCD Archives, Butler Papers, 10304/625/118, no. 118, letter Butler, 8 November 1939. Unger stayed in Cappagh from 3 February 1939 to 28 October 1939.
27 He was registered as a "textile maker". He may have been in the textile industry, but officially he had applied for a UCD place to study agriculture. NAI, DJ 69/80/93, 28 January 1939.

as having been "unofficially in charge" of the group) and his wife Elise,[28] the Aberbach brothers,[29] and Kurt Werner, his wife Lilli and their five-year-old son, Klaus Peter.[30] Hetty Staples, the Usshers' daughter, remembers the refugees' presence from her childhood days at Cappagh: "The young men would have helped other farmers with threshing days but mostly I think they worked on our estate. There was forestry going on and it was a mixed farm."[31] They were "housed and received food etc.", and in return "supplied farm labour and the woman [sic] was to cook meals and look after other household chores" (Horwitz),[32] but there was no language training and their contact with the local population was limited.

> Our little community, on top of a steep hill, was isolated from the main street, but, I found out, was widely known in the surrounding area. As a result visitors did call on us [...] There were middle-aged ladies of a "do-gooder" persuasion who brought presents, younger girls mostly curious how "foreign men" looked and behaved [...] occasionally some cultured society ladies who wanted to reminisce about the days they had spent in "beautiful romantic Austria".[33]

---

28 Stiegwardt had come to Ireland on 24 September 1938. The purpose and length of that visit is unclear. MAI, G2/0820. His arrival in Cappagh was recorded for 17 January 1939. http://www.waterfordmuseum.ie/exhibit/web/Display/article/373/3/Ardmore_Memory_and_Story__Troubled_Times_Austrian_Refugees.html: "Memories of Fritz Hirsch". On 19 June 1939, he married Elise Koppel, another Viennese refugee, in Edinburgh. They came back to Cappagh as a married couple in late June 1939. MAI, G2/0820 and G2/x/0028; also NAI, DJ 69/80/479, Kilkenny Garda to DJ, 8 July 1939.
29 In Vienna, Robert and Friedrich seem to have turned first to Cardinal Innitzer's aid organisation. Father Georg Bichlmaier is named as having recommended visas for Robert and Friedrich Aberbach. NAI, DJ 69/80/93, undated list of ICCR supporters handed in to the Department of Justice. For their emigration, however, the brothers had recourse to the Quakers' organisational capacities, at least in the advanced stage of their flight to Ireland. NAI, DJ 69/80/93, undated ICCR recommendation to DJ, listing the Aberbach brothers as having been "passed by Subcommittee Society of Friends" [sic].
30 Kurt Werner, a non-Jewish writer from Kassel, had married Jewish Lilli Robert in defiance of the ban on Jewish-Aryan marriages. The ceremony had to take place in Switzerland. The couple and their child Klaus Peter returned (or were made to return) to Kassel in September of that year as the Swiss authorities seem to have declared their presence in the country illegal. See Documents Diplomatiques Suisses, Vol. 11, no. 151, pp. 445–446. They made vain attempts to re-migrate to Switzerland in the following years. Stadtarchiv Kassel, personal file Werner family. In Ireland they were under the tutelage of Dillon's UCD Committee who placed them on a list of ICCR candidates. NAI, DJ 69/80/93, Ditchburn, 17 December 1938. On 2 February 1939, they were moved to Giant's Rock.
31 Hetty Staples email to authors, 10 August 2008.
32 Anselm Horwitz, email to authors, 20 January 2008.
33 Anselm Horwitz, email to authors, 1 February 2008.

The community dissolved when a new owner took over the whole Cappagh estate in October/November 1939. By that time some members had already left Giant's Rock.[34]

"Then we came to Enniskerry. Again a farmhouse, agricultural work, planting trees etc."[35] Fritz Hirsch and his family had left Ardmore together with the Strunz family, Kurt Adler and Gustav Beisser on 28 March 1939.[36] Their new residence was Onagh, a farm near Glencree about 10 km west of Enniskerry in the northern Wicklow Mountains. It was owned by T. Fitzpatrick and "equipped with hot and cold bath, dining room and all the amenities [...] of a country home". The local *Bray Tribune* further informed the public that the newcomers would be taught on two farms of over 200 acres. "The SVP are taking responsibility for their maintenance and the Agricultural Committee of the General Refugees' Committee [the ICCR] arranged with Mr Fitzpatrick for their accommodation and instruction."[37] The experience, however, was sobering. "Nothing ever happens here, except sheep are born or calves run away," one of the refugees remembered, contrasting it with the rich social life and convivial atmosphere of Ardmore.[38] The end came soon, possibly because the owner sold the estate in May 1939. For the Strunz family this meant another separation from Kagraners and the end of their participation in the agricultural project.[39]

The others remained agricultural workers, their minds still set on America. Newtown House in Termonfeckin near Drogheda, Co. Louth, was to house the next chapter of the group experiment. In 1922, Vida Lentaigne (née Haslam), daughter of an English Liberal politician, had bought Newtown House after her Irish husband's death. Today she is remembered in the region as a generous personality engaged in a flurry of community activities and employing many locals in her house, the gardens and on the fields.[40] In 1934, she successfully stood for

---

34 Anselm Horwitz left on 7 July 1939. MAI, G2/0492, G2 report, 5 September 1939. For the others see TCD Archives, Butler Papers, 10304/625/118, letter Butler, 8 November 1939.
35 Fritz Hirsch interview with authors, 14 November 2004.
36 G2 files of Hirsch (MAI, G2/0480), Strunz (MAI, G2/1827), Adler (MAI, G2/3190), Beisser (MAI, G2/0339).
37 *Bray Tribune*, 11 March 1939.
38 Siobhan Lincoln, "The Austrian Refugees", quoting one of the refugees. See http://www.waterfordmuseum.ie/exhibit/web/Display/article/373/3/.
39 They stayed for about a year with Diarmiud and Sheela Coffey at Granitefield, Cabinteely. MAI, G2/1827; for their time with the family see Erwin Strunz, Memoir. June 1989, unpublished, pp. 23–25.
40 Josephine O'Reilly, *The Hidden Gem*. London/New York/Toronto: Longmans, Green and Co. 1946, p. 70: "Newtown is a large Georgian house with a Georgian waste of space, in the form of a huge double hall and gallery reaching the ceiling which might quite happily have made three

Louth County Council as a candidate of the United Ireland Party, probably in opposition to what she conceived as de Valera's anti-British policy. Political and religious convictions prompted her to embrace the refugee cause. A convert to Catholicism, she co-founded and chaired the Catholic Council for Refugees (CCR, see chapter 6). In early May 1939 Kurt Adler came to Newtown House on her invitation.[41] Lentaigne and the CCR also succeeded in placing his father's name on the ICCR list, thereby enabling him to leave Vienna.[42] On 7 June 1939, the four members of the Hirsch family arrived at Termonfeckin;[43] Gustav Beisser, who had moved to Vallombrosa after his departure from Onagh, joined the group on 11 October 1939.[44] A few weeks later Wolfgang Eisenstaedt came; he too had been provisionally housed at Vallombrosa after his arrival in early August.[45] In spite of what two photos suggest about the extent of social contact between the Austrians and their hosts – one showing the Austrians performing a Tyrolean dance to an audience from the town,[46] the other portraying Kurt Adler and a local person in friendly poses at Newtown House[47] – it is doubtful if anything more than easy working relations developed between them.[48]

Privately, they "all more or less kept together and did not mix with the local people to a great extent", observed a G2 agent retrospectively.[49] The refugee community in Co. Louth lasted until spring 1940. By that time Vida Lentaigne was already engaged in a new project, which led to the four members of the Hirsch family and Gustav Beisser moving to the capital (see chapter 8).[50] After

---

rooms. It has five hundred acres of land, a beach, some woods, two tennis courts, a farm." On Vida Lentaigne (1890–1976) see also http://www.termonfeckinhistory.ie/page_39.html, Declan Quaile, "Vida Lentaigne" (first published in *Termonfeckin Historical Society*, Vol. 2007.).
41 MAI, G2/3190.
42 The rest of his family stayed in Vienna. See correspondence in MAI, G2/3190.
43 MAI, G2/0480.
44 MAI, G2/0339. At Vallombrosa he met the Karrach and the Fuchs families, who had been there since 20 March 1939. MAI, G2/0511-0512 and G2/0422.
45 MAI, G2/0398. By that time Josephine Lentaigne, Vida's daughter, had gone to England. As a consequence, her governess Mimi Höfer also left Termonfeckin. See MAI, G2/0485.
46 *Irish Independent*, 5 April 1940.
47 See MAI, G2/3190.
48 Declan Quaile told us during an interview in Termonfeckin on 18 June 2008 that "villagers did not know much about the newcomers' background – were they 'Jews' or 'spies'?".
49 There was one possible exception: Kurt Adler seems to have made friends with a Termonfeckin girl, but his father ended the affair by authoritatively sending him to a place that posed less risk of sexual partnerships: the male society of Mount St Benedict at Gorey, Co. Wexford (see below). MAI, G2/3190, G2 report, 13 February 1941.
50 After 1942, Lentaigne lived mainly in England, but during her stay in Termonfeckin other exiles came there from time to time. Georg Bernfeld and Otto Glaser, the two Blackrock College

September 1940, only Wolfgang Eisenstaedt stayed behind at Newtown House (see below).

On 20 September 1940, Kurt Adler arrived at Mount St Benedict in Gorey, Co. Wexford, [51] a place which has attracted scholarly attention from historians of Irish church history. The initiative to bring refugees to the Mount seems to have stemmed from the example of Downside Abbey, a Benedictine foundation in England under Abbot Siegbert Trafford, which had already acquired a reputation for engagement in refugee politics.[52] In the case of Mount St Benedict, however, attention has focused less on this aspect than on the personality of Dom John (religious name: Francis) Sweetman, a Wexford-born priest whose specific form of Benedictine Catholicism has made him unique in the late history of Irish O.S.B.[53] What Father Sweetman tried to initiate was a social experiment combining spiritual and practical work under spartan conditions. He was intimately linked with a number of Irish nationalist families and counted Theo and Matthew Dillon (see below) and Colum Gavan Duffy, for example, among his students at the boarding school in Gorey.

In the weeks following Adler's arrival, Herbert Unger and Kurt Staudt – both of whom had meanwhile taken part in another agricultural interlude in Co. Meath (see below) – also entered Sweetman's hermitic colony, as did the Aberbach brothers, all of them very probably on Theo Dillon's recommendation.[54] Evidence of their activities is limited. The focus must have been on practical work. We know at least that Unger, the Aberbachs and probably also Kurt Adler became more or less adept at woodwork in one of the work halls, which prepared them for their

---

students under the care of the CCR (see chapter 8), spent their summer holidays of 1940 at Newtown House. NAI, DJ 69/80/339 and DJ 69/80/585. Mimi Höfer also returned to Termonfeckin for a few months in 1940. MAI, G2/0485.

51 MAI, G2/3190.

52 Abbot Aidan Bellenger email to authors, 13 February 2008. The Abbot wrote that he could well imagine that Abbot Siegbert might "have been behind the Mount St Benedict contingent".

53 Aidan Bellenger, The Post-Reformation English Benedictines and Ireland: Conflict and Dialogue. In: Martin Browne and Colmán Ó Clabaigh (eds), *The Irish Benedictines. A History*. Columba Press: Dublin 2005, pp. 140–156. Dom Francis considered the Mount his "true home and monastery. He was the father figure, a resident landowner, providing work to many in the vicinity and encouraging local co-operative ventures, including a tobacco plantation. Family money had endowed the Mount and Sweetman continued to feel responsibility for its continuance. It was less a monastery than a hermitage and an austere one at that." Ibid., p. 154.

54 Unger stayed in Gorey from 10 October 1940 to 25 March 1941 (MAI, G2/0849), Kurt Adler from 20 September 1940 to 29 January 1941 (MAI, G2/3190); probably the Aberbach brothers went there as early as 1939. During the war they frequently returned after the others had left the colony. See data in MAI, G2/0308.

later employments in Dublin (see chapter 8).⁵⁵ The reasons for their departure from the Mount after only a few months are not clear. They may simply have followed a general move to the Irish capital at that time (see below), but there may also have been disputes within the colony.⁵⁶ The abandonment of the project at Mount St Benedict marked the end of a concept of communal emigration, which as we have seen was devised in Kagran but fell apart under the different conditions in Austria, England and Ireland.

It is doubtful if any of these amateur agricultural workers, apart from Wolfgang Eisenstaedt, saw the scheme as more than a fleeting period of their exiled existence, and there were growing doubts as to its possible further usefulness. Objectively, it had lost its original purpose. Of the 39 participants, only the Stiegwardt family succeeded in emigrating a second time, less because of the merits of their agricultural training than because of Stiegwardt's helpful contacts in the target country (see chapter 10). Kurt Kraus, Kurt Werner and Anselm Horwitz had already dropped out of the project at an early date.⁵⁷ They were placed in industries instead – whether because of their specific talents, which individual firms (and the Department of Commerce and Industry) had spotted in the pool of ICCR entrants, or because of the aid organisations' problems in accommodating them any longer, or both, is hard to know. Kraus's first address in Ireland had been Vallombrosa, where he stayed from the end of May to October 1939.⁵⁸ After that he was employed as works manager with Aibheise Eireannata Electric Co. of Ireland Ltd, Dunleer, Co. Louth – mainly, it seems, through the mediation of John B. Hamill, state solicitor for Co. Louth, who was deeply committed to giving practical help to refugees in other respects (see below).⁵⁹ On 28 January 1941, Kraus joined Recold Ltd, a refrigeration company in Dublin, as works supervisor.⁶⁰ Like Unger, Staudt and the Stiegwardts, the Werner family had departed from Cappagh on 16 October 1939. Intermittently accommodated at the Nugents' estate in Farrenconnell, they

---

55 Unger later described his work at the Mount as "design of handcraft and furniture". Herbert Unger, mimeographed CV, undated. Courtesy Klaus Unger.
56 Huggard's letters to Butler contain frequent references to dissension between host and exiles.
57 The employment of Robert Feldmann by a shoemaking enterprise in Edenderry, Co. Offaly, may also possibly be placed in such a context. See chapter 10.
58 See NAI, DJ 68/1/626 and DJ 69/80/93. Kraus himself claims that he spent a short time as an agricultural worker in Ireland, possibly in Termonfeckin. Kurt Kraus to authors, 8 June 2002.
59 For his role in bringing Kraus to Dunleer see correspondence in MAI, G2/0551.
60 See the respective work permits from the DI&C in December 1939 and January 1942 in NAI, DJ 69/80/93; also NAI, DJ 68/1/626, Garda report, 1 October 1945, and G2's report about his wartime career in Ireland. MAI, G2/0551.

made attempts to emigrate to the USA, but failed.⁶¹ In December 1940, Kurt Werner was hired as a cost accountant by General Textiles (or Gentex as it was popularly called), a Belgian cotton-spinning company in Athlone.⁶²

One interesting detail should be added. None of the agricultural trainees was a confessing Jew – whether because of sectarian reservations on the part of Christian helpers or because the Jewish aid organisation pursued a separate training project (or both) is an open question (see chapter 10).

Times at the demesnes and other places: workers, sojourners and their hosts

Lisa Fischer and her older sister Erika began their lives in Ireland in early February 1939.⁶³ Lisa's days were filled with challenging duties as a boarding student at St Margaret's Hall and then, in 1940, at Sligo High School. In 1941, she and Erica (who began spelling her name differently once she was in Ireland) were invited to spend their summer holidays at the home of Canon and Mrs Hipwell at the Rectory in Gort, Co. Galway – it was the beginning of a lasting association between the Hipwells and the two girls, particularly Lisa, who was effectively adopted by the Hipwells. There were a number of philanthropists in the towns and villages of rural Ireland who like the Hipwells opened their houses to individual refugees for weeks and months, for holidays or other purposes. Many of them belonged to the land-owning class. As a rule, some kind of work was expected in return for the hospitality tendered to the refugees, but it is often difficult to know whether they were serious agricultural workers or mere sojourners waiting for a chance of further emigration or for a more suitable job in Ireland. It seems that some former urbanites tested their hosts' magnanimity to a considerable extent.⁶⁴

---

61 NAI, DJ 69/80/93, note of 7 May 1940. After their departure from Cappagh in late September 1939 the family stayed at Farrenconnell until May 1940. Then they were moved to Dublin for half a year. See data in NAI, DJ 68/1/617.
62 The Werners shared a house with the Reid family at 2 Newton Terrace. George Eaton (The Old Athlone Society), email to authors, 9 December 2009. For Gentex, which had begun production in 1936, see Daly, *Industrial Development,* pp. 73, 84, 88, 110.
63 On the case of Lisa Fischer see Gisela Holfter, Marginalised Voices – Women in Irish Exile. In: *Yearbook for the Centre for German and Austrian Refugees.* Vol. 18. Leiden/Boston: Rodopi forthcoming 2017.
64 See, for example, Huggard's letters to Butler of 6 and 16 August 1941. TCD Archives, Butler Papers, 10304/597/774 and 777.

Termonfeckin: Wolfgang Eisenstaedt's farming experience in the old country had qualified him for more than a short-term apprenticeship. The list of items he brought with him – which included, apart from some everyday necessities, two saws, one broom, one spade, one pitchfork, one axe, and one wrench – reveals the kind of life he would have preferred in his new environment.[65] Vida Lentaigne entrusted him, *inter alia*, with her large poultry yard at Newtown House. He enjoyed board and lodging in the main building and received £3 pocket money per month from his hostess.[66] In the following years, his links with Termonfeckin strengthened, as indicated by his teaching music to local people and also by the fact that he alone visited the place after the war.[67] Basically, however, Eisenstaedt was known to be a "rather reserved individual" shunning frequent and intimate contacts with other people.[68] In spite of his growing familiarity with conditions in Termonfeckin and his relatively advanced age (in 1941 he was 50 years old), he did not give up his emigration plans, even when the coveted South American project came to nothing.[69] After 1943, he resigned himself to what he felt were the inescapable restrictions of life in Termonfeckin, the most distressing of which was the continuing separation from his fiancée. All his pleas for her to be allowed admission to Ireland met with stiff resistance from the Department of Justice.[70]

Another place where refugees were housed was Ballyalla, an estate near Ennis, Co. Clare. It belonged to Flora Vere O'Brien, descendant of a well-known political and artistic dynasty known for its philanthropic and social engagement.[71] ICCR committee members always found Flora helpful whenever a refugee had to be placed in an open house: it was well known that she found "it hard to make ends meet" and appreciated the weekly 10/6 which the ICCR paid her for each refugee.[72] It was at Ballyalla that Fritz and Ernst Hirsch spent some summer

---

65 Itemised list of Eisenstaedt's possessions in BLHA, Rep36A, F-359.
66 EA Berlin, no. 56.376, Lentaigne affidavit, 1 August 1958. The Hirsch brothers also received some money from Mrs Lentaigne at the start of their academic careers "in recognition of their work on her farm". TCD Archives, Mun/Sec./248,/ref/14, letter Chapter House, Christ Church Cathedral, 2 December 1940.
67 Declan Quaile email to authors, 22 November 2007.
68 MAI, G2/3190, G2 report, 13 February 1941.
69 For his failed emigration plans see MAI, G2/0398, Eisenstaedt to Friends Committee for Refugees, Bloomsbury House London, 10 December 1943.
70 NAI, DJ 69/80/468 documents his and his helpers' futile attempts to alter the DJ's position.
71 http://www.collectionscanada.gc.ca/obj/s4/f2/dsk3/OKQ/TC-OKQ-662.pdf. Susan E. Cahill, *Crafting Culture, Fabricating Identity. Gender and Textiles in Limerick Lace, Clare Embroidery and the Deerfield Society of Blue and White Needlework* [last accessed 2 December 2014].
72 TCD Archives, Butler Papers, 10304/597/781, Huggard to Butler, 9 April 1942.

months in 1940.[73] Later Fritz Hirsch recollected a "very pleasant experience" consisting of farm work in an intellectually inspiring atmosphere.[74] Apart from the Hirsch brothers, Flora temporarily housed Richard Wallach, Hans Morgenstern and Werner Schwarz, and possibly other refugees.[75] In 1939 Flora's brother, Hugh Vere O'Brien, lodged Hans Forell (see chapter 10) at his estate Monare on Foynes Island and in 1941 her sister Elinor offered hospitality there to Peter Lisowski and Werner Schwarz.[76]

Some refugees did their introductory course in agriculture in the Meath/Cavan border region with its large Protestant population. Two of them were Hans Morgenstern and Gerhard Hirschberg. They had been brought to Ireland through the same Protestant network, as we have seen, and their upkeep in the country was guaranteed by Joyce F. Nicholson, descendant of a land-owning Anglo-Irish family dating back to the 17th century.[77] Morgenstern and Hirschberg arrived at Balrath Bury in Co. Meath on 21 or 22 August 1939.[78] Hirschberg, like most others, considered his time in Ireland only as an interval before his passage to the USA: he had a temporary visa, and his prospects to begin a new life across the Atlantic looked promising, given Conrad Hoffmann's American contacts.[79] He and Morgenstern were given "hospitality for agricultural training", but this remained theoretical on account of Hirschberg's age and academic background. He left the estate four weeks later.[80] Morgenstern's engagement as an agricultural practi-

---

[73] MAI, G2/0480.
[74] Fritz Hirsch to authors, 31 October 2009.
[75] TCD Archives, Butler Papers, 10304/597/774, Huggard to Butler, 6 August 1941; 780, 10 May 1942. For Wallach see chapter 2 and 10.
[76] MAI, G2/0771, G2 report 26 September 1941.
[77] Peter Bamford, member of a neighbouring family, has described the house and family: "Balrath Burry (sic) was a monstrous long house with 21 windows across the front with a central front door. About all I remember of the house was the long passage going in both directions when you entered. The passage had windows on one side and what seemed like an untold number of similar doors opening into it [...]. It was built in the first half of the 1700s by Thomas Nicholson whose father was one of the '49' officers in the Royal Army and was granted land in Co Monaghan; these lands were sold and Balrath Burry bought in 1669. [...] The Irish Army took the house over as a barracks in 1939 and in accordance with well-established military precedent damaged it considerably. It was rebuilt in 1942 but cut down in size" http://www.bomford.net/IrishBomfords/Chapters/Chapter25/Chapter25.htm#25.3.1 _Neighbours_Further_Away_ [last accessed 7 September 2016].
[78] NAI, DJ 69/80/466, Kells Garda to DJ, 23 August 1939.
[79] The visa had been issued to him by the American Legation in Dublin. RCBL, JS, 4 February 1941. His continuing efforts to emigrate to the USA in 1940 and 1941 are documented in NAI, DJ 69/80/466.
[80] See undated DJ statement on him in NAI, DJ 69/80/466; further Cavan Garda to DJ, 7 August 1940 in the same file.

tioner looked more serious, but his life at Balrath Bury ended on 2 November 1939 when the Irish Army took over the Big House as a barracks – much to his chagrin, as he had "simply loved being there" and later felt "homesick for Kells and the people he knew there".[81] He continued his agricultural training at other estates in the Irish provinces, for example at the Mortimer family's demesne near Mullagh, Co. Cavan, until he was moved to Dublin, where he remained until 1943.[82]

Image 3: Gerhard Hirschberg.

The next stage of Hirschberg's exile was the Nugent family's estate at Farrenconnell, close to the southern border of Co. Cavan. The move had been arranged in talks between Joyce F. Nicholson and her friends Lady Nugent and her daughter Alison on the one hand and Kathleen Huggard on the other.[83] The Nugents' lineage dated back to Norman times, and the family had gained prominence through the actions of Alison's father, General Sir Oliver Nugent, acclaimed commander of an Ulster division in the Battle of the Somme. For several months Hirschberg was hardly involved in any real agricultural work, but was allowed a "free sojourn

---

81 TCD Archives, Butler Papers, 10304/597/776, Huggard to Butler, 13 August 1941. In the autumn he occasionally helped with farm work on the Nicholsons' estate. RCBL, JS, 9 September 1941.
82 TCD Archives, Butler Papers, 10304/597/774, Huggard to Butler, 6 August 1941; RCBL, JS, 4 June 1940; also correspondence in NAI, DJ 69/80/417. The Mortimers also lodged Kurt Stiegwardt and his wife for some time at their estate Lakeview (see below).
83 Benita Stoney's diary entry of 1 March 1994 records the recollections of her aunt Alison Nugent: "The Nicholsons came over to tea and [...] asked if they might bring their German refugee with them [...] and could Lady Nugent perhaps take him in. Alison and her mother had already agreed that they would take in a foreign refugee, so Gerhard came to Farrenconnell." Stoney email to authors, 23 March 2010.

in the countryside" by his generous hosts, with modest contributions from the Hebrew Christian Refugee Committee (2 shillings per month).[84] He left Farrenconnell in April 1941 when it became increasingly clear that, in spite of his and Conrad Hoffmann's efforts, his American visa would not be renewed, as the USA had barred immigrants with relatives in German-controlled areas.[85] These hopes indefinitely deferred, he tried to find occupation more in keeping with his qualifications.[86] His links to Farrenconnell however remained close (see chapter 11).

Another branch of the Nugent family was also involved with refugees. Alison Nugent's sister Theffania and her husband Robert V. Stoney housed Georg Liss (see chapter 5) at Rosturk Castle near Mulranny, Westport, Co. Mayo, soon after he had reached Ireland on an ICCR ticket. His time at Rosturk was spent waiting for a passage to the USA and doing practical work in the fields.[87]

It was probably through the Nugent family that Gerhard Hirschberg came to hear of Ludwig Heinsheimer, his wife Risa and their daughter Eva Maria (see chapter 2).[88] Like others, the Heinsheimers had been directed to Ireland through Hubert Butler's connections and the German Emergency Committee in London.[89] "Through the mediation of a committee we had received the invitation of a wealthy English-Scottish family on whose estate we were maintained. Being aliens we were prohibited from taking up an employment" (Risa Heinsheimer).[90] Their hosts were Gerald E. F. Tenison and his family, owners of a demesne at Lough Bawn with a history going back to 1690.[91] Their son remembers that the Heinsheimers "came from Hamburg and my parents had, I think, already notified the relief organisation in Dublin that we could accept a refugee Jewish family as a reasonably comfortable bungalow on the estate was vacant and could be

---

84 NAI, DJ 69/80/466, Garda to DJ, 21 April 1941. RCBL, JS, 5 March 1940 and 4 February 1941. The quotation is from a list of income written by Hirschberg. Wiedergutmachungsamt (WGA) Saarburg, no. 41.050. Translated by authors.
85 RCBL, JS, 4 April, 6 May, 1 July and 9 September 1941.
86 In 1942, he took up a job as tutor of languages in Dungarvan, Co. Waterford. Soon afterwards he gave it up, wishing to "obtain some employment in or near the city of Dublin". NAI, DJ 69/80/466, Garda to DJ, 11 January 1943.
87 See the few details on him in NAI, DJ 69/80/93.
88 The friendship between the Nugents and the Tenisons is mentioned in an email from Sir Richard Hanbury-Tenison, son of the former owner, to authors, 31 March 2009.
89 NAI, DJ 69/80/317, Garda J. Kenny to DJ, 22 March 1939; ICCR questionnaire filled in by Ludwig and Risa Heinsheimer, undated.
90 AdR, GZ 13237, Risa Heinsheimer to Hilfsfonds, 8 April 1977. Translated by authors. Thanks to Harald Miltner.
91 Sir Richard Hanbury-Tenison email to authors, 31 March 2009. G2 registered him as living in Lough House, Shantonagh, Castleblaney, Co. Monaghan. MAI, G2/0456 and 0457.

made available [...] my mother talked good German and was very friendly to the Heinsheimers."[92] Financially the situation remained precarious – the couple received only meagre grants from "the committee" (the ICCR). At least Eva Maria was given the opportunity of attending the Convent School of Middletown, Co. Armagh.[93]

Two others in the Tenisons' neighbourhood who helped the refugees were James Boylan (see chapters 4 and 11) and the Leslies. Shane Leslie was Winston Churchill's cousin and a Catholic convert since Home Rule days.[94]

Image 4: James Forrest drawn by Herbert Unger.

---

92 Sir Richard email to authors, 27 March 2009.
93 MAI, G2/0456 and 0457.
94 In a letter to Butler of 30 August 1941 Huggard refers to a refugee girl who was with the Leslies. TCD Archives, Butler Papers, 10304/597/778. This was probably Leopoldine Winter from Vienna, who left Austria in 1936 and was employed by Lady Leslie as a governess. She spent the first years of the war largely at Glasslough House, until early August 1941, when she married an Irishman and moved to Dublin. NAI, DJ 68/1/555. The Leslies had already played an important role in rescue operations for Belgian refugees in the First World War. See Elizabeth Quinn, Belgians in Ireland during the First World War: Social and Economic Aspects of a Forgotten Refugee Movement. Dublin: University College Dublin, BA thesis, 2007.

Image 5: Herbert Unger feeding pigs in Kingsfort.

Herbert Unger, Kurt Staudt, and Kurt and Elise Stiegwardt had withdrawn from the group experiment at Cappagh in October 1939.[95] Unger and Staudt were directed by the ICCR to Kingsfort near Moynalty, in the north western corner of Co. Meath, where they lived for almost a year on an estate owned by James Forrest, a bank manager.[96] The Stiegwardts were first moved to Lakeview, Mullagh, and then to nearby Cherrymount. Though they felt isolated in "our birdcage in (the) Meath desert", at least towards the end of their stay they were relatively close to Unger, Staudt and the Fuchs family, who after a short time at Vallombrosa were also accommodated at an estate in the Moynalty area.[97] The Fuchses left the Kells region in September 1940, when Lothar was hired as a teacher at St Gerard's

---

95 NAI, DJ 69/80/93, Waterford-Kilkenny Garda to DJ, 17 October 1939; further data in NAI, DJ 68/1/630.
96 MAI, G2/0849; NAI, DJ 68/1/630.
97 MAI, G2/041, Stiegwardt to Frankls, 3 February 1941. MAI, G2/0417. Translated by authors.

College, Bray (see chapter 8).⁹⁸ The Stiegwardts went to Dublin in early spring 1941, Elise expecting a baby.⁹⁹

One of the leading members of the Presbyterian Committee, Reverend R. Montgomery of Delvin, Co. Westmeath, spotted the place where the Frankl family from Berlin (see chapter 4) could prepare themselves for their future as agricultural workers in South America: Reynella, an estate of about 1,200 acres in Co. Westmeath, five miles from Delvin and twelve from Mullingar. It belonged to Richard Reynell and his sister Louise. The Frankls arrived at Reynella on 26 July 1939.¹⁰⁰ Their hosts offered an old Church of Ireland school building with kitchen, sitting room and two bedrooms, plus furniture, and two bicycles, one of which Heinz used on his rides to the farmhouses where he learned how to "plough with horses, milk cows, shear sheep, slaughter sheep and pigs and all aspects of harvesting" in the company of local agricultural workers.¹⁰¹ His father cycled on the other to Reynella House, where he became an adept at practical work, probably woodwork, and gardening.

Image 6: Kurt Staudt in Kingsfort.

They received no wages and lived on the weekly £2 grant from the Presbyterian Committee.¹⁰² The family was split up for some time while the younger son Gerd continued his education at Newtown School (see below) and

---

98 According to the registration dates in MAI, G2/0422 they stayed in Moynalty between September 1939 and September 1940. Their daughter Melanie, however, left the area in October 1939, because she had been accepted as a student at a school in Bray, probably St Gerard's College. See registration dates in NAI, DJ 68/1/755.
99 In Dublin they lived together with Unger at Berwick House, Rathfarnham. TCD Archives, Butler Papers, 10304/597/774, Huggard to Butler, 5 May 1941; also MAI, G2/0849. After the birth of the baby they were directed to Butler's Maidenhall. TCD Archives, Butler Papers, 10304/597/778, Huggard to Butler, 30 August 1941.
100 NAI, DJ 69/80/472, Mullingar Garda to DJ, 8 August 1939.
101 Heinz Frankl to authors, 8 October 2007.
102 NAI, DJ 69/80/472, Mullingar Garda to DJ, 8 August 1939. Their full income was probably higher. A G2 report of 2 December 1941 reveals that the whole family, including the parents, then living in Dublin, received £10 to cover their maintenance for five weeks. MAI, G2/0417.

then began an apprenticeship as an electrician.[103] In February 1941, with further emigration more doubtful than ever, and expecting a longer stay in Ireland, the family moved to Dublin, but Heinz still paid visits to Reynella: "I loved the countryside,"[104] he recalled in 2007, and he also remembered friendly neighbours and co-workers, all Catholics. For their first Christmas in Ireland they were invited by a local family. Heinz Frankl recalled that the family's daughter had travelled in Germany and was familiar with German Christmas traditions: "They wanted to make us feel at home so they fixed us up a German Christmas tree and played German Christmas songs. We all broke down and cried."[105] On Sundays there were invitations to the mansion, where the two Reynells asked them to take part in communal prayers with Protestant workers and then to share a private dinner with them. From July 1942 Heinz worked for Emma Howard, a Quaker, owner of a dairy, and her land-owning brother-in-law, in the village of Belmont near Clogham, Co. Offaly: dairy work, field work, easy-going social contacts that fostered a lifelong attachment to people and places.[106]

Most hospitable of all were Hubert Butler and his wife, in Kathleen Huggard's view "the few angelic beings on the earth who can get on with difficult refugees".[107] In 1941, they received Gustav Beisser and the Stiegwardt family at their estate of Maidenhall near Bennettsbridge, Co. Kilkenny; others who stayed at least temporarily included Werner Schwarz, Herbert Unger, Kurt Staudt, and Hans Morgenstern.[108]

---

103 Philip Jacob to authors, 26 November 2004. Gerd was apprenticed with Joseph Ch. Wicklow, Quaker and electrical contractor, from 1940 to 1945. EA Berlin, no. 3171.049, Bernhard Frankl, application to EA, 22 March 1958. In 1945, Wicklow married Mimi Höfer.
104 Heinz Frankl to authors, 8 October 2007. In Dublin he began an apprenticeship in the carpentry trade but this only lasted two months. NAI, DJ 69/80/472, Garda to DJ, 17 February 1941; also MAI, G2/0417 (he was again at Reynella on 2 April 1941).
105 "Exodus from Germany shows Shelby resident 2 sides of human nature", *The Daily Globe*, 11 July 1983.
106 Heinz Frankl to authors, 8 October 2007.
107 TCD Archives, Butler Papers, 10304/597/781, Huggard to Butler, 9 April 1942.
108 See various letters of Huggard to Butler in 1941 and 1942. TCD Archives 10304/597, 774, 778–79, 781–784. For a description of Maidenhall see Christopher Fitz-Simon, *Eleven Houses. A Memoir of Childhood*. Dublin: Penguin Ireland 2007, pp. 154–158; also Julia O'Faolain, *Trespassers. A Memoir*. London: Faber & Faber 2013, pp. 86–98 and Joseph Hone, *Wicked Little Joe*, Dublin: Lilliput 2009 – both authors spent time as paying guests in Maidenhall, Joseph Hone being almost adopted by the Butlers. The normal charge for taking care of a child in Maidenhall seems to have been £2.10.0 per week: see Hone, p. 65. This was more than the subsidy Butler got for the refugees, which amounted to only £1 per week for the whole Stiegwardt family. See TCD Archives, 10304/597/779, Huggard to Butler, 20 August 1941.

Students and teachers in the Irish provinces

No other Irish school rivalled the Quakers' Newtown School in Waterford for the number of German-speaking boarders.[109] Founded in 1798, Newtown School had been rescued from closure in 1925 thanks to its energetic new headmaster, Arnold Marsh.[110] Marsh brought with him much diverse experience.[111] From early on he supported refugees coming to Ireland, and Newtown's intake of at least a dozen students is unparalleled. Jürgen (George) Holländer stayed there from 1933 to 1938,[112] and others followed: Kurt Böhm (1934–1935), Käte Schulz (1934–1935), Peter Lisowski (1936–1938), Robert Weil (1939–1942), Gerd Frankl (1939–1942), Kurt Schwarz (1939–1944), Jochen Hengstenberg (1941–1946), Thomas Nachmann (1943–1945), Peter Strunz (1943–1948), Percy Schlesinger (1944–1949),[113] and Reiner Hengstenberg (1946–1951). The refugee pupils seemed to have fitted in well; they joined sports teams (excelling quickly at games previously unknown to them such as rugby and cricket: see below) and some were chosen as head boys.[114] The welcoming and open spirit of the co-educational boarding school was much appreciated: "Love it, it is marvellous" was a description of school life by Robert Weil in 1940.[115]

Newtown also employed three exiles as teachers. Käte Schulz (see chapter 1) came as a 21-year-old mature student in 1934 and was then appointed a full-time

---

109 All of them were boarders, apart from Kurt Schwarz, who seems to have lived with a member of the Jacob family, F.L. Jacob. See data in SFHD, Newtown School, Committee minutes 1925–1952.
110 Arnold Marsh, a Quaker from Ulster, had previously taught at the Friends' School in Lisburn. Financially independent following an inheritance, he heard about the school's difficulties and proposed to run Newtown school as his own financial responsibility. See Maurice J. Wigham, *Newtown School Waterford – A History 1798–1998*, Waterford: Newtown School 1998, p. 114.
111 Wigham, *Newtown School*, pp. 118–119.
112 Family recollections refer to Newtown School teachers paying for his passage to Australia in 1938. See http://www.naumburg-geschichte.de/geschichte/juden.htm#04 [last accessed 12 June 2016]. Holländer himself (who changed his name to George Holland in Melbourne) later gave money for the Holland Fund "to ensure that Newtown pupils who had no pocket money, as he had not, or were deprived in other ways, might be helped" (Wigham, *Newtown School*, p. 146).
113 Little is known about his family background. He was the son of a German couple (Julius and Erna Schlesinger) who had come to Ireland under unknown circumstances and had taken up residence in Youghal, Co. Cork. Newtown School, Committee minutes 1925–1952.
114 For example, Robert Weil: see Colin Walker, Robert Weil. In: Gisela Holfter (ed.), *German-speaking Exiles in Ireland 1933–1945*. Amsterdam/Atlanta: Rodopi 2006, pp. 133–147, 133.
115 Robert Weil's comparison with average school days in Germany ("I rather like it, it is quite nice, but...") and his emphatic preference for Newtown School is included in a number of his essays from 1940, collected as 'Father's Writings in 1940'. Thanks to Stephen Weil for providing a copy.

Image 7: Rugby 1934/35 (Jürgen 'George' Holländer and Kurt Böhm).

teacher trainee a year later. In 1938, she married her Newtown colleague Jack Shemeld. Headmaster Arnold Marsh would have liked to hire Werner Schwarz as her successor, but had to overcome a certain amount of opposition from the Department of Justice to employ him even for a few months in 1939–1940.[116]

---

[116] Schwarz was possibly entrusted with some unofficial duties until early 1940, when Marsh pleaded for help from the Jews Society's HCRC as the school could not "keep him any longer" – at least until such time as he could possibly be engaged as a fencing coach. RCBL, JS, 5 March 1940; also correspondence in NAI, DJ 69/80/340.

In 1936 Käte Müller-Lisowski (see chapter 1) was invited to teach Gaelic but did so only for three months.[117]

Image 8: Cricket 1940s (Jochen Hengstenberg & Kurt Schwarz).

Two other German-speaking refugees were employed as part-time teachers at the Benedictine Glenstal Abbey outside the village of Murroe, about twelve miles from Limerick. The Abbey's role in refugee affairs can be seen in the context

---

117 Wigham writes in *Newtown School Waterford*: "Her academic abilities did not altogether overcome the resistance of Irish youngsters," p. 132. On Käte Müller-Lisowski's single term of employment in 1936 see also Newtown School Archive, Executive Committee Minutes 1936–1939.

of its Continental links – it had been founded through the initiative of Belgian Benedictines – and of the exile topic in the history of Irish Benedictines as a whole.[118] In 1932, the order opened a secondary boarding school in an adjacent building,[119] and five years later Fr Matthew Dillon became its headmaster, presiding over a student body of fewer than 20 pupils.[120] His first tenure as headmaster was marked by the modernisation of the building and rapidly climbing student numbers to over a hundred within ten years.[121] Given this expansion, the need for a teacher of German may have grown, which Fr Matthew's brother, Theo Dillon, probably helped to satisfy.[122]

After an odyssey from Vienna via Zagreb, Italy and England, Ignaz Schulz came to Ireland a few days after the beginning of the war. The ICCR directed him first to Vallombrosa and then to a house in Bray.[123] There is no documentation to show why he, possibly a Catholic convert, was given employment as a part-time teacher at Glenstal.[124] On 11 May 1940, he was officially registered in Murroe.[125] Schulz lodged in a small house (a "hut" as he said), living on weekly pay of 1 shilling plus an ICCR grant.[126] He gave German lessons to a few students, but most

---

[118] In World War I, Dom Columba Marmion, the Irish abbot of the Belgian Benedictine community of Maredsous, brought the junior monks of the order to Ireland. See Mark Tierney, The Origins and Early Days of Glenstal Abbey. In: Martin Browne and Colmán Ó Clabaigh (eds), *The Irish Benedictines – A History*. Dublin: Columba Press 2005, pp. 163–176, 171. On the history of Glenstal see also Mark Tierney, *Glenstal Abbey. A Historical Guide*. 4th edition, Limerick: Glenstal Abbey Publications 2005. Other Benedictine groups who had found refuge in Ireland during that time were Benedictine nuns from Paris and the Irish Dames of Ypres. See William Fennelly, Monastic Exiles in Ireland. In: Browne and Ó Clabaigh (eds), *The Irish Benedictines*, pp. 177–191.
[119] Mark Tierney, Glenstal Abbey 1930–2004. In: Browne and Ó Clabaigh (eds), *The Irish Benedictines*, pp. 192–201.
[120] See ibid., p. 195 and Tierney, *Glenstal Abbey*, pp. 51–52. Dillon was headmaster from 1937 to 1948 and then from 1953 to 1961.
[121] See Tierney, *Glenstal*, p. 51 and Tierney, Glenstal Abbey 1930–2004, p. 195.
[122] Philip Tierney to authors, 12 December 2007.
[123] MAI, G2/0763. He was taken in by Mrs Brown of 4 Carlton Terrace, Bray.
[124] After the war he became a member of the Jacob Ehrlich Society and the Association of Jewish Refugees. AdR, 06/2290, Schulz to Berger, lawyer, 23 February 1957. In Ireland he rather implied that he was Catholic. It might have been relevant that he had been married to an Aryan Catholic wife and the wedding had been performed according to Catholic rites. The couple divorced in May 1941.
[125] MAI, G2/0763; AdR, 06/2290, court ruling (copy), 10 May 1941; Schulz to Hilfsfonds, 19 January 1957.
[126] MAI, G2/0763, Schulz to Franziska Schulz, 19 October 1940. Translated by authors. In the letter he complained that until September 1940 he had been living in an even more uncomfortable "hut". The low pay could perhaps provide a clue why Schulz had been given the job at Glenstal.

of his time was spent on book-keeping and other administrative work.[127] In his letters to his wife he complained about the permanent rain and his solitary existence in this "lonely region",[128] his only distraction a weekly shopping trip to Limerick by bicycle. He felt desperate when the bicycle broke down.[129] Problems were exacerbated when the Rector, in line with general immigration rules, thought it necessary to replace him as a teacher of German with an Irish national and give him office work instead; he feared the move might mean a drastic reduction in his salary.[130] His students retain an image of a marginal and dissatisfied man. They mainly recall him as an office worker and not as a teacher – he appeared "very quiet and unassuming", "kept very much to himself" and "always looked a bit lost".[131] In December 1942, he went to Dublin, taking residence in the Old Vienna Club (see chapter 8).

A few months later Ludwig Heinsheimer arrived, 55 years old at the time. Having long waited for a job, the Heinsheimers were ready to accept any offer, even if it meant a split in the family (which, as it turned out, lasted until 1946). In mid-1943 he began teaching German at Glenstal, earning £10 a month plus board and lodging.[132] Roughly at the same time, his wife found her first employment as a governess in Irish households, mainly teaching German to children in various places.[133] Former Glenstal School students mainly remember Heinsheimer as a riding teacher (with a preference for Vienna-style dressage, in marked contrast to most of his students, who were keen to career about the Glenstal estate, jumping fences and seeing how fast their horses could gallop)[134] and as the man in charge

---

John O'Callaghan, a former student, recalls that Heinsheimer and Schulz "were welcomed by Fr Matthew who had an eye for potential teachers who would work for little or nothing". Letter forwarded by Celestine Cullen to authors, 13 February 2008.
127 Mark Tierney, interview with authors, 5 January 2008. William Hederman, another student, remembers him "wheeling packages and other things on his hand trolley" along the floors. Hederman to authors (undated).
128 MAI, G2/0763, letters to Franziska Schulz, 19 October 1940, 5 March 1941. Translated by authors.
129 Ibid., letter of 19 October 1940. The repair cost him half his pay for a week.
130 Ibid., letter of 5 March 1941. Schulz blamed the Rector for having tried to replace him. Given the insecurity of his employment at the school, Schulz explored possibilities of emigrating to the USA in 1941. MAI, G2/0763, G2 report August 1941, in which it is said that he sought contact with the International Catholic Help for Refugees Committee in Washington.
131 Hederman to authors (undated); Mark Tierney, interview with authors, 5 January 2008.
132 See DJ 68/1/801 and DJ 69/80/317.
133 AdR, GZ 13237, Risa Heinsheimer to Hilfsfonds, 8 April 1977.
134 Celestine Brian Cullen, 27 November 2007; John O'Callaghan, 29 November 2007; William Hederman; R. O'Loughlin, 10 December 2007; Philip Tierney, 12 December 2007.

of the stables and the five horses. In that role he instilled a certain fear among the handlers of the horses as well as the schoolboys.[135] In Mark Tierney's recollection, Heinsheimer was what many Irish people would have considered typically "German": a man of exacting discipline, order and efficiency, the "best refugee ever in Glenstal", "bubbling with enthusiasm (and) energy", impressing his students with his sporting talents ("a brilliant horseman and skater"), and with an immaculate appearance. He "talked to all people" but kept his distance: he was "not involved with locals". The testimonies of his former students suggest that Heinsheimer was equipped with psychological reserves that enabled him more than others to come to terms with the rupture in his life.[136]

There were also religious Christian German-speaking immigrants to Ireland during the Nazi period – though to what extent they were refugees is debatable. Altogether 30 religious brothers, mostly missionaries and most of them Germans, came to Ireland before and during the war years.[137] Most noticeable among them were the thirteen members of the Dutch-German Society of the Divine Word Missionaries, who in 1939 congregated at Donamon Castle on the River Suck, Co. Roscommon, one of "the poorest bog areas" of Ireland (John Hennig).[138] Although the idea of establishing a branch of the Divine Word Missionaries in Ireland had developed years before the Second World War, the decision to purchase Donamon Castle in March 1939 was crystallised by the threat of German aggression and the prospect of an English involvement in war measures.[139] Catholic Ireland appeared a place where the brothers could at least temporarily evade conscription as soldiers or as medical staff in the Wehrmacht, or being interned as "enemy aliens" in England as had happened to members in World War I.[140] The Irish government

---

135 Mark Tierney, interview with authors, 5 January 2008.
136 Ibid.
137 NAI, DJ 69/80/475, hand-written memo for Costigan, DJ, 9 April 1940.
138 John Hennig, *Die bleibende Statt*, p. 149. For the missionaries see their G2 files and the identity cards and files of ten brothers in the Archivum Generale of the SVD (Societas Verbi Divini – in German *Steyler Missionare*) in Rome. We are grateful to Franz Bosold, Archivum Generale. Dermot Walsh, himself an SVD brother, has published extensive material in *Divine Word Missionaries in Ireland*. Rome: Apud Collegium Verbi Divini 1995.
139 SVD Archivum Generale, Analecta SVD-54, *Geschichte unserer Gesellschaft*, Vol. 2, p. 190; Walsh, *Divine Word Missionaries*, p. 32.
140 The personal files of the SVD Archivum Generale show that at least five, and possibly seven, Donamon brothers had been conscripted into the German army in the First World War. The order had been subject to house searches from 1937 in Germany, and some of the brothers, such as the headmaster of the Missionary house in St Wendel, P. Nikolaus Backes, were remanded in custody for several months that year. The missionary school there was closed in 1939, others in 1941. See also Holger Gast et al., *Katholische Missionsschulen in Deutschland 1887 – 1940*, Bad Heilbrunn: Klinkhardt 2013, pp. 47–48.

acceded to their applications on the usual condition that they would not become a "public burden".¹⁴¹ Bishop Dr Edward Doorly sanctioned the foundation of an SVD novitiate within his diocese of Elphin, and on 25 March 1939 the first three brothers moved in. The others followed before 1 September.¹⁴² Eight of the brothers had found their way to Roscommon from Hadzor, the English affiliation in Worcestershire, and the rest from Holland and Germany.¹⁴³ The three ecclesiastics at Donamon were training novices for SVD missions, while the lay brothers tried to sustain a self-sufficient lifestyle under wartime conditions. The new venture contributed to local employment, as carpenters, roofers, painters, electricians, joiners, and mechanics were needed to do necessary repair work to make Donamon Castle suitable for its new purpose.

In spite of the pressures that had made them move to Ireland, it is questionable if the Donamon brothers were refugees to the same extent as others portrayed in this study. Their exile was more voluntary. They considered their time at Donamon Castle no more than a temporary geographical move, working in a present and for a future for which their education and past experience had prepared them. Nor were they perceived as refugees by others. The Irish Secret Service even classified the brothers as "A" persons, i.e. Nazi sympathisers, a judgement based on bureaucratic routine rather than on concrete observation.¹⁴⁴ Local people primarily treated them with the respect and distance conventionally afforded to religious people in Ireland, that status outweighing the "foreignness"

---

141 NAI, DJ 69/80/475, DJ memo, 9 May 1940.
142 Walsh, *Divine Word Missionaries*, pp. 19, 21–26, 32–33; also NAI, DJ 69/80/475, reports of Garda, Roscommon to DJ.
143 See personal files, Archivum Generale; Walsh, *Divine Word Missionaries*, pp. 24, 31, 32, 64–65.
144 Adolph von Spreti was even accorded an 'A1' status ("particularly prominent" Nazi sympathiser). Two workers at industrial enterprises set up by refugees were also suspected of Nazi sympathies by G2. One was Florian Oberer of Wings in Galway (see below), who donated to the German Winterhilfswerk and attempted to organise Christmas ceremonies for some German internees at the Curragh Camp in 1942, as shown by two letters addressed to him by a prisoner of war in October and December of that year. See MAI, G2/0655. A handwritten note by a G2 agent revealed that Hempel and Oberer were discussing a "job" for the latter, probably to help the internees at the Curragh. Karl Rosulek of Les Modes Modernes (see below) was also believed to be a Nazi sympathiser. He came under observation by G2 because he seemed to be on familiar terms with the German spy Ernst Weber-Drohl and to have donated to the Curragh internees, see MAI, G2/0709, Weber-Drohl to Karl and Anastasia Rosulek, 15 December 1940, G2 report of 3 May 1941. Rosulek's donations to the Curragh internees required links with German sympathisers and authorities in Ireland. These activities, however, do not necessarily betray Nazi affinities. The names of correspondents in Oberer's and Rosulek's G2 files show that both had friendly links with German-speaking exiles and non-exiles alike.

recognisable from their German-accented English.¹⁴⁵ To John Hennig, who visited them during the war, their escape to Ireland and position there seemed far less fraught than his own.¹⁴⁶

Co. Roscommon was also host to one other immigrant who clearly was a refugee. 14-year-old Hans Kohlseisen had come to Ireland through the joint endeavours of the English Catholic Committee for Refugees from Germany and Dillon's UCD Refugee Committee. On 8 June 1939, he arrived in charge of two children – Andreas-Günter Dreyer from Cologne, aged seven, and Stefan Schmeltz from Vienna, who had just turned eight – who, like him, had been accepted under the June 'English quota' and guaranteed by Dillon's committee.¹⁴⁷ Schmeltz and Dreyer were adopted by John B. Hamill and his family, while Kohlseisen was directed to the Mantua Presbytery in Co. Roscommon. He spent almost all the war years there, doing, as he felt, misplaced agricultural work that failed to prepare him for further migration. At least to the adult chronicler, these years until 1944, when he finally went to Dublin, appeared as lost youth.¹⁴⁸ The adolescent had been set on a "blind passage" to rural Ireland, arriving there without proper support or a strategy concerning his educational future.

Most other German-speaking adolescents were given an opportunity to complete their secondary education at schools such as Clongowes Wood College, Naas, Co. Kildare, which vied academically with Blackrock College, St Gerard's College and Wesley College in or near the capital. The Jesuit Clongowes Wood College took in Gerhard P. Friedjung, Robert Dubsky and Hans V. Ledermann, who received board and a full secondary-school education, preparing at least the last two for subsequent academic careers (see chapter 11). The same may be said of Alfred Schulhof, who attended Ballina Technical School for one year (1939 to 1940) before his subsequent academic studies in Dublin.

---

145 Hennig, *Die bleibende Statt*, pp. 148–149; Walsh, *Divine Word Missionaries*, pp. 37–40.
146 Hennig came to Donamon Castle on the invitation of Adolph von Spreti, after the latter had taken issue with one of Hennig's articles in *The Standard*. Hennig, *Die bleibende Statt*, pp. 139, 148.
147 See correspondence in NAI, DJ 69/80/449; DJ 69/80/457 (Dreyer) and 458 (Schmeltz). Andreas-Günter Dreyer returned to Germany shortly after the war, joining his parents who had survived the war in England. Stefan Schmeltz was the son of a wealthy and well-known Viennese architect. His mother too lived in the UK in the war years. He stayed in Ireland until at least the 1950s. See below. Possibly, these accommodations had been arranged within the scope of Professor Mary Macken's work for children, referred to by Dillon in *Studies* 1939, p. 413. See also Kohlseisen, *Und ich reise immer noch – Die Geschichte des Hans Kohlseisen zwischen Gmünd, Stadlau und Irland*, pp. 73–74.
148 Kohlseisen, *Und ich reise immer noch*, pp. 75–88.

"It was all right when foreigners came along to start industries and give employment but [...]" – Exiles in provincial economies*

In the 1930s and 1940s, the industrial landscape of the Irish Free State began to take new shape. After Fianna Fáil's election victory of 1932, economic planners in Lemass's Department of Industry and Commerce took steps to implement a policy of self-sufficiency and decentralised, state-sponsored industrialisation by calling investors, managers and experts from the UK and Continental industrialised countries such as Germany, Czechoslovakia, and Belgium into the country. The following enterprises owed their establishment or at least an important developmental impulse to immigrants from Germany or countries threatened by German occupation:
- Les Modes Modernes Ltd (Galway)
- Wings Ltd (Galway)
- Hirsch Ribbons Ltd (Longford)
- Western Hats Ltd (Castlebar)
- Plunder and Pollack Ltd (Carrick-on-Suir, Co. Tipperary)
- McCowens Mouldings Ltd (Tralee, Co. Kerry).

Two further enterprises – Tipperary Glove Factory Ltd (Co. Tipperary) and Malbay Manufacturing Company Ltd (Miltown Malbay, Co. Clare) – engaged German-speaking refugees as key staff in their production processes. Five of the enterprises were located in the west of Ireland, where Fianna Fáil hoped to reverse the depopulation of impoverished rural areas.[149] The Control of Manufactures Act of 1932 and its 1934 amendment defined the limits of foreign economic involvement by giving Irish nationals in principle a majority of shares, especially those with voting rights, though in a number of cases this rule was undermined by a generous grant of non-voting shares and dividends to foreign investors.[150]

---

149 On rural poverty see Wills, *Neutral Island*, pp. 252–257.
150 Mary E. Daly, *Industrial Development*, pp. 81–89; Mary E. Daly, An Irish Ireland for Business? The Control of Manufactures Acts, 1932 and 1934. In: *Irish Historical Studies*, Vol. 24 (1984), pp. 246–272.

* The quotation is from W. Carrick, a leading spirit behind an anti-refugee motion in Galway in January 1939 (see below). He objected to "ordinary citizens unprepared to contribute anything to the welfare of the community" while there were "Galway people unemployed and badly off". See http://connachttribune.ie/galway-in-time-gone-by-a-browse-through-the-archives-of-the-connacht-tribune-31 – 1939: Objections to refugees/ [last accessed 20 May 2016].

To the immigrant former city dwellers the social fabric of an Irish country town must have posed enormous challenges, especially at the beginning.

> This was the first larger country town I visited. Talk about a "culture shock". The main street was full of two-wheeled carts and passenger traps drawn by a horse or donkey, trucks, cars, bicycles and people of all shapes and sizes over the road. There was a lot of joking and laughing. I did not understand a word. (Anselm Horwitz on arriving in Tralee).[151]

Conditions and local demography varied, as did individual reactions of the refugees. It made a difference if one lived in a larger town like Tralee, or in a village still devoid of banks, cinemas, hotels and modern sanitary facilities where daily personal contacts were inescapable and integration prospects possibly higher, or in a city like Galway or Cork where chances of making oneself less conspicuous were greater. The number of refugees played a role, as did the life perspectives of the newcomers. Horwitz, for example, originally planned to leave Tralee as quickly as possible, seeking an onward passage to the USA. Most other refugees however had come to these parts of Ireland hoping for a relatively safe and permanent economic existence in their new land: their resulting readiness to adjust more or less to new social realities also had a bearing on the immigrants' status in their new homes.

By the end of the 1930s, the Irish textile sector contained "significant foreign presence".[152] Jewish entrepreneurism in textiles was common all over Central Europe, especially in Vienna and the Sudetenland, where a disproportionately high percentage of such industries lay in the hands of Jewish (or formerly Jewish) owners. In Ireland, and specifically in Dublin, Irish-Jewish firms were also said to figure largely in the clothing manufacturing sector.[153] A man like Marcus Witztum, co-owner of a Dublin shop selling Viennese textiles and well-connected in the Continental sector, was able to identify potential candidates to set up their own industries or occupy leading positions in the new industries.[154] He could offer not only a life without Nazi harassment but also favourable economic conditions such as Irish social and wage standards, protective tariffs and quota regulations.[155]

---

151 Email to authors, 23 January 2008.
152 Daly, *Industrial Development*, p. 89.
153 Harris, *Dublin's Little Jerusalem*, p. 148.
154 The continental network that Witztum had built up in the 1930s comprised a number of persons, among them Ossias Teicher (see below) and Friedrich Roland. The latter tried to come to Ireland in 1939, arguing that he had helped Witztum to bring Austrian factories to Ireland. NAI, DFA 202/74, Murphy to DFA, 1 February 1939.
155 Daly, *Industrial Development*, pp. 66–67, 71, 81–89.

The Department of Industry and Commerce could use its licensing prerogative and discretionary power over tariffs and the other instruments mentioned above to establish factories at a distance from Dublin. In practice however site decisions did not depend on lofty strategic or social needs formulated in the Department – Lemass's new industries were "almost entirely located outside Gaeltacht areas"[156] – but rather on differentials of negotiating power including political patronage working in favour of competitive regional interest groups inside and outside Fianna Fáil.[157] They mostly ended as compromises between a political agenda formulated in Dublin or the regions and economic arguments. Refugees possessing economic capital or expertise were occasionally in a strong position to make their arguments heard in favour of a particular location (like A. Bayer, see chapters 1 and 6). A key "mover and shaker" in Lemass's circle and a strong proponent for industrial projects was Senator John McEllin from Balla, County Mayo, along with Witztum the most influential member of the head-hunting commission Lemass had set up in 1934. John McEllin and Sons, Ltd delivered material for the new factory buildings, a further demonstration of the close connection between Fianna Fáil and the building industry in general.[158] In addition McEllin occupied a seat on the board of directors in four of the industries mentioned above. Over the years he had formed a network of connections to influential Fianna Fáil politicians – de Valera was also counted among his friends – with common memories and convictions dating back to the old IRA days. McEllin's key role in the politics of Western industrialisation was highlighted by a lead article in the *Connacht Tribune* (4 March 1939) which ascribed the launch of the Hirsch factory in Longford and Western Hats in Castlebar to the political influence of this "energetic western representative" and the "loyalty of his countrymen". His status in the region also helped to boost the sale of shares in the new industries in which he was involved.[159] Indirectly, this helped to serve partisan interests. Fianna Fáil politicians in the region and in central positions were credited not only with having attracted jobs to a particular region, their associates in the new directorates also saw to it that members of "Republican" families were given preferential

---

156 Evans, *Seán Lemass*, p. 94.
157 Daly, *Industrial Development*, pp. 106–107, 114–116.
158 Statement by John C. McEllin, the Senator's nephew, made during a meeting between authors and citizens of Castlebar (Ernie and Susanna Sweeney, John C McEllin, Peggy Lee, former secretary to Walter Porges, John Garavan, retired Judge, and John Mee, former Mayor) on 14 and 15 June 2008 (henceforth described as Castlebar Meeting). See also an advertisement in *Irish Times*, 14 March 1941. The McEllin cases demonstrate that the "long-standing patronage network between the party and building merchants" (Evans, *Seán Lemass*, p. 94) was not only a Dublin phenomenon; see also Lee, *Ireland*, p. 193.
159 John C. McEllin at Castlebar Meeting, with authors, 14 June 2008.

employment opportunities. Even without hard evidence, the common assumption that political criteria played a role in distributing jobs frequently sufficed to give Fianna Fáil candidates an edge over competing political parties.¹⁶⁰

Les Modes Modernes, Wings and the exile community in Galway

Before the advent of Les Modes Modernes, Galway, in 1936 a small city of 18,294 inhabitants, had very few industrial establishments ("two fertiliser industries, a foundry, and a metal production site perhaps").¹⁶¹ Prior attempts to resurrect the traditional woollen mills in the city had failed.¹⁶² In summer 1935, Lemass announced the construction of a hat factory.¹⁶³ Plans had been in the making for months, but only approached realisation when Marcus Witztum's Continental forays led to Paris, resulting in Serge Philipson's trip to Galway (see chapter 1). Serge returned to Paris "full of enthusiasm", and a few weeks later he was put in charge of the new Galway hat factory as he was the "youngest partner [in Henri Orbach's Les Modes Modernes] and the last one to join the firm. It is the opportunity of a lifetime".¹⁶⁴ He arrived in Galway on 5 October 1937; his family stayed behind in Paris.¹⁶⁵ The foundation story of Les Modes Modernes as told by Rachel Philipson Levy describes the Orbach-Philipson angle, but there was another investor: Edmond Claessens, prominent Catholic politician and *grand patron* of Manufacture Moderne de Chapeaux in Verviers at the German-Belgian border.¹⁶⁶

---

160 This was common knowledge for example in the Castlebar region. Statement by Susanna Sweeney, author of an unpublished MA thesis on Western Hats, at Castlebar Meeting, 14 June 2008.
161 P. O'Dowd, local historian, interview with authors, 12 June 2008. In the census report for 1936 only 64 persons were employed in the textile industries (excluding dress). CSO, Census 1936, Vol. 7, group 06.
162 See summary of Bishop Dr Browne's and Lemass's speeches in *Irish Independent*, 19 July 1938; *Connacht Tribune*, 23 July 1938.
163 *Connacht Tribune*, 6 July 1935.
164 The story and all the quotations are taken from Rachel Philipson Levy, Memoir: An Odyssey Revisited, migs.concordia.ca/memoirs/levy/levy.html [last accessed 22 October 2014].
165 MAI, G2/x/0720.
166 Edmond Claessens, born on 28 September 1882 in Maastricht, was one of the most important economic and political figures in the border region between Germany and Belgium in the pre-war years. He was a leading member of the Catholic Party and, himself a fluent speaker of German, sat on the administrative board of the *Grenz-Echo*, the German-language journal that tried to influence the largely revisionist opinions of the German-speaking minority in favour of a

The genesis of the Witztum-Claessens connection remains unknown, but possibly it dates back to the time when the Witztum family settled in Antwerp (see chapter 2). As to the location of the new factory, some pressure on the part of the Department of Industry and Commerce was obviously needed to make the Orbach-Claessens group accept Galway.[167] The public learned from regional newspapers about the progress of negotiations between the Department of Industry and Commerce officers, the National Agricultural and Industrial Development Association (NAIDA) with its secretary Erskine Childers, the local Galway Industrial Development Association (GIDA) and the Belgian-French group. On 10 April 1937, it was announced that a hat factory would soon be established,[168] and five weeks later Orbach, Witztum and McEllin, among others, detailed optimistic job prospects: 100 hands would be needed at the beginning and no less than 600 at peak production.[169]

The capital of the company amounted to £60,000 to which the Orbach group contributed £40,000; the rest was to be subscribed by local investors.[170] The Board of Directors consisted of McEllin, Edmond Claessens, L. E. O'Dea, Orbach, and Marcel Goldberg, a German-Jewish cloth expert with Polish roots who arrived from France on 5 October to serve as an assistant managing director under Serge Philipson.[171] Witztum's head-hunting mission in Vienna supplied the production staff with Continental technicians, at least some of them Jewish: Wolf Zeiler, the works manager, Mathilde Schwenk, the chief designer, and Josef Miretinsky and Heinrich Bittgen, hat makers.[172] Then followed Austrian Karl Rosulek (in the war years, also his Czechoslovakian-born wife Anastasia Chvojkova) and Arnold Libin, a Belgian who became a finisher in the new factory.[173] Les Modes Modernes started production in the middle of August 1937 with 40 workers in premises on

---

pro-Belgian stance. From 1935 to 1939 he served in the Belgian Senate and occupied various local political functions in Heusy (a part of Verviers). He was a political prisoner in German detention camps in two world wars. Manufacture Moderne de Chapeaux had various branches in Belgium and other countries. For his career see obituaries in *Le Courrier* (Verviers), 15, 16 and 20 July 1954.
167 Daly, *Industrial Development*, p. 111.
168 *Galway Observer*, 10 April 1937.
169 *Galway Observer*, 22 May 1937.
170 *Galway Observer*, 5 June and 31 July 1937; *Irish Times*, 20 May 1937.
171 See list of employees in MAI, G2/x/0720.
172 Miretinsky returned to Vienna on 22 July 1938. WSLA, residential register of Vienna. For Bittgen see also WSLA register and NAI, DFA 10/2/18, list of Germans in Ireland, Co. Galway.
173 On Rosulek and Libin see list in MAI, G2/x/0720. Chvojkova came to Galway in December 1938 or January 1939. She and Rosulek were married in 1941. NAI, DJ 69/80/166.

Eyre Square, while a new building was under construction in Bohermore on the then north-eastern edge of the town opposite the New Cemetery.[174]

Even before its completion the new factory became a public issue. Dubliners had been given an opportunity of inspecting Galway hats in a showcase on St Stephen's Green.[175] "The Galway Hat Controversy" revolved around the question of whether the products of the semi-foreign enterprises were to be protected by import quota barriers. Outside Jury's Hotel, James Dillon, the deputy Fine Gael chairman, fulminated against the tariff privileges of the foreign investors ("exploiters"), mixing free-trade rhetoric with claims to have "those people sent back to the country from where they came".[176] A very different public event took place in Galway on 18 July 1938. Here the opening of Les Modes Modernes became a social affair with an official luncheon in the old Railway Hotel, the blessings of the Bishop of Galway, Michael Browne (a known supporter of Fianna Fáil) and Lemass praising the enterprise as a strategic operation at the beginning of a "transition age" towards industrialisation.[177]

The import quota against foreign competition and a contract with the Drapers' Chamber of Commerce guaranteeing the purchase of the full annual product (60,000 hats in 1938 and one million in 1939) laid the basis for Les Modes Modernes' market position. The Irish market was expected to absorb about one million hats annually ("In a few years time all the Irish cailins will be wearing hats made in the city of the tribes," it was said).[178] At the beginning the raw materials, mainly felt, had to be imported, but Marcus Witztum announced that in a few years the wool could be bought from Irish farmers and processed within Ireland.[179] The gravest problem at the beginning was accustoming Irish workers to an assembly-line production regime.[180] Most of them were paid on a low piecework

---

174 *Galway Observer*, 4 December 1937.
175 *Galway Observer*, 11 September 1937.
176 *Connacht Tribune*, 14 May 1938.
177 *Connacht Tribune*, 23 July 1938; *Irish Independent*, 19 July 1938. Philipson's daughter went to Galway with her mother for the event: "The hat factory was where the action was. There we met Miss Schwenk and Mr Zeiler, two Austrian employees of the factory, at supervisory levels…My father and Marcus Witztum were the best of friends, and Mrs. Witztum, Dola, took me under her wing. She really became my adopted mother when I arrived after the war at the age of 14." Rachel Philipson Levy email to authors, 2 November 2006.
178 *Connacht Tribune*, 8 January 1938.
179 *Connacht Tribune*, 8 January 1938.
180 This is what Rachel Philipson Levy remembers from conversations among her father's continental clientele in Galway. Email to authors, 2 November 2006. It seems that the new disciplinary regime met with some resentment, possibly directed against particular persons. See post-war complaints against Schwenk's role in factory life in NAI, DJ 68/1/601.

basis.[181] In summer 1938, 110 women and 54 male workers produced 1,200 hats a day, and there were hopes that 350 workers could reach an output of 3,500 hats a day. At this time Marcus Witztum recruited further candidates in post-*Anschluss* Vienna: Berta Mortl, hat maker,[182] Theodor Honig, who was to train local workers, his wife Else and their son, both of whom he had originally left behind in Leopoldstadt,[183] Katharina Hein,[184] Olga Bretholz,[185] Teresa (Therese) Dziewientnik,[186] Josef Storm, blockmaster, and Else Petersilka, his Viennese fiancée.[187] The last German-speaking refugee to join the workforce at Bohermore was Maria Marckwald (see below).[188]

Les Modes Modernes reached a leading position in the market for ladies' hats in wartime Ireland in spite of difficult periods.[189] The optimistic job expectations were not fully realised. On an average in the war years the total workforce comprised hardly more than 250 workers.[190] The strategic aim of replacing refugee managers by Irish nationals however took shape, at least at top management

---

181 This may have changed over the years. "Some members of the staff were on a normal method of pay, while others were on 'piece work', being paid for the amount of hats they produced. The girls on the normal week's wages were earning £1 – 15s, which after 18 months was raised to £2 – 5s. Those on piece work could earn between £2 – 10s and £3 per week. The men were also earning £2 – 5s. per week after 18 months." *Galway Independent*, 8 October 2014.
182 MAI, G2/0641; NAI, DFA 10/2/18, list of Germans in Ireland, Co. Galway.
183 NAI, DFA 202/43, O'Donnell, solicitor, to DFA, 25 January 1939; also data in MAI, G2/0494. He and Else, also Jewish, had owned a shop or enterprise in Vienna. They must have lost it during the phase of "wild Aryanisations" in early 1938. After her husband's departure in early August 1938 Else tried to follow him to Galway. On 20 April 1939, her name and that of her son were deleted from the residential register of Vienna. They went to Dublin at an unknown date before 1943 (see chapter 8), and Else too worked in the hat factory.
184 MAI, G2/0454.
185 MAI, G2/x/0720. Olga Bretholz left behind her husband Ossias Bretholz, a Galician Jew, who had to give up their flat in Dopplergasse (11th district) after her departure.
186 MAI, G2/x/0720; also WSLA, residential register of Vienna.
187 On both see MAI, G2/0823. Storm had left Vienna on 1 August 1938. WSLA, residential register of Vienna. Else Petersilka arrived in Folkestone on 14 December 1938 "to be married to Joseph Storm in London", and seems to have arrived for work in the factory a few months later. MAI, G2/x/0028.
188 One Olga Maria Dittrich was possibly also engaged by Les Modes Modernes. She came from Teschen, an area in Lower Silesia disputed between Poland and Czechoslovakia, and arrived in Galway on 6 January 1939 after her marriage to an Irishman one month earlier. NAI, DJ 68/1/514.
189 See Daly, *Industrial Development*, p. 90. In 1943, there was a strike of a moderate number of workers which the management met with a general lockout. *Irish Times*, 17 July 1943; *Connacht Tribune*, 10, 14, 21, 24, 31 July 1943. A critical situation is also indicated in an undated letter of Mathilde Schwenk ("Business bad but writer all right", as the G2 officer translated the gist of its text). MAI, G2/0775.
190 *Galway Independent*, 8 October 2014.

levels. In June 1942, the company secretary John McDermott took over the position of Philipson, who then helped to steer the enterprise from his Dublin office in 24 Suffolk Street.[191]

Wings Ltd, a smaller replica of Max Blaskopf's former zip-fastener enterprise in Vienna, also settled in Galway. In March 1939, production began in the very building on Eyre Square which Les Modes Modernes had deserted before their move to Bohermore.[192] The firm's beginning looked hopeful. The Irish state helped with a 40 per-cent protective tariff against Belgian and Czechoslovakian competition, and the newly 'Aryanised' "Ritsch" factory in Vienna sent the necessary materials to Wings to overcome initial production difficulties.[193] Wings, however, soon ran into such difficulties as to impact on the household budgets of its managers: "three families have to live off the factory," complained Grete Blaskopf.[194] In the winter of 1939 her tone became desperate: "Since March we have lived from hand to mouth and we three have to live on the same money that you have, and we have to pay a very high rent for the tiny house, as much as for my beautiful flat in Graz. And everything is very expensive, more so than before,"[195] and: "Hanna urgently needs a new coat. She came here with two old ones, and here with the weather and on her bike she has ruined them so much that they look ghastly. But we definitely cannot afford a new one."[196]

It had taken months for Kalman and Lowy to develop the necessary processing expertise and for Marcus Witztum to provide four Belgian machines that were indispensable for full production (and even when they were installed they did not work as planned).[197] The outbreak of the war meant there were no export opportunities.[198] The scarcity of imported raw materials, principally brass, created another difficulty, though later a new machine, made to the

---

191 Rachel Philipson Levy email to authors, 2 November 2006; John McDermott, the manager's son, interview with authors, 13 June 2008; NAI, DJ 68/1/600.
192 *Galway Observer*, 28 January 1939.
193 MAI, G2/0348, Grete Blaskopf to her parents, 28 October 1940. See also a reference to a claim of 5,162 Reichsmark plus £477 by "Ritsch" that had accrued from deliveries to Galway between 1 April and 3 August 1939. AdR, 06/7.146, Vol. 1, p. 45. Probably these deliveries were part of the compensation the Aryanisers in Vienna had granted to Blaskopf.
194 MAI, G2/0348, letter Grete Blaskopf, 6 December 1939.
195 MAI, G2/0348, Grete Blaskopf to parents, written in second half of 1939. Translated by authors.
196 MAI, G2/0348, Grete Blaskopf to her mother, end of October 1940. Translated by authors.
197 MAI, G2/0348, Grete Blaskopf to Blaskopf parents in Vienna, written in second half of 1939.
198 There had been hopes that products could be sold on the British market and in Europe. MAI, G2/2631, Helena Lowy to David Künstler, 3 January 1940; MAI, G2/0348, letter Grete Blaskopf, 28 October 1940.

specifications of Florian Oberer, helped to resolve this problem.[199] During the war the demand for zip fasteners sank further. On top of that, the company had to face cheap British competition forcing them to sell at levels barely above production costs.[200] "There are only enough orders to guarantee production for one to two weeks maximum [...] The workers are almost all unemployed [...] Many customers had to renounce zip fasteners completely, others order only a quarter of what they did in the previous year."[201] The unsteady flow of orders meant that the workforce had to be cut to a minimum and production peaks covered by overtime.[202]

Nevertheless, the difficulties of these refugees' exile in Galway did not appear to be primarily dictated by serious economic problems. The Blaskopf family could afford to buy a house, and Grete was not forced to work in the factory to augment the family income. The leading continental executives at Les Modes Modernes could dispose of satisfactory incomes,[203] and even when business was bad, Mathilde Schwenk declined a friendly offer of financial help saying that "up to now we have everything we need".[204] Even "normal" ICCR exiles and complete novices to the trade like the Marckwalds managed to make ends meet. After the Marckwalds' arrival in Ireland they had been briefly housed at Vallombrosa and then for another three months by the Jacob family in Tramore. On 25 July 1939, they moved to Galway because Maria had been offered a job at Les Modes Modernes, and in 1940 she was employed by Wings.[205] Her husband meanwhile failed to persuade the ICCR to support his wish to learn carpentry and open a business in Galway.[206] Instead the committee recommended that he attempt teaching German

---

199 *Irish Press*, 9 September 1942.
200 MAI, G2/0348, Grete Blaskopf to parents, 28 October 1940.
201 MAI, G2/0348, letter Grete Blaskopf, 28 October 1940. Translated by authors.
202 MAI, G2/0618, Marckward to his sister Sophie Cohn-Voss, 8 August 1940.
203 Oberer appears to have earned an annual salary of £1,000. NAI, DJ 68/1/680. In April 1939, Josef Storm in a lower position received between £8 and £10 per week. NAI, DJ 69/80/316, Storm to Ditchburn, 12 April 1939; Les Modes Modernes, To whom it may concern, 12 April 1939. At the end of the war Philipson earned the relatively large sum of £1,450 p.a. and Zeiler still £1,000 p.a. NAI, DJ 68/1/599 and 600.
204 NAI, DJ 69/80/316, letter Schwenk, undated. Translation by authors.
205 MAI, G2/0618, letter Marckwald, 8 August 1940. She was granted a permit to work for Les Modes Modernes from June to December 1939. NAI, DJ 69/80/93.
206 In early April 1940, his wife made a personal trip to Dublin in an effort to persuade the ICCR to intervene on his behalf at the DI&C, but learnt that the Department would not grant such an application. Fritz thought that the 'ladies' in Dublin were glad he and Maria had been accommodated in Galway, and that 'here their interest in our case has ended'. Niedersächsisches Landesarchiv Hannover (NLA), Nds. 110 W, Acc. 31/99, Marckwald to Slattery, 9 April 1940; ICCR to Margaret Shea, 15 April 1940.

to Irish people. Fritz knew that his chances of doing so in Galway, which he called a backwater ["*Nest*"], would be slim,²⁰⁷ but he complied, and with the help of a professor of German at the "wee university" (Marckwald), and of Margaret Shea and a Father Stephenson he at least succeeded in finding two students for a few weeks.²⁰⁸ After a meeting with Maud Slattery in Dublin, Maria let it be known at Wings that ICCR members had considered her weekly wage of £4 inadequate, and as a consequence the managers raised her pay by 10 shillings.²⁰⁹ Nevertheless their income was lower than that of other Austrian executives at Wings. Fritz contributed to the household budget by his teaching and by cultivating and harvesting their household garden.²¹⁰ Apart from that they had only limited savings which they did not want to spend prematurely.²¹¹ Nevertheless they were aware that they at least lived in better circumstances than many other exiles or than some of their Irish neighbours.²¹² Their situation seems to have improved after Wings moved to Dublin and Maria was again employed by Les Modes Modernes as a milliner and then as a designer.²¹³

Around the second half of 1941 plans matured to move Wings to Dublin, a logistically more suitable location than Galway. When these plans became known, Lemass was confronted with critical questions in the Dáil. He pointed to temporary wartime problems, especially to "the difficulty of arranging in Galway for speedy repairs and replacement of delicate machinery".²¹⁴ The guarded answer concealed that in reality the move was a setback for his Western development policy. The new site was at 9–10 Upper Liffey Street.

One ever-present conversational topic among the refugees in Galway had been the weather (Grete Blaskopf: "catastrophic", rain "lasting three quarters of a year"), but more pressing was their social isolation: "Our daily contacts are

---

[207] MAI, G2/0618, Marckwald to his mother, 24 April 1940.
[208] NLA, Nds. 110 W, Acc. 31/99, Slattery to Marckwald, 23 April 1940. NAI, DJ 69/80/93, Duff to ICCR, 17 June 1940.
[209] MAI, G2/0618, Marckwald to his mother, 24 April 1940.
[210] NLA, Nds. 110 W, Acc. 31/99, Marckwald CV, 10 October 1956. He may also have been briefly employed by Les Modes Modernes, which recorded his name as an employee beside his wife's. MAI, G2/x/0720. In NAI, DFA 10/2/18, list of Germans, Co. Galway, however, he is registered as unemployed.
[211] MAI, G2/0618, Marckwald to his mother, 24 April 1940.
[212] MAI, G2/0618, letter Marckwald, 8 August 1940.
[213] Her name appears in MAI, G2/x/0720. See also MAI, G2/0618 and NAI, DFA 10/2/18, list of Germans, Co. Galway. At the end of the war Maria earned a weekly £9 at Les Modes Modernes. NAI, DJ 68/1/589 and 590.
[214] DD, Vol. 86, 7 May 1942.

almost solely with Germans [...] Being alone is quite nice but not if it lasts for a year and no end is in sight."[215] In Galway there was no Jewish community – only six Jews had been counted in the whole county in the census of 1936 – and no synagogue.[216] The newcomers practised their religion privately, or went to Dublin for the High Holidays if possible.[217] Nevertheless, there seems to have existed a small Maccabi group.[218] Their isolation was, partly, self-imposed, but Grete Blaskopf lamented her domestic imprisonment at Margaret's Lodge, which she called a "winziges Häuserl" [dwarf house].[219]

As might be expected, subjective feelings of isolation fostered cohesion inside the exile community. Distances were short: every day they met in the factory, and privately a mere walk between Salthill and the town centre brought them together. Most had found accommodation in the streets surrounding Eyre Square,[220] the busy centre of the town with offices, banks, and private firms of solicitors and accountants.[221]

Social barriers were not hermetic. The presence of children, for example, could bridge social distance.[222] Among the adults the Marckwalds are reported to have had friendly relations with their landlords in Eyre Street, the family of William J. Concannon, a solicitor who also worked for James Joyce's mother-in-law Annie Barnacle. Fritz cultivated their garden with professional skill, having

---

215 MAI, G2/0348, letter Grete Blaskopf, 6 December 1939. Translated by authors.
216 *Galway Observer*, 8 April 1939.
217 Obviously, Helena Lowy had such private religious practice in mind when remarking that "Hans and I were praying the whole day" on Yom Kippur. Translated by authors. MAI, G2/2631, letter Helena Lowy, 2 October 1939.
218 MAI, G2/0348, letter Fritz Blaskopf, 7 December 1939.
219 MAI, G2/0348, letter Grete Blaskopf, 6 December 1939.
220 St Brendan's Terrace (Hein, Dziewientnik), Eyre Street (Marckwalds), Prospect Hill (Mortl, Bittgen), or beyond the Corrib but near the centre in University Road (Kalmans), or east of Eyre Square, Bohermore Road, not far from the factory site (Honigs, Miretinsky). Zeiler and Schwenk shared a house (1 Woodquay; in 1944 both moved to Riverside). Others had taken up residence in Salthill: the Storm family and Hein on Threadneedle Road, the Blaskopfs on Tailors Hill Road, the Lowys on St Marys Road, and Heinz and Alice Krotoschin in the Lenaboy area. The Rosuleks and Oberer rented flats in Eagle House on Shantallow Road. Philipson used to lodge in Galway's most renowned hotel, the Great Southern (nowadays the Meyrick) when he came on business trips from Dublin. Rachel Philipson Levy email to authors, 12 March 2008.
221 T. W. Freeman, Galway – the Key to the West. In: *Irish Geography*, Vol. 3 (1957), p. 199.
222 For example Hanna Blaskopf, who attended the local school. MAI, G2/0348, letter Grete Blaskopf, 6 December 1939. John McDermott remembers that he and the Storm children were playmates and that friendly links between their parents were maintained even after the Storms emigrated to Australia in 1947. Interview with authors, 13 June 2008.

been familiar with the trade from his childhood days in Erdeborn, with results that astounded their neighbours.²²³

At the same time fissures arose within the exile group. The insularity of their existence and the problems of the Wings company gave rise to tensions inside and outside the group. Among the three Wings-related families, some harboured animosities dating back to their pre-emigration time in Vienna and Antwerp. There was a split between the Witztums and Lowys on the one hand and Kalman, Oberer and Blaskopf on the other. Kalman and Oberer were suspected of planning to leave Wings and set up a separate enterprise,²²⁴ and Witztum and Lowy were accused of having deliberately excluded the Blaskopf parents in Vienna from their emigration scheme. The tensions produced accusations of incompetence and mobilised deeply rooted prejudices against Eastern-Polish Jews ("He cannot be changed: Polish remains Polish").²²⁵

These tensions should be seen also in the context of suspicions of the newcomers from the outside. In 1938, the presence of "Austrian experts" in the factory and in town was not a public issue, but in 1939 there was open expression of intolerance. At the monthly meeting of the County Libraries Committee in January 1939, the County Librarian remarked that "a number of German-speaking people – foreigners – living in Galway" had "frequently" called looking in vain for German books.²²⁶ Questions were raised: "Are they Aryan or Jew?" "Are they birds of passage or fixtures?" "They are German-speaking, but are they German-born?" The chairman, Mr Carrick, opined that "no books should be bought for outsiders of that description." Newspaper reports of the meeting fuelled a debate that reached beyond county borders.²²⁷ It was mainly about numbers: How many Jews were in town? First, the *Galway Observer* queried a Department of Industry and Commerce publication that quoted the census number of Jews for 1936 by adding a provocative question mark in its headline ("Six Jews in Galway?"), implying that in reality there were more.²²⁸ One Libraries Committee member had

---

223 MAI, G2/0618, Marckwald to his mother, 24 April 1940. See also DJ, 2013/50/5, William Concannon to DJ, 19 May 1945.
224 MAI, G2/2631, Helena Lowy to David Künstler, 3 January 1940. The suspicion was possibly not unfounded, as Kalman had already in Vienna expressed a wish to found a zip fastener factory of his own. IKG Vienna, Emigration Department, no. 36.692.
225 MAI, G2/0348, letter Grete Blaskopf, 28 October 1940. Translated by authors.
226 *Connacht Tribune* and *Galway Observer*, 28 January 1939.
227 For example, the Sligo-based *The People's Press*, 28 January 1939, reported on the incident in a tone sympathetic with Carrick's views.
228 *Galway Observer*, 28 January 1939.

it as a fact that "132 German-Jewish refugees" had been given permits to live in the town. The ICCR felt obliged to parry such charges and mollify public sentiment by having the correct numbers published in the *Connacht Tribune*: only 80 persons had been admitted to Ireland up to the end of January 1939; and in the same issue the paper cited some exiles saying that considerably fewer than 50 Catholic "aliens" were staying in Galway.[229]

Heinz and Alice Krotoschin and their two children (one born in Ireland in 1936) were the only German-speaking refugees in Galway living outside the social nexus of the two factories in the war years. Their Irish life up to 1940 was marked by various ruptures and changes. In 1935, Heinz's employment with the ink manufacturers W. & E. Haughton Ltd ended for unknown reasons. After that he and a British partner founded a mail-order business, selling their articles on Irish and English markets.[230] From 1937 to 1939 Krotoschin was also employed as a "commission agent" in the foreign trade branch of various enterprises, including Messrs Barlite Ltd, in Nenagh, Co. Tipperary.[231] The war cut his trade links with the Continent and forced him to look for other employment.[232] Nevertheless, the war seems to have improved the family's living conditions. In June 1940, Krotoschin was employed by Tofts Circus, the popular amusement carnival based in Galway, as a "free architect"; he also took over an agency for "building materials" and began buying credit-financed property for speculative purposes.[233] As early as late 1941, a foreign observer described him as a man living in "reasonable [sic] comfortable circumstances".[234] The family's situation took a turn for the worse in

---

[229] *Connacht Tribune*, 11 February 1939. See also *Connacht Sentinel*, 31 January 1939.
[230] *Visual History Archive*, interview with Henry Kent (=Heinz Krotoschin), 10 May 1996; MAI, G2/0111, Krotoschin, two hand-written G2 reports, undated; EA Berlin, no. 61.929, R 50–53, Alice Kent affidavit, undated; R64, Henry Kent affidavit, undated.
[231] See Garda reports in DJ 2013/50/406; also MAI, G2/0111, two hand-written G2 reports, undated.
[232] MAI, G2/0111, Krotoschin to Dublin Post Direction, 4 September 1939. In *Visual History* Kent claims that his ruin was caused by a failed delivery of sanitary products from the Continent at the beginning of the war for which he had paid in advance. For his futile attempts in early 1940 to find employment in the army or as a translator in the censorship office, see correspondence in MAI, G2/0111.
[233] See correspondence in MAI, G2/0111. The quotations are from *Visual History Archive*, interview with Henry Kent, 10 May 1996, and NA Washington, RG 84, Box 1, US Consulate report 12 December 1941. In Garda reports it was suggested that during the war he had bought several houses from the Irish Civil Service Building Society, which he intended to lease out. See DJ 2013/50/406.
[234] NA Washington, Consulate report 12 December 1941. He seems to have been able to buy a hotel in Salthill and a house on Rathgar Road, Rathmines. This is at least what G2 observers believed. MAI, G2/x/1091, col. 249; G2/0111, undated G2 report, probably December 1943.

1943 when Heinz's business was boycotted by Galway construction firms. Alice even recalled acts of physical aggression committed by nationalists, who accused them of pro-English sympathies.[235] It is unclear whether anti-Semitic overtones and/or the newcomer's supposedly robust business practices played a role. At any rate the situation appeared so critical that the Krotoschins decided to resettle in Dublin in January 1944.[236]

By that time Heinz Krotoschin had already changed his name, hiding his refugee and Jewish status behind a new identity – Henry Kay, officially changed to Henry Kent after the war.[237] It is possible therefore that he was the "Jew who was hardly able to speak English" but whose "name was that of an Irish family", whom S. Kelly, a County Councillor, speaking at a Galway County Council meeting in 1943, claimed to have met.[238] Following this debate, the County Council passed a resolution protesting against an alleged tendency among "Jews and other foreigners" to have their original names anglicised and thus adroitly slip into new identities.[239]

Happy exile in Cork?

Receiving migrants, foreigners and fugitives was part of the historical experience of Cork, Ireland's second largest city, which had approximately 93,000 inhabitants in 1936. The city housed a community of Jews who had fled from pogroms in Lithuania and numbered about 500 members at the beginning of the twentieth century. Close to 200 still lived there in the 1930s.[240] Corkonians had seen a number of refugees enter the country in 1938/1939 but only four permanently remained in town: Hans and Ines Mandl, Gerhard Schloss and his wife Elisabeth. Schloss, a baptised Protestant, had occupied various management positions in prestigious German companies.[241] After his dismissal at the end of 1938 and under the threat of detention he made serious efforts to emigrate by engaging the help of Quakers,

---

235 In an affidavit to the restitution court she even asserted that the situation in Ireland was as bad as in Germany. EA Berlin, no. 61.929, R12-19.
236 In Dublin they resided at 135 Rathgar Road, probably the house which they had bought during their profitable Galway years (see footnote 234). NAI, DJ 68/1/749 and MAI, G2/0111.
237 MAI, G2/x/1091, col. 249.
238 *Connacht Tribune*, 18 September 1943.
239 Ibid.
240 The Census of 1936 reported 202 Jews for Cork and Limerick combined, as well as boroughs in Co. Waterford. CSO, Census 1936, Religion and Birthplace. Table 6A.
241 MAI, G2/0746.

a Dutch support committee and German acquaintances in Ireland.[242] He came to Ireland as a coveted "constructeur" [sic] in the drawing office of Steel Ltd, Ireland's only steelworks, which started production on the fortified Haulbowline Island in August 1939.[243] Three months later, Hans Mandl began his career as a "highly paid" designer at the Sunbeam Wolsey knitting mill complex in Cork.[244] Mandl, married to Ines Hochmuth since 1936 (see chapter 2), had already worked as an agent for his father's textile business in London from 1930.[245] His wife left Vienna for good after the *Anschluss,* joining Hans in the British capital "for economic as well as political reasons".[246] On the eve of 2 September 1939, they made their crossing to Ireland. "Our intention was to get away for the week-end, maybe the war scare would blow over [...] When we arrived in Ireland war had broken out." Ines also remembers how people "advised us to contact Briscoe [...] He got us permission to stay and work in Ireland".[247] It seems that Briscoe found ways to persuade Sunbeam Wolsey Ltd to engage Mandl as a textile design expert and the Department of Industry and Commerce granted a permit.[248] On 28 November, they moved to a furnished flat at 27 Merchant Quays in the commercial heart of the town.[249]

Neither of the two couples experienced any financial difficulties during their time in Cork.[250] The letters that Gerhard and Elisabeth Schloss – she had joined

---

242 For his links to Hamburg Quakers see Staatsarchiv (SA) Hamburg, no. 3551-11, 2008/1, p. 44, Gerhard Schloss to Wiedergutmachungsamt Hamburg, 1 February 1957. The Enschede committee is mentioned in MAI, G2/0746, Schloss to committee, 25 January 1940. The Germans in Ireland were, among others, Mrs Stella Proctor, a relative and wife of a leading Dunlop official in Ireland. MAI, G2/0746, G2 report 1941, undated; SA Hamburg, no. 3551-11, 2008/1, Irish Steel to Gerhard Schloss, May-June 1939.
243 NAI, DFA 202/605, Irish Steel to DEA, 5 September 1939.
244 The Sunbeam Wolsey knitting mill complex specialised in silk hosiery and related textile articles and was the pivotal industrial enterprise in the northern part of the city. In mid-September 1939, Hans Mandl had negotiated employment conditions on a personal trip to Cork. NAI, DJ 69/80/529, Little, O'hUadhaigh and Proud, solicitors, to DJ, 23 September 1939.
245 NAI, DJ 69/80/529, Little, O'hUadhaigh and Proud to DJ, 14 September 1939.
246 Ines Mandl to authors, 11 October and 4 December 2004.
247 Ines Mandl to authors, 4 December 2004.
248 See correspondence between DJ and DI&C in NAI, DJ 69/80/529; also data in MAI, G2/0613.
249 In 1942, they moved to 64–65 St. Patrick's Street and in 1944 to 51 Grand Parade in central Cork. NAI, DJ 69/80/529.
250 Schloss earned £25 per month and after his second employment in November 1942 £10 per week. The factory had closed on 1 April 1941 for unknown reasons. It reopened in November 1942 when Schloss, who had meanwhile stayed in Dublin, was employed again. SA Hamburg, no. 3551-11, 2008/1, p. 24, Schloss to Wiedergutmachungsamt Hamburg, 1 February 1957. The Mandls could dispose of a regular monthly $500 grant from Ines's father Ernst Hochmuth in the USA besides Hans's income from Sunbeam Wolsey and – from November 1940 – Lee Hosiery Ltd in Cork. MAI, G2/0613 and NAI, DJ 69/80/529.

her husband on 15 December 1939[251] – addressed to her parents and others in Germany in 1940 are packed with glowing details about their comfortable life on Haulbowline Island.[252] In Ines Mandl's contemporary and later descriptions the words exile and refugee do not figure. The Mandls' early emigration to England and an expectation of joining their parents in the USA as soon as possible might have contributed to her perception. In Ines's memories her life in Cork was filled with studies at the public library (well-heated, in contrast to their flats), then at the Crawford Municipal Technical Institute, where she enrolled to study chemical technology.[253] In their free time the Mandls enjoyed the town's cultural life and took bicycle tours.[254] The two couples had few personal contacts with Corkonians outside their professional sphere. Neither did they have any contacts with the Jewish community (Ines Mandl: "We were not religious and did not attend synagogue") though she and her husband understood themselves in a cultural sense as Jewish. "We were never invited to the homes of co-workers, classmates or acquaintances and we did not invite them [...] We did not feel 'at home' as we had in England because we considered our stay temporary from the outset". However, there was no personal antagonism: "We encountered much more antisemitism [sic] amongst the Irish-Americans in New York than the Irish in Ireland."[255]

The exiles of Co. Tipperary

In June 2006, the *Munster Express* reported that "another link with Plunder and Pollack tannery was broken on the death of Hana Hitchman".[256] Hana's husband

---

251 NAI, DFA 202/605, Irish Steel to DFA, 5 September 1939.
252 They praised the mild climate on the "blessed island", their rented house, the garden, the furniture and the household equipment they had managed to rescue from confiscation. Their very positive responses have to be interpreted with some reservations as they cultivated a fiction that they had voluntarily chosen Ireland as their target country and not Great Britain, which they expected to be Germany's future enemy. This is at least what Schloss tried to impress on his addressees in the German ministries. MAI, G2/0746, letter Schloss, 8 January 1940.
253 Her husband also took part in evening courses in engineering, and both attended courses at Cork Art Institute. Ines Mandl passed exams in Spanish, thus adding another language to her French, English and German. Ines Mandl to authors, 8 December 2004.
254 On one of their tours to Kerry they "went out of (their) way to see an Austrian expatriate in Tralee who manufactured plastics": Anselm Horwitz (see below). Ines Mandl to authors, 8 December 2004.
255 Ines Mandl to authors, 8 December 2004.
256 *Munster Express*, 9 June 2006.

Fred Hitchman (Fritz Hitschmann) and his uncle had come to Carrick-on-Suir almost seven decades previously (see chapter 3). Their creation, Plunder & Pollack Ltd, had ceased to exist more than 20 years before Hana's death. The official 2008 website of the town records that "the closure of the Plunder & Pollack tannery in 1985 caused immense hardship in the town, as a significant proportion of the population [...] were employed there or were dependent on someone who was."

In 1943, the Irish Tourist Association announced that Carrick-on-Suir, once described as the second dirtiest Irish town, showed "unmistakable signs of growth: one has only to turn into one of the many narrow alleyways and lanes that branch off the modern main street, to find the complete Georgian or Tudor atmosphere". The I.T.A. also pointed to other cultural assets of the town, including a "neatly arranged" public park, two cinemas, and a Social and Literary Club.[257] Six years earlier when Fritz Hitschmann had visited the town to assess its suitability as a location for a tannery he would have observed mass unemployment and extensive poverty.[258] The "unmistakable signs of the growth" had come with the only industrial employer for many years, Plunder & Pollack.[259]

The foundation of the enterprise was part of attempts to revive the Irish leather industries that by the 1920s had become "virtually extinct, largely through the failure to meet British competition".[260] Seeking to lessen dependence upon imports from Britain, the new Fianna Fáil government introduced a system of protectionist import quotas to stimulate growth in the domestic tanning industry. The policy led to the establishment of a number of tanneries which mainly served the domestic market.[261] In Carrick-on-Suir a first step was taken in May 1935 when the Carrick-on-Suir Tannery Company was founded, its site at the old Condensed Milk Factory needing relatively little refurbishment.[262] Capital was provided by local subscribers, with the Department of Industry and Commerce acting as a credit guarantor to a London bank. An Irish Board of Directors ran the factory which provided

---

257 Irish Tourist Association (I.T.A.), General and Topographical Survey: *Carrick-on-Suir (1943)*. We are grateful to Mary Guinan-Darmody for providing a copy.
258 "Carrick Slums" in *Nationalist and Munster Advertiser* (*NMA*), 28 September 1935.
259 In 1943, the I.T.A. still recorded Plunder & Pollack as the only industrial employer in the town.
260 T. W. Freeman, *Ireland. A General and Regional Geography*. Reprinted with revisions. London: Methuen & Co. 1972, p. 218; D.J. Dwyer, The Irish Leather Industries of the Irish Republic, 1922–1955. A Study in Industrial Development and Location. In: *Irish Geography*, Vol. 4, no. 3 (1961), p. 176; also "The Tannery Industry" in *NMA*, 2 October 1935.
261 Dwyer, Irish Leather Industries, pp. 177–179.
262 *NMA*, 13 March 1935; also Carlos Hitschman to Richard Denny (forwarded to authors), 9 June 2008.

considerable employment.²⁶³ Remarkably, its productive capacities largely hinged on the skill of some Austrian experts as trainers of the mostly female local workforce – one of the first recruiting successes of the newly founded Witztum committee.²⁶⁴ Marcus Witztum himself became one of the six directors of the company.²⁶⁵

Of these Austrians only Anton Benesch remained in Carrick at the time when the company's assets were sold to Plunder & Pollack in 1938.²⁶⁶ By the end of October 1937, it had become known that negotiations concerning a new launch of the tannery project were under way, though Hitschmann's visit was not mentioned in the papers.²⁶⁷ Why Carrick-on-Suir? The availability of river water was an important factor,²⁶⁸ but Carrick also looked a logistically plausible site given its position midway between the company's principal offices at Cork's City Chambers, 4 Lapps Quay, and an agency serving their interests in Dublin.²⁶⁹ Plunder & Pollack Ireland Ltd was incorporated on 14 April 1938. Its capital base amounted to £100,000 divided into 400,000 ordinary shares of 5 shillings each.²⁷⁰

---

263 See data in NAI, TID, FD/1/17. In 1935, the workforce was calculated to comprise 150 persons (*NMA*, 7 December 1935), but it is doubtful whether this level was ever reached. See also NAI, DJ 69/80/717, Anton Benesch CV, 25 November 1947.

264 Sources on the number of Austrians are contradictory. In his CV of 25 November 1947 Benesch speaks of eight Austrians. More credible is a DJ file, according to which more than 20 Austrians were employed at the tannery. NAI, DJ 69/883. They had been recruited by Alfred Kreuzer who worked as a managing director of Carrick-on-Suir Tannery Company until the sale of the company's assets to Plunder & Pollack Ireland Ltd. He then returned to Austria. NAI, DJ 69/80/480, O'Shea, solicitors, to DJ, 26 July 1939.

265 See *Galway Observer,* 22 May 1937, where Witztum is described as the "promoter" and a present "director of the Carrick-on-Suir Leather Factory" (i.e. the Tannery Company); also DJ 2013/50/259, Garda report, September 1937.

266 Anton Benesch CV, 25 November 1947.

267 The *NMA* announced that a "taking over of the tannery by a new company and under new management" was in the offing. *NMA*, 30 October 1937.

268 Carlos Hitschman to Richard Denny (forwarded to authors), 9 June 2008; also Dwyer, Irish Leather Industries, pp. 182–184.

269 The agency was Messrs. Dowling and Marsh. See company account book. Courtesy Michael Coady.

270 *Stubbs Gazette*, 27 April 1938. In October 1938, Plunder & Pollack Leitmeritz was 'Aryanised'. Under the new legal circumstances the Board of Directors in Carrick-on-Suir decided on 16 January 1939 to transfer the 112,000 shares held by the Leitmeritz enterprise to Fritz Hitschmann in person. The Aryanisers in Leitmeritz disputed the registration before an Irish court which raised the question whether the laws of Ireland or Germany should prevail. The court granted an interim injunction, but this did not block the capital transfer. *Irish Times*, 21 January 1939. Among the Irish shareholders the names of Jack O'Connor and Joseph J. Dowley, leading representative of the local corn merchants E. Dowley and Sons and already a director and large investor in the old company, stand out. Company account book 1940.

The Leitmeritz investment was mainly in machinery, which became vital when the initial plan, limited to finishing off leather products, was replaced by a full production line.[271] The Board of Directors was chaired by George Crosbie. Among the other members were Fritz Hitschmann and Joseph J. Dowley.[272]

Meanwhile, Irma Hitschmann had already abandoned Vienna, seeking safety in her Prague flat.[273] Richard Hitschmann also fled there after the Aryanisation of the enterprise (see chapter 3).[274] Given this situation they and their younger brother Albert planned to join Fritz in Carrick-on-Suir.[275] The Department of Industry and Commerce supported the engagement of Richard and Albert, but Bewley's and Warnock's opposition led to delays that thwarted their attempts to leave Prague before the occupation on 13 March 1939. Irma Hitschmann succeeded in fleeing Prague on 29 March 1939.[276] She and Richard arrived in Ireland on 26 July 1939, but attempts to bring Albert to Co. Tipperary failed (see chapter 6).[277]

Plunder & Pollack became one of Ireland's largest leather producers, although the war created "difficulties in the supply of materials and machinery" and a tanning programme commensurate with existing capacities could not be launched until spring 1940.[278] The profit and loss account of that year showed a net profit of £9,120. In the war years this rate rose to an average in excess of £17,000, although it fell back to £13,469 in 1943.[279] The factory largely owed its market success to technical experience gained on the Continent. In 1943, the company introduced an advanced form of chrome belting as a tanning agent,

---

271 Carlos Hitschman to Richard Denny (forwarded to authors), 9 June 2008. Nicholas O'Neill, a leading executive of the firm, remembers that the Hitschmanns were given shares in exchange for machinery and technical knowledge at the time the company was founded. Richard Denny to Coady (forwarded to authors), 13 June 2008.
272 Company account book 1940.
273 The precise date of her flight to Prague in 1938 has not been found. It seems probable from the date of her first instalment of the *Reichsfluchtsteuer* (RFS) that she "legally" emigrated in July-August 1938. The full sum amounted to 13,965 Reichsmark. Landesarchiv (LA) Berlin B Rep. 025-01, nos. 68191/59 and 8556/59.
274 BA Bayreuth, no. 15.002.620, note Paul Hitchman, 5 October 1965.
275 She had applied to the German Legation in Prague for a passport. It was issued on 21 December 1938 and paved her way to Ireland. Copy of document in BA Bayreuth, 15.007.030.
276 BA Bayreuth, 15.007.030, Irma Hitchmann application sheet, 20 July 1967.
277 NAI, DFA 10/2/18, G2 list of Germans in Ireland, Co. Tipperary. From the correspondence in NAI, DFA 202/27 it seems however that Richard had already visited Ireland in November 1939. Fed up with delays caused by the authorities in Dublin, Albert Hitschmann found a way to emigrate to Bolivia in July 1939.
278 Company account book 1940.
279 Company account book 1940 to 1946.

which enabled them to produce at cheaper cost than their smaller competitors in the Irish market (Carlos Hitschman: "We were the first in Ireland (and) we were proud of Full Chrome Leathers, a term which later became quite general").[280] Production began in 1939 with only 45 workers, but employment figures rose steadily.[281] By modern standards the work was hard, and handling the poisonous chrome was a special health hazard.[282]

The knock-on effects of the Hitschmann factory reached into many Carrick families and elevated the Hitschmanns to the rank of public persons.[283] There is scant evidence of any anti-German, anti-Jewish or anti-refugee sentiments against the newcomers in Carrick-on-Suir, though some did exist.[284] The management tried to run the factory as a respected social institution. The annual factory dance was a community affair in the town, and when the Hitschmanns were present they tried to preserve a balance between proximity and aloofness.[285] They also helped Irish workers to rise in the company hierarchy.[286] In spite of their elevated position they eschewed any public display of wealth,[287] but though favouring a

---

[280] Carlos Hitschman to Richard Denny (forwarded to authors), 9 June 2008.
[281] Company account book 1939/1940.
[282] Richard Denny and Michael Coady, interview with authors, 10 June 2008.
[283] During and after the war the family circle in Ireland widened to include Hana (born Königova, another Czech refugee, whom Fritz married in 1944) and Fritz's brothers Paul and Albert. Paul had survived the war years in Holland and became an engineer there until he was called to Ireland by Richard and Fritz. Albert moved to Carrick-on-Suir in 1958 after a successful business life in Bolivia and Argentina. Carlos Hitschman to Richard Denny (forwarded to authors), 9 June 2008.
[284] Anti-Semitic or xenophobic sentiments were expressed in a letter of 11 September 1944 opposing Hitschmann's first application for naturalisation. NAI, DJ 68/1/574.
[285] Being invited to perform at the feast was a much coveted honour for every local band. Members of the Hitschmann family are remembered for making an appearance but "not necessarily of great length". Richard Denny and Michael Coady, interview with authors, 10 June 2008. A Garda report of 16 August 1945 described Fritz Hitschmann as a person "tactful in all his dealings with the public" and a "popular figure" in town. NAI, DJ 68/1/574.
[286] One post-war example was the Richard Hitchmann Scholarship. Richard Denny: "Richard put money aside to further educate the sons of his employees in order that they should take over from the German experts [...] I started college in 1964 in London. The college fee at the time was £250 p.a. for a foreigner [...] The average weekly wage at this time was a little over £8." Richard Denny email to authors, 13 June 2008.
[287] In the interview of 10 June 2008 Richard Denny and Michael Coady emphasised that the Hitschmanns "came to work by bike just as everyone else. [...] When times were hard they never spent money on themselves, they had the worst car in town (a Fiat 600), no trappings of wealth. The company car was an old Rover."

plain lifestyle and finding communication easy – the language was no barrier at all – they did not socialise much with the common people of Carrick. Carrickbeg House, where Fritz (locally known as Fred), Irma and Richard Hitschmann lived, was, and still is, a patrician mansion with a large garden, overlooking the whole town. Their economic independence accorded with their behaviour inside and outside Plunder & Pollack, meeting the criteria of what could be expected of a civil but distant "boss", Irish or non-Irish. The situation was not so easy for Fridolin Schrötter, Franz Reichelt and Anton Benesch, all three supervisors in the enterprise, due to the fact that they must have felt under a constant threat that they could be replaced by Irish nationals.[288]

In 1943, Tipperary Town, a market town with a few industries based on the processing of regional agricultural output, had 5,384 inhabitants. It vied with Carrick-on-Suir for the title of "Ireland's dirtiest" town, but as in Carrick, I.T.A. registrars discovered signs of recent improvement in the town centre.

Originally, the premises of the Tipperary Glove Factory Ltd on Nelson Street (nowadays St Michael Street) had been a workhouse, but had later been redeveloped as a textile factory.[289] Ernst W. Königsberger, the new general manager, then 54 years old, settled with his wife Gertrud in a flat on the top floor at 25 Henry Street, a side street to Main Street in the old and busy centre of the town, only a short walking distance from the factory.[290] Ernst earned £7 a week during the war.[291] To begin with Gertrud suffered from domestic isolation, while her husband "worked all day" in the factory.[292] The town had a cinema, but there were no theatres, social clubs or cultural societies.[293] Nevertheless, the Königsbergers

---

288 Fridolin Schrötter came to Carrick-on-Suir on 29 August 1938. NAI, DFA 10/2/18, Germans in Ireland, Co. Tipperary. The date may suggest that he had wanted to flee an area under immediate threat by German occupation. Franz Reichelt had arrived on 11 June 1938. Nicholas O'Neill remembers that Fritz Hitschmann had hired him from England and employed him as a consultant. On Anton Benesch see NAI, DJ 69/80/717, CV, 25 November 1947; also NAI, DFA 10/2/18, Germans in Ireland, Co. Tipperary.
289 I.T.A., *Survey: Tipperary Town, Co. Tipperary (1943)*. Courtesy Mary Guinan-Darmody.
290 Peter Kingshill, the Königsbergers' elder son, interview with authors during a joint visit to the town, 21 January 2007. Later they rented the whole house. Sophia Kingshill, Willi and Trudi Königsberger in Tipperary. In: Holfter (ed.), *Irish Context*, p. 54.
291 Niedersächsisches Landesarchiv Hannover (NLA) Nds. 110 W, Acc. 8/9, E. Kingshill CV, 16 November 1953; also Sophia Kingshill, Willi and Trudi Königsberger. In: Holfter (ed.), *Irish Context*, p. 53.
292 Peter Kingshill interview with authors, 21 January 2007. After the war his salary increased to a peak annual income of £877. NLA, Nds. 110 W, Acc. 8/90, 241/22, E. Kingshill affidavit, 14 June 1955.
293 I.T.A., *Survey: Tipperary*.

seem to have acclimatised quickly to their new surroundings.[294] Language was not a hurdle given their international contacts before their emigration. In particular their Protestantism, rediscovered in Ireland, helped to overcome barriers. Gertrud became an active member and (although possibly only after the war) a respected organist of the minority congregation. It was among these Tipperary Protestants that they gradually came to find "quite a circle".[295] In their free time they frequently enjoyed sorties by bike into the rural surroundings, which did not go unobserved by G2 agents who were especially suspicious about Ernst's camera and maps.[296]

Image 9: Tipperary 1939.

---

294 This is what Peter was impressed with in August 1939, when he and his brother came to Tipperary for a last family gathering. Kingshill, *Footnote,* p. 58. Peter Kingshill also remembered that by that time they were leading a "comfortable life". Interview with authors, 21 January 2007.
295 Peter Kingshill interview with authors, 21 January 2007. On the "circle" see also Sophia Kingshill, Willi and Trudi Königsberger. In: Holfter (ed.) *Irish Context,* pp. 53–54.
296 See correspondence in MAI, G2/0533. G2 knew that Ernst Königsberger sent the negatives to the Kodak shop in Dublin, Grafton Street, whose owner had signed an agreement that he would report all suspicious photos to the Service. G2 also discovered another seemingly suspicious

The Secret Service believed there was another cause for concern. In the course of 1942 the family began using the name "Kingshill" (a literal translation of "Königsberger").[297] Even if the change were only to avoid mispronunciation of their difficult German name, it was also a break with their German identity and a test of their new country's readiness to accept a new one. In October 1943, the Tipperary South Riding County Council unanimously passed a resolution in which they warned against "foreigners, mainly Jews" trying to have their names anglicised.[298] In this Tipperary followed the example set by Galway the previous month, as we noted. But Galway in turn had only copied another county – Longford.

Longford Ribbons

"No other factory was so closely connected with Longford as the ribbon factory,"[299] says local historian Jude Flynn, describing how Emil Hirsch's enterprise was remembered by Longford people born between the 1920s and the 1960s. Hirsch Ribbons Ltd was the first industrial establishment in the market town and remained an influential economic and social institution until its closure in 1976. From an investor's point of view the main advantages of Longford were its location at the crossings of road, railway and canal systems, its water supply from the Camlin River and the availability of a low-cost if untrained workforce. Originally, Galway had been selected as the site of Emil Hirsch's new ribbon factory. It was here that the Hirsch entourage had taken residence after their departure from Vienna – but Emil Hirsch thought Galway was "too wet and not good for silk", and decided for Longford, a county town of 3,807 inhabitants in 1936.[300]

In talks with the Hirsch family the Longford position was strongly represented by local interest groups – all of them with Fianna Fáil connections – who also invited Witztum and McEllin to visit the town in early February 1939 to

---

element in Ernst's background: he had been a staff officer in World War I. Ernst was however able to dispel any doubts about his loyalty. MAI, G2/0533, G2 report, 10 December 1942. See also correspondence in NAI, DJ 69/80/120.
297 The Königsbergers began to use the new name in 1940. NAI, DJ 69/80/120, Königsberger to DJ, 25 November 1940; further correspondence in the same file and in MAI, G2/0533.
298 See Keogh, *Jews in Twentieth-Century Ireland*, p. 173.
299 Longford historian Jude Flynn to authors, 16 June 2008.
300 Jenny Kenny and Desmond Hirsch, interview with authors, 9 November 2006.

Image 10: (from left) P. Goebl, H. Lintner, unknown, A. Goebl, F. Witztum, G. Klaar, E. Sonnenschein, M. Witztum, M. Hearne, Emil Hirsch, Elsa Hirsch.

assess local conditions.[301] On the national level the campaign was spearheaded by Erskine Childers, Fianna Fáil TD for Athlone-Longford and leading spokesman of Lemass's policy of industrialisation and capital import.[302] His connections with the decision-makers in the Department of Industry and Commerce and Department of Defence – the latter was to let a vacant section of Connolly Barracks as the site of the future factory – secured Longford's success.[303] All interested groups pointed to the high degree of unemployment, the various futile proposals for

---

[301] In talks with the Hirsch family the Longford side was represented by Hubert C. Wilson and Michael Hearne, Senator, whose family was later in charge of erecting parts of the factory. *Longford Leader*, 18 February and 22 July 1939, *Longford News*, 8 April 1939; also *Irish Press*, 18 February 1939; *Irish Times*, 18 and 24 February 1939. For the reconnoitring trip see *Irish Press*, 14 February 1939.

[302] Childers was a secretary of NAIDA between 1935 and 1938. In February 1939, he became secretary of the Federation of Irish Manufacturers (FIM). John N. Young, *Erskine Childers. President of Ireland. A Biography*. Gerrards Cross: Colin Smythe 1985, pp. 80–81, 92. He was considered as an "unofficial lobbyist" for the FIM inside Fianna Fáil. Kieran Allen, *Fianna Fáil and Irish Labour, 1926 to the Present*. London Chicago: Pluto Press 1997, p. 66; also Daly, *Industrial Development*, pp. 130–131.

[303] The site had gained notoriety in Longford as the former British prison for local and other Irish rebels during the Irish War of Independence (1919–1921).

industrial development in the past and a corresponding sense of pessimism in the town.[304] The Longford press vacillated between hailing the new industrial initiative as a singularly positive event and despairing about its viability.[305] In the national press the public was told that Hirsch and Co., a "world-famous firm", had left Vienna "bringing with them a large part of their plant and equipment" and giving jobs to 20 to 30, later to 80 to 100 people.[306] Again the papers were silent on the anti-Semitic causes of the Hirsch exodus, even if the mention of "political conditions in Austria" in the normally outspoken *Irish Press* was a clear message to most readers.[307]

Preparations for production went ahead unimpeded and were finished before the beginning of the war. By early May, the stock of ribbons and 21 looms had safely arrived in Longford[308] – eleven were immediately installed in a part of the barracks, the others were set up at an adjacent building constructed by Messrs Hearne, Building Contractors. Ernst Sonnenschein began recruiting a first group of workers in the Long Arms Hotel – ten young women to start with, but it was expected that employment figures would rise quickly as soon as full production started.[309] In 1940, an average level of 30 employees was reached, and in 1941 about 60 employees worked in the factory.[310]

The training of these workers had to be completed in a much shorter time than was common in Austria.[311] This is why Emil Hirsch and Witztum urged immigration authorities in Dublin to grant a visa and working permit to another former employee of the Austrian Hirsch factory, Pauline Goebl's sister Hedwig

---

304 The unemployment figure for Longford in 1939 was 393. *Longford News*, 1 July 1939. As to hopes pinned to the new factory project, see Childers in *Irish Press*, 14 February 1939 ("Longford has a very strong claim to a factory. The town has had a number of disappointments but it looks as if things will go well this time").
305 For the triumphant tone see *Longford News*, 18 February 1939 ("The New Factory"). But even after the decision for Longford had been made, there was a measure of disbelief ("There is now an attitude of contempt among the townsfolk towards those over-ballyhooed projects. Now they ask: Will they ever come, is it just bunk?"), *Longford News*, 5 March 1939. But the paper reassured its readers: "They will come." See also *Longford Leader*, 22 July 1939.
306 *Irish Press*, 18 February 1939; *Irish Independent*, 18 February 1939. In general the availability of disused barracks was a favourite argument in the competition of local groups for industrial developments. Daly, *Industrial Development*, p. 116.
307 *Irish Press*, 18 February 1939.
308 David Jones, then a young boy living in the neighbourhood of the factory in 1939, quoted in O'Connor, *Irish Government Policy*, p. 200.
309 *Longford News*, 10 June 1939.
310 *Longford Yearbook* 1940. For the 1941 figure see *Irish Times*, 31 December 1941.
311 Desmond Hirsch and Jenny Kenny, interview 9 November 2006.

Lintner (Emil Hirsch: "She has been in my factory in Vienna for about 20 years as forewoman, and is especially suitable for training people").[312] Hirsch Ribbons was incorporated as a limited company on 24 July 1939. Under the Articles of Association the share capital was fixed at £20,000.[313] Marcus Witztum, John McEllin, Emil Hirsch and Michael Hearne took seats on the Board of Directors. In 1942, the Department of Industry and Commerce informed the proprietors that the percentage of shares held by Emil Hirsch and Marcus Witztum and other "non-qualified" (i.e. non-national) shareholders contravened the terms of the Control of Manufactures Act. As a consequence, the limited company was split into two companies: Hirsch Ribbons Ltd in Longford produced ribbons and was contracted to sell them to Dublin-based Ribbons Ltd which traded them on the Irish market.[314]

Hirsch Ribbons Ltd started production at the end of October 1939. Before the war, the managers had hoped to "develop a considerable home trade, being the one factory in our line of production in this country. In addition we anticipate a good export trade" (Robert Hirsch).[315] The war destroyed these export options while demand on the home market for a non-essential product like ribbons suffered under the austere conditions of the wartime economy. In spite of these adverse economic circumstances, the annual gross profit steadily increased in the first ten years. Part of the merchandise produced by Hirsch Ribbons was sold to decorate the hats manufactured at Les Modes Modernes in Galway and Western Hats in Castlebar.[316] The companies were in profit by the second year of production and annual profits regularly exceeded £2,000 with the exception of 1943, 1944 and 1948. Total wage costs however remained stable at an average of £2,000 p.a. until 1948.[317]

---

[312] The factory managers considered Hedwig Lintner a substitute for Hirsch's relative Rosenberg who had gone to Australia. Witztum to Emil Hirsch, 24 March 1939; Emil Hirsch to Witztum, 3 May 1939; Irish Embassy to Hedwig Lintner, 6 June 1939. Courtesy Jenny Kenny.
[313] Memorandum of Articles of Association Hirsch Ribbons, Ltd. Courtesy Jenny Kenny.
[314] In the original configuration of Hirsch Ribbons Ltd, Emil Hirsch was the largest shareholder, followed by Robert Hirsch, Deborah Witztum, Ernst Sonnenschein ("B" shares). Among national "A" shareholders McEllin held the largest stake. In the new configuration Hirsch and the other "B" shareholders held a majority in the Dublin company but only a minority in the Longford company. The composition of the Board in Longford remained unchanged. See data in NAI, TID 1207/1340.
[315] The figures are taken from the account book of Hirsch Ribbons Ltd which is stored by the County Longford Historical Society. Courtesy Martin Morris.
[316] Esther Goebl, Alois Goebl's daughter-in-law, interview with authors, 16 June 2008.
[317] Hirsch Ribbons account book.

Longford was an entirely novel environment for George Clare, who perceived even Dublin on arrival as "fifty years back to what I was used".[318] Altogether twelve persons had thrown in their lot with Emil Hirsch's new enterprise apart from Emil Hirsch himself: his wife Elsa and his son Robert, Ernst and Elisabeth Sonnenschein, Alois and Pauline Goebl, Hedwig Lintner, Ludwig and Adolphine Kende and their daughter Erika, and Georg Klaar. But not all of them lived permanently in the town throughout the war years and afterwards. Emil Hirsch, the general manager, took up residence in Dublin, co-steering the commercial affairs of his enterprise from the upper floor of 24 Suffolk Street, while Robert Hirsch, Ernst Sonnenschein, Ludwig Kende, Alois Goebl and Georg Klaar organised production processes in Longford. At first they were accommodated in a rented house on Earl Street.[319] The task of training the new employees fell particularly on Pauline Goebl and Hedwig Lintner, who also joined the household community in Earl Street. Robert Hirsch was the managing director, Sonnenschein his principal engineer, and Ludwig Kende the chief designer, while Alois Goebl took care of the machinery.[320] Georg Klaar's position was undefined, but as a translator between the workers and the Austrians (only Robert Hirsch spoke English fluently at the beginning) he fulfilled an important role.[321]

The composition of the Earl Street household changed over the years. Robert Hirsch moved to Dublin once the opening phase had been successfully organised, coming to Longford only intermittently. When the enterprise was split he was especially concerned with organising the liaison between Longford and the Dublin office. Ludwig Kende also went to Dublin but not before 1943.[322] Georg Klaar left Longford in early 1941.[323] These movements led to a reshuffling of positions in the factory: Ernst Sonnenschein succeeded Robert Hirsch as manager ("he ran the factory"),[324] and Alois Goebl took Kende's position as chief designer.[325]

---

318 George Clare, questionnaire, 29 March 2005.
319 Text of tenancy agreement between the landlord and Robert Hirsch and others of March 1939; Hearne to Emil Hirsch, 3rd March 1939 (copies). Courtesy Jenny Kenny. Adolphine Kende and her daughter stayed in Dublin in the first years. MAI, G2/0522. It is possible that Elisabeth Sonnenschein came to Longford only when she and her husband had their own house on Dublin Road.
320 *Longford Leader*, 22 July 1939.
321 Margaret Canning, interview with authors, 16 June 2008; George Clare in questionnaire, 29 March 2005.
322 Desmond Hirsch and Jenny Kenny, interview with authors, 9 November 2006.
323 George Clare in questionnaire, 29 March 2005.
324 Desmond Hirsch and Jenny Kenny, interview with authors, 9 November 2006.
325 Esther Goebl, interview with authors, 16 June 2008.

The prospect of steady employment encouraged the two to put down roots in Longford: Sonnenschein bought Edenbawn on Dublin Road in July 1940, and the Goebl family acquired Vienna Lodge on Battery Road.[326] Hedwig Lintner, Goebl's sister-in-law, seems to have remained at their former residence on Earl Street.

The workforce of Hirsch Ribbons comprised mainly untrained 16-to-20-year-old women and girls, some local, others from within a six miles radius of the town.[327] One worker, Margaret Canning, who joined the factory in 1940 and stayed until 1976, remembers that "the work day started at 8am and finished at 5pm, 1 hour for lunch and one 15 minutes tea break. If you were late it would be deducted from your wages."[328] The managers were "hard people to work for and very tight", hard-fisted on pay rises ("they said we could not afford it"), averse to social events ("no summer outings, no Christmas dinners or dances, only chocolate boxes in the beginning at Christmas and that was gone too after few years"). She also tells of their opposition to unionisation: "It needed a public demonstration at Temperance Hall to make them give in."[329] On the other hand, she was satisfied with her job: "I enjoyed my days in the factory" and "we were all saddened" when the factory went into voluntary liquidation in 1976. Her job satisfaction obviously derived from non-monetary considerations. "I was glad to get work in the 1940's," "the girls were very nice," and she even compliments the "bosses" in hindsight as "fair" in their personal dealings with the staff.[330]

There was a large discrepancy between the wages of the local workers and those of the immigrant supervisors. On 3 May 1939, Emil Hirsch told Marcus Witztum that Hedwig Lintner's salary would amount to £5 weekly.[331] Margaret Canning was given 5/6 rising to ten shillings – a huge difference even given that Margaret was inexperienced to begin with and Lintner, non-Jewish and having little to fear in Nazi Austria, possibly had to be lured to Longford by an attractive wage offer. Her annual income of more than £200 was well above average in Longford at the time.

---

326 Sonnenschein had already made an application to build a house in early 1940. Longford Urban District Council, LUDC 1/11/9, minute book 9 January 1940. The exact date of their move to the house on Dublin Road could not be certified. Desmond Hirsch and Jenny Kenny, interview with authors, 9 November 2006. Vienna Lodge was bought later. In 1943, the Goebls' address was still in Earl Street. NAI, DFA 10/2/18, list of Germans in Ireland, Co. Longford.
327 Jude Flynn, interview with authors, 16 June 2008.
328 Margaret Canning, interview with authors, 16 June 2008.
329 As to the degree of unionisation, Margaret Canning mentioned that it took years until some employees ("not all") joined the ITGWU.
330 Margaret Canning, interview with authors, 16 June 2008; quotations are from Jude Flynn, *Fireside Tales from around Longford Town & County*, no. 2 (November 2004), pp. 54–55.
331 Emil Hirsch to Marcus Witztum, 3 May 1939. Courtesy Jenny Kenny.

Outside the factory, attitudes to the new arrivals probably echoed the euphoric reports in the two regional newspapers. David Jones remembers that immediately after the arrival of the newcomers his father, a Methodist minister, invited two of the "Austrian workers to tea as a welcome to Ireland [...] One of the visitors was a man in his thirties whose name was Sonnenschein."[332] An atmosphere of welcome and friendliness may have continued to reign, as many young women were seen flocking to the Longford Arms to be recruited by Sonnenschein. Before long, the newcomers became common sights on Longford streets. "Not particularly welcome, no antagonism either", George Clare summed up the prevailing mood.[333] They were "accepted", remembered David Jones.[334]

The Goebls' Vienna Lodge and the Sonnenscheins' Edenbawn on Dublin Road, both bungalows, had a deliberate air of privacy and distance. Their owners were first-generation strangers, psychologically and linguistically. The seclusion of the Goebls' house is remembered, likewise their economic self-sufficiency based on gardening and domestic farming, a common practice back home in Göpfritz. Like Marckwald in Galway, Alois Goebl turned his garden into a small business, making it a habit to sell the plums he grew to the girls in the factory – but they did not enter the house, as Canning remembers.[335] A social distance was felt by workers towards the "bosses" and their "German-ness", perceived as strictness and a perturbing commitment to hard work.[336] Possibly, the "otherness" of Ernst and Elisabeth Sonnenschein expressed itself in different forms. They seem to have had good links to the Anglo-Irish sector of Longford society, being members of the County bridge club and the golf club.[337] Both were

---

332 Quoted in O'Connor, *Irish Government Policy*, pp. 200–201.
333 George Clare in questionnaire, 29 March 2005.
334 O'Connor, *Irish Government Policy*, p. 244.
335 This is Margaret Canning's memory. Esther Goebl: "He loved the factory and his home and… Vienna Lodge. He had a Jersey cow, and hens and all kinds of vegetables, among them white cabbage for Sauerkraut, a small greenhouse. They were quite self-sufficient and house-proud." Interviews with authors, 16 and 17 June 2008.
336 In Esther Goebl's memory her father-in-law demonstrated his "German-ness" in that he "followed a clear routine every day, kept to it to the minute, was very exact" but also by other idiosyncrasies considered typically German. He "loved Frankfurter and Salami [...] Christmas would be celebrated on Christmas Eve [...], also St Nikolaus on 6 December [...] He also bought himself a VW, for his son and daughter-in-law as well."
337 The Sonnenscheins took part in inter-county bridge tournaments, probably after the war. The preference for bridge in an Anglo-Irish household is described in Patrick Campbell, *My Life and Easy Times*. London: Anthony Blond 1967, p. 64. In these years Elisabeth also rose to the captaincy of the Longford ladies' golf team. Desmond Hirsch and Jenny Kenny, interview with authors, and Martin Morris, interview with Padraic Gearty (forwarded to authors, 18 July 2008).

conscientious Jews, and it was noted in the town that they went to Dublin for Jewish holidays.[338]

In Longford the immigrants' Jewishness (or imagined Jewishness) had always been a hidden issue that was overlaid by the weight of the job argument. It surfaced however in 1943 when the economic situation became critical. On 17 July 1943, the Longford County Council wished to alert the Government and the other Irish County Councils "in the interest of the community" against the practice of usurping Irish names.[339] The proposer of the resolution, a Mr Dunne, believed that "Jews were gaining a certain control in the country in several ways". Mr Lynch, seconding him, argued that Jews had increased their share of industrial production of textiles in the country by 500 or 600 percent; he was also sure that they "have O'Connell Street of Dublin in their grip".[340] The Longford resolution was passed unanimously. The intriguing aspect is again that it was passed in a town whose only industrial enterprise was clearly owned by Jews. Ironically, in 1939 the *Longford Press* had hailed the advent of the newcomers in Longford. One of the saviours-to-be was addressed as "Mr. Sunshine".[341]

Under Western Hats

> *Myself, I am thinking of the local hat factory,*
> *Of its history and the eerie fact*
> *That in my small town I have never known*
> *Anyone who worked in it*
> *Or had anything to do with it at all;*[342]

History lies at the heart of Paul Durcan's poem "The Hat Factory". The poet is one who knows about the history of the hat factory, it fills his childhood memories and prompts the adult's reflections on the relevance of hats. His text is about the ironical juxtapositions of local production in the factory "down in the valley" and the universal purposes of hats, of people producing hats who had to flee from

---

338 Margaret Canning interview with authors. Their link to the Dublin Jewish Community is also shown by their burial at Dolphins Barn (Ernst on 11 August 1964, Elisabeth on 3 April 1974). Burial list of Jewish Community.
339 Longford County Council, minute book, 1942–1944, LCC/1/11, p. 111, special meeting, 17 July 1943. See also *Connacht Tribune*, 18 September 1943.
340 *Longford Leader*, 24 July 1943.
341 *Longford News*, 8 April 1939.
342 Paul Durcan, *A Snail in My Prime: New and Selected Poems*. London: The Harvill Press 1993, p. 19.

conditions that excluded anything that hats represent in the poem: diversity, freedom and tolerance. Aware of all this, the adult is perturbed by the fact that in spite of this knowledge he has never "known anyone who worked in it".

Between May and July 1939, a number of Czechoslovakians came to Ireland – Ernst Glass, Karl Polesie, Fred Schmolka, Siegfried Klepper, Fritz Konirsch, Franz Dielenz and their families, and Walter Porges – to seek protection under Western Hats, the name they aimed to give to the enterprise they were about to found in Castlebar, Co. Mayo. They had taken different routes across Europe to play roles in the future hat factory and the Irish network of Franz Schmolka. Their first port of call in Ireland was the capital. Schmolka's itinerary was erratic: for two or three months after his arrival in Dublin, where he was provisionally housed at Witztum's premises in 15 South Frederick Lane, he travelled back and forth between there and Verviers in Belgium.[343] Decisions on the production and capital structure of the new enterprise had to be reached in discussions with Senator Edmond Claessens, the Irish investors and the Department of Industry and Commerce.[344] As elsewhere, a critical problem was the training of a sufficient number of Irish workers. Since part of the machinery was to be imported from Belgium, a group of 40 Irish trainees, mostly young women, were sent to Verviers for a course supervised by Porges and Dielenz.[345] Simultaneously, Belgian workers in Castlebar were busy constructing the new building and its 300-foot factory chimney.[346] The capital structure of the new enterprise was explained to the public at a meeting chaired by a town councillor. It was set up in accordance with the recommendations of the Industrial Credit Company (ICC), the public bank that had been founded in 1933 to counter the lack of initial private capital and to encourage investment. On 28 April 1939, Western Hats Ltd was registered. The capital of £100,000 was to be divided into 50,000 cumulative preference shares of £1 each, and 50,000 ordinary shares of £1 each, with Edmond Claessens being the main individual subscriber, holding

---

[343] G2 gives three dates for Schmolka's entry and re-entry into Ireland: 9 January, 20 February and 15 March 1939. He may have gone a fourth time to Verviers, returning to Ireland on 24 April 1939. MAI, G2/1173.
[344] MAI, G2/1173, for example correspondence 19 January 1940..
[345] The course began in June 1939 and lasted at least until November 1939. Maura Ryan, former employee, online memorial text "Opening of the Hat Factory": http://www.mayo-ireland.ie/en/towns-villages/castlebar/history/the-hat-factory-opening.html [last accessed 10 April 2015]; also NAI, DFA 202/285, DI&C to DEA, 15 November 1939. See also *Mayo News*, 24 April 2007. http://www.mayonews.ie/index.phpoption=com_content&view=article&id=1444:when-castlebar-met-belgium [last accessed 10 April 2015].
[346] See also "Opening of the Hat Factory" and a critical discussion on the construction programme in DD, Vol. 76, 31 May 1939.

shares of £25,000.[347] The Board of Directors consisted of Claessens, McEllin, Franz Schmolka and Marcus Witztum; later additions were P. Sarsfield Brady, James Murphy and Dermot O'Dwyer, the company secretary.

The regional press celebrated the "magnificent new factory" as the beginning of "a new era in the industrial development of Castlebar, County town of historic Mayo".[348] Until that time the only industrial enterprise in the market town had been a bacon factory.[349] The new building was erected on what was locally known as Alice Quinn's Field on Newport Road, in a flat valley then somewhat outside the town centre. Production began in late August 1940, its energy requirements met by turf for fuel and water supply from nearby Lough Lannagh.[350] At first Western Hats produced only hoods for women, but from January 1941 men's felt hats were made too.[351] The German military offensive in Western Europe not only meant a loss of potential markets, it also meant that Claessens disappeared from the scene – all attempts to bring him to Ireland failed[352] – and that only £19,000 of his investment of £25,000 could be mobilised for imported machinery from Verviers.[353] Schmolka also failed to have machinery from Jureifi shipped to Castlebar.[354]

---

347 *Stubbs Gazette*, 3 May 1939, with a detailed list of subscribers. See also NAI, DFA 202/285, Ferguson, DI&C, to DJ, 21 June 1940; DJ, handwritten, 30 April 1940. The conditions of the Belgian capital investment had been discussed at a conference in Verviers with Witztum, Claessens and Schmolka in January 1940. Another participant was Ossias Teicher, a Jew with Galician roots, who Witztum had asked to write an expert report on the structure of the Castlebar factory. He also offered him a leading position in the factory (see below). MAI, G2/1733, Claessens to Western Hats, 19 January 1940; Schmolka to Teicher, 6 December 1939; Teicher to Fred Schmolka, 27 January 1940. NAI, DFA 202/285, letter DJ, 24 January 1940.
348 *Connaught Telegraph*, 14 September 1940.
349 In 1943, it employed 100 workers. T.W. Freeman, The Changing Distribution of Population in County Mayo. Lecture delivered on 29 January 1943. In: *Journal of the Statistical and Social Inquiry Society of Ireland*, Vol. XVII, part 1 (1942/43), Dublin, pp. 85–106, 102.
350 Ernie Sweeney, former employee, online memorial text "The Building of the Factory": http://www.mayo-ireland.ie/en/towns-villages/castlebar/history/the-hat-factory-building.html [last accessed 10 April 2015].
351 MAI, G2/x/0054, Dielenz to Wenzel Jaksch, 18 February 1941. A substantial number of the women's hoods were sold to Les Modes Modernes. *Galway Independent*, 8 October 2014.
352 Claessens and his wife fled to France and were engaged with Resistance activities that led to their arrest and internment. *Le Courrier*, 15 and 16 July 1954. See also correspondence in MAI, DFA 202/285.
353 NAI, DFA 202/285, Ferguson, DI&C, to DJ, 21 June 1940.
354 Schmolka wanted to arrange a meeting with a leading Jureifi manager in Ireland. MAI, G2/1173, Schmolka to Prodaska, 2 January 1940. It is very improbable that the meeting took place and even less probable that the machinery was shipped to Ireland before the effective interruption of trade with the Continent in spring 1940.

These setbacks led to curtailed production lines.[355] Originally, it was planned to create 400 jobs.[356] By March 1941, however, Western Hats employed only 160 workers, and in 1943 employment figures sank to 120, rising to 150 in 1944.[357]

In early 1940, the former Komotavians left their temporary Dublin residences and moved to the Mayo town. At the end of January, Porges, Fred and Steffka Schmolka, and the Dielenz, Polesie, Konirsch and Klepper families arrived by train, all taking up residence in the local Redmonds Hotel, only Porges and Cernik renting flats in Ellison Street.[358] Cernik was not only badly needed as electrician in the factory, but having been in Ireland since March 1934 he also acted as adviser to Schmolka.[359] The small exodus was not complete, however. Of the 23 people who belonged to the Komotau circle, seven remained in Dublin (Ernst and Else Glass, Gertrud Konirsch, and the Drechsler brothers, as well as Franz Schmolka and his wife). Franz Schmolka's absence was conspicuous. In March 1940, he seriously thought of emigrating to the USA. He accused the other directors of a "breach-of-contract", possibly because he would have liked to follow his brothers Paul (Pavel) and Hans and other members of the Schmolka family to New York.[360] The specific causes of the split must have been serious, as he had already transferred a sum of $18,000 to America to demonstrate his financial independence. Whether because Lemass refused to sign a leaving permit, or because the restrictions of US immigration policy began to be felt at that time, he had to remain in Ireland. It is within this context that his move to Castlebar

---

355 Hence one branch of production could not be installed as intended. Ossias Teicher (see above) had been assigned to head this department, but when it transpired that "due to the war it has been found impossible to obtain the necessary machinery", his services were no longer required. NAI, DFA 202/285, O'Dwyer, Western Hats, to DEA, 1 October 1941.
356 NAI, DFA 202/285, Ferguson to DJ, 21 June 1940.
357 "Opening of the Hat Factory"; note in *Irish Press*, 23 June 1944; T. W. Freeman, The Changing Distribution of Population in County Mayo, pp. 85–106, 102.
358 See the data in the G2 files of Dielenz, Klepper, Konirsch, Porges, Fred Schmolka.
359 Leo Cernik a former electrical engineer for the large German company AEG, had been working for the new sugar factories since 1934. In 1939, he briefly returned to Czechoslovakia, but after the occupation by German troops in March 1939 he came back to Ireland, together with his wife Julia. He was employed by Western Hats from 1 May 1939. See data in NAI, DJ 68/1/524; his entries in a questionnaire, MAI, G2/1078.
360 NAI, DFA 202/206, Boland note, 20 November 1940. Schmolka had his name put on the Czech quota for the USA in March 1940. On 3 March, numerous other members of the Schmolka family, who had been granted an Irish visa through Schmolka's and Witztum's influence, also emigrated to the USA (Hans, Paul, Helena, Peter, Vera Schmolka, and Hans's mother-in-law Eliska Sommer). List in MAI, G2/x/0789.

as late as December 1940, more than three months after the beginning of the first production stage, should be seen.[361] He took residence in the Imperial Hotel, intermittently enjoying the hospitality of other exiles who had meanwhile settled in the town (the Cernik and Konirsch families, for example).[362] It was only in the course of 1943 that he decided to rent a flat in Faulkner's House at the intersection of Main Street and Bridge Street.[363]

Gertrud Konirsch and the two Drechsler brothers stayed in Dublin throughout the war years, but remained in close touch with their relatives in Castlebar: it was through Gertrud, who was apprenticed as a clothes designer,[364] and Hanus and Frantisek Drechsler that "Uncle Franz" or "Uncle Walter" ordered commissions which could not be obtained in Mayo itself.[365] The other vital address in Dublin was 24 Suffolk Street, where Western Hats Ltd, Ribbons Ltd and Les Modes Modernes Ltd had rented an office linking production at their provincial sites to markets inside and outside Ireland.

When production started in August 1940 the Komotavians relinquished their temporary residence at Redmonds, renting houses or flats close to each other in the town centre. Dielenz and Konirsch with their families and Porges moved to Faulkner's House, Fred and Steffka Schmolka rented flats nearby in Main Street, and Ernst Glass lodged in Newtown Street.[366] Leo and Julia Cernik and Karl and Marie Polesie acquired houses on Newport Road within walking distance of the factory.[367] In the following years the Dielenz and Glass families, Fred and Steffka

---

361 See residential entries in MAI, G2/1173.
362 MAI, G2/1121, Erika de Leon (Schmolka) to Margarete Konirsch, 16 February 1941.
363 MAI, G2/1173. It is uncertain whether Erika Schmolka and her baby joined him at that time. Anny Giersch (née Polesie) remembers her as having been continually resident in Castlebar. Email to authors, 27 October 2008.
364 She was an apprentice with Margaret Brennan's Ladies Tailoring Establishment on 44 Dawson Street. NAI, DJ 69/80/591.
365 In particular, the G2 files of Schmolka and Konirsch are full of correspondence relating to such private and business commissions. They also speak of the close personal relations among their families. From the correspondence in MAI, G2/1173, it becomes clear that Hanus Drechsler especially acted as a kind of unofficial business agent for "Uncle Franz".
366 From the registration cards in their G2 files it is evident that the Dielenz, Konirsch, Polesie, Cernik, Klepper and Fred Schmolka families rented new and permanent flats at the end of July 1940, a few weeks before the opening of Western Hats. Porges had already moved to the new residence on 5 February 1940. NAI, DJ 68/1/615. A few weeks after the opening, Ernst Glass left Dublin for permanent lodgings in Castlebar. MAI, G2/1101.
367 MAI, G2/1149 and 1078. The Cerniks moved into Tully Farm, an old cottage with a stretch of land on Newport Road. NAI, DJ 68/1/524.

Schmolka and Porges also moved to the Blackfort area, as it was called.[368] In the eyes of locals the move changed the social character of the quarter. In spite of its mixed neighbourhoods it became known as 'Little Jerusalem', a name which indicates how strong was the psychological impact of the new occupants.[369] Architecturally, Blackfort consisted of a number of plain bungalows that had been built in the 1920s and 1930s on the western rise of Newport Road. Only the house which Walter Porges acquired in later years, a villa with a large garden adjacent to the entrance of the factory further down "in the valley", was different from the Blackfort norm.[370] The only family to stay outside the residential cluster on Newport Road and the centre were the Kleppers. They settled in a bungalow on Spencer Street on the eastern fringe of the town.[371]

Everything revolved around their work in the factory. Franz Schmolka held a key position in company management and daily operation processes. In various photos he, a "short man with sparkling eyes" (Maura Ryan), and dressed in a white coat, is portrayed as closely supervising the work of his employees. Walter Porges was the technical manager until October 1944, after which he seems to have taken over Schmolka's position as general manager.[372] The other exiled Komotavians headed various technical departments, as implied by their job titles: Dielenz was a "crank bumpers master",[373] Glass a "carding master",[374] Konirsch

---

368 The precise dates of their moves cannot be determined. Glass moved there in 1941. MAI, G2/1101. Probably Dielenz and his wife also bought a Blackfort home at that time. Mrs McLoughlin, one of their neighbours, interview with authors, Castlebar 16 June 2008. The couple still lived there in the 1950s. See their application sheet of 1956, Bezirksvertriebenenamt (BVA) Cologne, no. 53/2935 and 2936. In MAI, G2/1170, it is stated that Fred and Steffka Schmolka also occupied a house on Newport Road, but at an unknown date they rented a flat in Faulkner's House and later one in Burleigh House, a large Georgian mansion on Ellison Street.
369 Anny Giersch, email to authors, 28 October 2008.
370 Minutes of an inspection tour of the former factory premises, 14 June 2008 (in possession of authors).
371 MAI, G2/1117. Their bungalow was on Spencer Street; see also Doris Segal's memoir in Doorly, *Hidden Memories*, p. 76; MAI, G2/1081, Franz Dielenz to Wenzel Jaksch, 7 June 1942. In 1941, however, they seem to have lived for a short time in another house on nearby Station Road. MAI, G2/1117. Anny Giersch, email to authors, 28 October 2008. Whether the Kleppers' residential choice expressed a deliberate distance from the other Komotavians can only be speculated.
372 NAI, DJ 68/1/615, Garda report on Porges, 6 September 1945. His former secretary Peggy Lee: "He liked to see people working, had no time for idlers. Was a good time keeper and liked discipline, a joke at the right time, and honesty." She "enjoyed working for him and was not afraid of him at all", but "some of the workers might have been". Castlebar Meeting, 14 June 2008.
373 MAI, G2/1081.
374 MAI, G2/1101.

a "carbonisation master",[375] Klepper a "mixing master" in the spinning department,[376] Polesie a "dyemaster" in charge of the dye-house.[377] The loss of status is evident. Klepper, the former authorised signatory in Komotau, felt despair, as it was "clear that I cannot and must not even think of my former position" but he was "ready to fulfil the tasks I am allotted".[378] In fact he and the other "masters" had to learn technical processes they had formerly watched from afar in their offices, or of which, like Karl Polesie, they had been completely ignorant: dyeing in practice rather than in theory was something he had to learn from scratch.[379] Only Dielenz and Cernik could rely on some prior practical experience within the new structures.[380] Their work also incurred possible health risks.[381] In 1941, Franz Schmolka's salary amounted to an enormous £1,661 per annum before taxation.[382] Porges stated after the war that he had received a net annual income of £416 at the beginning of his work for Western Hats, which probably grew considerably in the following years.[383] Conceivably, the others earned somewhat less. The figures denoted a substantial drop of income in comparison with their earnings in Komotau, but they appeared generous to Irish eyes.[384] A state of near-poverty loomed for the families when a household had to live without a regular salary. The deaths of Karl Polesie in June 1942 and Fritz Konirsch two weeks later left their families in dire straits. Whereas Margarete Konirsch was "saved" by her marriage to Walter Porges in 1947, Marie Polesie and her six-year-old daughter had to live on a very meagre state and factory pension; their mainstay was the bungalow on Newport Road they had bought before Karl Polesie's death. Fifteen years later she still had no stable income and "barely manage(d) to eke out an existence by

---

375 MAI, G2/1121.
376 MAI, G2/1117.
377 Anny Giersch, email to authors, 19 August 2008.
378 MAI, G2/1117, letter Klepper, undated. Translated by authors.
379 He was employed for at least some time by Les Modes Modernes. MAI, G2/x/0720.
380 BA Bayreuth, no. 15.006.426, Walter Porges, undated affidavit: "From 1913 I have worked together with Mr Dielenz in the hat factory Hugo Reiniger and Co., Komotau […] We have been able to continue our cooperation in the hat factory Western Hats Ltd, Castlebar, Mr Dielenz as master and I as general manager." Translated by authors.
381 Fred Klepper had two accidents with the new machinery: he nearly lost two fingers, and his hand remained mutilated. BA Bayreuth, no. ZLA/6009633, Klepper CV undated; also Doorly, *Hidden Memories*, p. 76.
382 MAI, G2/1173, Arnold and McCarson Co. to Schmolka, 14 June 1941.
383 BVA, no. 4296/53, Walter Porges affidavit, 5 September 1957.
384 It is estimated that in the 1960s the weekly average pay of the workers at Western Hats still amounted to no more than £2 and half a shilling a week. Susanna Sweeney, email to authors, 30 October 2008.

occasional domestic work and letting of rooms".³⁸⁵ Eye witnesses agree that she bore her situation stoically.³⁸⁶

Inside the factory, labour relations were dictated by hierarchic rules separating workers from their superiors who were able to enforce industrial discipline on all levels, which many workers found hard to comply with.³⁸⁷ It can be imagined that workers were concerned, for example, by the prohibition of tea breaks or the fact that they were not allowed to attend mass during working hours. They had to pay for social events such as outings in summer. Christmas dinners and dances in the Travelling Friends Royal Hotel did not bridge the gap between "them" and "us", though they might have strengthened the workers' identification with "their" enterprise. There was also an awareness among workers that they had better jobs than their colleagues in the "dirty" bacon factory.³⁸⁸ Such assessments were important as wages at Western Hats were said to be very low, an assumption that was turned into a campaign against the "newly arrived German Jews", who had allegedly broken the Irish rules on a minimum wage.³⁸⁹

In general, the young did not find integration into their new surroundings difficult.³⁹⁰ Doris Segal (née Klepper) asserts in hindsight that as children they

---

385 BVA, no. 5311/53, Marie Polesie affidavit, 21 October 1957. Translated by authors. Also Mrs McLoughlin, interview with authors, 16 June 2008. In her later years she rented a flat in a nearby bungalow. Ernie Sweeney, interview with authors, 16 June 2008.
386 There were stories about her clothing ("she wore good clothes but very old") and about how neighbours politely tried to conceal their knowledge of her bad material circumstances. Views expressed at Castlebar Meeting, 14 June 2008.
387 Peggy Lee's memory of Walter Porges at Castlebar Meeting. In this connection it is possibly significant that Schmolka's application for naturalisation in January 1946 was delayed for more than two years, because Western Hats employees had not given "specific approval of the application". NAI, DJ 68/1/748, DJ note, 9 May 1946.
388 Ernie Sweeney at Castlebar Meeting, 14 June 2008.
389 After the war a Dáil Deputy singled out Western Hats as an example of exploitation and sweated labour in the new factories. DD, Vol. 99, 15 March 1946, col. 2642 and 2643. The issue was dropped because the Deputy could not present any concrete figures. The event was more than a local phenomenon and reflected a propensity to put forward irrational theories. On 25 August 1940, the American Ambassador David Gray cited an ex-IRA leader: "He says that [...] some four thousand Jews from Germany have got in here and established sweat shops cutting the minimum legal wage of eight shillings and sixpence in many cases to five shillings." It also appeared that "they have seduced some Catholic girls" and there was "a big undercurrent of pro-Hitler sentiment in the slums on the anti-Semitic issue, but not anti-British". Paul Bew (ed.), *A Yankee in de Valera's Ireland: The Memoir of David Gray*. Dublin: Irish Royal Academy 2012, p. 294.
390 Porges: "Dorli [Doris Klepper] has been invited to a nearby estate where there are two other children" and Gertrud Konirsch "has won the first prize at a tennis tournament". MAI, G2/1154, letter Porges, 30 August 1941. Translated by authors.

were not able to realise the full scope of what their parents were suffering. "I was a child and everything was an adventure and a challenge for me," even the climate, the damp bungalow, and the difficulties of heating it with turf that troubled her parents. At school "everybody was very nice to me. In fact they were all fighting over me, the Protestants and the Catholics."[391] She went to the Protestant School, a junior school, until she was ten, and then attended a Catholic convent school in the absence of an alternative. Anny Polesie completed her education at the convent school and the Glass children attended local primary schools. Sidney Glass found himself at the boys' Catholic vocational school, where as one of his former classmates fondly remembers he was "well integrated".[392]

Most had at least an elementary command of English (exceptions were Fred Klepper and Marie and Franz Dielenz).[393] In general, however, "everything was hard" for them, as Anny Giersch remembers.[394] There are isolated reports about the elders' contacts with local people, but generally these contacts were limited and did not extend beyond basic neighbourly relations.[395] One can easily picture the men's daily routine: their short walks to the factory and back to the nearby houses on Newport Road, the working hours; and the women's housebound life, with outings (mostly) to Mrs Wynne's shop opposite the Polesie house.[396] They felt a close-knit social family, within which the younger people naturally addressed all their elders as "Tante" (aunt) and "Onkel" (uncle): "They were our friends and we

---

391 Doorly, *Hidden Memories*, 1994, p. 76.
392 John Garavan at Castlebar Meeting, 14 June 2008.
393 The Polesies "spoke some English". Anny Giersch, email to authors, 19 August 2008. Porges was multi-lingual, with a reasonably good command of Czech, French and English apart from German. See data in BA Bayreuth, no. 1/6009639. Peggy Lee described his English as "good but not great". Castlebar Meeting, 14 June 2008. Franz and Marie Dielenz were not prepared for a foreign language by the schools they had attended, but after some years they were able to speak "some English". Translated by authors. BVA, no. 53/2935. Fred Klepper, who had grown up in Poland, was not able to speak English when he came to Ireland. Klepper: "Our Dorli babbles more than I (I do not really dare yet)." MAI, G2/1117, letter Klepper, undated. Translated by authors. At home Doris "helped him with his English", having "learned English as a child". Doorly, *Hidden Memories*, p. 76.
394 Anny Giersch née Polesie, email to authors, 19 August 2008.
395 Doris Segal remembered how her father, a former member of the Czech-nationalist gymnastics movement Sokol, was engaged by the Castlebar branch of the Local Defence Force as a trainer. Doorly, *Hidden Memories*, p. 77. It is also remembered that the Dielenz family cultivated relations with a family in the local Church of Ireland community, possibly in the post-war years. Mrs McLoughlin, interview with authors, 16 June 2008. She also remembered her neighbourly contacts with the Polesie family.
396 Mrs McLoughlin, interview with authors, 16 June 2008.

were very close,"³⁹⁷ and moreover tended to stick to everyday habits from their Continental past, to the mild astonishment of their Irish neighbours.³⁹⁸ Their religious difference from Catholic Castlebar, the shared experiences and memories of the past, the residential clustering round the factory, the discomforts of their daily lives in an Irish town, all encouraged a tendency to remain within a closed group. Even Walter Porges, who possibly came closest to adjusting to his new Irish existence – he especially enjoyed lonely walks in spite of the frequent rain³⁹⁹ – lived a private existence on the fringe of Castlebar society. He spent his private time mostly in his house on Newport Road, reading literature or listening to classical German music.

Western Hats was not the only industrial enterprise in Co. Mayo to be developed with the help of Czech industrialists. Albert Kröner, his parents, his brother-in-law Paul Ney, Rudolf Schwarz, and their families, had been invited to build up Western Cloths Ltd at Ballina (see chapter 3). In September 1938, the project had already been discussed between Albert Kröner and representatives of the Department of Industry and Commerce, Marcus Witztum and Senator McEllin during a joint visit to Les Modes Modernes in Galway.⁴⁰⁰ Kröner also engaged another expert, Robert Schüller, of Enzensdorf near Vienna.⁴⁰¹ Western Cloths Ltd

---

397 Anny Giersch, emails to authors, 19 August and 27 October 2008.
398 Strange activities like collecting hazelnuts and rosehips, making their own cheese, etc. were noted with some surprise among the local Irish. Mrs McLoughlin, interview with authors, 16 June 2008.
399 Peggy Lee at Castlebar Meeting, 14 June 2008. MAI, G2/1154, letter Porges, 30 August 1941: "The grass is so beautiful in August like it used to be in our old *Heimat* only in May." Translated by authors.
400 See a report in *Western People*, 29 October 1938. On the planning phase of the factory see also reports in *Irish Press*, 25 October 1938; *Irish Independent*, 25 October 1938; *Connaught Telegraph*, 5 November 1938. From these reports it is evident that the Minister of Justice, Patrick Ruttledge, one of the Co. Mayo T.D.s, played an important part in securing the factory for Ballina.
401 Schüller had been the owner of a small textile factory in Enzensdorf before its Aryanisation. NAI, DFA 202/58, DI&C to DEA, 28 December 1938; also data in MAI, G2/0764. According to the WSLA residential register he was in Dachau concentration camp but released at the beginning of January 1939. That he got to Ireland is surprising. DI&C was interested in him in late 1938 and required him as an expert weaver even if there were to be difficulties in regard to repatriation, "provided he is in fact a weaving expert and has not an unsatisfactory personal record". Bewley was to furnish a report and if he was satisfied, a visa was to be granted. Bewley's generally negative stance seems to have been taken into account: "If information is obtained which reflects adversely on the alien the permit should be held by the Minister Plenipotentiary and an objective report furnished." NAI, DFA 202/58, Seaġáin O'Catháin, DI&C, to Secretary, DEA, 28 November 1938. Different reports were accordingly obtained, not entirely in his favour but sufficiently so. On 12 August 1939, Schüller left Germany for England. It is not known when exactly he came to Ireland nor when he returned to England. According to the MAI file he was still in Ireland in December 1939.

was registered as a public company in August 1939. Its capital stock amounted to £300,000, divided into 150,000 preference shares at £1 and 600,000 ordinary shares at 5 shillings. Its directors were McEllin (chair), Albert Kröner, Paul Ney, Francis Sherry and Marcus Witztum.[402] Western Cloths was to produce cheap cloth, but obviously it did not progress beyond the initial stages of production. Its short existence is described in a summary statement by Kröner, according to which the project failed because of the outbreak of the war.[403] During the liquidation process the Kröner and Ney families were mainly concerned with organising their emigration to Latin America.[404] Rudolf and Eva Schwarz however remained on, making two further attempts to establish themselves as partners of new enterprises, at least in one case with the support of Marcus Witztum. Neither of them came to fruition. As the affidavits for the US were approved in late March 1941, they were able to leave the country on 16 June 1941.[405]

On Europe's fringe

According to a manager of the Malbay Manufacturing Company Ltd, Miltown Malbay, Co. Clare – where newly-wed Kurt Hainbach and Isabella Coutts arrived in mid-January 1939 – was "very lonely, and very far off the beaten track for anyone used to city life".[406] In 1943, the Tourist Association confirmed that the town had "little to interest" tourists, apart from its proximity to the nearby seaside resort Spanish Point and its "reasonably good accommodation". Between 700 and 800

---

402 See *Irish Press*, 23 August 1939; *Irish Independent*, 23 August 1939. MAI, G2/0771, letter of 30 October 1939. NAI, DFA 202/366, Belton to Walshe, 7 July 1939. Western Cloths was the name that came to be used in 1939.

403 MAI, G2/1123, Albert Kröner CV, undated. A letter by Rudolf Schwarz of December 1939 also suggests that the start of war was understood to be the cause of the "collapse" of Western Cloths (the German word "Zusammenbruch" is twice used in letters of 1939). MAI, G2/0771. The date of the formal closure of the factory in the second half of 1939 could not be established.

404 MAI, G2/1123, Albert Kröner to Franz Schmolka, 24 April 1940; Franz to Paul Schmolka, 25 April 1940. Albert emigrated to Argentina in early June 1940. See MAI, G2/x/0789. According to an affidavit by Katharina Ney (BA Bayreuth, no. 12.008.367, application sheet, 1 December 1961) Leo and Beate Kröner moved to Brazil in June 1940. A parallel to the Kröner-Ney case may have been that of Richard and Irma Jeric, who had come to Ireland via France and were expected to found a glass factory. They also gave up the project due to the war, and had to wait in Dublin until they were able to emigrate to Canada in April 1940. See correspondence in NAI, DJ 68/80/351.

405 On their various attempts to find partners for new enterprises, the last on Irish soil being a firm called Elms Manufacturing Co., see Rudolf Schwarz's correspondence in MAI, G2/0771.

406 NAI, DJ 69/80/275, Colbert, Company Secretary, to DI&C, 2 February 1939.

Image 11: Kurt and Isabella Hainbach.

people lived there at the time.⁴⁰⁷ The most prominent family in west Clare were the Hillerys. They owned a pub, a garage, a hackney service and one of the two dance halls with a cinema showing pictures twice weekly.⁴⁰⁸ In regional memory they are enshrined as a political dynasty closely connected with the Republican and Fianna Fáil strand of twentieth-century Irish history.⁴⁰⁹ Michael Hillery, former medical officer to the IRA in the War of Independence, was a political institution in west Clare. In Miltown Malbay he was a regular member of an informal Fianna Fáil circle that convened on Friday evenings to discuss local politics and influence community decisions. The circle included, among others, the village

---

407 I.T.A., *Survey: Miltown Malbay, County Clare (1942–1943)*. Freeman calculates that before the war about 700 people lived in Miltown Malbay. T. W. Freeman, *Ireland. A General and Regional Geography*. Reprinted with revisions. London: Methuen & Co. 1972, p. 389.
408 John Walsh, *Patrick Hillery: The Official Biography*. Dublin: New Island 2008, pp. 7–9.
409 Walsh, *Patrick Hillery*, pp. 8–13. Colin Hainbach, Kurt's son born after the war, interview with authors, 19 February 2009.

priest, and another director of the Company, Jeremy O'Driscoll.[410] The Manufacturing Company had been started in 1937 on locally-raised initial capital of about £4,000. Both directors sought contacts with the refugee population in London and succeeded in bringing a young Viennese textile expert to Miltown Malbay.[411] As in the other textile industries, the workforce consisted of newly-trained young women, 55 as an average in the war years, and possibly a few young men. In postwar years the workforce increased to over 100 employees.[412]

The Hainbachs took up residence on Main Street, renting a flat in the house of the local butcher.[413] Kurt, the new general manager, trained some young men, who had been pre-selected by the 'Friday Club', as machine experts in the factory.[414] He also replaced Margit Manswort, another Austrian expert worker who was about to join her husband in a Tipperary factory, with Mathilde Endeveld, Jewish and also from Vienna; she took up residence in their neighbourhood.[415] Isabella Hainbach, too, worked in the factory until her first child was born.[416] In the village, reaction to the newcomers was mixed. From what the Hainbachs later told their sons, there were isolated instances of pro-Nazi attitudes.[417] It appears that the Hillerys were the only family the Hainbachs mixed with socially.[418] Michael Hillery also

---

[410] Colin Hainbach, interview, 19 February 2009.

[411] See correspondence between the Jewish Aid Committee in London, who took care of both Hainbach brothers, the Irish High Commissioner in London and the departments in NAI, DFA 202/382. Possibly, O'Driscoll had also brought Margit Manswort to Miltown Malbay. See NAI, DJ 69/80/275, Ennistymon Garda to DJ, 24 February 1939.

[412] In Colin Hainbach's memory the workforce comprised about 120 workers. Interview with authors, 19 February 2009. See also Freeman, *Ireland*, p. 382.

[413] Mark Hainbach to authors, 29 January 2009; see also MAI, G2/0441.

[414] Colin Hainbach, interview with authors, 19 February 2009.

[415] In Vienna Endeveld had worked in a textile factory for five years before going to Switzerland and London. Here she met "our manager", probably Hainbach, at a time when there was "the question of Mrs. Manswort leaving". She was asked to come to Malbay "to keep the factory from closing down". NAI, DJ 69/80/275, unsigned letter by an official of the Company to Miss Rohan, 20 May 1939. In the following months, the Company and the DI&C were both strongly in favour of keeping her in Malbay, while the DJ feared that she could not be returned to the UK and might deprive a national of a job. See correspondence in the same file. She stayed however until 1945 (see chapter 11).

[416] According to a Garda report of 31 July 1940 she worked as a cutter, designer and finisher of knitted articles. MAI, G2/0441. After the birth of her first child in 1940 (a son) she stayed at home. A daughter was born in 1943, and a second son in 1945. Mark Hainbach to authors, 20 February 2009.

[417] "My mother often told me about a local policeman, to whom they had to report once week, who shocked her as a pro-Nazi." Mark Hainbach, interview with authors, 19 November 2004.

[418] Mark Hainbach to authors, 29 January 2009.

did Isabella Hainbach the favour of affording her occasional relief from village life by taking her to Dublin on his regular visits as a TD. Her husband however liked the outdoor life in the West and he "got along well with the people" (Mark Hainbach). The problems he faced were in the factory. In 1944, he confided to a colleague, whose G2 affiliation he could not know, that he "did not consider his salary and status as commensurable with the importance of his qualifications as a trade expert, more especially as he was well aware of the profits made by the Company over the past three years".[419] His dissatisfaction with his role in the factory management was one of the motives behind his abortive attempt to enlist in the British Army at the turn of 1943 to 1944 (see chapter 10).

The story of Anselm Horwitz is remarkable for various reasons. McCowens Mouldings Ltd, his creation, was conceived and realised on Irish soil by a young man of 22 years who had no prior entrepreneurial experience and had entered the country as a normal ICCR refugee, expecting (and expected) to leave for the USA as soon as possible.[420] The only resource he could draw on was a talent for technical engineering (see chapter 2). Realising that his agricultural lessons at Cappagh could hardly qualify him for a future life in New York City, the ICCR and the Department of Industry and Commerce accepted his wish to continue his technical studies. The place to do so was the Technical School in Tralee, County Kerry, then a town of little more than 10,000 people.[421] In Tralee "everybody – especially a person like me – was a little on edge. Ration books were issued for such essentials as tea and tobacco but also for other foods such as butter. White bread was prohibited […] Only the Military, police and essential officials incl. clergy could use their cars," but "no matter how the rest of the country did without we could get almost anything. If you knew the right people the black market supplied most things."[422]

He was directed to a lodging near the centre at 5 Strand View Terrace ("just a curving street with small houses on both sides") by James Enright, a public official in the County Council House and acquaintance of Maud Slattery.[423] Thanks to Enright's contacts, a romance with a local girl[424] and also an early mastery

---

419 MAI, G2/0441, G2 report 1944; also Mark Hainbach to authors, 29 January 2009.
420 NAI, DJ/69/80/93, application for a certificate of identity, 28 August 1940.
421 Horwitz wrote to Maud Slattery expressing his dissatisfaction with his life at Cappagh. Anselm Horwitz, email to authors, 20 January 2008.
422 Anselm Horwitz, email to authors, 23 January 2008.
423 Anselm Horwitz, emails to authors, 19, 22 and 31 January 2008. James's brother William, like Slattery, was from Waterford. Anselm Horwitz email to authors, 21 February 2008.
424 They married in November 1945. NAI, DJ 68/1/645.

Image 12: Anselm Horwitz.

of English, Horwitz quickly succeeded in making headway in the town and in forming associations with various groups of local people. One social nexus was a group interested in learning German from him,[425] and others formed around

---

[425] MAI, G2/0492, G2 report, 8 January 1942. Ironically, Horwitz counted among his Irish students one senior Garda officer, who wanted to prepare himself for an expected German attack on Ireland. Anselm Horwitz email to authors, 21 February 2008.

his fellow students at the Technical School, where he sought to "sharpen (his) skills in metal working" in the machine-shop.[426] Basically, however, he was "looking for a shop to start a business" in Ireland.[427] The production idea the resourceful young immigrant had in mind was plastics, a new-style industry that had not yet begun revolutionising everyday life in Ireland. The raw material for products such as combs, shoe horns and brush handles was abundantly available in Ireland: skimmed milk, its casein portions forming a necessary ingredient of galalith that in Central Europe was used in large quantities for the production of buttons. The idea, however, did not seem feasible: how to provide capital, get a licence, develop a production line?[428] Obviously, any answer to these questions could only be found in the capital. In early 1942, Horwitz got official permission to start a factory for the manufacture of plastics (provided that "the factory would be situated in Tralee").[429] During his frequent trips to Dublin he mostly stayed at Friedrich Hirsch's Old Vienna Club in Pembroke Street, where he met Barney Heron, a well-connected figure among the exiles (see above). Heron put him into contact with people in the circle of Lord Glenavy, predecessor of John Leydon as Secretary of the Department of Industry and Commerce and at that time Governor of the Bank of Ireland ("a key figure in Irish financial circles").[430] The story of the cooperation between the young exile and Ireland's chief banker, a strong upholder of Anglo-Irish traditions in the new state, is astonishing in its own right. McCowens Mouldings Ltd was founded in late 1942.

---

426 Anselm Horwitz emails to authors, 21 and 23 February 2008.
427 MAI, G2/0492, undated hand-written note, obviously addressed to his girlfriend. Until 1942, he was still thinking of the US option. NAI, DJ/69/80/93, application of 28 August 1940; also NAI, DJ 68/1/645. This casts some doubt on the tone of a letter to his parents in November 1939, which expressed a hope that he could stay in Ireland "forever" ("I like the country very much"). MAI, G2/0492. Translated by authors.
428 The following narrative is largely based on reminiscences contained in two long emails from Anselm Horwitz to the authors on 17 December 2008. All the quotations are from this text if not otherwise stated.
429 NAI, DJ 68/1/645.
430 Daly, *Industrial Development*, p. 65. As to the partnership between Glenavy and Horwitz, see a Garda report in NAI, DJ 68/1/645. Lord Glenavy (Gordon Campbell) had worked under Churchill in the Ministry of Munitions in World War I. After the war he returned to Ireland. In the Civil War his house was burned by the IRA; he narrowly escaped an execution. In the new state he was a Parliamentary Secretary in the Department of Industry and Commerce until 1932 when he resigned at Fianna Fáil's advent to power. In the 1930s he became a Governor of the Bank of Ireland and sat on the boards of a number of companies. See Campbell, *My Life*, pp. 16–18.

The Board of Directors consisted of Lord Glenavy (chairman), Thomas Martin (Dublin), Frank Daly (Cork) – who were also the three major shareholders – and Jim Bryce, managing director of the existing McCowens enterprise, which also provided premises in an unused part of a building on Edward Street. The Dublin office of the company was at 33/34 Anglesea Street, with Robert E. Whelan, one of Glenavy's staff, as secretary. Horwitz was the Technical Manager.[431] To begin with, the company bought casein sheets from the sole producers on the Irish market, an enterprise in Kanturk, Co. Cork, and converted them into combs in Tralee. It was a difficult undertaking as "the simplest items were not available, except an old used industrial boiler. Everything else had to be built from bits and scraps that I had to pick up in all sorts of places. The only help I could get was from the Technical School graduates." Production started in mid-1943 although Horwitz got his formal work permit only in March 1944.[432] The concept was successful. A distributor was found, Ticher & Co., whose owner, Kurt Ticher (see chapter 8), succeeded in placing "more and more orders", as combs were in great demand in wartime Ireland. But Horwitz's ambition reached beyond such modest beginnings. In the next phase, plastic articles were to be manufactured from the base material itself. Machinery was bought in Northern Ireland and installed in a newly erected building near a large creamery on Milltown Road. A licence was granted by the Department of Industry and Commerce. It is not known how long (if at all) plastics were produced under the new conditions, but it appears that the grant of a licence for this extended production was successfully contested by the owner of the Kanturk enterprise, a former IRA man, who had allegedly been given a monopoly for the production of casein from skimmed milk. "A meeting between Lord Glenavy, Thomas Martin and Robert E. Whelan with a couple of Government Ministers plus a retinue of Fianna Fáil Civil Servants" ended in "a great shouting match that brought up a whole lot of other, totally unrelated problems between the two camps". The strength of the opposition guaranteed "the end of my project as well as any future plans for MML". The outcome clearly revealed to what degree the idea of foreign engagements was dependent on the partisan interests and ideologies of Fianna Fáil. The exile from Vienna had unknowingly become part of an old but still-active imbroglio dating back to the origins of the Irish Free State. The battle lines lay between political favours extended to an "old comrade" and a man like Lord Glenavy, who customarily referred to de Valera and his Fianna Fáil followers

---

431 NAI, DJ 68/1/645. Anselm Horwitz, email to authors, 17 December 2008.
432 NAI, DJ 69/80/93, Tralee Garda to DJ, 9 January 1944.

as "ex-gunmen" unable "to understand even the rudimentary basis of economics".[433] It was a losing fight, which on a local scale replicated some typical elements of Lemass's economic rule in Emergency times. Though defeated in this battle, however, Anselm Horwitz had not yet abandoned all his entrepreneurial optimism (see chapter 11).

---

[433] Campbell, *My Life*, p. 32.

Chapter 8
Continental Dubliners

Many threads linked provincial exiles to Dublin. The capital was usually the gateway to Ireland and continued to exert a strong psychological and cultural pull on people who had grown up in urban environments. The centralisation of public offices and services in Dublin was of obvious practical relevance for people of alien status, and traffic conditions in wartime Ireland made travel to and from Dublin cumbersome and infrequent. By 1941, most agriculturalists among the newcomers had moved to the capital, as the revision of US immigration policy and the conditions on transatlantic seaways drastically impeded onward migration plans, thereby greatly reducing the attractiveness of continued agricultural training in the provinces. With the USA's entry into the war, prospects of moving there vanished entirely. Under these conditions, the exiles sought other means of supporting themselves in a country where they might have to stay for an indefinite period, if they could find no alternative way to leave. Of the 109 exiles who had spent some time in the provinces, about one third migrated to the capital for good during the war, joining those who had lived there from the beginning. Their total number was negligible, and their social circles too secluded and isolated to excite more than a fleeting and haphazard interest in wider society. Their wartime experiences, however, prefigured their further biographies in various ways and also contributed to the nuances of life in the capital.

First impressions of Dublin were not always favourable. It appeared "small and confined" – "slums and poverty such as I had never seen, not even in the poorest districts of Vienna, surrounded O'Connell Street, dirt and drunkenness almost everywhere one looked."[1] The shock Georg Klaar felt on entering the city is clear from the memoirs he wrote 40 years later. Before and during the Second World War, Dublin was indeed "much more like something from an earlier century than like the present day".[2] Nineteenth-century Dublin had been notorious for large-scale tenement housing and slums, and in 1939 the social geography of the city was still marred by large areas of derelict housing and conspicuous poverty.[3] Particularly appalling 'slumlands' were in parts of the Liberties, the northern

---

[1] George Clare (=Georg Klaar), *Last Waltz in Vienna: the Destruction of a Family 1842–1942*. London: MacMillan 1982 p. 234.
[2] Nuala O'Faolain, *Are you Somebody? The Accidental Memoir of a Dublin Woman*. New York: Henry Holt and Company 1996, p. 3.
[3] For a survey see Bryce Evans, *Ireland during the Second World War*. Manchester: Manchester University Press 2014, pp. 69–75.

side of the docklands, and various streets east and west of O'Connell Street.[4] Malnutrition, TB and alcoholism were rife, and infant mortality was high. The wasteland was too close to Dublin's smarter areas to be ignored, Gardiner Street and Dominick Street being only a few yards away from the lights of O'Connell Street. Passengers riding a tram or bus from Rathgar could not help noticing the slums abutting Aungier Street, nor could shoppers on Grafton Street or Henry Street avoid tenement dwellers, beggars or barefooted children. The conspicuous 'slumlands' offended the aesthetic and moral sense of affluent middle-class Dubliners, though some who had escaped poverty might have looked back to the street life with nostalgia.[5] The exiles had to get used to the constraints of the Emergency economy: limited mobility, energy shortages, a rationing regime exacerbated by inflated prices and comprising ever more everyday goods until its full introduction in 1942, and the black market.[6] Most able-bodied Dubliners used bicycles (which brought their thefts to the top of crime statistics), and the rest a curious variety of other vehicles predating the motor-age.[7] Petrol and coal rationing meant that only a skeleton bus and tram service was available for journeys between the suburbs and the centre. With coal hardly available, people resorted to turf for heating – a modestly efficient fuel, but moist, unwieldy, and also rationed from 1943 onwards. Gas too was rationed, and cooking severely restricted as a result.[8]

Continental urbanites may have found it harder than native Dubliners to get used to these conditions, given their former backgrounds and the economic difficulties they faced in Dublin during the war. Very few exiles, whether individuals or families, could live on the money they had been able to bring to Ireland.[9]

---

[4] Standing at the corner of Bishop Street and Aungier Street, one former Austrian refugee remembered in 2002: "All these were slums at the time when we came." See also Clair Wills, *That Neutral Island. A Cultural History of Ireland during the Second World War*. London: Faber and Faber 2007, pp. 258–262.
[5] O'Faolain remembers the fascination of what was then still Joyce's Dublin ("brown and dusty and dense with street life"). O'Faolain, *Are you Somebody?*, p. 19.
[6] Wills, *Neutral Island*, pp. 237–242, 246–253; Evans, *Ireland during the Second World War*, pp. 44–48, 69–75.
[7] John Ryan, *Remembering How We Stood. Bohemian Dublin at the Mid-Century*. Dublin: Gill and MacMillan 1975, p. 9; Benjamin Grob-Fitzgibbon, *The Irish Experience during the Second World War. An Oral History*. Dublin: Irish Academy Press 2004, pp. 53–55. Even residents in far-off Clontarf, such as Erwin Schrödinger, used the "humble bike" to reach the centre. TCD Archives, 10657/56/313–14, E.T.S. Walton to Ernest Pollard, 23 January 1966. See also Evans, *Ireland during the Second World War*, p. 56.
[8] Ryan, *Remembering How We Stood*, pp. 10–11; Wills, *Neutral Island*, pp. 247–248.
[9] One exception could have been Curt Heilfron. After the war he claimed that he "had never any support from anyone". NAI, DJ 69/80/538, Heilfron to Aliens Registration Office, 19 March 1948.

Whether they were completely financially dependent or relatively autonomous depended on factors including age, education, family relationships, work permits, job opportunities, Irish connections and plain chance.

"Only entrepreneurial partnership or agony"? Business ventures in exile

In late 1937, the Lisowski family had come to Ireland with £465, a small Volkswagen and some materials that Friedrich wished to use for a new business as an independent plumber. What he found, however, was a situation in which his previously highly regarded abilities were almost completely devalued.[10] Buying a site outside Cabinteely, Co. Dublin, substantially ate into their savings. Here Friedrich and 15-year-old Peter, who in July 1938 had to give up his schooling at Newtown School, erected a simple house and a shack for a workshop. It was here that they lived for nearly 20 years in relative isolation – only an Irish couple and refugee linguist Professor Ernst Lewy seem to have belonged to their social circle (for Lewy see chapter 9).[11] Likewise depressing was their economic situation. Instead of fully practising his old artisanship Friedrich "had to be satisfied with repair work".[12] He and Peter earned a little money in other ways, including pressing apple juice and making cider at harvest time, something Friedrich had already practised at Eden and now did again for owners of gardens in the Bray region.[13] He also invented and patented a turf stove, which was useful in

---

It seems that he had succeeded in retrieving some money from his German accounts which allowed him to buy two houses during the war and another in 1945. His statement ignores the support he and his wife received from their daughter and son-in-law. Ironically, in 1943 a G2 observer thought that the Heilfrons were badly off. MAI, G2/0453, G2 report, 12 February 1943.

10 In Ireland, each construction firm had its own specialist plumbers, while ready-made gutters and pipes were imported from England and then fitted by carpenters. Niedersächsisches Landesarchiv, Hannover (NLA), Nds. 110 W, Acc. 8/90, no. 269/11, text of application by Lisowski's lawyer, 15 February 1957; Friedrich Lisowski, undated CV: "A factory for making tins, which I also planned, failed because of insufficient capital." Translated by authors.

11 Eden Archive, Lisowski file, letter Käte Müller-Lisowski, 25 July 1953. In this letter however Käte takes pains to express that the Lewys were their "former" friends. Translated by authors.

12 NLA, Nds. 110 W, Acc. 8/90, no. 269/11, Friedrich Lisowski, undated CV. Translated by authors.

13 Verity Murdoch, the then twelve-year-old daughter of a neighbouring family, remembered the Lisowskis as deliverers of apple juice. Interview with authors, 26 November 2004; also her letter to authors, 20 March 2007. Peggy Moore-Lewy recalled that the Lisowskis tried to market the apple juice to Findlater, a well-known grocery chain in Dublin, but it did not sell. Interview with authors, 28 July 2005.

Emergency times when coal was scarce.[14] Nevertheless the family income fell dramatically, and only rose beyond £200 in 1944 and 1945.[15] Käte Müller-Lisowski tended the garden, their main source of food; an academic by profession, she also prepared her son for his school leaving certificate and gave some private lessons.[16] Despite financial pressures, the family more or less managed to support themselves independently in Ireland.

A few others had to survive more radical breaks with their past lives as businessmen. Unable in Ireland to find any position comparable to their former status, they had to try to establish themselves as producers of goods in the narrow niches left open to non-nationals by Irish regulations. This amounted to self-employment, in which they bore the financial risk. Ferdinand and Emilie Karrach made a success of their new existence. Kathleen Huggard called them "really the most satisfactory of all the refugees, have cost hardly anything and always been so grateful and helpful" (adding that they were "always trying to help other refugees").[17] In 1940, they set up a cottage industry, producing and selling craft articles (felted flowers, for example – "quite a nice thing", Emilie wrote her mother in Vienna),[18] and employing some Irish workers.[19] In April 1941, they were officially employed as "Viennese embroidery and handicraft" specialists by John Begley & Co., 10 Exchequer Street, and in May 1942 by J. Stanley & Son Ltd, 28 Parnell Square.[20] In 1943, they moved to London to join the war effort.[21] After their departure, another Viennese, Franziska Wiedmann, took over Ferdinand's position at Stanley & Son.[22] Less lucky than the Karrachs were Max Rund and David Nachmann. The Department of Justice allowed them a work permit only in 1943. Max Rund made and sold shades for electric lamps, while David Nachmann sewed

---

14 Eden Archive, Lisowski file, letter Käte Müller-Lisowski, 25 July 1953. In the interview of 26 November 2004 Verity Murdoch also confirmed the appeal of the new invention in the region.
15 In 1939–1940, Friedrich earned £42 p.a., in 1944–1945 £216. The figures are his own. See NLA, Nds. 110 W, Acc. 8/90, no. 269/11, Friedrich Lisowski, undated CV.
16 NLA, Nds. 110 W, Acc. 8/90, no. 269/12, Käte Müller-Lisowski CV, 4 June 1957.
17 TCD Archives, Butler Papers, 10304/597/778, Huggard to Butler, 13 August [1941].
18 Imperial War Museum London, G3/27/1, Emilie Karrach to parents, 19 September 1940.
19 Ibid. and Herbert Karrach to authors, 17 June 2016.
20 In departmental exchanges the Karrachs were described as employees, and in Ferdinand's visa application of 12 May 1945 he calls himself a "manager". NAI, DJ 69/80/16. Their son refers to his parents as "partners", indicating the importance of their position. Herbert Karrach email to authors, 4 October 2006 and in questionnaire, 30 November 2005.
21 NAI, DJ 69/80/16. For the motives behind their move to England, see chapter 10.
22 See DJ 69/80/198.

leather wallets and produced other fancy articles at his home, but the two former merchants continued to be dependent on charity funds.[23]

Opportunities in the capital were not necessarily better even for those exiles who were expected to assist industrial progress – like Leopold Schenk, who planned to produce and sell bicycle dynamos on Irish and other markets. Although he had been able to bring some capital, the enterprise did not take off.[24] He attributed this to wartime conditions that kept him from importing spare parts and expertise from his native Moravia, and to the fact that he had found no business partners. He was sure that in Ireland the business interests of "aliens" could only thrive through "entrepreneurial partnership[s]" with native businesses; otherwise "agony" loomed – as his countryman Rudolf Schwarz might have confirmed (see chapter 7).[25] Some partnerships of this kind had been established before 1939.[26] In most of them, Jewish partners, notably members of the Briscoe family, played a crucial role. Two expatriates had set a precedent: Marcus and Arnold Witztum, who established Viennese Knitted Goods & Co. together with Robert Briscoe in 1932.[27] A little later, in the mid-1930s, Abraham Bayer's handbag factory took in Irish partners and continued to expand, employing 54 workers at its new production site at the back of 181 Pearse Street.[28] Leather Articles Ltd had a capital basis divided between two Irish-Jewish shareholders, but required credit

---

23 In both cases Robert Briscoe had nudged the DJ towards a lenient attitude. NAI, DJ 69/80/302, Briscoe to DI&C, 11 February 1943; DI&C to Briscoe, 8 March 1943; NAI, DJ 68/1/712 and 713. For Nachmann, see NAI, DJ 69/80/128, DJ note, 12 October 1943; Nachmann to DJ, 22 August 1949.
24 For his financial capacities, see MAI, G2/0771, letter Rudolf Schwarz, 17 December 1939.
25 MAI, G2/1163 and 1164, letter Schenk, 2 December 1939.
26 Harry Cerniak (originally Harris Eikenbaum) should perhaps be mentioned here. Originally from Poland, then resident in Germany, he had fled to Antwerp in 1936 and came to Ireland in July 1939. In a later document he is described as having "formed" the textile enterprise Duncairn Clothing Factory Ltd, which in 1945 employed 40 Irish workers. NAI, DJ 68/1/705.
27 See DJ 2013/50/239 (Arnold Witztum) and 259 (Marcus Witztum). Robert Briscoe was a sleeping partner, and left the enterprise at an unknown date. Anna Adler, interview with authors, 13 September 2005. Naftali Witztum, the third brother, entered Ireland from Antwerp in 1936 (see chapter 2) and was employed as a designer and mechanic in 1939. NAI, DJ 68/1/605.
28 The other shareholders were Jacob Slotover, Morris Isaacson and Montague Buchalter, who also acted as directors. See NAI, TID 1207/300, minutes of meeting 21 November 1935. The success of the enterprise is demonstrated by its capital growth between 1940 and 1949. By the end of the 1940s, the Bayers and Elias Stiel had a controlling interest in the enterprise; although they were naturalised, this contravened the terms of the Control of Manufactures Acts. NAI, TID 1207/300, minutes of discussion between Briscoe and DI&C officers, 21 March 1946; hand-written list of directors and shareholders, 5 January 1949. For Bayer and his partners, see Nick Harris, *Dublin's Little Jerusalem*. Dublin: A & A Farmar 2002, p. 178 (here Abraham Bayer is called "Adolf Baer", possibly an assumed name). According to Harris, production at Pearse Street only started in 1942.

from Leib Margulies, which in effect made him a partner in the enterprise. He was also appointed managing director.[29] In 1941, the factory employed seven persons producing a variety of leather products at 8 Lower Ormond Quay.

Siegmund Liffmann had twice been denied a position as a manager of a Dublin firm, and was therefore dependent on help from "friends and relatives" or on casual work as a domestic or a "packer"[30] until 1942, when he was allowed to co-found the Belgrade Trading Company with premises at 31 Lower Ormond Quay. Liffmann's partner was George (Hymen) Rosenberg; each held shares of £2,500. In 1945, the enterprise, which specialised in the import of haberdashery, fancy goods and hardware, employed nine Irish nationals; Liffmann, also the managing director, drew a weekly salary of £10.[31] Leopold and Helena von Glasersfeld were co-founders of Eirecot Cotton Ltd, a textile enterprise manufacturing absorbent cotton wool products, which they ran jointly with their majority shareholders, four members of the Briscoe family, at Terminus Mills, Vergemount, Clonskeagh.[32] Their son became involved in an agricultural venture, Grove Dale Farm Co., which aimed to "acquire and develop farm lands, buildings and other property" in the Kilternan area, in the foothills of the Wicklow Mountains south of Dublin. The project, which fitted neatly into the government's tillage scheme, was realised through a partnership with William, Agnes and Barney Heron.[33] The Glaserfelds were mainly occupied with practical work on a farm which "had some 80 acres, half of which was arable land, the rest arid hillside. It was mixed farming, growing oats, barley, subsidized crops of wheat, potatoes, and cattle feed."[34]

---

29 Margulies earned £3 a week and 49% of net profits. MAI, G2/0619, Garda report, 22 January 1941. See also Harris, *Dublin's Little Jerusalem*, p. 179.

30 MAI, G2/0582, G2 officer hand-written note, 21 July 1942; NLA, Nds. 110 W, Acc. 890, no. 267/21, Siegmund Liffmann affidavit, 15 January 1957.

31 See NAI, CRO/1/D/1110. NAI, DJ 68/1/625, Garda report, 12 September 1945; DJ memorandum, 13 December 1945. Liffmann's contribution was probably funded from money he got from the sale of his furniture which had been misdirected to the USA and was auctioned off there (or possibly from grants from his brother-in-law Julius Silber). NAI, DJ 69/80/248, Briscoe to DJ, 17 September 1942.

32 Herbert, Henrietta, Wolf and Robert Briscoe. MAI, G2/0304, hand-written G2 report, 13 January 1941; also NAI, DJ 69/80/547, DJ to DI&C, June 1940. Leopold von Glasersfeld was also described as a director of the company.

33 NAI, CRO/1/D/10100; also advertisement in *Irish Independent*, 15 January 1941. For the beginnings of the project in 1939, see the description in Ernst von Glasersfeld, *Partial Memories: Sketches from an Improbable Life*. Exeter: Imprint Academic 2009, pp. 74–77, where he describes how his translation of poems by Rainer Maria Rilke laid the foundation of his friendship with William Hernon who then suggested a joint farming venture.

34 "For the first two years William and I did all the work; then we made enough money selling milk so that we could hire a boy, a 'chisler', to help." Von Glasersfeld email to authors, 2 August 2006; also von Glasersfeld, *Partial Memories*, pp. 87–90.

Photo: H.v.G.
Grovedale, County Dublin, 1942

Image 1: Ernst von Glasersfeld ploughing his farm.

The partnership concept also appeared viable for medical students who wished to establish themselves as practising doctors in Ireland (see chapter 6), as demonstrated by at least one case. In 1944, Ludwig Karrenberg was officially entered in the General Medical Register and seems to have commenced a partnership with an Irish doctor in the same year.[35]

Settled employees

A number of exiles in the Dublin area settled in occupations that had been guaranteed to them prior to their arrival in Ireland. This, however, did not necessarily entail an adequate income. On 4 July 1960, William Lewis (Wolf) Woolfson, President of the Lennox Street Hebrew Congregation, noted that the former rabbi

---

[35] NAI, DJ 69/80/406, Slattery to DJ, 18 October 1943; Secretary DJ to Slattery, 1 November 1944. Edeltraut Reinert, a fully qualified dentist in Ireland, was granted a work permit in 1941, and may perhaps have entered such a partnership. She had done most of her training in Dublin, having qualified from University College Dublin as a dentist in January 1938; she then went to Great Britain before returning to do a Master's degree in dental surgery in 1940. For her academic career see NAI, DJ 68/1/640; MAI, G2/2524, G2 report 23 October 1941.

of the congregation, Reverend Bernhard Holländer, had received an annual salary of £150 in the years 1938 to 1940, a sum which Woolfson thought "hardly sufficed to provide the minimum of existence" for the Reverend and his wife.[36] In the following years, Holländer's income was progressively raised (£200 in 1941–1942, and £250 in 1943–1945). Apart from his salary, he earned extra money from supplementary functions in the Dublin Jewish community.[37] Other officials employed by Dublin congregations also looked for additional sources of income.[38] Philip Moddel initially earned £180, a figure that was only moderately raised in the following years.[39] On 25 May 1942, he married Paula Margulies, and when she was expecting a baby in 1943, he applied for a position as a designer of leather fancy goods, but the Department of Justice, motivated by their old suspicions against foreign-born Jewish officials, refused a work permit.[40] Instead, Philip gave private music and German lessons, and his wife repaired clothing in a tailor's shop.[41] Exiles working as teachers at secondary schools also needed additional money to support their families. John Hennig was active in a number of fields outside his job at Belvedere College, which he took in late 1939: he gave German lessons, published articles in magazines and newspapers, taught part-time at Maynooth, and gave lectures and radio talks.[42] Lothar Fuchs, a former engineer, was employed as a maths teacher by St. Gerard's College, Bray, but the family income was supplemented through other sources.[43]

---

36 EA Berlin, no. 69.533, Woolfson hand-written affidavit, 4 July 1960.
37 Holländer taught at the new Hebrew School and charged extra fees for wedding services. See NAI, DJ 68/1/634, Garda report, 5 October 1945.
38 David Freilich's salary in 1940 was £104 and increased to £200 in 1945. He regularly borrowed money from his brother, Nandor, to support his family of four. Bayerisches Hauptstaatsarchiv Munich (BHSA), LEA files, F, no. 1344, Freilich to Bavarian Restitution Office, 6 July 1959.
39 EA Cologne, no. 420.613, Moddel to EA Berlin, 30 March 1957. In 1952, his annual income as choir leader was stated to be £234. Bundesstelle zur Entschädigung ehemaliger Bediensteter jüdischer Gemeinden (BEBJG), Cologne, no. II6-1091, Vol. I., Synagogue Chambers Adelaide Road affidavit, 16 June 1953.
40 NAI, DJ 69/80/496, Moddel to DI&C, 15 February 1943; DJ official to Ferguson, DI&C, 9 February 1943. For his marriage see Entschädigungsamt (EA) Cologne, no. 420.613, entry copied in General Registry Office, Dublin, 17 June 1953.
41 These jobs must have accounted for a large part of their earnings, as in 1948 their family income had risen to £404. EA Berlin, no. 420 613, Moddel to EA Berlin, 30 March 1957.
42 Gisela Holfter and Hermann Rasche (eds), *John Hennig's Exile in Ireland*. Galway: Arlen 2004, p. 37.
43 He was appointed as a school bursar in September 1940. See Brian Murphy, *St. Gerard's School 1918-1998*. Bray: Kestrel Books 1999, p. 126. The College allowed the family to lodge on school premises. The Fuchses must also have drawn income from handiwork for Ferdinand and Emilie Karrach's family business (see above). Imperial War Museum, G3/27/1, Emilie Karrach to parents,

Some of the exiles employed in industrial sectors seem to have earned slightly higher incomes. Peter W. Brandenburg, who patented a new filing system ('Easisee') which he, his wife and his daughter manufactured in their rented house in Furry Park Road, had signed a contract with Eason and Son Ltd, granting him £250 per annum. It was enough to "live halfway comfortably" in wartime Dublin.[44] Kurt Billig, a cement specialist, was probably in a comparable bracket,[45] while Eric Serff, an accountant at Kelly and Sheil Ltd, whose managers paid him £192 p.a. on average in the years 1937 to 1942, then found a job with the British radio assembly company Pye, Ireland Ltd, from whom he received about £260 p.a. to support his family of five.[46] Paul Boas seems to have owed his appointment in late 1939 as an Irish sales representative of the British firm Michelsons Ltd to the mediation of his son Hans (see chapter 4). Until 1943, he earned an average of £150 p.a.[47]

Job-seekers

On 9 April 1942, Kathleen Huggard observed: "They've all got some kind of work except for Dr Stiegwardt and the Hirsch boys."[48] A few months later she could have omitted the exceptions: the Stiegwardt family had taken what turned out

---

13 August 1941 (handwritten, 5 September 1941). The elder daughter Melanie may have also contributed to their income through her employment by J. L. Morton, 6 Fitzwilliam Square, until 1944 when she married. NAI, DJ 69/80/93. See also MAI, G2/0422.

44 See Denis Henderson, On Ruth Henderson and her parents, Peter and Else Brandenburg. In: Gisela Holfter (ed.), *Irish Context of Kristallnacht. Refugees and Helpers*. Irish-German Studies. Vol. 8. Trier: Wissenschaftlicher Verlag 2014, p. 68. EA Berlin, no. 252.909. K. Eason and Sons Ltd affidavit, 20 April 1954.

45 He represented his British-Irish construction firm as a "senior assistant" at his office in Molesworth Street. The multilingual Billig had worked for four years in Austria and five years in the Soviet Union. He had fled from Vienna in March 1938 and was granted entry and a work permit as a specialist in cement technology and a holder of various patents. His salary was the sole income for himself, his wife and his mother. MAI, G2/0345, telegram to Waller (London), 28 May 1941, telegram from Waller, 29 April 1941; MAI, G2/x/1091, G2 report, 18 June 1941.

46 Wiedergutmachungsamt (WGA) Cologne, no. A 295.472, Serff, undated CV; MAI, G2/0777, undated G2 report. See also MAI, G2/x/1091, G2 report, 11 July 1940, from which it appears that he earned about £5 a week. In Ireland, Erich Serff changed his name to Eric.

47 When Paul Boas died in December 1944, his widow's upkeep must have been largely dependent on Hans's allowances. EA Düsseldorf, no. 615.124, Michelsons Ltd affidavits, 22 August and 21 October 1957; NAI, DJ 68/1/715.

48 TCD Archives, Butler Papers, 10304/597/781. About a year later, however, Ignaz Schulz commented that "it was very difficult to get a special working permit". MAI, G2/0763, Schulz to secretary of Free Austria Movement (FAM), 5 March 1943.

to be the last transatlantic passage of German-speaking exiles from Ireland, and the two Hirsch brothers had begun to study at Trinity College Dublin (see below). Even at the time, her statement was not strictly accurate, since not all the other exiles had found jobs. Moreover, not all those who had succeeded in doing so were in secure employment: "some kind of work" covered a colourful variety of occupations from full-time posts to casual labour, with salaries ranging from satisfactory to poor, and while a few newcomers had achieved financial independence, others were making only a precarious livelihood, and several still relied to a greater or lesser extent on charitable funds.

Exiles who graduated from Irish universities in the war years seem to have passed quite easily into employment (except most medical students, as we shall see). Einhart Kawerau was enabled to continue his research work after his student days at TCD (see chapter 9). Sigurd Kawerau and Stefan Feric were employed by important enterprises after graduation from UCD,[49] and Robert Dubsky, who graduated from UCD in 1942, found a job as a civil engineer and later became assistant director of a department of the Turf Development Board, earning £260 p.a.[50] Generally, Irish employment policy was becoming more liberal, although this did not mean that exiles had unrestricted access to the labour market. The Department of Industry and Commerce still tried to slot "aliens" into positions that were uncontested by Irish nationals.

Erich Priebatsch had lived off his savings, together with a grant of 30 shillings a week from the Central Jewish Refugee Aid Committee and what he could earn from giving unofficial German lessons.[51] Not until 1942 did the Department of Industry and Commerce allow him to act as a textile agent for various firms on a commission basis; from November of that year he could "do without any support".[52] The woodwork industry offered opportunities for Herbert Unger, Bern-

---

49 Sigurd Kawerau took a degree in Commerce at UCD in 1938 and was then given a job by Bevan Lamb, the Quaker owner of a well-known jam factory. In 1945, he earned £3/10 per week. NAI, DJ 68/1/721. After completing his studies Feric was employed by a British confectionery concern, "testing foodstuff for canning". TCD Archives, Butler Papers, 10304/597/780, Huggard to Butler, 10 May 1942.
50 NAI, DJ 69/80/276, DI&C to DJ, 10 December 1942; NAI, DJ 68/1/593, Dubsky to DJ, 5 July 1945; Werner Röder and Herbert A. Strauss (eds), *Biographisches Handbuch der deutschsprachigen Emigration nach 1933*. Vol. I. Munich/New York/London/Paris: K.G. Saur 1980, p. 139.
51 MAI, G2/1680, G2 reports June and 15 July 1941.
52 He began an eleven-year employment as an agent for P. Faulkner & Sons (Ireland's "oldest packing enterprise"). EA Berlin, no. 431.019, Priebatsch CV, 22 February 1954. Translated by authors. See also NAI, DJ 69/80/191, Garda to DJ, 5 November 1942. His employment made him a "rich" man, at least in the eyes of Herbert Unger. MAI, G2/0849, Unger to Staudt, 28 March 1943.

hard Frankl and the Aberbach brothers (for the latter see footnote 64). After Unger had left Mount St Benedict he began attending design courses at the College of Technology's School of Architecture in Bolton Street, living on a weekly ICCR grant of 12s 6d.[53] In January 1942, he was granted a work permit and invited to join an enterprise founded by Barney Heron, a partner in Ernst von Glaserfeld's Grove Dale Farm Co. (see above). Heron had successfully marketed wooden clogs in times when leather was scarce. He now began producing prefabricated timber houses in his factory at Kingram Lane and later in Leixlip.[54] As Heron was mostly in Galway, it fell largely to Unger to run the factory.[55] At the beginning, his salary was a modest £1 per week but it seems to have climbed to £5 and 10% of profits in later war years.[56] It is questionable whether Bernhard Frankl earned as much. Until 1943 his family was dependent on charitable funds, and they "still lived in difficult circumstances", their son recalls, even after Bernhard found employment as an "instructor and helper in the production of woodcraft articles" and toy-making for Messrs. Woodcraft Products Co., 31 Avenue Road.[57]

Some years earlier, the exile sector had begun to generate its own jobs.

> I have [...] bought a house in Dublin but far from being a philanthropic move I have every hope that it will prove an excellent investment. It will be a residential club and the residents will pay their own way and are not limited to any nationality. The only advantage accruing to "refugees" will be the indirect one of enabling them to help each other and providing them with surroundings reminiscent [...] of old Vienna.[58]

This is how Vida Lentaigne, in early 1940, publicly explained the concept behind the establishment of the Old Vienna Club, perhaps fearing that her intentions would be distrusted. Physically, the building at 17 Pembroke Street contained club rooms, a restaurant, a kitchen, and rooms for boarding on the upper storey,

---

53 TCD Archives, Butler Papers, 10304/597/774, Huggard to Butler, 5 May 1941.
54 On Barney Heron's project, see also Christopher Fitz-Simon, *Eleven Houses – A Memoir of Childhood*. Dublin: Ireland Penguin 2007, p. 97. For Unger's permit see NAI, DJ 68/1/630.
55 Klaus Unger interviews with authors, 20 November 2004 and 15 November 2006; two undated CVs by Herbert Unger. Courtesy Klaus Unger.
56 NAI, DJ 68/1/630.
57 NAI, DJ 69/80/472, DI&C to DJ, 10 September 1943; Society of Friends House Dublin (SFHD), Heinz Frankl to Society of Friends Dublin, April 1998; Heinz Frankl to authors, 8 October 2007. Before 1943, Bernhard had begun an unpaid apprenticeship as a carpenter. NAI, DJ 69/80/472, Garda Dublin to DJ, 17 February 1941. Their financial predicament in these years was highlighted by Stella Webb, representing Quakers in the ICCR, asking the Quakers' Monthly Meeting to purchase two pairs of rubber boots from their poor relief fund in aid of the Frankls. SFHD, QA, MM 11 D 19.
58 *Drogheda Independent*, 20 April 1940.

with further rooms at nearby 6 Hatch Street. The Club's finances depended on the fees of its 60 non-resident and six resident members, the proceeds of the restaurant and the boarding rooms (£1 per week), and a small contribution from the Irish Co-ordinating Committee for Refugees. Lentaigne appointed Friedrich Hirsch as manager ("first caretaker"), and he ran the Club until it closed in 1946.[59] Most physical work rested on the shoulders of Marie Hirsch, but the Club also employed other exiles, for example Gustav Beisser and Ernst Einäugler, former agricultural trainees in Ardmore, who worked there as temporary waiters.[60]

The Unicorn restaurant opened in December 1940 at 11 Merrion Row.[61] Its Quaker owner, William Griffith, installed Erwin and Lisl Strunz as managers and Friedrich Lederer as an official "house steward", probably on the recommendation of the Irish Co-ordinating Committee for Refugees and through the mediation of the Strunzes' hosts, Diarmuid and Sheela Coffey. Each had a weekly salary of £5.[62] Jammet's restaurant at the corner of Grafton Street and Nassau Street, its owners themselves exiles of sorts, also recruited waiters from the pool of German-speaking exiles in Dublin. Einäugler worked here for some time in 1941 under conditions

---

59 MAI, G2/x/0450, published brochure on the OVC; also MAI, G2/0763, Ignaz Schulz to FAM, 5 March 1943.
60 Officially, Beisser was "assistant secretary" to Friedrich Hirsch. See MAI, G2/0480, Beisser to Hirsch family, 5 October 1941. MAI, G2/0397, Archer to Director of Censorship, 8 October 1940 (on Einäugler).
61 There were rumours that a possible Nazi influence in the Old Vienna Club had played a role in establishing the new "refugee club". MAI, G2/0397, anonymous H. N. to an unknown addressee, 9 September 1940. Such suspicions were afloat in the critical situation of mid-1940 (see below), but even G2 were sure that the members of the OVC "for the greater part seem to be genuinely anti-Nazi", although it was feared that "a Nazi may somehow gain admission". MAI, G2/x/0450, undated G2 report 1940.
62 SFHD, Friends' work with Jewish refugees brought to Ireland before second world war, anonymous, undated. For the link between Griffith and the Coffeys predating the establishment of the Unicorn, see Erwin Strunz, Memoir, June 1989, unpublished, pp. 25–26. On Lederer, see NAI, DJ 68/1/620, Garda report, 24 September 1945. As we have seen, Lederer, a former postal worker, had reached Ireland through an international network of socialist parties and trade unions (see chapter 2). In the course of 1939 the Abrahamson committee took over responsibility for his welfare. See correspondence in NAI, DJ 69/80/309. Through a note in the *Irish Press* of 9 March 1942, the public learned that three Austrian refugees (Lederer and the Strunzes) had been dismissed from the Unicorn because of excessive cost increases "at Mr. Griffith's expense". All three, however, retained their positions, as the whole staff threatened to resign in sympathy, and they received some compensation when the accusations turned out to be false. After this, Griffith seems to have engaged himself more directly in management affairs. TCD Archives, Butler Papers, 10304/597/780, Huggard to Butler, 10 May 1942; 784, Huggard to Butler, 2 October [no year, probably 1941/1942].

which Kathleen Huggard thought "very mean".⁶³ It is uncertain whether they were better for Friedrich and Robert Aberbach, who were also on the staff, but neither can have made a living solely from their work at the restaurant, since they continued to receive £1 a week each from the Irish Co-ordinating Committee for Refugees for at least some time after their departure from St Benedict, while Robert took other casual jobs.⁶⁴ Louis Jammet also engaged Walter Simon (see chapter 2) as an apprentice between October 1938 and July 1939, following initiatives from the young man's sponsor, Senator Patrick Hogan, and members of the Jewish community.⁶⁵

Dependants

Some exiles continued to rely on grants from charitable committees even after they had obtained temporary jobs. On that sliding scale of dependency were casual workers such as Gerhard Hirschberg, Hans Morgenstern, Werner Schwarz and Felix Samuel Kahn.⁶⁶

---

63 TCD Archives, Butler Papers, 10304/597/776, Huggard to Butler, 13 August 1941.
64 He was said to be working as a private language teacher; he was also a good sportsman, and it was believed that "for some time" he ran a private "gym school" in Dublin. MAI, G2/0308, undated G2 reports. The ICCR subsidies, £1 a week, were not granted beyond 1942, possibly because Robert, having learned woodwork techniques at Mount St Benedict, as his eldest son Paul reports, "began to sell his products to various stores including Woolworths where he met my mother, Sylvia, who was Assistant Buyer". Paul Auerbach to authors, 27 August 2010. The enterprise he and his brother Friedrich worked for in late 1942 also specialised in woodwork and toy production (Beltane Toys, Killiney). See list of permits in NAI, DJ 69/80/93. Friedrich continued to work in restaurants.
65 NAI, DJ 69/80/123, O'Catháin to DJ, 30 September 1938; Hogan to DJ, 19 April 1939. In 1939, the ICCR legalised his exile status on guarantees of the Abrahamson committee (CJRAC). For his entry into Ireland see also Dermot Keogh, *Jews in Twentieth-Century Ireland. Refugees, Anti-Semitism and the Holocaust*. Cork: University College Press 1998, p. 279, note 155. After his apprenticeship with Jammet's in July 1939, he was employed by Noel Huggard as a waiter at Ashford Castle. This ended at the beginning of the war, after which he was supported by the CJRAC with 30/- a week. As he had to pay 10/- for bed and breakfast, he had to live on £1 per week until his departure for the USA in 1940. MAI, G2/0207F, Simon to his mother in Sweden, 9 October 1939.
66 Felix Kahn had come from Worms/Rhine-Hesse where until 1912 his father had owned a paper factory. Felix and his mother lived on the proceeds of the sale, but possibly Felix had an income independent of his inheritance (in German documents he is described as a "merchant"). Karl and Annelore Schlösser and Dorothea Spille (eds), *Die Wormser Juden 1933–1945. Dokumentation*. CD-ROM 2002. As to his life in Dublin, there exist only few references in MAI, G2/x/1091. In a report of 14 September 1942 he is referred to as being maintained by the "Jewish refugee committee" after he had been "sacked" by Ross Studio at 3 St Stephen's Green.

After his move to Dublin in spring 1941 (see chapter 7), Gerhard Hirschberg lived off what he later termed "support money" from the Church of Ireland refugee committee except when he could find some short-term employment. The committee tried to place him in a variety of jobs: teacher at various secondary schools, translator in a camp for Italian prisoners of war, private tutor, helper for the YMCA in London, etc. – all to little or no avail.[67] In July 1944, he began studying for a Higher Diploma in Education at TCD.[68] Hans Morgenstern, after a few placements in the provinces (see chapter 7), tried to qualify as an electrical engineer, but was only sporadically able to support himself.[69] Werner Schwarz, who refused for unknown reasons to repeat his medical diplomas in Ireland, worked seasonally as a fencing instructor at schools, the Local Defence Forces or in the club sector. Otherwise, he lived on funds from the Church of Ireland refugee committee.[70]

Most dependent, though not necessarily in financial misery, were those older people and single women who were completely excluded from the labour market and entirely relied on charity or relatives throughout the war years: Richard Kappeler and his family, disadvantaged by Richard's age and the hurdles of the medical system in Ireland;[71] Ferdinand Goldschmidt and his wife Sidonie;[72] Elis-

---

67 RCBL, JS, 5 December 1939, 4 March, 9 September 1941, 13 January and 2 April 1942, 6 April and 7 September 1943.
68 RCBL, JS, 4 July 1944.
69 RCBL, JS, 4 February, 4 March and 6 May 1941. From these sources it seems that Morgenstern passed an engineering exam in 1941. In December 1941 and January 1942, Liffey Dockyard House employed him as an electrical engineer, but as no ships in the dockyards needed repair, he was dismissed after two months, too short a time to make him eligible for unemployment benefit. See correspondence between Garda, DI&C and DJ from December 1941 to February 1942 in NAI, DJ 69/80/417; also RCBL, JS, 2 December 1941 and 3 March 1942. A year later, Fritz Blaskopf gave him an intermittent job at Wings Ltd, 10–11 Upper Liffey Street, but his employment there seems to have been cut short by a trade union protest against his below-tariff wage. He probably wished to avoid the risk of losing trade union membership, since it seemed possible that he was about to find work at an industrial plant in England. RCBL, JS, 6 April 1943 (see chapter 10).
70 He was a fully qualified doctor, and was prepared to undergo an examination by Apothecaries Hall, but in line with general admission rules for doctors, the Hall's examination board demanded a preparatory training period of at least three years at an Irish university. RCBL, JS, 1 February and 6 June 1944. See further entries in RCBL, JS, 5 March 1940, 4 February 1941, 1 July 1941, 2 April, 7 July and 8 September 1942, 6 April 1943.
71 "No country needs doctors; in this respect it is the most miserable job in the world." MAI, G2/0510, letter Kappeler, 15 July 1941. Translated by authors. He, his wife and his mother-in-law Rosa Kobler continued to receive funds from the Church of Ireland refugee committee until the end of the war.
72 They depended on grants from relatives in the USA. See MAI, G2/0430, letter Ferdinand Goldschmidt, 2 October 1942 (see also chapter 9).

abeth Wiedmann, widowed since 14 December 1939;[73] Else Samter and Bertha Teichmann.[74] Berta Schwarz, although a widow, survived without charitable grants. Of Jewish birth, she had left Bremen together with her eleven-year-old son Peter at the end of 1938. It was believed in the Department of Justice that her dead husband's family had wished to separate her son from her. She came to Ireland in the first days of January 1939, thanks to her personal acquaintance with Conrad Hoffmann and his influence with the Protestant refugee committee,[75] and managed to eke out a narrow but independent existence by turning 57 Frankfurt Avenue into a boarding house and giving German lessons in the later years of the war.[76]

This survey covers some typical features of the exiles' economic situation in wartime Dublin. In general, distinctions between employees and autonomous artisans or entrepreneurs, or between secure employment and casual labour, which might have been important in their previous lives, had become more or less irrelevant compared to the question of sheer financial survival. This was a new and shocking experience, especially to former merchants or industrial managers and their families, whose post-emigration loss of status was combined with a dramatic drop in income. As they grew conditioned to their new circumstances, however, they might have noticed that an annual wage of £150 (which the President of the

---

73 In the first years of the war she relied on the assistance of relatives in New York. The G2 file on the Wiedmanns contains a large number of money orders directed to the family. An end to their help "would drive me to despair" and make it impossible "to pay my rent at the first next month", she told them on 16 April 1942. MAI, G2/1434. It seems, however, that she later managed to live in relative comfort from these American funds and the income her daughter earned from 1943 onwards (see above). See DJ 69/80/198. In 1945, she was said to have received £300 from her daughter and the American relatives. NAI, DJ 68/1/791.
74 Bertha Teichmann was supported by her daughter Ellen Ticher and her husband (see below). Else Samter seems to have lived on her own money during the first phase of her life as an exile. NAI, DJ 69/80/573, Solomons to DJ, 25 October 1939; also Detective Branch report, 10 April 1940. Later her maintenance was funded by the Jewish refugee committee. EA Berlin, no. 75780, Bartmann to EA Berlin, 19 March 1958. She could also count on the assistance of her sister Charlotte and Charlotte's husband Professor Hans Sachs (see chapter 9).
75 Her background is detailed in NAI, DJ 69/80/100. According to Peter Schwarz's recollection, it was not due to "racial tensions" that his father's family had opposed their move to Ireland, but because they feared that he would grow up in poverty ("Du nimmst das Kind in die Armut"). Peter Schwarz, email to authors, 16 July 2016.
76 It seems that the Church of Ireland refugee committee had turned over the house to her, obliging her to pay taxes and repair costs. At the end of the war, 57 Frankfurt Avenue housed eight persons. By that time she also taught German to classes of about ten students. NAI, DJ 68/1/685 (2013/50/659).

Lennox Street Hebrew Congregation had defined as a minimum subsistence level) was roughly what most general labourers in Ireland earned at the time (a number of exiles earned more, as we have seen; benefit payments on the other hand on average came to about £65 a year).[77] Even those exiles in the capital who were semi-employed or unemployed, and partially or fully dependent on charity or relatives, did not have to fear the kind of material deprivation they could observe among native Dubliners. Their fundamental predicament was of a different character. In 1941, Curt Heilfron brooded over his enforced idleness: "Our own life here is very quiet, or you could say monotonous. To spend one's days without useful work gives you a feeling of utter unhappiness."[78] In a letter to Elisabeth Wiedmann of 15 March 1941, Eva Schwarz commented on the dark underside of life in exile, on general indisposition and the development of anaemia: "I believe that we all have the same deficits and a doctor cannot help us."[79] Other exiles also passed through phases of psychosomatic illness,[80] and some had thoughts of suicide. Ernst Einäugler may have had one or more such crises.[81] David Nachmann, tormented by his continuing dependency, his self-reproaches over his wife's destiny and his failure to rescue her, tried to kill himself.[82] Others were protected by strong psychological resources and equipped with talents which allowed them at least temporarily to forget their estrangement. "We are quite well here if one only considers food and lodging as the traffic of life," wrote Adolf Adler. "However one

---

77 See Wills, *Neutral Island*, p. 259.
78 MAI, G2/0453, letter Curt Heilfron, 20 September 1941.
79 MAI, G2/1434. For Eva Schwarz, see chapters 3 and 7. For their correspondence, see also MAI, G2/0771, Eva Schwarz to Elisabeth Wiedmann, 26 November 1940.
80 In August 1941, Kathleen Huggard referred to Gustav Beisser's "complaint", which was "partly nerves and partly anaemia". TCD Archives, Butler Papers, 10304/597/778, 30 August 1941. She felt it was caused by his work situation at the Old Vienna Club. Even Gitla Bayer, well-settled and without any material worries, suffered from coronary problems and "nervous depression" in the war years. DJ 69/41, Bayer to DJ, 13 August 1945.
81 Kathleen Huggard reports on an occasion in 1940 when "we thought he had committed suicide". TCD Archives, Butler Papers, 10304/597/776, Huggard to Butler, 13 August 1941. See also also her letter to Butler on 2 October (1941 or 1942) in which she describes Ernst's temporary condition of disorientation. 10304/597/784.
82 EA Berlin, no. 322.992, Gerd Nachmann (David's son) to EA Berlin, 27 March 1967. For Nachmann's post-war suicide, see chapter 11. We know of at least one other person who committed suicide in exile (there may have been more, since in one case two exiles were buried on the same day): Elsa Höfler, who had previously suffered from depression. Her suicide in Limerick in October 1938 attracted considerable media coverage at the time. See Gisela Holfter, German-speaking Exiles 1933–1945 in Ireland – An Introduction and Overview. In: Gisela Holfter (ed.), *German-speaking Exiles in Ireland 1933–1945*. Amsterdam/New York: Rodopi 2006, pp. 1–19, 11.

must not think beyond that, then one enters fields of grey and dark uncertainties. But it is good that I do have sufficient mental distraction here in the city which lets me forget the many hours of brooding."[83] Richard Kappeler's health was affected "by long periods of idleness and financial anxiety",[84] but he was able to distract himself in phases of inactivity through his manifold interests and abilities (see also below). One of these became known to the Irish public. On 26 January 1942, the *Irish Times* published a photo story headlined "Sammy has a trainer. Austrian doctor volunteers." A seal, fondly named "Sammy", had been caught in a fishing net and was to be trained for shows in Dun Laoghaire (in a room to which it had to be carried almost daily in a wheelbarrow). Richard Kappeler, once "a collaborator of Professor Antonius, Superintendent of the Zoological Garden of Schoenbrunn, Vienna", had offered his services, which were gladly accepted. The story of "Sammy the Seal" hit the headlines in other papers, familiarising Irish readers with the personal background of Sammy's trainer.[85]

SAMMY HAS A TRAINER

AUSTRIAN DOCTOR VOLUNTEERS

By Our Animal Reporter.

Reading in last Thursday's *Irish Times* my suggestion that someone should train Sammy, the Dublin Zoo's new baby Lambay seal, an ideal man for the job instantly decided to take it on, and telephoned the Zoo at nine a.m. to volunteer his services.

He is Doctor Richard Kapeller, for many years a collaborator of Professor Antonius, Superintendent of the Zoological Gardens of Schoenbrunn, Vienna. When we met yesterday to talk about Sammy's future, I found the doctor, medium-sized, soft-voiced in his charming and almost perfect English, and with very dark, compelling eyes.

Image 2: Newspaper article 'Sammy has a trainer', *Irish Times*, 26 January 1942.

---

83 MAI, G2/3190, letter Adolf Adler, 22 August 1940. Translated by authors.
84 RCBL, JS, 13 January 1942.
85 See *Irish Times*, 26 January and 24 March 1942; *Irish Independent*, 13 January 1942.

New homes

Our survey of the exiles' social topography in the capital begins at their homes.[86] For some, this meant accommodation in boarding schools, universities, or houses owned by religious organisations or private persons, but others rented flats or houses on the residential market. A few found accommodation on their own, but most relied on the ICCR and the philanthropic societies for guidance, and partly for funding too.

Jewish refugees from Nazism might have been expected to settle in 'Little Jerusalem', the quarter north of the South Circular Road which owed its nickname to the influx of Lithuanian Jews before the First World War. By the 1930s, its character had fundamentally changed, its social and religious structure showing unmistakable signs of erosion, as affluent Jewish families had tended to move "over the bridge" to the larger Rathmines area, especially to Rathgar. "It was like the King leaving his Versailles, going out to see his people." This is how young Stanley Price described the difference between his grandparents' surroundings on elegant Kenilworth Square and his other grandparents' world in 'Little Jerusalem' with its "smell of horse-shit and boiled milk".[87] Nevertheless a nucleus of Jewish people still remained in the area, its infrastructure offering services like shuls, shops and the new Zion School and community offices in Bloomfield Avenue.[88]

In 1939, G2 drew up a list of functionaries serving at the most important shuls and synagogues:
- Adelaide Road: Nandor Freilich, Philip Moddel.
- Greenville Hall, Dolphins Barn: David Freilich, D. Garbarz (naturalised).
- Lombard Street: Emanuel Fischer.
- St. Kevin's Parade: Wirsberger (naturalised).
- Lennox Street: Bernhard Holländer, Abraham Gittleson (Irish).
- Walworth Road: Dayan Zalman Alony,[89] David Eichenstein.[90]

---

86 Unless otherwise noted, the following residential data are taken from G2 files in the MAI and the DJ 68/1 and DJ 69/80 series in the NAI.
87 Stanley Price, *Somewhere to Hang My Hat. An Irish-Jewish Journey*. Dublin: New Island 2002, pp. 42, 44.
88 See Stanley Waterman, Changing residential patterns of the Dublin Jewish community. In: *Irish Geography*. Vol. XIV, no. 1 (1981), pp. 41–50, 44.
89 Ray Rivlin, *Shalom Ireland. A Social History of Jews in Modern Ireland*. Dublin: Gill and Macmillan 2003, pp. 62–63.
90 In 1931, he had been called to Dublin by Chief Rabbi Herzog and others to be a cantor of the Lombard Street Congregation for five years. In 1936, he renewed his application for another tenure, which was granted despite opposition in the DJ. See DJ 2013/50/106.

- Rathmines: Bernstein (Irish).
- Swifts Row, Ormond Quay: Israel Frankel.

The aim was to show how important a role was played in Jewish community life by German speakers, naturalised or not:[91] at least five of the above (Nandor and David Freilich, Moddel, Frankel, Holländer), and probably more, came into this category. They had an Eastern-Jewish background and had been called to Ireland to fortify the ruling orthodoxy of the community.[92]

On first arrival, most of them lodged in the Portobello district, north of the South Circular Road, where the normal type of housing, two-storeyed buildings with a little front garden, was rather middle-class and refined.[93] Jacob Rosanowsky, a former senior cantor from Berlin, roomed with his niece at 7 Victoria Street. Bernhard Holländer and his wife Gertrud stayed at two addresses in Harrington Street in 1938 and 1939. Rabbi David Freilich, his wife Dina and their two children resided at the community centre in 33 Bloomfield Avenue. Rabbi Frankel, also a teacher of Hebrew at Zion Schools, lived with his wife Fanny in nearby Longwood Avenue. Emanuel Fischer, cantor at the Lombard Street shul, was first accommodated at 5 St Kevin's Parade. Philip Moddel, choir master at Adelaide Road Synagogue, may have frequently stayed at 33 Victoria Street, in the heart of 'Little Jerusalem', with the Margulies family, old acquaintances from his childhood days in Rechneigrabenstrasse, Frankfurt.

In due course, however, some of these officials of the community sought residences outside the traditional Jewish quarter. In May 1940, Moddel moved to nearby 89 Grove Park on the southern bank of the Grand Canal, sharing accommodation with Nandor Freilich, his partner at the Dublin Hebrew Con-

---

91 NAI, DJ 69/80/518.
92 David Freilich had done service in houses of the orthodox Adass Jeruschun and Ohel Jacob congregations during his time in Munich from 1929 to 1938. See entries in his police record of 31 October 1938. BHSA, no. 12438; also BEDJG, no. 22451, Israelite Community Munich affidavit, 6 March 1939. It is very likely that his brother Nandor was also orthodox. Before coming to Dublin on 21 February 1939 he had been engaged by the Jewish community of Zagreb for five years. *Jewish Chronicle*, 12 May 1939. For the orthodox background of others (Moddel, Fischer, Frankel), see chapters 4 and 6.
93 Cormac O'Grada, *Jewish Ireland in the Age of Joyce: A Socioeconomic History*. Princeton/Oxford: Princeton University Press 2006, p. 102.
94 Both were actively engaged in the Dublin Jewish Choral Society, founded in February 1940 and specialising in Hebrew and other folk singing. Nandor Freilich was one of the solo singers. *Jewish Chronicle*, 23 February 1940. They also shared a penchant for sports. Garret Moddel email to authors, 8 August 2005. Harris, *Dublin's Little Jerusalem*, p. 109. Nandor stayed at 89 Grove Park until his marriage to Eudice Buchalter in 1943, after which they bought a house in Vernon Grove, Rathgar.

gregation.[94] Between 1938 and 1941, the Holländers were recorded as tenants at 16 Leinster Square and then at 38 Grosvenor Square, while Bernhard continued to work as a rabbi for the Lennox Street Congregation in 'Little Jerusalem'. Emanuel Fischer also lodged at various addresses on Grosvenor Square until 1945.[95] David Freilich and Israel Frankel, on the other hand, retained their accommodation in the old Jewish quarter, probably because they were teaching at Zion School in Bloomfield Avenue. Otherwise, only the Margulies family and Abraham Wizniak,[96] also orthodox Jews of East-European origin, remained within the small and fragmenting world of 'Little Jerusalem', but in September 1943 the Margulies family too left the area,[97] buying a house in Sandymount (1 St. John's Road). In May 1944, their daughter Paula and Philip Moddel, her husband, became their neighbours.[98]

The Abrahamson committee, whose brief included finding adequate accommodation for the new residents, placed a number of them at Stein's Kosher Hotel at 6 Harrington Street, where other immigrants had found a first and, as a rule, short-term address before moving to private residences: Abraham Bayer, Paul and Karl Schnitzler, Leib Margulies, and later the Holländers, Nandor Freilich, Max and Hedwig Rund, Erich J. Priebatsch, Hermann Heymann, Walter Simon, Erwin Jakobi, Walter and Alice Storch, Else Honig and the Menkes family. Other addresses where several Jews found accommodation were, for example, 7 Harcourt Terrace (Philip Moddel, Walter Storch, Jacob Rosanowsky and Erich J. Priebatsch), 18 Westfield Road (the Rosenbergs and Runds), 19 Fergus Road, Terenure (David Nachmann and the Rosenbergs), 342 Harold's Cross Road (Adolf Mündheim and Thomas

---

95 He also retained his flat in St. Kevin's Parade. DD, Volume 108, 22 October 1947.
96 In January 1938, Abraham Wizniak was registered at 2 Walworth Road, living in dire circumstances and waiting for a chance to bring the rest of his family to Ireland, from where he hoped they could all emigrate to the USA. In October 1939, he moved across the Canal to 58 Terenure Road East before settling for a longer period at 111 Upper Rathmines Road in March 1940. MAI, G2/1690.
97 MAI, G2/0619. Originally, Margulies had lived for a short time at 34 Longwood Avenue; it was probably here that he first met the Harrises, with whom his family later came to have a close relationship. Harris, *Dublin's Little Jerusalem*, p. 179. He then moved to 81 Lower Leeson Street, probably in connection with the establishment of Leather Articles Ltd in central Dublin, returned to 'Little Jerusalem' when his family was finally reunited in late November 1938, after much lobbying by Quakers and representatives of the Jewish community. For these interventions see correspondence in DJ 69/1145; DFA102/229 and MAI, G2/0619.
98 The 1943 list of German residents, Co. Dublin (NAI, DFA 10/2/18), records the Margulies family as still at 33 Victoria Street. By 1947, they were recorded in Sandymount. DD, Volume 108, 22 October 1947. See also NAI, DJ 68/1/594 and 595. In June 1941, Philip Moddel had rented a flat at 7 Harcourt Terrace to be closer to his inner-city place of work, Adelaide Road Synagogue. He remained there for a year, after which he and Paula moved to 38 Lower Baggot Street, still near his synagogue. In May 1944, they were recorded as lodgers at 50 Sandymount Avenue.

Nachmann) and 38 Grosvenor Square (Otto Michael Falk and his old acquaintances from Schneidemühl/Pomerania, the Holländers).

All these places provided opportunities for mingling with Jewish Dubliners and taking part in communal Jewish life. Erich J. Priebatsch was recorded as a visitor to "a number of houses of leading Jews in Dublin for the purpose of dinner, etc".[99] Nick Harris remembers that such encounters were "not unusual", a few of them even leading to new Irish-German families.[100] The Jewish community, however, was not a closed society: Priebatsch, Moddel and others freely cultivated contacts with non-Jewish people. Nor was the newcomers' reception by Jewish Dubliners without traces of ambivalence. Heinz Krotoschin, while readily testifying to the material help he received from Dublin Jews, recalled that German "Jeckes" were treated less than sympathetically, a hint at least of the lingering reserve between traditionally orthodox Jewish Dubliners and the assimilated German newcomers.[101] The cordiality recalled by Nick Harris was perhaps primarily accorded to orthodox Jews like Bayer, Margulies or Moddel.

In the broad zone south of the Grand Canal, enclosing Harold's Cross, Ranelagh, Rathmines proper and Rathgar, these German-speaking Jews could have easily crossed paths with other German speakers, Jewish or not, although the exiles in the area, 67 or so excluding children, were no more than a speck within the total populace of about 40,000 living in Rathmines West and East.

Kenilworth Square was a focal point, consisting of two storey over basement houses with sash windows, fronted by porches and small hedged gardens, around a central green. In the quiet residential areas surrounding the Square to the north, east and west, in streets like Effra Road and Leinster Road, Leinster Square, Grosvenor Road and beyond Harold's Cross Road in Westfield Road and Kenilworth Park, the style of building was somewhat less exclusive, but still exuded a solid and quiet middle-class air. The atmosphere south-east of Kenilworth Square is vividly evoked in John Ryan's recollection. He remembers the "hushed calm" of his childhood days when he lived with his parents in a large

---

99 MAI, G2/x/1091, no. 181, undated G2 report. Among the people who invited him regularly was Eva Davies. Her daughter Joyce remembered that Priebatsch kept praising the quality of everything German, and pronounced German-made things to be generally superior. Joyce and Maurice Abrahamson interview with authors, 28 March 2012.
100 Harris, *Dublin's Little Jerusalem*, pp. 177–180.
101 Kent, Henry (= Heinz Krotoschin), *Visual History Archive*, 10 May 1996. Stephen Weil also recalls "the lack of connection they [the Scheyers] felt with the existing Irish Jewish community, Yiddish speaking, eastern European in origin, orthodox in practice, a community untouched by Goethe". Stephen Weil, "Children of Goethe": The Scheyer-Weil Family. In: Gisela Holfter (ed.), *The Irish Context of Kristallnacht. Refugees and Helpers*. Irish-German Studies. Vol. 8. Trier: Wissenschaftlicher Verlag 2014, pp. 23–28, 26.

Table 1: Exiles' residences in greater Rathmines (comprising the area south of the Grand Canal to Rathmines Road as far as Rathgar to the south, Ranelagh to the east and Harold's Cross Road to the west; excluding dependent adolescents and tenancies of less than one year), the superscript numbers after the addresses refer to the map on the next page.

Alice Hopf, Ludwig Hopf (+1939), Liselore Hopf (+1942)	65 Kenilworth Square[1]	1939 to 1943
Ferdinand and Sidonie Goldschmidt	65 Kenilworth Square[1]	1941 to 1944
Ernst and Marie Scheyer	67 Kenilworth Square[2]	1941 to 1945
Felix Kahn	79 Kenilworth Square[3]	1941/42 to 1945
Kurt and Adolf Adler	49 Garville Avenue[4]	1941 to 1943
Adolf Mündheim	342 Harold's Cross Road[5]	1942 to 1945 (visiting)
Elias Stiel	326 Harold's Cross Road[6]	1942 to 1945
Naftali Witztum[102]	18 Effra Road[7]	1936 to 1938
Hermann Heymann	18 Effra Road[7]	1939 to 1940
Bernhard and Gertrud Holländer	16 Leinster Square[10]	1939 to 1941
	38 Grosvenor Square[8]	1941 to 1945
Emanuel Fischer	15 (29, 26) Grosvenor Square[9]	1939 to 1945
Josefa Stein	4 Leinster Square[11]	1941 to 1942
Max and Hedwig Rund	28 Leinster Square[12]	1943 to 1945
Else, Theodor and Fritz Honig	234 Rathmines Road Lr[13] (in 1942 Castlewood Ave, near A.& L. Kende below)	1944
Adolphine Kende (Ludwig Kende joining about 1941)	35 Castlewood Avenue[14]	1939 to 1945
Else Samter	3 Palmerston Villas[22]	1939 to 1943
	178 Rathgar Road[15]	1943 to 1945
Rudi and Marianne Neuman	70 Upper Rathmines Road[16]	1939 to 1945
Kurt, Rosa and Sophie Billig	31 (37?) Grosvenor Road[17]	1939 to 1941
Berta Schwarz	57 Frankfort Avenue[18]	1939 (?) to 1945
Heinz and Alice Krotoschin	135 Rathgar Road[19]	1944 to 1945
Curt and Charlotte Heilfron	53 Highfield Road[21]	1939 to 1945
Hans and Charlotte Sachs	3 Palmerston Villas[22]	1939 to 1945
Ferdinand and Emilie Karrach	Dartry Road ('Dartmouth')[23]	1941 to 1943
Ernst and Hedwig Lewy, Esther Britz (née Lewy) and Georg Lewy	1 Cowper Gardens[24]	1939 to 1941
Siegmund Liffmann (and Rosa Liffmann from 1942)	6 Ormond Road[25]	1939 to 1945
David Nachmann	72 Palmerston Road[26]	1940 to 1941
Ludwig and Gisela Karrenberg	53 Mount Pleasant Square[27]	1939 to 1943 (?)
Philip Moddel	89 Grove Park[28]	1940 to 1941
Nandor Freilich	89 Grove Park[28]	1939 to 1943
	14 Vernon Grove[20]	1943 to 1945

---

102 His brothers Marcus and Arnold lived nearby in 14 Effra Road; Marcus and his wife Deborah were there from 1933 to about 1937; Arnold and his wife Eileen were at the same address from 1933 to 1945.

250 — Chapter 8 Continental Dubliners

Image 3: Map of Rathmines – Google maps (in accordance with their "fair use" guidelines).

red-brick house on Orwell Road, near the intersection of Rathgar Avenue and Rathgar Road.[103] From the point of view of an inner-city tenement-dweller, the area appeared "posh".[104] The urban landscape east of arterial Rathmines Road was more varied in character. In the zones south of Belgrave Square, typically on leafy Palmerston Road or its side roads such as Ormond Road or Cowper Gardens, or further south in Palmerston Villas, one finds the same kind of atmosphere and detached or semi-detached buildings as in Rathgar. In the district extending from Belgrave Square and Castlewood Avenue to the Grand Canal, comprising Ranelagh and Lower Rathmines, the buildings were more compact and "more modest, but still 'respectable'".[105]

The newcomers did not drift by chance into Rathmines. Exiles in search of accommodation could find a number of open houses and social attractions in the suburb. The majority of practising Jews used to frequent the new shul at 52 Grosvenor Road and other institutions of the Jewish community. David Nachmann wrote in a letter to his mother in Berlin: "I was with Thommy [sic] in the synagogue, and we thought a lot of the good old days with you. He diligently learns Hebraic [sic], and he does quite well."[106] Jewish ritual, in the synagogue as well as in host families, was obviously an important means of establishing a link between present and past. At the same time, Rathmines was known for its chequered inter-denominational neighbourhoods, the Protestant element being stronger than in other parts of Dublin.[107] The relatively easy relations between the local Church of Ireland and Jewish communities were shown, for example, by the fact that, before the new shul in Grosvenor Road was opened, the parochial

---

103 "The whole area…may, arguably, be the most perfectly intact, homogeneous, early Victorian, urban landscape we have." Ryan, *Remembering How We Stood*, p. 153.
104 Kevin C. Kearns, *Dublin Tenement Life. An Oral History*. Dublin: Gill and Macmillan 1994, p. 63.
105 Joseph Brady, Dublin at the Turn of the Century. In: Joseph Brady and Anngret Simms (eds), *Dublin through Space and Time (c. 900–1900)*. Dublin: Four Courts Press 2001, pp. 221–281, p. 270.
106 MAI, G2/0654, letter David Nachmann, probably September 1939. Translated by authors. At the time Thomas Nachmann was staying at 342 Harold's Cross Road, whose owners, the Eppel family, also housed Adolf Mündheim during his sojourns in Dublin. MAI, G2/0644.
107 Personal data collected by census officers for 1911 show that house owners in these streets were mostly well-off, with a Church of Ireland or, less frequently, Presbyterian religious background, many of their poorer tenants being Catholic servants or domestics. This can be concluded from random samples from Frankfort Avenue, Vernon Grove, Highfield Road, Garville Avenue. NAI, data of 1911 census. In the 1930s and 1940s, the proportion of Catholic house owners grew, as did the number of Catholics as a whole. The demographic shift can be seen from figures in the 1926 and 1936 censuses, which show that 6,295 Protestants lived in the area in 1926,

hall was used for Jewish services by permission of Reverend W.C. Proctor of the Harold's Cross Rectory.[108] He also conducted burial ceremonies for Ludwig Hopf and Hans Sachs, neither of whom had converted, at the then Protestant Mount Jerome Cemetery (see chapter 9).[109]

A centre of social activities was Grasmere, number 16 in quiet Zion Road opposite the Church of Ireland Zion Parish Church. It was owned by Kurt and Ellen Tichauer, both Protestants of Jewish origin who had already turned their backs on Germany in 1925. In the course of the ten following years, they had three children, Peter, Thomas and Ruth, and Kurt became a partner in O'Dwyer & Tichauer Ltd, Manufacturers' Agents and Importers, and also a director of Setiselle Ltd, Underclothes Manufacturers. The Tichauers were naturalised in 1936 and had their name officially changed to Ticher in 1939.[110] Outside his professional interests, Kurt gained a reputation as a silver collector and as a frequent host to former compatriots living in Ireland. In 1938–1939, endangered members of their extended family joined them in Rathmines: Bertha Teichmann, Ellen's mother, who lived in a little house not far from theirs, and Jochen and Reiner Hengstenberg, sons of Kurt's half-sister Trude Hengstenberg (who also came to Ireland after the war). Beyond the family circle, the Tichers hosted other expatriates at Grasmere: Otto Glaser, a boarder at Blackrock College, generally spent his holidays here or at other Ticher residences, and practically became an adopted son after he moved from his College to 16 Zion Road in December 1942,[111] Gisela Karrenberg frequently looked after Ruth, and Einhart Kawerau turned up in his holidays to spend time

---

falling to 5,381 in 1936. The Catholic population numbered 26,697 in 1926 and 33,766 in 1936. COS, Historical Censuses 1926 and 1936. Vol. 3, Table 12. The district's ambience of middle-class respectability was unaffected. Valuation figures support Haughton's opinion that Rathmines was a "middle-class residential district, with some larger detached houses in the southern part". Joseph P. Haughton, The Social Geography of Dublin. In: *The Geographical Review*. Vol. 39 (1949), pp. 257–277, p. 276. Interviewees who had spent their childhood and youth in Rathmines had similar memories. Patricia Moorhead and Séamus Ó Maitiú interviews with authors, 10 July 2009.
108 *Jewish Chronicle*, 28 October 1939.
109 When conducting the services, Proctor seems to have adhered to Christian practice. At Sachs's burial in April 1945 he gave a reading of Psalms 90. Sachs's widow, however, was satisfied that "all was done according to my husband's wishes." Quoted from a letter of Charlotte Sachs. Courtesy John Cooke.
110 See DJ 2013/50/107 and 159. The enterprise was located at 16 Parnell Square. It had a nominal capital of £10,000 and employed over 20 persons. NA Washington, RG 84, Box 1, Confidential report US Consulate Dublin, 16 March 1941.
111 NAI, DJ 69/80/585. Later Ticher described himself as Otto's official "guardian" ("with consent of his parents"). NAI, DJ 69/80/585, Ticher to DJ, 4 June 1946.

with Peter and Thomas.[112] Elisabeth Schloss was a regular visitor during her time in Dublin,[113] and Hans Reiss, whose German relatives had had business links with Ticher's enterprise before the war, spent practically every Sunday at Grasmere.[114] Other visitors were Georg Fäsenfeld, himself a helper of refugees,[115] Charlotte and Hans Sachs, Else Samter, Ludwig and Eva Bieler, the Scheyers, the Heilfrons, and the Neumans, most of whom lived within walking distance of Zion Road. The Tichers also helped some exiles to find an entry into the Irish business world. A special case was Julius ("Jusil") Silber (see chapter 4). A "keen businessman", whom Kurt Ticher seems to have met by chance in 1933,[116] he managed to find a place in Ticher's trade network comprising partners in London, on the Continent, including Germany, and in Ireland. After his arrival in London he made sporadic visits to Dublin for negotiations with firms involved in the Continental trade, on which occasions he stayed at Ticher's office.[117] Kurt Ticher also had a business relationship with Anselm Horwitz's McCowlings Moulding Ltd in Tralee (see chapter 7) and joined Siegmund Liffmann's Belgrave Trading Company as a junior partner in 1946.[118] Some exiles also called on his expertise to help sell a few rescued valuables, in order to make ends meet.[119]

A few exiles preferred to settle in the northern suburbs of Dublin, even if this meant they had to pass through the slum areas before reaching Drumcondra or

---

112 Peter Ticher email to authors, 28 March 2004; interviews with authors, 25 May 2004, 10 and 11 April 2007.
113 MAI, G2/0747, Elisabeth to Gerhard Schloss, 11 February 1943. She lived alone in Dublin for some months, during her husband's second period of employment at Irish Steel in Cork (see chapter 7), at times making daily bike rides to the Tichers.
114 Hans Reiss, *Erinnerungen aus 85 Jahren*. Göttingen: Petrarca 2009, pp. 108–110, 118, 152–156. In his unpublished memoir in English, Seven Years in Ireland, p. 29, Reiss recalls how he discussed at length with Kurt and Ellen Ticher what course of studies he should follow.
115 Fäsenfeld was not a refugee. In the 1930s, he was an important figure in German-Irish trade relations and part-owner of Roscrea Meat Factories Ltd. One of his temporary business partners in the company was Robert Briscoe. In 1939, Fäsenfeld was unable to bring Jewish relatives to Ireland in spite of his own and Briscoe's guarantees. See correspondence in NAI, DFA 202/366 and DJ 69/80/1; also Briscoe, Robert and Alden Hatch, *For the Life of Me*. Boston/Toronto: Little, Brown and Company 1958, pp. 261–265.
116 Peter Ticher interview with authors, 10/11 April 2007.
117 See correspondence in MAI, G2/0277. For his visits to Dublin between 1934 and 1939 see especially NAI, DFA 69/133; also NA Washington, Hickok, US Legation Dublin, to US Consul Francis Styles, 29 October 1942. It appears from a handwritten note that Silber worked in Ticher's office at 28 Parnell Square (whether this was part of the O'Dwyer & Tichauer premises or belonged to a different Ticher business is not certain).
118 NAI, CRO, 1/D/1110.
119 Michael Shire interview with authors, 28 April 2009. Shire passed on a letter from James Douglas to Kurt Ticher that mentions the latter's role as mediator in such transactions.

Clontarf.[120] Josef and Lucy Kalman seem to have permanently stayed at 76 Celtic Park Road in Beaumont.[121]

Some parts of Clontarf fringing Dublin Bay also attracted exiles.[122] An academic trio assembled here (see chapter 9): Leo Pollak and his wife lodged at 66 Hollybrook Road, Erwin Schrödinger's family was at 26 Kincora Road, and Schrödinger's colleague at the Dublin Institute for Advanced Studies, Walter Heitler, was almost next door, at 21 Seapark Road. The Schrödinger household frequently hosted a circle of young Austrian exiles comprising Alfred Schulhof, Stefan Feric and Mimi Höfer. Of the three, only Alfred Schulhof resided in the Schrödingers' neighbourhood, first in Ouldon Road and then at 37 Victoria Road.[123] Mimi Höfer's future husband, however, lived in the same street as the Schrödingers, at 38 Kincora Road. She used to visit both households, and felt like a daughter of the Schrödingers: it was Erwin Schrödinger who gave her away at her wedding in June 1945.[124] Further north, in Sutton, the Hennig family had, almost miraculously, found modestly priced accommodation in Burrow Road, which allowed the three daughters to roam freely on the beach behind their garden.[125]

The area south-east of Dublin, outside the densely built-up centre but within the capital's socio-geographical ambit, had long become more accessible since a regular train service connecting Bray and Dun Laoghaire with Dublin proper had commenced in the middle of the 19th century. It seems, however, that only Eric Serff and Franziska Wiedmann shuttled daily between residences in Dun Laoghaire and their work in the city. Many more exiles lived in the south-western suburbs for longer or shorter periods. They comprised:

---

120 Ruth Braunizer, Schrödinger's daughter, remembered her mother's frequent bike rides to the city. She would "on many a dark night... cycle through the slums into town and back. There was never a question of this being unsafe." Ruth Braunizer, Memories of Dublin – Excerpts from Erwin Schrödinger's Diaries. In: Gisela Holfter (ed.), *German-speaking Exiles in Ireland 1933–1945*. Amsterdam/New York: Rodopi 2006, pp. 265–274, 266.
121 MAI, G2/0096.
122 For the quality of housing here, see Brady, Dublin at the Turn of the Century, pp. 277–278
123 Schulhof entry in questionnaire, 5 November 2008.
124 See Elisabeth Guggenheimer's interview with Mimi Wicklow, née Höfer, 10 August 1987, University of Vienna, Zentralbibliothek für Physik; Braunizer, Memories of Dublin – Excerpts from Erwin Schrödinger's Diaries, pp. 273–274.
125 Walking along a road in Sutton with "splendid gardens", John Hennig had knocked at one of the doors. "The woman showed me the flat. It was ideal for us, and the rent was reasonable. But we had children. Boys or girls? Two girls. Oh, that was just fine; she was looking for company for her little daughter." John Hennig, "War". In: Gisela Holfter and Hermann Rasche (eds), *Exile in Ireland*. Galway: Arlen House 2004, pp. 53–73, 59. Margaret, the third daughter, was born in November 1942.

Image 4: Claire, Gabriele and Monica Hennig.

Image 5: Claire and John Hennig.

- pupils and boarders of secondary schools like St Gerard's College (Melanie and Annaliese Fuchs), Blackrock College (Otto Glaser, Georg Bernfeld, Walter Lewin), Avoca School, Blackrock (Dietrich Scheff), Loreto College School, Dalkey (Marianne Lönhardt and Irma Karfunkelstein) and Hall School, Monkstown (Ottilie Schwarz);
- those who could afford a comfortable lifestyle in suburban surroundings, such as Emil and Elsa Hirsch or Leopold and Helena von Glasersfeld;[126]
- people such as Ernst von Glasersfeld and his wife, the Fuchs family, and the Lisowskis (and, possibly, Edeltraut Reinert) who were economically tied to the area;
- others whose temporary or permanent unemployment compelled them to reside in communal houses like Vallombrosa or Roseville Home.[127]

Summing up, one notes that many of these suburbanites were middle-aged or old, married and able to dispose of a regular and guaranteed income. They obviously preferred the ambience and "hushed calm" of Rathgar or other outer areas to the bustle of street life in the centre.

The lure of the city

The young, the unmarried, and those dependent on charity tended to inhabit the city centre. Lighted at night, in contrast to blacked-out Belfast, the city appealed to the young and single. Here they could be independent, and had access to universities, secondary schools, hospitals, help organisations, and offices, with new social connections, places to meet informally and better opportunities to learn English. They resided in parts of the city reaching from the southern and eastern

---

[126] The von Glasersfelds lived in a Monkstown hotel and then in the exclusive Kilcroney Sports Club. Emil and Elsa Hirsch had also chosen accommodation outside the city, though not as far as the other exiles in the 'railway townships'. In June 1939, they bought a house at 52 Nutley Park/ Stillorgan Road, an indication that Emil was about to withdraw from business affairs (which were increasingly overseen by his son).

[127] Ferdinand Karrach and his wife, for example, lived at Vallombrosa for most of 1939, and with the Kappelers at Roseville Home between November 1939 and April 1940 (and then again for two weeks in late December 1940). Herbert Karrach, The Karrach Family. In: Gisela Holfter (ed.), *The Irish Context of Kristallnacht. Refugees and Helpers*. Irish-German Studies. Vol. 8. Trier: Wissenschaftlicher Verlag 2014, pp. 43–50, 47. In 1940, when Ferdinand found a job (see above), they moved to the city centre (16 Lower Mount Street). They returned to Roseville for the Christmas season in 1940, see MAI, G2/0511 and 0512.

fringes of the Grand Canal to the Upper Pembroke area, the eastern environs of St Stephen's Green, and as far as Trinity College and the Liffey.[128] Flat swapping was quite common among the city-dwelling refugees,[129] partly because they kept a look-out for affordable rooms, as did the hospitality services of the committees, on their behalf: Kathleen Huggard ruefully noted that the committees treated them "like babies doing all their planning for them & shoving them round without consulting them".[130]

One major reason for this clustering was the number of secondary schools and universities in the area (younger children were mostly placed at primary schools near their parents' homes in the suburbs).[131] A lot of secondary students attended Wesley College on St Stephen's Green, which was run by Methodists, but was also open to Jewish students: Georg Pick (from April 1939 to July 1941), Hans Reiss (September 1939 to 1940), and Hans Menkes (1939–1940). Presbyterian St Andrew's College at Wellington Place was attended by Herbert Karrach (1939 to late 1942) and Peter Schwarz,[132] and the Church of Ireland's High School in Harcourt Street by Jochen Hengstenberg (September 1939 to September 1941).

---

128 A few middle-aged, married and self-sufficient commuters were attracted to the Upper Pembroke area, which was relatively close to the city. In 1939–1940 Fritz Lederer lived at 8 Merlyn Park, Ballsbridge, as a neighbour of his guarantor William Norton (see chapter 2), but in 1940 he moved to 21 Ely Place, which was nearer his workplace, the Unicorn. Robert Donath (see chapters 2 and 9) roomed in Serpentine Avenue, Homelee 2, from November 1938. The Boases lived at 36 Morehampton Road and stayed there until Paul gave up his job at the end of 1943; then they were listed at an address even closer to the city centre (42 Lower Leeson Street). The Blaskopf family took up residence at 70 Waterloo Road in refined Ballsbridge. NAI, DFA 10/2/18, list of Germans, Co. Dublin.
129 The G2 file of the Aberbach brothers listed no fewer than eight flat swaps between 1941, the time when they came to Dublin from Mount Benedict, and 1944. They regularly switched between the Pembroke-Leeson Street area and Sandycove.
130 TCD Archives, Butler Papers, 10304/597/777, Huggard to Butler, 16 August 1941. In a letter of 30 June 1940 from Bernhard Frankl to his (unknown) "dear friends" it is noted that the ICCR had relocated "Freddie" Aberbach to another address. The tone of the letter makes clear that the decision was not to Aberbach's liking. MAI, G2/0308.
131 They included the daughters of John and Claire Hennig (Gabriele, Monica and Margaret), who attended Santa Sabine School, a Dominican convent in Sutton, and Ruth March, daughter of Erwin Schrödinger and Hilda March, a pupil of Holy Faith Convent, Clontarf. Jewish children – the sons and daughters of the Bayer and Krotoschin families, for example – presumably also attended a school in the Jewish centre of Dublin (very probably Zion National School which had been set up on Bloomfield Avenue in 1934).
132 Berta Schwarz's son, aged eleven on their arrival in Ireland, got his first schooling at Baymount Preparatory Boarding School in Clontarf before entering St Andrew's. NAI, DJ 69/80/100, Garda to DJ, 8 February 1939.

Three exiled girls studied at Wesley College, which had been co-educational since 1911 ("in name rather than in practice", thought Hans Reiss):[133] Eva Maria Pick (November 1940 to 1942), Doris Brünn (June 1939 to 1942),[134] and Renate Scheyer (1939–1940), while others were sent to girls-only schools: Liselore Hopf (to Alexandra College, Earlsfort Terrace, from 1939 to 1941) and Anna Maria Tuchmann (Loreto College, St Stephen's Green, 1937 and 1938); St Margaret's Hall School on Mespil Road educated Erica Fischer (January to September 1939), her sister Lisa (January 1939 to January 1940) and Eva Maria Pick (from November 1943).

The German school system had ill prepared these students for the peculiarities of Irish secondary schooling. Apart from grappling with the new language, they had to adjust to the rules and conventions of boarding schools, which differed greatly from the separation of school and family life they were used to in their homelands. Other unfamiliar factors were the school uniforms, the prefect system, the pervasive role of religious ritual in Irish confessional schools, the different styles of teaching and communication between teachers and students, the strict gender rules, and the much more important role of sports. Moreover, unlike German *Gymnasien*, these schools considered it a prime function to prepare their senior students for entrance and scholarship examinations to a university, rather than primarily impart a classic body of *Bildung*.[135]

---

[133] Hans Reiss, Seven Years in Ireland (unpublished).

[134] The daughter of the head of an insurance company in Vienna, Doris Brünn had been under the tutelage of the Swedish Mission and came to Ireland on a *Kindertransport*. She expected to be reunited with her mother in New York as soon as possible. See correspondence in NAI, DJ 69/80/362.

[135] Our assessment follows Hans Reiss's memories of his experiences at Wesley College, the most exhaustive description of the differences between German and Irish school systems. See his *Erinnerungen,* pp. 103–108; also Hans Reiss, "Wesley College". In: Seven Years in Ireland (unpublished); Hans Reiss, My Coming to Ireland. In: Gisela Holfter (ed.), *The Irish Context of Kristallnacht. Refugees and Helpers.* Irish-German Studies. Vol. 8. Trier: Wissenschaftlicher Verlag 2014, pp. 35–41. Other memoirs are less detailed. Hans Menkes seems to have enjoyed his months at the College and even tried to learn Irish. See his interview, *Visual History Archive,* 18 July 1996. On the other hand it is said that Marianne Lönhardt suffered under the discipline of the Sisters at Loreto School, Dalkey. See Barbara Esser, *Sag beim Abschied leise Servus.* Vienna: Kremayr & Scheriau 2002, pp. 191, 203. The role of sports is emphasised in Reiss's memoirs (see his *Erinnerungen,* pp. 106–107), but it also fascinated Lisa Fischer, the student at St Margaret's Hall. See entries in her 1939 diary, quoted in Gisela Holfter, Marginalised Voices – Women in Irish Exile. In: *Yearbook for the Centre for German and Austrian Refugees.* Vol. 18, Leiden/Boston: Rodopi forthcoming 2017. Individual teachers are remembered for their idiosyncrasies by Reiss (*Erinnerungen,* pp. 104–105). Peter Schwarz recalled that in general "teaching at St Andrew's was excellent" (email to authors, 6 July 2016), but also that his early interest in science had to survive the lessons of his teacher at the College. Peter Schwarz, An Anecdotal Biographical Note. March 1996 (unpublished).

In the years 1938 to 1945, over 40 exiled German-speaking students enrolled in University College Dublin, Trinity College and other colleges, among them some who had graduated from secondary schools in Dublin or elsewhere in Ireland.[136]

Table 2: Exiles and places of tertiary education in Dublin, 1939 – 1945.

Name	University, College	Discipline	Years
Kurt Adler	TCD	Medicine	1941 to 1947
Hanus Drechsler	TCD	Science, Geography	1940 to 1943 1945 to 1946
Lisa Fischer	TCD	Modern Languages	1943 to 1944
Ernst Hirsch	TCD	Science Veterinary College	1942 to 1946
Fritz Hirsch	TCD	Science	1942 to 1946
Liselore Hopf	TCD	Science	1941 to 1942
Herbert Karrach	TCD	Physics, Medicine	1942 to 1943
Einhart Kawerau	TCD	Medicine	1934 to 1940
Wolfgang Pappenheim	TCD	Medicine	1944 to 1947
Georg Pick	TCD	Theology	1943 to 1944
Hans Reiss	TCD	Languages	1940 to 1945[137]
Dietrich Scheff	TCD	unknown	1939
Heinz Scheyer	TCD	Medicine	1937 to 1942
Renate Scheyer	TCD	Languages	1941 to 1945
Peter Schmolka	TCD	unknown	1939 to?
Ottilie Schwarz	TCD	Modern Languages	1942 to 1945
Gertrud Schwarz	TCD	unknown	1940
Peter Schwarz	TCD	Physics, Chemistry	1944 to 1948
Robert Weil	TCD	Languages	1942 to 1946
Georg Bernfeld	UCD	Physics	1942 to 1946
Frantisek Drechsler	UCD	Mechanical Engineering	1940 to 1943 1945 to 1946

---

136 This number does not include John Hennig, who studied architecture in UCD for some semesters, or Ernst Scheyer, who was allowed to participate in Commerce lectures in TCD. For a full picture of all German-speaking refugee students in the timeframe 1933–1945 one would need to take into account also the medical students who came to Ireland in the early years of Hitler's regime (see chapter 1). Another German student at TCD was Franziska Brill, born in Berlin in 1917. She had a German father and an Irish mother, but it is unclear if she came to Ireland as a refugee in 1936. See MAI, G2/0368. The same may be said of Irma Karfunkelstein, born in Berlin in 1923, who arrived in Ireland in 1935 to stay with relatives in Bray, Co. Wicklow. After attending Loreto Convent she also went to Trinity College. See NAI, DJ 69/80/688.
137 He was awarded a B.A. degree in 1943 and PhD in 1945.

Table 2: (continued).

Name	University, College	Discipline	Years
Robert Dubsky	UCD	Civil Engineering	1939 to 1942
Stefan Feric	UCD	Medicine, Therapeutics	1939 to 1941
Otto Glaser	UCD	Physics, Chemistry	1943 to 1946
Ernst Hirsch	UCD	Agriculture	1940 to 1941
Fritz Hirsch	UCD	Agriculture	1940 to 1941
Ludwig Karrenberg	UCD	Medicine	1939 to 1944
Sigurd Kawerau	UCD	Commerce	1936 to 1938
Hans V. Ledermann	UCD	Medicine	1937 to 1939
Richard Marx	UCD	Medicine	1939 to 1943
Edeltraut Reinert	UCD	Dentistry	1936 to 1938
Karl Steiner[138]	UCD	Medicine	1941 to 1942
Robert Steiner	UCD	Medicine	1938 to 1941
Anna Maria Tuchmann[139]	UCD	Medicine	1939 to 1942
Josef Wolfgarten[140]	UCD	Medicine	1938 to 1939
Peter Lisowski	College of Surgeons	Medicine	1942 to 1946
Gerhard Rosenberg	College of Surgeons	Medicine	1939 to 1941
Josefa Stein	College of Surgeons	Medicine	1939 to 1942
Otto M. Falk	National College of Arts	Arts	1944 to 1946
Eva Maria Pick	Technical School Rathmines	Secretarial course	1943 to 1944
Georg Pick	Technical School	Electrical Engineering	1941 to 1942
Alfred Schulhof	Technical School Kevin Street	Engineeering	1940 to 1944
Herbert K. Unger	Technical School Bolton Street	Architecture	1941 to 1944

---

138 Steiner, son of a "wealthy Austrian family", originally wanted to join his emigrant father in the USA. MAI, G2/0484, G2 report 7 September 1939. Before he moved to the capital, he had been provided with accommodation as an ICCR-maintained guest at the house of Colonel Hughes, an acquaintance of Hubert Butler, in Fethard, Co. Tipperary.

139 It is not known when Anna Maria Tuchmann began studying at UCD. In February 1939, UCD President listed her as a student of medicine, residing in the Loreto Order's residential hall on 77 St Stephen's Green and probably living on ICCR grants. NAI, DJ 69/80/31, Coffey to Roche, 9 February 1939. See also MAI, G2/0848.

140 Wolfgarten, born on 5 April 1914, came to Ireland in February 1938, obviously in retreat from anti-Catholic repression in the *Reich*, to study at UCD and prepare himself for a missionary career (he was maintained by an African Missionary society). In a G2 file it is said that his entry had been supported by President Coffey – a hint that possibly at UCD the open door policy shown to

A number of refugee students lived on grants and scholarships. Some successfully obtained sizarships or scholarships – Einhart Kawerau, Hans Reiss, Robert Weil, Heinz and Renate Scheyer, Peter Schwarz and Herbert Karrach – which meant that they were freed from fees and had to pay less for board.[141] Most, however, still needed the continued support, whether full or partial, of the religious charity groups and the ICCR to cover costs; others had to ask their *alma mater* for deferment of fees.[142] Stefan Feric and Hans V. Ledermann roomed at the Jesuits' University Hall in Hatch Street.[143] Anna Maria Tuchmann remained at Loreto Residence Hall during her studies at UCD until she moved to the National Maternity Hospital in mid-1941. Some medical students enrolled at the College of Surgeons to escape the higher fees at UCD or TCD.[144] Aspiring doctors lodged at the Royal City of Dublin Hospital in Upper Baggot Street, the National Maternity Hospital in Holles Street or the Rotunda Hospital during their practical training.[145]

What also attracted exiles to the city was the growing social scene. Its focal spot was the Old Vienna Club (see above).[146] Some exiles took up residence in the Club, though rarely for longer than a year. As a rule, the Club hosted temporary residents waiting either for employment, or private rooms, or permits for

---

Catholic students began earlier than in mid-1938 (see chapters 6 and 9). In his student days he lodged at a "private hotel" on Harrington Street (Stein's Kosher Hotel?) and from January 1942 at 19 Brighton Avenue, Rathgar. In G2 circles it was assumed that he could have been of Jewish origin. At the end of his medical studies in June 1944 he left for England (see chapter 10). MAI, G2/240; G2/x/1091, 27 October 1942.

141 Again Hans Reiss provides the most detailed description of TCD scholarships in general and his own academic achievements in particular (especially in his Seven Years in Ireland). For UCD scholarships, only one case (Otto Glaser) can be documented. See note in *Irish Times*, 11 November 1943. The Hirsch brothers, non-boarders, sought admission to TCD because the National University had demanded tuition fees which they could not afford. See TCD Archives, Mun/Sec/248/ref/14, The Chapter House, Christ Church Cathedral, to Provost TCD, 2 December 1940.

142 One such case was Richard Marx. Even as late as 1959, he owed UCD part of his tuition fees. District government Düsseldorf, no. 235.139, Karsten, lawyer, to District government Düsseldorf, 23 June 1959.

143 NAI, DJ 69/80/93.

144 See Price, *Somewhere to Hang My Hat*, pp. 116, 156.

145 This had to be paid for. An example: the medical student Karl Steiner asked the Church of Ireland refugee committee for a grant, as residence fees at the Upper Baggot Street Hospital were very high. RCBL, JS, 9 September 1941.

146 Among the students intermittently residing at the Old Vienna Club, the names of Bernfeld, Feric, Sigurd Kawerau, Georg Pick, Schulhof, Karl Steiner, Kohlseisen, Unger and Marx are on record. The gender restrictions in the Club rules were not strictly enforced, as Mimi Höfer roomed in Club premises from 1 October 1940 to 21 October 1941. MAI, G2/0485.

the UK.[147] Austrians from the provinces also lodged here during their visits to Dublin (for example, Anselm Horwitz or Ludwig Heinsheimer).[148] The Club restaurant offered Viennese meals at reasonable prices, a welcome change also to some native Dubliners from "the usual cabbage and bacon we had".[149] In 1943, Ignaz Schulz, looking back on his ten-weeks' board in the Club, noted that they had had "two nice Christmas parties, one evening there was some dancing, also good music, singing and so on" in a pseudo-Viennese atmosphere.[150] A few months later he listened to "an interesting lecture about Red Cross work".[151] In early 1943, however, he noted that, in general, cultural events like "lectures, recitations, conversation and such like" had become rare, obviously due to changes in the lives of the young exiles since 1941, such as onward emigration to the UK or the increasing demands of work and academic studies.[152]

These new circumstances may also have accounted for the early closure of the Dublin Overseas Club in 1941–1942.[153] Supported by the Quakers and run by its secretary and organiser Harold Douglas (Senator James Douglas's son), it offered lectures and performances dealing with various countries, among them some

---

147 Two examples: Richard Marx stayed at the Club to bridge the time until his departure for the UK, see MAI, G2/2097; also registration card and telegram Huggard to Medical Department Bloomsbury House, 10 April 1943. Ignaz Schulz boarded here between his departure from Glenstal Priory (see chapter 7) and his passage to the UK in 1944. See correspondence in MAI, G2/0763.
148 See correspondence in G2/0492 (Horwitz) and G2/0456 and 0457.
149 Memory of an exile's wife who wished to remain anonymous.
150 According to Ignaz Schulz the Club management served inexpensive "native Viennese cooking, genuine Vienna taste". He also noted that the rooms were "clean and comfortable". MAI, G2/0763, Schulz to secretary FAM, 5 March 1943. Since wine was not always available, a typical Viennese "Heurigen" atmosphere could be difficult to stage. Sherry was served instead. Interview Fritz Hirsch with authors, 14 November 2004. The original rules of the Club had outlawed any alcoholic drinks. G2/x/0450.
151 MAI, G2/0763, Schulz to FAM, 20 November 1943.
152 MAI, G2/0763, Schulz to secretary FAM, 5 March 1943. One memorable event had been a public discussion in 1940 on "Ireland and Austria". See Paul Dubsky, The Dubsky Family. In: Gisela Holfter (ed.), *The Irish Context of Kristallnacht. Refugees and Helpers*. Irish-German Studies. Vol. 8. Trier: Wissenschaftlicher Verlag 2014, pp. 57–64, 60.
153 In a letter of 5 February 1941, a Rosy Newey had already anticipated the imminent closure of the Dublin Overseas Club premises. MAI, G2/0510. A G2 agent referred in mid-1942 to the "late Overseas Club". MAI, G2/x/1091. The exact date and causes of the closure are uncertain. George Lewy blamed the disproportionately strong influence of some Jewish members for its premature end. George Moore-Lewy, Yesterday. In: Esther Moore & George Moore-Lewy, A Sister and Brother Remember – Wechterswinkel to Dublin and a Little Beyond. Unpublished and undated, p. 62. Thanks to Anne Mossop and Anne Lindsay.

exiles' home countries (Austria, for example).[154] Such events were staged every three to four weeks in "The Country Shop" at 23, St Stephen's Green.[155] 57 German-speaking exiles of all groups were listed as members.[156] Some senior exiles belonged to the Dublin Overseas Club board of active "Fellows": Ernst Scheyer, Adolf Adler, Richard Kappeler, Hans Sachs, and Philip Moddel, among others.[157] Another facility was the ICCR's Refugee Social Club, where exiles and their Irish supporters, Quakers as a rule, could informally meet for discussions and other social activities. The Quaker Monthly Meeting had granted the use of its Tea Room in Eustace Street, and during the founding year, 1941, the Club's meetings took place there every fortnight from 7.45 to 11 pm.[158]

The lure of the city was not confined to demarcated places where exiles met only exiles. Dublin, like other capitals of neutral states, offered social and cultural attractions that made it one of the more exciting places of war-torn Europe. Though hurdles stood in the way of participation (language, money, the problems of public transport, age, different cultural interests, and so on), individual exiles crossed social boundaries, helping to give Dublin "a certain international atmosphere".[159] The Unicorn catered for a mixed clientele of Dubliners and non-Dubliners, who sought to enjoy a Viennese atmosphere and a "very high standard of continental cooking". It was said that "people would go there for coffee and

---

154 The DOC probably catered mainly for members from "First World" countries. Another Overseas Club in Leeson Street provided social opportunities for 50 to 60 Asian and African students who stayed in Ireland during the war. It was run by Frank Duff's Legion of Mary and was opened on 13 July 1940. It is not known how it was institutionally related to the Club at 23 St Stephen's Green, nor how long it lasted. Its programme provoked the rage of the Catholic episcopate. See Finola Kennedy, *Frank Duff - A Life Story*. Burns & Oats: London/New York, 2011, pp. 165–166.
155 A typical DOC program at "The Country Shop" was a "Musical Evening of the Nations" which was staged by representatives of twelve nations. It was initiated by Moddel, the "musical lecturer" within the DOC's Fellowship, and the Austrian refugees, including Adolf Adler and Richard Kappeler, were asked to form an "Austrian Preparatory Committee". MAI, G2/3190, Adler to Kappeler, 27 January 1941.
156 See names in two lists compiled by the G2. MAI, G2/x/0540, G2 report, 13 November 1940.
157 Scheyer seems to have been an organiser and initiator of DOC events, and Hans Sachs gave one or more lectures. Kappeler, a man of many talents – the *Irish Independent* called him a "novelist, poet and essayist" (13 January 1942) – performed at a number of "musical lectures" with violin accompaniment. MAI, G2/0510, Scheyer to Kappeler, 26 February 1941, and other correspondence. It is very probable that Rosa Kobler, his mother-in-law, also took the stage at the Dublin Overseas Club.
158 SFHD, MM, D 19, 7 February, 7 March, 10 April, 9 May, 11 July, 12 September, 11 October, 7 November, 12 December 1941.
159 Patrick Kavanagh, quoted in Terence Brown, *Ireland. A Social and Cultural History 1922–2002*. 2nd edition. London: Harper Perennial 2004, p. 165.

sit for hours."¹⁶⁰ While Lisl Strunz worked in the kitchen or stood at the door explaining the continental dishes (according to her husband she had no practical "idea of cooking, or business management"), Erwin discussed the merits of French wines with his "Dublin notables", and made music: "During Christmas 1940, when all the lights had gone out over Europe, I played my guitar in the restaurant and sang Christmas carols and folk songs in eight languages."¹⁶¹ He later claimed that "it wasn't long before 'The Unicorn' restaurant became the most famous restaurant in Ireland."¹⁶² Possibly, Jammet's eclipsed the Unicorn as to formality, culinary quality and prices. Some regarded it as the "best restaurant this side of the Atlantic from the fall of France to the Liberation".¹⁶³ Among the regulars in both restaurants were writers, actors and artists such as members of the White Stag Group, self-styled modernisers who had come from the UK at the beginning of the war to become what Wills called perhaps the "most adventurous and active of the new wartime ventures".¹⁶⁴ Robert Hirsch and Serge Philipson, who reached some prominence in the developing art scene of the capital, would come to the Unicorn from their office rooms at nearby 24 Suffolk Street, and both

---

160 Maurice Craig in Grob-Fitzgibbon, *Irish Experience*, p. 114.
161 The quotations are from Erwin Strunz, Memoir, June 1989, unpublished, p. 25; Strunz, "An Escape from Hell", *Irish Times*, 19 December 1988; Peter Strunz, letter to *Irish Times*, 18 May 2007. Denis K. Henderson, son of Ruth Henderson (née Brandenburg), called the Unicorn "this peaceful artists' and writers' Mecca". Letter to *Irish Times*, 24 May 2007.
162 Strunz, Memoir, June 1989, p. 25. He supports his sweeping claim with an impressive catalogue of celebrities: "We had all the creme [sic] of Irish Society, the government, the leaders of literature and all the famous women writers, like Kate O'Brien, Maura Lafferty, Ethel Mannion, as well as the theatre people – the famous Micheál MacLiammóir and Hilton Edwards of the Olympia and Lord Longford and his wife Lady Christina of the Gate Theatre. We also were patronized by the leading painters of that time, like O'Sullivan, Jack Yates [sic], Kernoff and others. Other prominent guests were Randolph Churchill, the grand-nephew of Winston Churchill, Elizabeth Taylor and Walt Disney, the man who invented Mickey Mouse, beside the landed gentry of Ireland." Ibid., pp. 25–26.
163 Ryan, *Remembering How We Stood*, p. 46. See also Máirtín Mac Con Iomaire, Hidden Voices from the Culinary Past: Oral History as a Tool for Culinary Historians. In: S. Friedland (ed.), *Food and Language*. DIT, School of Culinary Arts and Food Technology, online conference paper 2010 http://arrow.dit.ie/cgi/viewcontent.cgi?article=1008&context=tfschcafcon [last accessed 24 November 2015]: "The leading French chefs, the brothers François and Michel Jammet, opened a restaurant in Dublin in 1901, which up to its closure in 1967 remained one of the best restaurants serving haute cuisine in the world."
164 Wills, *Neutral Island*, p. 283. Erwin Strunz, "Escape from Hell", *Irish Times*, 19 December 1988; Fitz-Simon, *Eleven Houses*, pp. 167–168. Yvonne Jammet herself was counted as a White Stag painter. See Máirtín Mac Con Iomaire, Louis Jammet. In: James McGuire and James Quinn (eds), *Dictionary of Irish Biography*. Cambridge: Cambridge University Press 2009, Vol. 4, pp. 956–958.

were also regulars at Jammet's.[165] Younger exiles, however, could have hardly afforded frequent visits to a restaurant like Jammet's. A casual suggestion in a letter of 1941, "we could meet in the city at a place you like – Bewley's, Savoy, and so", shows what would have been within their range.[166]

Exiles and modernisers would also flock to the new Gate Theatre (on the grounds of the Rotunda Hospital) and the larger Gaiety, where the MacLiammóir/Edwards Company performed from 1940 onwards. Especially the Gate Theatre catered for an audience fascinated with continental avant-garde theatre. Hans Reiss and the younger von Glasersfeld and his wife were ardent theatre goers, the latter undertaking long trips from their farm at Kilternan, by bus and horsetrap, to be present at performances and their after-parties.[167] They found access to a circle of people closely affiliated with the Gate: Lord Gordon Glenavy (see chapter 7), a member of its Board and Michael Scott who had helped with its lease and architecture; and they were friendly with writers Edward Sheehy, Denis Johnston, and Patrick Kavanagh, as well as theatre people like Shelagh Richards, Micheál MacLiammóir and Hilton Edwards.[168] The circle also included political representatives such as Erskine Childers and John Betjeman, the official British Press Attaché.[169] John Hennig deserves special

---

[165] Philipson was one of the art collectors called the "Three Musketeers". See Roisin Kennedy, *The Emergency. A turning point for Irish Art?* www.irishabroad.com/Culture/VisualArts/emergency.asp [last accessed 14 March 2016]. The two others were Louis Jammet himself and Victor Waddington, owner of an important gallery in South Anne Street which exhibited many modern paintings of Irish artists. Robert Hirsch was treated as a special guest at Jammet's, with a table reserved for him. Desmond Hirsch and Jenny Kenny interview with authors, 9 November 2006.

[166] MAI, G2/0813, Rosy Newey to Josefa Stein, 10 November 1941. The Savoy at 16–19 Upper O'Connell Street, considered Dublin's most "luxurious 'atmospheric' cinema" of the time, had on its first storey a "popular restaurant". Marc Zimmermann, *The History of Dublin's Cinemas*, Dublin: Nonsuch 2007, pp. 154–155. It was favoured, for example, by Stefan Feric and Erich J. Priebatsch. MAI, G2/0409, G2 report 13 November 1944; G2/1680, G2 report 15 July 1941.

[167] To Ernst von Glasersfeld, the Dublin theatres "at that time" were "the best in the English-speaking world". Email to authors, 2 August 2006. Reiss recollected his various forays into the cultural life of the capital and specifically remembered attending a performance of *Hamlet* at the Gate as well as meetings with Elizabeth Bowen and John Betjeman. Reiss, *Erinnerungen*, pp. 129–130; also Hans Reiss, Sieben Jahre in Irland 1939–46: Mein Weg in die Germanistik. In: *Jahrbuch der Schillergesellschaft*. Vol. 40 (1996), pp. 409–432, 421; on the theatres, see also Wills, *Neutral Island*, p. 305.

[168] Von Glasersfeld, *Partial Memories*, pp. 83–84, 90–91; von Glasersfeld email to authors, 12 May 2006. On Johnston, see Wills, *Neutral Island*, pp. 195–198.

[169] Young, *Erskine Childers*, p. 103; von Glasersfeld, *Partial Memories*, pp. 66–69. For Betjeman's network see Grob-Fitzgibbon, *Irish Experience*, pp. 109–110; von Glasersfeld email to authors, 12 May 2006; Wills, *Neutral Island*, pp. 185–187.

mention. His intellectual approach transcended the interests of that liberal intelligentsia – which Ernst von Glasersfeld called a "closed society" – and branched into many fields of indigenous culture, some to be found outside the capital. Nevertheless he mingled in these circles and fully appreciated their works.[170] One of his acquaintances was Erina Brady, who may also be included in this mixed panel of exiles and modernisers.[171] Nowadays, she is considered one of the pioneers of modern Irish dance, whose basics she had learned in Germany before 1933. In 1940, she founded the Irish School of Dance Art at 39 Harcourt Street, and moved in the Bohemian circles and "salon atmosphere" (Schrödinger) of the capital, closely observed by G2 agents who mainly knew her as an organiser of "Bottle and Pyjama parties".[172] She, too, frequently left Dublin, trying to take modern dance to the provinces.[173] She was not, however, a refugee in a narrow sense,[174] as is clear from the array of persons she mixed with in Dublin, including 'real' refugees such as John Hennig and Eva Bieler[175] as well as John Betjeman and R.M. Smyllie of the *Irish Times* – and also Eduard Hempel, the German Minister, and his wife.[176]

---

170 His autobiography *Die bleibende Statt* documents his wide range of interests in Irish history, society and culture, including its modernist variants (like the paintings of Jack Yeats, for example). Noteworthy also is his collaboration with Irish abstract artist Mainie Jellett, co-founder in 1943 of the Irish Exhibition of Living Art, and Máirín Allen, a lecturer in the history of art at the National College of Art, for an evening on "European Art" in January 1943. *Irish Press*, 25 January 1943. See also Monica Schefold, Childhood Memories in Ireland from 1939–1956. In: Gisela Holfter (ed.): *German-speaking Exiles in Ireland 1933–1945*. Amsterdam/New York: Rodopi 2006, pp. 249–264, 262–264.
171 Brady, born on 29 May 1891, was the daughter of an Irish father, a former priest, and a German mother, and grew up near Frankfurt/Main. It seems the family moved to Switzerland when Hitler came to power. See Deirdre Mulrooney, Erina Brady: Irish/German Harbinger of Modern Dance to 1940s Ireland. In: Sabine Egger (ed.): *Cultural/Literary Translators – Selected Irish-German Biographies II*, Irish-German Studies 9. Trier: WVT 2015, pp. 11–29, 16. In Switzerland Brady did some work for the Irish Legation at the League of Nations, before coming to Ireland shortly before the war.
172 Mulrooney, Erina Brady, p. 23.
173 Christopher Fitz-Simon remembers a stay in Butler's Maidenhall, where she, wearing a leopardskin coat and a black beret, came to teach her Kilkenny pupils some elements of modern dance production. Christopher's mother thought that "it must be a dreadful step down for her to be running classes in provincial towns in Ireland and dancing the part of a squaw in a semi-professional production of *The Merry Widow* in Dublin." Fitz-Simon, *Eleven Houses*, p. 168.
174 Thanks to her Irish father she had been "indoctrinated" with Irish language, history and geography; furthermore, as Mulrooney also points out, unlike other refugees she was not chiefly seeking safety but was on a private and professional mission – "to set up Ireland's first ever school of modern dance [...] specifically Mary Wigman's *Ausdruckstanz*". Mulrooney, Erina Brady, p. 16.
175 She was familiar in the refugee scene thanks to her acquaintance with Hennig and received assistance from some of the refugees. Eva Bieler, for example, found students for her. MAI, G2/0467, Lotte and Hans Sachs to John and Claire Hennig, 8 February 1941.
176 See Mulrooney, Erina Brady, p. 20.

Dotted with many social opportunities, the city space produced encounters, sought or unsought, with persons of contrasting experiences, status and outlook. In principle, the social zones of exiles on the one hand and representatives of the German Legation or the *Auslandsorganisation* of the Nazi party were separate, the former tending to assemble in places like the Old Vienna Club, the Unicorn, etc., the latter in the Red Bank restaurant on d'Olier Street, for example.[177] Each side was suspicious of the other. Most exiles, having been declared stateless up to 1941, saw no need to communicate with the personnel of the German Legation, but in places like the Palace Bar or Pearl Bar on Fleet Street, frequented by "literary fringemen [...], diplomats, spies, refugees, chancers of many descriptions", an exile might have easily found himself next to Carl Petersen, the notorious press attaché of the German Legation.[178] The same could happen in a Wicklow Mountain retreat known to have been a favourite resort of Germans,[179] or at the Gresham Hotel in O'Connell Street.[180] Accidental meetings at such places were embarrassing, but acrimony could ensue when members of the Legation tried, or were believed to have tried, to cross the line to 'exile territory'. Dublin was one of the hotspots of wartime espionage activities, with spy talk rampant in many settings.[181] In such an atmosphere, stories of transgressions abounded. For example, it was said that a German diplomat's wife had wished to become a member of the Old Vienna Club.[182] Mistrust also thrived within the exile community itself. John Hennig in particular attracted a lot of attention. A "friendly German national"

---

177 For the Red Bank see R. M. Douglas, The pro-Axis underground in Ireland, 1939–1942. In: *Historical Journal*. Vol. 49, no. 4 (2006), pp. 1155–1183, 1161, footnote 19.
178 Peter Kavanagh, *Beyond Affection. An Autobiography*. New York: Peter Kavanagh Hand Press 1977, p. 52. In the quoted sentence, the term "refugees" also comprised refugees from Britain, who would have generally frequented the Shelbourne Hotel (see Campbell, *My Life*, p. 150). For the Palace Bar, see Wills, *Neutral Island*, pp. 75–78 and Maurice Craig's memory that the "whole of intellectual life was mostly polarized" there. Grob-Fitzgibbon, *Irish Experience*, p. 114. Hans Reiss, a good friend of Maurice Craig, remembers meeting R. M. Smyllie, the *Irish Times* editor, in a pub, but only to get a renewed engagement as the TCD columnist for the *Irish Times*. Reiss, *Erinnerungen*, pp. 135–136 (see also chapter 9).
179 For an awkward encounter of Schrödinger with Hempel in 1944, see Grob-Fitzgibbon, *Irish Experience*, p. 117–118. Hans Reiss also remembers a chance meeting with Hempel and his wife in a hotel in the Wicklow Mountains. Reiss, *Erinnerungen*, pp. 153–154. Some such encounters could have taken place at the Kilmacurragh Park Hotel, which had been owned by a German Nazi named Charles Budina, who left Ireland with other members of the German colony on 11 September 1939. In the war years the hotel was run by an Irish caretaker.
180 For the Gresham, see Mark Hull, *Irish Secrets. German Espionage in Wartime Ireland 1939–1945*. Dublin: Irish Academic Press 2004, p. 31. Exiles too could occasionally be seen at the hotel.
181 Wills, *Neutral Island*, pp. 147–162.
182 The attempt was successfully blocked. MAI, G2/0339, G2 report 25 September 1940.

informed G2 at the end of April 1940 that "Joannes [sic] Hennig, German [...] was worthy of attention." Hennig's subsequent movements were closely monitored. For example, when he was invited on a trip to Connemara that summer and notified his local garda station, one of his travel group was contacted and asked to report afterwards.[183] A year later it was seen as "very suspect" that the Hennigs' landlord was an officer in the Local Security Force at Sutton and that Claire Hennig was supposed to be Jewish, "but she is not".[184] Two years later, another warning about Hennig was issued: "A friend who has been on visiting terms with the above told me 'it [the Hennigs' home] is a meeting place for many Germans'."[185] A former boarder of the Old Vienna Club still believes that it was a nest of spies with Friedrich Hirsch its mastermind.[186] There are also stories of encroachments by German officials into the 'exile territory' of the Unicorn.[187] It can easily be imagined that the Legation and the NSDAP *Auslandsorganisation*, fearing anti-German propaganda in Ireland, tried to find an entry into the exile community by keeping track of exiles and especially their residential changes in Dublin.[188] The Old Vienna Club and the Unicorn were places certain to be visited for inspection or provocation, but in the tense political atmosphere of wartime Dublin, both sides acted cautiously. Potential confrontations were handled "unofficially" and did not provoke any public attention. On 17 December 1940, the German Legation made an effort to win over Erwin Schrödinger to the German regime. The physicist, tongue in cheek, proceeded to request an official apology for this approach, stating that he would prefer a breach between him and the embassy.[189] The Legation seems to have succeeded, however, in recruiting some support from a few non-Jewish employees in the new factories (see chapter 7).

---

183 MAI, G2/0467, see also Holfter/Rasche, *John Hennig's Exile*, pp. 32–34.
184 MAI, G2/0467, undated note, probably March 1941.
185 MAI, G2/0467, handwritten note, 2 February 1942: the "many Germans" were later identified as Hans Sachs and Ludwig Bieler – "both ok as far as known". Ibid.
186 Hans Kohlseisen, *Und ich reise immer noch - Die Geschichte des Hans Kohlseisen zwischen Gmünd, Stadlau und Irland*. Ed. by Margarete Affenzeller and Gabriele Anderl. Vienna: Mandelbaum 2015, pp. 89–91.
187 Hempel and company paid a visit to the restaurant. Whether or not this was intended as provocation, it was perceived as an "invasion of the sanctity of the Unicorn by warmongers". The unwelcome guests did not enjoy their meal. Strunz may have intentionally over-salted it, as D.K. Henderson wrote in a letter to *Irish Times*, 24 May 2007. See also Fitz-Simon, *Eleven Houses*, p. 167.
188 Gerry Mullins, *Dublin Nazi No.1. The Life of Adolf Mahr*. Dublin: Liberties Press 2007, pp. 94–95.
189 Entry in Schrödinger's diary, quoted by Braunizer, Memories of Dublin - Excerpts from Erwin Schrödinger's Diaries. In: Holfter (ed.), *German-speaking Exiles*, pp. 268–269.

Any apprehensions on the part of the exiles concerning political exposure were unfounded. Feeling obliged to respect their host country's neutrality, and aware of the reverberations an ideological stance might cause among the divided Irish public, these natural anti-Nazis abstained from any public anti-Nazi pronouncements, though they must have felt repelled by what they knew of the subterranean movements of the IRA or Fascist sympathisers. One exception, however, can be documented. In the first weeks of his Irish life, Peter Brandenburg was provoked by an anti-Semitic diatribe from George Griffin, leading member of various groups of Irish Fascists in the war years, who had polemicised against the allegedly pernicious role of Jewish (and alien) moneylenders in Irish society.[190] On 24 October 1939, Brandenburg wrote a private letter to Griffin, in which he ("a stranger in the country and without any political ambitions") suggested a personal meeting "for humanity's sake", at which "these matters could be settled in a reasonable way".[191] Contrary to Brandenburg's intentions, Griffin gave the letter to the Aliens Registration Office and also informed An Garda Síochána. The meeting took place at Brandenburg's Dublin flat in 22 Upper Cross Road, Rialto, on 30 October. It ended inconclusively, as did the whole incident, although it led to Brandenburg coming under increased suspicion as an "anti-Hitlerite", as noted by one especially enlightened G2 agent. The result of intensified observation in November and December was unspectacular. It was said that Brandenburg avoided notice, went to work, and otherwise stayed at home.[192]

---

190 Hull, *Irish Secrets,* pp. 96–100.
191 The letter had been seized by the censors and was sent to G2. See correspondence in MAI, G2/0014.
192 MAI, G2/x/1091, no. 204.

Chapter 9
Academics in Exile

Academia at its best transcends borders. International links, education and awareness of research developments around the world were (and are) of vital importance, especially in the sciences. These networks played a crucial role when in 1933 shockwaves of threats, forced suspensions, early retirements and large-scale dismissals of formerly cherished scholars reverberated through all German universities and led to an avalanche of desperate attempts to find new positions. The signs of the new age were read correctly by Albert Einstein, who extended a stay in the USA, started in December 1932, and remained there permanently following Hitler's ascent to power in January 1933. Others held on to their positions with varying success for a year or longer. At first, academics (as other civil servants) who had fought in the war were exempt from the new legislation introduced on 7 April 1933 (see chapter 1). The so-called *Frontkämpferprivileg* (privilege for front line soldiers) lasted until September 1935 when the Nuremberg Laws ('Erste Verordnung zum Reichsbürgergesetz') eliminated the *Frontkämpferprivileg* and with it the chance for people with Jewish backgrounds to retain their positions. There were very few exceptions. Even before 1935, there were different interpretations; sometimes decisions were influenced by the specific area of expertise. In rare cases protests by colleagues played a role. None of the academics who came to Ireland still had, at the time of flight, the benefit of their former positions, though most had received (steadily decreasing) pensions, and a few had previously found temporary refuge in other exile destinations. Strauss and Szöllösi-Janze estimate that about 15% or, in absolute numbers, 1,100–1,500 of German professors had emigrated by 1940.[1] In a more recent study, Grüttner and Kinas calculate the proportion as 19.3%, including the small number of academics who left German universities voluntarily due to political convictions.[2] Some found

---

[1] Herbert A. Strauss, Wissenschaftsemigration als Forschungsproblem. In: Herbert A. Strauss et al. (eds), *Die Emigration der Wissenschaften nach 1933*. Munich et al: Saur 1991, pp. 7–23, 10. Also Margit Szöllösi-Janze, Wir Wissenschaftler bauen mit — Universitäten und Wissenschaften im Dritten Reich. In: Bernd Sösemann (ed.), *Der Nationalsozialismus und die deutsche Gesellschaft*. Stuttgart: Deutsche Verlags-Anstalt 2002, pp. 155–171, 159.
[2] Michael Grüttner and Sven Kinas, Die Vertreibung von Wissenschaftlern aus den deutschen Universitäten 1933–1945. In: *Vierteljahrshefte für Zeitgeschichte*. Vol. 55 (2007), pp. 123–186, 141. According to their study, which closely analysed two thirds of German universities, over 60% of the dismissed professors emigrated and of the ones remaining over 20% were killed by the Nazis or committed suicide (ibid., p. 143). Overall, 71.8% were Jewish or 'non-Aryan', 8.8% had a

new work places, and some, such as Erwin Schrödinger (see below) were even sought after, but for many, the process was very difficult indeed.³

Personal interventions were made by some foreign scholars and by German-speaking scholars already abroad, such as Albert Einstein. A number of organisations came together to help academics in need, most notably the Society for the Protection of Science and Learning, founded in London in 1933 as the Academic Assistance Council (AAC) by a small group including William Beveridge,⁴ Leo Szilard,⁵ A.V. Hill⁶ and Ernest Rutherford.⁷ The aim was to provide short-term grants for refugee lecturers as well as trying to assist them in finding new employment. Much of the day-to-day work was done by the administrator Esther (Tess) Simpson.⁸ The funds of the AAC were raised mainly by appeals

---

'non-Aryan' spouse, and the others were dismissed mainly due to their political engagement or strong church affiliation (ibid, p. 144).

3 See for example comment by Walter S. Cook, New York University, Institute of Fine Arts: "Hitler is my best friend; he shakes the tree and I collect the apples." Quoted in Klaus Fischer, Die Emigration deutschsprachiger Physiker nach 1933. In: Strauss (ed.), *Die Emigration der Wissenschaften nach 1933* (following W. M. Clay, Weimar in America. In: *The American Scholar.* Vol. 55 (1985/1986), p. 120).

4 William Beveridge (1879–1963), Indian-born British economist and social reformer who studied in Oxford and was director of the London School of Economics from 1919 to 1937. From early on Beveridge was interested in the causes of unemployment and he is best known for his 1942 report on 'Social Insurance and Allied Service', which was the basis for the reform of the Welfare State under the Attlee government in 1945. While in Vienna in spring 1933 he became aware of the plight of German academics with Jewish background through Leó Szilárd, and upon his return to England instigated the founding of the AAC. He gained the support of numerous leading academics in Britain, and of the Royal Society which provided office space and a first address for funds in May 1933.

5 Leó Szilárd (1898–1964), Hungarian physicist who got his PhD in Berlin and became Max von Laue's assistant. In early 1933, he emigrated to Vienna and then to England, and in 1938 he got a position in the USA. He later came to prominence as the instigator of the 'Manhattan Project', the race for the atomic bomb.

6 Archibald Vivian Hill (1886–1977) was a British physiologist and biophysicist who received the Nobel Prize for Physiology and Medicine in 1922. He was a founding member and vice-president of the AAC.

7 Born in New Zealand in 1871, Ernest Rutherford did his postgraduate studies at the Cavendish Laboratory in Cambridge. He gained the chair in physics at McGill University in Canada in 1898 before moving to Manchester in 1907. A year later he won the Nobel Prize for Chemistry. In 1919 he returned to Cambridge as director of the Cavendish Laboratory, a position he held until he died suddenly in 1937. He is regarded as the father of nuclear physics and was the first president of the AAC.

8 Esther (Tess) Simpson (1903–1996) received a first-class degree in German and French from Leeds University. She worked in Germany, France and Austria and briefly in Geneva with the World Alliance of YMCA, a position she gave up in 1933 to work for a third of her former salary

to the academic community (all academic staff of the London School of Economics agreed to have a percentage of their salary go towards the AAC funds, a measure that was adopted some six years later to a smaller extent in Trinity College, Dublin). Of special impact was an event in the Albert Hall in October 1933 with a speech by Einstein. As the need for support for refugee scholars grew, the Academic Assistance Council was formally re-established in 1936 as the Society for the Protection of Science and Learning (SPSL), with an advisory council, executive committee, grants allocation committee, and a small secretariat. By the outbreak of the war in 1939, some 2,000 scholars had been registered with the Society, the German refugees now being joined by those from Austria, Italy, Spain and a few from Soviet Russia.[9] The SPSL was able to aid at least 900 of them.[10]

Another active group, but with less importance for academics who came to Ireland, was the Emergency Committee in Aid of German Scholars, which was based in New York. Also in the USA was the Rockefeller Foundation, which was mainly interested in extremely distinguished academics.[11] The *Notgemeinschaft Deutscher Wissenschaftler im Ausland* (Emergency Society of German Scholars Abroad)[12] contributed to the relief efforts by providing a direct connection between desperate academics and possible positions at universities abroad through their 'List of Displaced German Scholars 1936' as well as their 'Supplementary List of

---

for the AAC. Some 45 years later she retired, having barely taken any holidays; she kept in contact with many of "her" refugees up to the end of her life. See Jean Medawar and David Pyke, Obituary Esther Simpson. *The Independent*, 24 December 1996, p. 8. For further information see R. M. Cooper, *Refugee Scholar: Conversations with Tess Simpson*. Leeds: Moorland Books 1992 and Katharina Scherke, Esther Simpson und die Aktivitäten der SPSL (Society for the Protection of Science and Learning) im Zusammenhang mit der Emigration deutschsprachiger Wissenschaftler zwischen 1933–45. In: J. M. Ritchie (ed.), *German-speaking Exiles in Great Britain*. The Yearbook of the Research Centre for German and Austrian Exile Studies, Vol. 3. Amsterdam/New York: Rodopi 2001, pp. 121–130.

9 The Royal Commission on Historical Manuscripts, *Report on the Records of the Society for the Protection of Science and Learning, 1933–1987*. London 1988, p. 1.

10 David Zimmerman, The Society for the Protection of Science and Learning and the Politicization of British Science in the 1930s. In: *Minerva*. Vol. 44, no. 1 (2006), pp. 25–45, 30.

11 Among the smaller aid committees were the Jewish Professional Committee and the Comité international pour le placement des intellectuals réfugiés in Geneva, which took the broader remit of looking after refugees of professional classes, including doctors and lawyers. Neither seems to have played a role for refugees who came to Ireland.

12 It was founded in 1933 by Philipp Schwartz. Starting in Zürich it moved to London in December 1935, but had hardly any funds for relief and was generally concerned with investigations of openings, successfully so in South America and the Near East, especially Turkey.

Displaced German Scholars 1937', both published in London.[13] Most of the senior academics who made it to Ireland can be found there: on the 'List of Displaced German Scholars 1936' we find Walter Heitler (p. 97), Ludwig Hopf (p. 52), Hans Sachs (p. 58) and Erwin Schrödinger (p. 101), as well as Hans Motz (p. 99) and Alfred Bloch (p. 36). The 'Supplementary List' from autumn 1937 features Ernst Lewy (p. 12), who had been in Ireland since June of that year, and Peter Paul Ewald (p. 13), who was at that stage in Belfast. The information given on the academics (155 names are included on the Supplementary List alone) was organised according to subject and included former university, academic rank, special areas of expertise and whether and where a new (temporary) placement had been found. Information was also given about when they were born, if they were married and how many children they had, as well as their previous employment history. There were some issues in terms of accuracy, as it was hardly possible to keep track of all individual movements.[14]

Not on the list were later exiles to Ireland such as Leo Pollak, Victor Ehrenberg and Ludwig Bieler who were employed in Prague and Vienna, and thus still out of Hitler's reach.

One needs to keep in mind that at the time academic unemployment was a major issue in most countries – not only in Germany but also even in the USA,[15] which was regarded as a country potentially willing to accept refugees. In Germany in the 1930s the oversupply of university lecturers had reached a stage where there were three fully qualified candidates (meaning that they had obtained not only a PhD but also the necessary second qualification, the *Habilitation*, another independently researched thesis demanded by German universities) for every position and in some subjects even seven candidates per position. That was one reason why Max Planck, Schrödinger's predecessor and one of Germany's best

---

13 Herbert A. Strauss et al. (eds), *Emigration – Deutsche Wissenschaftler nach 1933. Entlassung und Vertreibung*. List of Displaced German Scholars 1936. Supplementary List of Displaced German Scholars 1937. The Emergency Committee in Aid of Displaced Foreign Scholars, Report 1941. Berlin: Technische Universität Berlin 1987.
14 See ibid., appendix. The entry on Ernst Lewy for example includes Finnish and Hungarian languages as well as Sanskrit among his academic specialities, and also classifies him as "unplaced" and "since 1937: London", which was untrue, as in reality he was then in the west of Ireland working on a project with a grant from the SPSL. On the Supplementary List Lewy was named as one of only three academics within Philology; one of the other two was Julius Pokorny, who did not come to Ireland, but thanks partly to Irish support was able to stay in Germany until 1943 before finally emigrating to Switzerland. See below.
15 See Herbert A. Strauss, Vorwort. In: Strauss et al. (eds), *Emigration – Deutsche Wissenschaftler nach 1933*, p. VI.

known and esteemed academics, who tried to help several dismissed colleagues, did not see any chance for public intervention on behalf of the beleaguered academics.[16]

With respect to refugee scholars who came to Ireland, the source material available is quite different from that for many other 'ordinary' exiles. In most cases it is comparatively easy to establish the outlines of their lives before 1933, especially the academic milestones, thanks to their own publications, published letters and material in university archives. From the beginning, there was a different awareness of the scholars, seen as individuals rather than part of the mass of Jewish and 'non-Aryan' emigrants. It is no accident that the first publications in the emerging field of exile studies focused on the academics and their support organisations.[17] In German and international exile studies the exile of scientists and academic teachers from Nazi Germany and their reception in other countries has been a favoured topic since the 1980s.[18] An important result of this research was the *International Biographical Dictionary of Central European Emigrés*, a collective work by international historians, which has documented about 9,000 biographies,[19] among them a disproportionately high number of German-speaking academics[20] but also many other intellectuals and artists. 17

---

16 As shown by his often quoted answer to fellow physicist Otto Hahn's question whether a public appeal should be issued: "Wenn heute 30 Professoren aufstehen und sich gegen das Vorgehen der Regierung einsetzen, dann kommen morgen 150 Personen, die sich mit Hitler solidarisch erklären, weil sie die Stellen haben wollen." (If today 30 professors stand up and protest against the actions of the government, then there will be 150 people showing solidarity with Hitler tomorrow as they want the positions), Otto Hahn, *Mein Leben*. Munich: Bruckmann 1968, p. 145.

17 Norman Bentwich, *The Rescue and Achievement of Refugee Scholars*. The Hague: M. Nijhoff 1953. He also wrote They Found Refuge. London: Cresset Press 1956; William Beveridge, *A Defence of Free Learning*. Oxford: Oxford University Press 1959.

18 See for example Strauss et al. (eds), *Die Emigration der Wissenschaften nach 1933*; Klaus Fischer, Vom Wissenschaftstransfer zur Kontextanalyse — oder: wie schreibt man die Geschichte zur Wissenschaftsemigration? In: Rainer Erb and Michael Schmidt (eds), *Antisemitismus und jüdische Geschichte: Studien zu Ehren von Herbert A. Strauss*. Berlin: Wissenschaftlicher Autorenverlag 1987; Mitchell G. Ash and Alfons Söllner (eds), *Forced Migration and Scientific Change. Emigré German-speaking Scientists and Scholars after 1933*. Cambridge/New York/Melbourne: Cambridge University Press 1996.

19 Herbert A. Strauss and Werner Röder (eds), *International Biographical Dictionary of Central European Emigrés 1933–1945*. Munich et al.: K.G. Saur 1983.

20 Stefan L. Wolff estimates that of the total half million emigrants, 2,000–3,000 (less than 1%) were university scholars. See Wolff, Die Emigration von Physikern während des Nationalsozialismus – ein Geschichtsansatz mit vernetzten Biographien. In: Peter Zigman (ed.), *Die biographische Spur in der Kultur- und Wissenschaftsgeschichte*. Jena: IKS Garamond 2006, pp. 101–115, 101.

of them are recorded as having found reception in Ireland before 1945[21] – not an insignificant number, relative to the size of the country and the total number of its Continental immigrants. Indeed, this research project on refugees in Ireland started with John Hennig thanks to his achievements in Irish-German studies,[22] and initial publications in the context of our research mostly dealt with exiles who had some impact on Irish academia, such as Hans Sachs, Ernst Scheyer, Ernst Lewy, Ludwig Bieler and, of course, Erwin Schrödinger. Schrödinger held a special position among the refugees, as we will see in the section below on the newly founded Dublin Institute of Advanced Studies. Earlier and far more scattered activities at the Irish universities will however be considered first.

At Irish universities

From early on, there was some contact between the Academic Assistance Council (AAC) and Irish universities.[23] More importantly, among the most active members of the Irish Co-ordinating Committee for Refugees (see chapter 6) were university professors, notably Theo Dillon of University College Dublin (UCD) and Robert William Ditchburn (see chapter 6) of Trinity College Dublin (TCD). Ditchburn especially was in close contact with the Academic Assistance Council and later SPSL from the early 1930s onwards thanks to his prior study in Cambridge and contacts with Ernest Rutherford among others. During 1934 he played host to Alfred Bloch (see below in Trinity section) and in July of that year he attempted to form an 'Irish Committee',[24] though seemingly without much success. On 11 February 1935, he received an enquiry from the AAC regarding a letter of appeal and whether it would be worthwhile to circulate it at "the Dublin Colleges". Ditchburn replied by first pointing out the differences between TCD/University of Dublin and the constituent colleges of the National University of Ireland in Dublin, Cork and Galway; he then continued with an assessment of potential support at each institution:

---

21 Though some of them mistakenly, as they only came after 1945, such as Gerhard Bersu, Hans Deutsch (who both went to Northern Ireland) and Immanuel Jakobovits. On the other hand, Kurt Roger had been in Ireland already for some weeks in 1939 (see chapter 10).
22 See Gisela Holfter and Hermann Rasche (eds), *Exil in Irland*. Trier: WVT 2002, and G. Holfter and H. Rasche (eds), *John Hennig's Exile in Ireland*. Arlen: Galway 2004.
23 See for example Bodleian Library, University of Oxford, files of the Society for the Protection of Science and Learning (hereafter SPSL), 127/1/243.
24 See SPSL 127/3/5, R.W. Ditchburn, 3 July 1934.

> My friends and I are of the opinion that it would definitely be worthwhile sending an appeal to members of the staff of Trinity College and that it would not be worthwhile sending it to people in Galway. About Cork and University College [Dublin] our opinions are very divided.[25]

Ditchburn also advised asking the Provost of Trinity (E. J. Gwynn) for a brief letter commending the appeal, and possibly inviting him to serve on the general committee. All suggestions were positively received by the AAC, and its general secretary Walter Adams also informed Ditchburn of a planned letter to be published on March 13, with the signatures of Lord Londonderry, Lord Halifax, Stanley Baldwin, Lord Crewe, Lord Maston and Lord Cecil already secured. Lord Iveagh (the Chancellor of Trinity College) was also to be approached. Ditchburn meanwhile talked to Dr Gwynn and got his support, as he describes in a letter to Adams of 6 March 1935. Ditchburn however remained unsure about the National University of Ireland. He was quite aware of local sensitivities, and his assessment of de Valera is especially interesting – it seems that already at this early stage both de Valera's empathetic personal stance and his outwardly more political manoeuvring were recognised:

> I think that a few people (including the provost) will sign a covering note to your letter to the staffs of the Irish Universities. The difficulty is getting people from the National University to sign. I have to approach people through other people and this means a good deal of delay. However I think it is worth waiting another week before deciding to make this local appeal solely from Trinity people to Trinity people. A joint appeal would look so much better.
>
> In the letter to the papers the phrase Great Britain should be replaced by "Great Britain and Ireland" if it is sent to the Irish newspapers.
>
> I do not know whether you are asking De Valera to sign as Chancellor of the National University. I think it would be worth doing so. Perhaps you might ask that if he was unable to sign himself he should suggest somebody else who would sign on behalf of the National University. He is very keen on trade relations with Germany and might not like to give his name but I think he would be privately sympathetic to your appeal.[26]

In the end, the Chancellor of TCD did not reply in time to appear on the public letter in March 1935. Meanwhile, although Ditchburn got one of the NUI professors (possibly Theo Dillon) to approach Dr Coffey about the appeal for displaced German scholars, it is not clear whether Coffey decided to support it or not. In any case, the appeal was postponed when the Council decided to limit the emergency financial grants at the end of the academic year 1935/1936 and instead to concen-

---

25 SPSL 52/4/30f., Ditchburn to Adams, 22 February 1935.
26 SPSL 52/4/34 & 34r, Ditchburn to Adams, 6 March 1935.

trate on longer term fellowships, partly in cooperation with the Rockefeller Foundation. The idea behind this was to support the most distinguished or promising German scholars, at the cost of others who, it was recognised, "will have to be left to their own resources, if necessary to return to Germany or to abandon hope of an academic career".[27] This approach was in later years to become less restrictive. With ever increasing marginalisation of Jewish and 'non-Aryan' academics, the pressure to emigrate grew, and eventually the overall funding situation and the willingness to take in foreign scholars improved to some extent. For younger academics especially, however, it was generally personal connections (often those of their supervisors) that helped them to enter a new academic environment abroad. In the case of academic refugees to Ireland there was a mixture of well known, distinguished scholars and others at the beginning of their careers, as will be seen in the following section introducing the activities of the individual universities and specifically the refugee scholars themselves.

Trinity College

R.W. Ditchburn was not only engaged with organising institutional support, he was also host in 1934 to the first academic refugee accepted into Ireland, Alfred Bloch. Born 30 years previously into an orthodox Jewish family in Franconia in southern Germany, Bloch had attended a Jewish primary school in his city of birth, Weiden, where he received very intensive tuition, being in a class of only two students.[28] Following schooling in Regensburg and Bayreuth, he studied at the Technical University of Munich, where he was one of the very few Jewish students.[29] He gained a first class degree with distinction in 1928,[30] then a doctorate of engineering in 1932.[31] While continuing to work as an assistant at the

---

27 SPSL 52/4/43f.
28 Historisches Archiv, Technische Universität Munich (hereafter HATUM), Personalakten. Studierende. Bloch, Alfred, Lebenslauf 23 June 1925.
29 According to Wolfgang A. Herrmann, there were only 35 Jewish students at the Technical University in 1929, about 1%; see Herrmann, *Technische Universität München – Die Geschichte eines Wissenschaftsunternehmens*. Berlin: Metropol 2006, p. 242.
30 HATUM, Personalakten A. Bloch. The files show that Bloch's first-class degree received an additional "mit Auszeichnung" (with distinction) following the proposal of 31 May 1928 by one of Bloch's lecturers, Dr Johann Ossanner, who argued that Bloch was only 0.3 grades away in his average from gaining the distinction and, if permitted, he would upgrade some results achieved during the exams to arrive at the necessary average. There was unanimous approval for this proposal.
31 Again first class with distinction, see HATUM, PromA Bloch, A.

university,[32] he was appointed by the German State Railways as research engineer, and invented an advanced system of railway signalling. An academic career seemed possible,[33] but Hitler's ascent nullified such chances, and his contract could not be extended after July 1933. Following a short period as a technical adviser in the private sector, Bloch went to Great Britain in the summer of 1934 with his parents and younger sister. Thanks to the connection made by the Academic Assistance Council (AAC), in late October he went on to Trinity College Dublin, as a guest of R. W. Ditchburn, who had written to the AAC that he could offer hospitality to an unmarried refugee scholar in his College rooms, which were not much used by Ditchburn. Like all married fellows and professors he lived outside College with his family, as women (except the Provost's wife) were not allowed to live in College.[34] The arrangement suited the unmarried Bloch, and also provided him with free meals in College. His time in Dublin, until the summer of 1935, led to at least some tangible outcomes in the form of inventions and articles,[35] as well as an M.Sc. degree from Trinity, all of which probably helped him obtain a position at the General Electric Company (GEC) Research Laboratories at Wembley, where he remained for the rest of his working life.[36] Hoping to take advantage of a preference in certain Irish circles for non-British

---

32 Obituary Professor Alfred Bloch. In: *AJR Information* (July 1979), p. 10.
33 Since November 1929 Alfred Bloch had been an Assistant in Technical Mechanics. His PhD had been praised as outstanding (see report 17 June 1932, HATUM, PromA Bloch, A). The appreciation of his work is also evident in the reference by Professor Ludwig Föppl for his assistant. He praises Bloch's work as excellent and also emphasises his skills at tutorials with several hundred students, but records that due to regulations the contract could not be renewed after 31 July 1933. See SPSL 241/11/411, testimonial by Ludwig Föppl, 1 June 1933.
34 See SPSL 241/11/448, Ditchburn to AAC, 11 September 1934. In his letter to AAC shortly afterwards (on 20 September 1934) Ditchburn goes into more detail about how this could work in practice: "I have two problems waiting for someone who understands photo-cells and if he would tackle one of them I could tell the Board that his presence in my laboratory would cost the college very little. Also the professor of applied mathematics (Dr McConnell) would be interested in his work. He would be willing to help in every way he could I am quite sure. I should hope also to enlist the friendly sympathy of the professor of engineering."
35 Some were communicated to the Royal Irish Academy, some were published, for example: On the Frequency Response of Photronic Cells. In: *Review of Scientific Instruments*. Vol. 6, no. 6 (1935), p. 173. His inventions included a range-finding gadget for cameras which he planned to patent with Zeiss, see SPSL 241/11/478, handwritten note on visit by Ditchburn, 9 April 1935.
36 See Obituary Professor Alfred Bloch, p. 10.

technical experts,[37] Ditchburn had tried to find a position for him in Ireland, but to no avail.[38]

In 1936, a year after the departure of Alfred Bloch, Hans Motz, a 26-year old Viennese refugee, came to stay in Dublin for a longer period. When asked decades later in a questionnaire what he had known about the country to which he was emigrating (and from what sources), Motz's answer was short: "Nothing".[39]

Image 1: Hans Motz.

While still at school, Motz had already been politically engaged as a member of the '*Sozialistische Mittelschüler*' (Socialist Middle School Students) (1924–1927). Later during his studies at the Technische Hochschule in Vienna he was active

---

[37] "It is just possible that some opening might occur for him here. The country is short of technicians and some of the ultra-nationalists here feel that they show their independence of England by employing German or American technicians when there is no Irishman available. Of course, as an Englishman I do not entirely approve of this attitude but I am not unwilling to exploit it in a case like this if I got an opportunity." SPSL 241/11/452, Ditchburn to Adams, 20 September 1934.
[38] As he mentioned in his communication to the AAC, there were also a number of unemployed Germans looking for work who had previously been engaged in the Shannon scheme in Ireland. See SPSL 241/11/478.
[39] Zentrum für Antisemitismusforschung, TU Berlin archive, microfiche material, questionnaire Hans Motz, dated 6 June 1975, for Herbert A. Strauss, Werner Röder project (published version *International Biographical Dictionary of Central European Emigrés 1933–1945*, Vol. II, part 2: L-Z, The Arts, Science, and Literature. Munich/New York/London/Paris: K.G. Saur 1983, p. 837).

in the '*Sozialistischer Studentenbund*' (Socialist Student Union) (1927–1934).[40] He became part of Hermann Mark's[41] research group at the University of Vienna, where he obtained his first degree in engineering in 1932, and in 1935 he received an Austrian PhD. Already in July 1934 he had made contact with the AAC, pointing out that, though he was not a German but an Austrian Jew, his situation was not much better, as "in Austria Jewish people not officially but practically are no more accepted at any academic service."[42] In response, the Dublin research facilities and accommodation were mentioned to him. At that stage, however, he was still covered by a scholarship in France at the Laboratoire de Physique in Besançon. In 1936, with Mark's support[43] and through the connections of the AAC, he finally came to Ireland, officially as a student at TCD, joining Ditchburn's laboratory. His delight about the move is evident in his report to the AAC about his new surroundings:

> I wish to thank you very much for having arranged my coming to Trinity College. I am completely happy here for general and personal reasons. Prof Ditchburn is the most charming man I can imagine, the problem he gave me to work at is the most interesting I have dealt with till now and the conditions of work are the most satisfactory I ever had.

---

40 See Johannes Feichtinger, *Die Wiener Schule der Hochpolymerforschung in England und Amerika – Emigration, Wissenschaftswandel und Innovation*. Graz: University of Graz 2001, p. 44. www.uni-graz.at/johannes.feichtinger/OESHpF_Projekt.pdf [last accessed 1 April 2016].

41 Hermann Mark (1895–1992), originally from Vienna, had started his research in Berlin and Ludwigshafen. In 1932 he became Chair and Director at the Chemical Institute of Vienna University. He left Austria in 1938 and went to live in Canada after short transit stays in Switzerland, France and England. See Wolfgang L. Reiter, Die Vertreibung der jüdischen Intelligenz: Verdoppelung eines Verlustes – 1938/1945. In: *Internationale Mathematische Nachrichten*. Vol. 187, no. 55 (August 2011), pp. 1–20, 5. Among his assistants was Max F. Perutz who had left for Cambridge in 1936; he was awarded the Nobel Prize for Chemistry in 1962. Mark himself went on to the US and founded the Institute of Polymer Research at Polytechnic Brooklyn.

42 SPSL 335/5/161–276, 177A Hans Motz, Hans Motz to AAC, 31 July 1934. His daughter Anna Motz remembers a poignant visit to Vienna in 1984 when her father told her in the University that he had witnessed brutality there in the early 1930s and told her how a fight ensued after all Jewish students had been asked to leave. Email to authors, 6 August 2015. A letter from mathematician Karl Menger to Oswald Veblen, 27 October 1934 is also illuminating about the situation for mathematicians in Vienna; "First of all the situation at the university is as unpleasant as possible. Whereas I still don't believe that Austria has more than 45% Nazis, the percentage at the universities is certainly 75% and among the mathematicians I have to do with, except, of course, some pupils of mine, not far from 100%." Quoted in Sanford L. Segal, *Mathematicians Under the Nazis*. Princeton/Oxford: Princeton University Press 2003, p. 69.

43 In the 1975 questionnaire for Röder/Strauss, Motz also mentions a recommendation by Leó Szilárd. Zentrum für Antisemitismusforschung, TU Berlin archive.

The Board allowed me to have my lunches and dinners in the Common room of the Staff and so I made acquaintances with interesting personalities. I appreciate very much the calm and serene atmosphere of this College. Lying just in the middle of a turbulent storm it is an oasis of calm and concentration of thought. It is lovely situated in a large park with wide sporting places. My rooms look out upon beautiful trees and flower beds.[44]

The positive impression was mutual. Ditchburn worked hard behind the scenes to keep the talented young academic. To improve his dire financial situation, Motz received £20 in August 1936 from the AAC, and also seems to have been supported by the Jewish community in Dublin.[45] He obtained a Master of Science degree in 1937, but his attempts to obtain a position in England failed. In July 1938 things looked up: he was offered a position in Trinity,[46] but opted for a better paid job in London offered by Standard Telephones and Cables.[47] He had been making regular visits to Austria to see his family,[48] and as his attempt to get Irish visas for his parents had failed, this move also gave him a better chance to look after them: when he moved to the UK his mother joined him the same year (his father having meanwhile died in Vienna).[49]

The minutes of TCD board meetings show that political developments had started to leave a mark on their debates by the time Motz arrived. Discussions about the attendance of a TCD member at the Heidelberg University 550th anniversary celebrations in June 1936 show an increasing reluctance to observe academic

---

44 SPSL 335/5/192, Hans Motz to AAC, 12 June 1936.
45 See Strauss, Röder (eds), *International Biographical Dictionary of Central European Emigrés 1933–1945*, p. 837, also Röder/Strauss microfiche material in Zentrum für Antisemitismusforschung, TU Berlin archive. In the questionnaire, Hans Motz answers that it was the offer of help from the Jewish community in Dublin that prompted his departure at that specific time, and that the reason for choice of country was the offer of hospitality by Trinity College. It is unclear, however, what links Motz had established with the Jewish community and what form the help took. In the SPSL files there is a reference to a letter from Edwin Solomons in Dublin to Neville Laski (a prominent British barrister and president of the Board of Deputies of British Jews at the time), asking for help for Hans Motz (after he had already arrived in Dublin). Laski passed this on to the AAC, and A. J. Makower, Chairman, Professional Committee for Jewish Refugees, then replied to Edwin Solomons that the AAC should be his first port of call and that they had assisted Motz previously. SPSL 335/5/161–276, 205, 206.
46 See TCD Archives, Mun/V/5/25, Minutes TCD Board meetings from 1934 until December 1941, 11 June 1938: Dr Motz was appointed an assistant in the Physical Laboratory at a salary of £250 for the ensuing academic year 1938/9.
47 See Feichtinger, *Die Wiener Schule*, p. 46.
48 See NAI, DFA, 102/244, Dr Hans Motz. In 1937, he was even issued a Document of Identity for his forthcoming trip by the Department of External Affairs as he had lost his Austrian passport.
49 SPSL 335/5/257.

niceties in contacts with universities in Nazi Germany.⁵⁰ Whilst on 22 January 1936 it was decided that Dr Ernest Alton was to represent Trinity at Heidelberg's celebratory events from 27 to 30 June, a decision confirmed by a meeting on 3 March, the matter was brought up again at the Board meeting on 21 April (possibly due to developments at University College Dublin, see below) and following a vote (9 votes to 3 with Dr Alton among the 3 dissenters) the decision was reversed. The board meeting on 6 May decided that not even a letter of congratulation should be sent to Heidelberg University.⁵¹

Relations with Heidelberg were to be strengthened in a quite different way, some three years later, as a result of some concerted initiatives on behalf of refugees. In spring 1939, Trinity College was to benefit from two such actions, one initiated externally and one internally, affecting two German refugee scholars of international standing in their respective fields, serologist Hans Sachs of Heidelberg, and mathematician Ludwig Hopf who came from Aachen.

Germany's leading serologist – Hans Sachs

The external development which led to Hans Sachs coming to Ireland came via the Medical Research Council of Ireland, which was established in 1937,⁵² with Robert Farnan, a close friend of Éamon de Valera and professor of midwifery at University College Dublin, as its first chairman, and Joseph W. Bigger, professor of bacteriology and preventive medicine at Trinity, as honorary secretary. The aim of the Medical Research Council was to fund original scientific work and, on occasion, bring in international talent in fields lagging in Ireland, often in close cooperation with their British counterparts. Following a consultation with the British Medical Research Council and the SPSL, which again played a crucial liaison role, Hans Sachs, formerly Germany's leading serologist, was offered a

---

50 Heidelberg was not only the oldest and one of the best known universities in Germany, it was also a stronghold of the NSDAP. See Steven P. Remy: *The Heidelberg Myth: The Nazification and Denazification of a German University*. Cambridge, Mass.: Harvard University Press 2003.
51 TCD Archives, Mun/V/5/25. Trinity College was acting similarly to most British universities in this case. William Beveridge describes in his autobiography the "vigorous discussion [that] raged in the letter columns of *The Times* as to whether or not such invitations should be accepted" (W. Beveridge, *Power and Influence*. London: Hodder and Stoughton 1953, p. 237). He himself argued against it in a letter to *The Times* on 22 February 1936: "The facts of persecution in Germany are naked and undisguised."
52 See also Caoimhghin S. Breathnach, The medical sciences in twentieth-century Ireland. In: *Irish Journal of Medical Science*. Vol. 169, no. 3 (July–September 2000), pp. 221–225, 225.

grant to come to Ireland on 8 February 1939.[53] He was known as the author of several hundred publications and co-editor of the *Zeitschrift für Immunologie und experimentelle Therapie*. In Ireland he was hailed as a famous scientist of European repute who had been "the right-hand man of that genius and benefactor of mankind, Prof. Ehrlich".[54] Born in 1877, the son of one of the wealthiest coal mine-owners in Upper Silesia (who was also a local politician in Kattowitz), Sachs excelled at school and went on to study medicine in Freiburg, Breslau and Berlin.[55] He received his PhD in Leipzig in 1900 (following in the footsteps of Paul Ehrlich, whose doctoral dissertation had been accepted in Leipzig 22 years earlier). In 1905, Sachs married Adelheid Charlotte Grelling (generally called Lotte), aged 20, seven years younger than her husband, from a well-off academic Berlin family.[56] At this stage Sachs had been Paul Ehrlich's assistant in Frankfurt at the *Institut für Experimentelle Therapie* for five years, the Institute having been founded only a year before he joined. In the year of his marriage he became an academic member of the Institute, sharing the joy over Ehrlich's Nobel Prize in 1908 – and himself increasingly recognised, thanks to many well-received publications.[57] In 1907, he became titular professor and in 1914 associate professor at

---

[53] For more details see Horst Dickel, Hans Sachs. In: Holfter (ed.), *German-speaking Exiles*, pp. 183–213, 199.
[54] Kees van Hoek ('Spectator'), Leader Page Parade. *Irish Independent*, 6 February1943, p. 2.
[55] For more detailed background on Hans Sachs, his flight to Ireland and his life there see Horst Dickel, Hans Sachs; John Cooke, Hans and Charlotte Sachs. In: Holfter (ed.), *German-speaking Exiles*, pp. 215–248.
[56] Her father Richard Grelling, a lawyer, journalist and co-founder of the German peace society, and her brother Kurt Grelling, a mathematician and philosopher, had been engaged in public dispute about the causes of World War I, starting with Richard Grelling's publication of *J'Accuse! Von einem Deutschen* (1915) and Kurt's response *Anti J'accuse – Eine deutsche Antwort* (1916). Her mother came from a well-to-do Berlin Jewish family that had a long record of philanthropy (see Cooke, Hans and Charlotte Sachs, pp. 218, 239), her grandmother Ida Simon for example having bequeathed 300,000 Reichsmark to fund medical treatment for poor women – an enormous sum to which her family added another 200,000 Reichsmark (cf. Yvonne Schwittai and Matthias David, Die Geschichte der Frauenkliniken der Charité. In: Matthias David, Andreas Ebert (eds), *Geschichte der Berliner Universitäts-Frauenkliniken: Strukturen, Personen und Ereignisse in und außerhalb der Charité*. Berlin/New York: de Gruyter 2009, pp. 27–51, 41).
[57] Publications by Hans Sachs include the following: *Die Hämolysine und ihre Bedeutung für die Immunitätslehre*. Wiesbaden: Bergmann 1902; contributions to Paul Ehrlich's *Gesammelte Arbeiten zur Immunitätsforschung*. Berlin: August Hirschwald 1904; (with Paul Ehrlich) *Über die Beziehung zwischen Toxin und Antitoxin und die Wege ihrer Erforschung*. Leipzig: G. Fock 1905; *Die Hämolysine und die cytotoxische Sera. Ein Rückblick auf neuere Ergebnisse der Immunitätsforschung*. Wiebaden: Bermann 1907; *Über die Beziehung des Kobragiftes zu den roten Blutzellen* (Müncher Medizinische Wochenschrift). Munich: Lehmann 1908; (with Alfred Klopstock),

Frankfurt University. A year later, when Ehrlich died, Sachs became deputy director of Ehrlich's now world-famous Institute. Sachs's main areas of research were in serodiagnostics, looking at questions of immunology and relations of toxins and antitoxins. Thanks to his work with Walter Georgi, leading to the discovery of the 'Sachs-Georgi Reaction',[58] his name became "a household word in laboratory technology", associated with "one of the first simple and reliable flocculation tests for syphilis".[59]

Image 2: Hans Sachs.

In 1920, the family (a son and daughter had been born in 1906 and 1909 respectively) moved to Heidelberg, where Sachs had been appointed to the post of professor for immunology and serology at Germany's oldest university. He took charge of the immunisation research unit at the 'Institut für Experimentelle Krebsforschung' (Institute of Experimental Cancer Research), and in 1930 he became the director of the newly founded 'Institut für Serologie' and a member of the prestigious Kaiser Wilhelm Society. He was now acknowledged as an internationally leading researcher in his field and a capable administrator, and several decades later was still remembered with gratitude as a great teacher of scientific

---

Methoden der Hämolyseforschung. Berlin et al.: Urban & Schwarzenberg 1928 and *Probleme der pathologischen Physiologie im Lichte neuerer immunbiologischer Betrachtung.* Vienna: Julius Springer 1928.

58 See Hans Sachs and Walter Georgi, Zur Serodiagnostik der Syphilis mittels Ausflockung durch cholesterinierte Extrakte. In: *Medizinische Klinik.* Vol. 14, no. 33 (1918), pp. 805–809.

59 Obituary Hans Sachs. In: *The Lancet.* Vol. 245 (28 April 1945), p. 547.

methods.⁶⁰ He was also among the first German academics to be invited back into international research activities after World War I when he worked for the League of Nations on the commission for the standardisation of serodiagnosis of syphilis. Sachs had become "a centre of attraction" for academics from many countries and he "did much to enhance the reputation of the Heidelberg medical faculty".⁶¹ All this helped when Hitler came to power in 1933. Although initially dismissed, Sachs was reinstated and could continue to lecture and lead his research institute, thanks to the intervention of some eminent Heidelberg colleagues such as Ludolf von Krehl and the then dean of the medical school, Richard Siebeck, who referred to Sachs as "Germany's leading serologist".⁶² The reprieve ended, however, in autumn 1935; following the Nuremberg Laws he was formally pensioned off. He was one of ten (out of 35) directors of the Kaiser Wilhelm research institutes forced to step down since 1933. This time, there were few attempts by colleagues to help him, since it was feared such attempts might endanger the very existence of research institutes.⁶³ It was clear that for Sachs there was no chance of a meaningful academic future in Germany. Sachs hoped for a position in England, where his daughter emigrated in 1936, and wrote to his contacts there. The SPSL tried to follow up on these efforts, but no secure position or fellowship emerged.⁶⁴ Furthermore, it was difficult for Hans and Lotte to obtain their passports.⁶⁵ A young assistant at the Heidelberg institute who had joined the SS, Otto Westphal (himself later a well-known scientist, who still recalled many decades later how important Sachs's teaching had been for his career),⁶⁶ turned out to be loyal and helpful, both on the night of *Kristallnacht* and afterwards, when emigra-

---

60 A. L. Copley, Opening Address of the President of the Society. In: H. H. Hartert and A. L. Copley (eds), *Theoretical and Clinical Hemorheology: Proceedings of the Second International Conference*. Berlin/Heidelberg/New York: Springer 1971, pp. 2–4, 2f. Alfred Lewin Copley (1910–1992) was one of Sachs's PhD students and internationally recognised, not only as a scientist but also as an artist.
61 Obituary Hans Sachs, p. 547.
62 Rudolf Vierhaus and Bernhard vom Brocke (eds), *Forschung im Spannungsfeld von Politik und Gesellschaft: Geschichte und Struktur der Kaiser-Wilhelm-/Max-Planck-Gesellschaft*. Stuttgart: Deutsche Verlags-Anstalt 1990, pp. 105–108.
63 Ludolf von Krehl at least did try again in a letter to Max Planck, but Planck advised restraint. See Rüdiger Hachtmann; *Wissenschaftsmanagement im 'Dritten Reich' – Geschichte der Generalverwaltung der Kaiser-Wilhelm-Gesellschaft*, Vol. 2. Göttingen: Wallstein 2007, pp. 405f.
64 See SPSL 544/3 and Dickel, Hans Sachs, pp. 195–196.
65 Dorothee Mußgnug, *Die vertriebenen Heidelberger Dozenten*. Heidelberg: Winter 1988, p. 153.
66 "From him I learned about the basics of what I needed for my work. He also had an excellent library, maybe one of the best in Germany where I tried to keep up with the latest news in the field of immunology." Otto Westphal, About the History of the MPI for Immunobiology. In: Klaus

tion became more urgent than ever.[67] Another particularly helpful figure was the British Consul-General in Frankfurt, Robert T. Smallbones, who in late November issued visas on his own authority to avoid further delays. While experiencing the almost complete despoliation of their financial assets by the German authorities, the Sachses were at least able to send abroad a considerable amount of furniture and books, and were finally able to leave Germany in the last week of 1938, arriving in Harwich on 27 December. The first weeks in London were marked by uncertainty, and at this stage it was not clear where they would live. When in early February 1939 he received the Irish offer, Sachs did not immediately agree, but it quickly became clear that there would be no avalanche of alternative options. On 20 April 1939,[68] Hans and his wife Lotte arrived in Ireland, together with Lotte's sister Elsa Samter (see chapters 4, 8 and 11).[69] It seems their previous knowledge of Ireland was negligible, perhaps based mainly on the memoirs of nineteenth-century traveller Hermann Fürst Pückler.[70] Hans and Lotte started settling into their new home at 3 Palmerston Villas in Rathmines, greatly helped by having their own furniture, piano and much of Sachs's famous library. His friend Kees van Hoek (writing as 'Spectator' in the *Irish Independent*) noted that they had recreated their Heidelberg home in Dublin:

> The very name-plate on his Rathmines door was that of his Heidelberg house. No other Dublin house had quite like his that atmosphere of Continental culture; his furniture and all the wall-covering bookcases to the graceful porcelain in which coffee was served, it remained Heidelberg, transplanted to Dublin.[71]

Eichmann (ed.), *The Biology of Complex Organisms – Creation and Protection of Integrity*. Basel: Springer 2003, pp. 63–76, 63–64. In turn, Lotte Sachs supported him in his denazification trial in June 1946. See Generallandesarchiv Karlsruhe, BRM 348, Vol. 1.

67 See Frank Moraw, Die nationalsozialistische Diktatur. In: Andreas Cser et al. (eds), *Geschichte der Juden in Heidelberg*. Heidelberg: Guderjahn 1996, pp. 440–555.

68 In a number of studies on Jewish-German scholars and the repression they suffered, the year of his emigration to Ireland is given as 1936: see for example Reinhard Rürup, *Schicksale und Karrieren – Gedenkbuch für die von den Nationalsozialisten aus der Kaiser-Wilhelm-Gesellschaft vertriebenen Forscherinnen und Forscher*. Göttingen: Wallstein 2008, pp. 310–313, 312, Rüdiger Hachtmann, *Wissenschaftsmanagement im 'Dritten Reich'*, p. 405 and others – probably all following the information given in Strauss and Röder (eds), *International Biographical Dictionary of Central European Emigrés 1933–1945*, p. 1007.

69 Incidentally, his name might have been somewhat familiar to people in Ireland, as 'Hans Sachs' was also the name of a successful thoroughbred that won a number of races and made headlines in the mid-1930s. In the German context the name is mainly known as a medieval '*Meistersinger*', a 'master singer' and song writer who was immortalised as the leading character in Richard Wagner's *Die Meistersinger von Nürnberg*, premiered in 1868.

70 See Cooke, Hans and Charlotte Sachs, pp. 223 and 242.

71 Kees van Hoek ('Spectator'), Leader Page Parade. *Irish Independent*, 27 March 1945.

In many ways, they were very well off, with a large flat in nice surroundings, a grant of £500 per annum and some domestic help.[72] Work also provided some stability, though Sachs missed the emphasis on teaching,[73] and found the standard of laboratory equipment and team support not equal to what he had been used to in Heidelberg.[74] But as van Hoek emphasised, Sachs "continued to devote his rarely matched brilliance and untiring energy to his medical research which benefited his adopted country".[75] As well as continuing his publication output[76] and attending conferences, his work included testing some 30,000 blood samples from volunteers of the Local Defence Force.[77] Sachs's work contributed considerably to establishing the Irish Blood Transfusion Council in 1942 and raising

---

72 See Cooke, Hans and Charlotte Sachs, pp. 225–226.
73 In a letter to a fellow émigré he says that to be engaged only in research work is perhaps "the worst job one may have". MAI G2/S/54, Sachs to Lehmann, 21 June 1940. He also reflected in a private notebook on his own working style, and the psychological and practical importance of linked teaching and research as he had known it in the German university system. In Dublin he experienced "what I had avoided in my life – reliance on research work alone" (Notebook 4 July 1940, see Cooke, Hans and Charlotte Sachs, p. 232).
74 These elements were particularly crucial in his field: "I believe that generally I know how to make the best of a situation. But laboratory activity cannot be carried on by oneself, without contact with anyone and to all appearances thrown back on oneself for all practical support. This arises from the fact that my field of work, serology, depends on being organised on a large-scale, serial basis. So I cannot bring anything properly to completion. I go about my work like Tantalus and Sisyphus." (ibid.) Another entry in October 1942 confirms that the situation has not improved: "Nothing has basically changed in my situation [...]. My work situation continues with all its restrictions and impossibilities. I suffer from that. I see on the one hand that my qualifications for research work are no longer sufficient, and on the other want of stimulation or of any possibility for professional partnership." (ibid.) Visitors to his laboratory also remarked on its basic nature. The cold and draughty surroundings particularly were noticed. Van Hoek makes a point of it in both his articles about Sachs: in the article of 6 February 1943 he describes "a self-concocted skullcap against the draughts" worn at Sachs's laboratory in TCD, and in his other article he records that Sachs "fortified himself with screens and a skull cap against Dublin draughts" (Spectator, *Irish Independent*, 27 March 1945). Hans Reiss, too, remembered decades later Sachs's small office where it was freezing during winter time. Email to authors, 8 March 2003.
75 Spectator, *Irish Independent*, 27 March 1945.
76 For example, Hans Sachs, Salt Concentration in Blood-grouping Technique. In: *The Lancet*. Vol. 239, no. 6190 (18 April 1942), pp. 473–474; there his readers were informed of his present affiliation ("From the Department of Bacteriology, Trinity College, Dublin, Ireland"), and next to his name the place where he did his PhD was noted and in brackets and in capitals "Lately Professor of Serology and Immunology in the University of Heidelberg" - a statement by both him and the journal about his rightful place, some three years after he started work in Trinity.
77 Kees van Hoek remembers: "I often went to chat with him, watched him in his laboratory work at Trinity College, as with deft fingers balancing test tubes he worked his methodical way through some 30,000 blood tests of our L.D.F." Spectator, *Irish Independent*, 27 March 1945.

awareness of differences of blood groups among the Irish population – which has a much higher prevalence of blood group O and considerably lower occurrence of blood group A than on the Continent or in England.[78]

Life was not all about work. Thanks partly to his wife Lotte, in Dublin Hans Sachs was quickly integrated into a social network mainly consisting of other refugees such as the Hennigs, Bielers and Heilfrons – and the Tichers, who had come to Ireland before 1933 (see chapter 8). Music was a special bond – John Hennig writes of little concerts that took place every Monday at 3 Palmerston Villas, with Hans Sachs playing piano and Ludwig Bieler singing, often Schubert songs.[79] Ellen Ticher also often arranged "lovely house music".[80] Contacts with work colleagues were also good. John Cooke, Hans' and Lotte's grandson, points out, however, that their last few years in Ireland were depressing. 1942 especially would have been a very difficult year, with their daughter Ilse giving birth to a still-born child in February, and in September the terrible news that Lotte's brother Kurt had been deported east from a prison camp in France and was beyond help.[81]

Health problems also took an increasing toll, and on 23 March 1945 Hans Sachs died of heart failure following an operation. Following his death, the many letters his widow received showed how much his presence in Ireland had been appreciated. Among them was one from Ernest Alton who had been originally supposed to go to Heidelberg. Now Provost of Trinity since 1942, he wrote that

---

[78] See also *Irish Journal of Medical Science*. Vol. 172 (April 1940).
[79] See Holfter and Rasche (eds), *John Hennig's Exile in Ireland*, p. 31.
[80] As Sachs described it in his speech on the occasion of Bertha Teichmann's (Ellen Ticher's mother's) birthday. The speech shows his humorous side and linguistic abilities and includes a self-ironic reference to his work (for the full text see Cooke, Hans and Charlotte Sachs, pp. 59, 244–245):
"When I got the kind invitation to tonight's dinner I was wondering. I was wondering what might be happening. I am well aware that Dr. and Mrs. Ticher like to spend the weekend evenings in their cosy home in Grasmere where all the people of Dublin, the British Isles and the Continent go in and out at any time and where the Tichers sometimes arrange lovely house music if they are not too busy in attending the Saturday dances at the Gresham or elsewhere. Tonight, however, they renounce all pleasure and comfort, only entertaining their guests at Jammet's restaurant. […] But Mrs Teichmann has another merit which we should not forget. Without Mrs Teichmann no Mrs Ticher, without Mrs Ticher no Peter, no Thomas, no Ruth Ticher. The grandchildren have a real father as I have doubtlessly proved by blood-grouping tests."
[81] See Cooke, Hans and Charlotte Sachs, pp. 231 and 245. See also Abraham S. Luchins and Edith H. Luchins, Kurt Grelling: Steadfast Scholar in a Time of Madness. In: *Gestalt Theory*. Vol. 22, no. 4 (2000), expanded 2001 as an internet publication http://gestalttheory.net/archive/kgbio.html [last accessed 27 October 2015].

Sachs "was highly esteemed and valued for his work [...] he had won the affection of all who had contact with him – both professors and students".[82] All major newspapers, North and South, recorded his death: the *Belfast Telegraph*, *Irish Times* and *Irish Press* carried obituaries on 26 March, and on 27 March a longer appreciation by Kees van Hoek appeared in the *Irish Independent*.

Ludwig Hopf – Einstein's first assistant

The internal TCD initiative mentioned previously was set in motion five days before the Medical Research Council decided to invite Hans Sachs to Trinity. On Friday 3 February 1939, a meeting of Junior Fellows and Professors was held in the Common Room, to consider a proposal that the Board of the College should be requested "to appoint to a temporary position on the College staff a Refugee of distinction (chosen from the many now available)".[83] The question of a financial guarantee was also discussed, resulting in two resolutions that were passed unanimously: (1) to appoint a refugee to a temporary position on the staff of the University, and (2) that there were to be invitations

> to members of the College staff, whose emoluments from the College exceeded £500 per annum, to guarantee the salary of such a refugee to the extent of ½ per cent of said emoluments on the understanding (a) that the Board would not call on the guarantee in any year in which they considered that the salary could be made fair charge on the Cista Communis, and (b) that the Board would not, under any circumstances, call on the guarantee in more than three years in all.[84]

The "Refugee of distinction" who was to benefit from this resolution was Ludwig Hopf.

---

[82] See Cooke, Hans and Charlotte Sachs, p. 235. Especially noteworthy is Irish microbiologist William Hayes's experience with Hans Sachs in TCD: "Sachs initiated me into the mysteries of serology and it was from him that I first learnt that what the text books say and the latest hypotheses proclaim are usually grossly over-simplified approximations to reality. Together we studied the nature of an unusual human serum that was falsely positive in the Wassermann Reaction; when heated to destroy the human complement, this serum inactivated the haemolytic properties of the standardised guinea pig complement used in the test. All the ideas in this research came from Sachs's great knowledge and experience, but he generously insisted on my being senior author of the paper that followed - my second publication." Bruce Holloway and Paul Broda: William Hayes 1913–1994. In: *Historical Records of Australian Science*. Vol. 11, no. 2 (December 1996), pp. 213–228, 215.
[83] TCD Archives, Mun/Sec/248/ref/2.
[84] TCD Archives, Mun/Sec/248/ref/9.

Born on 23 October 1884 in Nürnberg into a family of well-established hop merchants, Hopf had studied mathematics and physics at the best German universities at Berlin and Munich and in Zurich from 1903 onwards, and was clearly a good candidate.[85] He had completed his dissertation under Arnold Sommerfeld,[86] one of the most esteemed mathematicians of his time, in Munich in 1909. During this time, he had also worked closely with Paul Ewald and Peter Debye. After being introduced to Albert Einstein by Sommerfeld in September 1909 he became Einstein's assistant in Zurich and Prague, before moving in 1911 to Aachen where he completed his *Habilitation* in 1914. The connections to Sommerfeld and Einstein, who thought very highly of Hopf and also shared his love of music, remained. In 1923, Hopf became full professor for mathematics and mechanics at the Technical University in Aachen. Following his hydrodynamic studies for his PhD and *Habilitation* he turned to aerodynamics during WWI, working closely with the key figures of the time, Richard Fuchs and Theodore von Kármán.[87] Later, he published on the theory of relativity and made his name as an author in a series on 'understandable science'.[88] His long list of publications also includes two papers jointly authored with Einstein[89] and one with Sommerfeld.[90]

Hopf proved his administrative abilities as Dean of the Faculty of Science. He was at the helm of the *Außeninstitut* (the External Institute, representing humanities and social sciences at the Technical University in Aachen) and also took charge of Kármán's Aachen Institute for Aerodynamics when Kármán was on sabbatical.

---

85 For more information on Ludwig Hopf's background see Gisela Holfter, Ludwig Hopf (1884–1939). In: Ian Wallace (ed.), *Voices in Exile*. Amsterdamer Beiträge zur Germanistik. Leiden/Boston: Brill/Rodopi 2015, pp. 113–140.
86 See also Michael Eckert, *Arnold Sommerfeld. Science, Life and Turbulent Times, 1868–1951*. New York: Springer 2013 on the importance of Sommerfeld who, together with Max Planck, Albert Einstein and Niels Bohr, is regarded as one of the founding fathers of modern theoretical physics and an unequalled teacher and supervisor.
87 Ludwig Hopf and Richard Fuchs's book *Aerodynamik* (Berlin: Schmidt 1922) was the key text on the topic for many years.
88 *Relativitätstheorie*. Berlin: Julius Springer 1931; *Einführung in die Differentialgleichungen der Physik*. Berlin: de Gruyter 1933; *Materie and Strahlung*. Berlin: Springer 1936.
89 Albert Einstein and Ludwig Hopf, Über einen Satz der Wahrscheinlichkeitsrechnung und seine Anwendung in der Strahlungstheorie. In: *Annalen der Physik*. Vol. 33 (1910), pp. 1096–1104. Also Einstein and Hopf, Statistische Untersuchung der Bewegung eines Resonators in einem Strahlungsfeld. In: *Annalen der Physik*. Vol. 33 (1910), pp. 1105–1115.
90 Ludwig Hopf and Arnold Sommerfeld, Über komplexe Integraldarstellung der Zylinderfunktionen. In: *Archiv der Mathematik und Physik*. Vol. 3, no. 18 (1911), pp. 1–16.

Image 3: Ludwig Hopf.

Already in his student days in Munich he had been popular as an outstandingly gifted teacher. He was an excellent musician, interested in art and in psychology (he introduced Einstein to C.G. Jung) and had a happy home life. His wife Alice also came from Nürnberg, and he got on so well with his parents-in-law, Dr Ferdinand and Sidonie Goldschmidt,[91] that they eventually moved to Aachen, lived next door and were part of his social circle.

In April 1933, Hopf was suspended, as he was accused of being a communist. While this accusation was not upheld, he was officially dismissed in January 1934 because of his "non-Aryan origin", despite having been a *Beamter*, a public servant since 1914 and active in World War I[92] and despite support from the Faculty of Science in Aachen.[93] His greatest concern was for his five children, Hans (born in 1913), Peter (1915), Arnold (1916), Dieter (1918), and his youngest, the only daughter, Liselore (1921). Both Sommerfeld and Einstein supported his attempts to emigrate from 1933 onwards, but without much success until 1939.[94]

---

[91] Ferdinand Goldschmidt had been an esteemed physician in Nürnberg and author and editor of several publications on the public health service.

[92] See Ulrich Kalkmann, *Die Technische Hochschule Aachen im Dritten Reich (1933–1945)*. Aachen: Verlag Mainz 2003, especially pp. 120–140.

[93] RWTH Aachen archive, Carl Wieselsberger, Dean, on behalf of the Faculty of Science, no date; see also Holfter, Ludwig Hopf, p. 125.

[94] See Hebrew University Jerusalem, Einstein Archive, no. 13/346, Einstein to Kármán in Pasadena, 25 February 1939: "All attempts so far to do something here for Hopf did not lead to anything. We also tried in vain to get his very good and popular books published [here]. But it is clear to me that we can't leave him in the frying pan. It seems to be clear to me now that despite his good academic reputation no university will take him as he is not young enough anymore. Don't you

Hopf was distraught to be expelled from "the only community to which one actually belongs", but remained initially ambivalent regarding leaving Germany.[95] The continuing and growing exclusion hurt,[96] but he kept working on his research.[97] He also found solace in music, playing (as he had previously done with Albert Einstein) with his son Dieter, a gifted violinist. They occasionally played Hopf's favourite piece of music, the Largo of Bach's *Violin Sonata No 5 in F minor*.[98]

The events of *Kristallnacht* led to Hopf's son Arnold (apparently pretending to be his father) being brought to the KZ. He was released three weeks later because he could demonstrate the possibility that he would emigrate to Kenya. Rescue efforts for Hopf by fellow physicists and mathematicians intensified, notably by Sydney Goldstein and Geoffrey Ingram Taylor in Cambridge and Paul Ewald, a fellow Sommerfeld pupil and refugee who had found a position at Queen's University Belfast. At last, in late January 1939, the longed-for offer from the SPSL reached Hopf at his home in Eupener Strasse 129 in Aachen:

> I have the pleasure of letting you know that my Committee has decided to make you a grant at the rate of £250 a year, in the first instance for four months from the date of arrival in

---

think that it is somehow possible to organise some irregular teaching position for him, whether at a university or by organising a lecture circuit? He is such a wonderful teacher and has surely improved his English in the meantime sufficiently for this. Dear Karman, I am totally isolated here and have no connections to academics. But Hopf worries me to the core. If you give me any links I would be happy to write everywhere." Translated by authors.

95 "Going abroad would mean exile for me. I would only do this if forced, so that the children have a home again," Hopf to Sommerfeld, 24 May 1933. In: Arnold Sommerfeld, *Wissenschaftlicher Briefwechsel*, Vol. 2. edited by Michael Eckert and Karl Märker. Berlin/Munich: Deutsches Museum/Verlag für Geschichte der Naturwissenschaften und der Technik 2004, p. 386.

96 His exclusion from the 'Physikalische Gesellschaft' was particularly painful at official events such as the one organised for Arnold Sommerfeld's 70th birthday in December 1938. As he writes consolingly, however, on 3 December 1938 in his congratulation letter to Sommerfeld: "Forget for a few days all gloom! I'll surely be there for your 75th and 80th." Deutsches Museum Munich archive. Thanks to Michael Eckhart.

97 See also Paul P. Ewald, Prof. Ludwig Hopf. In: *Nature*. Vol. 145, no. 3671 (9 March 1940), p. 380: "More recently, Hopf studied the methods of solving linear differential equations in separate domains with the view of finding the relation between the corresponding solutions. A first paper appeared in 1935, and important applications were to follow."

98 Hopf to Sommerfeld, 28. June 1933, in Sommerfeld, *Wissenschaftlicher Briefwechsel*, p. 390. Music was clearly an important part of his identity, and one that he thought of as particularly German – in the same letter he mentions the most wonderful records he got from his mother-in-law, with Bach's D minor piano concert, which, he says, conjures up the "heretical thought" that he must be after all "a real German" whereas the current rampage is more part of the "Slavic-Barbaric-Bolshevik world".

Great Britain, to enable you to continue research if possible with Professor Taylor and Professor Jones in Cambridge.[99]

The Home Office agreed to allow Hopf's research work, and advised that he should apply through the nearest British Consul to the British Passport Control Officer in Berlin. In early March, however, it became clear that authorisation for Hopf's wife Alice was missing. After this was rectified, Ludwig, Alice and Liselore Hopf left Germany, arriving in London on 26 March 1939 and staying at 105 Finborough Road, SW10 for the first few days before arriving in Cambridge on 1 April. By then, two of their sons were in England, one in the USA and one in Kenya. Three weeks later Dublin became an option. On 22 April, A.J. Leventhal, Secretary to the Registrar of the University of Dublin, Trinity College, informed the SPSL that it had been decided that subject to a satisfactory interview, they wanted to invite Professor Ludwig Hopf "to act as a special lecturer in Mathematics for 12 months at a salary of £300".[100] In Trinity, as it was thought that Hopf was still in Aachen, some difficulty was anticipated as regards the interview ("we can't really send a member of our Staff to Aachen") and it was proposed that Hopf was to travel to London in late May when TCD Provost Dr Thrift was to be there.[101] Given the new situation, Hopf could travel from Cambridge to Dublin instead, and informed the SPSL with obvious delight on 15 May 1939 that he had been accepted.[102] He indicated that he hoped to go over soon, in early June, but as his first salary from TCD was only to be paid in September he needed an extension of the SPSL grant, which was duly made. By the middle of June, however, the permission of the Irish government was still outstanding. Trinity asked Hopf to send his CV. The delay was mainly due to Trinity College; as late as 7 July the Registrar wrote to the Minister of Justice stating that Hopf, while his professional qualifications seemed "unexceptional", was undoubtedly a mathematician of great and special attainments. The problem was that rumours of Nazi connections had come to the ears of the Trinity Board:

> We do not know, however, anything about his political associations. He is, according to his own accord, of Hebrew extraction, though he is not now an active member of that religious community. It has been presented to us that a certain number of Nazi agents are connected with Aachen, and we think it right to draw your attention to the fact that Dr Hopf comes from Aachen. We would be glad to know he has no political ties of an undesirable or extreme

---

99 SPSL 503/3/416, David Cleghorn Thomson to Ludwig Hopf, 27 January 1939.
100 SPSL 503/3/438.
101 SPSL 503/3/441, E. H. Elton, Registrar, TCD, to Assistant Secretary, 28 April 1939.
102 SPSL 503/3/445f., Hopf to SPSL, 15 May 1939.

type. We have not had any reason to believe that he has such ties, and the one interview I myself had with him gave me the impression that he was a Professor and nothing else.[103]

Despite these potential misgivings permission was granted and on 17 July the Hopf family (now consisting of Ludwig, Alice and Liselore Hopf and Alice's parents Sidonie and Ferdinand Goldschmidt who had followed to England) arrived in Dublin. Ten days later Hopf informed the SPSL that his appointment in Ireland had been approved by the Government, and he and his family had settled down at his new address in 65 Kenilworth Square, Rathmines. As much as possible, he kept in contact with former friends and colleagues on the Continent (for example writing to his cousin that he was now in a "very beautiful, very famous and very expensive corner of Europe" and that he hoped now to be in a position to start publishing again),[104] and got to know fellow academics in exile in Ireland such as Hans Sachs. While worrying about his sons in England after the war broke out, he busied himself planning his lectures, which started in October, and trying to improve his English.[105] It seems to have taken a while before colleagues from his new academic home opened their doors to social events; it was not until mid-November that he and Alice were for the first time invited to tea.[106] But overall, and despite being in reduced material circumstances, he settled quickly in his new life and enjoyed his lecturing.[107]

---

103 NAI, DJ 69/80/429, Alton, Registrar TCD to Minister of Department of Justice, 7 July 1939. One could speculate that the "Nazi agents connected with Aachen" might refer to Jupp Hoven and (or) Helmut Clissmann, who were viewed with distrust. For some background on Clissmann and Hoven see Mervyn O'Driscoll, *Ireland, Germany and the Nazis – Politics and Diplomacy, 1919–1939*. Dublin: Four Courts 2004, pp. 250–251.
104 ETH-Bibliothek Zürich, Hochschularchiv, Hs 621: 725–726, Ludwig Hopf to Heinz Hopf (a fellow scientist who knew the Schrödingers), 18 November 1939.
105 As he wrote to Otto Blumenthal, his former colleague and friend in Aachen (and then in exile in the Netherlands) on 24 September 1939: "My lectures will begin in 4 weeks time; I have plotted a lot of them and hope to have enough self-confidence (or impudence) to go on." Letter in the papers of the Blumenthal family: thanks to Volkmar Felsch for providing a copy. The Hopf family appears frequently in the recently published diaries of Otto Blumenthal (1876–1944) who was killed in November 1944 in Theresienstadt concentration camp.
106 Ludwig Hopf to Arnold Hopf, 16 November 1939. Thanks to Willie Walshe and the Hopf family in Kenya.
107 He wrote to his cousin in Switzerland that it was astonishing how far one got with boldness in the use of a foreign language, mentioning also that his grant covered food, but not clothing: see ETH-Bibliothek Zürich, Ludwig Hopf to Heinz Hopf, 18 November 1939. Hans Reiss recalls a lunch in Hopf's flat during which Hopf expressed his disappointment that he had only a few students in his classes and hoped that more would in due course attend his lectures. Reiss email to authors 23 June 2015.

On 21 December 1939, however, only some five months after his arrival in Ireland, Ludwig Hopf died from thyroid failure after a short illness. Again and again after his death, the contrast was recalled between his happy and successful life on the one hand and on the other the hardship he had suffered, but which he had not let define him. His wife Alice wrote to Theodore von Kármán that he was not aware he was dying and did not suffer, but that she was grieved that he had enjoyed living so much and he would still have had so much to say and give. The eulogies at his funeral were fittingly given by Hans Sachs and Erwin Schrödinger. Schrödinger emphasised that Hopf's life could be called "a happy one. His lodestar was truth. The finding of knowledge was what he strained all his nerves for," and that "[h]e was a friend of the great geniuses of his time, indeed he was one of them." Even after "[g]loomy clouds shadowed the last year of his life" Hopf

> never complained of his lot. A Bavarian by birth, attached to the cheerful Rhineland for many years, his gay and joyful spirit was unabatable. He soon began to love this country which had received him with such kindness, and to love a people whose mentality he felt to be akin to his own. He would have continued to call himself a happy man, had it pleased Providence not to take him away from us.[108]

Sachs chose to speak in German, "the old common mother tongue", and drew parallels between their experiences:

> A shared fate led us to this beautiful and hospitable country. Here he attempted to find a new future with gratefulness and fresh hope. Only here did we first meet.
>
> But our short period of togetherness was enough to get an insight into a life sustained by pure sincerity and joyful hope. The beautiful humanity that was his own, may also have brought about the great success in research and teaching that he enjoyed as an esteemed academic.[109]

Again, it was the SPSL to whom the desperate and grieving family turned. Daughter Liselore was now fifteen, and her mother Alice also looked after her parents, Sidonie and Dr Ferdinand Goldschmidt, both of them in their seventies and invalids due to very bad sight and hearing, but fortunately supported by a small annuity from a relative in the US. There were no financial resources for Hopf's widow and daughter. A solution for the immediate future was found through an

---

108 Script of Erwin Schrödinger's eulogy at Ludwig Hopf's grave, 26 December 1939. Thanks to Volkmar Felsch for the copy from the Blumenthal family papers.
109 Script of Hans Sachs's eulogy at Ludwig Hopf's grave, 26 December 1939, thanks to Willie Walshe. Translation by authors.

act of generosity by Trinity College and Erwin Schrödinger,[110] who agreed to continue Hopf's lectures for the second part of the academic year while the income of £150 was paid to Alice Hopf. She hoped that at the end of this arrangement she and the remaining family in Dublin could move back to England in order to be with her sons. Despite numerous attempts and letters to the Under Secretary of State at the Home Office by the SPSL over the next months, things did not work out as desired: the timing was unfortunate.[111]

Schrödinger and others had hoped that the SPSL could provide a guarantee and financial support, but their remit allowed funds to be used only on behalf of displaced scholars who were likely to be re-absorbed into academic life.[112] Trinity College helped again, this time by providing a position for Alice Hopf as Assistant Lecturer in German, despite her lack of experience and training;[113] she also taught German at a girls' school and tried to make ends meet by renting out rooms at their residence in 65 Kenilworth Square.[114] Two years later, in September 1942, Liselore Hopf, who had just started studying sciences at Trinity College, died from polio.[115] Hans Hopf, Ludwig and Alice's oldest son, was now, like his brother Peter Paul Hopf, in steady employment in London (the other brothers being in

---

110 Schrödinger wrote very modestly about the situation on 26 May 1940 to Nancy Searle, SPSL: "It was the generosity of Trinity College Dublin by which the first emergency arising for Professor Hopf's wife and daughter through his sudden death could be met. My own contribution consisted only in helping to remove formal difficulties by an undertaking that was in itself an honour and a pleasure for me." SPSL 503/3/493.

111 Though initially prospects looked promising, in mid-May 1940 fears of a German invasion of Britain prompted orders to intern all male (and later also female) aliens, including refugees: to take in more refugees was for the time being out of the question.

112 SPSL 503/3/494, Nancy Searle to Erwin Schrödinger, 3 June 1940.

113 "I have not learned too much, not a real thing. I made my 'Abitur' thirty years ago, which was in this time quite a good and not very usual thing for a woman in Germany; but I fear, I have forgotten all the things I learned at this time and also afterwards during a few University Terms. Perhaps I remember a little more of all the lectures and courses of general cultural importance I heard during the last years (before Hitler) together with my husband [...] I think I could work everywhere as a German assistant of any kind with a German teacher or at any institute." SPSL 503/3/482, Alice Hopf to Nancy Searle, 30 April 1940.

114 See MAI, G2/0495 Ludwig Hopf, Alice Hopf to her sons Hans and Peter, 3 January 1942. At this stage the Scheyer family had already been neighbours at no.67 for several months (see chapter 8). Alice Hopf also mentions 'Annemarie' who is a great help in the household, but also causes delays due to unpunctuality – this is probably Mimi Höfer (see chapters 1, 7 and 8).

115 Possibly contracted following a visit to the dentist. The first polio epidemic occurred in 1942 and continued into the following year. In all, 487 cases and 133 deaths were notified to the Department of Health, a fatality rate of 27.3%. See Laurence M. Geary, The 1956 polio epidemic in Cork. In: *History Ireland*. Vol. 14, no. 3 (2006), pp. 34–37.

the US and Kenya respectively) and made a fresh attempt to get his mother and grandparents to England through the SPSL, but was unsuccessful.[116] Only in late October 1943 was it possible for Alice Hopf to move to Great Britain.[117]

There are a number of similarities between the experiences of Hans Sachs and Ludwig Hopf. Both were very gifted and dedicated academics, at the forefront of new developments in their specific fields, in contact with and esteemed by world leaders in science who are still household names today. In socio-economic and religious terms the parallels are also striking – they both came from well-off, established Jewish backgrounds though neither of them seems to have placed great emphasis on religion. Arguably, the academic life was what they both believed in, including a love of German culture and specifically music. In many ways Ludwig Hopf and Hans Sachs epitomised the very best of the country that broke up their families and robbed them of their nationality, their academic careers, and their homes.

Neither had the slightest connection to Ireland; England or the USA would have been more likely (and desired) options for both of them – and both went to England for a short time and received their call to Ireland from there. For neither was it an ideal position, but for both it was the best, indeed the only one available. Notwithstanding the crucial support from Trinity, both were basically thrown on their own resources in circumstances very different from what they had been used to (though Sachs had some support and was clearly appreciated – and Hopf would probably have been drawn into the orbit of the Dublin Institute of Advanced Studies if he had still been alive when it was founded in 1940). In any case both quite quickly established helpful links with the academic German-speaking refugee community – and supported others in turn. Both brought family members with them, both died prematurely. It seems very fitting that both are buried in Mount Jerome Cemetery, less than a hundred metres apart.

There seems little awareness, whether at Trinity or beyond, of either Sachs or Hopf, nor of any of the other academics who came to Trinity. This also goes for the support that was extended from Trinity, notably by individuals such as Robert Ditchburn, but also joint College activities, specifically the invitation to a 'refugee of distinction'.

---

116 SPSL 503/3/498, E. Cooper, Home Office (Aliens Department), to Nancy Searle, 23 November 1940. It did not help that Hans Hopf had been severely injured while on duty as an air raid warden in December 1940 when both his legs were crushed: he spent more than a year in hospital.
117 Her parents, Sidonie and Ferdinand Goldschmidt, stayed behind in Dublin, Ferdinand dying there only a few months later in early 1944 and Sidonie then living alone in the Rathburn Nursing Home on Dartry Road, Rathgar, until the end of the war when she too went to England (see chapter 10).

The presence of young refugee scholars and students who for shorter or longer periods taught or studied in Trinity during the 1933–1945 period seems similarly to have been forgotten.

One of these was Gertrud Baumgarten. A multilingual legal secretary in Berlin, she lost her position after 1933 due to her Jewish background. Moving to friends in Italy in 1936, she eventually managed to obtain a good position and re-establish herself. In July 1938, her parents Paul and Helena Baumgarten joined her in Rome and the plan was to open a guesthouse with the furniture brought from their large Berlin flat.[118] Just six weeks later, however, the decree of 7 September stipulated that "alien Jews" had to leave Italy within six months (see chapter 5). Baumgarten wrote later that it was thanks to the "kindness of the Vatican" that they were able to get to Ireland.[119] Though their visas were granted in February 1939 it was not until July that they arrived. After two months in a cottage in the country in Mullach, Co. Meath, they received permission to move to Dublin. There being no exchange students from Germany for 1939–1940 in Trinity College, Gertrud was appointed as Assistant Lecturer in German at the request of Professor Liddell. She was to give six lectures per week during term at a remuneration of 8/- per lecture,[120] the first of several refugees in this position. The same conditions applied to her successor Einhart Kawerau (see chapter 1) who had finished his medical studies at TCD in 1940 and was appointed in April that year, after Gertrud Baumgarten had left Ireland on 4 March 1940 to travel with her parents to the USA via Great Britain and Italy.[121] Kawerau himself was replaced after only three months, in July 1940, by Ludwig Hopf's widow, as mentioned previously (a year later he was appointed Assistant to Professor William Fearon in biochemistry for Trinity Term, his remuneration now at the considerably more generous rate of £250 per annum).[122] After Alice Hopf left the Assistant Lecturer position in

---

118 Landesamt Berlin, no. 375770 – 375771, Gertrud Baumgarten.
119 See ibid. Translated by authors. A letter from Maud Slattery of the ICCR to DJ on 16 February 1939 also indicates strong support for them: "These three cases are guaranteed by Catholic Committee and are very specially recommended." NAI, DJ 69/80/304 Paul, Helena, Gertrud Baumgarten. We were not able to find details of the specific link between the Vatican and Catholic Committee (which must have been at that time the University College Catholic Committee for German and Austrian Refugees). This link also benefited one other refugee to Ireland, Richard Marx (see chapter 5).
120 See TCD Archives, Mun/V/5/25, TCD Board meeting minutes, 2 October 1939.
121 See NAI, DJ 69/80/304.
122 According to Walter Moore, Schrödinger's partner Hilde March originally also taught German in TCD, but resigned to allow Alice Hopf to take up the position (Walter Moore, *Schrödinger – Life and Thought*. Cambridge: CUP 1989, p. 359). There are no references to either her employment or her resignation in the minutes of the TCD Board meetings.

Trinity College in 1943, it was taken on by Hans Reiss, who had seemingly been in competition with yet another refugee, John Hennig, for the post. Reiss had the advantage of having been in TCD for his studies and having his tutor canvass on his behalf.[123] Reiss had come from Mannheim to Ireland in August 1939 and was supported by the Methodist Refugee Committee, specifically Edith Booth, and the Ticher family (see chapter 8). Thanks to his hard work he had been successful in the TCD scholarship competition and obtained first a Sizarship and shortly afterwards a University Scholarship which came with a grant of £20 a year. Encouraged by John Hennig, he started writing about German cities, initially his home town Mannheim, and sent an article to the *Times Pictorial*, a weekly subsidiary of the *Irish Times*. It was printed and he was allowed to continue, receiving two guineas for each article.[124] Years later, in 1944, he took over the weekly column of the 'T.C.D. Correspondent' in the *Irish Times* from Conor Cruise O'Brien.[125] Thanks to his articles, his scholarship, then £30, the Moderatorship Research Prize worth £25 per annum and £66 from his teaching position, he was able to live independently at last. Alongside Hans Reiss, Gerhard Hirschberg, a refugee lawyer, was teaching for two hours per week in 1945 (see also chapter 7).[126] After Reiss left Ireland in 1946, Ernst Scheyer, also a lawyer by training and profession, held the position until 1958, having gained experience by teaching German at school level at St Andrew's (see chapters 8 and 10). He was to become a much respected and influential lecturer in German at TCD, and today a prize for the two TCD students obtaining the highest marks in German in the Junior Freshman honour examination is still named after him.[127]

Another refugee who found an anchor at Trinity at least temporarily in 1941 and 1942 was Robert Donath (see chapters 3 and 6), who had obtained a PhD in History before he became a journalist. Donath managed to publish a few articles in Irish newspapers and gave lectures on international politics. In October 1941, he was appointed to arrange pamphlets in the library at a salary of £2 10/- a week for one year, the money being contributed not by Trinity College but by friends

---

123 See Hans Reiss, Seven Years in Ireland. Unpublished memoir in English, pp. 59–60.
124 In his English memoir Reiss recalls that he first wrote about cities which he had visited, and then, with the help of travel guides which he found in the TCD library, about any German city, p. 48.
125 Reiss, *Erinnerungen*, p. 133. R.M. Smyllie, the editor of the *Irish Times*, had seemingly had his nephew, Tim Sheehan, in mind for this role, but Sheehan recommended his friend Hans Reiss, cf. p. 135.
126 See NAI, DJ 69/80/466.
127 For more information on him see Holfter, Ernst Scheyer. In: Holfter (ed.), *German-speaking Refugees*, pp. 149–169.

through Senator James Douglas.[128] In his case, both Trinity and UCD offered him some employment: he had a similar position in UCD as in Trinity from February 1941 onwards. One should also keep in mind that apart from the lecturers and researchers, there was a considerable presence of refugee students in Trinity College Dublin – at least 25 refugee students were at TCD in the period during 1933–1945. Not quite so many but also a substantial number studied at University College Dublin (see chapter 8).

University College Dublin and the National University of Ireland in Cork, Galway and Maynooth

As compared to Trinity College, there seems to have been less awareness of the refugee problem among the academics of the colleges of the National University of Ireland in Dublin, Cork, Galway and Maynooth in the early years, and the few attempts in Cork and Galway actively to help beleaguered colleagues in the crucial time 1938–1939 were not particularly successful – but, contrary to Ditchburn and his Trinity colleagues' negative assessment of Galway, at least some efforts were made there as well, as we shall see.[129] The issue of Heidelberg was raised here too. Like Trinity College, University College Dublin (UCD) had received an invitation to send a representative to the 550th anniversary of the Foundation of the University of Heidelberg, to take place 27–30 June 1936. At the Senate Meeting on 12 March 1936 Prof. Conway proposed and Prof. Ó Máille seconded the resolution that a representative should be appointed (at this stage, still the course on which Trinity seemed set). However, on a show of hands, there were only eight in favour, twelve voted against, and the motion was lost. As a compromise, the Senate unanimously adopted a motion proposed by Denis J. Coffey (the president of UCD since its new beginning in 1909 to 1940, who, incidentally, had shown a strong preference for the German academic system)[130] and seconded by Ó Máille, that a Congratulatory Address should be forwarded. Rev. Timothy Corcoran (eminently

---

128 TCD Archives, Mun/V/5/25, TCD Board meeting minutes, 1 October 1941. In December 1940, Douglas had written to W.E. Thrift, Provost of TCD, to ask whether Donath could take over the position of German lecturer, normally held by a German exchange student but at that stage occupied by Alice Hopf. TCD Archives, Mun/Sec/248/ref/11.
129 No evidence could be found of any activities in Maynooth, though it should be stated that John Hennig gave occasional German classes there (see chapter 8).
130 See Mary Macken, Dr Denis J. Coffey President of University College, Dublin, 1909–1940. In: *Studies: An Irish Quarterly Review*. Vol. 29, no. 114 (June 1940), pp. 177–186, 181.

qualified as he had won gold medals for English and Latin verse in his university days)[131] undertook to draft the Address.

More importantly, in 1938, when the situation in Germany worsened and exclusion for academics with Jewish backgrounds became legally enforced in Austria, a concerted effort began, especially on behalf of students, and was to have a considerable impact on Irish policy due to de Valera's involvement as Chancellor of the National University of Ireland, as mentioned previously (see chapter 6). At the meeting of the Standing Committee of the University College on 6 July 1938 the question was tabled whether the university could aid Austrian professors and students "pressed by the existing difficulties". The decision was taken to recommend to the Senate meeting, taking place the next day, that

> £1,000 should be set aside from the funds of the University to make provision for certain distinguished Austrian Professors (not political refugees) to be asked to give courses of lectures in the three Constituent Colleges (one term) and that the Presidents of the three Colleges should act as a special Selection Committee.[132]

The "authorities" of University College Dublin also indicated that they were prepared to admit twelve selected Austrian students, without payment of lecture, entrance or conferring fees.

The Senate meeting approved the proposals,[133] and the UCD initiative also had an impact on the constituent colleges in Galway and Cork. At the subsequent Senate meeting, on 27 October 1938, it was reported from University College Galway that at the meeting of its Standing Committee on 13 July 1938 it had adopted a similar policy, agreeing to accept six Austrian students in the coming academic year and to exempt them from all fees except the College fee. Likewise, at the Senate meeting on 8 December 1938, the Registrar reported receipt of a letter dated 23 November 1938 from the president of University College Cork, stating that the governing body of that College had also decided to consider "sympathetically" applications for admission from Austrian students.[134]

---

131 Offaly Historical and Archeological Society, Reverend Dr Timothy Corcoran, S. J., D. Litt. 2 September 2007. https://www.offalyhistory.com/reading-resources/history/famous-offaly-people/rev-dr-timothy-corcoran-s-j-d-litt [last accessed February 2016].
132 NUI, Registrar's Office, Standing Committee Minutes, 23 October 1935 to 8 March 1939, 6 July 1938. The explicit exclusion of political refugees is a clear indication that the University was only prepared to support academics persecuted on perceived religious or racial grounds – and had no interest in anyone who could be viewed as a potential troublemaker.
133 NUI, Registrar's Office, Minutes of Senate, Vol. XVII, 19 May 1938 to 26 October 1939.
134 There had already been a personal initiative from Cork in 1933. Among the university files of the SPSL there is one relating to correspondence with a professor of University College Cork, Louis P. W. Renouf, who wrote in response to a notice in *Nature* and offered "both working and

Galway accordingly responded positively when approached by a student named Wilhelm Mann, born in Mannheim in 1916, who was not allowed to finish his chemistry studies in Heidelberg, and could claim personal links to Galway through one of his ancestors, Dr August Bensbach.[135] Initially, things seemed promising. In mid-September 1938, Thomas Dillon, the professor for chemistry in Galway, wrote to Mann's aunt that her letter to University College Galway's president had been forwarded to him and he would be very glad to have her nephew as a student in his department. Better still, he indicated that the College was prepared to waive payment of all fees, although he felt it his duty to warn her that if "Mr Mann is interested in physical chemistry Galway would not suit him as we have no physico-chemical institute here and work only at organic chemistry".[136] As Mann also had the support of Dutch friends who had agreed to pay for his board and lodging in Galway, everything seemed settled. This was further confirmed by a telegram from Galway in November 1938. Mann himself then wrote to the Department of Justice presenting his case, enclosing the correspondence from Galway and requesting a permit to enter Ireland, adding that he would stay only for a limited time as he had prepared his emigration to the US. He stated that he had a US quota number and was only waiting for an affidavit. All to no avail: a few days later John Duff from the Department of Justice wrote at length to Thomas Dillon presenting the restrictive policy of his department, and explaining that the Minister of Justice would not grant a visa to Mann, but only

---

rough living quarters for about half the year, unfortunately most of it during late autumn and winter" some 60 miles from Cork (SPSL 127/1/243, L. Renouf to C. S. Gibson, 13 June 1933). This research station (probably at Lough Hyne near Baltimore where scientific research has been carried out since the late 19th century; see also the publication by T. Kearney, *Lough Hyne: The Marine Researchers - in Pictures*. Skibbereen: Skibbereen Heritage Centre 2011) could, according to Renouf, be of special interest to a displaced botanist due to the lichens and marine algae, or provide interesting problems for a biochemist. He also offered the possibility of staying in his house for the remainder of the year, helping his two sons with Latin, Mathematics, Chemistry, Physics and French, as well as German, during part of the day. Renouf indicated that there might be a chance to use the facilities at UCC during the rest of the day, and very much regretted that he was not in a position to give any pecuniary assistance (SPSL 127/1/246–249, Renouf to Gibson, 1 August 1933). Nothing seems to have come of this offer.

135 NAI, DJ 69/80/139, Wilhelm Mann, Charlottenstr. 3a, Mannheim to DJ, 27 November 1938. August Bensbach, a graduate in Medicine of the University of Heidelberg and author of a *Sketch of German Literature*, was appointed to the professorship in Modern Languages at Queen's College (as it then was), Galway from 1848 to 1866. He became a Vice-President of the Royal Galway Institution for the promotion of Polite Literature, Science, and Antiquities in 1851. He died in Germany in 1868, two years after his return from Ireland.

136 Ibid., Thomas Dillon to Louise Lefor, 14 September 1938.

to the twelve originally agreed students for UCD and then some further cases through the ICCR:

> As Wilhelm Mann is a Jew it is very probable that he would be deprived of his German nationality if he left Germany and that he would become a refugee in this country. You will appreciate that there are objections to the admission of refugees who would compete with Irish nationals in professions and employments. The Minister has agreed to admit not more than 12 refugee students to University College, Dublin, and he has since agreed to admit a limited number of refugees of other classes for whose maintenance in this country arrangements will be made by the Irish Co-Ordinating Committee for German and Austrian refugees. The Minister is not prepared to consider any application for the admission of a refugee (other than students for University College, Dublin) unless the application is supported by the Irish Co-Ordinating Committee. If you are anxious that Wilhelm Mann should be admitted, I am to suggest accordingly that you get in touch with the Irish Co-Ordinating Committee.[137]

A letter was dispatched to Mann the same day from the Department of Justice, stating only that the minister had communicated with Thomas Dillon regarding the matter referred to in his letter. It is not clear whether Mann ever got this, or whether an attempt to involve the ICCR took place, as in April 1939 Mann was still hoping for an answer to his November request.[138] In any case, he never got to Ireland (but managed to escape to China instead).[139]

After the decision regarding the twelve refugee students allowed to come to Dublin was grudgingly accepted by External Affairs and Justice (after the intervention by the Taoiseach in early September 1938),[140] Theo Dillon immediately seized the opportunity and managed in the same month to get a visa granted without any lengthy application process or paper trail – he simply telephoned the Department of External Affairs "to enquire as to whether a visa would be granted to one Stefan Friedrich Feric, an Austrian national, who was to come to

---

137 Ibid., Duff, DJ to Thomas Dillon, 2 December 1938.
138 The file contains only a desperate telegram from Mann, dated 5 December 1938 ("Please answer urgently my request to enter Galway for studies till my final emigration to USA permit necessary as soon as possible") and a much later letter ("Dear Sir, Referring to your letter of the 2nd December 38 I want to ask if you kindly could give me any answer regarding the matter of my letter of the 27th Nov. 38", ibid., Mann to DJ, 24 April 1939), but no further reply to these pleas: see ibid.
139 See Gregor Eisenhauser's obituary of Wilhelm Mann, Fast alle Schanghai-Emigranten reisten weiter. Er blieb. *Tagesspiegel*, 16 November 2012 and also Ulrike Unschuld, *You banfa - Es findet sich immer ein Weg: Wilhelm Manns Erinnerungen an China 1938 – 1966*. Berlin: Hentrich & Hentrich 2014.
140 See NAI, DFA 102/438 Admission to Ireland of Austrian Students for purpose of attending Lectures at University College, Dublin, DEA to DJ, 7 September 1938 and see chapter 6.

the National University as a medical student".[141] As External Affairs had never heard of Feric they called the Department of Justice, only to ascertain "that they likewise had no papers to anybody of that name", but given the recent development they concluded it had to be in the context of the UCD initiative, and Dillon was advised to call Justice directly. A subsequent phone call from Justice to External Affairs made clear that no objection to the granting of a visa would be raised, and requested that the British Consulate at Vienna was to be wired and informed of the situation.[142] Feric arrived in Dublin in early November 1938 (see chapters 2 and 8).

Ernst Lewy – a linguist with rare abilities

Ernst Lewy was an eminent linguist who was probably the first academic refugee at UCD to appear before the general public. In early 1939 students and interested outsiders alike were invited to a special lecture taking place at UCD: "University College Dublin – Professor Lewy (formerly of the University of Berlin) will deliver an introductory lecture on 'the Structure of the Indo-European Languages' on Friday Next, Jan. 20th, at 4 p.m., in the Physics Lecture Theatre. The Lecture will be Open to the Public."[143] Afterwards, the event was reported upon further,[144] and the *Irish Press* printed a photo and some details about the background of the linguistic scholar: under the headline "German Professor's Dublin Lecture", readers were informed that Ernst Lewy was a victim of the "'non-aryan' movement" of the Nazis and that he had left Berlin three months previously in order to teach a course in linguistics in UCD. It was noted that the "German refugee professor [...] seemed more at ease in the Irish language than in English".

The information given in the *Irish Press* article was only partly correct. Ernst Lewy had indeed been a professor in Berlin, but he had arrived in Ireland as early as June 1937, partly in order to learn Irish, although he stayed mainly in Ennistymon, Co. Clare, rather than on one of the islands or in a traditional Gaeltacht

---

141 NAI, DFA 102/465 Application for Visa to enter Ireland of Stefan Friedrich Feric, Austrian National, memo Belton to Secretary, 27 September 1938.
142 See ibid.
143 *Irish Independent*, 18 January 1939, p. 10.
144 See *Irish Independent*, 21 January 1939, p. 13: "Lecture on Linguistics.
Prof. Ernst Lewy, former Professor of General Linguistics at Berlin University, began a series of lectures on linguistics at University College, Dublin, yesterday, when he spoke on 'the Structure of the Indo-European Languages'. Prof. Lewy, who is a distinguished linguist, has made a special study of the structure of various languages. He speaks Irish."

area. With regard to his knowledge of English, while Lewy seemed more at home reading than speaking the language, he had extensive linguistic abilities generally: he could speak German, French, Italian, Spanish, Russian, Swedish, Hungarian, Finnish, Mordvinic, Mari, and Basque, and had a reading knowledge of Latin, Greek, English and Sanskrit. No doubt his spoken English had also improved thanks to his stay in Ennistymon. After a reunion with his wife Hedwig and son Georg in 1938 after almost eight months of separation and a few months together in Galway they moved to Cowper Gardens in Rathmines. There they were joined in late August 1939 by Ernst and Hedwig's daughter Esther Britz, née Lewy, whose admittance to Ireland had been discussed together with that of the Austrian students and the Pick children. Later, in 1941, the family moved outside Dublin, to Woodtown Park[145] in Rathfarnham, where Lewy was to live until his death in 1966.

Ireland had not been an obvious choice for Lewy. Born in Breslau in 1881, the youngest in a large Jewish family, he studied in Breslau, Munich and Leipzig before being awarded a PhD in Breslau in early 1905 for his thesis on 'Old Prussian Personal Names'.[146] From 1905 onwards he continued his studies in Berlin, concentrating on general linguistics and Finnish-Ugric languages. His lecturers included Wilhelm Schulze and two professors who had links to Ireland: Franz Nikolaus Finck (who had spent several months on the Aran Islands) and Heinrich Zimmer, the Orientalist and first professor of Celtic Studies. While Lewy seems to have had no interest in Celtic Studies at the time, he did make contact with some of the Irish students in Berlin, who would prove to be of great importance to his life in Ireland later. Following his *Habilitation* ('On Finno-Ugric word and sentence connection') he lectured without a post in Berlin, and two of his students, Wolfgang Steinitz[147] and Walter Benjamin,[148] went on to make names for themselves, though in

---

145 Owned by Arnold Marsh, the headmaster of Newtown School (see chapter 6).
146 Gisela Holfter, Akademiker im irischen Exil: Ernst Lewy (1881–1966). In: *German Life and Letters*. Vol. 61, no. 3 (July 2008), pp. 361–385.
147 Wolfgang Steinitz (1905–1967) was a member of the Central Committee of the SED (1954 to 1958), and from 1954 to 1963 he was Vice-President of the Academy of Science of the GDR. Among his achievements was the collection of German folksongs: his *Deutsche Volkslieder demokratischen Charakters aus sechs Jahrhunderten*, published in Berlin 1954 and 1962, and in West Germany in 1979 as 'Der große Steinitz', influenced songwriters in East and West. His relationship with Lewy was to last up to his death, though after the war it became complicated and difficult: see chapter 11 and Gisela Holfter, Ein Fallbeispiel zur Rückkehrproblematik aus dem Exil – Ernst Lewy (1881–1966). In: A. Goodbody et al. (eds): *Dislocation and Reorientation*. Amsterdam/New York: Rodopi 2009, pp. 139–151.
148 Walter Benjamin had been a student of Lewy's in 1914, some years before Steinitz. In 1920 Benjamin wanted to start a new journal, to be called 'Angelus Novus', and he hoped that Lewy would be among the contributors. Lewy responded positively, but, following a visit by Benjamin

very different areas. During the First World War Lewy was deemed unsuitable for active service due to a deformed foot, but from 1915 onwards he supported the war effort in his own way – with linguistic studies in prisoner of war camps.[149] Until 1923 he was able to continue his research privately in the huge but long-neglected 18th-century former provost's house he and his wife Hedwig[150] had purchased in northern Bavaria in 1914 thanks to inherited money. Having lost his fortune in the inflation he returned to Berlin to lecture during term time, and in 1925 he was appointed as 'extraordinary professor', but was paid for his teaching only as a part-timer. In 1929 he received the prestigious research award of the Harry Kreismann Foundation, which was welcome not least due to the generous prize money of 10,000 marks. Finally, in July 1931 Lewy was appointed to the coveted tenured position of associate professor in Berlin, which came with an appropriate salary, and at last the first professor for Finno-Ugric languages in Germany had seemingly attained professional and financial security. Academically, he was fascinated by comparing structures and words between a huge array of mainly lesser-known languages and was a strong proponent of Wilhelm von Humboldt's ideas about language and its influence on the mental development of peoples.[151] Long research stays in Hungary, Finland and the French and Spanish parts of the Basque country enabled him to improve his wide language skills further. His standing among his colleagues is reflected in his appointment as joint director

---

and his friend Gershom Scholem to Lewy's home in Wechterswinkel in September 1921, relations cooled. Even in later years, however, Lewy came to Benjamin's mind in the context of Humboldt. In a letter to Hugo von Hofmannsthal in August 1925 he recalled his former lecturer: "Working on Humboldt leads me directly to my student days, when I was studying his linguistic writings in a seminar under the direction of a personally very strange man who was almost grotesquely congenial to the later Humboldt's contemplative genius." Walter Benjamin, *Briefe I*. Edited and annotated by Gershom Scholem and Theodor W. Adorno. Frankfurt a. M.: Suhrkamp 1978, pp. 400f. Translated by authors.

149 In this context Lewy contributed to a publication edited by Wilhelm Doegen (who was in charge of the research project among the prisoners of war): *Unter fremden Völkern. Eine neue Völkerkunde*. Berlin: Otto Stollberg 1925, with articles on Roma and Sinti ('Die Zigeuner', pp. 167–176) and on his own area of research, tribes speaking Finno-Ugrian languages in Russia ('Die Finnisch-Ugrischen Stämme im europäischen Rußland', pp. 212–232). Some of his recordings of prisoners of war for Carl Stumpf's project to establish a "voice-museum of the nations" from 1915 onwards are still accessible. See also http://www.lautarchiv.hu-berlin.de/ [last accessed 1 April 2016].

150 Hedwig Ludwig, born in 1883 in Breslau into a Protestant family. They had two children, a daughter Esther born in January 1911 and a son Georg in May 1922.

151 Regarding his place within linguistics see Utz Maas, *Verfolgung und Auswanderung deutschsprachiger Sprachforscher*, Vol. II, G-P (Q). Osnabrück: Secolo 2004, pp. 265–275.

of the Institute of Indo-Germanic Studies in the autumn of 1932, but everything changed with Hitler's ascent to power and he was suspended in May 1933.

A contact he made in September 1933 at the Third International Congress of Linguistics in Rome proved to be of great importance for his emigration. Egyptologist Alan Gardiner[152] promised him every assistance. Accordingly Gardiner wrote in early October 1933 to the Academic Assistance Council and asked for a copy of their questionnaire in order to forward it to Lewy who was at this stage near San Sebastian. Lewy had made a strong impression on Gardiner and was clearly well regarded by his colleagues: "I heard on all hands that Prof. Lewy was a man of the very highest ability, and I both liked him and found him extremely interesting on all matters of philology."[153]

The initial assessment on behalf of the Academic Assistance Council was positive but reserved, as Lewy's wish for travel and research abroad was seen as difficult to facilitate, and there were many others in more desperate circumstances.[154]

Like Ludwig Hopf and Hans Sachs, Lewy seems to have been comparatively well off financially in the first years of the Nazi regime, but again, this does not tell the full story of threatened withdrawal of income. His previously safe existence as a public servant also became precarious. Like Sachs, Lewy was reinstated after his initial dismissal thanks to a campaign organised by his colleagues Julius von Farkas (Director of the Hungarian Institute at Berlin University where Lewy held his professorship) and Max Vasmer (Director of the Institute for Slavic Studies), who made sure that Lewy's international standing and contacts, for example with Emil Nestor Setälä, the linguist and former Finnish minister for Foreign Affairs, were made known to the new rulers in the education ministry.[155]

---

[152] Alan Gardiner (1879–1963), Oxford Egyptologist, had a special empathy for Lewy's position. His own father-in-law was Jewish and Gardiner had spent many years studying in Berlin under renowned scholars Kurt Heinrich Sethe and Adolf Erman.

[153] SPSL 310/1/27, Alan Gardiner to General Secretary Academic Assistance Council, 5 October 1933.

[154] See SPSL 310/1/29, Allen Mawer, Provost University College London, to C. S. Gent, Academic Assistance Council, 4 November 1933.

[155] Julius von Farkas to Fritz Hartung, 24 July 1946, on his and Vasmer's endeavours on behalf of Lewy. In: István Futaky, Die Gründung der ersten deutschen Institute für Finnougristik im Spiegel des Briefwechsels zwischen Julius von Farkas und Max Vasmer. In: *Finnisch-Ugrische Mitteilungen*. Vol. 20 (1997), pp. 135–155, 147. The reasons for the decision by the Ministry of Education in Lewy's case are discussed in detail by Hans-Christian Jasch in his article: Das preußische Kultusministerium und die "Ausschaltung" von "nichtarischen" und politisch mißliebigen Professoren an der Berliner Universität. In: *forum historiae iuris, erste europäische Internetzeitschrift für Rechtsgeschichte* (25 August 2005), pp. 45–46 and 51. http://www.forhistiur.de/zitat/0508jasch.htm

Lewy therefore continued to receive a professorial income of 11,080 Reichsmark p.a. until 1935. In November 1934, he was one of the few Jewish professors who had not seen active service in World War I to swear allegiance to Adolf Hitler (the 'Hitler oath' was requested for the military and civil servants from August 1934 onwards; previously the oath had referred to the people, fatherland, constitution and laws of Germany). Inevitably, however, he was finally suspended in October 1935 and officially retired on 31 December 1935.[156] In 1936 and 1937 he received his pension of 4,986 Reichsmark; the payments ceased altogether only in March 1938,[157] when he had been in Ireland for nine months and after his wife and son had joined him there. Before that, Spain had been the main focus for the family, specifically the Basque country where Lewy had already spent considerable time and where he had sent his books into the care of Professor Pere Bosch-Gimpera (1891–1974), Rector of the university in Barcelona (whom Lewy knew from Bosch-Gimpera's time in Berlin in 1921).

Image 4: Ernst Lewy

[last accessed 1 April 2016]. There are also interesting insights into the situation at the Kaiser-Wilhelms-Universität during the Nazi regime by Max Vasmer from 1948, published by Marie-Luise Bott, *Die Haltung der Berliner Universität im Nationalsozialismus. Max Vasmers Rückschau 1948*. Berlin: Humboldt-Universität 2009. http://edoc.hu-berlin.de/series/geschichte-hu/1/PDF/1.pdf [last accessed 1 April 2016]. Max Vasmer himself was named by Lewy as one of the few older Berlin scholars to be trusted: in a letter to the SPSL of 7 October 1945 (SPSL 310/1/292), Lewy calls Vasmer "courageous" and stresses that he behaved decently towards him. This positive assessment is further evidenced in his outrage about Wolfgang Steinitz's rather negative description of Vasmer: see his letter to Julius von Farkas, 16 April 1948, in Futaky, Die Gründung, p. 154.
156 Humboldt-Universität Berlin archive, Personalakten Ernst Lewy 140/91.
157 See Landesverwaltungsamt Berlin, file Ernst Lewy, E1, Ernst Lewy to Entschädigungsamt Berlin, 2 June 1951.

In the summer of 1936, when his wife Hedwig and son Georg had moved to Switzerland with the intention of going to Spain later on and meeting him there, Lewy stayed in Copenhagen with the Danish linguist Viggo Brøndal (1887–1942) who, together with his colleague, physicist Niels Bohr, tried to develop a plan for Lewy with the assistance of the SPSL. He would be in Denmark until autumn 1936, then travel at the expense of the Danish committee to Spain, where he would spend six to eight months, supported by the SPSL. Then Lewy "would gladly come to England, taking a strong interest in Celtic languages".[158] In the end, as a result of advice by Brøndal and thanks to positive references obtained in England, Lewy secured a scholarship through the SPSL given by an 'anonymous' donor – in fact, Alan Gardiner, who intended the money specifically for Lewy. The idea was that he "should be discouraged from taking too many separate schemes of study and should settle down to one good piece of work".[159] This one good piece of work did come about – it was to be called *Bau der europäischen Sprachen* (The Structure of European Languages). What seems remarkable is that it appeared – in German – in Ireland, in 1942, published by the Royal Irish Academy. One can assume that this was thanks to the same group that had helped to secure his lectureship in UCD in January 1939. His subsequent appointment as lecturer in UCD in February 1939[160] was probably the result of a longstanding academic network that included Osborn Bergin[161] and Canon Patrick Boylan[162] (see chapter 6) and possibly also Myles Dillon,[163] all former students in Berlin who had now become influential academ-

---

158 SPSL 310/1/41, Viggo Brøndal to Walter Adams, AAC, 13 July 1936.
159 SPSL 310/1/81, SPSL to Provost Allen Mawer (1879–1942), 15 January 37.
160 SPSL 310/1/213, Lewy to SPSL, 23 January 1939.
161 Osborn Bergin (1873–1950) remained among Lewy's closest friends. He met Lewy when he studied Old Irish in Berlin in 1904 under Heinrich Zimmer, and went on to Freiburg where he obtained his PhD under the supervision of Rudolf Thurneysen in 1906. From 1909 onwards he was the first professor of Early and Medieval Irish at UCD. In 1940 he became Schrödinger's counterpart as the director of the School of Celtic Studies at the Dublin Institute for Advanced Studies, but stepped down after one year.
162 See also Michael Bertram Crowe, A Great Irish Scholar: Monsignor Patrick Boylan. In: *Studies*. Vol. 67, no. 267 (Autumn 1977), pp. 201–211. Crowe refers to the acquaintances Boylan made in Berlin after the war such as Osborn Bergin, Myles Dillon, Thomas McLoughlin and "Levy" – it is likely that this in fact refers to Ernst Lewy.
163 Myles Dillon (1900–1972) had been in Berlin after WWI (on his time there see Joachim Fischer and John Dillon (eds), *The Correspondence of Myles Dillon, 1922-25: Irish-German Relations and Celtic Studies*. Dublin: Four Courts 1999. Lewy does not seem to have been a close contact of Dillon's, and is not mentioned in his letters). After teaching for a few years in Trinity Dillon moved to UCD in 1930 and taught Sanskrit and comparative philology (before leaving for the US in 1937). Upon his return to Ireland in the late 1940s he worked at the School of Celtic Studies at DIAS, from 1960–1968 as its director.

ics in Ireland. Throughout the war years Lewy gave lectures and taught courses at UCD in European Languages, Comparative Philology, Sanskrit, Old-Slavonic, and Finno-Ugric languages. His seminars took place, as he wrote to the SPSL in 1945, "of course always with very few students as these subjects are outside the common curriculum". Despite this, he notes gratefully, the courses "were kept on".[164]

A brief interlude

The best known of all refugees who came to Ireland and one almost synonymous with de Valera's project of a Dublin Institute of Advanced Studies (DIAS) was Erwin Schrödinger. While his background and work for the DIAS will be described in more detail below, it was at UCD that he lectured first, tiding him over after his arrival in Ireland in October 1939 until the DIAS was officially launched. Accordingly he gave lectures in UCD from November 1939 onwards.[165] He was rewarded with an honorary doctorate from the National University, conferred on 11 July 1940.[166]

"Certain distinguished Austrian Professors"

It took over a year until the Senate's decision regarding Irish lecture tours by Austrian academics was implemented. Up to 1939 the University College Catholic Committee for German and Austrian Refugees (which involved key figures such as Theo Dillon, Canon Boylan and Mary Macken) was the only Catholic relief committee, which resulted in it being somewhat overwhelmed and drawn into all aspects of refugee work: up to June 1939 it was responsible for the recommendation of all Catholic refugees (see chapter 6).[167] In the summer of 1939, the Irish Catholic Council for Refugees was founded, leaving the University College Catholic Committee to concentrate on academic refugees. Attempts to get academics to come to Ireland to give lectures at the National University of Ireland were resumed in August 1939. The timing, just before the outbreak of the war, was crucial. The academics mainly concerned were Ludwig Bieler, Carla Zawisch and Victor Ehrenberg. Of these, only Ludwig Bieler was to stay long-term, and

---

164 SPSL 310/300, Lewy to Skemp, 19 November 1945.
165 See *Irish Independent*, 4 November 1939, "Former Professor in Vienna Lectures in Dublin". De Valera's presence at his first lecture was duly recorded, as was Schrödinger's tribute to Irish mathematician William Rowan Hamilton.
166 See NUI, Minutes of Senate, Vol. XVIII, Senate Meeting 16 May 1940.
167 T. W. T. Dillon, The Refugee Problem, p. 413.

this only after overcoming many obstacles and mainly thanks to the efforts of his wife Eva, UCD's president Denis Coffey, and de Valera. Carla Zawisch could not come at all, although at one stage she seemed to have an advantage over Bieler (see below). Victor Ehrenberg (who was German rather than Austrian) was probably the most eminent. He was originally supposed to lecture at the National University of Ireland from October 1939 to June 1940, firstly in Dublin, then in Cork and Galway.[168] In the end, however, his time in Ireland was short, only one term rather than the envisioned year.[169] He found that there was insufficient support in Ireland compared to better opportunities opening up in Great Britain where his family was, and there were also difficulties in getting entry and exit visas to travel between Great Britain and Ireland. Again, Ehrenberg was an acknowledged authority in his field. Born in November 1891 in Altona (Elbe) near Hamburg, of an old German-Jewish family, mostly schoolmasters and professors, after an initial preference for architecture he had studied Classics and Ancient History in Göttingen and Berlin, under Eduard Meyer (brother of the renowned Celtic scholar Kuno Meyer) among others. From spring 1929 he was extraordinary professor for Greek History and Epigraphy at the German University in Prague, in June 1934 he became an ordinary professor and in 1936 he added a new subject to his teaching portfolio: History of the Near East. His publication list in 1938 contains numerous books, over 40 articles and many book reviews.[170] As a scholar seeking a position abroad it was to his advantage that one of the books, *Alexander and the Greeks*, had been published in Oxford in 1938. Having taken out Czech nationality, he had an advantage over other displaced scholars from Germany and Austria, and he also enjoyed the support of many colleagues. On 30 November 1939 Esther Simpson of the SPSL wrote to Leo Liepmann of the Oxford Committee for Refugee Relief: "We have been having an enormous amount of correspondence about Professor Victor Ehrenberg and we are hoping to be able to help him."[171] At that stage Ehrenberg

---

168 NAI, DFA 202/543.
169 NAI, DFA 202/424, Question of facilities for Aliens for purpose of giving lectures in National University.
170 Some of them rather short, such as *Alexander und Ägypten*. Leipzig: J. C. Hinrichs'sche Buchhandlung 1926, 59pp; *Karthago*. Leipzig: J. C. Hinrichs'sche Buchhandlung 1927, 48pp; and *Vom Beginn der Geschichte Europas*. Prague: Taussig & Taussig 1929, 23pp; other works were *Die Rechtidee im frühen Griechentum*. Leipzig: S. Hirzel 1921; *Neugründer des Staates*. Munich: C. H. Beck 1925; *Der griechische und der hellenische Staat*. Leipzig 1932; and his volume *Ost und West*. Brünn: Rudolf M. Rohrer 1935.
171 Very positive opinions about him include the following: H. J. Wade Gery, Wadham College Oxford, praised the "brilliance of his historical generalizations and of his characterizations of moments and tendencies of history"; William Scott Ferguson, Cambridge, emphasised that

and his family were already in England, having left Prague a month before Hitler invaded. In early 1940 his SPSL grant was renewed for another three months and he was appointed visiting lecturer at the National University of Ireland, but it quickly became clear that the agreed arrangement – one term in Dublin, then Cork, then Galway, for £100 each – resulted in two households and the need for a continuation of the SPSL grant as Ehrenberg found "life in Ireland is extremely expensiv [sic], much more than in England." He was staying in a boarding house "as the College has no accommodations whatever for that purpose."[172] Home Office permission to return to England was crucial for his stay in Ireland, but, following his return in June 1940 to Cambridge where his family was,[173] lack of a British exit permit hindered his teaching in Ireland. In spring 1941, just after the last instalment of his SPSL grant, he obtained a teaching position at Carlisle Grammar School, and in the end, Ehrenberg was able to build a successful career in Newcastle upon Tyne and London.[174]

Another academic who was supported by UCD was Ludwig Bieler. He left Austria on 12 March 1938, the day of Hitler's *'Machtergreifung'*, due to his political convictions. He wrote to the SPSL that he had good reasons to leave as he was known "as a true follower of the Austrian government and a strong enemy of the

---

Ehrenberg "is unquestionably one of the best of the students of Greek history of his generation in Germany. He is a man of breadth of view as well as exact knowledge. I have found his books unusually stimulating." Karl Viëtor, then already at Harvard University, described him as an extremely efficient and able teacher who was very highly thought of among his colleagues. M. L. W. Laistner, Cornell University, considered him one of the best continental ancient historians of his generation, sentiments echoed in statements by William Westermann, Columbia University, New York ("his work as a scholar is excellent"), and Jakob Larsen, University of Chicago ("one of the ablest scholars in the field"). Three professors (Josef Dobias, A. Salao and K. Svobak) from Charles University Prague, Ehrenberg's main work place, expressed their appreciation of his "extensive and deep-rooted learning" and also "his outstanding teaching abilities", and went on to state that his "pure character and his prominent qualities both of a man and scholar made him an excellent and desirable friend and colleague". SPSL 252.

172 SPSL 252, Ehrenberg to Simpson, 13 April 40. See also his letter on 5 May 1940 along the same lines.

173 NAI, DJ 69/80/516 Victor Ehrenberg.

174 He published academic books on different aspects of ancient history in English and became co-founder and guiding spirit of the London Classical Society. His contributions to classical studies in England where he stayed until his death in 1975 were widely acknowledged. Both sons followed in their father's footsteps: the elder son, Geoffrey Elton, became Regius Professor of Modern History in Cambridge and was knighted. Victor's other son, Lewis, became Professor of Physics and later Professor of Higher Education at Surrey and in 1994 the first Professor of Higher Education at University College London (and his son, Ben Elton, has become a well-known comedian and playwright).

National socialists, and, at least I had no more hope for any career as a scholar".[175] Bieler went to Switzerland and found a first refuge at the Séminaire de Philologie Classique at the Université de Fribourg. Bieler had been born on 20 October 1906 in Vienna into a Catholic family. His university education had taken place in Vienna, Tübingen and Munich, where he read classical and German philology. After gaining his PhD in 1929 he became an assistant at the Patristic Department of the Academy of Letters in Vienna; he also taught in schools, and was an instructor in Greek at the University of Vienna, where in 1936 he took an extra unsalaried post lecturing in classical philology. From 1934 he also worked at the National Library of Vienna, becoming a provisional librarian in 1935 and a full librarian in 1937. His academic career seemed promising: in 1937, the year he received his *Habilitation*,[176] he was designated for the professorship of classics when there was hope that a Catholic University of Salzburg could be established[177] (the actual re-establishment of a university in Salzburg was to take place only in 1962).

In his questionnaire for the SPSL of 4 July 1938 he named Ireland after England and before the USA and Canada as his preferred countries of emigration. Less than a fortnight later he applied for one of three assistantships in classical philology in Belfast, but without success. His private situation changed that year, when he met his future wife Eva, seven years his junior, the only child of renowned paediatrician Albert Uffenheimer and his wife Elisabeth.[178] According to Ludwig and Eva's daughter Elizabeth, they came together in Switzerland while Eva was trying to pack a suitcase and could not shut the lid: "Along came Ludwig Bieler to return a book he'd borrowed. Eva asked him to sit on the case so she could close it. Bieli (we always called him that) being very methodical unpacked,

---

175 SPSL 292/3/142. In his article about his Latin teacher Dr Joseph Pavlu, 'A Viennese Schoolmaster', Bieler writes that he "left a home in which I could no longer be my own master". In: *Studies: An Irish Quarterly Review*. Vol. 37, no. 148 (December 1948), pp. 440–446, 446.
176 See also Franz Römer, Sonja Schreiner, Ein Österreicher in Irland – Ludwig Bieler. In: Evelyn Adunka et al. (eds), *Exilforschung: Österreich. Leistungen, Defizite & Perspektiven*. Vienna: Mandelbaum forthcoming 2017.
177 SPSL 292/3/128.
178 Albert Uffenheimer (1876–1941), an acknowledged specialist in paediatrics, author of numerous publications and co-editor of the journal *Monatsschrift für Kinderheilkunde*, was sacked as Director of the children's clinic in Magdeburg. Following a short exile in London he got a position in 1940 in the USA at the newly founded Catholic Siena College in Albany. He died following a heart attack in 1941. His standing in medical circles can be seen in the appreciations following his death: obituaries appeared for example in the *New York Times*, 10 April 1941, *The Siena News*, 25 April 1941 and the *Siena College Yearbook* 1941. In 2001 a square in Magdeburg was named after him.

repacked and closed the suitcase, by which time 'they were in love'."[179] Things did not, however, go smoothly. Bieler was in contact with both the *Notgemeinschaft deutscher Wissenschaftler im Ausland* and the SPSL, where he had previously sent papers and testimonials. Having had no reply, he enquired of the SPSL in December 1938 about the chances of finding a position in Great Britain, this time from Paris where he had moved after nine months in Switzerland. The swift answer was not encouraging:

> You had not heard further from us because we have not been able so far to find a possible opening for you. Conditions are now not at all easy and your subject is rather difficult to place. We shall go on doing our best on your behalf, but in the meantime if you have any contacts in U.S.A. we would recommend you to get in touch with them without delay, as there are better prospects in that country than in Europe.[180]

The Catholic Committee for Refugees in London also worked on his behalf, as did the Bishop of Chichester, George Bell. Bieler applied for the Chair in Latin at Queen's University in Belfast, without much hope. The invitation to Ireland promised a solution, but before Bieler could get there, war broke out and he was interned by the French authorities as an enemy alien.[181] In desperation, Eva appealed to Denis Coffey in UCD:

> I have not yet told you that my husband resigned a post as a professor for Latin, Greek and German at a Missionschool of the Fathers of the Holy Heart in Clairefontaine (Belgium) – a post for which he had already got his labour–permit and which he ought to begin in September. He resigned at once when he had got the call for the National University of Ireland on the 1st of August 1939. So <u>all</u> for us two depends now from the visa and the permit for Ireland. We will be so very very grateful to you for all your efforts in Dr Bieler's behalf.
>
> <u>For God's sake, help him!!</u>
>
> Many thanks for all your kindness. Yours gratefully Eva Bieler[182]

---

179 Elizabeth Bourke, née Bieler, 12 May 2005, quoted in Hermann Rasche, Ludwig Bieler. In: Holfter (ed.), *German-speaking Exiles*, p. 171.
180 SPSL 292/3/166, Esther Simpson to Ludwig Bieler, Hotel Palissy, 24 rue Du Dragon, Paris Vie, 20 December 1938.
181 Sean Murphy, Paris Legation to DEA, 21 September 1939: "I may state for your general information in connection with the applications for visas by German and Austrian nationals, that as a result of decrees taken by the French Government, all adult male subjects of the 'German Empire' have been put in concentration camps. Ex-Austrian nationals seem to belong to this category and Dr. Bieler is at present in a camp at Rosières (Somme)." NAI, DFA 202/424 Question of facilities for Aliens for purpose of giving lectures in National University.
182 NAI, DFA 202/424 Question of facilities for Aliens for purpose of giving lectures in National University, Eva Bieler to Denis Coffey, 23 September 1939.

Coffey strenuously pursued the question of admittance for them and for Carla Zawisch. In fact, it seems to have been entirely due to his perseverance that Ludwig Bieler was allowed in, as all relevant departments seemed to agree that he should no longer be allowed to come. The following memo to Joseph Walshe, Secretary of the DEA, clearly states the position:

> I had a long talk with Dr Coffey the other day in the matter. He agreed that, as Bieler was in an internment camp in France, no action could be taken regarding his entry to Ireland. Since then, however, Bieler has been released, so that the matter can be re-opened.
>
> Carla Zawisch is, of course, free to come if her entry is authorised.
>
> The question of the two aliens was discussed at the recent conference in the Department of Justice. The representatives of the Department of Justice, the Department of Industry and Commerce, and the Department of Defence, were all agreed that Dr Coffey's application in respect of Bieler should be refused. It was generally agreed that, from now on, the only aliens that should be admitted to this country should be technical experts required for industrial purposes and recommended by the Minister for Industry & Commerce. A case might be made for Carla Zawisch, if she could obtain a valid re-entry permit into France or some other country so as to ensure that, if necessary, she could be sent out of this country at any time. This is essential in the case of this alien, as she is at the moment in straitened financial circumstances and the possibility of her becoming a public charge in this country could not be overlooked. If permission were granted for her entry, it would, accordingly, only be on condition that she would remain in this country for the period of her employment with U.C.D., and would return to France or whatever country she had her re-entry visa for immediately thereafter.
>
> Dr. Coffey made a very strong case for the need of the two aliens in question in the University, and I would not be surprised if he were to approach the Taoiseach in the matter.[183]

Indeed, de Valera seems to have weighed in. Only a few days later, a note in quite different terms was dispatched from the Department of Justice to the Department of the Taoiseach,[184] and both Bielers accordingly arrived on 28 February in Ireland. As Ludwig's profession the registration recorded "Prof of Philosophy". They settled at Hazelbrook, Kimmage Road East in Terenure.

In spring 1940 Bieler got a visiting lectureship at University College Dublin. He seems to have become a popular public figure, partly on account of his musical skills (when a position was being sought for him, violin teacher had been the first possibility mentioned).[185] He managed to make a niche subject such as mediae-

---

183 NAI, DFA 202/424, 25 October 1939, no signature.
184 NAI, DFA 202/424, DJ to Department of the Taoiseach, 27 October 1939, stating that Justice would not be opposed to giving a visa to Bieler, provided that DI&C agreed.
185 See SPSL 292/3/173, Pater Wilfried OSB, Prinknash Abbey, Gloucester, to Headmaster, Appleforth College, York, 23 January 1939.

val Latin exciting for the general public as indicated by a newspaper notice in January 1941 under the heading "Interesting Lectures":

> An interesting series of lectures is being given during this term on Tuesday afternoons at 3.30. The lecturer is Dr. Ludwig Bieler, and his subject, "An Introduction to Mediaeval Latin." So far, there has been a good attendance at the lectures, which is not surprising, as the matter contained in Dr. Bieler's discourses has a special advantage in being somewhat out of the ordinary, and therefore likely to appeal to the curious and to all seekers of knowledge.[186]

Bieler himself summarised his war years in Ireland very positively in a letter to the SPSL in June 1945:

> Dear Mr Skemp,
>
> Many thanks for your letter of May 28th. I feel really ashamed that I never wrote to the Society for several years. So is human nature – when all goes well. And it did go well with us. Although I am not settled, if this means permanent employment, I have enjoyed the comforts of a steady and normal life all these years – and remote from the horrors of war, too. My appointment with the National University – still on the basis of a Visiting Lectureship – has been extended from year to year, and has just now been extended again until June, 1946. I have reasonable prospects that the University will keep me and give me a more permanent appointment – now that peace has come. I should indeed like to stay. I have found congenial work here and made the best of the years of scientific isolation. The Dublin Institute of Advanced Studies has published a Catalogue of Manuscripts relating to St Patrick, which I had drawn up during the first two years of my stay; the Historical Manuscripts Commission will soon bring out a major opus of mine: a Textgeschichte, edition of and commentary on the Libri Epistolarum of St. Patrick. I have also had an opportunity of contributing to a number of periodicals and have repeatedly been approached as an expert in matters of Palaeography and mediaeval studies.
>
> In order to give a human touch to this scientific report, I may mention the fact that we have two Irish born Children, a boy of three years and a girl of fifteen months.
>
> I only wish that all your protégés could send you equally satisfactory reports, but I am afraid they have not all been quite so lucky.[187]

Clearly Bieler managed to make the best of his initially precarious situation, with only £200 from a series of lectures to rely on.[188] He was fortunate in fitting the description issued in July 1938 by the UCD Senate of a refugee scholar who could

---

186 University College Notes. *Irish Times*, 27 January 1941, p. 3.
187 SPSL 292/3/193, Ludwig Bieler to Secretary of the SPSL, 2 June 1945.
188 See NUI, Minutes of Senate, Vol. XVII, Meeting 13 July 1939. The same amount was stipulated for Victor Ehrenberg's lectures.

assemble and edit "selected source-texts, A.D. 600–800 down to 1700–1900, illustrative of the historical, linguistic, literary and other work of Irish Scholars, Soldiers, and other public figures, especially in Central and Western Europe"[189]. Although not initially significant in Bieler's life, this was to become one of his major occupations in later years,[190] and he forged connections not only in UCD but also with the Dublin Institute of Advanced Studies, thanks to his work on St Patrick.[191] Becoming an authority on Ireland's patron saint[192] was certainly an excellent path to integration in the host country. Bieler also seems to have been of an outgoing and gregarious nature, more so, for example, than Ernst Lewy, who valued individual discussions and exchanges at a certain distance. In fact, Ludwig Bieler was one of the few who visited Lewy regularly out in Rathfarnham and thought nothing of walking there.[193]

Academics who did not come

Dr Carla Zawisch,[194] who had hoped to come to UCD to give lectures in histology, was in the end unable to secure the French re-entry visa demanded by the

---

189 NUI, Minutes of Senate, Vol. XVII, Senate Meeting 7 July 1938. This had been in addition to their intention to support academic refugees who could give lecture courses in the three Constituent Colleges.
190 In later years he was entrusted by the director of the National Library with the task of collecting information about Irish manuscripts found outside Ireland: cf. John Hennig, The Lasting Abode. In: Holfter and Rasche (eds), *John Hennig's Exile in Ireland*, p. 67.
191 Ludwig Bieler, *Codices Patriciani Latini – A descriptive catalogue of Latin Manuscripts*. Dublin: Dublin Institute for Advanced Studies 1942 (see also the announcement in the *Irish Press*, 4 September 1942).
192 Ludwig Bieler's numerous publications on St Patrick include: The mission of Palladius. A comparative study of sources. In: *Traditio*. Vol. 6 (1948), pp. 1–32; *The Life and Legend of St. Patrick: Problems of Modern scholarship*. Dublin: Clonmore & Reynolds 1949; *St Patrick and the Coming of Christianity*. Dublin, Melbourne: Gill 1967. His identification with St Patrick, which seems to have gone so far that he called his house 'St. Patrick's', was due in part to his perception of St Patrick as a foreigner in Ireland like himself, speaking a language that was not his mother tongue: cf. Dr Ludwig Bieler, An Appreciation. *Irish Times*, 12 May 1981.
193 Peggy Moore-Lewy, interview with authors, 28 July 2005.
194 Carla Zawisch-Ossenitz (1888–1961) had a privileged upbringing and initially opted for a musical career, studying violin and conducting. After an illness she turned to medicine and was assistant at the histology department in Vienna. It is possible she met Theo Dillon during his time in Vienna. Having published numerous studies she got her *Habilitation* in 1934. Following the *Anschluss* in March 1938 she was imprisoned for six weeks, allegedly for having made negative remarks to students about the NSDAP and for her active membership of the Catholic "St. Lukas Gilde" which she had helped to found in 1932, and her teaching permission was withdrawn.

Department of Justice.¹⁹⁵ It is clear that the decision in October 1939 by Justice, External Affairs and Industry and Commerce to allow in only "technical experts required for industrial purposes and recommended by the Minister for Industry & Commerce" did not help her case.¹⁹⁶ At the same time, the possibility that she might become "a public charge" following her engagement at UCD applied to almost all other refugee academics, especially after the start of war. Perhaps the apparently more positive attitude of the departments, indicating that she would be admitted provided the French visa was forthcoming, led Coffey to pursue his attempts to get an immediate permission less vigorously in her case than in Bieler's – and then it was too late.¹⁹⁷

There were also plans for and discussions about a number of other academics apart from Dr Zawisch who in the end did not come for various reasons. One was Julius Pokorny, who did visit Ireland after 1933 but did not remain. A colourful Austrian academic who had obtained the chair of Celtic Studies in Berlin in 1920, Pokorny was suspended in 1933 as non-Aryan, due to his Jewish grandparents, then reinstated like Lewy (a good friend of his) and Sachs, and finally dismissed in 1935, although in more favourable circumstances than others.¹⁹⁸ Acquainted with Roger Casement, Douglas Hyde and Éamon de Valera among others, he was a strong supporter of Irish nationalism, and his case aroused special sympathies in Ireland. President Hyde mentioned the matter in a meeting with Hempel, but further intervention by Hyde or de Valera, as expressly requested by Pokorny during a visit to Ireland in September 1938, was seen as potentially interfering with the internal administration of another country, and Hyde felt unable to ask

---

195 See handwritten note 13 February 1940: "this alien has not been able to secure a French re-entry visa and consequently our visa has not been granted", NAI, DJ 69/80/549.
196 NAI, DFA 202/424, 25 October 1939.
197 She was able to escape to France before going on to Madrid and in 1943 to the USA. After the war she returned to Austria, obtained a position at Graz University in 1947 and was later appointed the first female professor there. See also Alois Kernbauer, Carla Zawisch-Ossenitz. Eine biographische Skizze der ersten Professorin an der Karl-Franzens-Universität in Graz. In: Alois Kernbauer and Karin Schmidlechner-Lienhart (eds), *Frauenstudium und Frauenkarrieren an der Universität Graz*. Graz: Akademische Druck- &. Verlagsanstalt 1996, pp. 265–270.
198 See also Pól Ó Dochartaigh, *Julius Pokorny, 1887–1970: Germans, Celts and Nationalism*. Dublin: Four Courts 2004, and for a quite critical assessment of his nationalistic sympathies see Joachim Lerchenmueller, *'Keltischer Sprengstoff' – eine wissenschaftsgeschichtliche Studie über die deutsche Keltologie von 1900 bis 1945*. Tübingen: Niemeyer 1997. Pokorny himself wrote on 24 March 1938 to Douglas Hyde that he "never had any Jewish intercourse nor any sympathy for Jews – they are quite foreign to me" and further states that he had given "such great services to the German empire during the war and have always been a patriotic and even fanatic nationalist". NAI, Pres/2002/7/4 Julius Pokorny.

for his reinstatement as Professor in Berlin despite requests by Eoin MacNeill and Liam Gogan in April 1939.[199] In August 1939, it was decided between External Affairs and Justice that "in view of his outstanding position in the world of Celtic studies" Pokorny should be able to obtain a visa "at any time he desires to visit this country".[200] This offer was kept open after the beginning of the war and is likely to have contributed to Pokorny's relatively unmolested position in Berlin until 1943, when, after a few months in hiding in Vienna and Freiburg, he managed to escape to Switzerland.[201]

Another scholar who had long-established links to Ireland and was supposed to come to the country in connection with Celtic studies research was Rudolf Hertz. Suspended in 1933 and reinstated in 1934, he was able to stay on at Bonn University until 1938 despite having had a Jewish grandfather. Hertz was the pupil of Rudolf Thurneysen, acknowledged as the main authority of the time on Old Irish, and had himself achieved recognition in Celtic Studies with his publications on Old and Middle Irish. In Ireland it was Prof. Kathleen Mulchrone of University College Galway who engaged with External Affairs in September 1939 about getting Hertz admitted to Ireland.[202] She was referred to Dr Coffey and the University College Refugee Committee, and followed up her initiative at the Standing Committee in October.[203] At the Senate meeting on 7 December the decision was postponed and further reports requested, and in April 1940 it was decided not to invite him[204] – probably due to travel restrictions at that stage. Like Pokorny, Hertz was able to live more or less unmolested until 1943, after which he was enlisted in forced labour assignments from which he fled in September 1944. He then survived in hiding, and returned to lecture at Bonn University after the end of the war.[205]

Another academic who it was intended would lecture in UCD was Wilhelm Winkler, who was removed as Professor of Statistics in the University of Vienna

---

199 NAI, Pres/2002/7/4, 21 September 1938 and 3 April 1939.
200 Correspondence DEA to DJ 17 August 1939 and subsequent agreement by DJ on 22 August 1939 and in later years up to September 1942; see NAI, DJ 69/80/506.
201 In Switzerland Pokorny soon settled in Zurich where he died in 1970. Even there, the support from Ireland ensured a special standing – a recommendation from de Valera seems to have helped him to obtain a special position with the Swiss authorities, as mentioned in eulogies by Johannes Hubschmidt and Irish ambassador Frank Biggar at Pokorny's funeral; see NAI, Pres/2002/7/4.
202 See NAI, DFA 202/504.
203 See NUI, Minutes of Senate, Vol. XVII.
204 See NUI, Minutes of Senate, Vol. XVIII.
205 See Lerchenmueller, 'Keltischer Sprengstoff', p. 426.

in April 1938 for refusing to divorce his Jewish wife. His case is especially interesting as he came highly recommended (with a strong reference from Cardinal Innitzer[206] and praised as "one of the best statisticians alive" by Joseph A. Schumpeter),[207] and had prior connections to Irish academics.[208] Winkler was a devout Catholic who had married a Jewish woman and had five children to provide for.[209] His case also shows the difficulties Bewley still tried to create even for academic refugees: although instructed by Walshe in "urgent" communication on 9 February 1939 to issue a visa to Winkler or "to furnish a full report to the Department immediately",[210] Bewley took no immediate action. On 22 February, Dillon received a letter from Winkler informing him that Bewley now requested to see "the permission of my ministry" first – whereas he had thought that "both actions could run besides each other; the wish of the Irish Legation would not have been very great, because I couldn't think to go to Ireland without the permission of my Government". Given that Winkler was supposed to start lecturing in March and obviously needed the Irish permit before he could approach the Belgian and English authorities for a visa, he was understandably desperate. Dillon at once forwarded Winkler's letter to Walshe, clearly stating that he was losing patience with the Irish Minister Plenipotentiary in Berlin: "Bewley is becoming more unreasonable than ever."[211] Dillon was given an invented excuse

---

206 Innitzer called him a "Catholic of excellent reputation" (catholicum optimae famae) and asked in his Latin recommendation from 11 July 1938 that he be supported. NAI, DJ 69/80/274.
207 Alexander Pinwinkler, *Wilhelm Winkler (1894–1984) – eine Biographie*. Berlin: Duncker & Humblot 2002, pp. 330f.
208 In a letter dated 29 July 1938 to a Mr Lyon of UCD he refers to a past encounter where they knelt side by side in the Cathedral of Mexico City; see NAI, DJ 69/80/274.
209 Winkler's situation was similar to John Hennig's and Ludwig Bieler's – his wife was Jewish and he refused to divorce her. Because of that he lost his university position in April 1938. See also Pinwinkler, *Wilhelm Winkler*, p. 312.
210 See NAI, DFA 202/114. For added urgency Walshe informed Bewley that "I am to add that the Minister for Justice is particularly anxious that there should be no undue delay of any kind in this case." This 'anxiety' might be because this was another case where de Valera was in the background – when the Registrar of the National University informed DJ about the Senate's decision to appoint Winkler he emphasised: "I may add that an Taoiseach was present, as Chancellor of the University, at the meeting of the Senate at which this decision was reached." NAI, DJ 69/80/274, Alex McCarthy to Costigan, 4 February 1939.
211 Ibid., Dillon to Walshe, 25 February 1939.

for the delay, External Affairs wired to Bewley on 1 March demanding action,[212,213] and a visa was provided the same day. It is unclear why Winkler did not in the end come to Ireland.[214]

Then there was Austrian art historian Dr Otto Pächt who was to give two lectures at UCD on 30 and 31 January 1940 on the history of painting.[215] Pächt was at the time a refugee in London and lectured at the Courtauld Institute and the Warburg Institute, and was supposed to be the guest of Dr Furlong, director of the National Gallery.[216] He applied for a permit to enter Ireland and special permission to bring his slides along. While the University had already fixed the time and

---

212 "My minute 202/7 of 9th February has visa yet been granted Wilhelm Winkler Stop If not please wire today cause of delay", ibid., telegram DEA to Berlin, 1 March 1939.
213 "You will be glad to hear that Professor Winkler has now his visa. Some delay was inevitable in this case as the Department of Justice wished us to confirm officially that Professor Winkler would be allowed to return periodically to Germany." Ibid., Walshe to Dillon, 2 March 1939. Walshe's excuse is clearly wrong, as DJ had already advised DEA on 11 February that "[t]he visa may be made valid for any number of journeys within one year from the date of issue," ibid. The reason for this was the stipulation that Winkler had to be back in Austria every two months in order not to endanger his pension and his family.
214 Alexander Pinwinkler suggests that the lack of support from F. A. Hayek (then at the London School of Economics) would have been one of the key reasons for Winkler's failure to emigrate, following Feichtinger's argument (Johannes Feichtinger, *Wissenschaft zwischen den Kulturen. Österreichische Hochschullehrer in der Emigration 1933–1945*. Frankfurt a. M.: Campus 2001, pp. 226f.); see Pinwinkler's article Wilhelm Winkler und der Nationalsozialismus 1933–1945. In: Rainer Mackensen (ed.), *Bevölkerungslehre und Bevölkerungspolitik im 'Dritten Reich'*. Wiesbaden: Springer 2004, pp. 165–182, 174. Winkler had however (finally) obtained both an offer of lectures and a visa for Ireland, entirely without Hayek's help. Pinwinkler's extensive biography of Winkler includes other reasons why emigration to Ecuador or Ireland was not feasible – one son being sick and one son not being furnished a visa (see *Wilhelm Winkler*, p. 321) – though it is unclear whether this visa was for Ecuador or Ireland (mail to authors, 25 February 2016). Given that Winkler seemingly wanted to come alone and return to Austria every two months, neither should have been an obstacle to making use of his Irish visa. Winkler however remained in Vienna, and after the war was reinstated and appointed as chair of Statistics.
215 See NAI, DFA 202/424, A. J. O'Connell, Secretary and Bursar at UCD to External Affairs, 24 January 1940.
216 See NAI, DJ 69/80/618. It seems that George Furlong was also instrumental in enabling Otto Pächt to leave Austria in 1936. Pächt, a Jewish art historian from Vienna, had been dismissed from his position in Heidelberg in 1933 and returned to Austria. Furlong's invitation led to Pächt working at the Warburg Institute in London from 1937. See also Ulrike Wendland, *Biographisches Handbuch deutschsprachiger Kunsthistoriker im Exil*. Vol. 2, L-Z, de Gruyter Saur 1999, pp. 479f. George Furlong had studied in Munich and Vienna where he received his PhD in 1928, and had been appointed director of the National Gallery in Dublin in 1935; his interest and support for refugees is also evident in Hubert Butler's notes. See TCD Archives, Butler Papers 10304/625/118.

lecture rooms, it seems that communication with the relevant authorities (and indeed with Pächt himself, who only heard about it less than two weeks before the scheduled lectures, on 19 January) was left a little late. While the Irish officials sorted things out between DEA and Justice within a day, due to a missing exit visa from Great Britain the lectures had to be cancelled.[217] No reason was given for the visa not being issued, despite Belton from DEA calling his British colleagues.[218]

Another academic who did not come to Ireland was Dr Kurt Sitte, a former assistant at the Physics Department of Prague University. Born in the Sudetenland, Sitte was not a member of any party, but tried to promote good relations between Germans and Czechs, and had close contact with Beneš. According to a letter written by Alfred Peres of the Czech Refugee Trust Fund in London to Erwin Schrödinger in December 1939, Sitte's wife Hedwig was Jewish, but he had refused to divorce her. He had been arrested by the Gestapo on 15 March 1939, the day of Hitler's occupation of Czechoslovakia, released after two months, but then taken to Buchenwald concentration camp.[219] Schrödinger passed on the letter to the Department of the Taoiseach, which in turn sent it on to the Department of Justice, which then raised enquiries with the Department of External Affairs. Sitte, who numbered Max Planck among his referees, was seen as very promising, and correspondence between Schrödinger and the different departments shows that there was general support for him to be allowed temporary entry to Ireland, as a stepping stone to the UK. The SPSL eventually promised to support him and to approach the Home Office once Sitte was in Ireland,[220] but the British Home Office refused him the necessary re-entry permit.[221]

---

217 See also notice in *Irish Times*, 30 January 1940 that his lectures "are unavoidably cancelled".
218 See NAI, DFA 202/424.
219 NAI, DJ 69/80/600.
220 After initially championing Sitte's admission to Ireland, Schrödinger had informed the Department of the Taoiseach that he was no longer pursuing the case, following a negative response from the SPSL regarding their ability to support Sitte (see correspondence DT to DJ 16 February 1940). Following SPSL's decision to grant £200 to Sitte, however, Schrödinger wrote again, indicating that he would be glad if the case could be re-opened. He stated that he had no personal relations with Sitte, but had been acting as mediator "impelled by compassion for a worthy colleague who, as I am told, is suffering from the terrible persecution which I myself have been lucky enough to escape" (NAI, DJ 69/80/600, Schrödinger to Moynihan, 12 March 1940).
221 NAI, DFA 202/710 Dr Kurt Sitte. Sitte and his wife survived Buchenwald concentration camp. In 1948 he went to the USA and later to Brazil. He caused headlines around the world when he was arrested in July 1960 in Israel for espionage. He had worked as Head of the Physics Department at the renowned Technion Institute of Technology in Haifa and was accused of working for the Czech Secret Service.

The Dublin Institute of Advanced Studies (DIAS)

Image 5: Schrödinger portrait by Seán Keating.

Among the numerous academics who came to Ireland, Erwin Schrödinger has a special role. He was and is by far the best known exile in Ireland.[222] His coming to the country can be attributed first and foremost to Éamon de Valera.

De Valera had long cherished an ambition to accelerate scientific research in Ireland along the lines he thought most important – mathematics/physics and the study of Irish.[223] In order to achieve this, he planned to create a Dublin Institute of

---

[222] There are still annual Schrödinger lectures in Trinity College, the University of Limerick named a building after him, and there was even a call to have a statue erected in Merrion Square in his honour: http://www.politics.ie/forum/education-science/213857-why-no-statue-schroedinger-dublin.html [accessed 18 March 2016]. For publications about his time in Ireland see for example Ruth Braunizer, Memories of Dublin – excerpts from Erwin Schrödinger's diaries. In: Gisela Holfter (ed.), *German-speaking Exiles in Ireland 1933–1945*. Amsterdam/New York: Rodopi 2006, pp. 265–274 and Walter Moore's biography *Schrödinger – Life and Thought*. Cambridge: CUP 1989. For a fictionalised approach to Schrödinger's time in Dublin see Neil Belton, *A Game with Sharpened Knives*. London: Weidenfeld & Nicolson 2005 (translated into German as *Das Spiel mit geschliffenen Klingen*. Frankfurt/Main: S. Fischer 2007).
[223] William McCrea argues that while reasons for founding the Celtic School were obvious, for Theoretical Physics they were fourfold: a) the tradition of leading figures produced by Ireland in the past, above all Sir William Rowan Hamilton; b) it was a field in which fundamental advances were being made; c) it called for no prohibitively expensive equipment; and d) it was an area in which de Valera was interested. See William McCrea, Eamon de Valera, Erwin Schrödinger and the Dublin Institute of Advanced Studies. In: *Bulletin of the Department of Foreign Affairs*. Vol. 1037 (May/June 1987), pp. 12–14, 13. It is often forgotten, however, that de Valera had initially

Advanced Studies, modelled along the lines of the Institute of Advanced Studies in Princeton,[224] which had been founded in 1930 and had become Albert Einstein's new work domain. Accordingly, de Valera saw it as vital to find researchers who could provide a strong initial impetus and ensure academic development at a world-class level.[225] Schrödinger fitted that bill admirably, although under normal circumstances it is unlikely that he would have ever come to Ireland. Born in Vienna in 1887, by the 1930s he could look back on a career and scientific discoveries that had brought him into the inner circle of the best known and most influential physicists of the twentieth century. Following brief appointments in Jena, Stuttgart and Breslau, he moved to Zurich in 1921 as professor of theoretical physics. In 1927, he succeeded Max Planck in the coveted chair of physics at Friedrich-Wilhelms-Universität in Berlin (though he had not been the first choice: Ludwig Hopf's supervisor Arnold Sommerfeld had turned down the post, preferring to stay in Munich). In 1933, however, the new political developments in Germany poisoned his time in Berlin. While he was not an outspoken opponent of the Nazis, he had no time for their policies, and left Germany when an opportunity arose.[226] This came through Frederick Lindemann, an Oxford professor of physics (known to many as 'the Prof') who had come to Berlin looking for suitable candidates among the threatened academics to go to England.[227] Schrödinger's

---

planned to have medicine as a third area of research: this was discussed during Schrödinger's first trip to Dublin on 19–21 November 1938. See NAI, S10602A, minutes of the meeting on 21 November between de Valera, Schrödinger, Conway from NUI, McConnell from TCD and Walshe from External Affairs, 23 November 1938.

224 The spread of subjects at the Princeton Institute was considerably broader than what was envisaged for Dublin, encompassing Schools of Historical Studies, Mathematics, Natural Sciences and Social Science.

225 Edmund Taylor (E. T.) Whittaker in Edinburgh had originally been the key person in de Valera's plans, and he continued to advise de Valera on the project. A meeting with him in Dublin on 8 April 1939 led de Valera to conclude that the "men of international reputation" who were to lead the Princeton-modelled institute were to be Conway, Whittaker and Schrödinger, as Max Born and Einstein were not available. Note NAI, S13013A, 12 April 1938.

226 As Schrödinger wrote in September 1939 to F. G. Donnan (professor of chemical engineering at University College, London, who had studied in Belfast and obtained his PhD in Leipzig), he saw it as his "duty to withdraw from this government and thus, for the moment, from this people, all assistance whatsoever, in order to do what we can to make this shameful system collapse". P. K. Hoch and E. J. Yoxen, Schrödinger at Oxford: A hypothetical national cultural synthesis which failed. In: *Annals of Science*. Vol. 44, no. 6 (1987), pp. 593–616, 611.

227 Frederick Lindemann was an English physicist who studied in Berlin before WWI and became an influential scientific adviser to Winston Churchill, especially in the 1940s. Having been appointed to a professorship in Oxford in 1919 he also became the director of the Clarendon Laboratory where he managed to place a number of Jewish academics from Germany after 1933.

maternal grandmother was English and he had visited England as a child: he was fluent in the language and he knew the country, although he could be very critical about the living conditions there. In 1928, during a visit to Cambridge and London, he wrote:

> What depresses me here in England so much is the anodyne, dispassionate gentlemanly atmosphere. You have to say 'I am sorry' all the time, constantly cover up everything you want to say, because nudity is frowned upon here in every sense. I feel as if I'm tied up. On top of that, uncomfortable rooms, the gruesome cold in all rooms of the house, and added a terrible cold and coughing (but this is already abating).[228]

Nonetheless, when Lindemann offered him the chance to go to Oxford, he took it. He was elected a Fellow of Magdalen College, and in addition received a two-year financial grant from the British company Imperial Chemical Industries (ICI). Shortly after his arrival in November 1933, news broke that jointly with Paul Dirac he was to receive the Nobel Prize for Physics, principally for his 1926 publications on wave mechanics.[229] In 1934, he was offered a professorship in Princeton which he turned down, mainly for financial reasons, a key point being the question of pensions for him and his wife Annemarie (Anny).[230] Anny and Erwin Schrödinger's marriage was somewhat unorthodox; Erwin in particular had many affairs, which were largely tolerated by Anny. It raised eyebrows that Schrödinger had brought to Oxford fellow physicist Arthur March and his wife Hilde, with whom he had a liaison which led to her pregnancy. Their daughter Ruth was born in Oxford in May 1934, a few weeks after Schrödinger's return from a visiting lectureship in Princeton.

Although Oxford was not perfect for Schrödinger (nor Schrödinger for Oxford, not least because of his domestic set-up),[231] it still came as a surprise when he

---

He had many critics, however. According to Max Born, Lindemann was a "mediocre physicist, but a remarkable personality and a remarkable snob". Max Born, My Life. London: Taylor & Francis 1978, p. 260.
228 Schrödinger to Paul Ehrenfest (Leiden), 12 March 1928. In: Karl von Meyenn (ed.), *Eine Entdeckung von ganz außerordentlicher Tragweite – Schrödingers Briefwechsel zur Wellenmechanik und zum Katzenparadoxon*, Vol. I. Berlin/Heidelberg: Springer 2011, p. 450. Translated by authors.
229 Schrödinger, Quantisierung als Eigenwertproblem (Erste Mitteilung [First Paper]). In: *Annalen der Physik*. Vol. 4, no. 79 (1926), pp. 361–376; this was followed by three more papers in the *Annalen der Physik*, published later that year.
230 See Moore, *Erwin Schrödinger*, pp. 293f.
231 Oxford could not match Berlin academically and Schrödinger missed the passionate interest of lecturers and students, as Karl Popper recalled (see Hoch and Yoxen, Schrödinger at Oxford, p. 595). The specific atmosphere in Oxford with a strong emphasis on formalities and college life was at times combined with a disregard for the sciences (Hans Motz, who came to Magdalen a

accepted a professorship in Graz in 1936.²³² As Anny Schrödinger recalled later: "It never occurred to us that this step might turn out to be rather foolish, even dangerous. Many of our friends shook their heads and soon we understood their attitudes. In March 1938 Austria was invaded."²³³ Initially, Schrödinger tried to appease the new regime, and wrote an open letter which was published in the Graz newspaper *Tagespost* on 30 March 1938,²³⁴ entitled "Bekenntnis zum Führer" ("Commitment to the Führer").²³⁵ Explaining that he had been one of the people who had not until recently understood the right course, but now embraced the German offer of peace ("deutsche Friedenshand"), he declared that for an old Austrian who loved his country there could be no question but that each 'No' vote in the upcoming referendum on the annexation of Austria would be tantamount to racial suicide ("völkischen Selbstmord"). Less than a fortnight later – just after the landslide plebiscite on 10 April 1938 in favour of the *Anschluss* – Schrödinger was dismissed from his post as honorary professor in Vienna. It seems that at

---

few years after Schrödinger, doubted whether most of the Fellows "knew who he [Schrödinger] was", ibid., p. 602). Furthermore, there was little understanding for Schrödinger's unconventional marital situation, ibid., p. 608 and Moore, *Schrödinger*, p. 298.

232 Just prior to the Graz offer he was offered the Darwin chair in Edinburgh and initially seemed enthusiastic, but then declined, explaining that the pull from his homeland was too strong. Other personal factors might also have played a role, as might the delay by the Home Office in processing the application for permanent residence. Moore, *Schrödinger*, p. 319. Max Born was appointed to the Darwin chair instead of Schrödinger.

233 Anny Schrödinger, Notes on Events leading up to Professor Schroedinger's coming to Dublin in 1939. Copies of her account can be found in the DIAS archive, Admin 40 and the Dokumentationsarchiv des Österreichischen Widerstandes (DÖW), Vienna.

234 See Wolfgang L. Reiter, 1938 und die Folgen für die Naturwissenschaften. In: Friedrich Stadler (ed.), *Vertriebene Vernunft II – Emigration und Exil österreichischer Wissenschaft 1930–1940*, Vol. 2. Münster: Lit 2004, pp. 664–680, 675–676.

235 "Die Hand jedem Willigen. Bekenntnis zum Führer – Ein hervorragender Wissenschaftler meldet sich zum Dienst für Volk und Heimat" ([Offering] the hand to everyone willing. Commitment to the Führer. An outstanding scientist reporting for duty for the nation and homeland). Translated by authors. This letter might not have become widely known, but a subsequent article in *Nature* on 21 May 1938 ensured international publicity. Schrödinger felt quite aggrieved, as he wrote five years later to Max Born – not because of the included translation of the last paragraph ("Well-wishing friends who overestimate my importance consider it right that the repentant confession which I made to them should be made public. I too belong to those who seize the outstretched hand of peace, because sitting at my writing desk, I have misjudged to the last the real will and destiny of my land. I make this confession readily and joyfully. I believe it is spoken out of the hearts of many and I hope in doing this to serve my country"), which he himself seems to have passed on to *Nature* at their request, but due to the information in the article that he "will continue to occupy the chair of theoretical physics", which, as it turned out, was wrong. See Hoch and Yoxen, Schrödinger at Oxford, pp. 609–610.

least to begin with the new regime acted against him not because of his departure from Berlin in 1933, but rather because of his outspokenness against Nazi sympathisers while in Graz,[236] although publication of his open letter had averted a threat to revoke his citizenship.[237] It was clear, however, that his position was precarious and that an offer of a safe haven would be most welcome. In Dublin meanwhile it was understood that time was of the essence and that a covert approach was required. Anny Schrödinger describes the chain of messages as follows: de Valera to Whittaker, Whittaker to Max Born (now established in a professorship in Edinburgh, a position Schrödinger had turned down), Born to Richard Bär (in Zurich) who had a Dutch friend on the way to Vienna who went to see Anny's mother and wrote down a few sentences, "approximately running like that: Mr de Valera intends to create an Institute for Advanced Studies. Would you be principally prepared to take up a post there. No signature – nothing",[238] which Anny's mother sent with her next letter. The Schrödingers' reaction was suitably clandestine: "We read the few lines over and over again – then put a match to it and burnt it." Later, Anny Schrödinger went to meet Bär and passed on her husband's "definite answer: 'Yes'".[239] The voluminous files in the National Archives on the Institute of Advanced Studies contain details of the negotiations in Dublin

---

[236] See Archiv Auswärtiges Amt Berlin (AAA), R 100007, Abt. Deutschland, Az. 83-76 Ausbürgerungen, Vol. 11. German Consulate Graz to Department of Foreign Affairs Berlin, 24 January 1938, about the proposed employment of a German professor who had been in prison for insulting Hitler. Allegedly Schrödinger was the only one in favour of this appointment, and declared that Hitler only ruled by violence whereas there was still freedom in Austria. The Consulate called for Schrödinger's immediate expatriation. Surprisingly, enquiries from the Gestapo in Berlin following the proposal in Graz were inconclusive as there was "a lack of personal details and his last address is not known. There is no information where Schrödinger worked or where relatives of his are living". Gestapo Berlin to Department of Foreign Affairs Berlin, 23 February 1938. Translated by authors.
[237] A previous letter by Schrödinger and his personal appearance at the German Consulate in Graz were not seen as sufficient. AAA, R 100007, Az. 83-76 Ausbürgerungen, Vol. 11, German Consulate Graz to Department of Foreign Affairs Berlin, 17 March 1938. On 30 March, however, the German Consulate Graz forwarded his "contrite confession" from the *Grazer Volksblatt* to the Department and argued that for formal and legal reasons it would no longer be possible to revoke his citizenship – but added that the question of withdrawing his professorship might still be addressed by the local administration. Translated by authors. Schrödinger's letter had quite a negative impact on his supporters in England. He himself defended his "certainly quite cowardly statement" to Albert Einstein in July 1939 arguing "I *wanted* to remain free – and could not do so without great duplicity," Moore, *Schrödinger*, p. 338.
[238] Anny Schrödinger, Notes on Events leading up to Professor Schroedinger's coming to Dublin in 1939, p. 1.
[239] Ibid., pp. 2–3.

and Edinburgh.[240] While de Valera and Schrödinger had come to an understanding, however, the Institute had yet to be established.

On 26 August 1938, Schrödinger was dismissed from Graz, a development that considerably increased the tension. He and Anny went to Rome (assisted by Schrödinger's membership of the Papal Academy) and wrote to de Valera, who telephoned immediately and asked Schrödinger to meet him in Geneva, where he was on League of Nations business, the Schrödingers' trip being facilitated by the Irish Legation in Rome. Following a return to Oxford in October and November 1938, Schrödinger accepted a short-term position in Ghent, while in Dublin preparations for the establishment of the Institute continued. De Valera ensured that travel documents were to be available as soon as needed.[241] The Schrödingers were seen by External Affairs as "aliens whose entry has been recommended by the Co-ordinating Committee for Refugees, and the Minister is particularly anxious that they should be in a position to travel to this country as soon as possible".[242] It is interesting that despite the clear eagerness of de Valera (who was Minister of External Affairs as well as Taoiseach) to speed up the process, even this prized specialist and his wife still needed the recommendation of the ICCR, following the established rule that admission would only be granted to those (limited and numbered) cases that the committee decided on. The travel group was somewhat unusual, consisting of Erwin and Anny Schrödinger, Hilde March, and her and Schrödinger's daughter Ruth (who had both joined Erwin and Anny in spring 1939 in Belgium), and a visa for Hilde March was accordingly required. This difficulty was resolved, as de Valera had already anticipated the need for personal involvement.[243] Interestingly, unlike Erwin and Anny, March was not to

---

240 See NAI, S10602A, specifically Whittaker's letters to de Valera 25 April 1938, 4 and 25 May 1938.
241 DEA informed the Paris Legation on 17 January 1939 that as directed by the Minister (i.e. de Valera), visas for travel to Ireland by Erwin Schrödinger and his wife, at present in Ghent, were to be granted immediately on application. Despite worries that the Department of Justice would not sanction any deviation from normal rules, it had been arranged that "in the peculiar circumstances of this case, the passports, although expired, will be recognised as valid for the purpose of entry into Ireland," NAI, DFA 202/525.
242 Ibid.
243 See NAI, DFA 202/525. Schrödinger wrote to de Valera from Ghent on 29 January 1939 indicating that thanks to Walshe's help with passport difficulties, his and Anny's visas should be settled in a few days. "But in the case of our friend, Frau Hildegund March from Innsbruck, you advised me, Sir, to apply to yourself. She has now joined us here in Ghent and I should be very thankful for a visa to be issued to her by your Minister in Paris, enabling her to enter Eire, as soon as the necessity may arise in connection with our removal. For several reasons I feel uneasy, until we, all three of us, possess the necessary documents for sailing any moment." He went on

be counted as one of the 20 ICCR cases of "guaranteed adults", something that caused confusion among the civil servants, as did the fact that she was coming to Ireland without her husband.[244] Schrödinger became alarmed at the slow progress of the planned Institute of Advanced Studies[245] and the reported opposition to its establishment, but he was immediately reassured by de Valera, who optimistically indicated that the legislation was to be enacted before Christmas, and also mentioned that he had organised a lecturing appointment for Schrödinger at UCD for the autumn.[246] Following the outbreak of war, Schrödinger and his entourage finally travelled to Ireland in early October 1939.[247]

---

to reassure de Valera that Hilde March did not intend to seek work of any kind: "I take personal responsibility for her entertainment as well as for her never causing any trouble to you, Sir, or to your country."

244 See for example NAI, DJ 69/80/46, J. E. Duff, DJ, to Maurice Moynihan, 24 November 1938: "As you know, a quota of twenty has been allotted to the Co-Ordinating Committee to be filled with cases of what we call 'guaranteed adults', that is persons who are anxious to escape from Germany or Austria and whose maintenance is guaranteed here by responsible citizens. The Professor has asked for an extra-quota case, but as the Taoiseach is interested I did not refuse and probably the Professor is under the impression that no difficulty is likely to arise. At the same time I felt that it was extremely peculiar that a request should be made for facilities for this lady to abandon her family for the somewhat inadequate reason that she would be of assistance to Frau Schroedinger in establishing a home here." The Taoiseach's office confirmed a fortnight later that Hilde March was indeed not to be considered in connection with the quota. Ibid. The probable reason was that, whereas a case could be made for Schrödinger being a refugee, given his dismissal, no argument could be put forward on behalf of Hilde March in this respect.

245 As de Valera wrote to Schrödinger: "It was unusual for a Bill to be opposed on its First Reading," NAI, S10602A, 15 July 1939. The discussion in the Dáil on 6 July was initiated by General Richard Mulcahy: see Institute for Advanced Studies Bill, 1939 – Second Stage, http://oireachtasdebates.oireachtas.ie/debates%20authoring/DebatesWebPack.nsf/takes/dail1939070600011 [last accessed 1 April 2016].

246 NAI, S10602A, Schrödinger to de Valera 29 July 1939 and de Valera to Schrödinger 31 July 1939.

247 The outbreak of the war interrupted direct passenger service between Belgium and Ireland and also invalidated British visas for the Schrödingers (whose Irish visas were due to expire on 20 September 1939). Once again de Valera's personal intercession was necessary: see NAI, S10602, Schrödinger to de Valera, 15 September 1939. Schrödinger's mere presence provided much-needed reassurance to a young fellow-exile who came to Ireland in circumstances of far greater insecurity and, crucially, with his family's destiny still in limbo – John Hennig. Hennig describes in his memoir the fraught time of arrival in Folkestone where a Jewish man took his own life after being prevented from leaving the ship. Hennig was led into the immigration office along with another family: "The husband's name was called out first: 'Schrodinger' [sic]. 'Forgive me if I ask a stupid question,' I said when he came back, 'but would you be the great Schrodinger?' 'Whether or not I am great, I don't know,' he answered. 'I am a physicist, and like you, I am travelling on to Dublin.' It must be a good omen, I thought, to emigrate in such good company." Holfter and Rasche (eds), *John Hennig's Exile in Ireland*, p. 54.

In their first days in Ireland the extended family stayed in the Caledonian Hotel in the city centre, before moving out to 45 Victoria Road in Clontarf for several months. In early November Schrödinger commenced his lectures at University College Dublin (being paid £200), and in December de Valera arranged a special grant for the Royal Irish Academy so that they could pay Schrödinger for research work and lectures at a rate of £1,200. Although some creative accounting was required, this was duly approved by the Academy and the Department of Finance,[248] and on 1 April 1940 Schrödinger was appointed to a temporary professorship.

While there were occasional discussions of potential opportunities to leave Ireland at least temporarily (whether for the US, Canada or India), on the whole Schrödinger clearly appreciated his surroundings.[249] His residence from July 1940 onwards at 26 Kincora Road in Clontarf, close to the sea,[250] soon became a regular meeting place for young scholars and refugees. Among them was Stefan Feric (see chapters 2 and 8) who had met Schrödinger in 1939 at the Old Vienna Club and was immediately invited to Schrödinger's home where he became a frequent visitor, and often found himself with other German-speaking guests or some of Schrödinger's students. According to his recollections the discussions in Schrödinger's study (or in the summer in the back garden) were wide-ranging. He also remembered going on cycle tours with Schrödinger.[251] Anny also wrote to her mother about holidays with Erwin spent cycling, whether into the nearby Wicklow Mountains or on longer trips in the South of Ireland.[252] The simplicity of the life, the natural surroundings and the friendliness of the people appealed to

---

[248] Finance was prepared to insert the necessary provision for the extra cost in the 'Vote for Miscellaneous Expenses' in 1940–41: NAI, S10602A, memo, 18 December 1939.

[249] "Neither now nor in any future should I willingly leave this beautiful little boat which Mr. de Valera is steering through the heavy gale – nor where I feel so happy." NAI, S10602B, Schrödinger to Walshe, 26 July 1940.

[250] As Anny Schödinger wrote to her mother, they had never, not even in Zurich, lived in such a nice place. MAI G2/0760, letter, 30 August 1940. While Ruth seems to have made the most of living only a few hundred metres from the sea in Clontarf and went swimming, her father was not a keen swimmer, preferring bike trips. See University of Vienna, Zentralbibliothek für Physik der Universität Wien, Stefan Feric interview with Elisabeth Guggenberger, 10 August 1987.

[251] University of Vienna, Zentralbibliothek für Physik, Feric interview, 10 August 1987. Excursions with students were not unusual at the time. Walter Heitler remembers in his obituary for Schrödinger that in Zurich in the 1920s, every Sunday was spent walking in the hills with the Schrödingers, followed by a glass of wine (or maybe two) in a nice country inn. See Walter Heitler, Erwin Schrödinger. In: *Biographical Memoirs of Fellows of the Royal Society of London.* Vol. 7 (1961), pp. 220–225, 223.

[252] See MAI G2/0760, for example Anny Schrödinger to Elisabeth Bertel, 11 August 1940.

him. He was also interested in theatre and the arts, and soon became a member of the Dublin Arts Club.[253] Also, the academic atmosphere in Dublin, with a tendency to "foster width of interest and the indulgence of curiosity" was congenial for Schrödinger, according to William McCrea, who records that intellectually Schrödinger and Dublin "took to each other right from the start".[254]

Schrödinger was occupied mainly with the establishment of the Institute of Advanced Studies. There was some opposition to the scheme from farmers' representatives – as late as May 1940 the project was still coming under fire in Senate discussions.[255] Professor Michael Tierney, professor of Greek and later president of UCD, also had reservations. He criticised especially "the bringing together of two matters which have really no relation to each other at all, [...] and the attempt [...] to produce research work under the close supervision and direction of any Ministry, whether it be the Ministry of Education or the Ministry of Finance".[256] Continuing his indictment, he exclaimed that these points "are not my objections alone. I believe if the Taoiseach were to consult almost anybody in either of the two universities in Dublin he would find that nobody really likes this combination of mathematical physics and Celtic studies except the Taoiseach himself. It is his own idea and nobody else, as far as I am aware, likes it or wants it." In the same debate Ernest Alton of Trinity argued against the strong involvement of the Department of Finance, but in essence he gave it his (and Trinity's) support, and credited de Valera with possibly having "lit a little lamp of learning and hope,

---

253 See Arthur James McConnell's interview with Elisabeth Guggenheimer, 10 August 1987, Zentralbibliothek für Physik der Universität Wien.
254 William McCrea, Eamon de Valera, Erwin Schrödinger and the Dublin Institute. In: C. W. Kilmister (ed.), *Schrödinger – Centenary Celebration of a Polymath*. Cambridge: CUP 1989, pp. 119–135, 132–133.
255 Senator John Joseph Counihan, a member of the Agricultural Panel of the Senate, argued: "I think this sum of £30,000 or £40,000 a year, which it is proposed to spend in setting up this school of advanced Celtic studies, could be much better spent in building halls in the small towns and villages of the country where organised studies could be carried on. The money would be much better spent in supplying these halls with small libraries, with books, periodicals, papers and magazines, and it would be much more to the material, intellectual and moral advantage of the rural population and be a very much more effective way of spending the money than spending it on the establishment of this school of advanced Celtic studies. But, of course, that will not appeal to the professors. That is the farmer's point of view." (Ibid.).
256 Seanad Éireann Debate, Vol. 24, no. 14, Institute for Advanced Studies Bill, 1939 – Second Stage, http://oireachtasdebates.oireachtas.ie/debates%20authoring/debateswebpack.nsf/takes/seanad1940051500004?opendocument [last accessed 7 March 2016]. At this Senate discussion of the second reading of the proposed bill, de Valera as the current Minister for Education had the opportunity to speak at length about the advantages and background of the proposed institute.

which may yet be able to cast a gleam of light across the whole of the world". Helena Concannon, professor of history at University College Galway, invoked Kuno Meyer, who had researched evidence that Ireland had benefited in earlier times from scholars brought there by war, and had been "splendidly repaid" for its hospitality. She argued that "the distinguished European scientists" who had already arrived (clearly referring to Erwin Schrödinger) had "hastened the maturing of plans the Taoiseach already cherished for an institute of advanced studies" and "will repay no less richly the welcome we give them".[257]

The resistance possibly surprised de Valera (who had informed E. T. Whittaker in early May 1940 that the bill had passed through all stages at the Dáil, and expressed his hope that it would go through the Senate "with equal, or perhaps greater ease")[258] but in no way changed his plans. In the end the scheme was approved, and on 19 June the *Institute for Advanced Studies Act, 1940* was passed to make provision for the establishment and maintenance in Dublin of an Institute for Advanced Studies consisting of a School of Celtic Studies and a School of Theoretical Physics.[259] Work could finally begin. At the first meeting of the Governing Board of the School of Theoretical Physics on 21 November 1940, Schrödinger was appointed director. While the premises of the School of Theoretical Physics were being prepared for their new tenants at 65 Merrion Square (no. 64 being reserved for the School of Celtic Studies), Schrödinger commenced two courses on quantum theory in the premises of the Royal Irish Academy at Academy House on Dawson Street.

Overall, Schrödinger was very happy in Ireland. As Anny wrote to Arnold Sommerfeld in May 1942:

> There is only good news from us. Erwin really must have been born under a particularly lucky star. That he was brought by a lucky coincidence in the right moment to this beautiful island – for that we can't thank providence enough. The result was that Erwin has become unbelievably productive again as he has been able to dedicate himself to scientific research work fully and under ideal conditions. As there is no greater joy for a scientist one has to

---

[257] Ibid., Colcannon (1878–1952) echoed Alton's sentiments about the contrast of the darkness of the world around and the light of learning and asked for "a prayer of gratitude to God, because in the midst of the terrible tempest which has set almost the whole world reeling on its foundations, and strewn its seven seas with shipwrecks and corpses, we can have peace enough, tranquillity and leisure of mind enough to take thought for other things besides war and its havoc, for construction rather than destruction, for the things of the mind and the spirit rather than for the cult of that brutal materialism which has before our eyes sent its own shrines crashing, and carried its own appalling retribution."
[258] DIAS archive, Admin /39, de Valera to Whittaker, 2 May 1940.
[259] For the full text see http://www.acts.ie [last accessed 19 March 2016].

say that Erwin once again landed on his feet. The research institute grows and is thriving which delights everyone involved there and also causes joy and satisfaction for the noble founder. You can imagine that in these difficult times the ruler of a country – even if only a small one – has more than enough worries; therefore it is especially noteworthy (doubly fortunate) that Mr de Valera takes part to such an extent in the development of an academic research institute which was founded only thanks to himself.[260]

That the research institute was thriving was thanks not only to Schrödinger (and de Valera) but also to Walter Heitler, another German émigré academic, whose important contribution gets little recognition.[261] Heitler's name had already been mentioned by Whittaker in May 1938 in a letter to de Valera – "a much younger (age 34) but extremely brilliant man [...] If Schrodinger and Heitler could both be got, Dublin would be the most important centre of mathematical physics in the world".[262]

Heitler's move to Ireland followed his release from internment in Britain, which he had spent in three camps, including one on the Isle of Man. Born on 2 January 1904, the son of a professor of engineering in Karlsruhe, Heitler came to physics almost by chance, following a friend's recommendation, when he was at a loose end after his *Abitur*.[263] Following studies in Karlsruhe and Berlin, Heitler joined Sommerfeld's institute in Munich. Under the supervision of Karl Herzfeld he finished his PhD in 1926, and that autumn went to Copenhagen (the main centre of physics research apart from Munich and Göttingen) with a grant from the Rockefeller Foundation, before joining Schrödinger as an assistant in Zurich.[264] Schrödinger generally preferred to work alone, so Heitler's time in spring and summer 1927 was spent mostly with another young physicist in receipt

---

260 Deutsches Museum Munich archive, Anny Schrödinger to Arnold Sommerfeld, 24 May 1942, thanks to Dr Michael Eckert. Translation by authors.
261 See Lochlainn O'Raifeartaigh and Günther Rasche, Walter Heitler 1904–81. In: Ken Houston (ed.), *Creators of Mathematics: The Irish Connection*. Dublin: University College Dublin Press 2000, pp. 113–121; Cormac O'Raifeartaigh, An Irishman's Diary. *Irish Times*, 29 December 2004 and Neasa McGarrigle, Walter Heitler, the forgotten hero of Éamon de Valera's science push. *Irish Times*, 15 October 2015.
262 NAI, S10602A, Whittaker to de Valera, 25 May 1938.
263 See Karl von Meyenn (ed.), *Eine Entdeckung von ganz außerordentlicher Tragweite*, Vol. 1, p. 223. Also interview Walter Heitler by John L. Heilbron, 18 March 1963, Center for History of Physics of the American Institute of Physics, https://www.aip.org/history-programs/niels-bohr-library/oral-histories/4662-1 [last accessed 18 March 2016].
264 A potential move to Zurich by one of Sommerfeld's students (and possibly even Heitler) had already been discussed by Schrödinger and Sommerfeld in spring 1926 though at that stage Schrödinger expressed reservations regarding Heitler's statistical approach. See Schrödinger to Sommerfeld, 11 May 1926. In: Sommerfeld, *Wissenschaftlicher Briefwechsel*, Vol. 2, pp. 253–4.

of a Rockefeller grant, Fritz London.[265] Their collaboration proved fruitful – they calculated the bonding of H_2 molecules in terms of quantum physics, building on Schrödinger's wave equation. This discovery of valence bonding laid the foundation for much of modern chemistry.[266] In autumn 1927, London accepted an assistantship in Berlin offered by Schrödinger, who had just been appointed Planck's successor,[267] while Heitler went on to Max Born's famous institute in Göttingen, where he worked as Born's assistant and completed his *Habilitation*. He began to be in international demand, and was invited as guest professor to Columbus, Ohio in 1931 and to Moscow in 1932 (a time he looked back to in horror in his memoirs, due to the beginnings of a food crisis in the Soviet Union and a "mental muzzle which could not have been more repugnant").[268] In 1933, his promising career in Göttingen came to an abrupt halt, as he was Jewish. According to Einstein, when Lindemann went to Berlin to look for promising scholars suffering under the new regime, he had originally considered both Fritz London (who also had Jewish background and had been, like Heitler, Hopf and Fröhlich, one of Sommerfeld's students in Munich) and Heitler – and was surprised instead by Schrödinger's interest.[269] While London eventually decided to move to Oxford, Heitler settled in Bristol where Nevill Mott (previously a student of Bohr's in Copenhagen and of Born's in Göttingen, then lecturer in Manchester and Cambridge) had just been appointed to a new chair in theoretical physics and started a research group where a number of the refugee physicists found sanctuary.[270]

---

[265] Fritz London (1900–1954) was also a student of Arnold Sommerfeld and then became the assistant of Peter Paul Ewald in Stuttgart before moving to Zurich. Continuing to Berlin with Schrödinger, he left with him for Oxford in 1933. When London's three-year grant there ran out, he went to Paris before accepting a professorship at Duke University in North Carolina in 1939.

[266] Max Born rather pointedly writes that though the publication by Heitler and London was fundamental, for a further development of their theory Linus Pauling was awarded the Nobel Prize for Chemistry, whereas Heitler and London did not receive one for Physics. See Albert Einstein and Max Born, *Briefwechsel 1916–1955*. Munich: Langen Müller 2005, p. 191.

[267] At this stage, Heitler's relationship with Schrödinger was still somewhat distant – he writes to London in September 1927 that he was invited by Courant to join him, Schrödinger and Niels Bohr in Arosa skiing – but that he would prefer to go with London instead of with the 'fat cats'. See Meyenn (ed.), *Eine Entdeckung von ganz außerordentlicher Tragweite*, Vol. 1, p. 439.

[268] Walter Heitler, Lebenserinnerungen (1981, unpublished), access thanks to Günther Rasche, Zurich. Translated by authors.

[269] Einstein wrote on 30 May 1933 from Oxford to Max Born (who due to his Jewish background had been suspended and moved to Italy in May 1933). Albert Einstein and Max Born, *Briefwechsel 1916–1955*, p. 190.

[270] Heitler seems to have obtained his position in Bristol thanks to Max Born. See Nancy Greenspan, *The End of the Certain World: The Life and Science of Max Born*. New York: Basic Books 2005, p. 183. Nevill Mott saw him as the most distinguished of the many refugees who

Heitler received a three-year fellowship worth £450, awarded thanks to the SPSL, Nevill Mott and the generosity of the Wills family. At first Heitler stayed with Mott, who later recalled him as "deeply unhappy at having to leave the German-speaking world", although he cheered up later.[271] Thanks to a glowing reference from the SPSL, stating that his work in Bristol in theoretical physics "has proved to be of extremely great importance",[272] Heitler got a permanent permit from the British Home Office in 1936. He was thus able to get his sister Annerose[273] to England when the situation in Germany became worse, and also, after *Kristallnacht*, his brother Hans, who had been interned in a concentration camp, and their mother.[274] He only had a temporary position, however, and chances of obtaining a professorship in England were slim and not improved by his alien status. Heitler therefore accepted a position at the DIAS (though only as Assistant Professor: it took until 1945 before he was made Senior Professor, equal to Schrödinger). This enabled him to provide for his family long-term, especially his sister and mother as well as his English fiancée, who all followed him to Ireland.[275] The Heitlers arrived in Ireland at Dun Laoghaire on 23 June 1941, and soon settled at 21 Seapark Road in

---

came there at the time. See Nevill Mott, Walter Heinrich Heitler 1904–1981. In: The Royal Society (ed.), *Biographical Memoirs of Fellows of the Royal Society*, Vol. 28. Bristol: Stonebridge 1982, pp. 141–151, 143.

271 Ibid.

272 SPSL 330, Home Office file 432, General Secretary SPSL to Home Office, 25 February 1936.

273 Dr Annerose Heitler, born in Berlin in 1896 before the family moved to Karlsruhe where her two younger brothers Hans and Walter were born. She studied in Karlruhe, Berlin and Heidelberg where she obtained a PhD in 1920, and became a teacher at the commercial college in Baden-Baden, teaching German, French, history, business studies, correspondence, mathematics, accounting and marketing. See Hans Schadek, Das jüdische Kinderheim 'Sonnenhalde' in Bollschweil bei Freiburg 1935–1939. Zur Geschichte des Heims (I) und seiner Leiterinnen, der Kinderärztin Dr. med. Elisabeth Müller (II) und der Handelsschullehrerin Dr. phil. Annerose Heitler (III). In: *Zeitschrift des Breisgau-Geschichtsvereins „Schau-ins-Land"*. Vol. 126 (2007), pp. 203–261, 248. In April 1933, like Walter, she lost her position due to her Jewish religion. In 1935, she founded a home for Jewish children in Bollschweil near Freiburg in the Black Forest together with paediatrician Dr Elisabeth Müller. In October 1938, Annerose joined her brother in Bristol.

274 Ottilie Heitler was born in 1876 in Kolin, Bohemia, and was fourteen years younger than her husband Adolf who died in August 1937.

275 His family, however, was also the main reason that it took over six months before he came to Dublin (he received Schrödinger's offer on 10 December 1940). Initially, there was the worry whether his brother could keep his position in Bristol without him. Moreover, the offered salary of £400 was less than what Heitler received in Bristol (£450). See MAI, G2/0760, his letter to Schrödinger, 11 December 1940.

Clontarf, close to the Schrödingers, though they preferred a more withdrawn lifestyle than the vivacious Austrian.[276]

Walter Heitler had come just in time to join the opening events of the newly founded Institute. In his autobiographical notes, he recalls the general set-up and the contrast between expectations and means – but also the uniqueness of the endeavour given world affairs at the time:

> The institute consisted of two sections: theoretical physics and Celtic Studies. It wasn't to cost much money but was supposed to achieve the highest level of scientific achievement. It was housed in one of the beautiful old Georgian houses, not like the concrete-glass monstrosities of today. The heating worked via open fires, built from turf that was provided in ample supply, though the fires had to be maintained by oneself. Probably the Dublin Institute was the only one in the world at that time where the study of pure science was pursued and where it was possible to do so.[277]

Heitler contributed to the inaugural lectures of the DIAS in July 1941, speaking fittingly on modern theoretical physics. Paul Ewald came down from Belfast and de Valera attended many sessions, as did academics from the different universities; to Heitler it seemed a remarkable start for the new scientific institution.[278] That Schrödinger was delighted with the new recruit is clear from a letter to his friend Max Born, Heitler's former employer:

> Having had Heitler here for some time, I feel I must thank you particularly for recommending him so strongly. He is a most valuable asset in *every* respect. When scientifically at least equal to his 'milk-brothers' [sic] London (I mean that brothership with respect to their first great achievement), as a man and as a teacher he is incomparably better. Indeed, he has a marvellous gift of understanding the difficulties and objections of another person.[279]

---

276 Denis Henderson (grandson of Peter & Else Brandenburg and son of Ruth Henderson, née Brandenburg) recalls "a most reclusive lifestyle" with Ottilie very much the domineering matriarch. Unpublished note on Heitlers and Strunzes, Dublin, sent to authors 29 November 2015.
277 Heitler, Lebenserinnerungen, p. 18. Translated by authors.
278 See also Walter Heitler's impressions of the Dublin Institute of Advanced Studies in *Scoil an Léinn Cheiltigh, Tuarascáil Leathchéad Blian: School of Celtic Studies, Fiftieth Anniversary Report 1940–1990*. Dublin: Dublin Institute of Advanced Studies 1990, pp. 28–29. Heitler continued to be very impressed by Éamon de Valera and his support and kept in contact with him after leaving Ireland in 1949. On his frequent return trips (his sister and mother stayed in Dublin) he always visited de Valera. See ibid. p. 29 and Lebenserinnerungen, p. 18. In both texts Heitler also quotes a sentence by de Valera on understanding nature: "I wish the Lord had made it a bit easier for us."
279 Schrödinger to Born, 5 October 1941. In: Meyenn (ed.), *Eine Entdeckung von ganz außerordentlicher Tragweite*, Vol. 2, p. 580.

Heitler was not the only international appointment sought for Dublin. From the beginning, the Institute was outward-looking. Dr Wolfgang Hepner of the Department of Mathematical Physics at Birmingham University and a Chinese physicist, Dr Hwan-Wu Peng, who worked in Edinburgh with Max Born, were invited to join as research fellows, but due to visa problems their appointments were delayed.[280] Other young affiliated scholars were James Hamilton, who had worked with Paul Ewald at Queen's University Belfast, and Sheila Power, originally from Galway, who had also worked in Edinburgh with Born and held an assistant lectureship at University College Dublin.

Criticism of the Institute continued. On 10 April 1942, Myles na gCopaleen in his *Irish Times* column 'Cruiskeen Lawn' objected to the costs ("nothing but the Best is good enough for the Institute of Advanced Studies"), questioned the results, and ended with a solemn warning that "unless we are careful this Institute of ours will make us the laughing stock of the world."[281] Schrödinger and Heitler nevertheless continued their work unperturbed. The Institute's first international colloquium took place from 16 to 29 July 1942. It was characterised by high-profile speakers who delivered what would now be called cutting-edge contributions, and a unique atmosphere, both stimulating and relaxed. Paul Dirac spoke on 'Quantum Electrodynamics', his Cambridge colleague Arthur Eddington on 'The combination of Relativity Theory and Quantum Theory'. William McCrea, then Head of Mathematics at Queen's in Belfast, remembers that these "two usually painfully shy individuals became unwontedly relaxed and sociable", and emphasises that all of the approximately 50 participants (himself included) found the event "a rare intellectual refreshment at a time when war made them feel so isolated".[282] The success of this and following events can be attributed to a large extent

---

280 Their names appear alongside Heitler's in correspondence between DJ and DEA from 1 April 1941 onwards. It took until February 1942, however, before the British allowed Hepner to come to Dublin- see NAI, DFA 202/1299- and it is unclear whether in fact he ever did come. Peng did come, however, later in 1941, and stayed until 1943 as a scholar, working closely with Heitler and James Hamilton. He returned to Edinburgh for two years and in 1945 he was appointed Assistant Professor in Dublin before leaving for China in 1947.
281 *Irish Times*, 10 April 1942. Myles (a pen name used by Brian O'Nolan who published his novels *At Swim-Two-Birds* and *The Third Policeman* under the name Flann O'Brien) was particularly exercised that "the first fruit" of the Institute was the effort to show "that there are two Saint Patricks and no God" – the latter referring to Schrödinger proving that one cannot establish a first cause. While Schrödinger was not much concerned about this (and remained on good terms with Brian O'Nolan), others in the Institute took exception to the passage, and the editor of the *Irish Times* had to give his assurances through the Institute's solicitors that the Institute would not be mentioned in the column again. See Moore, *Schrödinger*, p. 379.
282 McCrea, de Valera, Schrödinger and the Dublin Institute, p. 132.

to Schrödinger's excellent contacts and the impression he and Heitler managed to create, together with Éamon de Valera (who was often present, attending as many sessions as he could) that the pursuit of knowledge did still matter. It was also helpful that collaborators and friends such as Max Born and Paul Ewald[283] were close by in Edinburgh and Belfast, and were involved and supportive of the whole endeavour from the start.[284]

Image 6: Paul Ewald, Max Born, Walter Heitler, Erwin Schrödinger in Dublin

---

283 Schrödinger's friendship with Paul Ewald (1888–1985) dated back to his time in Stuttgart in the winter of 1920/21. Anny also travelled up to Belfast for regular visits.
284 Though Born found it distasteful to be "neutral" in the conflict with the Nazis and was worried that it would seem he was consenting to that attitude when participating in the summer colloquium, he also wanted "to keep science out of and above all political struggle", and was very keen to meet up with Schrödinger. Born to F.G. Donnan, Oxford, 4 May 1943. See Hoch and Yoxen, Schrödinger, p. 612.

While the speakers at the colloquiums and seminars were international, the audience comprised many Irish academics and students and at times also the interested public – the astonishing number of 400 attending Schrödinger's lectures was even remarked upon by the American magazine *Time*:

> Only in the precarious peace of Eire could Europe today provide such a spectacle. At Dublin's Trinity College last month crowds were turned away from a jampacked scientific lecture. Cabinet ministers, diplomats, scholars and socialites loudly applauded a slight, Vienna-born professor of physics.[285]

These lectures which Schrödinger gave in February 1943 on the topic "What is life?" were published a year later[286] as a book which sold more than 100,000 copies and became one of the most influential scientific publications of the twentieth century. It subsequently inspired James D. Watson, Francis Crick and Maurice Wilkins in their work on the structure of DNA.[287]

Just a few weeks after Schrödinger's lecture, yet another refugee, Leo Wenzel (Vaclav) Pollak, was asked to meet Éamon de Valera.[288] Following that meeting, Pollak wrote a memorandum that eventually led to the establishment of a third school at the Institute of Advanced Studies, the School for Cosmic Physics.[289] While the new School was only established after the war, by 1943 Pollak was already having a very considerable impact in his work for the Irish Meteorological Service.

When Leo Pollak arrived in Ireland in late October 1939, the 51-year-old academic had already had a varied and distinguished career. Born in Prague in 1888, he studied physics and geophysics at the German University from 1906 to 1910. In 1911 he became a demonstrator at the University and made the acquaintance of Albert Einstein, who had just moved to Prague (and possibly also of Ludwig

---

285 *Time*, 5 April 1943.
286 Erwin Schrödinger, *What is life? The Physical Aspect of the Living Cell*. Based on lectures delivered under the auspices of the Dublin Institute for Advanced Studies at Trinity College, Dublin in February 1943, Cambridge: Cambridge University Press 1944.
287 Joachim Pietzsch, The Nobel Prize in Physiology or Medicine 1962 – Perspectives, Nobel Media AB 2014. http://www.nobelprize.org/nobel_prizes/medicine/laureates/1962/perspectives.html [last accessed 27 March 2016].
288 See handwritten note to Pollak that de Valera wished to see him that very evening, DIAS archive, Admin/39, 29 March 1943.
289 Memo from Pollak proposing establishment of School of Geophysics (later School of Cosmic Physics), NAI, S14207A, 7 April 1943. The School opened in 1947 with Leo Pollak as its director, Lajos Jánossy and Hermann Brück being appointed the same year (see chapter 11).

Hopf).²⁹⁰ In 1912, Pollak obtained his PhD, and two years later he was made assistant. From December 1914 he was in military service, first at the front, but in February 1916 he was appointed commander of the meteorological stations at Trento and later Levico, where he organised some 200 observers and their assistants, instigating the use of new methods and constructing several meteorological instruments himself, some of which were introduced in both the Austrian and the German armies and later patented.²⁹¹ He married Johanna Dittrich, a high school teacher with a PhD, in 1920. In 1927, he was appointed extraordinary professor of the Institute for Geophysics and Meteorological Observations, and only two years later he became full professor and director of the Institute. From 1935 to 1936 he also served as Dean of the Natural Science Faculty. More than 100 publications resulted from his theoretical and experimental studies, and he also held eight patents, six of which related to meteorological instruments. In early November 1938, less than two months after Germany annexed the Sudetenland, Pollak contacted the SPSL as he saw the approaching danger with regard to his position in Prague. For his emigration he favoured English-speaking countries, naming England, Scotland, Ireland, Canada and the USA.²⁹² While the prospects for astronomers were not particularly good, a potential opening in Ireland's fledgling meteorological service had already been flagged by the SPSL to one of Pollak's

---

290 It was Pollak who brought together Einstein and his early collaborator Erwin Freundlich following a visit to the Berlin observatory. Einstein was eager to have astronomers examine his theory on the influence of gravity on the deflection of light, and following Pollak's suggestion, Freundlich took up the challenge with great enthusiasm. See Lewis Pyenson, Einstein's early scientific collaborations. In: Russell McCommach (ed.), *Historical Studies in the Physical Sciences*. Princeton/London: Princeton University Press 1976, pp. 83–124, especially pp. 105–106. It was the possible appointment of Freundlich in Prague that rekindled their acquaintance in 1935. See Hebrew University of Jerusalem, Albert Einstein Archives, 19–118, Pollak to Einstein, 21 March 1935 and Einstein to Pollak, 10 April 1935. It is likely that Pollak's Jewish family background led to his name appearing on a black list and hence his need to leave Czechoslovakia, although according to an article in the *Irish Times*, his facilitating of Freundlich's appointment in Prague in 1937 was to blame (An Irishman's Diary, 15 September 1948 – which mainly focused on Pollak's leather coat).
291 SPSL 336/3/357, CV Dr Leo Wenzel Pollak. He was awarded an order of merit (*Goldenes Verdienstkreuz am Bande der Tapferkeitsmedaille*) for the impact of his constructions for the aviation service. Incidentally, more than 20 years later in Ireland, he met his former opposite number, S. P. [Sidney Percival] Peters. Peters was a colleague in Foynes, and it transpired that Pollak "had cracked the British code and was listening in to Peter's wind and weather reports". Lorna Siggins, Met Magicians cast a cold spell. *Irish Times*, 8 December 1986.
292 SPSL 336/3/355, Leo Wenzel Pollak, General Information, 8 November 1938. Under languages, English features before Czech (German being his first language).

academic contacts in Great Britain.²⁹³ The position, however, was only open to candidates below a certain age, and Pollak was too old to qualify.

In late November, Professor Brunt from Imperial College London indicated to the SPSL that they could "afford the facilities" for Leo Pollak.²⁹⁴ A personal grant was also available, as the SPSL could put a certain amount of money raised for Czech refugees in general towards funding university teachers.²⁹⁵ On 10 February 1939, Leo and Johanna Pollak arrived by plane in Croydon. After their arrival in London, however, it transpired that the grant could be paid for only six months rather than a year, and Pollak accordingly continued his search for employment. In this situation it was a fortunate development that a few months later the Irish meteorological position was re-advertised, this time with an age limit of 55 years, making Pollak eligible.²⁹⁶ His application was successful,²⁹⁷ but it was not until October that he received confirmation.²⁹⁸ On 28 October 1939, the Pollaks entered

---

293 "If Professor Pollak is a meteorologist too, there might be some chance in Ireland. In any case I enclose a copy of an advertisement which has appeared in the press." SPSL 336/3/426, Simpson to Dr A. Beer, University of London Observatory, 1 November 1938.
294 SPSL 336/3/432, Brunt to SPSL, 28 November 1938.
295 SPSL 336/3/434, Simpson to Beer, 30 November 1938.
296 The SPSL actually knew about this position previously, thanks to Hans Motz, who wrote about it confidentially while he was at Trinity College Dublin on 3 August 1937. At that stage the age limit was still 28. See SPSL 335/5/227.
297 Before his appointment in Ireland Pollak had an interview with the Civil Service Commission in Dublin on 25 July 1939. SPSL 336/3/460, Pollak to Thomson, SPSL, 3rd August 1939. After that he was informed by the Director of the Irish Meteorological Service, A. H. Neagle, that he had been given the job. Pollak to SPSL; 7 October 1939. He seems to have been reasonably confident of getting the position following the interview, which caused dismay among unsuccessful competitors. The Austrian Dr Hermann von Socher, the dismissed director of the *Übungs-Sternwarte* (the former public observatory) of the University of Berlin, who was staying in the same London hotel as Pollak and his wife at the beginning of their time in England, had also applied for the Irish position, but unsuccessfully. Socher regarded this as another proof that Irish politics were being undermined by "leftfront and Jewish" tendencies, to the detriment of a genuinely Catholic Ireland (it should be noted however that Pollak states in his CV that he was baptised five days after his birth, and was brought up a Catholic). Socher repeatedly wrote to the Archbishop of Dublin in summer 1939 seeking to "counteract this bold attempt to establish a bolshevist cell of reliable men under the guise of this (and other planned) scientific institutions". See Socher to Archbishop Byrne, 3 August 1939 (also 24 August and 3 September 1939), Diocesan Archives Dublin, files Archbishop Byrne. It is not known whether there was any answer. Socher, who received his PhD in 1928 and had since been at the *Übungs-Sternwarte*, was elected Fellow of the Royal Astronomical Society in January 1939, but would not have had the same academic and international standing as Pollak. Socher managed to re-establish himself after the war at the university observatory in Vienna.
298 On 11 October 1939 he wrote to the SPSL "I am very glad to be able to inform you that I have now received my appointment for the Meteorological Service in Eire. I have been asked to make

Ireland and were given a permanent permit. A problem experienced by many exiles, whether and how to get their furniture and books to Ireland, reached huge proportions in his case, exacerbated by the rather short notice of his appointment. In the end he managed to get his books and materials transferred,[299] which was much appreciated in Ireland where resources still had to be accumulated.[300]

The background to Pollak's appointment was a change to the Irish Meteorological Service (later to be called Met Éireann). It was founded only in 1936, as a result of the requirement to provide accurate weather information for transatlantic aviation. Until then the British Meteorological Office had run Ireland's weather observation stations and forecasts, and for the next few years it continued to provide personnel and services, but when in 1939 the first transatlantic service started, landing in Foynes, County Limerick,[301] Ireland urgently needed to recruit and train its own cadets and assistants. This was the task performed by Leo Pollak and his colleagues.[302] The Pollaks moved to Foynes in early December 1939 and stayed there until May 1940. During these months, Pollak seems to have been very successful in infecting his students with "his enthusiasm for meteorology".[303]

---

arrangements to start with my duties in Dublin on October 16th. I am extremely happy having obtained this post, which gives me excellent opportunities to carry on with my researches, and I am most grateful to you that you have made all this possible."

299 Pollak received the £150 needed for his furniture and books after some negotiation. See William Beveridge's memoir about the SPSL, *A Defence of Free Learning*. Oxford: Oxford University Press 1959, p. 64. In this context one needs to keep in mind that the funding guideline adopted by the SPSL for individual refugee scholars was £182 a year (£250 for a couple). Ibid., p. 37.

300 "Our furniture has now arrived and I am very happy to have my books at hand again, and so is Director Nagle who thinks it a very valuable addition to the library of the institute, as there are books and journals not available here and now. They will be of great use to me and my collaborators especially at Foynes, where I am going to instruct the young meteorologists." SPSL 336/3/474, Pollak to Simpson, 30 November 1939.

301 Foynes was chosen after a national survey by pioneer aviator Charles Lindbergh, to enable a direct Atlantic route from Great Britain to New York within the range of the American and British flying boats. See Tom Keane, *Establishment of the Meteorological Service in Ireland – The Foynes Years, 1936–1945*. Varsity: n. p. 2012, p. 3.

302 Apart from S. P. Peters (one of the British staff in Foynes who helped get the Irish Met Service going: see fn. 291), the person mainly involved was Dr Mariano Doporto, a Republican refugee from the Spanish Civil War. In contrast to Pollak who was remembered as "very formal", Doporto "sparkled with fun". Keane, *Establishment of the Meteorological Service in Ireland*, p. 61. Doporto went on to become the second director of the Irish Meteorological Service in 1948.

303 F. E. Dixon, Obituary Prof L. W. Pollak. In: *Nature*. Vol. 205 (30 January 1965), p. 448; Tom Keane, *Establishment of the Meteorological Service in Ireland*, p. 61.

In May 1940, the Pollaks returned to Dublin to take up permanent residence in 66 Hollybrook Road in Clontarf, close to the Schrödingers and Heitlers (see chapter 8). In Dublin, Pollak directed and developed the Climatological Division of the Irish Meteorological Service (one of the three main Meteorological Centres at the time, with Foynes and Valentia Observatory being the other two) and lectured cadet officers in the Meteorological Service Headquarters at 14/15 Andrew Street. Pollak enjoyed teaching, and even gave Trinity students lectures in Meteorology without payment.[304] His work was seen as extremely important. Met Service Director Austen Nagle[305] and subsequently the Department of Industry and Commerce made a special case for his naturalisation in late 1940, though this did not come to anything during the war, due to G2 resistance to any naturalisations in that time for security reasons.[306] Leo Pollak and his wife eventually gained Irish citizenship in 1947.[307]

Pollak's contribution to the Irish Meteorological Service was "tremendous" according to Fred E. Dixon, one of the first seven meteorological cadets.[308] With his ability to invent new techniques and more refined instruments, and his push to evolve new techniques of recording meteorological data with improved punchcards,[309] as well as with his books and materials and his teaching, he contributed significantly to the budding Irish Meteorological Service being internationally recognised as efficiently run and competent.[310]

---

304 TCD Archives, Mun/V/5/26.
305 Nagle argued that out of a total of 65 staff (in July 1940), only Pollak, Doporto and "a British Officer on loan" (i.e. Peters) could be regarded as sufficiently experienced to deal with emergency conditions (and therefore needed protection). Keane, *Establishment of the Meteorological Service in Ireland*, p. 82.
306 See MAI, G2/1152, Ferguson, DIC to Walshe, DEA, 9 October 1940 and Archer to Walshe, 2 December 1940.
307 See NAI, DJ 68/1/914 and 68/1//915.
308 Dixon had already met Pollak in April 1939 when he attended lectures on Dynamical Meteorology given by Professor Brunt in Imperial College, London, where Pollak tried to perfect his English. See F. E. Dixon, Professor Leo W Pollak. In: Keane, *Establishment of the Meteorological Service in Ireland*, appendix XI, pp. 159–160, 159.
309 Friedrich Kistermann argues that Pollak deserves a place in the history of data processing and refers also to contemporary acknowledgement of Pollak's ground-breaking work. See Friedrich Kistermann, Leo Wenzel Pollak (1888–1964): Czechoslovakian Pioneer in Scientific Data Processing. In: *IEEE Annals of the History of Computing*. Vol. 21, no. 4 (1999), pp. 62–68, 65. See also Desmond John Clarke, Honorary Degrees Conferred by Dublin University. *Irish Times*, 5 July 1963.
310 See Seán Lemass in Dáil Éireann, 23 February 1944: "Our meteorological service at the present time is mainly employed in connection with civil aviation services. I think it is true to say that it has been very efficiently run, so efficiently that it has established an international recognition for competency. I have received from other Governments that have had contact with our

Another refugee academic, Friedrich Mautner, who only joined DIAS in 1944, should also be mentioned briefly. Born in 1921 in Vienna, he had emigrated to the UK after the *Anschluss*. Like thousands of other refugees he was interned in autumn 1940, and was shipped to Australia on HMT *Dunera*. From September 1940, at Hay Camp 7, Felix Adalbert Behrend, who later became a leading scholar at the University of Melbourne, taught Mautner pure and applied mathematics; Mautner reached a standard which in Behrend's opinion corresponded to a second-year university course, and furthermore studied various mathematical and physical topics on his own.[311] On his return to the UK Mautner gained a BSc at Durham University, and in 1944 obtained an assistantship with Paul Ewald at Queen's University Belfast. From there he went on to Dublin, becoming a visiting scholar at the Institute for Advanced Studies in 1944. Clearly he did not need much time to settle in at DIAS: within a year of his arrival, a joint publication with Erwin Schrödinger appeared. In 1946 he went on to Princeton University, where he obtained his PhD in 1948.[312]

Overall assessment

The academic refugees generally had a quite specific and often privileged route into Ireland, thanks to their international connections and organisations specifically devoted to their aid, first and foremost the Society for the Protection of Science and Learning. From the Irish side, the Irish Co-ordinating Committee

---

service very substantial praise of its efficiency. We are, of course, in a key position so far as the meteorological services in Europe are concerned. All weather comes from the west, and the efficiency of the meteorological services in all European countries depends very largely on the efficiency of the service in this country. Consequently, it helps to enhance our prestige internationally when our meteorological service is fully developed and efficiently run." Keane, *Establishment of the Meteorological Service in Ireland*, p. ix.

311 See Hans Lausch, Mathematics in detention. In: *Gazette of the Australian Mathematics Society*. Vol. 33, no. 2 (May 2006), pp. 95–103, 97.

312 Mautner and Schrödinger, Infinitesimal Affine Connections with Twofold Einstein-Bargmann Symmetry. In: *Proceedings of the Royal Irish Academy*. Vol. 50 (1945), pp. 223–231. As Heitler wrote in his obituary for Schrödinger, who was throughout his life "a lone worker", this is a rare example of a publication under Schrödinger's joint authorship. He took no research students, except while in Dublin, and even there, Mautner was one of very few. See Heitler, Erwin Schrödinger, p. 225. Mautner later became a professor at Johns Hopkins University in Baltimore. Mautner's Lemma, the Mautner phenomenon and Mautner Group are named after him, and his representation theory of reducible p-adic groups is seen as especially important.

for Refugees was far less important than in cases of 'ordinary' refugees (though individual members such as Theo Dillon and especially Ditchburn played a role, the latter personally accommodating Alfred Bloch and Hans Motz in his college rooms, as referred to at the beginning of this chapter).[313] Even for academics, some of whom had good contacts in Ireland, getting permits to come to the country was not always straightforward, and was at times subject to delay or obstruction as in the case of Wilhelm Winkler.

For universities, the results of immigration were not profound. The number of scholars was few, and their appointments were made only reluctantly and often restricted to lecturing for a few terms. The untimely death of Ludwig Hopf at 55, after only a few months in Ireland, and the relative isolation of Hans Sachs and his death in 1945 meant that their impact was limited. Only Ludwig Bieler experienced a mostly successful transition from Vienna to Dublin in wartime (and, as we will see later, to several decades of contribution to Irish academic life – though not without interruptions). Even he, however, mentions "the years of scientific isolation" despite "the congenial work found" and "making the best of [it]".[314] While at TCD the great majority of refugee scholars were scientists, at the National University Colleges their disciplines were far more diverse, with particular strengths in the Arts and Humanities.

Notwithstanding the generally temporary nature of their appointments, the few academics who came to Ireland did have an effect. Writing about two series of lectures by Bieler and Ehrenberg in spring 1940, the *Irish Times* pointed out that these refugee scholars

> are obtaining in Ireland the opportunity denied to them in their native countries. As we remarked earlier in the year, when Professor Erwin Schrödinger delivered lectures on wave mechanics, the fact that we are one of the nations turned to for sanctuary in itself makes us proud, but later on, when the influence of such men as these is fully felt, we will be not so much proud but grateful.[315]

After 1945, the next generation of refugee scholars, those who were students during the war years, came through the universities, but almost all of them were eventually to leave Ireland (see chapter 11).

---

313 See NAI, DJ 69/80/51. From September 1938 to July 1939, Ditchburn also undertook the education of a refugee boy, Dietrich Scheff, under the guardianship of the German Jewish Aid Committee in London, and shouldered the financial burden involved. Scheff became a pupil at Avoca School in Blackrock and lived with the Ditchburn family at 18 Rosmeen Park, Sandycove. Later he briefly became a student in Trinity College (see chapter 8).
314 See previously quoted SPSL 292/3/193, Bieler to Skemp, Secretary of the SPSL, 2 June 1945.
315 *Irish Times*, 15 April 1940.

The situation and role of refugees at the Dublin Institute of Advanced Studies (DIAS) was quite different. There is no doubt that the success of DIAS resulted from the expertise and international contacts of the German-speaking refugee scholars (this became even more obvious after the war ended: see chapter 11). Their influence can be measured on an international basis.[316] To Ireland, a country previously isolated from most major research developments, they brought some of the world leaders of theoretical physics, a subject which in the first half of the twentieth century was seen as the discipline that would define the future (a belief shattered for many by the terrible impact of the atom bomb). In terms of exile studies, DIAS was acknowledged in one of the earliest studies on academic refugees, Norman Bentwich's 1953 publication *The Rescue and Achievement of Refugee Scholars*. Bentwich refers to DIAS in the context of five "remarkable movements" of group rescues: Turkey; the transfer of the Warburg Institute from Hamburg to London; the establishment of a "University in Exile" which formed a department of the New School for Social Research in New York; the Institutes of Advanced Studies in Princeton and Dublin; and the academics who found refuge in academic institutions in Israel.[317] In the vast literature about academic refugees, Bentwich's reference to DIAS is one of the few acknowledgements of the sanctuary Ireland provided.

The importance of the émigré scholars in setting up the Dublin Institute has been acknowledged by DIAS itself,[318] but not yet fully researched, though this is slowly changing.[319] It should be accepted, however, that DIAS remained

---

[316] "Most important centers for research on unified field theory in the 1930s until the early 1950s were those around Albert Einstein in Princeton and Erwin Schrödinger in Dublin," Hubert Goenner, On the History of Unified Field Theories. Part II (ca 1930 – ca 1965). In: *Living Review in Relativity*. Vol. 5, no. 17 (2014), p. 7. http://www.livingreviews.org/lrr-2014-5 [accessed 24 July 2015].

[317] Norman Bentwich, *The Rescue and Achievement of Refugee Scholars*. The Hague: M. Nijhoff 1953, p. 42.

[318] School of Theoretical Physics, *50 year report*. Dublin: Dublin Institute of Advanced Studies 1990. Luke Drury, Senior Professor at the School for Cosmic Physics, argues that the "academic diaspora were of course essential to the establishment of the Dublin Institute for Advanced Studies" and points out "it is clear from the few internal memos that have survived that a working language of the senior staff was German; Pollak, Brueck, Schroedinger, Heitler etc would naturally communicate in German when writing or talking to each other although of course when others were involved, or in communications to the external environment, they all used English." Luke Drury, email to authors, 1 October 2015. Professor Drury later kindly provided a photo of a thick file from Leo Pollak entitled "Umbau und Ausstattung" (Reconstruction and equipment) relating to 5 Merrion Square (where the School of Cosmic Physics was housed), adding later that it included notes in German as well as some mixed language notes such as "Besprechung mit Board of Works".

[319] There is currently a PhD study underway by Neasa McGarrigle, Trinity College Dublin on "The establishment of the Dublin Institute for Advanced Studies 1939–1947".

a relatively isolated phenomenon in Irish academia as a whole. A contrast can be drawn with another "group rescue" undertaking named by Bentwich, that which took place in Turkey.[320] Reisman argues that the 300 or so academics and 50 technicians and support staff who found refuge there "totally transformed Turkey's higher education in the sciences, professions, humanities, and the arts. They also re-engineered its public health, library, legal, engineering, and administrative practices."[321] This was clearly not the case in Ireland, where existing academic structures were far superior, and already well integrated in Western European and British academic networks. Other relevant differences were in the sheer numbers involved, and also in clustering and the timing of immigration. By the end of 1933 some 30 émigré professors had already arrived in Turkey. This immediate establishment of a cluster of refugee academics, provided with well-remunerated positions as well as good research facilities and contracts of mostly five-year periods, is in stark contrast to the slowly growing number of exiles in Ireland and their temporary appointments; the scale of Turkish modernisation instigated through German exiles in a vast number of areas, including health care, architecture, education and industrial development, greatly surpassed the rather patchy developments in Ireland.

Nevertheless, Éamon de Valera's vision and interest in creating a hub of internationally connected and high-level research showed what could be done on a smaller scale. The refugee scholars played their part, as acknowledged at least academically in the considerable number of refugees appointed members of the Royal Irish Academy: Erwin Schrödinger had already been elected an honorary member in 1931, before he had received his Nobel Prize; Leo Pollak was elected in 1941 (the same year as Max Born was appointed Honorary member); Walter Heitler in 1943; Ludwig Bieler in 1947; John Hennig in 1948; and Ernst Lewy, eventually, in 1962 (and strangely as an Honorary member despite his ongoing residence in Dublin).

---

320 On exile in Turkey see Philipp Schwartz and Helge Peukert (eds), *Notgemeinschaft - Zur Emigration deutscher Wissenschaftler nach 1933 in die Türkei*. Marburg: Metropolis-Verlag 1995; Christopher Kubaseck and Günter Seufert (eds), *Deutsche Wissenschaftler im türkischen Exil*. Würzburg: Ergon 2008; and Arnold Reisman, *Turkey's Modernization. Refugees from Nazism and Atatürk's Vision*. Washington D.C.: New Academia 2006.
321 Reisman, *Turkey's Modernization*, p. 10.

Chapter 10
Transit Lives

One condition of Irish refugee policy agreed by policy makers and the ICCR had been an expectation that the people within its purview would leave the country as soon as possible. The expectation turned out to be unduly optimistic, as became clear even before the war.[1] From 1938, many hopeful migrants, especially those without adequate financial means, found entry difficult even to second-choice Latin American countries.[2] Then, within a few months after September 1939, the intensifying maritime warfare not only meant that fewer passenger ships were sailing, with consequently reduced availability of places aboard, but also made such travel perilous. The sea passages became even more life-threatening with the growing involvement of the USA on the Atlantic seaways after spring 1941 and especially after their formal entry into the war in December of that year. Added to such risks was the growing restrictiveness of US immigration policy.[3] By mid-1940 and then again in spring 1941 admission rates fell to about 25% of the relevant entrance quotas under the influence of isolationist and anti-Semitic forces, especially in the State Department and the consular services.[4] Canada, Australia and New Zealand also closed their doors after the beginning of the war.[5] Possibilities thus became limited for the many who had been poised for a second emigration. The following table does not include those persons whom Irish law enforcement authorities expelled from the country against their will. We have counted 14 cases of such "illegal" entries from the UK after November 1938. All of them passed the border controls, but were not granted permission to stay, and generally had to return to the UK within weeks.[6] The table also omits legal visitors – for example, refugees from the Continent who were in Britain or Northern Ireland and who

---

[1] For an example of such optimism, see Ditchburn's memorandum of 7 March 1939, which expresses expectations that the ICCR would soon be able to send many temporary exiles elsewhere ("There are only a few cases in which the Committee anticipates real difficulty"). NAI, DFA 243/9.
[2] For an overview see Patrick von zur Mühlen, The 1930s: The End of the Latin American Open Door Policy. In: Caestecker/Moore (eds), *Refugees from Nazi Germany*, pp. 103–108.
[3] In a letter of 8 December 1939, Belton, DEA, reported that the ICCR had listed about 20 refugees who wished to go to the USA, but the DEA thought it hopeless "at present" to "approach" US authorities on the matter. NAI, DFA 202/637.
[4] See Bat-Ami Zucker, *In Search of Refuge. Jews and US Consuls in Nazi Germany 1933–1941*, London, Portland: Valentine-Mitchell 2001, pp. 97–100.
[5] Paul R. Bartrop (ed.), *False Havens The British Empire and the Holocaust*. Lanham, New York, London: University of America Press 1995, pp. 79–98 (Canada), 127–57 (Australia), 187–210 (New Zealand).

either wished to see exiled relatives or friends in Ireland or had other reasons for visiting Ireland. At the end of their visits they returned to the UK or proceeded to other countries.[7]

While waiting to leave, these migrants filled their Irish days investigating possible routes, securing affidavits from consular services of the USA and other countries, approaching family members, relatives and friends in the target countries for guarantees, booking tickets and raising funds for passage costs and landing money – all this within narrow time limits as affidavits might lapse,

---

[6] One example was Peter Irsa, a 21-year-old Silesian who had been engaged by Colonel Robert Prioleau, Easkey, Co. Sligo, to take care of his two children. The DJ refused to grant a permit, which meant he had to go back to England on 10 May 1939 after two months in Sligo. For the details see NAI, DJ 69/80/363.

[7] Before the beginning of the war such short-term entries were possible for applicants from the Continent too. Thus, non-Jewish Anna Lederer from Vienna was able to visit her divorced Jewish husband Friedrich Lederer in Dublin a few weeks before the war and then return to Vienna. NAI, DJ 69/80/309. Peter and Konrad Königsberger came over from England to spend time with their parents in Tipperary. See Kingshill, *Footnote*, p. 58. Wolfram Kawerau and his mother repeatedly visited Einhart and Sigurd before the beginning of the war and Wolfram's emigration to Australia. His mother returned to Germany. TCD Archives, Mun/Sec/248/ref/16.

As before 1939 (see chapter 1), visitors and refugees to Ireland included a few prominent figures. Among the 44 refugee visitors we could identify, was the ballet group of Kurt Jooss, which performed twice in Dublin in 1939, to great acclaim (see "The Revolt is Essence of Ballets Jooss", *Irish Press*, 28 March 1939 and "The Art of Kurt Jooss – The Ballet at its Best", *Irish Independent*, 7 November 1939). Another artistic visitor was Austrian composer Kurt Roger who had studied music alongside Arnold Schönberg and then taught at the Vienna Conservatoire from 1923 to 1938. In late 1938, he emigrated to London where at a private musical evening he met Lady Irene Congreve, who invited him to her home Mount Congreve in Waterford for some weeks in August 1939 while he was waiting for his passage to the USA. During his time in Waterford he composed the only known musical trace of German-speaking refugees in Ireland – the "Irish Sonata" for viola and piano, opus 37. This proved also to be the beginning of a lifelong love story, as a young viola player from Belfast was visiting her sister in Waterford and tried out the piece. She premiered it in Belfast in 1942 (reviewed very favourably in the local newspaper under the heading "Refugee's Work Played at Belfast Recital") – and married its composer in 1948 in the USA. See Joy Roger Hammerschlag, Kurt Roger 1895–1966 (Belfast 1997, unpublished) and interview with authors, 6 March 2012. Exiled German historian Veit Valentin, who had found temporary refuge at University College London thanks to the SPSL, came on a holiday trip to Killarney in July 1939, was much impressed by the landscape and found the people he encountered remarkably "un-English" – talkative, funny and quite musical. Valentin to Lien Kalkschmidt, 17 July 1939, NL Eugen Kalkschmidt, Monacensia Munich. Translated by authors. Information thanks to Dr Klaus Seidl who is working on a biography of Valentin. Another notable visitor was Rudolf Rocker (1873–1958), a leading German anarchist who had been in US exile for years and came to Dublin on 14 October 1942, an unknown detail in the history of anarchism. No further evidence on the aims and course of the visit could be found. MAI, G2/x/1091, 14 November 1942.

Table 1: Transmigrants, 1933–1938, 1939 to 1945[8]

Destination/year	1933–1938	1939	1940	1941	1942	1943	1944	January-May 1945
Germany	1[9]							
USA	4[10]	2	28[11]	6				
Brazil			7					
Argentina			1		3			
Canada			3					
Australia	1[12]	2						
Kenya		1						
New Zealand	1[13]							
United Kingdom	10[14]	6	4	16	8	9	7	1
Denmark		1						
Total	17	12	43	22	11	9	7	1

---

8 Names and departure dates, 1939 to 1945.
United Kingdom
1939. Dietrich Scheff: 3 July, Julius Steinberger: 10 May, Gahr-Goldstein family (Peter and Hilda Gahr, Friederike Goldstein): 2 September, Julius Silber: 22 November. 1940. Erwin Jakobi: 6 June, Walter Storch: 6 June, Eva Schenkel: 10 January, Susanne Fantes: 6 January. 1941. Gustav Beisser: 18 November, Georg Klaar: unknown, Ernst Einäugler: 13 August, Elkin family (Boris, Anna): 18 November, Georg Liss: 18 November, Marianne Lönhardt: 31 May, Rosenberg (Gerhard, Else, Marianne, Michael): 6 October, Schwarz family (Rudolf, Eva): 14 June, Kurt Staudt: 7 August, Antonin Vesely: unknown, Robert Steiner: 3 December. 1942. Billig family (Kurt, Sophie, Rosa): 17 January, Doris Brünn: 16 February, Karola Schönberg: 4 December, Christa Schreiber: 14 September, Josefa Stein: 25 September, Karl Steiner: 19 September. 1943. Otokar Engländer: 1 March, Alice Hopf: 29 October, Karrach family (Ferdinand, Emilie): 29 July, Richard Marx: 9 April, Hans Morgenstern: 7 August, Georg Pick: 14 October, Eric Serff: unknown, Anna Maria Tuchmann: unknown. 1944. Feldmann family (Robert, Stefanie, Margaretha, Hertha): 21 April, Ignaz Schulz: 27 February, Josef Wolfgarten: 3 June, Heinz Scheyer: 2 November. 1945. Gertrude Konirsch: 9 April.
United States
1939. Hans Forell: 19 June, Paul Wessely: 6 August. 1940. Alfred Bacher: 2 September, Baumgarten family (Paul, Helena, Gertrud): 4 March, Siegfried Dziewientnik: 27 February, Hermann Heymann: 20 September, Hans V. Ledermann: 6 June, Olga Schlesinger: 18 July, Schmolka family (Hans, Paul, Helena, Peter, Vera): 7 March, Kurz family (Benjamin, Golda, Diana): 28 May, Walter Lewin: 20 September, Menkes family (Karl, Valerie, Hans): 3 April, Schwab family (Julius, Gertrud): 30 April, Schwarz family (Theodor, Irma, Gertrude): 20 September, Walter Simon: 1 May, Aaron Stein: 20 May, Richard Wallach: 21 May. 1941. Stefan Lendt: 31 March, Bedrich and Ludwig Salz: 14 February, Schenk family (Leopold, Hedwig and child): 24 June.
Brazil.
1940. Kröner family (Leo, Beate): June, Ney family (Paul, Katharina, Peter, Robert): unknown, Hans Wilmersdörfer: 5 June.

quota rules might change, and nobody knew how long their arrangements might take. It could be weeks or even months before they could finally board a ship from an English port, usually Liverpool, and face the risks of a transatlantic passage.

A second fundamental condition of refugee policy had made the charity societies responsible for arranging emigration for people under their care. The task primarily fell into the remit of the ICCR's emigration branch under its "able and energetic"[15] secretary, Oscar Singer.[16] Unfortunately, the committee's activities have yet to be fully researched, in particular the international links of the denominational societies and the ways they, and the various external informants, interacted with the Singer office.

The forms of help available to the few Catholic transients between 1939 and 1942 are especially unclear. Candidates may have looked for help to the St Vincent

---

Argentina.
1940. Albert Kröner: 5 June. 1942. Stiegwardt family (Kurt, Elise, one son): 15 July.
Australia.
1939. Gerhard Harant: 28 August, Konrad Topper: August.
Canada.
1940. Frantisek Dostal: 10 August, Jeric family (Richard, Irma): 29 April.
Denmark.
1939. Gerhard Jaffe: 7 September.
Kenya.
Alfred Singer: 29 April.
9 Gustav Amsterdam, January 1935. Alice Krotoschin (see chapter 1) also returned to Germany in October 1937, but after a visit to her husband who was in England for New Year she was not allowed back into Germany. Granted a short visa for Berlin in July 1938 to settle family affairs after her mother's suicide, and realising that she would not be allowed to stay longer, she took her son, who had meanwhile stayed in Germany, back to Ireland. See EA Berlin, no. 61.929, R50-54.
10 Viktor Hähnlein, his wife and two children (1935).
11 The relatively high number of emigrants to the USA in 1940 was possibly due to the fact that at least some of them were classified within the US country quota for Ireland of that year. This is indicated by the passage of the Menkes family to the USA. Later John Menkes thought that his family's passage had been due to their being filed within the high Irish quota in 1940. See *Visual History Archive*, Hans (John) Menkes, 18 July 1996.
12 Jürgen (George) Holländer (1938).
13 Kurt Brehmer.
14 Wilhelm Emanuel, Otto W. Nelki, Ernst Sommer (1934), Paul and Karl Schnitzler (1935), Alfred Bloch (1935), Kurt Böhm (1935), Hans Motz (1938), the two domestics Bina Wallach and Ilse Lönhardt (1938).
15 NAI, 243/9, Ditchburn memorandum, 7 March 1939.
16 Singer was manager of the Carlow Sugar Factory from 1926 to 1933. He and his Irish wife then returned to Austria but emigrated to Italy after the *Anschluss*. In May 1938, they came back to Ireland and he obtained Irish citizenship. See DJ 2013/50/2640 and DFA 102/339.

de Paul Society which "circularised its correspondents in many countries for help in emigration",[17] or to the newly founded Catholic Council for Refugees, or to the ICCR, but there is no clear evidence. We know very little about the circumstances of Paul Wessely's move to the USA in late August 1939,[18] or Walter Lewin's in September 1940,[19] or about the Stiegwardts' perilous passage to Argentina in mid-1942, the date itself signalling how dissatisfied they were with their exile life in Ireland.[20] We do know that Hans V. Ledermann went from Clongowes Wood College to New York in 1939 with guarantees offered by Jesuits who had already brought him to Ireland.[21] It may also be assumed that Oscar Singer (see above) did much to make possible his brother Alfred's employment as a railway engineer by the British Colonial Service in Kenya in 1939.[22]

As we have seen, the Church of Ireland's Jews Society and its refugee committee had settled a number of persons in the broad sector of affiliated Protestant families and institutions.[23] The critical question was whether Conrad Hoffmann

---

[17] NAI, 243/9, Ditchburn memorandum, 7 March 1939.
[18] Originally a participant in the Ardmore project, he stayed at Vallombrosa between May and August 1939. His guarantor on the US side was an aunt living in Florida. NAI, DJ 69/80/93, Mulcahy, Bray Garda to DJ, 22 August 1939; see also G2/x/0028.
[19] See NAI, DJ 69/80/270.
[20] In early 1941, they had moved to Dublin, frustrated with farm work and still enthralled with the US option. In the capital they lived on ICCR grants and Kurt's infrequent German lessons. TCD Archives, Butler Papers, 10304/597/774 and 783, Huggard to Butler, 6 August and 5 September 1941. The CCR, the SVP or another Catholic organisation may have established contact with a priest who seems to have acted as a guarantor on the Argentinian side (see chapter 7). See MAI, G2/0820, Stiegwardt to Padre Jose Gomez, 2 July 1942. The ICCR was also involved in negotiations (a telegram of 20 May 1942: "Transit visa granted Stiegwardts writing – Slattery". MAI, G2/0820).
[21] In May 1939, he had concluded his studies at UCD. Originally, he had planned to return to Ireland for another study period at UCD (see NAI, DFA 202/29, DJ to DEA, 14 August 1939), but by November 1939 he wished to stay in the USA where he had been reunited with his parents. Thanks to the on-going support of the Jesuits, he was able to enrol at Loyola University in Chicago ("I feel very happy at Loyola University, just as I always did under the care of the Jesuits"), Ledermann to Rev. Francis Talbot, New York, 5 November 1939; also further correspondence between Fra Fergal McGrath, Clongowes Wood College, Rev. Francis Talbot and Rev. George L. Warth. Courtesy Harold Browne, Williamsburg (Virginia).
[22] Alfred Singer had made his passage from Vienna to Ireland through his brother's mediation. Oscar also maintained him in Ireland between late January and April 1939. Alfred, who had worked for a long time as a civil engineer for Austrian Railways, was then employed by the British Colonial Office as a railway engineer in Kenya. See correspondence in NAI, DJ 69/80/101.
[23] For the Picks see chapter 8; for Hirschberg chapter 7. Olga Schlesinger had enlisted the help of the Swedish Mission and the Gildemeester Aktion to implement her flight to Ireland and then, she hoped, to the USA where her two sons had already gone. In Ireland she lived on HCRC funding and was housed by Miss Piggott in Greystones. In 1940, while residing in Dublin, she

Image 1: Stiegwardts in Argentina.

---

was allowed to sell gloves she knitted herself and flowers in the city centre to enable her to pay the passage money. See AdR, VA, no. 29.622; MAI, G2/x/0028; RCBL, JS, 5 March, 4 June, 2 July 1940; see also NAI, DJ 69/80/254. Richard Wallach, the Viennese teacher, stayed with Flora Vere O'Brien at her estate near Ennis, Co. Clare from mid-July 1939 to mid-May 1940, being guaranteed and maintained by the Presbyterian Refugee Committee. MAI, G2/0868 and correspondence between local Garda and DJ in NAI, DJ 69/80/415. It seems however that responsibility for his planned exit to the USA was passed to the larger HCRC in spring 1940. RCBL, JS, 6 May and 4 June 1940. Between December 1938 and June 1939 Hans Forell had been accommodated by Hugh Vere O'Brien at his estate Monare on Foynes Island, Co. Limerick, and then for a few weeks by

could provide affidavits. He failed to do so in the cases of the two Picks and Hirschberg,[24] but succeeded in sending HCRC-supported Forell, Schlesinger and Wallach to the USA.[25] On 6 June 1939, HCRC minutes recorded that cheques had been drawn not only for Forell, but also for the passage costs of Konrad Topper and Gerhard Harant.[26] These were the only persons whom the HCRC helped to send to Australia before the beginning of the war.[27] Obviously, their second emigration was part of a planned family project.[28] In late 1938, the ICCR had already appealed to the Australian government to grant visas to refugees from Ireland.[29] The government in Canberra only reacted after the HCRC had opened channels to guarantors in the country and provided the landing money.[30] Topper's guarantor and first address after his arrival in Australia was the St

---

Alison Nugent at Farrenconnell, Co. Cavan. RCBL, JS, 3 November 1938, 2 February 1939; see also MAI, G2/x/0028 and NAI, DJ 69/80/57. Gerhard Jaffe, a Jewish teacher from Berlin, had come to Ireland from Denmark on 2 July 1939. He stayed only two months in Dublin, being maintained by the HCRC. He returned to Denmark on 7 September, wishing to find an academic post in Norway and later in the USA. See NAI, DJ 69/80/272; RCBL, JS, 6 July 1939.

24 For the Picks see RCBL, JS, 4 February, 1 July 1941 and 2 December 1941. For Hirschberg RCBL, JS, 6 May, 1 July and 9 September. In the Pick case, it must have been relevant that a family reunion became impossible when Heinrich Pick, their father, was unable to get to the USA.

25 For Forell see MAI, G2/x/0028; for Schlesinger RCBL, 5 March 1940; NAI, DJ 69/80/254; Wallach, RCBL, JS, 6 May and 4 June 1940; NAI, DJ 69/80/415. Obviously, they benefited from visa rules that were still liberal in the early war months, and from the fact that Forell and Schlesinger were to join family members who had already fled to the USA. The financial help of the HCRC is apparent from various entries in RCBL, JS minutes for 1939 and 1940.

26 RCBL, JS, 6 June 1939.

27 Topper had been brought to the country through the Swedish Mission-HCRC link (see chapter 2). In Ireland the HCRC had him briefly lodged at Miss Piggott's address in Greystones (see above), and then at a house in nearby Delgany, Co. Wicklow. NAI, DFA 202/331, DEA to Irish HC London, 9 June 1939. Gerhard Harant had stayed with the Power-Steele family at 74 Highfield Road/Rathgar (see chapter 6). NAI, DFA 202/348 and DJ 69/80/144.

28 In the Quaker index stored at Friends House, London, Topper is recorded as having emigrated to Australia together with his wife and son, whom Topper had obviously left in the care of English Quakers before coming to Ireland. SFHL, FCRA/16: Alphabetical Index. Gerhard Harant had also temporarily separated from his parents and his younger brother in London. Both were reunited with their families at their English port of departure.

29 Presumably in December 1938, Joseph Glynn had approached the Australian Prime Minister for help, both as President of the Irish Council of the St Vincent de Paul Society and as a leading member of the ICCR. Online Research Guide of National Archives of Australia (NAA), Correspondence between J. A. Glynn and Prime Minister. Signature A461, R449/3/5.

30 The "landing money" of £160 which the Australian authorities demanded for Harant's entry was procured through a fund-raising fete organised by the HCRC. RCBL, JS, 4 May and 6 July 1939.

Thomas Rectory in North Sydney,[31] while the Harants' entry was supported by the Australian-Jewish Welfare Society and a prominent Jewish family within its ranks.[32]

It was widely believed that confessing Jews were in a better position than non-Jews, as they could count on an efficient international network of helpers. This view seemed to be supported by Leonard Abrahamson's account, printed in the *Jewish Chronicle* in December 1941 (see chapter 6). Abrahamson told the public that among the "sixty-odd" exiles "many" had been "re-emigrated" to the USA or Latin America by the Central Jewish Refugee Aid Committee (CJRAC).[33] Abrahamson emphasised the active role of the CJRAC in engineering these passages, but not all confessing Jews necessarily owed their emigration to CJRAC initiatives. Benjamin Kurz, for example, co-owner of A. Kurz & Co. Ltd, a company that sold optical instruments from an office in 57 Middle Abbey Street, Dublin,[34] or Stefan Lendt, the Viennese lawyer, may have organised and financed their "re-emigration" themselves.[35] We may however be reasonably sure that several of the emigrants to the USA in 1940 made use of the financial and logistical support

---

31 NAA, list from Quarantine Service report on passengers of SS Otranto, Department of Health, 15 August 1939. For this we are indebted to Julia Church who kindly scanned documents stored in the National Archives of Australia. The only subsequent entries in the HCRC minutes relating to Topper are from 7 October 1941 and 13 January 1942. They document his gratitude for the help he had received from the HCRC.

32 Julia Church email to authors, 7 April 2014.

33 *Jewish Chronicle,* 19 December 1941.

34 In late July 1938, Kurz, a manufacturer of optical instruments in Vienna, had applied to found an Irish head office for his enterprise. It was incorporated on 15 February 1939 with the legal advice of Herman Good. Benjamin, his wife Golda and their daughter Diana lived in a flat in Monkstown and from January 1940 at 1 Orwell Gardens in Jewish Rathgar. It is unclear if they had all originally planned to move to the USA, as a later text by Diana implies, or if Benjamin wanted to bring his family there while hoping to return to Ireland himself. See Diana Kurz interview with *Centre for Austrian Studies Newsletter,* University of Minnesota, Vol. 12, no. 2, p. 6; NAI, DJ 69/80/230.

35 For Stefan Lendt see chapter 2. He had come to Ireland via Switzerland through the lobbying of Michael Noyk and the support of Padraic Colum (in the USA) and James Joyce (then in Zurich: he knew Noyk from his time in Paris). Lendt's efforts to reach the Americas were at first unsuccessful, and he had to stay in Dublin for almost two years. His independence from the community infrastructure is indicated by his addresses: he stayed first at Noyk's flat in Grafton Street, then lodged at 3 Mountjoy Square and 1 Cambridge Terrace, an address he shared with Stefan Feric. MAI, G2/0571. Lendt lived off grants from family members in Switzerland, and seems to have organised his own emigration (see his telegrams in the same file).

of Abrahamson's committee, as well as Jewish families. Examples were Julius Schwab and his wife Gertrud from Fürth, Bavaria,[36] and the families of the Viennese doctors Karl Menkes[37] and Aaron Stein,[38] as well as Hermann Heymann,[39] Walter Simon[40] and Siegfried Dziewientnik,[41] all three also from Vienna. Hans Wilmersdörfer from Munich, who had originally wanted to settle in the USA, also seems to have turned to the CJRAC for help in emigrating to Brazil, where he planned to join his parents.[42]

Exit Great Britain

"If a war starts I will not stay here. I shall join the British army at the first opportunity." Few statements could have been more shocking to Ernst Klaar than his

---

36 The admittance of Julius, a scientific chemist, and Gertrud had been advocated by their old acquaintance "Dr. Good" - probably Herman Good, at that time Honorary Secretary of the Jewish Representative Council for Eire – and was guaranteed by the CJRAC. They stayed first with Rudi and Marianne Neuman at 70 Upper Rathmines Road; in February 1940, they moved to 22 Belgrave Road, Rathmines. NAI, DJ 69/80/424.
37 See NAI, DJ 69/80/416; John Menkes, A Didactic Autobiography. In: *Journal of Child Neurology*, 2001, Vol. 16, no. 3, pp. 191–198, 192; also Hans (John) Menkes, *Visual History Archive*, 18 July 1996.
38 In late 1938, Phyllis Helen Moss, described as a friend of James Joyce's family, had gone to Vienna to help Jewish candidates emigrate to England, Ireland or the USA by teaching them English. "Her first pupil was a young physician for the Vienna fire department, Dr Aaron Stein, whom she married in 1939." The couple entered Ireland on the 'English quota', spending more than a year in Blackrock, Co. Dublin, at a property owned by Mrs. E.A. Moss, who was obviously closely related to Phyllis. See http://articles.philly.com/1995-04-08/news/25687073_1_leopold-bloom-bloomsday-james-joyce [last accessed 6 June 2015].
39 MAI, G2/0474.
40 NAI, DJ 69/80/123, Dillon to Duff, 29 January 1940; Walter Simon to Immigration Office Dublin, 12 May 1965.
41 Dziewientnik, as we saw in chapter 2, had been in Dachau. He was guaranteed by the CJRAC and given a visa to Ireland in April 1939. During his few months in Ireland he received help and hospitality from his sister Teresa, who worked at Modes Modernes in Galway. NAI, DJ 69/80/356; WSLA, residential register of Vienna.
42 After the Aryanisation of Max Wilmersdörfer Ltd, of which Hans was a one-third partner, and the November Pogrom, he was sent to Dachau and stayed there till 21 December 1938. He was freed through the involvement of Edwin Solomons, President of the Dublin Hebrew Congregation. In the Irish capital he lived on CJRAC funding and the meagre remains of his former assets, and stayed longest in the household of Arthur Seale, owner of a textile shop in Westmoreland Street. See texts in Bayerisches Landesentschädigungsamt (BLEA), no. 24.152; MAI, G2/x/0028; departmental correspondence in NAI, DFA 202/488 and DJ 69/80/16. For his wish to emigrate to the USA see NAI, DJ 69/80/163, Vera Law to DJ, 8 December 1938.

son's determined "To hell with Irish neutrality" (or so George Clare remembers).⁴³ Georg made his declaration in Dublin in November 1938, but when, some months later, Britain did go to war, he remained in neutral Ireland. Leaving aside obedience to his irate father, other factors might have dampened Georg's initial enthusiasm for the fight. In September 1939, the British government installed tribunals which, beginning their work at the beginning of October, classified "aliens" not by their possible usefulness to the war effort but by the danger they posed. In 1939, only a minority of refugees were interned, but in spring and summer 1940, huge numbers, indiscriminately classed as "enemy aliens", were sent to camps in Britain, Canada and Australia. Internment drastically decreased in the course of the year, but remained a spectre that deterred those Austrians and Germans who had found refuge in Ireland from attempting to join the British Army. Georg Klaar might have been alerted to the hazards of a move to the UK by a case such as Julius Silber's. He had to leave Ireland under the new restrictions at the beginning of the war, as it was feared that he, now addressed as "Israel Julius J. Silber", could not be deported if he were allowed to "take up residence for any considerable period".⁴⁴ Though he volunteered for the British Army, he was interned on the Isle of Man, and was released only at the end of 1941.⁴⁵ Significantly, it seems that no other male refugee except for Peter Gahr crossed the Irish Sea in the first two years of the war.⁴⁶

"They have no prospects here," Kathleen Huggard told Hubert Butler on 16 August 1941, concluding that "the best plan" would be to go to the UK.⁴⁷ By that time there was at least the option of joining the unarmed Auxiliary Military Pioneer Corps or certain technical units; enlisting in the British Army however was still prohibited.⁴⁸ Kurt Staudt, Herbert Unger, Ernst Einäugler, Gustav Beisser, Georg Liss, Georg Klaar, Hans Morgenstern, Karl Steiner and Kurt Stiegwardt considered

---

43 Clare, *Last Waltz in Vienna*, pp. 277.
44 NAI, DFA 69/133, Duff, DJ to Garda, 12 January 1940; also Duff to Garda, 7 November 1939 in the same file.
45 NLA, Nds. 110 W, Acc. 8/90, no. 339/6, Julius Silber affidavit, 15 September 1960; Peter Ticher interviews with authors, 10 and 11 August 2007; Thomas Ticher to authors, 23 August 2004. Sir Stephen Silver, Silber's son, email to authors, 10 January 2010. Most internees were released in 1940 and 1941, the majority finding a job in war industries or enlisting with the Pioneers. Wolfgang Muchitsch, *Mit Spaten, Waffen und Worten. Die Einbindung österreichischer Flüchtlinge in die britischen Kriegsanstrengungen 1939–1945*. Vienna, Zurich: Europa Verlag 1992, p. 13.
46 Gahr went to England the day before the British declaration of war, together with his wife and mother-in-law Friederike Goldstein. It is not certain whether he was interned. MAI, G2/x/0028.
47 TCD Archives, Butler Papers, 10304/597/777, Huggard to Butler, 16 August 1941.
48 Muchitsch, *Spaten*, pp. 11–12, 30–57.

signing up with the Pioneers,⁴⁹ but there were obstacles: Herbert Unger, having relatives in Berlin, did not meet entry requirements, as citizens of the Old *Reich* were generally excluded from service with the Pioneers.⁵⁰ Others emigrated elsewhere (Steiner, Stiegwardt), or failed a medical test (Morgenstern).⁵¹ Einäugler, Beisser, Staudt, Liss and Klaar, however, did go to England, entering the Pioneer training camps in the second half of 1941.⁵²

In 1943, the British Army finally opened its ranks to refugee Pioneers and those who had not yet seen military service, including those living in Ireland or the Dominions. In late December of that year, Kurt Hainbach applied to the British War Office. Summoned to the Recruitment Office in Belfast for an examination of his case, he left Miltown Malbay on 4 February without informing his company of his intentions. He returned on 8 February. On 20 March, he was arrested on the charge that he had wilfully and illegally deserted his position as a company manager, in violation of Section 20 of the Offences against the State Act.⁵³ After his interrogation and dismissal of the charge he gave up any further attempts to join the Army. Others were more successful.⁵⁴

---

49 Karl Steiner intended to join the Pioneers after his original plan to emigrate to the USA had failed. TCD Archives, Butler Papers, 10304/597/783, Huggard to Butler, 5 September 1941. For Stiegwardt see TCD Archives, 10304/597/782, Huggard to Butler, 7 May 1941; for Georg Pick see NAI, DJ 69/80/7, Huggard to DJ, 7 October 1941.
50 TCD Archives, Butler Papers, 10304/597/784, Huggard to Butler, 2 October 1941. Huggard considered him "quite unsuited for the Pioneers". TCD Archives, 10304/597/777, Huggard to Butler, 16 August 1941.
51 TCD Archives, 10304/597/774, Huggard to Butler, 6 August 1941.
52 For the dates of their moves to the AMPC camps see footnotes to above table of migrants.
53 Hainbach's Belfast expedition is documented in MAI, G2/0441.
54 On 27 February 1944, Ignaz Schulz volunteered for the Army, obviously with success. MAI, G2/0763. The circumstances of his Irish life had already been critical in Glenstal, as we have seen, and it was at the very end of that time that he first tried to enlist in the British Air Force. For the whole of 1943, he resided in the Old Vienna Club looking for work, but he "could not (even) find [...] a casual job", and was one among "many other men [...] waiting, unemployed and inactive". Translated by authors. The quotations are from letters to his former wife, 6 February 1943, and to the Free Austrian Movement in London, 5 March 1943. The brothers Hanus and Frantisek Drechsler enlisted as members of the associated Czech Military Mission. Hanus, having received his B.Sc. from TCD on 1 July 1943, offered his services to the War Office and left Ireland in October 1943. See MAI, G2/1082 and G2/x/0102; NAI, DJ 69/80/678, McGuire, Garda, to DJ 24 January 1944, M.A. Hogan to DJ, 29 March 1945. His younger brother, a Bachelor of Engineering and an Assistant Lecturer at UCD, began his military service only in April 1945 and then served as a technician with the Royal Electrical and Mechanical Engineers (REME). Mary Drechsler to authors, 24 May 2010. NAI, DJ 69/80/678, Little, O'hUadhaigh & Proud to DJ, 28 December 1945.

The need for manpower in the British war economy since 1941 had opened doors into war-related industries and civilian sectors of the economy, creating jobs for thousands of Irish workers, mostly young men.[55] Among them were also the family of Kurt Billig,[56] Ferdinand and Emilie Karrach,[57] Robert and Stefanie Feldmann,[58] Hans Morgenstern[59] and Eric Serff,[60] wanting to join the war effort (as was the main motivation for the Karrachs) or expecting higher salaries after they had received work permits and visas from the British Permit Office in Dublin.

In November 1944, the Irish monthly *The Bell* called attention to the fact that "the number of doctors we produce is out of all proportions to our needs".[61] The skills of graduates from Irish medical schools were not required in Ireland,

---

55 See "The vanished generation", Wills, *Neutral Island*, pp. 309–343.
56 See the telegram exchanges between Billig and his brother in London in MAI, G2/0345. James Waller, one owner of Delap and Waller, persuaded the Home Office to accede to a work permit.
57 Ferdinand seems to have wanted to go to England as early as summer 1941. See a reference in TCD Archives, Butler Papers, 30409/597/777, Huggard to Butler, 16 August 1941. The Karrachs moved to London in August 1943. NAI, DJ 69/80/16. Their son Herbert Karrach remembers that they left Ireland because Emilie blamed the Irish government for refusing to grant a vital visa to her parents and because they wanted to join the war effort. Herbert Karrach email to authors, 4 October 2006; also MAI, G2/0511 and 0512. See also Emilie's letters to her parents. Imperial War Museum, G3/27/1. In 1944 and 1945, the Karrachs were employed by the US Forces in England. Ferdinand worked as a doorman in an officers' club and his wife in a factory. NAI, DJ 69/80/16, visa applications for Ireland, 12 May 1945. Herbert Karrach email to authors, 4 October 2006.
58 It has not been possible to investigate the Feldmanns' story in Austria. In Edenderry, the central shoemaking town in Co. Offaly, Feldmann was employed by the Edenderry Shoemaking Co., founded in 1935, but it is unknown when his employment began and how long it lasted. In 1942–1943 the economic situation of the family must have been precarious, as the 1943 list of Germans, Co. Offaly, described him as an "unemployed former shoemaker". NAI, DFA 10/2/18. Although he was given a new permit in 1943, the family left Ireland the following year, obviously looking for more secure employment in the UK. NAI, DJ 69/80/93.
59 MAI, G2/0640. TCD Archives, Butler Papers, 10304/597/781, Huggard to Butler, 9 April 1942, all of them documenting efforts to provide Morgenstern with a job; also RCBL, JS, 3 March, 2 April 1942, 6 April and 7 September 1943. These efforts failed, but his tireless supporters in the HCRC and ICCR tried to place him in the British armament industry. On 17 August 1943, he took the boat for England to work in a gun factory at Woolwich.
60 MAI, G2/0777, telegram Ministry of Aircraft Production, 31 May 1943. He could expect an income three times as high as with Pye, Ireland. See two G2 reports, one undated, the other from 17 May 1943, in MAI, G2/0777. It may also have been the prospect of a higher income that led Robert Dubsky, a civil engineer engaged by the Turf Development Board, to apply for a post in British industries in 1944. NAI, DJ 69/80/276, certificate of identity, 15 August 1944. He stayed in Ireland however after he had married an Irish girl in June of that year. Paul Dubsky, The Dubsky Family. In: Holfter (ed.), *Irish Context*, p. 60.
61 *The Bell*, November 1944, pp. 119–128, 119.

concluded the writer of the article, and an additional factor was the problem of raising capital to purchase a practice (or to become a partner: see chapter 8). The British wartime economy provided an outlet for many of "Eire's Surplus Doctors", and in their wake a number of qualified exiles also found employment beyond the Irish Sea. In Britain, doctors were in high demand for assistantships and junior appointments in hospitals, the military and the Public Health Department. Even Richard Kappeler and Werner Schwarz, two doctors who had refused to re-qualify in Ireland, would probably have been accepted, if the former had not suffered from health problems[62] and the latter had not been assigned to an Emergency Hospital in Newcastle, a region that was declared one of the "prohibited areas".[63] Gerhard Rosenberg however returned to the UK, equipped with an Irish graduation diploma and expecting to open a practice in Guildford, Surrey.[64] Others who left Ireland for England were Robert Steiner,[65] Karl Steiner,[66] Josefa Stein,[67] the two nurses Christa Schreiber[68] and Anna Maria Tuchmann,[69] Richard Marx,[70] Heinz Scheyer[71] and Josef Wolfgarten.[72]

---

[62] RCBL, JS, 13 January 1942.
[63] RCBL, JS, 1 February 1944. From an interview with Elsa Peile on 11 November 2004 it appears that he managed to find a position in the UK after the war.
[64] It is unclear if this was his first engagement as a doctor. His wife is recorded as having returned to Ireland on 13 September 1943. MAI, G2/x/0102.
[65] He departed without his fiancée Gertrud Konirsch, whom he visited several times during the war years. See DJ 69/80/182. In March 1945, they were married in Sheffield, where Steiner had joined the staff of the United Sheffield Hospitals. BA Bayreuth, no. 15.000.813, Steiner (née Konirsch) CV, 22 February 1961.
[66] He became a junior doctor in a hospital in Maidstone, Kent. RCBL, JS, 8 September 1942; MAI, G2/x /0102.
[67] She practised at the Liverpool Heart Hospital. MAI, G2/x /0102 and NAI, DJ 69/80/240.
[68] Her entry to Ireland as a children's nurse in December 1938 had been organised by her future employers, the Crowley family, who had close affiliations to Fianna Fáil, and whose influence prevailed over Bewley's opposition. She found a job in a British hospital in September 1942 but returned to Ireland in 1943 to marry Sigurd Kawerau. She was then employed as a technical assistant at Adelaide Hospital. See correspondence in NAI, DFA 102 /437 and DJ 69/80/138.
[69] She was engaged by a hospital in Grimsby in 1943. MAI, G2/x/0102; G2/2097, Huggard to Medical Department, Bloomsbury House, 10 April 1943.
[70] He accepted an offer to practise at a hospital in Weston-super-Mare, Somerset. MAI, G2/2097.
[71] He had qualified as a medical doctor in June 1942 and worked at various hospitals in Dublin until his departure for the UK in 1944, where he was employed at Woodland Hospital, Harwich. See NAI, DJ 69/2404.
[72] Wolfgarten left on 3 June 1944 after having qualified as a doctor. MAI, G2/0240.

Exit Northern Ireland?

Remarkably, no German-speaking exile in from the South of Ireland seems to have gone to find employment in Northern Ireland where both war-related and other industries were booming. The training farm at Millisle, Co. Down, was a Northern Irish and Jewish variant of the agricultural training scheme south of the border, in which confessing Jews did not take part. Millisle Farm had been founded in July 1939 through the initiative of the Belfast Hebrew Community and the Newtownards Rural Council, which granted land for the erection of buildings. Like other similar projects, it was run by members of the Belfast community and aimed to qualify the trainees for agricultural and practical employment overseas.[73] In the first two years of its existence, an average of between 90 and 100 Jewish refugees were continuously in training. The number of participants from the South, however, was low. They were channelled to the Farm through transborder cooperation between the Farm organisers and Abrahamson's Central Jewish Refugee Aid Committee (CJRAC).[74] In mid-1939, the CJRAC proposed a list of 13 candidates from those it was assisting.[75] It was also prepared to contribute £1,125 to their maintenance costs and then a further £1,000 towards building and equipment expenses.[76] In fact, six of the candidates, Hans Wilmersdörfer, Karl, Valerie and Hans Menkes, Walter Simon and Aaron Stein, had already left Ireland for the Americas, as we have seen, and in the event, only Ernst and Marie Scheyer, Walter Storch, Erwin Jakobi, David and Thomas Nachmann and Adolf Mündheim were assigned for the project. They arrived at Millisle on 7 June 1940 – if on a completely voluntary basis is an open question. Few of them were well qualified for the agricultural and practical work they had to do at the Farm. Mündheim, who was to some extent prepared for the work at the Farm by his past experience, may have been the only one who looked on the episode as more than an experiment: at least it must have been a relief after his purposeless time in the South.[77] At the

---

73 *Jewish Chronicle*, 14 July 1939. Non-Jewish members, too, seem to have been originally included in the plan. *Jewish Chronicle*, 26 May 1939.
74 *Jewish Chronicle*, 19 December 1941, 7 February 1944.
75 Ernst and Marie Scheyer, David Nachmann, Adolf Mündheim, Hans Wilmersdörfer, Karl, Valerie and Hans Menkes, Walter Simon, Aaron Stein, Walter Storch, Frederick [sic] Lederer and Erwin Jakobi. PRONI, HA-8-787.
76 Ibid.
77 Before June 1940 he had sometimes stayed in Dublin, at 46 Upper Mount Street, and also with Simon Eppel's family at 342 Harold's Cross Road (MAI, G2/0644), and at other times at the Boylans' house in Tiravera, Glasslough. Barred from employment in Boylan's enterprise or anywhere

Farm he appears to have been seriously engaged in training programmes, and is remembered by a former Millisle participant as the co-designer of a daring engineering project, the so-called Mundheim Monument, two twin-gabled buildings housing various workshops.[78] It seems the main impetus for the scheme came from the Abrahamson committee in order to support Millisle Farm on an ongoing basis and reduce its local liabilities, rather than from the Department of Justice.[79] Its timing remains puzzling given that since Churchill had become Prime Minister in early May 1940, male German-speaking refugees were being fairly indiscriminately interned, due to the panic over "fifth columnists" after the seizure of Belgium. Perhaps it was assumed that those who had already suffered in concentration camps would be spared further detention. In fact, Storch and Nachmann, both former prisoners in German concentration camps, were interned shortly after their arrival, and stayed in a camp until November 1940.[80] Ernst and Marie Scheyer hastily returned to Dublin in early September, after their son Heinz had been warned that they too would be interned, and perhaps also because they hoped to emigrate to the USA.[81] If Walter Storch and Erwin Jakobi were interned and how long they stayed in Millisle is uncertain.[82]

Altogether, 111 people, almost one third of all refugees in Ireland in 1939, had succeeded in leaving the country by May 1945. Then the war was over. Within a few weeks, Hans and Ines Mandl, Else Samter and Otto Michael Falk left Ireland to join their families in the USA. And the others?

---

else, his livelihood had to be guaranteed through grants from a brother and an American cousin. NAI, DJ 69/80/251, Garda to DJ, 25 April 1939.

78 Robert Sugar, Millisle Farm, *The Jewish Monthly*, October 1990, pp. 26–29. In Maggie Boylan's notebook there is an entry from August 1941 referring to his residence at an address at Hatch Street (possibly the Old Vienna Club guesthouse, which would indicate that he only temporarily returned to Dublin).

79 DJ had prepared official Deportation Orders but these were not issued.

80 For Storch see NAI, DJ 69/80/439, Home Office to DJ, 14 November 1940; for Nachmann EA Berlin, Gerd/Gerald Nachmann affidavit, 27 March 1967.

81 See Holfter, Ernst Scheyer. In: Holfter (ed.), *German-speaking Exiles*, pp. 155–156. Also further correspondence in NAI, DJ 69/80/121. For the Scheyers' lingering hopes for an exit to the US, see MAI, G2/0733, Ernst Scheyer to Maurice Bisgyer, 25 May 1940 (less than two weeks before their journey to Millisle). They left Millisle on 2 September 1940, expecting to board a ship to America in October 1940 (together with their daughter Renate who was then still studying in England). See NAI, DJ 69/80/121, Garda to DJ, 3 September 1940 and S.E.C. Kendrick, American Consulate General Dublin to Ernst Scheyer, 21 September 1940. But they stayed in Ireland, now having their daughter with them.

82 At least we know that Walter Storch stayed in Belfast where his sister Alice had already lived for some years. In 1943, he tried to re-enter Eire for a two-week holiday, but contrary to practice in other similar cases the DJ refused his visa application. See correspondence in NAI, DJ 69/80/439.

Part III **After the War**

Chapter 11
Refugees Revisited

Stay on, go back to the old countries, venture a second emigration? These were the questions facing the refugees in 1945, and for the group as a whole the issue took about 15 years to play out. Within that timespan at least 120 persons, including children, left Ireland, among them 23 returning to Austria, West Germany and West Berlin – added to those who had left Ireland up to 1945 this raised the number of known trans-migrants to 223. At least 107 persons stayed in Ireland, most of them to the end of their lives. Choices arose from very individual deliberations and circumstances, but a few general patterns emerge from the different stories.

To begin with, plans may have been influenced by wartime experiences, but assessments of personal opportunities inside and outside post-war Ireland soon took precedence. Whether or not such opportunities could be realised depended on factors such as age, education and contacts. "The young person [...] is not only who he is, but also who he will be,"[1] wrote Jean Amery, reflecting on the potential of the younger refugees, with their "short past" and "long future". Time was on their side, the future offering possibilities that would dim their memories of the past: "The storm has come over us and passed away. We have to face a new life, looking forward to new harvests. We cannot always be tied up to the past; and pity only brings us back to a nasty and cruel experience which we like to forget."[2]

Educated in Ireland

Most of the younger refugees had been spared the strenuous efforts of their elders, often in vain and usually without local qualifications and connections, to enter the Irish labour market. Their primary task of learning the language was accomplished quite easily, in most cases, through communication with their Irish peers, and after that they were mainly occupied with study, exams, and preparation for a career. After the war, they could decide on their own futures (and felt lucky to be able to do so, especially in comparison with the war and post-war experiences of their peers in Germany or Austria). Marriage or work, or both, often led to a deep integration into Irish society. Ernst Hirsch and

---
1 Jean Amery, *At the Mind's Limits. Contemplations by a Survivor of Auschwitz and its Realities.* Bloomington: Indiana University Press 1980, p. 57.
2 SFHD, Lisl Strunz, speech to a Yearly Quaker Meeting.

Image 1: Frank Drechsler.

Frank (Frantisek) Drechsler obtained professorships at TCD – Hirsch as an internationally acknowledged specialist in veterinary medicine and Drechsler in economics[3] – while others embarked on business careers in post-war Ireland: Robert Dubsky played a leading role in Irish-Austrian trade and cultural relations (see further below); Fritz Hirsch was a director of firms in the chemical industry;[4]

---

[3] Ernst Hirsch's career: 1946 graduation from TCD, employment by Department of Agriculture and Dublin Corporation as a specialist vet, postgraduate studies in various European countries, Junior Lecturer at Veterinary College, 1951 professorship TCD, 1957 Permanent Lecturer at Veterinary College, 1960 Senior Lecturer for pathology and haematology at Veterinary College. He also co-edited the *Veterinary Journal*. See laudatio *Silbernes Ehrenzeichen* award, Austrian Bundesministerium für Auswärtige Angelegenheiten, Vienna 1982. Frank Drechsler, having first concluded his service in the exiled Czech Army and then his academic studies at UCD, went to the USA but returned to Ireland in 1953, by then a Catholic convert. He became a lecturer at UCD in the Electrical and Electronic Engineering Department, and from 1964 was consecutively Head of Industrial Management and Head of the School of Business Studies at the TCD School of Business. In the early 1990s, he was among the founders of the Irish Czech and Slovak Society. Summarised from: letters and emails from Mary Drechsler, Frank's daughter, to authors; NAI, DJ 69/80/678; also Daniel Samek, *Czech-Irish Cultural Relations 1950–2000*. Prague: Centre for Irish Studies, Charles University 2012 (online), pp. 39, 58.

[4] As early as his student days, Fritz Hirsch had worked as a salesman. In 1946, he received a B.Sc. in Chemistry, Bacteriology and Physics from TCD. Demand for chemists in industry being high at the time, he became a director of a small washing-powder company. In the following 60-odd years Fritz was mainly engaged in enterprises producing textiles and articles associated with the fashion trade. See laudatio *Silbernes Ehrenzeichen* award, Austrian Bundesministerium für Auswärtige Angelegenheiten, Vienna 1982. Fritz Hirsch to authors, 3 August 2010.

Stefan Feric continued his career in food processing;[5] Kurt Schwarz studied radio engineering at the Technical School, Kevin Street, and then began an apprenticeship as an electrician;[6] Kurt Kraus became an innovative refrigeration engineer in the new business of pasteurised milk;[7] Peter Strunz entered what his father termed "a most successful" career as a "sales manager in a large Irish firm";[8] Robert Aberbach founded a photography business in the city centre of Dublin;[9] Herbert Unger excelled as an architect;[10] and Otto Glaser is ranked as one of the leading entrepreneurial spirits of the technical modernisation which had a huge impact on the Irish economy from the late 1950s onwards.[11]

Hanus Drechsler, brother of Frank, emigrated to the USA, one among the thousands of young Irish who were boarding the boats to escape what was still

---

5 In 1963, he described his position in the business as a *Konsulent* (consultant). AdR, Hilfsfonds, Feric to Hilfsfonds für politisch Verfolgte, 24 October 1963.
6 He lived on ICCR funds in the first post-war years. NAI, DJ 69/80/413, Garda Siochana to DJ, 3 December 1947. He undertook a number of trips abroad but remained in Ireland at least until the early 1950s.
7 His technical competence and Continental links enabled him to contribute to developing the new market in Ireland. A founding member of the Rotary Club of Waterford and leading member of the Waterford Chamber, he became a public figure in the south east of Ireland. See Rotary Club Waterford homepage; see also *Irish Times*, 17 April 1951, 7 October 1959. The quotation is from *Munster Express* online, 24 July 2008.
8 See "Memories of Erwin Strunz". In: http://www.waterfordmuseum.ie/exhibit/web/Display/article/373/3/Ardmore_Memory_and_Story__Troubled_Times_Austrian_Refugees.html. [last accessed 23 November 2014], first published in *Ardmore Journal* 1989.
9 Paul Auerbach, Robert's eldest son, to authors, 27 August 2010; also correspondence in NAI, DJ 69/80/93.
10 After completing his academic studies, Unger became (from 1946 to 1955) an assistant architect in the head office of Michael Scott, Ireland's most influential 20th century architect. He commenced his public service career in the Office of Public Works (1955–1956); in the following decades he alternated between functions within Dublin Corporation and Dun Laoghaire Corporation. Among the public buildings that he helped design were the Berkeley Library of TCD and the interior of the Curragh Camp Church. He retired as the borough architect for Dun Laoghaire in 1981. He was also a part-time lecturer in the history and theory of architecture at the National College of Art and Design for 20 years. See Klaus Unger, On Herbert Unger. In: Holfter (ed.), *Irish Context*, pp. 29–34; further an undated CV of Herbert Unger and interviews with Klaus Unger.
11 After graduating from UCD, Glaser (who also developed links to the Dublin Institute of Advanced Studies) was employed as an assistant engineer by the Department of Post and Telegraph, providing services at Irish airports. He co-founded and managed innovative telecommunications firms such as Technico Ltd and Telectron Ltd, with 1100 employees overall, and he served as chairman of AT&T Ireland and Alcatel Ireland among other activities. Questionnaire Dr Otto Glaser 15 June 2004 and Peter Ticher interviews with authors, 25 May 2004 and 10/11 April 2007.

an economically backward society in post-war Ireland. Those young refugees who moved on had the advantages of a sound academic education and a good command of English, acquired during their Irish years. Among them were a remarkably high number of young medical practitioners, who had completed a full academic programme, which in principle would have allowed them to practise in Ireland, but were seeking better professional opportunities in the UK. Again, their departure was only a part of a general exodus of young Irish doctors that had already begun during the war, as we have seen. Foreign Jewish doctors, whether academically qualified or not, often felt they had no chance of being employed by Catholic hospital boards or founding a general practice.[12] By the mid-1950s, all the German-speaking medical students had left the country, apart from Marianne Neuman who at that time was studying medicine at the College of Surgeons.[13] Herbert Karrach, Wolfgang Pappenheim, Peter Lisowski, Kurt Adler and Manfred Bayer all went to England soon after the war.[14]

Among the last to leave was Einhart Kawerau. In 1954, he gave up his research work in biochemistry at TCD and accepted an appointment as Senior Lecturer at St Mary's Hospital, a branch of the Medical Department of the University of London.[15]

---

12 See O'Grada, *Jewish Ireland*, p. 213; Price, *Somewhere to Hang My Hat*, pp. 115–116.

13 For her background and entry into Ireland in April 1939, see chapter 4, footnote 10. For examination results see notes in *Irish Times*, 10 July and 18 December 1951, 4 September 1952. Her life-long contribution to Irish medicine and especially her devotion to the St John Ambulance Brigade is acknowledged in an obituary in the *Irish Times*, 5 April 2008.

14 After his graduation from TCD, Karrach entered the medical service of the British Colonial Department. From the mid-1950s he was a medical officer and a Christian missionary in Africa and Asia. Herbert Karrach email to authors, 4 October 2006. Nothing is known about Wolfgang Pappenheim's post-war career. He had come to Ireland in early 1944, obviously to complete his medical studies in Dublin, and went to the UK in 1947. Paul Weindling to authors, 9 June 2004. In the same year Peter Lisowski began practising as a doctor at a Liverpool hospital after having finished his general medical exam and gained a specialist qualification as a gynaecologist. In the mid-1950s, he moved to Birmingham where he became a lecturer at the Anatomical Institute of the University. His subsequent international academic career took him to places such as Ethiopia, Hong Kong, and Australia. See NLA. Nds.110 W, Acc. 31/99, no. 232.812, Peter Lisowski undated CV. Kurt Adler, a graduate from TCD in 1947, also worked at a Liverpool hospital. In 1950, he and his Irish wife emigrated to Canada. From 1957 on, he was employed for 23 years as medical health officer and director at the Chinook Health Unit in Fort Macleod, Alberta. Note in *Irish Times*, 8 July 1947; obituary in online *Fort MacLeod Gazette*, 11 October 2010. Manfred Bayer, Abraham and Gitla Bayer's Offenbach-born son, also qualified as a doctor and emigrated to England after the war. See Harris, *Dublin's Little Jerusalem*, p. 178.

15 In 1967, he and his family emigrated to Canada where he became head of Clinical Chemistry at Hamilton General Hospital, Ontario. See obituary in *The Lancet*, 22 February 1975, p. 469.

Medical practitioners were by no means the only ones to leave post-war Ireland for a career in the UK or elsewhere. Robert Weil (married to Renate Scheyer since 1948) and Hans Reiss successfully continued their academic careers in the United Kingdom and further afield.[16] Peter Schwarz was appointed Assistant Lecturer in chemistry and awarded a PhD by TCD in 1953 before being appointed to a professorship of chemistry, specialising in physical chemistry, and becoming Vice-Dean of the Science Department at the University of Edinburgh, where he remained for many years.[17] Ernst von Glasersfeld and his wife had their farm project dissolved in July 1946; in the 1950s Ernst started his career as philosopher and radical constructivist, a field in which he gained great distinction, working first in Italy and from 1966 in the USA.[18] Georg Bernfeld, a physicist, emigrated to South Africa. Georg Strunz, a biochemist, went to Canada, a country whose liberal immigration laws and economic opportunities also attracted Kurt Adler, Sigurd Kawerau, an educator, and Alfred Schulhof, an electrical engineer.[19] In the

---

[16] Robert Weil concluded his postgraduate studies at Trinity with a B.Litt. in 1950. He and Renate had moved to Northern Ireland in the late 1940s, and Renate started teaching in 1947 at Victoria College, Robert in 1948 at Methodist College Belfast (where Renate then taught part-time from 1958 until 1976, the last four years as Head of German). In 1973, Robert received a call from Queen's University Belfast, where he became Lecturer and then Senior Lecturer for Modern Languages in the Department of Education. See Colin Walker, Robert Weil. In: Holfter (ed.), *German-speaking Exiles*, pp. 133–147; Stephen Weil, 'Children of Goethe': The Scheyer-Weil Family. In: Holfter (ed.), *Irish Context*, pp. 27–28 and email Stephen Weil to authors, 15 June 2016. In October 1946, when TCD did not renew his contract as lecturer in German literature, Hans Reiss became an assistant lecturer at the School of Economics and Political Science, University of London. Reiss, *Erinnerungen*, pp. 54–55. His appointment in London was followed by professorships in Montreal and Bristol.
[17] Peter Schwarz, An anecdotal autobiographical note, March 1996.
[18] NAI, DJ 68/1/602. On their life after 1946 in Europe and the USA see von Glasersfeld, *Partial Memories*, pp. 109–212. Isabel died in 1969, Ernst von Glasersfeld in 2010; in the Afterword to the *Partial Memories* (pp. 263–266) Josef Mitterer mentions that von Glasersfeld, together with Thomas Kuhn, was rated the most influential philosopher in a recent study of researchers in Science Education. Also of interest is the assessment of his philosophical achievement and standing in his German memoir *Unverbindliche Erinnerungen* in the "Nachwort" [afterword] by Heinrich Mitterer (pp. 235–240). Material and videos, specifically on Glasersfeld's concept of radical constructivism, are available via the online Ernst von Glasersfeld archive: http://www.evg-archive.net/en/. Glasersfeld maintained that his time in Ireland had a strong impact on his thinking, and that his interest in constructivism developed partly from reading James Joyce's *Finnegans Wake*. Email to authors, 12 May 2006.
[19] After graduation from Blackrock College, Georg Bernfeld studied at UCD and was appointed as a part-time teacher of Maths and Physics at the College of Technology, Bolton Street, in December 1946. NAI, DJ 69/80/339; *Irish Times*, An Irishman's Diary, 6 October 2011. From this text

mid-1950s, Jochen Hengstenberg resolved to further his journalistic career in the USA. Otto M. Falk, the art student, had gone there already in 1946 before moving to Israel a few years later.[20]

Image 2: Peter Schwarz and his mother Berta.

---

it appears that he must have left Ireland by 1954–1955. Georg Strunz was still an adolescent at the time when his elder brother Peter started a business career (see above). After his graduation from TCD with a B.A. in 1959 he emigrated to Canada, where he became a biochemist "in charge of a four provinces research laboratory, besides lecturing at the university". See source in footnote 8. After his retirement from the Canadian Forest Service in 1999, he was able to pursue artistic interests. See http://charlottestreetarts.ca/index.php/site/full-event-details/111. Sigurd Kawerau continued working as a clerk for Bevan Lamb after the war. In 1956, he and his wife Christa (née Schreiber) migrated to Edinburgh, a move that was "forced upon me by economic circumstances", as he explained in 1961. The quotation is from one of Kawerau's letters to DJ in April 1961. NAI, DJ 68/1/721. Later they went to Mills Haven, Strathcona County, Canada – in both places he worked as a teacher of German in primary and secondary schools. Alfred Schulhof was employed by a Dublin firm in 1946. In the early 1950s, he and his Irish wife emigrated to Canada, probably in search of better economic opportunities. See correspondence in NAI, DJ 69/80/359.

20 After his exams at Newtown School, Jochen Hengstenberg (John Heston after 1961) had been apprenticed as a journalist and then studied at the London Academy of Dramatic Art. Back in Ireland he worked as a writer of comedy serials for RTE. In 1955, he emigrated to the USA. John Heston CV, email to authors, 24 October 2007 and questionnaire 29 October 2007. Brian Hengstenberg, his younger brother, left Ireland a few years later. He went back to Westphalia, resettling near their parents' former residence in Wuppertal. In 1946, Otto Michael Falk was reunited with his parents in New York after his graduation from the National College of Art. In 1950, he moved to a Kibbutz and in 1957 to Moshav Sde Warburg. Besides his agricultural activities he has devoted himself to painting. http://www.ginagallery.com/gallery/showArtistBiography.asp?ArtistId=117 [last accessed 1 January 2015]; see also text in *Holocaust Memorial Day 2009 Booklet*, p. 18.

Image 3: Einhart, Maria and Sigurd Kawerau (left to right).

Growing old – in Ireland?

By contrast, exiles born before 1890 had seen their achievements and settled social existence ruined before their entry into Ireland. Nearing retirement age around 1945, and lacking the range of options available to their younger fellows, their post-war lives were a tale of vanishing job opportunities and reliance on what was left of their family networks after the Holocaust and exile. Some had tried to support themselves in extremely difficult circumstances during the war years and continued to do so after 1945, until sickness and age forced them into retirement. Friedrich Lisowski, Siegmund Liffmann and Ludwig Heinsheimer all spent their last years with their sons or daughters in Ireland and the UK.[21] Else Samter joined her daughter in the USA in mid-September 1945.[22] Max and Hedwig

---

21 Liffmann's Belgrave Trading Company was dissolved in 1955, but he and his wife could count on the assistance of his two daughters and his brother-in-law until his death in January 1958. NAI, CRO/1/D/1110; NLA, Nds. 110 W, Acc. 8/90, no. 267/21, Liffmann and German Legation Dublin affidavits, 15 January 1957; Peter Ticher interview with authors, 25 May 2004. Friedrich Lisowski kept up his installation business in Cabinteely into the 1950s. In 1956, a cardiovascular disease stopped his work. After that, he and his wife largely lived with their son in England. NLA, Nds. 110 W, Acc. 31/99, no. 232.812, Peter Lisowski undated CV. Heinsheimer ran some small agencies ("Agenturen"), with his daughter Eva Maria as "general assistant", in the early post-war years, while his wife still worked as a governess in various households. See correspondence in NAI, DJ 69/80/317; also AdR, Hilfsfonds, GZ 13.237, Risa Heinsheimer to Hilfsfonds, 8 April 1977.
22 NAI, DJ 69/80/573.

Rund departed in August 1946 to live with other exiled family members in New York.[23] The only elderly person without a family refuge at the end of his working life was Erich J. Priebatsch (see chapter 4).[24] Several of the older refugees suffered from coronary diseases, and some died comparatively young. There was a perception among their families and their doctors that this was attributable to the trauma of the Nazi period and the experience of exile, and although it is difficult to verify such opinions, many would have subscribed to what Doris Segal said about the deaths of her parents: though they had "escaped the worst under the Nazis, the tragedy had taken its toll on them. They died relatively early, in their sixties."[25]

Those still of working age at the end of the war had the option of further emigration. This could be successful, as the example of Gerhard Hirschberg demonstrates (though he and his Irish wife returned to Ireland in the 1960s),[26] but had its risks, as the long-term effects of persecution and displacement could lead to an inability to integrate either in Ireland or further afield.[27] As a rule, those with jobs, such as Wolfgang Eisenstaedt or Lothar Fuchs, remained in Ireland and continued working in their wartime professions.[28] The

---

[23] Max Rund seems to have had economic expectations in connection with his emigration, but in 1952 he was recorded as living on welfare payments. NAI, DJ 69/80/302, Rund to DJ, 7 March 1946. EA Berlin, no. 310.868, City of New York Welfare Department, 4 February 1952, and other correspondence.

[24] An affidavit at the Irish Department of Finance showed that in 1947 he had an income of £394, in 1952 of £623; in his last year it dropped to £333. See Irish Department of Finance, correspondence in EA Berlin, no. 431.019.

[25] Doorly, *Hidden Memories*, p. 77. Evidence of illness related to persecution and exile can be found in a number of personal documents and official death certificates submitted to restitution agencies after the war by exiles or their relatives to substantiate claims for compensation.

[26] Gerhard Hirschberg emigrated to the USA after the war and was employed as a librarian at Chicago University, and then again in the 1950s when he seems to have made a "good career". But at the beginning of the 1960s he and his wife Alison Nugent (married since 1947) returned to Farrenconnell permanently. On Hirschberg's and Nugent's post-war lives see NAI, DJ 69/80/466, DI&C employment permit for Hirschberg at TCD, 8 June 1945, Hirschberg to Irish Consul Chicago, 10 May 1948, and other correspondence in the same file. Benita Stoney, email to authors, 23 March 2010; *The Anglo-Celt*, 26 November 2008, obituary Alison Nugent Hirschberg; WGA Saarburg, no. 41.050, Hirschberg application sheet for restitution, 28 December 1953.

[27] David Nachmann made two futile efforts to establish himself in Montreal, where his eldest son lived. In Canada he committed suicide. EA Berlin, no. 322.992, Gerd Nachmann to EA Berlin, 27 March 1967.

[28] Wolfgang Eisenstaedt moved to Dublin in February 1945. He was employed first as a maker of wooden toys at the shop of Kurt Adler's wife Maura (Moira) at 36 Fenian Street, then as a carpenter; in the 1950s he became a self-employed upholsterer and joiner with an income that sufficed to

Karrachs returned to Ireland after their contribution to the British war effort, and resumed their former occupations.[29] Others in less secure or lower-paid employment, such as the Frankls and the Kalmans, tended to leave Ireland as soon as possible.[30]

On 15 December 1945, the *Irish Independent* ran an advertisement announcing that the Unicorn, continuing under the management of Erwin and Lisl Strunz, would open new rooms "for the entertainment of private parties". In fact, the new Unicorn did not pass beyond the planning stage. This failure – which was probably partly due to a conflict between William Griffith and the Strunzes – caused serious financial difficulty for both Strunz and Lederer. In July 1947, after an unsuccessful experiment running a restaurant in Kildare Street and nine months of unemployment, Friedrich Lederer moved to Wales where he found a job in the hotel business.[31] Strunz also seems to have played with the idea of onward migration, but the whole family had put down roots in Ireland – their two sons were still at school – and Erwin found work first as a manager of a bakery and from 1950 onwards as a representative for Bewley's Café.[32] The Hirsch family's Old Vienna Café also closed after Marie Hirsch's death in 1945. A year later, Vida Lentaigne sold the establishment.[33]

---

feed his family (wife and daughter). NAI, DJ 69/80/468, DI&C to DJ, 10 September 1945. EA Berlin, no. 56.376, Convent of Sacred Heart, Mount Anville, Dundrum, affidavit 27 May 1958; Eisenstaedt affidavit 13 March 1960. Lothar Fuchs also stayed in Ireland. His oldest daughter had married an Irishman in 1944, as previously mentioned, and he remained a "main teacher" at St Gerard's School. MAI, G2/0422; Brian Murphy, *St. Gerard's School 1918–1998*, Bray: Kestrel Books 1999, pp. 133, 135. For his musical activities, see a note in *Irish Times*, 9 April 1953.

[29] Ferdinand and Emilie Karrach returned to Dublin in 1945, becoming partners of the craft shop they had been involved with until 1943. It seems that their business thrived through links to Austrian partners whom Ferdinand knew from his Continental days. NAI, DJ 69/80/16, visa applications Emilie and Ferdinand Karrach, 12 May 1945; questionnaire filled in by Herbert Karrach, 30 November 2005; Herbert Karrach, email to authors, 4 October 2006.

[30] The Frankl family emigrated to the USA in mid-1947. Bernard found a job as a cutter of car seats in Cincinnati enabling him to buy a small house in the town. He, his wife and Heinz later moved to Shelby, Ohio. Josef Kalman, the dissatisfied manager at Wings, and his wife also left Ireland soon after the end of the war, and reached what their nephew calls a "lower middle class" status in the USA. Rudi Lindner email to authors, 21 December 2007. Two other middle-aged emigrants to the USA were Alice and Heinz Krotoschin (see below).

[31] NAI, DJ 68/1/620.

[32] Strunz, Memoir, June 1989, unpublished, pp. 26–28.

[33] Fritz Hirsch interview with authors, 14 November 2004.

Women in exile

Although women shared the feelings of alienation common to all refugees, their experiences of exile were in many cases somewhat different.[34] Gender convention dictated that a woman's place was in the home, rather than earning money (at least in bourgeois households). This was particularly so in Ireland, a largely Catholic society, where a marriage bar for female teachers at National Schools, introduced in 1932, had been extended throughout the Civil Service (and was not abolished until 1973) and women's access to industrial or public employment had been curtailed.

Some women overcame the restrictions, the largest group being those employed in the 'refugee factories' of Longford and Galway. Although most of the middle-aged wives among the exiles kept to traditional roles, three managed to pursue their former career interests: Käte Müller-Lisowski, who had given up her lectureship at Berlin University following her marriage to Friedrich Lisowski in 1920, but continued to publish articles in academic journals,[35] and the two teachers Lisl Strunz and Annerose Heitler.[36] Lisl Strunz and Marie Hirsch became their respective husbands' business partners and Maria Marckwald, Risa Heinsheimer and Paula Moddel supplemented family income through various activities outside their husbands' fields of work.[37]

It is important to stress the crucial contribution of women who worked in the home and were largely responsible for organising the private and social lives of their families. They had of course done so before emigration, but under the pressures of adjusting to a strange environment, these concerns took on new importance. Here again there were obvious differences, often relating to financial circumstances. It is likely, for example, that Käte Müller-Lisowski found her life in Ireland (see above) more demanding than most wives of managers in the

---

34 For two case studies of female exiles see Gisela Holfter, Marginalised Voices – Women in Irish Exile. In: *Yearbook for the Centre for German and Austrian Refugees*, Vol. 18, Leiden/Boston: Rodopi forthcoming 2017.
35 An early article appeared in the *Etudes Celtiques*, fasc. III, June 1938, pp. 46–70. See *Life and Works of Käte Müller-Lisowski*. CELT, Corpus of Electronic Texts (University College Cork), compiled by Beatrix Färber. The text also makes clear, however, that she was unable to have any academic text published in the war years, probably due to the domestic obligations she had to shoulder in that time.
36 For Strunz see chapter 2; for Annerose Heitler see chapter 9.
37 In 1946, Helena Lowy applied for permission from the DI&C to found a shop for mending ladies' and children's stockings. The application was only granted in 1948, and it is unclear whether she actually started her business. See NAI, TID 1207/2165.

'refugee factories' (Grete Blaskopf, for example) or those of academics, whose husbands earned enough money to secure a comfortable living for their families. Even for the more financially secure, however, circumstances could change dramatically if the husband died, as can be seen from the wartime cases of Margarete Konirsch and Alice Hopf (see chapters 7 and 9). In cases where widows had grown-up children in the UK or USA, their chief wish was generally to join them (see the examples of Alice Hopf, Else Samter, Charlotte Sachs, Rosa Liffmann and Gertrud Königsberger), although Berta Schwarz stayed in Ireland (see chapter 8 and below). Annerose Heitler also remained in the country, though her brother Walter Heitler left for Switzerland (see below). She had developed links with Alexandra College during the war,[38] and became a permanent member of its staff in 1948.[39] Her mother Ottilie, who stayed in Dublin, died there shortly before her 96th birthday, outliving her daughter by five years. She is remembered by her son as a very religious person.[40] Both she and Annerose had domestic help and were materially quite well off, but seem to have been rather socially isolated, despite their own generosity and goodwill towards others.[41]

Image 4: Ottilie Heitler – unknown artist.

---

38 Through Walter and Kathleen Heitler, contact had been made with Honor Stuart, a teacher there, leading initially to an informal arrangement with the school. Interview Honor Stuart with authors 18 June 2007.
39 See Anna V. O'Connor and Susan M. Parkes, *Gladly learn and gladly teach. A history of Alexandra College and School, Dublin 1866–1966*, Tallaght: Blackwater Press 1984, p. 205.
40 Walter Heitler, Lebenserinnerungen (unpublished, courtesy of Günther Rasche), p. 1.
41 Denis Henderson, The Heitlers and the Strunzes, unpublished recollections, 2015. See chapter 9.

Image 5: Lisa Fischer.

Turning to the young female refugees (such as Sabina Wizniak, Eva M. Heinsheimer, Erika Kende, Mimi Höfer, Melanie Fuchs, Esther Britz, Doris Klepper, Anny Polesie, Lisa and Erica Fischer, Gertrud Konirsch, Christa Schreiber), most of them married. A few of the husbands were fellow exiles or English, but the majority were Irish, meaning that the wives blended more easily into Irish society under their new names. When Lisa Lynn (née Fischer) died, aged only 22, following complications when she gave birth to twins, nothing in the newspaper article announcing her death gave any indication of her refugee background.[42] Several of the women went with their husbands to live abroad – as did many of their Irish counterparts of the time. Erica Fischer for example moved to Australia after working in Dun Laoghaire's Cottage Home for some years. Esther Britz (Ernst and Hedwig Lewy's daughter), who had started working in Arnotts department store in Dublin before the end of the war, went to England with her husband Frank (they got married in 1951, a few months after Esther's brother Georg married Peggy, Frank's sister).[43] Eva Maria Pick, who remained single, was employed as a "general office worker" with the *Irish Times* until at least 1953, and in 1955 emigrated to Toronto where

---

[42] "Death of Mrs. E. Lynn, The Knather, Ballyshannon", *Donegal Democrat*, 26 July 1947. Lisa, referred to throughout the article as Mrs Lynn, is described as a former governess in Ballyshannon, whose "charming manner and jovial personality endeared her to all those whose privilege it was to have been acquainted with her". The only hint might have been that the attendance at her funeral was "representative of classes and denominations".
[43] Interview with Peggy Moore-Lewy, 28 July 2005.

she seems to have worked as a secretary.⁴⁴ Franziska ("Frances") Wiedmann supported herself and her mother through employment in the textile business after her father's death at the beginning of the war – in the 1947 naturalisation list she was described as a "designer and director".⁴⁵ Some of the women continued an independent career after marriage: Renate Scheyer, for example, in Northern Ireland (see above, footnote 16). Ruth Brandenburg had acquired some practical knowledge of filing systems even before her emigration (see chapter 8). After the war, she and her father continued to produce 'Easisee' in their own workshop, now in Castle Avenue, Clontarf. After her marriage to an Irish husband and the birth of their two children, she may to some extent have withdrawn from this and other family businesses, but following the deaths of her parents in 1955 and her husband in 1959, it fell mainly to her to keep 'Easisee' and the other products on the market. She often started work "at 6.a.m. to make plates for her two Rotaprints, then attending to the needs of her customers for Leitz, Kalle and Easisee during office hours" and spent "the evening, till midnight, servicing Vari-Typers".⁴⁶

Leaving the outposts

Many of those who worked in the provinces, although their jobs might be secure and well-paid and their social status respectable, decided after the war that it was time for a change. The younger refugees were among the first. In September 1945, the Werner family moved from Athlone to Dublin, where Kurt was employed by a firm of accountants.⁴⁷ A few months later Kurt and Isabella Hainbach also went to the capital, leaving their difficulties in Miltown Malbay behind them.⁴⁸ Ines and

---

44 See data in Hessisches Hauptstaatsarchiv Wiesbaden (HHSA), file group 518, no. 6.848; also correspondence in NAI, DJ 69/80/7.
45 DD, Volume 108, 22 October 1947. See also correspondence in NAI, DJ 69/80/198.
46 Denis Henderson, On Ruth Henderson and her parents, Peter and Else Brandenburg. In: Holfter (ed.), *Irish Context*, pp. 65–72, 70.
47 In 1951, Kurt went to London, while Lilli eked out an existence for herself and Klaus Peter, student at St Andrew's Christian Brothers School, through a number of jobs plus welfare payments and her husband's assistance, until she settled in a more remunerative post as surgery assistant in the mid-1950s. NAI, DJ 69/80/93, Werner to DJ, 26 July 1947; further correspondence in DJ 68/1/617.
48 It seems that economic difficulties of the Malbay Manufacturing Co. hastened their departure. It was noted at the time that "work at the factory became very slack" – a situation which led to the dismissal of Mathilde Endeveld, who also moved to Dublin. NAI, DJ 69/80/272, Garda Síochána Ennistymon to DJ, 29 October 1945. For Endeveld's move to Dublin see MAI, G2/0400, G2 note of 3 December 1945.

Hans Mandl realised their long-time aspiration to emigrate to the USA, both well-qualified for their future careers in the new country.[49]

Most other exiles with executive positions in the 'refugee factories' were in their fifties when the war ended.[50] In Galway, Les Modes Modernes was in the mid-1950s still "the most unexpected concern to a visitor", where "hoods are received from Castlebar and transformed into the finished article".[51] At that time, however, only a few of the exiled German speakers still lived and worked in Galway: five at most, our research suggests, out of a wartime population of 29 refugees.[52] The exodus had begun during the war years, when Wings transferred to Dublin, and Serge Philipson (see chapters 7 and 8) and Else Honig and her son moved to the capital.[53] In 1947–1948, Josef and Else Storm emigrated to Australia with their two children.[54] The Marckwalds returned to Waterford in 1948, where Fritz was finally offered a position more commensurate with his former commercial activities. They stayed there for the rest of their lives.[55] Heinrich Bittgen returned to Austria

---

[49] Hans worked as a designer and production manager for US textile companies before setting up his own company (H. A. Mandl Co.). His wife began a successful academic career, leading to a professorship of chemistry at Columbia University. Their early passage to America also led to a reunion with their parents who had been living in New York since 1941. Ines Mandl to authors, 11 October and 8 December 2004. For details on their careers see Werner Röder and Herbert A. Strauss (eds), *International Biographical Dictionary of Central European Emigrés 1933–1945*. Volume II / Part 2: L-Z, The Arts, Science, and Literature. Munich et al.: K. G. Saur 1983, p. 767; also entries on Ines Mandl in the Strauss/Röder collection, stored at Technical University Berlin.

[50] Ernst Königsberger, somewhat older, continued as a general manager in Tipperary until he suffered a stroke in 1950. After his death in October 1954, his wife Gertrud joined one of their sons in England. The Tipperary factory was closed in 1960. NLA, Nds. 110 W, Acc. 8/90, no. 241/22, Ernst Königsberger to German Legation Dublin, 16 November 1953; Gertrud Königsberger CV, 14 June 1955; DJ affidavit, 24 May 1955. Konrad Kingshill, *On the Precipice of Prejudice and Persecution*. Bloomington: Authors House 2008, p. 86.

[51] T.W. Freeman, Galway - the Key to the West. *Irish Geography*, Vol. 3, 1957, p. 204.

[52] Teresa Dziewientnik had married an Irishman in late August 1940. NAI, DJ 68/1/512. At an unknown date Wolf Zeiler, the former supervisor, also moved to Dublin, where he stayed mostly in the Jewish sector. He seems to have owned one or more laundrettes. Anna Adler interview with authors, 13 September 2005; Anna Adler to authors, 3 January 2010. It is unknown whether Olga Bretholz, Bertha Mortl, and Katharina Hein were still in Galway by the 1950s.

[53] MAI, G2/0494.

[54] John McDermott interview with authors, 13 June 2008.

[55] The employer was Waterford Glass Ltd. NLA, Nds. 110W, Acc. 31/99, Fritz Marckwald affidavit, 2 October 1948. The file documents Fritz's earlier endeavours to find other jobs. In Waterford he also became a partner in H. Kneisel and Co., a jewellery shop. NAI, TID 1207/3148. Memory of Philip Jacob in text of *Holocaust Memorial Day 2009 Booklet*, Dublin: Holocaust Educational Trust of Ireland 2008, p. 22.

in 1947, Karl Rosulek and his wife in 1949,[56] and Mathilde Schwenk a few years later.[57]

At the end of the war, the tiny exile community of Longford was still to a great extent economically and socially dependent on the Hirsch factory. In 1949, the owners concluded an extra-judicial settlement in which they waived physical restitution of their former enterprise in favour of compensation for its Aryanisation: the compensation must have strengthened the capital basis of their Irish undertaking.[58] Members of the family itself, however, only occasionally visited the town. Emil and Elsa Hirsch had moved to Dublin during the war, and after 1945 their son was preoccupied with his new business (see below), although he still held capital in the Longford enterprise.[59] The management of the factory lay in the hands of Ernst Sonnenschein (who also owned some shares at the end of the 1950s) and Alois Goebl.[60] The Goebls struck deeper roots in local society than either the Hirsch or Sonnenschein families, after the arrival of Alois Goebl Jr. in 1946 and his marriage to an Irish girl a few years later.

In Carrick-on-Suir, the Hitschmanns maintained a continuous presence, although members of the family spent time in Dublin, too. Their stronger links to the region were the result not only of their capital stake in Plunder & Pollack, but the involvement of family members in the enterprise – after Fritz Hitschmann's death in 1963 his brothers Albert and Paul as well as Albert's son Carlos took over important management positions.

After the war, Dublin-based Wings Ltd largely lost its character as an Austrian exile company. Josef and Lucie Kalman emigrated to the USA (see above), and Fritz and Grete Blaskopf returned to Vienna (possibly accompanied by their daughter).[61] They later claimed the complete restitution of their Vienna enterprise, which still produced zip fasteners in the same building at Lindengasse 56 and with much of the old workforce as in 1938. It seems that Florian Oberer followed the Blaskopfs to Vienna,[62] and only Hans and Helena Lowy remained in

---

56 For both see data in WSLA, residential register of Vienna.
57 Information provided by Tony Conneely, Galway, 25 March 2008.
58 See WSLA, VEAV-837/1, *Vereinigte Bandfabriken* to Bezirksamt VI, 15 November 1946; text of accord of 13 April 1949 and other correspondence in AdR-0606/5.426/3 and 3.0901/3; FLD 194-XII-1774.
59 Jenny Kenny and Desmond Hirsch interview with authors, 9 November 2006.
60 NAI, TID 1207/1340; Hirsch Ribbons account book, pp. 81, 85.
61 The Blaskopfs were registered in Vienna on 13 June 1949. The WSLA residential register does not record Hanna Ruth as a returning exile. During the war she had worked "for some time" as an apprentice with Miss Brennan on Dawson Street (like Gertrud Konirsch). See also data in NAI, DJ 68/1/703 and 704.
62 Oberer was registered on 28 December 1953. WSLA, residential register of Vienna.

Ireland. Shortly after the war, Hans tried to return to his professional roots by applying for a licence to open a dental laboratory in Dublin, but this was refused. He then resumed his wartime position with Wings Ltd, working as a "full time manager" until the closure of the factory.[63]

The Castlebar Komotavians of the older age group had pinned their hopes on a speedy return to the Sudetenland and a new life within a multi-ethnic state. "I am a Czechoslovakian citizen residing in this country," Franz Schmolka asserted in 1942.[64] In the same year, he offered to take part in post-war planning.[65] In November 1944, with Hitler's troops withdrawing from Eastern Central Europe, he was received by Jan Masaryk, foreign secretary of the two exile governments since 1940, to discuss plans for the future of Czechoslovakian industry.[66] On 31 December 1944, he stepped down from his post as general manager of Western Hats and moved to 33 Pembroke Park in Dublin, hoping to establish profitable trade links between Ireland and Czechoslovakia. In 1945, he was appointed as a director of the newly founded Irish-Czechoslovakian Trade Company, along with two other familiar figures of the Witztum circle, Senator Michael Hearne and John McEllin.[67] This probably signified that he had given up hopes of returning to the Sudetenland, given its occupation by the Red Army after the liberation of Prague in May 1945. On 7 June 1945, by which time Komotau had been almost completely deserted by its former majority population of Germans, a ruling of a Czechoslovakian district court turned the old factory over to a provisional national administration. On 15 April 1947, legal ownership was returned to Schmolka, but probably in view of the new power structures in Czechoslovakia, this did not alter his decision to stay in Ireland: in January 1946, he had applied for an Irish passport, in

---

[63] Hans was allowed to practise only as a dental technician with no direct contact with patients. See correspondence between the Lowys and the DI&C in NAI, TID 1207/2344 and 2165; TID 158/782, Wings to IDA, 24 September 1954.

[64] MAI, G2/1173, Schmolka to Sir Kingsley Wood, British Chancellor of the Exchequer, 16 April 1942.

[65] See Schmolka's correspondence with the exiled government's Czech Economic Advisory Association (CEAA) in 1942, especially MAI, G2/1173, CEAA to Schmolka, 14 April 1942.

[66] *Irish Times*, 5 November 1944. About a month later, he wished to participate in a CEAA conference in London dealing with the new post-war order. His closeness to the Beneš government is also apparent from NAI, DJ 69/80/678, Little, O hUadhaigh & Proud to G. Boland, 28 December 1945.

[67] NAI, DJ 68/1/748, DJ report, 15 February 1946; NAI, DFA 202/206, D&IC to DEA, 9 February 1945. Future Irish-Czech trade connections were also indicated by the London exile government's appointment of Leo Cernik as an "Official Representative of the Prague International Fair". NAI, DJ 69/80/67, Cernik to DJ, 21 February 1947.

October 1947, he and his wife had their names changed to Smolka and in January 1948 both were naturalised in Ireland – events which provided the formal justification for the district court of Chomutov to decide on 18 March 1948 that Smolka had forfeited his right of ownership. On 26 June 1948, the Czechoslovakian Ministry of the Interior proclaimed the nationalisation of the old hat factory and its amalgamation into the state company Tonak,[68] following the Communist take over in Czechoslovakia in February of that year. This development also thwarted all plans for new trade projects between the two countries.[69]

Smolka's failure illustrates a pattern: in view of their age and the developments in their homeland the only realistic option for the Komotavians was to stay in Ireland. In the 1950s, their numbers in Castlebar thinned. Franz Smolka died on 3 August 1952. At an unknown date Fred and Steffka Schmolka moved to Dublin. Other 'masters' left because their employment in the factory had ended, or because they dreaded the loneliness of old age in provincial Ireland. Although their children had attended the primary schools in Castlebar, for secondary and tertiary education the parents looked further afield. In December 1950, Fred Klepper, then 58 years old, developed an allergy from his work in the spinning department of Western Hats.[70] A few months later, he and his wife moved to Dublin to look for new employment and re-unite with their daughter Doris, whom they had sent as a boarder to Hall School in Monkstown in 1944. In the capital they seem to have lived on Fred's work as a *Handelsagent* ("commercial agent"). His death in February 1955 at the age of 62 was a disaster for his widow ("Today I am completely without means [...], old, deaf, sick and unable to work. Due to persecution and emigration I have developed a coronary disease")[71], who died not

---

68 Nevertheless, Smolka made a last attempt to reclaim his lost property. That claim was denied on 23 March 1950 by the district court of Chomutov. Our survey of the story of the hat factory in post-war Chomutov relies on copies of three court rulings by the Chomutov district court of 7 June 1945, 15 April 1947 and 23 March 1950, and a summary of developments concerning the factory after 1945 by an unknown author – all stored in Litomerice District archive, branch Most (Lit-Most), file group 149, box 1. We are grateful to Maria Hughes for her translation of these texts.
69 It was only in the more liberal 1960s that trade missions between Dublin and Prague were established. See Daniel Samek, *Czech-Irish Cultural Relations 1950–2000*. Prague: Centre for Irish Studies, Charles University 2012, pp. 44–45.
70 Doorly, *Hidden Memories*, p. 76. In general, Klepper had not been happy in his work "due to conditions imposed by a bullying manager", as the Protestant Dean of Tuam testified to the DJ in 1946. NAI, DJ 68/1/731.
71 See Margarete Klepper's description of her husband's job in BA Bayreuth, no. 1/600.9633. The quotation is from Margarete Klepper affidavit, 11 November 1955, in the same file. Translated by authors.

long afterwards, aged 63. Ernest (formerly Ernst) Glass's chronic health problems also compelled him to give up his position with Western Hats. Like the Kleppers, the Glasses went to Dublin, where they made a living as self-employed owners of a small import firm ("Glassimpag", 25 Rockville Avenue, Terenure).[72]

Image 6: Dielenz return to Nuremberg.

From Franz Dielenz's wartime correspondence with the leaders of the exiled Sudeten Social Democratic Party in London it emerges that he and his wife Marie took a lively interest in the politics of that exile scene, hoping that activists and leaders of the Sudeten German party would be allowed to play a political role in the future state.[73] These hopes were frustrated, as already mentioned. In February

---

[72] Ernest Glass CV, 6 November 1958, BA Bayreuth, no. 16.011.012.
[73] Dielenz was closely associated with the dominant splinter group of the exiled Social Democracy in London, led by Wenzel Jaksch, who played a prominent part in the post-war integration of former Sudeten Social Democrats into the West German SPD. In a letter of 7 June 1942 Dielenz

1956, Franz, still described as a foreman, and Marie officially declared their intention to return. "We have been living in the West of Ireland, in Castlebar, and have been welcomed here as German people" – words the other Komotavians probably would not have used – but were now looking forward to spending the rest of their lives "in the midst of relatives and hundreds of old and young friends of the former Sudeten homeland".[74] On 29 November 1956, they were granted German citizenship and on 22 July 1960, after 22 years in exile, they were welcomed by relatives and friends at Nuremberg railway station. They spent the rest of their lives in Fürth, Nuremberg's neighbouring town, where many expelled Komotavians had settled after their expulsion in 1945. Among these were both anti-Nazis and ex-Nazis of 1938, all of them now the Dielenz's neighbours.

In Castlebar, Annie Polesie and the Glasses' daughter and son had gone.[75] The exile community had shrunk to Marie Polesie and Walter Porges, who could still be "seen about the outskirts of the town with his small dog. He remained on while all the others left the town."[76]

Overall, the pockets of German-speaking industrialists in various parts of Ireland were a temporary one-generation phenomenon. After their roles in the factories ended almost all of the owners and developers disappeared from the provinces. Marcus Witztum, the man who had brought most of them to Ireland, died on 21 May 1948.[77] The story of the factories themselves lasted longer (see further below).

Restitution and compensation

Many middle-aged or older exiles, especially those previously supported by the ICCR, barely managed to scrape by during the immediate post-war years. After a considerable period of waiting, they may have hoped to receive compensation from those successor states that officially accepted responsibility for the persecution and expulsion of their former citizens. While the German Democratic Republic refused to provide compensation, legislation in West Germany and Austria entitled

---

spoke on behalf of Siegfried Klepper, whom he had won as a second Irish subscriber to the monthly Social Democratic *Freundschaft* ("Friendship"). MAI, G2/1081; see also MAI, G2/1117, handwritten G2 report, 7 June 1942.
74 BVA Cologne, no. 53/2935, Franz Dielenz, undated CV. Translated by authors. The term *Werkmeister* (foreman or supervisor) is used in the application sheet, 9 February 1956, in the same file.
75 Anny Giersch email to authors, 27 October 2008.
76 M. Mullen email to authors, 8 May 2007.
77 See DJ 2013/50/259.

former emigrants from the *Reich*, including those Germans who had been expelled from their homelands after 1945 (Eastern Germans as well as Sudeten Germans, for example), to apply for material restitution for lost assets including goods and property, and for financial compensation for other losses arising from interrupted and ruined careers, loss of health etc.[78] A large number of the Irish exiles commissioned lawyers to claim their rights before a bewildering array of regional restitution and compensation courts (*Wiedergutmachungsämter, Entschädigungsämter,* a *Bezirksvertriebenamt* in Cologne, for example) and via a special Federal institution dealing with former officials of Jewish congregations. Altogether, more than 70 such proceedings for compensation were initiated by Irish exiles before West German and Berlin civilian courts. Compensation came too late for those who had already died by the late 1950s. Many claimants and their lawyers found the bureaucratic process cumbersome, and its outcome an inadequate recognition of moral guilt. Legal restrictions reduced a number of material claims; financial settlements in general failed to match the real losses involved while non-material losses such as deprivation of childhood, tradition, identity – and most painful of all, the murder of beloved family members – remained excluded from the process. Academic reviews of the compensation rules have been mostly critical.[79] Nevertheless, the lump sums and regular pensions helped to stabilise incomes, even if the real losses could never be effectively compensated.

Home and identity

Die Melodie	The melody
„Weißt du es noch?" Das ist ein Lied	"Do you still remember?" It is a song
Gespielt auf alten Saiten	Played on old chords
Aus gilben Noten kommt Musik	From yellowed notes comes music
Vergangener Gezeiten.	Of former times.

---

[78] The *Bundesergänzungsgesetz zur Entschädigung für Opfer der nationalsozialistischen Verfolgung* (Federal supplementary law on compensation for victims of Nazi persecution), to give its full title, was passed in 1953 (and in 1956 was republished as *Bundesgesetz zur Entschädigung für Opfer der nationalsozialistischen Verfolgung*). It was intended as a uniform and extended instrument to compensate victims of Nazi Germany, in contrast to the uncoordinated legislation since 1949 such as the *Gesetz zur Wiedergutmachung nationalsozialistischen Unrechts* (Law on compensation for victims of Nazi injustice) passed in Bavaria, Hesse, Baden-Württemberg and Bremen.
[79] This is especially true of the Austrian system of *Wiedergutmachung*. See Brigitte Bailer-Galina, Die Opfergruppen und deren Entschädigung. In: Politische Bildung (ed.): *Wieder gut machen? Enteignung, Zwangsarbeit, Entschädigung, Restitution*. Innsbruck, Vienna: Studien-Verlag, 1999, pp. 90–96 and http://www.demokratiezentrum.org/fileadmin/media/pdf/opfergruppen.pdf.

Dort saugt die Wurzel die dich speist	There is the root which feeds you
Mit Kraft fürs Aufrechtstehen	Giving you strength to stand upright
Und die das Müdsein niederkämpft	And fight your tiredness
Vorm neuen Weitergehen	Before a new advance.
Es ist die rechte Melodie	It is the right melody
Im Heute Deiner Sorgen	In today's worries
Wohl dem, der sie bewahren kann	Blessed is he who can preserve it
Bis auf ein bessres Morgen.	Until a better tomorrow.
	(translated by authors)

Richard Kappeler's poetic elegy, composed in 1941, sprang from an urge to commemorate particular aspects of the *Heimat* as healing forces in an exiled existence, and provides a striking alternative to Lisl Strunz's text, quoted previously.[80] Even if not all exiles shared Kappeler's feelings – others assiduously tried to banish anything German from their Irish lives[81] – none could have extinguished all traces of their past identity. Denis Henderson recalls with pleasure how his grandparents retained some "unusual foreign customs" like "hanging the bed linen out of the upstairs windows every Saturday morning to air" or "scrubbing the front garden path on a weekly basis".[82] Other elements retained from a vanished world were the Königsbergers' tile stove, the gardening practices of the Marckwalds, the Brandenburgs and the Goebls, and German-Austrian Christmas traditions, often celebrated on Christmas Eve (Herbert Unger made a point of celebrating a German family Christmas, including the inevitable "O Tannenbaum").[83] The refugees' basic diet remained German, as far as possible under Irish conditions – "Please next week no sauerkraut," Stefan Feric once desperately pleaded, seeking a change to the customary menu on his visits to the Kappelers.[84] It seems that cultural differences made them distinctive if not exotic in Ireland, as, later, their new Irish identities made them distinctive in Germany or Austria – complexities that could have generated a feeling of "living in the third person" (Don DeLillo, *Americana*).

---

[80] See footnote 2.
[81] One story remembered in present-day Castlebar has it that Mrs Polesie refused to accept a lift in a German car. Story told at Castlebar Meeting, 14 June 2008.
[82] Denis Henderson, On Ruth Henderson and her parents, Peter and Else Brandenburg. In: Holfter (ed.), *Irish Context*, pp. 65–72, 68.
[83] Klaus Unger interview with authors, 20 November 2004. For other examples of Unger's attachment to German culture see Klaus Unger, On Herbert Unger. In: Holfter (ed.), *Irish Context*, pp. 31–32.
[84] MAI, G2/0409, Feric to Kappeler, 25 January 1941.

The real test of their German-ness came after the war. Return was a painful process, readjustment difficult or impossible, under the combined pressures of disturbing and still raw memories of persecution at the hand of the state, neighbours and society, traumatic revelations of parents' and other relatives' deaths in the Holocaust, material conditions in war-ravaged Germany and Austria in the post-war years, and political reversals in East Germany and post-war Czechoslovakia, both ruled by the Red Army.

"Ours are mostly young people, and I fully hope that some day they will go back to their parents and help to build up a new Germany and work for friendly relations with their experience of both countries and their happy memories of British [sic] friends."[85] Kathleen Huggard's mid-war dreams only partially came true. Only two of the refugees, Annelies Becker and Georg Pick, embraced the kind of political mission she probably had in mind.[86] Among the older generation we have counted about 20 exiles who for various reasons decided to return to West Germany or Austria, but apart from Adolf Adler, who left Ireland in 1947, none went before the 1950s, near the end of their careers, or in old age.[87]

Those who stayed in Ireland often developed other links to their former *Heimat*. From its beginnings in the early 1960s, the Irish-Austrian Society has

---

[85] TCD Archives, Butler Papers, 10304/597/781, Huggard to Butler, 9 April 1942.

[86] Georg Pick went to London at the end of 1943 to study theology and prepare himself for a future role in post-war Germany. In 1946, he continued his studies at the University of Basel. He was then employed by the Bonn office of Moral Re-Armament, the non-denominational international peace movement founded as the Oxford Group in 1921. Annelies Becker took part in relief work with the Quakers, who employed her in West Germany and Vienna until well into the 1950s, and then in other countries. Two others returned for purely private reasons: Hans Kohlseisen went to Austria in 1949 to see his dying mother. He and his Irish family remained there, initally because they lacked resources to return to Ireland. Kohlseisen, *Und ich reise immer noch*, pp. 113–137. For Brian Hengstenberg, Jochen's younger brother, see footnote 20.

[87] Bertha Teichmann returned to Berlin in 1954 to be reunited with her daughter's family who had survived the war. See NAI, DJ 69/80/119. In 1953, Adolf Mündheim gave up his place in a Jewish Home for the Infirm and Old in Dublin to join his brother in France. In 1957, he went to West Germany, where he lived in a hotel in Baden-Baden. NAI, DJ 69/80/251, Mündheim to Garda, 11 March 1958. Richard and Alice Kappeler emigrated to the USA together with Alice's mother Rosa Kobler in May 1947. Health problems prevented Richard from practising as a doctor in New York, and in the 1950s he returned alone to Vienna, where he died in 1968. AdR, Hilfsfonds Alt, no. 28.311, application 31 May 1957 and letter 1 October 1959. The Krotoschins (=Kents) went to Belfast, probably because Henry wanted to take exams qualifying him to register as a member of the Royal Institute of British Architects before moving to New York. In the USA he became a successful and wealthy architect. After his wife's death he returned to Europe, initially to Zurich and in 1979 back to his native city Berlin. Hilary Chaplin to authors, 24 April 2008. As mentioned before, Marie Hirsch had died in Dublin in 1945, and her husband returned to Vienna for good in September 1955. WSLA, residential register of Vienna.

aspired to "promote closer ties of friendship and understanding between the peoples of Ireland and Austria".[88] Its cultural programmes have mainly served the needs and interests of its Irish members, many of whom have a specific rapport with Austria.[89] The Society's official website lays some emphasis on the claim that the "origins of the Society go back to the early nineteen forties", without expanding upon its genesis: leading positions in the Society have been held by Robert Dubsky, Otto Glaser, Ernst and Fritz Hirsch – who had entered Ireland roughly at that time.[90] Attempts to organise the Austrian exiles in Ireland had indeed begun before the war, and Robert Dubsky had supposedly already suggested the formation of such a group in early 1939,[91] but this could not be accomplished during the war. On 1 November 1943, the Moscow Declaration officially declared Austria Hitler's "first victim", thereby legitimising a separate Austrian history after the war. It was within this context that plans emerged to organise an Austrian exile group in Ireland as a partner to the London-based Free Austrian Movement. A few days after the Moscow Conference Fritz Blaskopf, a leading spirit among Irish-Austrians, was called upon by the Free Austrian Movement to form an Irish cohort behind the idea of building up a "new Austria".[92] The concept provoked critical discussion among the Austrians in Ireland,[93] and was rejected at

---

88 Irish Austrian Society homepage http://www.austria.ie/about-ias [last accessed 15 July 2016]. On 2 October 1960, the *Sunday Independent* announced the imminent foundation of the Society on 14 October. In 1969, its membership was almost 200. *Irish Independent*, 19 January 1969.

89 Its counterpart in Vienna, the Austro-Irish Society, was founded in 1969 "in response to the needs created by an influx of Irish people coming to work for the UN organisations and for Semperit". The predecessor of that institution was the Irish Club in Vienna, which had been set up in the 1950s by Mary Kohlseisen (wife of Hans Kohlseisen) and Marigold Slocock. "The Society provided a point of contact for the Irish at a time when there was no resident Ambassador in Vienna." Austro Irish Society homepage http://www.austro-irish.at/node/1 [last accessed 15 July 2016]. Semperit is an international Austrian corporation which since 1967 has produced tyres in Dublin.

90 Robert Dubsky was an Acting Vice President, Otto Glaser a President, Ernst Hirsch a Treasurer and his brother Fritz a leading programme developer, to take a sample of their functions from time to time within the IAS.

91 See laudatio *Silbernes Ehrenzeichen* award, Austrian Bundesministerium für Auswärtige Angelegenheiten, Vienna 1982.

92 MAI, G2/0763, Ignaz Schulz to Free Austrian Movement, 20 November 1943.

93 MAI, G2/0348, Fritz Blaskopf to Free Austrian Movement, 23 November 1943. The Free Austrian Movement had been founded at the end of 1941 as an umbrella organisation for various Austrian exile groups: its aims were to form an Austrian fighting unit and to establish an independent Austria after victory over Hitler. See Wolfgang Muchitsch, *Mit Spaten, Waffen und Worten. Die Einbindung österreichischer Flüchtlinge in die britischen Kriegsanstrengungen 1939–1945*. Vienna/Zurich: Europa 1992, pp. 98–100.

the time, but showed that at least some Austrians were in favour of establishing a separate group identity.[94] It was only after the war that such ambitions, now linked with plans to further Irish-Austrian trade interests, were revived among the Austrians still remaining in Ireland. A central figure was Robert Dubsky, who in 1946 gave up his position at the Turf Board to "join the commercial world".[95] He was appointed as an unofficial Austrian Trade Delegate in Dublin by the Austrian Chamber of Commerce, and helped build up entrepreneurial networks between the two countries.[96]

Austria and Ireland had a number of features in common: Catholicism, small nation status, abstention from military organisations in the Cold War, an advanced role in international peace-keeping initiatives, the liberalisation and internationalisation of policies and markets. Key players in the Austrian-Irish narrative also shared a number of characteristics: educated in Irish schools and universities, professionally established, married to Irish wives and essentially defining themselves as Irish – Robert Dubsky, for example, had "no doubts about Ireland being the home country of choice".[97]

As noted above, many of the Austrian exiles considered Germany as the prime offender, a belief that made it easier to reconnect with the country that had expelled them only a few years earlier. It was psychologically harder for refugees from the Old *Reich* to reconnect with Germany. For example, as far as we know none of the exiles was involved in Operation Shamrock, a government-backed Red Cross scheme which between 1946 and 1948 brought over 500 German children from their devastated homes to Ireland. It might have been discredited in the eyes of the exiles as it followed a similar proposal put forward by the Save the German Children Society, founded in 1945 and viewed with suspicion as a semi-political anti-British organisation in which German spy Hermann Goertz,

---

94 MAI, G2/0348, Blaskopf to Free Austrian Movement, 23 December 1943.
95 Paul Dubsky, The Dubsky Family. In: Holfter (ed.), *Irish Context*, pp. 57–64, 61.
96 Otto Glaser, Brief Review of the Austrian Colony in Ireland 1938 – 1955. In: Paul Leifer and Eda Sagarra, *Austro-Irish Links through the Centuries*. Vienna: Diplomatic Academy 2002, pp. 127–130. Glaser links the origins of the Irish Austrian Society to Dubsky's wartime and post-war contacts with the Austrian exile scene in London. That theory is repeated in Muchitsch, *Spaten*, p. 45. Dubsky must indeed have played a pivotal role within the foundation process of the IAS. The Society's offices were at the same address as Dubsky's official address as Trade Representative (121 St Stephen's Green). For his entrepreneurial links, see Paul Dubsky, The Dubsky Family. In: Holfter (ed.), *Irish Context*, pp. 62–63.
97 Paul Dubsky, The Dubsky Family. In: Holfter (ed.), *Irish Context*, pp. 57–64, 57.

among others, was active.⁹⁸ Nor, it seems, did any German-speaking exiles take part in another project, the hosting of 84 displaced Jewish children in 1948–1949 at Clonyn Castle, Delvin, Co. Westmeath, prior to their passage to Israel,⁹⁹ although John and Claire Hennig invited about 20 children, concentration camp survivors brought to Ireland after the war by Dr Robert Collis, and even considered adopting one.¹⁰⁰ The Irish-German Society, founded in October 1951 under the presidency of Dr Proinnsias O'Suilleabhain,¹⁰¹ had Dr Rudi Neuman on its first provisional committee, while Berta Schwarz was elected to the executive committee, but German exiles clearly played a less important role in this Society than Austrian exiles in the Irish-Austrian Society. Its members, which soon numbered more than 400, had a very diverse background, including for example Helmut Clissmann, a former *Abwehr* agent,¹⁰² and Dr Kathleen Murphy, one of the founders of the Save the German Children Society.

Individual former German émigrés, however, were active in promoting German-Irish relations. Berta Schwarz helped organise student exchange schemes between West Germany and Ireland, as well as being involved in the Irish-German Society. She was also very active in the German Goethe Institut that was opened in Dublin in 1960.¹⁰³ At university level, Ernst Scheyer's influence as a teacher of German in Trinity College has been noted,¹⁰⁴ and through his broadcasts on Ireland with the popular Berlin-based radio station RIAS he contributed to a broader understanding of Irish current affairs in Germany. John Hennig became a founding father of Irish-German Studies, having "to all intents and purposes

---

98 Hermann Goertz, the principal German espionage officer in wartime Ireland, was secretary of the Save the German Children Fund from 1946 to 1947. NAI, Taoiseach's Office, S13301. See also Cathy Molohan, *Germany and Ireland, 1945–1955: Two Nations' Friendship*. Dublin: Irish Academic Press 1999, pp. 44–61.
99 *Jewish Chronicle*, 14 May 1948, 4 February 1949 and Keogh, *Jews in Twentieth-Century Ireland*, pp. 209–216.
100 See Monica Schefold, Childhood Memories in Ireland from 1939–1956. In: Holfter (ed.), *German-speaking Exiles*, pp. 252–253 and Deutsche Nationalbibliothek Frankfurt Exilarchiv, Felix Meyer Papers, Felix Meyer to John and Claire Hennig, 6 October 1945.
101 See *Irish Times*, 25 October 1951 and 11 November 1955.
102 See also Mark Hull, *Irish Secrets – German Espionage in Wartime Ireland 1939–1945*. Dublin: Irish Academic Press 2003.
103 Peter Schwarz, An anecdotal autobiographical note, March 1996. On 14 May 1963, she was honoured by the West German state with a *Bundesverdienstkreuz* for her unceasing efforts. Peter Schwarz, email to authors, 7 July 2016.
104 See chapter 9 and Gisela Holfter, Ernst Scheyer. In: Holfter (ed.), *German-speaking Exiles*, pp. 156–157.

[created] the field of Irish-German literary relations"[105] with the dozens of articles he wrote about Irish-German links from the Middle Ages up to the 1940s.[106]

Though few exiles were willing to return permanently to their former countries, nearly all felt a strong urge at least to visit, to see their former homes and often to show their children where they had grown up[107] – but "the occasional visit was enough", as Klaus Unger describes his father's ambivalent reactions.[108] There are some reports of unpleasant encounters.[109] Garret Moddel, commenting on his father Philip's frequent trips to Germany, notes that although Philip himself had been expelled and his family had barely managed to survive Nazi Germany he "harboured a soft spot for Germany and things German", but when confronted with a difficult situation, memories of the original wound sprang up and he swore never to come back again. "But of course he did."[110]

Brokers of modernity?

What part did the exiles play, during the war and afterwards, in the economic, social and cultural transformation – one might say Europeanisation – of Irish society?

One influence can be traced within the tiny Jewish fringe of Irish society which in 1936 comprised 3,749 persons in a population of almost 3 million.[111] In the Dublin community, German-speaking functionaries played an important part in professionalising community services. Bernhard Holländer, Ishmael Fisher (formerly Emanuel Fischer) Nandor and David Freilich and Philip Moddel provided inspiring religious and social leadership, their Eastern European Ashkenazism and ortho-

---

105 Patrick O'Neill, *Ireland and Germany – A Study in Literary Relations*. Peter Lang: New York 1985, p. 10.
106 Over 50 of these articles are collected in Holfter, Rasche (eds): Exil in Irland - John Hennigs Schriften zu deutsch-irischen Beziehungen, Trier: WVT 2002.
107 Mary Drechsler remembered her father's love of "the landscape, the food, the dark bread which he always brought home when he had been abroad, he showed us [...] the beauties of his old Bohemian landscape – these things". Mary Drechsler interview with authors, 8 November 2004.
108 Klaus Unger, On Herbert Unger. In: Holfter (ed.), *Irish Context*, pp. 29–34, 32.
109 Desmond Hirsch and Jenny Kenny told us in an interview on 9 November 2006 that in 1960 their father Robert Hirsch came home after a visit to Austria in a very dejected mood, probably after personal confrontations in his former home country. Herbert Karrach felt on his visits to Vienna in post-war years that Austrians considered themselves victims of German Nazism without any sense of guilt. Herbert Karrach questionnaire filled in 30 November 2005. Sabina Wizniak recalled an unpleasant encounter with a woman in Berlin. See Mary Rose Doorly, *Hidden Memories*, p. 64.
110 Garret Moddel email to authors, 12 September 2005.
111 CSO report for 1946, Volume 3, Table 1a.

doxy suiting the religious sensibilities of most congregationists. After the war, they vanished one by one from the Jewish scene of the capital, a process matching the general demographic decline of congregations (in 1946 the Jewish population peaked at 3,907, and progressively sank to 3,255 in 1961 and 2,633 in 1971).[112] Bernhard Holländer was a typical case. As the President of the Lennox Street Hebrew Congregation stated, it was "on account of its bad financial position" that the Congregation "was obliged to reduce the Rev. Hollander's salary. This made him decide to leave for Israel in the autumn of 1950."[113] By that time other community servants had already left Ireland in search of jobs in larger, British Jewish communities.[114] Only two German-born community officers were still in place by the end of the 1950s, Immanuel Jakobovits, Chief Rabbi of Ireland from 1949, and Philip Moddel. Both emigrated in 1958.[115] Moddel's departure must be seen on the one hand as a reaction to the drain of community members that affected even Dublin's large Adelaide Road Synagogue.[116] On the other hand his interests and activities surpassed his duties as a community servant. His son's opinion is that Ireland had been "stifling any opportunity he had to interact with a larger musical community", although he had "good friends there, including someone in the political establishment [...] and a moderately successful small business".[117]

---

112 CSO report for 1991, Volume 5, Table 1.
113 BEBJG Cologne, no. 921/53, Woolfson affidavit, 4 July 1960. It seems that the newly founded state of Israel did not attract many of the refugees who had come to Ireland. Apart from the Holländers only the cases of Otto M. Falk and the Margulies family have come to our notice (see above and footnote 118).
114 Ishmael Fisher went to Belfast in early October 1947, assuming functions in the large Belfast community (and possibly also seeking a medical post). David Freilich, Rabbi of the Dublin Hebrew United Congregation since 1941, followed a call of the community of Gateshead-on-Tyne a few months later. Israel Frankel departed in early 1950.
115 Jakobovits was born in Königsberg in 1921. In 1937 he emigrated to England. During his tenure as Chief Rabbi of Ireland he edited the Irish-Jewish Yearbook. He then became a Rabbi of the Fifth Avenue Synagogue, New York. Röder, Strauss (eds), *International Biographical Dictionary of Central European Emigrés 1933–1945*. Volume II / Part 1: A-J, pp. 329f.
116 In the *Irish-Jewish Yearbook* of 1992–1993 the time between the 1940s and 1960s is termed "the golden period" of Dublin's Jewish life, but it is doubtful if this is really true of the 1950s. In an official online text it is stated that the seat holders of the Dublin Hebrew Congregation had sunk from 365 in 1944 to 294 in 1953. *Irish-Jewish Yearbook* 1992–1993, p. 19. www.jewishgen.org/jcr-uk/Ireland/dublin1_hc/index.htm [last accessed 3 May 2013].
117 Garret Moddel to authors, 12 September 2005. See also BEBJG Cologne, no. II6-1091, Vol. 1. Moddel CV, 22 September 1966. Moddel's father-in-law Leib Margulies and his wife also emigrated to the USA, living for at least some time at the Moddels' house in Anaheim, California, before moving to Israel in 1964. HHSA, no. 34.962-94A, Lionel V. Lee Margulies affidavits. For the residential references see also BEBJG Cologne, no. II6-1091, Vol. 2, NAI, DJ 68/1/594 and 595.

Image 7: Graves Ernst and Marie Scheyer.

It may be speculated if the loss of German officials at the end of the 1940s was also linked with the splitting of the Jewish Progressive Congregation Dublin from the Dublin Hebrew Community in 1946. The establishment of a liberal Reform Community was a step towards aligning Irish Jewry with movements already established in modern Continental and British Judaism. On the other hand, the development may have weakened the position of orthodox traditionalists and of their official representatives, some of them German speakers, as we have seen. Details of the conflict leading to the schism became known to readers of the *Jewish Chronicle*. According to its Irish correspondent, it came about through the influence of representatives of London's Reform Jewry, who apparently succeeded in moulding autonomous trends in Dublin into an organised opposition to the hitherto dominant bearers of orthodox tradition in Ireland.[118] Some of the German-speaking Jews

---

[118] *Jewish Chronicle*, 22 June 1945. A visit by Maurice Barron from London seems to have played an important role in the founding process. The opposition's strongest voice was the former Chief Rabbi's. See Isaac Herzog's critique of the Liberals and their reply in *Jewish Chronicle*, 24 May and 7 June 1946.

exiled in Ireland, steeped in the tradition of continental Reform Judaism, supported or at least sympathised with the new ideas. Their names can be gleaned from their graves in the Progressive Community cemetery in Woodtown, Rathfarnham.[119] Some played an influential role in the foundation of the Reform Community. Joan Finkel, daughter of one of the founders, remembers that Ernst Scheyer, Hans Borchardt, and Rudi Neuman were among the instigators, and that others such as Hana and Fred Hitchman and Fred and Steffka Schmolka were donors to the new synagogue project.[120] Kurt and Ellen Ticher also contributed.[121] The wedding of Robert Weil and Renate Scheyer in July 1948 was the first to be celebrated at the newly established Progressive Jewish Synagogue in Dublin.

Rudi Neuman was twice elected as Vice Chairman of the congregation.[122] Like orthodox Jews in previous decades, the Reformists were in need of external functionaries, and again, German-speaking former refugees were summoned to answer the need. Rudolph Brasch, exiled in London, not only helped to found the new Congregation, but also became its first Minister.[123] In March 1947, he was succeeded by Jakob Kokotek who served the Progressive Dublin Community until July 1951.[124]

It is tempting to look for other traces of "influence" by German-speaking exiles on the developing Europeanisation of Irish society. We have already noted how Dublin's social life was given a "special dash" by "English and European

---

119 The following were buried here: Johanna Boas, Hans Borchardt, Annerose and Ottilie Heitler, Else and Emil Hirsch, Irma, Fritz, Richard and Paul Hitchman, Rudi and Marianne Neuman, Ernst and Marie Scheyer, Fred and Steffka Schmolka. List provided by Jewish Museum, Walworth Road. Courtesy Raphael Siev. Very probably, more exiles would have preferred a burial at a Reform cemetery if one had existed earlier, according to Marianne Neuman. Interview with authors, 12 July 2004.
120 Hans Borchardt, son of a Jewish dentist in Berlin Charlottenburg, had been employed by a major enterprise specialising in surgical and dental instruments. He emigrated to England in September 1934 after the enterprise had been Aryanised. He knew the country well from former visits and became an English citizen in 1935. As an agent for a firm that imported gloves from the west of Ireland he frequently crossed the Irish Sea, and chose in 1939 to make his home in Ireland. Joan Finkel interview with authors, 28 April 2009; Renee Borchardt, Hans Borchardt's wife, interview with authors, 6 August 2009. See also EA Berlin, no. 310.601. On Ernst Scheyer's involvement see Holfter, Ernst Scheyer. In: Holfter (ed.), *German-speaking* Exiles, pp. 159–160.
121 See memorial plaque in Progressive Synagogue.
122 *Jewish Chronicle*, 9 May 1947 and 18 March 1949.
123 Brasch was born on 6 November 1912. He fled from Berlin to London in 1938; in 1944 he was elected a Rabbi of the North London Synagogue. *Jewish Chronicle*, 30 August, 20 September, 22 November 1946. 30 January 1948; Röder, Strauss (eds), *International Biographical Dictionary of Central European Emigrés 1933–1945*. Volume II / Part 1: A-J, p. 85.
124 Born on 22 June 1911 in Bedzin, Poland, he had been a Rabbi in a Silesian town from 1934 and was forced into exile after November 1938. BEBJG Cologne, file Kokotek. undated CV; *Jewish Chronicle*, 9 May 1947, 6 February 1948.

exiles",[125] how these Continentals took part in the avant-garde discourse of the capital in the war years and afterwards, and how the small group of exiled academics familiarised their students, their colleagues and the Irish public with Continental trends in their respective disciplines. Such "influence" can be discovered outside the capital too. This is how Norman Freedman recollects the subtle impact of German, Austrian and Czech workers in Tuam, Co. Galway during World War II:

Image 8: Wedding Robert Weil and Renate Scheyer.

We grew up hearing the music of Schubert and Mozart and the voice of Richard Tauber from records and radio. The Czech musical influence came in the sound of popular pieces like Dvorak's Slavonic Dances and Smetana's The Bartered Bride. My mother learned how to prepare and cook the Hungarian dish, goulash, from Mr Kaplan. We developed a taste for

---

125 See also Brown, *Ireland*, p. 165. Wills remarks on the modernising "injection of energy brought by small groups of refugees from Britain and elsewhere in Europe" into the cultural life of Dublin. Wills, *Neutral Island*, p. 13. Similar impressions of a groundswell of cultural and social modernisation in the war years are contained in Grob-Fitzgibbon's oral history project of 2004.

sauerkraut and for frankfurters [...] We heard German, Czech and Hungarian spoken. The smell of paprika, of cigars and of continental cooking wafted about.[126]

Contributions to economic modernisation may also be traced in the careers of young exiles, but the reach of these achievements beyond their immediate personal and entrepreneurial environments is hard to assess – with the possible exception of Otto Glaser's innovative telecommunications firms (see above) and Peter and Ruth Brandenburg's 'Easisee', which according to its inventor was used by "more than 500 firms in Eire, including the Army for their Stores [...] and the L.S.F. [Local Security Forces]" and had been installed all over the country by 1943.[127]

More objective criteria are available on the role of those factories that would not have flourished in the Irish provinces without their German-speaking founders. Their growth was part of the foundation story of Irish industrialisation from the 1930s onwards. In specialised sectors of the textile industry these factories became leading and innovative players in the national market, but their profitability, which depended to a large extent on a protective tariff policy, declined in the post-war period. The open-market reforms brought in by Lemass's first government at the end of the 1950s and further liberalisation in the 1960s dealt a deathblow to such companies, exposed to new competitors on the home market and lacking export successes, although some limped on for years before their final collapse.

Les Modes Modernes stopped production in June 1972, by which time only about 30 workers were still engaged in making hats there. The premises in Bohermore were sold for £67,000 to a subsidiary of the Guinness Group.[128] Today, the site has vanished beneath a car park and a leisure centre. It is still remembered by older people, but otherwise neither it nor Wings Ltd and its site on Eyre Square have left any traces in the city.[129]

In 1976, after 37 years in Longford, Hirsch Ribbons came to an end, which in Robert Hirsch's view was due to debts, inflation, rising costs and a lagging demand for Hirsch products.[130] At its closure, the factory still employed 23 workers.[131] The old building in Longford with its distinctive roof has been turned into a training centre, but there is still a house called Vienna Lodge, there is a grave of the Goebl family in the Catholic cemetery, the older generation can still tell their stories

---

126 *Irish Times*, An Irishman's Diary, 2 June 2010.
127 NAI, DJ 69/80/345, Brandenburg to DI&C, 22 December 1943.
128 *Connacht Sentinel*, 13 and 27 June, 25 July 1972; *Irish Times*, 22 July 1972.
129 Peter O'Dowd interview with authors, 12 June 2008.
130 *Longford Leader*, 3 September 1976.
131 *Longford Leader*, 20 August 1976 ("Sad Day for Hirsch").

of the factory, and the County Longford Historical Society is trying to keep its memory alive.

Western Hats closed in 1981, putting roughly 70 employees out of work. Taking a walk through the empty and wall-less halls of the "old factory" is a minor health risk now, with leaking roofs, broken glass and splintered remnants of factory equipment. In this derelict place, it takes an effort to imagine that not so many years ago hundreds of people were busy producing hats here. Nevertheless, the memory of the factory has been kept vividly alive in the region. When the large tower was torn down, an event that was felt to symbolise an end to industrial history in Mayo (and Ireland) and a shift to a globalised service economy, there was a boom in oral history projects in the town.[132]

Plunder & Pollack closed in 1985. After the war, especially in the 1950s and 1960s when net profits in some years climbed beyond the £30,000 margin, it was a significant economic and social force in the region.[133] In 1975, it still employed 266 men and 34 women. A decade later, only 148 remained. The tannery's closure raised the unemployment rate in Carrick to 50–60 per cent.[134] The factory retains a local presence: the Tannery Bar, a pub at Sean Kelly Square near the entrance to the former factory area, is decorated with a panoramic mural depicting a stylised production scene and a poem by the Carrick-born writer Michael Coady:

> Carrick leather earned renown
> Far beyond this little town
> As good as workers ever made
> Praise to all who plied the trade.

---

[132] Local historians like Maura Ryan and Ernie and Susanna Sweeney, the first two both former employees of Western Hats, collected their own and other workers' memories, presenting them in local forums, on the internet and to an academic audience. Castlebar pupils interviewed their grandparents for a school project, and local artists were inspired by the factory and its history. Most of these commemorations paid explicit attention to the Jewish-foreign part of the foundation story. See http://www.mayo-ireland.ie/en/towns-villages/castlebar/history/the-hat-factory-opening.html (Ryan, The Opening of the Hat Factory); http://www.mayo-ireland.ie/en/towns-villages/castlebar/history/the-hat-factory-building.html (Sweeney, Building of the Hat Factory); http://www.sip.ie/sip019E/grparnts/hatfactory.htm [last accessed 12 July 2016]. Susanna Sweeney wrote an MA thesis at NUI Galway about the situation of female workers at the factory (Women in Business: Heads for Hats, 2006), and visual artist Amanda Rice recreated factory traditions as part of an art project in 2014 and worked on a radio documentary about the hat factory.

[133] Company account book for the years until 1965. Richard Denny and Michael Coady interviews with authors, 10 June 2008.

[134] See notes in *Irish Times*, 6 October 1975, 5 March 1979, 6 February 1980, 12 September 1986.

In Tralee, Anselm Horwitz and his wife had successfully integrated in local society, but emigrated to Ontario in September 1955 after the failure of Anselm's second enterprise, a joint venture with an English firm. Its owners

> had a plastics factory in England and transferred the operation to Tralee. After a great start the English representatives on the Board of Directors managed – behind my back – to run the operation into bankruptcy [...] to claim tax credits in England. I had gained a lot of experience and succeeded without further trouble in the New World.[135]

Wings Ltd was prevented from "making any headway" after the war by the revolution of production methods in the USA, the lack of raw materials in Ireland, and increasing competition by foreign and national competitors. In the 1950s, however, a takeover by L. B. Koppel ("managing Director of Zipp Fastener Co. Ltd, London, and one of the founders of the zip fastener industry in Europe") provided fresh capital, opening new market opportunities and leading to an increased number of employees.[136] How long the company upheld its market position is unclear.

Abraham Bayer's Irish Leather Goods Ltd persisted at least until its founder's retirement.[137] By the end of the war Leib Margulies' Leather Articles Ltd employed six men and 17 women, all Irish nationals. In 1946, Margulies, who had become an Irish citizen, acquired substantial shares, which he later sold for £6,900. He then emigrated to the USA (see above), and nothing further is known of the factory's history.[138]

In November 1945, Kurt Hainbach and Robert Hirsch founded an innovative textile enterprise, Pallas Manufacturing Ltd, with Hainbach its "technical and production manager".[139] Among their suppliers was a "socialist" knitwear co-operative founded in 1966 by Father James McDyer in Glencolmcille, Co. Donegal. Hainbach had been involved in the founding of the co-operative, revisiting the leftist ideas of his youth. He died in 1970; Pallas Manufacturing Ltd however has continued to flourish, with two members of the Hainbach family still acting as owners and directors.[140]

---

135 Anselm Horwitz email to authors, 18 February 2008.
136 NAI, TID 158/782, Wings to IDA, 24 September 1954.
137 Harris, *Dublin's Little Jerusalem*, p. 178. From a note in *Irish Times*, 17 November 1967, it appears that the factory existed until 1965.
138 HHSA, no. 34.962-94A, Lionel V. Lee Margulies affidavit, 7 May 1964. See also data in NAI, DJ 68/1/594.
139 NAI, DJ 68/1/633, memo in DJ, 26 November 1946.
140 *Irish Times*, 29 March 1952, 10 September 1953, 18 February 1954 ("A new idea in knitwear – and it's Irish"), 17 April 1967. Kurt's sons Mark and Colin interviews with authors, 19 November 2004 and 19 February 2009. James McDyer, *Father McDyer of Glencolumbkille. An Autobiography*.

Although with this one exception the 'refugee factories' failed to meet the later challenges of competitive markets, it would be a mistake to dismiss their modernising influence in the post-war period. The creation of local jobs was a great boon at a time when high unemployment in the provinces meant that many younger Irish women and men had to move to larger cities or emigrate.[141] The factories transformed the economies of county towns, but innovation was not confined to the economic sphere: traditional cultural and social values too were modified through the influence of the factories. Since they employed numbers of young women, female lifestyle patterns in particular were changed.

And the academics?

The end of the war also had repercussions, of course, for the academic refugees. For one thing, it led to more potential openings abroad. As for other exiles, there were questions whether a return to Germany, Austria or Czechoslovakia was possible or desirable. Max Born, the close collaborator of Schrödinger and Heitler, who eventually decided to return to Germany from Edinburgh, reflected on the dilemma in a way that is equally relevant to the refugees in Ireland:

> It is not quite easy to understand why, even for ourselves. Germany had been in the grip of the most horrible gang of criminals which ever came to power in the whole of recorded history; the German people had submitted to them without resistance and fought a cruel war for them; we had lost numerous relatives and friends through the Nazi terror, heard terrible tales of concentration camps and the murder of millions of Jewish people and we witnessed the overthrow of peaceful nations. Yet in spite of all this, there remained an inextinguishable[142] homesickness for the German language and landscape. On the other hand, Scotland had invited and accepted us, given us nothing but kindness, opened our minds

---

Dingle: Brandon 1982, pp. 81–82, 103. http://www.whai.ie/company/the-pallas-manufacturing-company-limited-11307/ [last accessed 3 February 2016].

141 This is borne out by the rise in population of Galway, Castlebar, Longford and Carrick-on-Suir between 1936 and 1946: Castlebar had 4,826 inhabitants in 1936, more than 4,900 in 1946. The figures for Longford were 3,807/4,020, Galway 18,294/20,370, Carrick-on-Suir 4,840/4,859. COS, Historical Censuses for 1936 and 1946. Volume 1, Tables 13. In general, emigration figures from areas with urban employment opportunities were lower than the national average. See Mary E. Daly, *The Slow Failure. Population Decline and Independent Ireland, 1922–1973*. Madison: University of Wisconsin Press 2006, pp. 44–45.

142 "unüberwindliches Heimweh" is the expression Born uses in the original German version of his autobiography, *Mein Leben: Die Erinnerungen eines Nobelpreisträgers*. Munich: Nymphenburger 1975, p. 377.

to the ways of democracy and political fairness, and widened our horizon by making us members of the great British community of nations, the Commonwealth. But still we were not Scots and would never be. Germany meant for us a struggle between hatred and love, Scotland between love and strangeness. Thus the choice was difficult. In the end the decision was helped by rather trivial factors of a practical, financial nature.[143]

On the other hand, refugees could now claim Ireland as their permanent home by applying for citizenship (which had not been possible during the war). New positions in Ireland became available to some academics – while for others, current appointments came to an end. John Hennig, for example, not only lost his position as German teacher in Belvedere but also his part-time teaching post in Maynooth which, he was informed, had to be filled by a cleric.[144] In September 1945, he was employed by the Dun Laoghaire Vocational Education Committee on a part-time basis before obtaining a position as records officer and librarian for Bord na Móna and later ESB, continuing his research in the evenings and at weekends.[145] A professorial appointment was offered in Heidelberg, but a return to Germany seems to have been too unpalatable.[146] Indeed, when the Hennig family left Ireland in 1956, partly to take over the firm of John Hennig's deceased father-in-law, Hennig preferred to live in Basle and make a daily border crossing from Switzerland to Germany, where the firm was located, rather than live in Germany. The family's move was also for the sake of better prospects for their three daughters, and can be seen as part of the broader Irish emigration phenomenon, a result of the economic situation in Ireland at the time.[147]

Even for Ludwig Bieler, employment after the war was not as smooth as had been expected. Like their friends the Hennigs, the Bielers acquired Irish citizenship after the war, but Bieler, who had so positively summarised his time in Ireland in 1945 and expressed his hope for a permanent position, had his appointment with the National University of Ireland in Dublin terminated on 31 December 1946. Instead he got a temporary, non-pensionable appointment as archivist in the National Library. Seeking a better position in England,

---

143 Max Born, *My Life*. London: Taylor & Francis 1978, p. 281.
144 Holfter and Rasche (eds), *John Hennig's Exile in Ireland*, p. 73.
145 Hennig's election in 1948 as a member of the Royal Irish Academy was thus an acknowledgement of academic work done under most difficult circumstances in addition to his day job and family commitments.
146 The offer, conveyed by Hans Reiss, came from renowned German philosopher Karl Jaspers, reinstated at Heidelberg University (having been dismissed under the Nazis due to his Jewish wife). Email Hans Reiss to authors, 27 September 2000.
147 Erica Becker (John Hennig's youngest sister) to authors, 12 July 2001.

the USA, Canada or the Dominions, he turned again to the SPSL,[148] and thanks to their efforts was offered a position at Notre Dame University where he spent the academic year 1947–1948 as Assistant Professor of Classics. The time proved sufficient for the difficulties in Dublin to be resolved, and when Bieler returned to Ireland in 1948 he was able to resume teaching at University College Dublin, first as Assistant College Lecturer, then College Lecturer. Once established, he stayed in Ireland despite several offers from elsewhere. On 14 January 1960, he was finally appointed Professor of Palaeography and Late Latin. Since the end of the war he had been systematically working his way through European libraries during his summer breaks, cataloguing Hiberno-Latin Manuscripts. He became internationally known as the founder of *Scriptores Latini Hiberniae* and received honorary doctorates from Trinity College, Dublin (1970), Ludwig Maximilian Universität, Munich (1972) and Glasgow University (1975). Apart from being elected a member of the Royal Irish Academy, he also became corresponding member of the Medieval Academy of America, and a member of the Institute for Advanced Studies in Princeton, the Austrian Academy of Sciences, the British Academy, and the Royal Dublin Society.[149] When he died on 2 May 1981 it meant "the end of a fruitful era in Irish Latin studies" for his colleagues, former students and friends.[150] Although his central position in Irish culture had much to do with his chosen area of study (and also, perhaps, with his outgoing personality), Bieler's involvement and acceptance in Irish life showed how much the refugees could and did contribute if allowed.

The question of returning to Berlin University (now in the Soviet sector) arose for linguist Ernst Lewy who was 64 years old in 1945. His feelings about returning were ambivalent, but there is no doubt that he would have welcomed the invitation.[151] Although contact was re-established in September 1946, nothing further happened, due partly to oversight, partly to Lewy's age and state of health, and also to the new political situation in Berlin and at the university (and the academic and political ambitions of his former student Wolfgang Steinitz).[152] A guest

---

148 SPSL 292/3/200, Ludwig Bieler to Secretary of the SPSL, 1 January 1947. A letter in the SPSL file by Professor P. Semple from University College Dublin makes it clear that Bieler was appreciated by his colleagues: "We [...] regret deeply that the financial and other difficulties of the war years and post-war period have prevented us from finding a permanent post for him." SPSL 292/3/203, P. Semple to Ilse Ursell, SPSL, 27 February 1947.
149 For more details see Hermann Rasche, Ludwig Bieler, pp. 176, 180–181.
150 Dr Ludwig Bieler, An Appreciation. *Irish Times*, 12 May 1981, p. 4.
151 See ABBAW, Vol. 20 Max Vasmer papers, Hedwig Lewy to Max Vasmer, 15 August 1946.
152 See Holfter, Ein Fallbeispiel zur Rückkehrproblematik aus dem Exil, pp. 141–151.

professorship did not materialise either, despite a glowing reference from Wilhelm Wissmann.[153] At this stage political considerations had become even more important. Lewy's friends in Ireland, however, supported him, and in February 1947 he was appointed to a newly created professorship in linguistic science at the Royal Irish Academy.[154] According to Arnold Marsh's appreciation of Lewy in the *Irish Times*, his appointment came as a surprise to him:

> He was astonished to read in the paper one day that the Royal Irish Academy had appointed him to a professorship in its chair of General Linguistics. He had never heard of such a chair outside Berlin, and rang up the Academy to ask what it meant.
>
> The Academy had never heard of it either and had no chairs of anything, but was making enquiries. Apparently an eminent person had instructed the Minister for Finance to make provision in his estimates for the salary for this office for Dr. Lewy, and the Minister had done so, assuming that all was arranged, but the eminent person or his agents had forgotten to arrange anything. No matter, it was arranged. The benefaction was of the greatest help and was given the greatest help and he was deeply grateful. He had nothing to live on except support from relief funds.[155]

A lingering feeling of displacement stayed with Lewy.[156] He lived fairly reclusively, though he passed on his extraordinary knowledge and gift for languages to many

---

153 Archive Humboldt-Universität zu Berlin, Personal-Akten des b.a.o. Prof. Ernst Lewy, Vol. 140, Lewy, Ernst, 1930/1948, Personalnachrichten Blatt 25.
154 Royal Irish Academy, *Minutes of Proceedings, Session 1946–47.* Meeting 24 February 1947, p. 4.
155 [Arnold Marsh] Dr. Ernst Lewy – An Appreciation. *Irish Times*, 29 September 1966. Gerhard Bersu (1889–1964), another refugee, originally from Frankfurt/Oder (who had been in exile in Britain and Northern Ireland since 1937), was also appointed by the Royal Irish Academy as professor of archaeology in 1947, the same year as Lewy. He stayed in Dublin until 1950, returning to Germany when he was reappointed to his former position as director of the Roman-Germanic Commission, one section of the German Archaeological Institute in Frankfurt/Main. In addition to Lewy's and Bersu's new positions, a professorship of Mathematical Logic was founded at the Academy and filled by Jan Łukasiewicz, who had been Professor of Philosophy at the University of Warsaw. From Warsaw he and his wife fled to Germany in 1944, then to Switzerland, and after the war while in precarious employment in Brussels, he was offered a chance to go to Ireland by a Polish-speaking Irishman "as the Irish government was anxious to give a position to some Polish scholars". He accepted "in gratitude and joy" and was appointed in September 1946 (see his CV in Metalogicon. Vol. VII, no. 2 (1994), http://web.mclink.it/MI2701/rivista/1994ld/lukasiewicz94ld.pdf [last accessed 5 April 2016]). Altogether, there were only four professorships of the Royal Irish Academy –all filled by refugees, starting with Schrödinger in 1940.
156 In a poem he sent to Finnish linguist Emil Öhmann in 1964, he states that Dublin has not become his home: "Es ist eine fremde Stadt / In der ich leben musste / So gut es auch war / Für mich und die meinen / Dass wir hier leben durften" (It is a foreign city, in which I had to live, as good as it was, for me and mine, that we could live here). Thanks to Doris Wagner, Turku; excerpt

young visiting linguists, mostly from Germany. Shortly before his death, Lewy visited Hubert Butler in Maidenhall, Co. Kilkenny, who asked him about his relationship with Germany. Lewy found it "a difficult question I could not answer so quickly as it is necessary in conversation", and responded some days later in writing. In fact he replied twice, in German and in English. His German answer refers to his cherished belief in the close connection between language and nation, in the tradition of Wilhelm von Humboldt, emphasising that therefore his relationship with Germany is at once very friendly and close and very difficult, and stressing that his ambivalence would be far from unique, as many exiles were in the same situation. His English answer focuses more on the difficulties of coming to terms with the horrors of Nazi Germany – and does not absolve the Western powers of blame:

> The discovery that the language of a nation is connected with the mentality of this nation, a doctrine transferred to me by some of my teachers, discovered by the german-prussian [sic] philosopher-linguist WvHumboldt, and the cornerstone of my work, I could not forget, and was not to be changed at all. But the things having happened in Germany, how could one overlook them, and how could one forget them? I owe my life only to my wife who expelled me from home, I would have stayed there because I pitied the Germans, under the horrid rule of MM (Monkey Moustache) that eventually they accepted that rule as a law? [sic] I had not expected. But I could have accepted it because in an enigmatic way the western powers who had anything the German governments had asked for, gave it to MM.[157]

Leo Pollak's relationship with Czechoslovakia was far less ambivalent than Lewy's with Germany: at the end of the war he immediately applied for repatriation,[158] but in fact, like Lewy, he remained in Ireland for the rest of his life. He re-established Dunsink Observatory in collaboration with Hermann Brück, and in 1947 became head of the DIAS's new School of Cosmic Physics, which had been officially established on 26 March of that year at 5 Merrion Square.[159]

---

from her IVG Shanghai 2015 paper "Es ist eben keine Heimatstadt, nicht meine Heimatstadt, in der ich geworden war." Zu den Emigrationsschwierigkeiten des deutschjüdischen Linguisten und Volkskundlers Ernst Lewy (1881–1966) in Irland.
157 TCD Archives, Butler Papers, 10304/597/879, Lewy to Butler, 11 October 1965.
158 SPSL 336/3/497, Questionnaire Leo Pollak for Society for the Protection of Science and Learning, 25 May 1945.
159 See Thomas Murphy and James R. McConnell, De Valera and the Foundation of the School of Cosmic Physics. In: *Scoil an Léinn Cheiltigh, Tuarascáil Leathchéad Blian: School of Celtic Studies, Fiftieth Anniversary Report 1940–1990*. Dublin: Dublin Institute of Advanced Studies 1990, pp. 32–34, 32: "Pollak was a controversial figure. He held the view that in Ireland the importance of

Physics was now housed in two buildings on opposite sides of the square, one for each of the two schools: Theoretical Physics, under Erwin Schrödinger, Walter Heitler and John Lighton Synge, and Cosmic Physics, run by Hermann A. Brück[160] (astronomy), Leo Pollak (geophysics, director of the School) and Lajos Jánossy[161] (experimental Cosmic Ray research). Of the six senior professors who created an internationally acknowledged research institution, three had come to Ireland as refugees during the war and two more had very similar backgrounds (Hermann Brück found asylum in Cambridge and Lajos Jánossy left Berlin for London in 1936, also for political reasons). All were internationally experienced, Synge having lectured in Toronto for five years and then having had appointments at several US universities, and Lajos Jánossy having studied in Vienna and Berlin, then been to Birkbeck and had a position at Manchester University before his appointment in Dublin. When he left for Hungary in 1950, a newspaper commentary made clear that the DIAS and specifically the presence there of many foreigners was still controversial. Under the title 'The School of Cosmic Physics', the *Irish Independent* editorial argued as follows:

> If Dr. Janossy's decision to leave us be final it will to some extent redress the national balance in the School of Cosmic Physics. When last the citizens were told anything about the personnel of this mighty institution – more than three years ago – the academic staff consisted of thirteen persons – two Germans, one Austrian, one Greek, one Frenchman, one Hungarian, one Czechoslovakian, one Egyptian, one Indian, two Chinese – and two natives. What this interesting gathering may have been doing for the Irish nation we cannot say. We

---

meteorology was not fully recognised and that there was no proper teaching of the subject at university level. This view, conveyed probably by Schrödinger, impressed de Valera who returned to the idea of a School in the Institute for geophysical subjects." Viktor Franz Hess, an émigré from Graz, living in New York, had been de Valera's first choice for the school of Cosmic Physics (which would have brought together in Ireland the two Austrian winners of the Nobel Prize in Physics), but Hess decided to stay at Fordham University.

160 Hermann Brück (1905–2000) was born in Berlin and studied in Kiel, Bonn and Munich, where he obtained his PhD under the supervision of Arnold Sommerfeld. Following his time at the observatory in Potsdam he was obliged to leave Germany in 1936, but received help from the Vatican where he got a temporary position at the observatory, and a year later went to Cambridge. Following his appointment in Dublin, initiated by an invitation from de Valera in 1946, he became a Member of the Royal Irish Academy in 1948.

161 Lajos Jánossy (1912–1978) was born in Budapest, but lived mostly abroad from the age of six. In Berlin he studied under Werner Kohlhörster (1887–1946) and according to Thomas Murphy and James R. McConnell (De Valera and the Foundation of the School of Cosmic Physics, pp. 32–34, 33) he obtained his PhD there. He returned to Hungary in 1950 as deputy director at the Cosmic Radiation Department at the Central Research Institute for Physics, after his mother and stepfather (the philosopher György Lukács) returned from exile in Moscow.

do know that they are costing us £21,000 this year: the two other branches of the Institute of Advanced Studies claim the rest of the £55,000 which the taxpayer has to provide.[162]

The editorial went on to urge that the School should be wound up as speedily as possible so that funds might be released for better purposes.

The question of the actual impact of the DIAS upon Ireland had been raised before, the point being made that while the Institute was internationally well connected, links within the country were less defined. Leopold Infeld, who co-authored *The Evolution of Physics* with Albert Einstein, described his impression of the impact of the DIAS after a visit in 1949:

> The Institute, which draws students from all parts of the earth, has put the name of Ireland on the world map of scientific achievement. Yet its influence upon its own country, upon Irish intellectual life and universities, is small. In its cloistered isolation the institute is a miniature of Ireland itself, whose problems and fights as a nation are not those of the rest of the world.[163]

To an extent this was a natural result of former allegiances and collaborations – or lack thereof. The Ireland of the 1930s and 1940s was to a large extent provincial and anti-intellectual, and a complete overhaul and modernisation of science education thanks to one rather unusual research institute would have been too much to expect. In fact, there was interest in and active collaboration with the Institute from Irish academics involved in the natural sciences at UCD and TCD. The benefits were also felt by Irish students who made use of the international links of the Continental researchers. Austria, especially, became a temporary home for a number of Irish students[164] who went on to become leading academics in their fields. Moreover, the link with Zurich developed into a meaningful and lasting connection for the DIAS thanks to Walter Heitler. When in late 1945 Schrödinger resigned (which was front page news in Irish newspapers),[165] Heitler became the second director of the School of Theoretical Physics and, until his departure in 1949, took on the administrative duties that Schrödinger had found increasingly onerous. When Heitler was offered the chair of theoretical physics in Zurich, whose first incumbent had been Einstein, he accepted only

---

162 *Irish Independent*, 25 August 1950.
163 Leopold Infeld, Visit to Dublin. In: *Scientific American*. Vol. 181, no. 4 (October 1949), pp. 11–15, 11.
164 See also Elisabeth Guggenheimer's interview with Mary Reynolds, the long-time technical assistant at the DIAS, 10 August 1987, Zentralbibliothek für Physik, Universität Wien.
165 Prof. Schroedinger Resigns School Directorship. *Irish Press*, 17 December 1945, p. 1, and Dr Schroedinger Resigns (with photo). *Irish Times*, 17 December 1945, p. 1.

after careful consideration, though the arguments were clearly in favour of the move.[166] He liked the idea of teaching again rather than doing only research, was attracted by the considerably higher income, and felt that the DIAS, having been founded by a politician, was easy prey for the political opposition. He also admitted longing to leave the small country where he had spent the war when it had been impossible to go elsewhere.[167] Ireland had however become a home of sorts, and he kept his Irish citizenship even after he became eligible for Swiss citizenship.

As for Schrödinger, he continued his research[168] and his involvement with the arts and cultural scene in Dublin,[169] and in 1949 he even published a book of poetry in German and English, including translations of poems by Irish writers W. B. Yeats, John Millington Synge and George Darley.[170] There seems no doubt that overall he was very happy in Ireland. He looked back on his time in the country with great fondness. In his autobiographical notes, where he divides his life into distinct periods, he wrote:

> The fifth period (1939–56) I shall call 'My Long Exile', but without the bitter association of the word, as it was a wonderful time. I would never have got to know this remote and beautiful island otherwise. Nowhere else could we have lived through the Nazi war so untouched by problems that it is almost shameful. I can't imagine spending seventeen years in Graz 'treading water', with or without the Nazis, with or without the war. Sometimes we would quietly say amongst ourselves: 'Wir danken es unserem Führer' ('We owe it to our Führer').[171]

---

166 See Lochlainn O'Raifeartaigh and Günther Rasche, Walter Heitler 1904–81. In: Ken Houston (ed.), *Creators of Mathematics: The Irish Connection*. Dublin: University College Dublin Press 2000, pp. 113–121, 119.
167 Heitler, Lebenserinnerungen, p. 23. In later life Heitler became very attracted to philosophical and anthropological ideas about science. His list of philosophical publications and lectures runs to 69 items between 1960 and 1980, including several books. His leadership and contribution at the DIAS was appreciated, as demonstrated when Schrödinger finally decided to return to Austria: Heitler was asked whether he would consider coming back to Dublin and resuming the directorship, but refused.
168 His attempts to solve the question of a unified field theory, though widely reported in Irish newspapers in January 1947, were unsuccessful and led to a temporary falling out with Einstein. See Moore, *Schrödinger*, pp. 424–435.
169 For example, when Hilton Edwards and Micheál MacLiammóir performed *Hamlet* in Denmark, he recommended the production to Niels Bohr. See Schrödinger to Bohr, 3 June 1952, Meyenn, *Eine Entdeckung von ganz außerordentlicher Tragweite*, Vol. 2, p. 658.
170 Erwin Schrödinger, *Gedichte*. Godesberg: Helmut Küpper 1949.
171 Erwin Schrödinger, Autobiographical Sketches. In: *What is Life* with *Mind and Matter & Autobiographical Sketches*. Cambridge: Cambridge University Press 2012, pp. 165–184, 182–183.

By 1946,[172] however, offers had already come from Austria, and the pull to return increased.[173] Schrödinger informed de Valera ("to whose personal protection I owe my salvation from the wreck of Central Europe") that he had received an inquiry from the Austrian government about resuming his academic activities in Vienna, stating that the main reason he was considering the approaches very seriously was because of "the question of pensions".[174] The same year Schrödinger wrote to Sommerfeld from Dublin:

> Whether I return? Sooner or later, most certainly. Since this Nazi plague, thank God, has been utterly defeated, I trust myself again to say how deeply I feel connected to the German intellectual culture, because, say what you like, it is the fundamental and leading one in our modern time, just as the Hellenic one was, from which we have sprung. The culture of the enslaved Greece has already outlasted the power of the victorious Roman cavalry by half a millennium. Likewise imperishable is the German.[175]

Returning for Schrödinger always meant Austria, not Germany, and in 1956 he left Dublin for Vienna.[176] He was given a dignified farewell, with many parties and lunches including one with the president Seán T. O'Kelly, and de Valera even went to the boat to see him off. Schrödinger lectured again in Vienna for a few semesters, but in 1960 his health deteriorated further and he died in January 1961.

After his death, Anny returned to Dublin and took some soil from their former home in Clontarf, which she brought back to Alpbach for his grave.[177]

---

172 Arthur March (Hilde's husband) had already discussed with Felix Hurdes, the Austrian Minister for Education, the possibility of Schrödinger coming to work with him in Innsbruck in 1946 – while at the same time indicating to Schrödinger that living standards in Austria were still not good enough for a long-term move, so the ideal solution might be a guest professorship. At this stage Hilde March and Ruth had left Dublin to live with Arthur, a move that seems to have been especially hard on Ruth who was often ill. Zentralbibliothek für Physik, Wien, March to Schrödinger, 24 October 1946.
173 According to Stefan Feric this was already very strong in 1950, but Schrödinger did not want to disappoint de Valera. See interview, 10 August 1987, Zentralbibliothek für Physik der Universität Wien.
174 Zentralbibliothek für Physik der Universität Wien, Schrödinger to de Valera, 28 April 1946.
175 Sommerfeld, *Wissenschaftlicher Briefwechsel*, Vol. 2, p. 596, Schrödinger to Sommerfeld, 15 July 1946. Translated by authors.
176 John Hennig, incidentally, who had arrived the same day as Schrödinger, left in the same year. He retained his Irish citizenship and the anglicised version of his first name until the end of his life.
177 Zentralbibliothek für Physik der Universität Wien, Feric interview, 10 August 1987.

Bibliography

A Primary sources

Austria

Archiv der Republik, Vienna (AdR)
Property declarations 1938–1939 (Adler, Blaskopf, Klaar, Harant, Heinsheimer, Hirsch, Horwitz, Kalman, Kappeler, Kende, Kobler, Menkes, Schlesinger, Sonnenschein, Wallach, Wiedmann).
Finanzlandesdirektion Vienna, personal files (Adler, Hainbach, Heinsheimer, Wiedmann).
Hilfsfonds Alt, personal files (Aberbach, Heinsheimer, Emil Hirsch, Kappeler, Schulz).
Abgeltungsfonds, personal files (Heinsheimer, Robert Hirsch, Wallach).
Neuer Hilfsfonds Grün, personal files (Robert Hirsch, Karrach, Sonnenschein, Strunz).
Vermögensverkehrsstelle, personal files (Blaskopf, Emil Hirsch).

Wiener Stadt- und Landesarchiv (WSLA)
Residential register of Vienna.
Handelsgericht, personal files (Blaskopf, Heinrich Hainbach, Emil Hirsch).

Archiv der Evangelischen Kirche in Österreich (AEKOe)
Administrative files of Schwedische Israelmission (Swedish Mission).
Files of Swedish Mission, personal files (Deutsch, Erika and Liselotte (Lisa) Fischer, Höfer, Mörtl, Neumann, Platz, Schwarz).

Diözesanarchiv, Vienna (DA, Vienna)
Letters of Cardinal Innitzer.
BA Innitzer, cass. 17.
Pater Ludwig Born Papers.

Israelitische Kultusgemeinde, Vienna (IKG, Vienna)
Emigration Department, personal files (Braun, Fried, Hein, Kalman, Menkes, Seinfeld, Stein, Storch, Teicher).

Dokumentationsarchiv des Österreichischen Widerstands, Vienna (DÖW, Vienna)
Personal files (Richard Wallach; Annemarie Schrödinger, 'Notes on Events leading up to Professor Schroedinger's coming to Dublin in 1939').

Zentralbibliothek für Physik, University of Vienna
Schrödinger Papers.
Interviews Stefan Feric, Arthur James McConnell and Mary Reynolds with Elisabeth Guggenberger.

Bundesministerium für Auswärtige Angelegenheiten, Vienna
Honorary awards Ernst Hirsch, Ludwig M.F. Hirsch and Patricia Glaser.

Czech Republic

Staatliches Gebietsarchiv Litomerice, Most (SOA Litomerice, Most)
Hat factory Chomutov (Apitz, Unger, formerly Reiniger).

Staatliches Gebietsarchiv, Plzen
People's register Plzen: Hanus and Frantisek Drechsler.
Krajsky soud v PlziA III, Oddeleni c. VI. A 193: Drechsler factory.

Germany

Archiv des Auswärtigen Amtes, Berlin (AAA)
R 100007, Abt. Deutschland, Az. 83-76 Ausbürgerungen, vol. 11.

Archiv der Berlin-Brandenburgischen Akademie der Wissenschaften (ABBAW)
Wolfgang Steinitz Papers.
Max Vasmer Papers.

Archiv der Odenwald Schule, Heppenheim
Correspondence Kawerau, Hedwig Lewy and Paul Geheeb.

Bundesarchiv (BA)
Amt Rosenberg: file Ernst Lewy.

Bundesarchiv, Bayreuth (BA, Bayreuth)
Personal files Dielenz, Glass, Klepper, Porges, Steiner (née Konirsch), Konirsch, Polesie, Smolka, Schmolka, Hitschmann, Kröner.

Bundesarchiv, Ast. Zehlendorf
File Ludwig Karrenberg.

Regierungspräsident Köln, Bezirksvertriebenenamt (BVA, Cologne)
Personal files Dielenz, Glass, Klepper, Porges, Polesie, Smolka.

Brandenburgisches Landeshauptarchiv, Potsdam (BLA, Potsdam)
Files Krotoschin, Lisowski, Heilfron, Nachmann, Edelmann, Tichauer, Samter.

Deutsches Exilarchiv 1933–1945, Deutsche Nationalbibliothek Frankfurt
John Hennig Papers and Felix Meyer Paper.

Diözesanarchiv, Berlin (DA, Berlin)
Annual Reports of Hilfswerk beim Bischöflichen Ordinariat Berlin 1939–1941; DAB I 1–6: Eisenstaedt; DAB I 1–89: Correspondence between Hilfswerk and Raphaelsverein.

Document Centre, Berlin
File Ludwig Karrenberg.

Eden Archiv, Oranienburg
Files Lisowski family.

Evangelisches Zentralarchiv, Berlin (EZA, Berlin)
File group 51: Ecumenical archive: correspondence on Conrad Hoffmann.

Haus der Geschichte, Offenbach/Main
Jewish register: files Bajer, Bulka, Stiel.

Historisches Archiv Technische Universität, Munich (HATUM)
File Alfred Bloch.

Landesarchiv, Berlin (LA, Berlin)
Restitution files Heilfron, Boas, Hitschmann, Hopf, Kawerau, Lewy, Liffmann, Priebatsch.
    Sabine Halle Papers.

Universität Heidelberg, Archiv
File Sachs.

Stadtarchiv, Kassel
Registration data Curt and Lilli Werner.

Staatsarchiv, Hamburg (SA, Hamburg)
Jerusalem Community, Hamburg.
Restitution file Schloss.

Zentrum für Antisemitismusforschung, Technische Universität, Berlin (ZfA, Berlin)
Visual History Archive, USC Shoah Foundation. Institute for Visual History and Education (John Menkes, Henry Kent).
Questionnaires, International Biographical Dictionary of Central European Emigrés 1933–1945 project (Röder/Strauss).

Hochschularchiv Rheinisch-Westfälische Technische Hochschule Aachen (RWTH Aachen archive)
Hopf papers.

Humboldt Universität, Archiv, Berlin
File Ernst Lewy.

Deutsches Museum, Munich
Sommerfeld papers (including letters Ludwig Hopf, Erwin and Annemarie Schrödinger).
Sommerfeld Collection (letters Hopf, Erwin and Annemarie Schrödinger).

Bundesstelle zur Entschädigung der Bediensteten jüdischer Gemeinden, Cologne (BEBJG, Cologne)
Restitution files Freilich, Holländer, Moddel, Kokotek.

Bayerisches Hauptstaatsarchiv, Munich
Restitution file Freilich.

Bayerisches Landesentschädigungsamt, Munich (BLE, Munich)
Restitution files Wilmersdörfer, Schwarz.

Wiedergutmachungsamt, Saarburg
Restitution file Hirschberg.

Niedersächsisches Hauptstaatsarchiv, Hannover (NLA, Hannover)
Restitution files Königsberger, Liffmann, Lisowski, Marckwald, Silber.

Hessisches Hauptstaatsarchiv, Wiesbaden (HHSA, Wiesbaden)
Restitution files Margulies, Pick.

Wiedergutmachungsamt, Cologne (WGA, Cologne)
Restitution files Moddel, Serff.

Entschädigungsamt Arnsberg
Restitution file Pick.

Entschädigungsamt, Berlin (EA, Berlin)
Restitution files Brandenburg, Priebatsch, Eisenstaedt, Frankl, Holländer, Rosenberg, Rund, Samter, Nachmann, Borchardt, Baumgarten, A. Kent (née Krotoschin).

Staatsarchiv Baden-Württemberg, Ludwigsburg
Restitution file Sachs.

Generallandesarchiv Baden, Karlsruhe
Restitution file Sachs.

Wiedergutmachungsamt, Bremen
Restitution file Schwarz.

Entschädigungsamt, Düsseldorf (EA, Düsseldorf)
Restitution files Boas, Marx.

Republic of Ireland

National Archives of Ireland (NAI)
Department of External Affairs (DFA).

Department of Justice (DJ).
Department of Industry and Commerce (DI&C).
Department of An Taoiseach (DT).

Military Archives, Dublin (MAI)
G2 files.

County Longford Historical Society, Longford
Hirsch Ribbons Ltd. account book.
Minutes Longford County Council 1943.
Minutes Longford Urban District Council 1939–1940.

Diocesan Archives, Dublin
Files Archbishop Edward Byrne.

National Library of Ireland (NLI)
Robert Briscoe Papers.
Rosamond Jacob Papers.

Representative Church Body Library, Dublin (RCBL)
Minutes Jews Society, 1933–1945.
Jews Society's Annual Reports, 1937–1947.

Society of Friends House Library, Dublin (SFHL, Dublin)
File groups 073, 074, 077, 079, 080, 082, 083.
Committee minutes Newtown School 1925–1952.
1936–1937 MSS Box IV, no.4.
Newtown and Mountmellick Old Scholars Association.
Monthly Meetings Committee: MM II D 19, 24.
"Friends' work with Jewish refugees brought to Ireland before second world war" - anonymous,
    undated.
Yearly Meetings, 1939–1941.
Yearly Meetings Committee (Executive), 1929–1942.

Red Cross Archives, Dublin
Minutes Central Council and Executive Committee, 1939–1941.

Irish Jewish Museum, Dublin
Burial lists Dolphin's Barn and Woodtown cemeteries.
Martin Gotha Papers.
Rabbi Isaac Herzog letter.

Royal Irish Academy (RIA)
Minutes of proceedings, session 1946–1947.
Minutes of proceedings, session 1961–1962.

Trinity College Dublin (TCD)
TCD Board meetings 1934 to 1943.
Hubert Butler Papers.
Estella Solomons Papers.
Arland Ussher Papers.
Arnold Marsh Papers.

National University of Ireland, Registrar's Office
Minutes of Senate.
Standing Committee Minutes.

Dublin Institute of Advanced Studies Archive (DIAS)
Annual reports.
Administration 1937–1940.

Newtown School Archive
Executive Committee Minutes 1936–1939.
Committee minutes Newtown School 1925–1952.
Photo collection.

Irish Tourist Association (ITA)
Wartime reports on Carrick-on-Suir, Tipperary, Miltown Malbay, Longford.

Houses of the Oireachtas
Dáil and Seanad Debates 1933–1950.

Central Statistics Office (CSO)
Census Reports 1926, 1936, 1946.

Israel

The Hebrew University of Jerusalem, Albert Einstein Archive
Letters Einstein, Hopf, Pollak.

United Kingdom

University of Oxford, Bodleian Library
Society for the Protection of Science and Learning (SPSL): 52 (University Appeal), 127 (Universities), 241 (Bloch), 252 (Ehrenberg), 292 (Bieler), 310 (Lewy), 327 (Ewald), 330 (Heitler, home office 432), 335 (Motz), 336 (Pollak), 340 (Sitte), 503 (Leopold [Ludwig] Hopf), 544 (Sachs).

Public Record Office of Northern Ireland (PRONI)
HA 8/787 Millisle project; HA 8/69; COM/17/3/1–5.
Imperial War Museum, London
Photo collection; letters Karrach family.

Lambeth Palace Library, London
George Bell Papers.

Society of Friends House Library, London (SFHL, London)
FCRA/16, 24, 25 series.

London Metropolitan Archives (LMA)
ACC/2793/01/09/023: Ireland. 69/1–35.

Switzerland

International Missionary Council, Geneva
Minutes International Missionary Council relating to the International Committee on the Christian Approach to the Jews and Dr Conrad Hoffmann.

Geheeb-Archiv, Ecole d'Humanité, Hasliberg, Golden
Correspondence Hedwig Lewy.

USA

National Archives at College Park, Maryland
General Records of the Department of States 1930–1939, Central Files (RG 59).
Foreign Service Posts, Department of States, General Records 1936–1948 (RG 84).

California Institute of Technology (Caltech)
Theodore Kármán Papers.

Correspondence and Interviews

Louise Abels, David Abrahamson, Joyce and Maurice Abrahamson, Anna Adler, Myrtle Allen, Paul A. Auerbach, Frank Baigel, Annelies Becker, Desmond Beckett, Dom Aidan Bellenger, G. Bernstein, Renee Borchardt, Sean Boylan, Ruth Braunizer, Kurt Brehmer, Joanna Cahir, Margaret Canning, Mary Casey, Hilary Chaplin, Hel Chavasse, George Clare, Michael Coady, Dairine Coffey, Tony Conneely, John Cooke, Celestine B. and Niall Cullen, Bridget Curley, Christopher Dillon OSB, Richard Denny, Luke Drury, Paul Dubsky, George Eaton,

Barbara Esser, Marie Therese (Dillon) Farrell, Gisela Faust, Nuala Feric, Joan Finkel, Heinz Frankl, Jude Flynn, John Garavan, Padraic Gearty, Anny Giersch, Otto Glaser, Ernst von Glasersfeld, Esther Goebl, Joy Roger Hammerschlag, Ivor Hamrock, Colin Hainbach, Helen M. Hainbach, Mark Hainbach, Sir Richard Hanbury-Tenison, Noel Healey, Denis Henderson, Bill Herdeman, John Heston (Hengstenberg), Desmond Hirsch, L.M.F. Hirsch, Carlos Hitschmann, Anja Hollaender, Anselm Horwitz, Philip Jacob, Herbert Karrach, Sir Richard Keane, Jennifer Kenny, Konrad Kingshill, Peter and Sophia Kingshill, Christian Knüppel, Peggy Lee, Catriona Lennon, Siobhan Lincoln, Noel Magner, Ines Mandl, John McDermott, John McEllin, John Mee, Garret Moddel, Grace Moloney, Peggy Moore-Lewy, Patricia Moorhead, Martin Morris, Anna Motz, Verity Murdoch, Brian Murphy OSB, Placid Murray OSB, Jiri Nebesky, John O'Callaghan, Colman O'Clabaigh OSB, Sister Deirdre O'Connor, John O'Donnell, Paedar O'Dowd, R. O'Loughlin, Séamus Ó Maitiú, Ursula Owen, David Parsons, Elsa Peile, Rachel Philipson-Levy, H. Platz, Declan Quaile, Fr Peter Queally, Günther Rasche, Hans Reiss, Hilary Rosenblatt, Stuart Rosenblatt, Monica Schefold, Otto Schindler, Alfred Schulhof, Monika Schulte, Robert Schurmann, Peter Schwarz, Michael Shire, Raphael Siev, Ivor Shorts, Sir Stephen Silver, Hetty Staples, Myles and Benita Stoney, Honor Stuart, Ernie and Susanna Sweeney, Thomas and Peter Ticher, Mark and Philip Tierney OSB, Ilse Tysh, Klaus Unger, Deborah Vietor-Englaender, Ernst von Glasersfeld, Alena Wagnerova, Bina Wallach, Bernadette Walsh, William and Geraldine Watts, Anne Webber, Stephen Weil, Paul Weindling, Otto Westphal, Margaret Wynne, Anní Zakon, twelve German-speaking elders of Chomutov (Czech Republic).

Private Papers

Maggie Boylan's notebooks (thanks to Sean Boylan).
Hubert Butler Papers, Maidenhall, Kilkenny (thanks to Julia Crampton).
Lisa Fischer, Diary 1939 and photos (thanks to Margaret Wynne).
Fred Hainbach, 1920–1950. A Memoir. 2002 (thanks to Mark Hainbach).
Walter Heitler, Lebenserinnerungen, privately held Zurich (thanks to Günther Rasche).
Denis Henderson, The Heitlers and the Strunzes, unpublished recollections, 2015.
CV Hildegard Holländer-Wollesen, Christoph Holländer.
Hopf family papers (thanks to Willie Walshe).
Moore, Esther and George Moore-Lewy: A Sister and Brother Remember – Wechterswinkel to Dublin and a Little Beyond. Unpublished and undated (thanks to Anne Mossop and Anne Lindsey).
Minutes of shareholders' meetings of Plunder & Pollak between 1940 and 1965 (provided by Michael Coady).
Hans Reiss, Seven Years in Ireland (thanks to Hans Reiss).
Joy Roger Hammerschlag, Kurt Roger 1895–1966, 1997 (thanks to Joy Roger Hammerschlag).
Erwin Strunz, My connection with the Kagran Group 1938. Butler Papers, Maidenhall, Kilkenny.
Erwin Strunz, Memoir. June 1989 (thanks to Freda Mishan and Bob Strunz).
Peter Schwarz, An anecdotal biographical note. March 1996.
Peter Ticher, The Tichers and their collection and research of Irish Georgian silver, 2003 (thanks to Peter Ticher).
Robert Weil [Notes, 1940] (thanks to Stephen Weil).

Questionnaires of the University of Limerick German-speaking exiles in Ireland project:
George Clare, Kurt Brehmer, Otto Glaser, John Heuston (Hengstenberg), Herbert Karrach, Ines Mandl, Hans Reiss, Alfred Schulhof, Heinz Shire, Ivor Shorts (for Sabina Wizniak), Peter Schwarz, Ernst von Glasersfeld.

Newspapers

Ireland
Irish Independent, Irish Times, Irish Press, Cork Examiner, Waterford Standard (1938–1939), *Connaught Telegraph* (1938–1939), *Connacht Tribune* (1937–1940, 1943), *Galway Observer* (1937–1939), *Bray Tribune* (1938–1939), *Drogheda Independent* (1939–1940), *Dundalk Examiner* (1938–1939), *Dungannon Observer* (1939), *The Nationalist and Munster Advertiser* (1935, 1937–1938), *Longford News* (1939–1940), *Longford Leader* (1939–1941), *Church of Ireland Gazette* (1938–1945), *The People's Press*, Sligo (1938–1939).

Germany
Edener Mitteilungen, Oranienburg (1927–1933), *Tagesspiegel* (2012).

Italy
The Siena News (1941).

United Kingdom
Jewish Chronicle (1933–1950), *The Independent* (1996).

USA
Time (1943), *New York Times* (1941).

B Literature

1 Secondary literature

Aalen, F.H.A./Kevin Whelan (eds): *Dublin City and County: From Prehistory to Present*. Studies in Honour of J. H. Andrews. Dublin: Geographical Publications 1992.

Alexander, Gabriel: Die Entwicklung der jüdischen Bevölkerung in Berlin zwischen 1871 und 1945. In: Shulamit Volkov/Frank Stern (eds), *Tel Aviver Jahrbuch für Deutsche Geschichte*. Vol. 20 (1991), pp. 287–314.

Alexander, Gabriel: Die jüdische Bevölkerung Berlins in den ersten Jahrzehnten des 20. Jahrhunderts: Demographische und wirtschaftliche Entwicklungen. In: Reinhard Rürup (ed.): *Jüdische Geschichte in Berlin*. Berlin: Edition Hentrich 1995, pp. 117–148.

Allen, Kieran: *Fianna Fail and Irish Labour, 1926 to the Present*. London/Chicago: Pluto Press 1997.

Aly, Götz/Wolf Gruner/Susanne Heim/Ulrich Herbert/Hans-Dieter Kreikamp/Horst Möller/Dieter Pohl/Hartmut Weber (eds): *Die Verfolgung und Ermordung der europäischen Juden durch das nationalsozialistische Deutschland 1933–19451*. Vol. I. Munich: Oldenbourg 2008.

Anderl, Gabriele/Dirk Rupnow: *Die Zentralstelle für jüdische Auswanderung als Beraubungsinstitution. Nationalsozialistische Institutionen des Vermögensentzuges*. Österreichische Historikerkommission. Vol. 20, no. 1. Vienna (et al.): Oldenbourg 2004.

Anderl, Gabriele/Edith Blaschitz/Sabine Loitfellner/Mirjam Triendl/Niko Wahl: *"Arisierung" von Mobilien*. Österreichische Historikerkommission. Vol. 15. Vienna et al.: Oldenbourg 2004.

Armitage, Ernest: *Wesley College Dublin 1845-199: An Illustrated History*. Dublin: Wesley College 1995.

Ash, Mitchell G./Alfons Söllner (eds): *Forced Migration and Scientific Change. Emigré German-speaking Scientists and Scholars after 1933*. Cambridge/New York/Melbourne: Cambridge University Press 1996.

Bailer-Galina, Brigitte: Die Opfergruppen und deren Entschädigung. In: Politische Bildung (ed.): *Wieder gut machen? Enteignung, Zwangsarbeit, Entschädigung, Restitution*. Innsbruck, Vienna: Studien-Verlag, 1999, pp. 90–96 and http://www.demokratiezentrum.org/fileadmin/media/pdf/opfergruppen.pdf.

Bailer-Galanda, Brigitte/Eva Blimlinger/Susanne Kowarc: *"Arisierung" und Rückstellung von Wohnungen in Wien*. Österreichische Historikerkommission. Vol. 14. Vienna et al.: Oldenbourg 2004, pp. 91–152.

Barkai, Avraham: *Vom Boykott zur "Entjudung". Der wirtschaftliche Existenzkampf der Juden im Dritten Reich 1933–1943*. Frankfurt/M.: Fischer 1988.

Barton, Brian: *Northern Ireland in the Second World War*. Belfast: Ulster Historical Foundation 1995.

Bartrop, Paul R.: *False Havens. The British Empire and the Holocaust*. Lanham/New York/London: University of America Press 1995.

Beer-Heidrich, Lotte: *Einwohnerbuch Leitmeritz und Pokratitz vor Mai 1945*. Nürnberg: C. Beer 1989.

Behan, A.P.: Up Harcourt Street from the Green. In: *Dublin Historical Record*. Vol. 47, no. 1 (1994), pp. 24–45.

Beiner, Guy: *Remembering the Year of the French. Irish Folk History and Social Memory*. Madison: The University of Wisconsin Press 2007.

Bellenger, Aidan: An Irish Benedictine Adventure: Dom Francis Sweetman (1872–1953) and Mount St. Benedict, Gorey. In: W.J. Sheils/D. Wood (eds): *The Churches, Ireland and the Irish. Papers read at the 1987 Summer Meeting and the 1988 Winter Meeting of the Ecclesiastical History Society*. Oxford: Blackwell 1989, pp. 401–415.

Bellenger, Aidan: The Post-Reformation English Benedictines and Ireland: Conflict and Dialogue. In: Martin Browne/Colmán Ó Clabaigh (eds): *The Irish Benedictines. A History*. Dublin: Columba Press 2005, pp. 140–56.

Belton, Neil: *A Game with Sharpened Knives.* London: Weidenfeld & Nicolson 2005 (translated into German as *Das Spiel mit geschliffenen Klingen.* Frankfurt a.M.: S. Fischer 2007).
Benjamin, Walter: *Briefe I.* Edited and commented by Gershom Scholem/Theodor W. Adorno. Frankfurt a.M.: Suhrkamp 1978.
Bentwich, Norman: *The Rescue and Achievement of Refugee Scholars.* The Hague: M. Nijhoff 1953.
Bentwich, Norman: *They Found Refuge.* London: Cresset Press 1956.
Benz, Wolfgang: *Flucht aus Deutschland. Zum Exil im 20. Jahrhundert.* Munich: dtv 2001.
Berghahn, Marion: *Continental Britons: German-Jewish Refugees from Nazi Germany.* Oxford/Hamburg/New York: Berg 1988.
Bermann, Armin: *Die sozialen und ökonomischen Bedingungen der jüdischen Emigration aus Berlin/Brandenburg 1933.* opus.kobv.de/tuberlin/volltexte/2009/2194/pdf/bergmann_armin.pdf [last accessed 17 February 2016].
Beveridge, William: *A Defence of Free Learning.* Oxford: Oxford University Press 1959.
Beveridge, William: *Power and Influence.* London: Hodder and Stoughton 1953.
Bieler, Ludwig: A Viennese Schoolmaster. In: *Studies.* Vol. 37, no. 148 (December 1948), pp. 440–446.
Bieler, Ludwig: *Codices Patriciani Latini – A Descriptive Catalogue of Latin Manuscripts.* Dublin: Dublin Institute for Advanced Studies 1942.
Bieler, Ludwig: The Mission of Palladius. A comparative study of sources. In: *Traditio.* Vol. 6 (1948), pp. 1–32.
Bieler, Ludwig: *The Life and Legend of St. Patrick: Problems of Modern Scholarship.* Dublin: Clonmore & Reynolds 1949.
Bieler, Ludwig: *St Patrick and the Coming of Christianity.* Dublin, Melbourne: Gill 1967.
Bloch, Alfred: On the Frequency Response of Photronic Cells. In: *Review of Scientific Instruments.* Vol. 6, no. 6 (1935), p. 173.
Bohnke-Kollwitz, Jutta et al. (eds): *Köln und das rheinische Judentum. Festschrift Germania Judaica 1959–1984.* Cologne: J.P. Bachem 1984.
Booth, Lionel: *Dublin Central Mission 1893–1993.* Dublin: n.p. n.d. 1993.
Born, G. V. R.: The Wide-Ranging Family History of Max Born. In: *Notes and Records of the Royal Society of London.* Vol. 56, no. 2 (May 2002), pp. 219–262.
Bott, Marie-Luise: *Die Haltung der Berliner Universität im Nationalsozialismus. Max Vasmers Rückschau 1948.* Berlin: Humboldt-Universität 2009. http://edoc.hu-berlin.de/series/geschichte-hu/1/PDF/1.pdf [last accessed 17 February 2016].
Botz, Gerhard: The Jews of Vienna from the "Anschluß" to the Holocaust. In: Herbert A. Strauss (ed.): *Hostages of Modernization. Studies on Modern Antisemitism 1870–1933/39. Austria - Hungary - Poland – Russia.* Current Research on Antisemitism. Vol. 3, no. 2, Berlin/New York: de Gruyter 1993, pp. 836–854.
Botz, Gerhard/Ivar Oxaal/ Michael Pollak/Nina Scholz (eds): *Eine zerstörte Kultur. Jüdisches Leben und Antisemitismus in Wien seit dem 19. Jahrhundert.* 2nd edition. Vienna: Czernin 2002.
Bourke, Eoin: Irland, George Clare und die Kagran Gruppe. In: Sandra Wiesinger-Stock/Erika Weinzierl/Konstantin Kaiser (eds): *Vom Weggehen. Zum Exil von Kunst und Wissenschaft.* Wien/Budapest: Mandelbaum 2006, pp. 102–112.
Brady, Joseph: Dublin at the Turn of the Century. In: Joseph Brady/Anngret Simms (eds): *Dublin through Space and Time (c.900–1900).* Dublin: Four Courts Press 2001, pp. 221–281.

Brandstetter, Thomas/Ulrich Troitzsch (eds): *Hugo Theodor Horwitz. Das Relais-Prinzip*. Vienna: Löcker 2007.
Breathnach, Caoimhghin S.: The Medical Sciences in Twentieth-Century Ireland. In: *Irish Journal of Medical Science*. Vol. 169, no. 3 (July–September 2000), pp. 221–225.
Brenner, Michael/Rainer Liedtke/David Rechter: *Two Nations: British and German Jews in Comparative Perspective*. London Leo Baeck Institute/Tübingen: Mohr/ Siebeck 1999.
Brophy, James M.: Rezeption Daniel O'Connells und der irischen Emanzipationsbewegung im vormärzlichen Deutschland. In: *Marx-Engels Jahrbuch 2011*, Berlin: Akademie 2012, pp. 74–93.
Brown, Terence: *Ireland. A Social and Cultural History 1922–2002*. 2nd edition. London: Harper Perennial 2004.
Bühnen, Matthias/Rebecca Schaarschmidt: Studierende als Täter und Opfer bei der NS-Machtübernahme an der Berliner Universität. In: Christoph Jahr (ed.): *Die Berliner Universität in der NS-Zeit*. Vol I: Strukturen und Personen. Wiesbaden: Franz Steiner 2005, pp. 143–178.
Caestecker, Frank/Bob Moore (eds): *Refugees from Nazi Germany and the Liberal European States*. New York/Oxford: Berghahn Books 2010.
Cahill, Susan E.: *Crafting Culture, Fabricating Identity. Gender and Textiles in Limerick Lace, Clare Embroidery and the Deerfield Society of Blue and White Needlework*. http://www.collectionscanada.gc.ca/obj/s4/f2/dsk3/OKQ/TC-OKQ-662.pdf [last accessed 17 February 2016].
Clay, W. M.: Weimar in America. In: *The American Scholar*. Vol. 55 (1985/86), pp. 119–128.
Cohen, Gary B.: *Education and Middle-class Society in Imperial Austria 1848–1918*. West Lafayette: Purdue University Press 1996.
Compass, *Industrie und Handel, CSR*. 1925. Vienna: Compass Verlag 1925.
Compass, *CSR*, 1938. Vienna: Compass Verlag 1938.
Compass, *Industrielles Jahrbuch Protektorat*, 1939. Vienna: Compass Verlag 1939.
Coogan, Tim Pat: *Wherever Green Is Worn*. London: Arrow Books 2000.
Cooper, R. M.: *Refugee Scholar: Conversations with Tess Simpson*. Leeds: Moorland Books 1992.
Copley, A. L: Opening Address of the President of the Society. In: H. H. Hartert/A. L. Copley (eds): *Theoretical and Clinical Hemorheology: Proceedings of the Second International Conference*. Berlin/Heidelberg/New York: Springer 1971, pp. 2–4.
Corbach, Dieter: *Die Jawne zu Köln. Zur Geschichte des ersten jüdischen Gymnasiums im Rheinland. Ein Gedenkbuch*. Köln: Scriba 1990.
Crowe, Michael Bertram: A Great Irish Scholar: Monsignor Patrick Boylan. In: *Studies*. Vol. 67, no. 267 (Autumn 1977), pp. 201–211.
Daly, Mary E.: The Economic Ideals of Irish Nationalism: Frugal Comfort or Lavish Austerity? In: *Eire-Ireland*. Vol. 4 (1994), pp. 77–100.
Daly, Mary E.: *Industrial Development and Irish National Identity, 1922–1939*. New York: Syracuse University Press 1992.
Daly, Mary E.: *The Slow Failure. Population Decline and Independent Ireland, 1922–1973*. Madison: University of Wisconsin Press 2006.
Daly, Mary E.: *Dublin, the Deposed Capital*. Cork: Cork University Press 1985.
Darton, Lawrence: *An Account of the Friends' Committee for Refugees and Aliens, first known as the German Emergency Committee of the Society of Friends 1933–1950*. [London:] Friends Committee for Refugees and Aliens 1954.

Department of Local Government and Public Health: *Annual Report of the Registrar-General 1940.* Dublin: Stationery Office 1941. http://www.cso.ie/en/media/csoie/releasespublications/documents/birthsdm/archivedreports/P-VS,1940.pdf [last accessed 8 July 2016]).
Dickel, Horst: *Die deutsche Außenpolitik und die irische Frage von 1932 bis 1944.* Frankfurter Historische Abhandlungen. Wiesbaden: Steiner 1983.
Dickel, Horst: Hans Sachs. In: Gisela Holfter (ed.): *German-speaking Exiles in Ireland 1933–1945.* Amsterdam/Atlanta: Rodopi 2006, pp. 183–213.
Dillon, T. W. T.: Slum Clearance: Past and Future. In: *Studies.* Vol. 34, no. 133 (1945), pp. 13–20.
Dillon, T. W. T.: The Refugee Problem. In: *Studies.* Vol. 28, no. 111 (1939), pp. 402–414.
Dillon, T. W. T.: The Society of St. Vincent de Paul in Ireland, 1845–1945. In: *Studies.* Vol. 34, no. 136 (1945), pp. 515–521.
Diner, Dan/Gotthard Wunberg (eds): *Restitution and Memory. Material Restoration in Europe.* New York/Oxford: Berghahn Books 2007.
Ditchburn, Robert: *Catalogue of the Papers and Correspondences of Robert William Ditchburn, Frs. (1903–1987).* University of Reading, Special Collections NCUACS 6/5/88, 1919-ca.1988. http://www.nationalarchives.gov.uk/a2a/records.aspx?cat=006-ncuacs6588&cid=0#0 [last accessed 1 April 2016].
Ditchburn, Robert: The Refugee Problem. In: *Studies.* Vol. 28, no 110 (1939), pp. 275–292.
Dixon, F. E.: Obituary Prof. L. W. Pollak. In: *Nature.* Vol. 205, no. 4970 (1965), p. 448.
Dixon, F. E.: Professor Leo W. Pollak. In: Tom Keane: *Establishment of the Meteorological Service in Ireland -The Foynes Years, 1936–1945.* Appendix XI. Varsity: n.p. 2012, pp. 159–160.
Dohrn, Verena/Gertrud Pickhan (eds): *Transit und Transformation. Osteuropäisch-jüdische Migranten in Berlin 1918–1939.* Göttingen: Wallstein 2010.
Doorly, Mary Rose: Sabina Wizniak Shorts. In: Gisela Holfter (ed.): *The Irish Context of Kristallnacht. Refugees and Helpers.* Irish-German Studies. Vol. 8. Trier: WVT 2014, pp. 109–120.
Douglas, R. M.: The pro-Axis Underground in Ireland, 1939–1942. In: *Historical Journal.* Vol. 49, no. 4 (2006), pp. 1155–1183.
Duggan, John P.: *Herr Hempel at the German Legation in Dublin 1937–1945.* Dublin: Irish Academic Press 2002.
Durcan, Paul: *A Snail in My Prime: New and Selected Poems.* London: The Harvill Press 1993.
Dwyer, D. J.: The Leather Industries of the Irish Republic, 1922-'55. A Study in Industrial Development and Location. In: *Irish Geography.* Vol. 4, no. 3 (1961), pp. 175–189.
Eckert, Michael: *Arnold Sommerfeld. Science, Life and Turbulent Times, 1868–1951.* New York: Springer 2013.
Ehrenberg, Victor: *Alexander and Ägypten.* Leipzig: J. C. Hinrichs'sche Buchhandlung 1926.
Ehrenberg, Victor: *Der griechische und der hellenische Staat.* Leipzig: B.G. Teubner 1932.
Ehrenberg, Victor: *Die Rechtidee im frühen Griechentum.* Leipzig: S. Hirzel 1921.
Ehrenberg, Victor: *Karthago.* Leipzig: J. C. Hinrichs'sche Buchhandlung 1927.
Ehrenberg, Victor: *Neugründer des Staates.* Munich: C. H. Beck 1925.
Ehrenberg, Victor: *Ost und West.* Brünn: Rudolf M. Rohrer 1935.
Ehrenberg, Victor: *Vom Beginn der Geschichte Europas.* Prague: Taussig & Taussig 1929.
Ehrlich, Paul (ed.): *Gesammelte Arbeiten zur Immunitätsforschung.* Berlin: August Hirschwald 1904.
Eichmann, Klaus (ed.): *The Biology of Complex Organisms – Creation and Protection of Integrity.* Basel: Springer 2003, pp. 63–76.
Einstein, Albert/Max Born: *Briefwechsel 1916–1955.* Munich: Langen Müller 2005.
Einstein, Albert/Ludwig Hopf: Statistische Untersuchung der Bewegung eines Resonators in einem Strahlungsfeld. In: *Annalen der Physik.* Vol. 33 (1910), pp. 1105–1115.

Einstein, Albert/Ludwig Hopf: Über einen Satz der Wahrscheinlichkeitsrechnung und seine Anwendung in der Strahlungstheorie. In: *Annalen der Physik*. Vol. 33 (1910), pp. 1096–1104.
Erlanger, Simon: *„Nur ein Durchgangsland". Arbeitslager und Interniertenheime für Flüchtlinge und Emigranten in der Schweiz 1940–1949*. Zurich: Chronos 2006.
Evans, Bryce: *Seán Lemass: Democratic Dictator*. Cork: The Collins Press 2011.
Evans, Bryce: *Ireland during the Second World War*. Manchester: Manchester University Press 2014.
Ewald, Paul Peter: Prof Ludwig Hopf. In: *Nature*. Vol. 145, no. 3671 (1940), pp. 379–380.
Fanning, Bryan: *Racism and Social Change in the Republic of Ireland*. Manchester: Manchester University Press 2002.
Feichtinger, Johannes: *Die Wiener Schule der Hochpolymerforschung in England und Amerika – Emigration, Wissenschaftswandel und Innovation*. Graz: Uni Graz 2001. http://www.uni-graz.at/johannes.feichtinger/OESHpF_Projekt.pdf [last accessed 17 February 2016].
Feichtinger Johannes: *Wissenschaft zwischen den Kulturen. Österreichische Hochschullehrer in der Emigration 1933–1945*. Frankfurt a.M.: Campus 2001.
Felber, Ulrike/Peter Melichar/Markus Priller/Berthold Unfried/Fritz Weber: *Ökonomie der Arisierung. 1: Grundzüge, Akteure und Institutionen. Zwangsverkauf, Liquidierung und Restitution von Unternehmen in Österreich 1938 bis 1960. Ökonomie der Arisierung. 2: Wirtschaftssektoren, Branchen, Falldarstellungen. Zwangsverkauf, Liquidierung und Restitution von Unternehmen in Österreich 1938 bis 1960*. Österreichische Historikerkommission. Vol. 10.1/10.2. Vienna et al.: Oldenbourg 2004.
Fennelly, William: Monastic Exiles in Ireland. In: Martin Browne/Colmán Ó Clabaigh (eds), *The Irish Benedictines – A History*. Dublin: Columba Press 2005, pp. 177–191.
Ferriter, Diarmaid: *Judging Dev. A Reassessment of the Life and Legacy of Eamon de Valera*, Dublin: Royal Irish Academy 2007.
Fischer-Seidel, Therese/Marion Fries-Dieckmann (eds): *Der unbekannte Beckett: Samuel Beckett und die deutsche Kultur*. Frankfurt am Main: Suhrkamp 2005.
Fischer, Joachim: *Das Deutschlandbild der Iren 1890–1939: Geschichte, Form, Funktion*. Heidelberg: Winter 2000.
Fischer, Joachim: Ernst Toller and Ireland. In: Richard Dove and Stephen Lamb (eds), *German Writers and Politics, 1918–39*. Warwick Studies in the European Humanities. Basingstoke/London: MacMillan 1992, pp. 192–206.
Fischer, Joachim/John Dillon (eds): *The Correspondence of Myles Dillon, 1922–25: Irish-German Relations and Celtic Studies*. Dublin: Four Courts 1999.
Fischer, Klaus: Die Emigration deutschsprachiger Physiker nach 1933. In: Herbert A. Strauss (ed.): *Die Emigration der Wissenschaften nach 1933*. Munich/London/New York/Paris: K.G. Saur 1991, pp. 25–72.
Fischer, Klaus: Vom Wissenschaftstransfer zur Kontextanalyse — oder: wie schreibt man die Geschichte zur Wissenschaftsemigration? In: Rainer Erb/Michael Schmidt (eds): *Antisemitismus und jüdische Geschichte: Studien zu Ehren von Herbert A. Strauss*. Berlin: Wissenschaftlicher Autorenverlag 1987, pp. 267-293.
Fitz-Simon, Christopher: *The Boys. A Biography of Micheal MacLiammoir and Hilton Edwards*. Dublin: New Island Books 2002.
Fleetwood, John: *History of Medicine in Ireland*. Dublin: Richview Press 1951.
Freeman, T. W.: Galway - the Key to the West. In: *Irish Geography*. Vol. 3 (1957), pp. 194–205.

Freeman, T. W.: The Changing Distribution of Population in County Mayo. In: *Journal of the Statistical and Social Inquiry Society of Ireland.* Vol. XVII, no. 1 (1942/1943), Dublin, pp. 85–106.
Freeman, T. W.: *Ireland. A General and Regional Geography.* Reprinted with Revisions. London: Methuen & Co. 1972.
Frei, Norbert/Josef Brunner/Constantin Goschler (eds): *Die Praxis der Wiedergutmachung. Geschichte, Erfahrung und Wirkung in Deutschland und Israel.* Göttingen: Wallstein 2009.
Friedenberger, Martin: *Fiskalische Ausplünderung: die Berliner Steuer- und Finanzverwaltung und die jüdische Bevölkerung 1933–1945.* Berlin: Metropol 2008.
Friedländer, Saul: *Nazi Germany and the Jews: the Years of Persecution, 1933–1939.* New York: Harper Collins 1997.
Frisius, Hildegard/Marianne Kälberer (eds): *Evangelisch getauft – als Juden verfolgt. Spurensuche Berliner Kirchengemeinden.* Berlin: Wichern 2008.
Futaky, István: Die Gründung der ersten deutschen Institute für Finnougristik im Spiegel des Briefwechsels zwischen Julius von Farkas und Max Vasmer. In: *Finnisch-Ugrische Mitteilungen.* Vol. 20 (1997), pp. 135–155.
Gallagher, Tom: *Portugal, a Twentieth-Century Interpretation.* Manchester: Manchester University Press 1983.
Ganglmair, Siegwald: Österreicher in den alliierten Armeen, 1938 bis 1945. In: *Truppendienst.* No. 6 (1990), pp. 523–528.
Garner, Steve: *Racism in the Irish Experience.* London: Pluto Press 2004.
Gast, Holger, et al.: *Katholische Missionsschulen in Deutschland 1887 – 1940.* Bad Heilbrunn: Klinkhardt 2013.
Gavan Duffy, Colum: George Gavan Duffy. In: *Judicial Studies Institute Journal.* Vol. 2, no. 2 (2002), pp. 1–30.
Geary, Laurence M.: The 1956 polio epidemic in Cork. In: *History Ireland.* Vol. 14, no. 3 (2006), pp. 34–37.
Gibney, Frank: *Tralee Urban District Planning Scheme. Town and Regional Planning Acts 1934–1939.* Tralee: typescript December 1939.
Girvin, Brian: *The Emergency. Neutral Ireland 1939–1945.* London: MacMillan 2006.
Glanz, Franz: *Gedenkbuch Göpfritz a.d. Wild.* Göpfritz: Selbstverlag 1930.
Glasersfeld, Ernst von: online archive: http://www.evg-archive.net/en/.
Glettler, Monika/Lubomir Liptak/Alena Miskova (eds): *Geteilt, besetzt, beherrscht. Die Tschechoslowakei 1938–1945, Reichsgau Sudetenland, Protektorat Böhmen und Mähren, Slowakei.* Essen: Klartext 2004.
Goenner, Hubert: On the History of Unified Field Theories. Part II (ca 1930 – ca 1965). In: *Living Review in Relativity.* Vol. 5, no. 17 (2014), p. 7. http://www.livingreviews.org/lrr-2014-5 [accessed 24 July 2015].
Gold, Hugo: *Die Juden der Judengemeinden Böhmens in Vergangenheit und Gegenwart.* Brünn, Prague 1934.
Golding, G. M.: *George Gavan Duffy 1882–1951 – A Legal Biography.* Dublin: Irish Academic Press 1982.
Goldstone, Katrina: 'Benevolent helpfulness'? Ireland and the International Reaction to Jewish Refugees, 1933–9. In: Michael Kennedy/Joseph M. Skelly (eds): *Irish Foreign Policy 1919–1966.* Dublin: Four Courts Press 2000, pp. 116–136.
Gray, Tony: *The Lost Years. The Emergency in Ireland 1939–45.* London: Warner Books 1998.
Greenspan, Nancy: *The End of the Certain World: The Life and Science of Max Born.* New York: Basic Books 2005.

Griffin, Timmy (ed.): *Tralee's Old Stock Reminiscence*. Compiled by Mick O'Neill. Part II. Tralee 2003.
Grob-Fitzgibbon, Benjamin: *The Irish Experience during the Second World War. An Oral History*. Dublin: Irish Academic Press 2004.
Grübel, Monika/Georg Mülich (eds): *Jüdisches Leben im Rheinland. Vom Mittelalter bis zur Gegenwart*. Cologne/Weimar/Vienna: Boehlau 2005.
Gruner, Wolf: Die Reichshauptstadt und die Verfolgung der Berliner Juden 1933–1945. In: Reinhard Rürup (ed.): *Jüdische Geschichte in Berlin*. Berlin: Edition Hentrich 1995, pp. 229–266.
Gruss, Peter: Geleitwort. In: Reinhard Rürup: *Schicksale und Karrieren – Gedenkbuch für die von den Nationalsozialisten aus der Kaiser-Wilhelm-Gesellschaft vertriebenen Forscherinnen und Forscher*. Göttingen: Wallstein 2008, pp. 9–12.
Grüttner, Michael/Sven Kinas: Die Vertreibung von Wissenschaftlern aus den deutschen Universitäten 1933–1945. In: *Vierteljahrshefte für Zeitgeschichte*. Vol. 55 (2007), pp. 123–186.
Grüttner, Michael: *Studenten im Dritten Reich. Geschichte der deutschen Studentenschaft 1933 – 1945*. Sammlung Schöningh zur Geschichte und Gegenwart. Paderborn: Schöningh 2000.
Hachtmann, Rüdiger: *Wissenschaftsmanagement im 'Dritten Reich' – Geschichte der Generalverwaltung der Kaiser-Wilhelm-Gesellschaft*. Vol 2. Göttingen: Wallstein 2007.
Hahn, Judith/Rebecca Schwoch: *Anpassung und Ausschaltung. Die Berliner Kassenärztliche Vereinigung im Nationalsozialismus*. Berlin: Hentrich & Hentrich 2009.
Hamilton, Hugo: Blind Eye – Film Script. In: Gisela Holfter (ed.): *The Irish Context of Kristallnacht. Refugees and Helpers*. Irish-German Studies. Vol. 8. Trier: WVT 2014, pp. 121–132.
Hammel, Andrea/Anthony Grenville: Introduction. In: *Yearbook of the Research Centre for German and Austrian Exile Studies*. Vol. 16 (2015), pp. xi–xv.
Hasberg, Wolfgang: Siegfried Kawerau (1886–1936). In: Michael Fröhlich (ed.): *Die Weimarer Republik. Portrait einer Epoche in Biographien*. Darmstadt: Primus 2002, pp. 293–304.
Häsler, Alfred A.: *Das Boot ist voll. Die Schweiz und die Flüchtlinge 1933–1945*. Zürich: Ex Libris 1967.
Haughton, Joseph P.: The Social Geography of Dublin. In: *The Geographical Review*. Vol. 39 (1949), pp. 257–277.
Heim, Susanne/Beate Meyer/Francis R. Nicosa (eds): *"Wer bleibt, opfert seine Jahre, vielleicht sein Leben". Deutsche Juden 1938–1941*. Göttingen: Wallstein 2010.
Heimatkreis Komotau (ed.): Geschichte der Juden in Komotau. In: *Komotauer Jahrbuch*. Vol. 6 (2001), pp. 102–111.
Heitler, Walter: [My Impression of Dublin Institute of Advanced Studies]. In: *Scoil an Léinn Cheiltigh, Tuarascáil Leathchéad Blian: School of Celtic Studies, Fiftieth Anniversary Report 1940–1990*. Dublin: Dublin Institute of Advanced Studies 1990, pp. 28–29.
Heitler, Walter: Erwin Schrödinger. In: *Biographical Memoirs of Fellows of the Royal Society of London*. Vol. 7 (1961), pp. 220–225.
Hennig, John: Irish-German Literary Relations. In: *German Life and Letters*. Vol. 3 (1950), pp. 102–110.
Hepp, Michael (ed.): *Die Ausbürgerung deutscher Staatsangehöriger 1933–45 nach den im Reichsanzeiger veröffentlichten Listen*. 3 Volumes. Munich/New York/Paris/London: Saur 1988.
Herrmann, Wolfgang A.: *Universität München – Die Geschichte eines Wissenschaftsunternehmens*. Berlin: Metropol 2006.

Hess, Volker: Die medizinische Fakultät im Zeichen der „Führeruniversität". In: Christoph Jahr (ed.): *Die Berliner Universität in der NS-Zeit.* Vol I: Strukturen und Personen. Wiesbaden: Franz Steiner 2005, pp. 37–48.
Heumos, Peter: *Die Emigration aus der Tschechoslowakei nach Westeuropa und den Nahen Osten 1938–1945. Politisch-soziale Struktur, Organisation und Asylbedingungen der tschechischen, jüdischen, deutschen und slowakischen Flüchtlinge während des Nationalsozialismus. Darstellung und Dokumentation.* Munich: Oldenbourg 1989.
Hirnschall, Franz: *Beiträge zur Geschichte von Göpfritz a.d.Wild.* Göpfritz: Buschek 1979.
Hoch, P. K./E. J. Yoxen: Schrödinger at Oxford: A hypothetical national cultural synthesis which failed. In: *Annals of Science.* Vol. 44, no. 6 (1987), pp. 593–616.
Hoensch, Jörg/Stanislaw Biman/Lùbomir Liptak (eds): *Judenemanzipation – Antisemitismus – Verfolgung in Deutschland, Österreich-Ungarn, den Böhmischen Ländern und in der Slowakei.* Essen: Klartext 1999, pp. 175–194.
Hoerder, Dirk/Yvonne Hebert/Irina Schmitt (eds): *Negotiating Transcultural Lives. Belongings and Social Capital among Youth in Comparative Perspective.* Göttingen: V & R unipress 2005.
Hogan, J. J.: Mary M. Macken. An Appreciation. In: *Studies.* Vol. 39, no. 155 (Sepember 1950), pp. 315–318.
Holfter, Gisela (ed.): *German-speaking Exiles in Ireland 1933–1945.* Amsterdam/New York: Rodopi 2006.
Holfter, Gisela (ed.): *The Irish Context of Kristallnacht. Refugees and Helpers.* Irish-German Studies. Vol. 8. Trier: WVT 2014.
Holfter, Gisela/Hermann Rasche (eds): *Exil in Irland. John Hennigs Schriften zu deutsch-irischen Beziehungen.* Trier: WVT 2002.
Holfter, Gisela/Hermann Rasche (eds): *John Hennig's Exile in Ireland.* Arlen: Galway 2004.
Holfter, Gisela/Hermann Rasche: "Was ausgewandert sein heißt, erfährt man erst nach Jahrzehnten" – John Hennig im (irischen) Exil. In: Ian Wallace (ed.): *Fractured Biographies.* German Monitor. Vol. 57. Amsterdam/New York: Rodopi 2003, pp. 55–85.
Holfter, Gisela: Akademiker im irischen Exil: Ernst Lewy (1881–1966). In: *German Life and Letters.* Vol. 61, no. 3 (July 2008), pp. 361–385.
Holfter, Gisela: Ein Fallbeispiel zur Rückkehrproblematik aus dem Exil – Ernst Lewy (1881–1966). In: A. Goodbody et al. (eds): *Dislocation and Reorientation.* Amsterdam/New York: Rodopi 2009, pp. 139–151.
Holfter, Gisela: *Erlebnis Irland.* Trier: WVT 1996.
Holfter, Gisela: Ernst Scheyer. In: Gisela Holfter (ed.): *German-speaking Exiles in Ireland 1933–1945.* Amsterdam/New York: Rodopi 2006, pp. 149–169.
Holfter, Gisela: German-speaking Exiles 1933–1945 in Ireland, an Introduction and Overview. In: Gisela Holfter (ed.): *German-speaking Exiles in Ireland 1933–1945.* Amsterdam/New York: Rodopi 2006, pp. 1–19.
Holfter, Gisela: "He was a Friend of the Greatest Geniuses of his Time – Indeed, He Was One of Them" - Ludwig Hopf (1884–1939). In: Ian Wallace (ed.): *Voices in Exile. Essays in Memory of Hamish Ritchie.* Amsterdamer Beiträge zur Germanistik. Leiden/Boston: Brill/Rodopi 2015, pp. 113–140.
Holloway, Bruce/Paul Broda: William Hayes 1913–1994. In: *Historical Records of Australian Science.* Vol. 11, no. 2 (December 1996), pp. 213–228.
Hopf, Ludwig/Arnold Sommerfeld: Über komplexe Integraldarstellung der Zylinderfunktionen. In: *Archiv der Mathematik und Physik.* Vol 3, no. 18 (1911), pp. 1–16.
Hopf, Ludwig/Richard Fuchs: *Aerodynamik.* Berlin: Schmidt 1922.

Hopf, Ludwig/Richard Fuchs: *Einführung in die Differentialgleichungen der Physik*. Berlin: de Gruyter 1933.
Hopf, Ludwig/Richard Fuchs: *Materie and Strahlung*. Berlin: Springer 1936.
Hopf, Ludwig/Richard Fuchs: *Relativitätstheorie*. Berlin: Julius Springer 1931.
Horgan, John: *Seán Lemass. The Enigmatic Patriot*. Dublin: Gill & Macmillan 1997.
Horner, Arnold: The Dublin Region, 1880–1982: An Overview on its Development and Planning. In: M. J. Bannon (ed.): *A Hundred Years of Irish Planning*. Dublin: Turoe Press 1985, pp. 21–76.
Hull, Mark: *Irish Secrets. German Espionage in Wartime Ireland 1939–1945*. Dublin: Irish Academic Press 2004.
Hull, Mark: Perdition's Guests: Irish in Germany during World War II. In: Claire O'Reilly/Veronica O'Regan (eds): *Ireland and the Irish in Germany: Reception and Perception*. Baden-Baden: Nomos 2014, pp. 45–62.
Jacob, Philip: *The Religious Society of Friends and the „Helpers" Side*. In: Gisela Holfter (ed.): *The Irish Context of Kristallnacht. Refugees and Helpers*. Irish-German Studies. Vol. 8. Trier: WVT 2014, pp. 75–80.
Jasch, Hans-Christian: Das preußische Kultusministerium und die "Ausschaltung" von "nichtarischen" und politisch mißliebigen Professoren an der Berliner Universität. In: *forum historiae iuris, erste europäische Internetzeitschrift für Rechtsgeschichte* (25.8.2005) http://www.forhistiur.de/legacy/zitat/0508jasch.htm [last accessed 17 February 2016].
Jochem, Gerhard: *Mitten in Nürnberg. Jüdische Firmen, Freiberufler und Institutionen am Vorabend des Nationalsozialismus*. Nürnberg: Edelmann 1998.
Johnson, David: *The Interwar Economy in Ireland*. Dundalk: Dundalgan Press 1985.
Jones, Emrys: *A Social Geography of Belfast*. London: Oxford University Press 1960.
Jüdische Gemeinde Halle (ed.): *300 Jahre Juden in Halle. Leben, Leistung, Leiden, Lohn*. Halle: Mitteldeutscher Verlag 1992.
Kalkmann, Ulrich: *Die Technische Hochschule Aachen im Dritten Reich (1933–1945)*. Aachen: Verlag Mainz 2003.
Kalter, Frank Kalter (ed.): Migration und Integration. In: *Kölner Zeitschrift für Soziologie und Sozialpsychologie*. Special edition. Vol. 48. Wiesbaden: Verlag für Sozialwissenschaften 2008.
Keane, Tom: *Establishment of the Meteorological Service in Ireland - The Foynes Years, 1936–1945*. Varsity: n.p. 2012.
Kearney, T.: *Lough Hyne: The Marine Researchers - in Pictures*. Skibbereen: Skibbereen Heritage Centre 2011.
Kearns, Kevin C.: *Dublin Tenement Life. An Oral History*. Dublin: Gill and Macmillan 1994.
Kellerhoff, Sven Felix: *Kristallnacht: Der Novemberprogrom 1938 und die Verfolgung der Berliner Juden 1924 und 1945*. Berlin: Berlin Story 2008.
Kennedy, Finola: *Frank Duff - A Life Story*. Burns & Oats: London/New York, 2011.
Kennedy, Michael: *Ireland and the League of Nations, 1919–1946. International Relations, Diplomacy and Politics*. Blackrock: Irish Academic Press 1996.
Kennedy, Roisin: *The Emergency. A Turning Point for Irish Art?* www.irishabroad.com/Culture/VisualArts/emergency.asp [last accessed 14 March 2016].
Kennedy, Seán (ed.): *Beckett and Ireland*. Cambridge: Cambridge University Press 2010.
Keogh, Dermot: *Ireland and Europe, 1919–1948. A Diplomatic and Political History*. Cork/Dublin: Hibernian University Press 1988.

Keogh, Dermot: *Jews in Twentieth-Century Ireland. Refugees, Anti-Semitism and the Holocaust.* Cork: University College Press 1998.
Keogh, Dermot: *Twentieth-Century Ireland. Nation and State.* Dublin: Palgrave Macmillan 1994.
Keogh, Niall: *Con Cremin: Ireland's Wartime Diplomat.* Cork: Mercier Press 2006.
Kernbauer, Alois: Carla Zawisch-Ossenitz. Eine biographische Skizze der ersten Professorin an der Karl-Franzens-Universität in Graz. In: Alois Kernbauer/Karin Schmidlechner-Lienhart (eds): *Frauenstudium und Frauenkarrieren an der Universität Graz.* Graz: Akademische Druck- u. Verlagsanstalt 1996, pp. 265–270.
Kettler, David/Zvi Ben-Dor (eds): *The Limits of Exile.* Berlin/Madison: Galda 2010.
Kincaid, Andrew: Memory and the City. Urban Renewal and Literary Memoirs in Contemporary Dublin. In: *College Literature.* Vol. 32, no. 2 (2005), pp. 16–42.
Kistermann, Friedrich W.: Leo Wenzel Pollak (1888–1964): Czechoslovakian Pioneer in Scientific Data Processing. In: *IEEE Annals of the History of Computing.* Vol. 21, no. 4 (1999), pp. 62–68.
Klusacek, Christine and Kurt Stimmer: *Leopoldstadt.* Vienna: Kurt Mohl 1978.
Annette Kolb/René Schickele, *Briefe im Exil 1933–1940.* Edited by Hans Bender. Mainz: v. Hase & Koehler 1987.
Knowlson, James: *Damned to Fame: The Life of Samuel Beckett.* New York: Grove Press 1996.
Knüppel, Christoph: Aus der Scholle festem Grunde wächst dereinst die Freiheitsstunde. Gustav Landauer und die Siedlungsbewegung. In: Erich-Mühsam-Gesellschaft (ed.): *Von Ancona bis Eden. Alternative Lebensformen.* Lübeck: Erich-Mühsam-Gesellschaft e.V. 2006, pp. 45–66.
Krejcova, Helena: Spezifische Voraussetzungen des Antisemitismus und antijüdische Aktivitäten im Protektorat Böhmen und Mähren. In: Jörg Hoensch/Stanislav Biman/Lubomir Liptak (eds): *Judenemanzipation – Antisemitismus – Verfolgung in Deutschland, Österreich-Ungarn, den Böhmischen Ländern und in der Slowakei.* Essen, 1998, pp. 175–194.
Krist, Martin: *Vertreibungsschicksale. Jüdische Schüler eines Wiener Gymnasiums 1938 und ihre Lebenswege.* Vienna: Turia und Kant 1999.
Krohn, Claus-Dieter (ed.): *Handbuch der deutschsprachigen Emigration 1933 – 1945.* Darmstadt: Primus 1998.
Kubaseck, Christopher, Günter Seufert (eds): *Deutsche Wissenschaftler im türkischen Exil.* Würzburg: Ergon 2008.
Lausch, Hans: Mathematics in detention. In: *Gazette of the Australian Mathematics Society.* Vol. 33, no. 2 (May 2006), pp. 95–103.
Lee, Joseph J.: *Ireland, 1912–1985.* Cambridge: Cambridge University Press 1989.
Leichsenring, Jana: Die Auswanderungsunterstützung für katholische 'Nichtarier' und die Grenzen der Hilfe. Der St. Raphaelsverein in den Jahren 1938–1941. In: Susanne Heim/Beate Meyer/Francis R. Nicosia (eds): *"Wer bleibt opfert seine Jahre, vielleicht sein Leben." Deutsche Juden 1938–1941.* Hamburger Beiträge zur Geschichte der deutschen Juden. Vol. XXXVII. Göttingen: Wallstein 2010, pp. 96–114.
Leichsenring, Jana: *Die Katholische Kirche und ihre Juden: Das Hilfswerk beim bischöflichen Ordinariat Berlin 1938–1945.* Berlin: Metropol 2007.
Infeld, Leopold: Visit to Dublin. In: *Scientific American.* Vol. 181, no. 4 (October 1949), pp. 11–15.
Lerchenmueller, Joachim: *'Keltischer Sprengstoff' – eine wissenschaftsgeschichtliche Studie über die deutsche Keltologie von 1900 bis 1945.* Tübingen: Niemeyer 1997.

Lewy, Ernst: Die Finnisch-Ugrischen Stämme im europäischen Rußland. In: Wilhelm Doegen (ed.): *Unter fremden Völkern. Eine neue Völkerkunde.* Berlin: Otto Stollberg 1925, pp. 212–232.

Lewy, Ernst: Die Zigeuner. In: Wilhelm Doegen (ed.): *Unter fremden Völkern. Eine neue Völkerkunde.* Berlin: Otto Stollberg 1925, pp. 167–176.

Lill, Rudolf: *Südtirol in der Zeit des Nationalismus.* Konstanz: UVK 2002.

London, Louise: *Whitehall and the Jews, 1933 –1948. British Immigration Policy, Jewish Refugees and the Holocaust.* Cambridge: Cambridge University Press 2000.

Longford Yearbook 1940. Longford: T. & Mac Manus 1940.

Luchins, Abraham S./Edith H. Luchins: *Kurt Grelling: Steadfast Scholar in a Time of Madness.* 2001. http://gestalttheory.net/archive/kgbio.html [last accessed 27 October 2015].

Ludlow, P. L.: The Refugee Problem in the 1930's. The Failures and Successes of Protestant Relief Programmes. In: *English Historical Review.* Vol. 90, no. 356 (1975), pp. 564–603.

Ludwig, Hartmut: *Die Opfer unter dem Rad verbinden. Vor- und Entstehungsgeschichte, Arbeit und Mitarbeiter des "Büros Pfarrer Grüber".* PhD dissertation. Berlin 1988.

Lukasievicz, Jan: Curriculum Vitae. In: *Metalogicon.* Vol. II, no. 2 (1994), http://web.mclink.it/MI2701/rivista/1994ld/lukasiewicz94ld.pdf [last accessed 17 February 2016].

Maas, Utz: *Verfolgung und Auswanderung deutschsprachiger Sprachforscher.* Vol. II: G-P (Q). Osnabrück: Secolo 2004, pp. 265–275.

Mac Con Iomaire, Mairtin: Hidden Voices from the Culinary Past: Oral History as a Tool for Culinary Historians. DIT, School of Culinary Arts and Food Technology, online conference paper 2010 http://arrow.dit.ie/tfschcafcon/5/ [last accessed 24 November 2015].

Mac Laughlin, Jim: *Location and Dislocation in Contemporary Irish Society. Emigration and Irish Identities.* Cork: Cork University Press 1997.

Macken, Mary: Dr. Denis J. Coffey President of University College, Dublin, 1909–1940. In: *Studies.* Vol. 29, no. 114 (June 1940), pp. 177–186.

MacManus, Ruth: *Dublin, 1910 – 1940. Shaping the City and Suburbs.* Dublin: Four Courts Press 2002.

Maderegger, Sylvia: *Die Juden im österreichischen Ständestaat 1934–1938.* Vienna/Salzburg: Geyer 1973.

Marciniak, Kataryna: *Citizenship, Exile, and the Logic of Difference.* Minneapolis/London: University of Minnesota Press 2006.

Mautner, Friedrich Ignaz/Erwin Schödinger: Infinitesimal Affine Connections with Twofold Einstein-Bargmann Symmetry. In: *Proceedings of the Royal Irish Academy.* Vol. 50 (1945), pp. 223–231.

Maxwell, Alison/Shay Harpur: *Jammet's of Dublin 1901–1967.* Dublin: Lilliput 2012.

McCarthy, Kevin: An Introduction to Robert Briscoe's Extraordinary Immigration Initiative, 1933–1938. In: Gisela Holfter (ed.): *The Irish Context of Kristallnacht. Refugees and Helpers.* Irish-German Studies. Vol. 8. Trier: WVT 2014, pp. 81–88.

McCarthy, Mark: Writing Ireland's Historical Geographies. In: *Journal of Historical Geography.* Vol. 28 (2002), pp. 534–553.

McCrea, William: Eamon de Valera, Erwin Schrödinger and the Dublin Institute of Advanced Studies. In: *Bulletin of the Department of Foreign Affairs.* Vol. 1037 (May/June 1987), pp. 12–14.

McCrea, William: Eamon de Valera, Erwin Schrödinger and the Dublin Institute. In: C. W. Kilmister (ed.): *Schrödinger – Centenary Celebration of a Polymath*, Cambridge: Cambridge University Press 1989, pp. 119–135.

McGuire, James/James Quinn (eds), *Dictionary of Irish Biography*. Cambridge: Cambridge University Press 2009.
Meinl, Susanne/Jutta Zwilling: *Legalisierter Raub. Die Ausplünderung der Juden im Nationalsozialismus durch die Reichsfinanzverwaltung in Hessen*. Frankfurt/New York: Campus 2004.
Mejstrik, Alexander/Therese Garstenauer/Peter Melichar/Alexander Prenninger/Christa Putz/Sigrid Wadauer: *Berufsschädigungen in der nationalsozialistischen Neuordnung der Arbeit. Vom österreichischen Berufsleben 1934 zum völkischen Schaffen 1938–1940*. Österreichische Historikerkommission. Vol. 16. Vienna/Munich: Oldenbourg 2004.
Menkes, John: *After the Tempest*. McKinleyville, CA: Fithian Press 2003.
Meyenn, von Karl (ed.): *Eine Entdeckung von ganz außerordentlichen Tragweite – Schrödingers Briefwechsel zur Wellenmechanik und zum Katzenparadoxon*. Vol I. Berlin/Heidelberg: Springer 2011.
Milgram, Avraham: *Portugal, Salazar and the Jews*. Jerusalem: Yad Vashem 2011.
Molohan, Cathy: *Germany and Ireland, 1945–1955: Two Nations' Friendship*. Dublin: Irish Academic Press 1999.
Moore, Walter J.: *Erwin Schrödinger- Life and Thought*. Cambridge: Cambridge University Press 1989.
Moraw, Frank: Die nationalsozialistische Diktatur. In: Andreas Cser et al. (eds): *Geschichte der Juden in Heidelberg*. Heidelberg: Guderjahn 1996, pp. 440–555.
Moser, Jonny: *Demographie der jüdischen Bevölkerung Österreichs 1938–1945*. Schriftenreihe des Dokumentationsarchivs des österreichischen Widerstands. Vol. 5. Vienna 1999.
Moser, Jonny: Die Gildemeester-Auswanderungshilfsaktion. In: Dokumentationsarchiv des österreichischen Widerstands (ed.): *Yearbook 1991*, pp. 115–122.
Mosse, Werner (ed.): *Second Chance. Two Centuries of German-speaking Jews in the United Kingdom*. Tübingen: Mohr Paul Siebeck 1991.
Mott, Neville: Walter Heinrich Heitler 1904–1981. In: The Royal Society (ed.), *Biographical Memoirs of Fellows of the Royal Society*, Volume 28, Bristol: Stonebridge 1982, pp. 141–151.
Muchitsch, Wolfgang: *Mit Spaten, Waffen und Worten. Die Einbindung österreichischer Flüchtlinge in die britischen Kriegsanstrengungen 1939–1945*. Vienna/Zurich: Europa 1992.
Muchitsch, Wolfgang: Österreichische Flüchtlinge in Irland 1938–1945. In: Dokumentationsarchiv des österreichischen Widerstands (ed.): *Yearbook 1994*, pp. 33–45.
Müller-Arends, Dietmar/Ulrich Kalkmann: Ludwig Hopf. In: Klaus Habetha (ed.): *Wissenschaft zwischen technischer und gesellschaftlicher Herausforderung: die RHTW Aachen 1970–1995*. Aachen: Einhard 1995, pp. 208–215.
Mullins, Gerry: *Dublin Nazi No.1. The Life of Adolf Mahr*. Dublin: Liberties Press 2007.
Mulrooney, Deirdre: Erina Brady: Irish/German Harbinger of Modern Dance to 1940s Ireland. In: Sabine Egger (ed.): *Cultural/Literary Translators – Selected Irish-German Biographies II*, Irish-German Studies 9. Trier: WVT 2015, pp. 11–29.
Murphy, Brian: *St. Gerard's School 1918–1998*. Bray: Kestrel Books 1999.
Murphy, Gerard: Theobald Wolfe Tone Dillon 1898–1946. In: *Studies*. Vol. 35, no. 138 (June 1946), pp. 145–152.
Murphy, Thomas/James R. McConnell: De Valera and the Foundation of the School of Cosmic Physics. In: *Scoil an Léinn Cheiltigh, Tuarascáil Leathchéad Blian: School of Celtic Studies, Fiftieth Anniversary Report 1940–1990*. Dublin: Dublin Institute of Advanced Studies 1990, pp. 32–34.
Mußgnug, Dorothee: *Die vertriebenen Heidelberger Dozenten*. Heidelberg: Winter 1988.

Nevin, Donal (ed.): *Trade Union Century*. Cork and Dublin: Mercier Press 1994.
Nevin, Donal: *Trade Unionism and Change in Irish Society*. Dublin: Mercier Press 1980.
Nitsche, Jürgen/Ruth Röcher (eds): *Juden in Chemnitz: Die Geschichte der Gemeinde und ihrer Mitglieder*. Dresden: Sandstein 2002.
Nixon, Mark: *Samuel Beckett's German Diaries 1936–37*. New York: Continuum Publishing Group 2011.
Nixon, Mark: The German Diaries 1936/37: Beckett und die moderne deutsche Literatur. In: Marion Dieckmann-Fries/Therese Seidel (eds): *Der unbekannte Beckett. Samuel Beckett und die deutsche Kultur*. Frankfurt am Main: Suhrkamp, pp. 138–54.
Nolan, Aengus: *Joseph Walshe, Irish Foreign Policy 1922–1946*. Cork: Mercier Press 2008.
Ó Dochartaigh, Pól: 'A shadowy but important figure': Rudolf Thomas Siegfried. In: *The Tripartite Life of Whitley Stokes (1830–1909)*. Dublin: Four Courts 2011, pp. 29–43.
Ó Dochartaigh, Pól: *Julius Pokorny, 1887–1970: Germans, Celts and Nationalism*. Dublin: Four Courts 2004.
O'Brien, Eoin: 'From the Waters of Sion to Liffeyside'. The Jewish Contribution: Medical and Cultural. In: *Journal of the Irish Colleges of Physicians and Surgeons*. Vol. 10 (January 1981), pp. 107–119.
O'Connor, Anna/Susan M. Parkes: *Gladly Learn and Gladly Teach. A History of Alexandra College and School, Dublin 1866–1966*. Tallaght: Blackwater Press 1984.
O'Connor, Siobhán P.: *Irish Government Policy and Irish Public Opinion toward German-speaking Refugees in Ireland, 1933–1945*. PhD thesis Limerick 2009.
O'Donoghue, David: *The Devil's Deal. The IRA, Nazi Germany and the Double Life of Jim O'Donovan*. Dublin: New Island 2010.
O'Donoghue, David: *Hitler's Irish Voices*. Belfast: Beyond the Pale Publications 1998.
Ó Drisceoil, Donal: *Censorship in Ireland 1939–1945*, Cork: Cork University Press 1996.
O'Driscoll, Mervyn: *Ireland, Germany and the Nazis. Politics and Diplomacy, 1919–1939*. Dublin: Four Courts Press 2004.
O'Driscoll, Mervyn: The 'Jewish Question', Irish Refugee Policy and Charles Bewley, 1933–1939. In: Guðmundur Hálfdanarson (ed.): *Racial Discrimination and Ethnicity in European History*. Pisa: PLUS, Università di Pisa 2003, pp. 139–154. https://www.academia.edu/1065493/The_Jewish_Question_Irish_Refugee_Policy_and_Charles_Bewley_1933-39" [last accessed 17 February 2016].
Ó Faoláin, Seán: The Price of Peace. In: *The Bell*. Vol. 10, no. 4 (July 1945), pp. 281–290.
O'Grada, Cormac: *Jewish Ireland in the Age of Joyce: A Socioeconomic History*. Princeton/Oxford: Princeton University Press 2006.
O'Neill, Patrick: *Ireland and Germany – A Study in Literary Relations*. Peter Lang: New York 1985.
O'Raifeartaigh, Lochlainn/Günther Rasche: Walter Heitler 1904–81. In: Ken Houston (ed.), *Creators of Mathematics: The Irish Connection*. Dublin: University College Dublin Press 2000, pp. 113–121.
Offaly Historical and Archaeological Society: Reverend Dr Timothy Corcoran, S.J., D. Litt. 2 September 2007. https://www.offalyhistory.com/reading-resources/history/famous-offaly-people/rev-dr-timothy-corcoran-s-j-d-litt [last accessed 1 February 2016].
Ökumenischer Rat der Kirchen: *Die zehn Aufbaujahre 1938–1948. Arbeitsbericht des Ökumenischen Rats der Kirchen über seine Aufbauzeit*. Amsterdam: Ökumenischer Rat der Kirchen 1948.

Osterloh, Jörg: Judenverfolgung und „Arisierung" im Reichsgau Sudetenland. In: Monika Glettler/ Lubomir Liptak/Alena Miskova (eds): *Geteilt, besetzt, beherrscht. Die Tschechoslowakei 1938–1945, Reichsgau Sudetenland, Protektorat Böhmen und Mähren, Slowakei*. Essen: Klartext 2004, pp. 211–228.

Otruba, Gustav: Der Anteil der Juden am Wirtschaftsleben der böhmischen Länder seit dem Beginn der Industrialisierung. In: Ferdinand Seibt (ed.): *Die Juden in den böhmischen Ländern*. Lectures by Collegium Carolinum in Bad Wiessee, 27 to 29 November 1981. Munich: Oldenbourg 1984, pp. 209–268.

Pammer, Michael: *Jüdische Vermögen in Wien 1938*. Österreichische Historikerkommission. Vol. 8. Vienna et al.: Oldenbourg 2003.

Parkes, Susan M. (ed.): *A Danger to the Men? A History of Women in Trinity College 1904–2004*. Dublin: Lilliput 2004

Pauley, Bruce: Political Antisemitism in Interwar Vienna. In: Herbert Strauss (ed.): *Hostages of Modernization. Studies on Modern Antisemitismn 1870–1933/39. Austria - Hungary - Poland – Russia*. Current Research on Antisemitism. Vol. 3, no. 2. Berlin/New York: de Gruyter, 1993, pp. 811–835.

Pietzsch, Joachim: The Nobel Prize in Physiology or Medicine 1962 – Perspectives, Nobel Media AB 2014. http://www.nobelprize.org/nobel_prizes/medicine/laureates/1962/perspectives.html [last accessed 27 March 2016].

Pinwinkler, Alexander: *Wilhelm Winkler (1894–1984) – eine Biographie*. Berlin: Duncker & Humblot 2002.

Pinwinkler, Alexander: Wilhelm Winkler und der Nationalsozialismus 1933–1945. In: Rainer Mackensen (ed.): *Bevölkerungslehre und Bevölkerungspolitik im 'Dritten Reich'*. Wiesbaden: Springer 2004, pp. 165–182.

Prunty, Jacinta: *Dublin Slums 1800–1925. A Study in Urban Geography*. Dublin: Irish Academic Press 1998.

Prusin, Alexander Victor: *Nationalising a Borderland. War, Ethnicity, and Anti-Jewish Violence in East Galicia, 1914–1920*. Tuscaloosa: The University of Alabama Press 2005.

Puirseil, Niamh: *The Irish Labour Party, 1922–1973*. Dublin: University College Press 2007.

Pyenson, Lewis: Einstein's early scientific collaborations. In: Russell McCommach (ed.): *Historical Studies in the Physical Sciences*. Vol. 7. Princeton/London: Princeton University Press 1976, pp. 83–124.

Quaile, Declan: Mrs. Vida Lentaigne 1894–1976. Termonfeckin Biographies. First published in *Termonfeckin Historical Society Review*. No. 7 (2007). http://www.termonfeckinhistory.ie/page_39.html [last accessed 19 February 2016].

Rasche, Hermann: Ludwig Bieler. In: Gisela Holfter (ed.): *German-speaking Exiles in Ireland 1933–1945*. Amsterdam/New York: Rodopi 2006, pp. 171–182.

Reisman, Arnold: *Turkey's Modernization. Refugees from Nazism and Atatürk's Vision*. Washington D.C.: New Academia 2006.

Reiter, Wolfgang L.: Die Vertreibung der jüdischen Intelligenz: Verdoppelung eines Verlustes – 1938/1945. In: *Internationale Mathematische Nachrichten*. Vol. 187, no. 55 (August 2011), pp. 1–20.

Reiter, Wolfgang L.: 1938 und die Folgen für die Naturwissenschaften. In Friedrich Stadler (ed.), *Vertriebene Vernunft II – Emigration und Exil österreichischer Wissenschaft 1930–1940*. Vol. 2. Münster: Lit 2004, pp. 664–680.

Remy, Steven P.: *The Heidelberg Myth: The Nazification and Denazification of a German University*. Cambridge, Mass.: Harvard University Press 2003.

Reuband, Karl-Heinz: Life Histories: Problems and Prospects of Longitudinal Designs. In: Jerome M. Chubb/E. K. Scheuch (eds): *Historical Social Research. The Use of Historical and Process-Produced Data*. Stuttgart: Klett 1980, pp. 235–263.

Reutter, Lutz-Eugen: *Katholische Kirche als Fluchthelfer im Dritten Reich. Die Betreuung von Auswanderern durch den St. Raphaelsverein*. Recklinghausen/Hamburg: Paulus 1971.

Rivlin, Ray: *Shalom Ireland. A Social History of Jews in Modern Ireland*. Dublin: Gill and Macmillan 2003.

Röder, Werner/Herbert A. Strauss (eds): *Biographisches Handbuch der deutschsprachigen Emigration nach 1933. Vol. I.: Politik, Wirtschaft, Öffentliches Leben*. Munich/New York/London/Paris: K. G. Saur 1980.

Röder, Werner/Herbert A. Strauss (eds): *Biographisches Handbuch der deutschsprachigen Emigration nach 1933 (International Biographical Dictionary of Central European Emigrés 1933–1945 Vol. 2. The arts, sciences, and literature)*. Pt. 1. A – K. Munich/New York/London/Paris: K.G. Saur 1983.

Röder, Werner/Herbert A. Strauss (eds): *Biographisches Handbuch der deutschsprachigen Emigration nach 1933 (International Biographical Dictionary of Central European Emigrés 1933–1945 Vol. 2. The arts, sciences, and literature)*. Pt. 2. L - Z. Munich/New York/London/Paris: K.G. Saur 1983.

Roehm, Eberhard/Jörg Thierfeder: *Juden, Christen, Deutsche*. 7 Volumes. Stuttgart: Calwer 1992–2007.

Rosenstock, Werner: Exodus 1933–1939. A Survey of Jewish Emigration from Germany. In: *Yearbook Leo Baeck Institute*. Vol. 1, no. 1 (1956), pp. 373–390.

Roth, Andreas: *Mr. Bewley in Berlin. Aspects of the Career of an Irish Diplomat 1933–1939*. Dublin: Four Courts Press 2000.

Rückl, Steffen: Studentischer Alltag an der Berliner Universität 1933 bis 1945. In: Christoph Jahr (ed.): *Die Berliner Universität in der NS-Zeit. Vol. I: Strukturen und Personen*. Wiesbaden: Franz Steiner 2005, pp. 115–142.

Rumbaut, Ruben: Ages, Life Stages and Generational Cohorts. Decomposing the Immigrant First and Second Generations in the USA. In: *International Migration Review*. Vol. 38, no. 3 (2004), pp. 1160–1205.

Rürup, Reinhard: *Schicksale und Karrieren – Gedenkbuch für die von den Nationalsozialisten aus der Kaiser-Wilhelm-Gesellschaft vertriebenen Forscherinnen und Forscher*. Göttingen: Wallstein 2008.

Sachs, Hans/Alfred Klopstock: *Methoden der Hämolyseforschung*. Berlin et al.: Urban & Schwarzenberg 1928.

Sachs, Hans/Paul Ehrlich: *Über die Beziehung zwischen Toxin und Antitoxin und die Wege ihrer Erforschung*. Leipzig: G. Fock 1905.

Sachs, Hans/Walter Georgi: Zur Serodiagnostik der Syphilis mittels Ausflockung durch cholesterinierte Extrakte. In: *Medizinische Klinik*. Vol. 14, no. 33 (1918), pp. 805–809.

Sachs, Hans: *Die Hämolysine und die cytotoxische Sera. Ein Rückblick auf neuere Ergebnisse der Immunitätsforschung*. Wiesbaden: Bergmann 1907.

Sachs, Hans: *Die Hämolysine und ihre Bedeutung für die Immunitätslehre*. Wiesbaden: Bergmann 1902.

Sachs, Hans: *Probleme der pathologischen Physiologie im Lichte neuerer immunbiologischer Betrachtung*. Vienna: Julius Springer 1928.

Sachs, Hans: *Über die Beziehung des Kobragiftes zu den roten Blutzellen*. Müncher Medizinische Wochenschrift. Munich: Lehmann 1908.

Sachs, Hans: Salt Concentration in Blood-grouping Technique. In: *The Lancet*. Vol. 239, no. 6190 (18 April 1942), pp. 473–474.
Sacks, Paul Martin: *The Donegal Mafia: an Irish Political Machine*. New Haven: Yale University Press 1976.
Sapper, Manfred/Wolfgang Weichsel/Anna Lipphardt (eds): *Impulses for Europe. Tradition and Modernity in East European Jewry*. Berlin: BWV 2008.
Schadek, Hans: Das jüdische Kinderheim 'Sonnenhalde' in Bollschweil bei Freiburg 1935–1939. Zur Geschichte des Heims (I) und seiner Leiterinnen, der Kinderärztin Dr. med. Elisabeth Müller (II) und der Handelsschullehrerin Dr. phil. Annerose Heitle (III). In: *Zeitschrift des Breisgau-Geschichtsvereins „Schau-ins-Land"*. Vol. 126 (2007), pp. 203–261.
Scherf, Konrad: *Die metropolitane Region Berlin. Genese und Niedergang, Revitalisierung und Innovation*. Vienna: Verlag der österreichischen Akademie der Wissenschaften 1998.
Scherke, Katharina: Esther Simpson und die Aktivitäten der SPSL (Society for the Protection of Science and Learning) im Zusammenhang mit der Emigration deutschsprachiger Wissenschaftler zwischen 1933–45. In: J. M. Ritchie (ed.): *German-speaking Exiles in Great Britain*. The Yearbook of the Research Centre for German and Austrian Exile Studies, Vol. 3, Amsterdam/New York: Rodopi 2001, pp. 121–130.
Schilde, Kurt: *Bürokratie des Todes. Lebensgeschichten jüdischer Opfer des NS-Regimes im Spiegel von Finanzamtsakten*. Berlin: Metropol 2002.
Schlösser, Karl/Annelore Schlösser/Dorothea Spille (eds): *Die Wormser Juden 1933–1945*. Dokumentation. CD-ROM 2002.
School of Theoretical Physics: *50 year report*. Dublin: Dublin Institute of Advanced Studies [1990].
Schmitt, Hans: *Quakers and Nazis. Inner Light in Outer Darkness*. Columbia/London: University of Missouri Press 1997.
Schrödinger, Erwin: *What is life? The Physical Aspect of the Living Cell*. Based on lectures delivered under the auspices of the Dublin Institute for Advanced Studies at Trinity College, Dublin in February. Cambridge: Cambridge University Press 1944.
Schrödinger, Erwin: Quantisierung als Eigenwertproblem (Erste Mitteilung [First Paper]). In: *Annalen der Physik*. Vol. 4, no. 79 (1926), pp. 361–376.
Schulz, Thilo: *Das Deutschlandbild der Irish Times 1933–1945*. Frankfurt am Main: Peter Lang 1999.
Schwartz, Philipp/Helge Peukert (eds): *Notgemeinschaft - Zur Emigration deutscher Wissenschaftler nach 1933 in die Türkei*. Marburg: Metropolis-Verlag 1995.
Schwarz, Peter/Siegwald Ganglmair: Emigration und Exil 1938–1945. In: E. Talos, E. Hanisch/W. Neugebauer/R. Sieder (eds): *NS-Herrschaft in Österreich. Ein Handbuch*. Vienna: öbv & hpt 2000, pp. 817–850.
Schwittai, Yvonne/Matthias David: Die Geschichte der Frauenkliniken der Charité. In: Matthias David/Andreas Ebert (eds): *Geschichte der Berliner Universitäts-Frauenkliniken: Strukturen, Personen und Ereignisse in und außerhalb der Charité*. Berlin/New York: de Gruyter 2009, pp. 27–51.
Schwoch, Rebecca (ed.): *Berliner jüdische Kassenärzte und ihr Schicksal im Nationalsozialismus: ein Gedenkbuch*. Berlin: Hentrich & Hentrich 2009.
Segal, Sanford L.: *Mathematicians Under the Nazis*. Princeton/Oxford: Princeton University Press 2003.
Söllner, Alfons: 'Exilforschung' as Mirror of the Changing Political Culture in Post-War Germany. In: David Kettler/Zvi Ben-Dor (eds): *The Limits of Exile*. Berlin/Madison: Galda 2010, pp. 65–77.

Solomons, Estella: *Portraits of Patriots – with Biographical Sketch of the Artist by Hilary Pyle.* Dublin: Allen Fidges & Co. 1966.
Sommerfeld, Arnold: *Wissenschaftlicher Briefwechsel.* Vol 2. Michael Eckert/Karl Märker (eds). Berlin/Munich: Deutsches Museum/Verlag für Geschichte der Naturwissenschaften und der Technik 2004.
Spielhofer, Sheila: *Stemming the Dark Tide.* York: Ebor Press 2001.
Storr, Katherine: *Excluded from the Record: Women, Refugees and Relief, 1914–1929.* Bern: Peter Lang 2010.
Strauss, Herbert A. et al. (eds): *Emigration – Deutsche Wissenschaftler nach 1933 Entlassung und Vertreibung, List of Displaced German Scholars 1936 Supplementary List of Displaced German Scholars 1937 The Emergency Committee in Aid of Displaced Foreign Scholars, Report 1941.* Berlin: Technische Universität Berlin 1987.
Strauss, Herbert A. et al. (eds): *Die Emigration der Wissenschaften nach 1933. Disziplingeschichtliche Studien.* Munich et al.: K. G. Saur 1991.
Strohmeyer, Armin: *Annette Kolb. Dichterin zwischen den Völkern.* Munich: dtv 2002.
Swanton, Daisy L.: *The Lives of Sarah Anne Lawrenson and Lucy O. Kingston – Emerging from the Shadows (Based on Personal Diaries, 1883–1969).* Dublin: Attic 1994.
Sweeney, Suzanna: *Women in Business. Heads for Hats.* Unpublished MA thesis. University of Galway 2006.
Szöllösi-Janze, Margit: Wir Wissenschaftler bauen mit — Universitäten und Wissenschaften im Dritten Reich. In: Bernd Sösemann (ed.): *Der Nationalsozialismus und die deutsche Gesellschaft.* Stuttgart: Deutsche Verlags-Anstalt 2002, pp. 155–171.
Tierney, Mark: *Glenstal Abbey. A Historical Guide.* 4th edition. Limerick: Glenstal Abbey Publications 2005.
Tierney, Mark: The Origins and Early Days of Glenstal Abbey. In: Martin Browne/Colmán Ó Clabaigh (eds), *The Irish Benedictines – A History.* Dublin: Columba Press 2005, pp. 163–176.
The Royal Commission on Historical Manuscripts: *Report on the Records of the Society for the Protection of Science and Learning, 1933–1987.* London 1988.
Tobin, Robert: *The Minority Voice. Hubert Butler and Southern Protestantism, 1900–1991.* Oxford (et al.): Oxford University Press 2012.
Trinks, Ulrich: Die Schwedische Mission in der Seegasse. http://www.christenundjuden.org/artikel/geschichte/58-trinks-die-schwedische-mission-in-der-seegasse [last accessed 19 February 2016].
Unknown: Obituary Albert Uffenheimer. In: *Siena College Yearbook.* (1941).
Unknown: Obituary Hans Sachs. In: *The Lancet.* Vol. 245 (28 April 1945), p. 547.
Unknown: Obituary Professor Alfred Bloch. In: *AJR Information* (July 1979), p. 10.
Unschuld, Ulrike: *You banfa - Es findet sich immer ein Weg: Wilhelm Manns Erinnerungen an China 1938 – 1966.* Berlin: Hentrich & Hentrich 2014.
Venus, Theodor/Alexandra-Eileen Wenck: *Die Entziehung jüdischen Vermögens im Rahmen der Aktion Gildemeester. Eine empirische Studie über Organisation, Form und Wandel von "Arisierung" und jüdischer Auswanderung in Österreich 1938–1941. Nationalsozialistische Institutionen des Vermögensentzuges.* Österreichische Historikerkommission. Vol. 20, no. 2. Vienna et al.: Oldenbourg 2004.
Vierhaus, Rudolf/Bernhard vom Brocke (eds): *Forschung im Spannungsfeld von Politik und Gesellschaft: Geschichte und Struktur der Kaiser-Wilhelm-/Max-Planck-Gesellschaft.* Stuttgart: Deutsche Verlags-Anstalt 1990.

Villani, Cinzia: Fra tolleranza e persecuzione, Ebrei in Alto Adige, Trentino e Bellunese. In: *Geschichte und Region/Storia e regione*. Vol. 6 (1997), pp. 295–308.
Voigt, Klaus: *Zuflucht auf Widerruf. Exil in Italien 1933–1945*. 2 Volumes. Stuttgart: Klett-Cotta 1989 and 1993.
Walker, Colin: Robert Weil. In: Gisela Holfter (ed.): *German-speaking Exiles in Ireland 1933–1945*. Amsterdam/New York: Rodopi 2006, pp. 133–148.
Walsh, Dermot: *Divine World Missionaries in Ireland*. Rome: Apud Collegium Verbi Divini 1995.
Walsh, John: *Patrick Hillery: The Official Biography*. Dublin: New Island 2008.
Waterman, Stanley: Changing residential patterns of the Dublin Jewish community. In: *Irish Geography*. Vol. XIV, no.1 (1981), pp. 41–50.
Weiner, Louis (ed.): *The Jews of Czechoslovakia*. 3 Volumes. New York: The Jewish Publication Society of America 1984.
Weinzierl, Erika: *Prüfstand. Österreichs Katholiken und der Nationalsozialismus*. Unter Mitwirkung von Ursula Schulmeister. Mödling: St. Gabriel 1988.
Weinzierl, Erika: *Zu wenig Gerechte. Österreicher und Judenverfolgung 1938–1945*. Vienna: Styria 1997.
Wenisch, R./E. Krakauer: Geschichte der Juden in Komotau. In: Hugo Gold (ed.): *Die Juden und Judengemeinden Böhmens in Vergangenheit und Gegenwart*. Vol. 1. Brünn/Prague: Jüdischer Buch und Kunstverlag 1934, pp. 299–304.
Werner, Charlotte M.: *Annette Kolb. Biographie einer literarischen Stimme Europas*. Königstein: Ulrike Helmer 2000.
Westphal, Otto: About the History of the MPI for Immunobiology. In: Klaus Eichmann (ed.): *The Biology of Complex Organisms – Creation and Protection of Integrity*. Basel: Springer 2003, pp. 63–76.
Wigham, Maurice J.: *Newtown School Waterford – A History 1798–1998*, Waterford: [Newtown School] 1998.
Wills, Clair: *That Neutral Island. A Cultural History of Ireland during the Second World War*. London: Faber and Faber 2007.
Wlaschek, Rudolf M.: *Juden in Böhmen. Beiträge zur Geschichte des europäischen Judentums im 19. und 20. Jahrhundert*. Munich: Oldenbourg 1997.
Wolff, Stefan L.: Die Emigration von Physikern während des Nationalsozialismus – ein Geschichtsansatz mit vernetzten Biographien. In: Peter Zigman (ed.): *Die biographische Spur in der Kultur- und Wissenschaftsgeschichte*. Jena: IKS Garamond 2006, pp. 101–115.
Woodward, Guy: *Culture, Northern Ireland & the Second World War*. Oxford: Oxford University Press 2015.
Wyman, David S.: *The Abandonment of the Jews. America and the Holocaust, 1941–1945*. New York/London: The New Press 1984 (new edition 2007).
Wyman, David S.: *Paper Walls: America and the Refugee Crisis, 1938–1941*. New York: University of Massachusetts Press 1968.
Yaakov, Ariel: *Evangelizing the Chosen People. Missions to the Jews in America, 1880 – 2000*. Chapel Hill/London: The University of North Carolina Press 2000.
Young, John N.: *Erskine Childers. President of Ireland. A Biography*. Gerrards Cross: Colin Smythe 1985.
Zimmerman, David: The Society for the Protection of Science and Learning and the Politicization of British Science in the 1930s. In: *Minerva*. Vol. 44, no. 1 (2006), pp. 25–45.

Zimmermann, Marc: *The History of Dublin's Cinemas*, Dublin: Nonsuch 2007.
Zimmermann, Volker: *Die Sudetendeutschen im NS-Staat. Politik und Stimmung der Bevölkerung im Reichsgau Sudetenland (1938–1945)*. Essen: Klartext 1999.
Zucker, Bat-Ami: *In Search of Refuge. Jews and US Consuls in Nazi Germany 1933–1941*. London, Portland: Valentine-Mitchell 2001.

2 Personal recollections and autobiographies

Amery, Jean: *At the Mind's Limits. Contemplations by a Survivor on Auschwitz and its Realities*. Bloomington: Indiana University Press 1980.
Anonymous. *The Noyk Story 1890–1965. A Record of Achievements over 75 years*. Dublin: Noyek 1965.
Becker, Annelies: *Tread Softly: Scenes from My life*. The Library: May 1999. http://homepage.tinet.ie/~interfriendpublisher/tread.html [last accessed 19 February 2016].
Behrendt, Gideon *Mit dem Kindertransport in die Freiheit. Vom jüdischen Flüchtling zum Corporal O'Brian*. Frankfurt/M.: Fischer 2001.
Belau, Detlef/Anja Hollaender: Familie Dr. Otto Hollaender http://www.naumburg-geschichte.de/geschichte/juden.htm#04 [last accessed 12 June 2016].
Benson, Sylvia: *Down Memory Lane*. Tel Aviv: Self-published 1977.
Benson, Asher: *Jewish Dublin: Portraits of Life by the Liffey*. Dublin: A. & A. Farmar 2007.
Bernstein, Mashey: *A Portrait of Jews in Ireland*. Presented by Maurice Abrahamson in Memory of Professor Leonard Abrahamson. Dublin 1971.
Bew, Paul (ed.): *A Yankee in de Valera's Ireland: The Memoir of David Gray*. Dublin: Irish Royal Academy 2012.
Born, Max: *Mein Leben: Die Erinnerungen eines Nobelpreisträgers*. Munich: Nymphenburger 1975.
Born, Max: *My Life*. London: Taylor & Francis 1978.
Braunizer, Ruth: Memories of Dublin – excerpts from Erwin Schrödinger's diaries. In: Gisela Holfter (ed.): *German-speaking Exiles in Ireland 1933–1945*. Amsterdam/New York: Rodopi 2006, pp. 265–274.
Briscoe, Robert/Alden Hatch: *For the Life of Me*. Boston/Toronto: Little, Brown and Company 1958.
Butler, Hubert: *The Children of Drancy*. Dublin: The Lilliput Press 1988.
Butler, Hubert: *Escape from the Anthill*. Mullingar: The Lilliput Press 1985.
Campbell, Patrick: *My Life and Easy Times*. London: Anthony Blond 1967.
Clare, George: *Last Waltz in Vienna: the Destruction of a Family 1842–1942*. London: MacMillan 1982.
Cooke, John: Hans and Charlotte Sachs. In: Gisela Holfter (ed.): *German-speaking Exiles in Ireland 1933–1945*. Amsterdam/New York: Rodopi 2006, pp. 215–248.
Couturié, Sylvia: *No Tears in Ireland. A Memoir*. New York: The Free Press 2001.
Crowley, Elaine: *Dublin Girl. Growing up in the 1930s*. New York: Soho 1996.
Deutscher Bundestag, Wissenschaftliche Dienste, Abteilung Wissenschaftliche Dokumentation (ed.): *Aufzeichnungen und Erinnerungen. Vol. 2: Curt Becker, Franz Marx, Ernst Paul, Hans Schütz, Elisabeth Schwarzhaupt, J. Hermann Siemer, Anton Storch*. Boldt: Boppard am Rhein 1983.

Doorly, Mary Rose: *Hidden Memories. The Personal Recollections of Survivors and Witnesses to the Holocaust Living in Ireland*. Dublin: Blackwater Press 1994.
Douglas, Glynn: Norah Douglas and the Belfast Committee for German Refugees. In: Gisela Holfter (ed.): *The Irish Context of Kristallnacht. Refugees and Helpers*. Irish-German Studies. Vol. 8. Trier: WVT 2014, pp. 89–101.
Dubsky, Paul: The Dubsky Family. In: Gisela Holfter (ed.): *The Irish Context of Kristallnacht. Refugees and Helpers*. Irish-German Studies. Vol. 8. Trier: WVT 2014, pp. 57–64.
Englaender, Otokar: *Geschichten aus der Geschichte meines Lebens*. Self-published 1971. (Archived in the Institut für jüdische Geschichte Österreichs).
Eppel, Cissie: *A Journey into our Ancestry. Chronicles of the Rosenheim, Levy, Eppel Families*. Jersey: Benny Linder 1992.
Esser, Barbara: *Sag beim Abschied leise Servus – Eine Liebe im Exil*. Vienna: Kremayr & Scheriau 2002.
Falk, Otto Michael: Michael Falk. In: *Holocaust Memorial Day 2009 Booklet*, Dublin: Holocaust Educational Trust of Ireland 2009, p. 18.
Fitz-Simon, Christopher: *Eleven Houses. A Memoir of Childhood*. Dublin: Penguin Ireland 2007.
Flynn, Jude: Hirsch Ribbons. In: *Fireside Tales from around Longford Town and County*. No. 2 (November 2004), pp. 53–55.
von Förster, Heinz/Ernst von Glasersfeld: *Wie wir uns selbst erfinden. Eine Autobiographie des radikalen Konstruktivismus*. Heidelberg: Carl Auer 1999.
Glasersfeld, Ernst von: *Unverbindliche Erinnerungen. Skizzen aus einem fernen Leben*. Vienna: Folio 2008 (in English: *Partial Memories: Sketches from an Improbable Life*. Exeter: Imprint Academic 2009).
Gaughan, J. A. (ed.): *Memoirs of Senator James G Douglas, Concerned Citizen*. Dublin: University Dublin College Press 1998.
Glaser Otto: Personal, Cultural and Academic Links. In: Paul Leifer/Eda Sagarra (eds): *Austrian-Irish Links through the Centuries*. Vienna: Diplomatic Academy of Vienna 2002, pp. 101–142.
Gross Eva: *A Kinder Story*. Belfast: privately published 2003.
Hahn Otto: *Mein Leben*. Munich: Bruckmann 1968.
Harris, Nick: *Dublin's Little Jerusalem*. Dublin: A. & A. Farmar 2002.
Hedenquist, Göte: Meine Begegnung mit Adolf Eichmann. In: *Schweden-Österreich*. No. 2 (1988), pp. 7–10.
Hedenquist Göte: *Undan förintelsen – Svensk hjälpverksamhet i Wien under Hitlertiden*. Kristianstad: Verbum 1983.
Heitler, Walter: Interview by John L. Heilbron, 18 March 1963. Center for History of Physics of the American Institute of Physics. https://www.aip.org/history-programs/niels-bohr-library/oral-histories/4662-1 [last accessed 18 March 2016].
Heitler, Walter: *Lebenserinnerungen*. Privately held, Prof Günter Rasche, Zurich.
Henderson, Denis: On Ruth Henderson and her Parents, Peter and Else Brandenburg. In: Gisela Holfter (ed.): *The Irish Context of Kristallnacht. Refugees and Helpers*. Irish-German Studies. Vol. 8. Trier: WVT 2014, pp. 65–72.
Hennig, John: *Die bleibende Statt*. Bremen: privately published 1987 (2 chapters translated as John Hennig, The Lasting Abode. In: Gisela Holfter/Hermann Rasche (eds): *John Hennig's Exile in Ireland*. Galway: Arlen 2004, pp. 53–86).
Hirsch, L. M. F./Erwin Strunz/Siobhan Lincoln: Ardmore – Memory and Story. First published in: *Ardmore Journal* (1989).http://www.waterfordmuseum.ie/exhibit/web/Display/

article/373/3/Ardmore_Memory_and_Story__Troubled_Times_Austrian_Refugees.html [last accessed 11 April 2016].

Jesenska, Milena: *Alles ist Leben. Feuilletons und Reportagen 1919–1999*. Ed. by Dorothea Rein. Frankfurt/M.: Neue Kritik 1984.

Kapralik, Charles J.: Erinnerungen eines Beamten der Wiener Israelitischen Kultusgemeinde. In: *Leo Baeck Institute Bulletin*. Vol. 58 (1981), pp. 52–78.

Karrach, Herbert: The Karrach Family. In: Gisela Holfter (ed.): *The Irish Context of Kristallnacht. Refugees and Helpers*. Irish-German Studies. Vol. 8. Trier: WVT 2014, pp. 43–49.

Kavanagh, Peter: *Beyond Affection. An Autobiography*. New York: Peter Kavanagh Hand Press 1977.

Kearns, Kevin C.: *Dublin Tenement Life. An Oral History*. Dublin: Gill and Macmillan 1994.

Kent, Henry (= Heinz Krotoschin): Interview with Bettina Kaufmann, 10 May 1996. *Visual History Archive*, USC Shoah Foundation, The Institute for Visual History and Education [accessed through Zentrum für Antisemitismusforschung TU Berlin].

Kingshill, Konrad: *On the Precipice of Prejudice and Persecution*. Bloomington: Authors House 2008.

Kingshill, Peter: *Footnote – A Memoir*. London: Self-published 2007.

Kingshill, Sophia: Willi and Trudi Königsberger in Tipperary. In: Gisela Holfter (ed.): *The Irish Context of Kristallnacht. Refugees and Helpers*. Irish-German Studies. Vol. 8. Trier: WVT 2014, pp. 51–56.

Klemperer, Victor: *I Shall Bear Witness: The Diaries of Victor Klemperer 1933–41*. London: Phoenix 1999.

Knowlson, James and Elizabeth (eds): *Remembering Beckett. Uncollected Interviews with Samuel Beckett and Memories of Those who Knew Him*. London: Bloomsbury 2006.

Kohlseisen, Hans: *Und ich reise immer noch - Die Geschichte des Hans Kohlseisen zwischen Gmünd, Stadlau und Irland*. Ed. by Margarete Affenzeller/Gabriele Anderl. Vienna: Mandelbaum 2015.

Kurz, Diana: Diana Kurz drawings on the Holocaust. Interview with Daniel Pinkerton. In: Center for Austrian Studies, University of Minnesota (ed.): *Austrian Studies Newsletter*. Vol. 12, no. 2 (2000), pp. 6–7.

McDyer, James: *Fr McDyer of Glencolumbkille. An Autobiography*. Dingle: Brandon 1982.

Marcus, David: *Oughtobiography: Leaves from the Diaries of a Hyphenated Jew*. Dublin: Gill and MacMillan 2001.

Marcus, David: *Buried Memories*. Cork: Marino Books 2004.

Menkes, John: A Didactic Autobiography. In: *Journal of Child Neurology*. Vol. 16, no. 3 (2001), pp. 191–198.

Menkes, John: Interview, 18 July 1996. *Visual History Archive*, USC Shoah Foundation, The Institute for Visual History and Education [accessed through Zentrum fuer Antisemitismusforschung TU Berlin].

Menkes, John: Interview with Connie Martinson (13 October 2003). Claremont Colleges Digital Library. http://ccdl.libraries.claremont.edu/cdm/ref/collection/cmt/id/512 [last accessed 19 February 2016].

O'Brien, Maire Cruise: *The Same Age as the State*. Madison: The University of Wisconsin Press 2004.

O'Faolain, Julia: *Trespassers. A Memoir*. London: Faber & Faber 2013.

O'Faolain, Nuala: *Are You Somebody? The Accidental Memoir of a Dublin Woman*. New York: Henry Holt and Company 1996.

O'Reilly, Josephine: *The Hidden Gem*. London/New York/Toronto: Longmans, Green and Co. 1946.
Philipson-Levy, Rachel: *Memoir: An Odyssey Revisited. Au fil du souvenir*. Holocaust Survivor Memoirs. Vol. 15d. Ed. by Montreal Institute for Genocide and Human Rights Studies. http://migs.concordia.ca/memoirs/levy/levy.html [last accessed 19 February 2016].
Price, Stanley: *Somewhere to Hang My Hat. An Irish-Jewish Journey*. Dublin: New Island 2002.
Reiss, Hans: Sieben Jahre in Irland 1939–46: Mein Weg in die Germanistik. In: *Jahrbuch der Schillergesellschaft*. Vol. 40 (1996), pp. 409–432.
Reiss, Hans: *Erinnerungen aus 85 Jahren*. Göttingen: Petrarca 2009.
Reiss, Hans: My Coming to Ireland. In: Gisela Holfter (ed.): *The Irish Context of Kristallnacht. Refugees and Helpers*. Irish-German Studies. Vol. 8. Trier: WVT 2014, pp. 35–41.
Remmel, Herbert: *From Cologne to Ballinlough*. Aubane: Aubane Historical Society 2009.
Ryan, John: *Remembering How We Stood. Bohemian Dublin at the Mid-Century*. Dublin: Gill and MacMillan 1975.
Schefold, Monica: Childhood Memories in Ireland from 1939–1956. In: Gisela Holfter (ed.): *German-speaking Exiles in Ireland 1933–1945*. Amsterdam/New York: Rodopi 2006, pp. 249–264.
Schrödinger, Erwin: Autobiographical Sketches. In: *What is Life with Mind and Matter & Autobiographical Sketches*. Cambridge: Cambridge University Press 2012, pp. 165–184.
Sheridan, Peter: *44: Dublin Made Me*. New York: Viking 1999.
Solomons, Bethel: *One Doctor in His Time*. London: C. Johnson 1956.
Sweeney, Ernie/Maura Ryan: Castlebar Hat Factory (also: The Building of the Factory; The Opening of the factory). http://www.mayo-ireland.ie/en/towns-villages/castlebar/history/the-hat-factory.html [last accessed 19 February 2016].
The Holocaust Memorial Day Committee in association with the Department of Justice, Equality and Law Reform: *Learning from the Past - Lessons for Today*. Dublin: Holocaust Educational Trust of Ireland 2008, 2009, 2010, 2011, 2012. http://hetireland.org/app/uploads/2015/02/HMD2008.pdf, http://hetireland.org/app/uploads/2015/02/HMD2009.pdf, http://hetireland.org/app/uploads/2015/02/HMD2010.pdf, http://hetireland.org/app/uploads/2015/02/HMD2011.pdf, http://hetireland.org/app/uploads/2015/02/HMD2012.pdf [last accessed 19 February 2016].
Unger, Klaus: On Herbert Unger. In: Gisela Holfter (ed.): *The Irish Context of Kristallnacht. Refugees and Helpers*. Irish-German Studies. Vol. 8. Trier: WVT 2014, pp. 29–34.
Weil, Stephen: "Children of Goethe": The Scheyer-Weil Family. In: Gisela Holfter (ed.): *The Irish Context of Kristallnacht. Refugees and Helpers*. Irish-German Studies. Vol. 8. Trier: WVT 2014, pp. 23–28.
White, John D.: *The Dublin Hebrew Congregation, Adelaide Road Synagogue, Dublin 2, 1892–1999*. Dublin: The Congregation 1999.
Wigoder, Geoffrey: *In Dublin's Fair City*. Jerusalem: World Zionist Agency 1985.
Zuckmayer, Carl: *A Part of Myself: Portrait of an Epoch*. Translated by Richard Winston/Clara Winston. New York: Carroll & Graf 1984.

Index of Names (main text)

Aberbach, Friedrich 38, 159, 162, 238, 240
Aberbach, Robert 36, 38–39, 159, 162, 238, 240, 367
Abrahamson, Leonard 109, 123, 139, 247, 355–56, 361–62
Adams, Walter 276
Adler, Adolf 161, 243–44, 249, 263, 386
Adler, Alfred 49
Adler, Kurt 52, 155, 160–62, 249, 259, 368–69
Alony, Dayan Z. 245
Alton, Ernest 282, 288, 331
Améry, Jean 365

Bär, Richard 327
Baker, Joshua 123
Baldwin, Stanley 150, 276
Barnacle, Annie 191
Baumgarten, E. 136
Baumgarten, Gertrud 298
Baumgarten, Helene, née Pohly 298
Baumgarten, Paul 298
Bayer, Abraham 25, 102–03, 117, 183, 232, 247–48, 397
Bayer, Gitla née Bulka 25
Bayer, Manfred 25, 368
Beach, Sylvia 95
Becker, Annelies 20, 113, 134, 386
Beckett, Samuel 1–2, 157
Behrend, Felix A 344
Beisser, Gustav 155, 160–61, 172, 239, 357–58
Bell, George 314
Belton, John A. 322
Belton, Patrick 106
Beneš, Edvard 322
Benesch, Anton 198, 201
Benjamin, Walter 305
Bensbach, August 302
Bentwich, Norman 117, 346
Benz, Wolfgang 3, 6
Berger Hammerschlag, Alice 150
Bergin, Osborn 309
Bernfeld, Georg 256, 259, 369

Betjeman, John 265–66
Beveridge, William 271
Bewley, Charles 44, 100, 110–11, 120, 124–25, 199, 320–21
Bewley, Ernest 113
Bewley, Susan E. 113
Bieler, Eva, née Uffheimer 253, 266, 288, 313–14
Bieler, Ludwig 253, 273, 275, 288, 310–18, 345, 347, 399–400
Billig, Kurt 32, 236, 249, 359
Billig, Rosa 249
Billig, Sophie 249
Bittgen, Heinrich 185, 378
Blaskopf, Fritz 33, 46, 48, 189–92, 379, 387
Blaskopf, Grete née Schwarz 46, 188–92, 375, 379
Blaskopf, Hanna Ruth 188
Blaskopf, Max 33, 46, 188
Bloch, Alfred 273, 275, 277–79, 345
Boas, Hans 90, 236
Boas, Johanna, née Philippsthal 89–90
Boas, Mathilde 90
Boas, Paul 89–90, 236
Böhm, Kurt 21, 173
Bohr, Niels 309, 334
Booth, Edith W 138, 299
Borchardt, Hans 393
Born, Max 247, 327, 334, 336–38, 398
Bosch-Gimpera, Pere 308
Boylan, James 89–90, 169
Boylan, Patrick 129, 309–10
Brady, Erina 266
Brady, Sarsfield P. 212
Brandenburg, Else, née Liebmann 77–78, 236, 385
Brandenburg, Peter W. 77, 236, 269, 377, 395
Brandenburg, Rolf 77
Brandenburg, Ruth 77, 236, 377, 395
Braunizer, Ruth, née March 325, 328
Brasch, Rudolph 393
Brehmer, Kurt 20, 113–14
Bretholz, Olga 187
Briscoe, Herbert 95

Briscoe, Robert 27, 95, 100, 114–16, 121–22, 139, 195, 232
Britz, Esther 111, 249, 305, 376
Brondal, Viggo 309
Browne, Michael 186
Brück, Hermann A. 402–03
Brünn, Doris 56, 258
Brunt, David 341
Bryce, Jim 226
Bulka, Chana 14
Bulka, Emmi 14
Butler, Hubert 9, 51–52, 114, 138, 146, 157, 168, 172, 357, 402
Butler, Peggy, née Guthrie 52, 172
Buxton, Rodan 21
Byrne, Edward 135

Cadbury, Emma 50
Campbell, Mary 51
Canning, Margaret 208–09
Carrick, W. 181, 192
Casement, Roger 318
Cecil, Lord 276
Cernik, Julia 214
Cernik, Leo 213–14, 216
Childers, Erskine 185, 204, 265
Churchill, Winston 169, 362
Claessens, Edmond 71–72, 144, 184–85, 211–12
Clare, George (Klaar, Georg) 9, 31, 34, 39, 44–46, 50, 76, 207, 209, 228, 356–58
Clissmann, Helmut 389
Coady, Michael 396
Coffey, Denis J. 110, 276, 300, 311, 314–15, 318–19
Coffey, Diarmuid 239
Coffey, Sheela 239
Cohen, Maurice 123
Colbert, John P. 95
Collis, Robert 389
Concannon, Helena 332
Concannon, W. J. 191
Conway, Arthur W. 300
Cooke, John 288
Corcoran, Timothy 300
Costigan, Daniel 111
Coudenhove-Kalergi, Richard von 94

Crewe, Lord 276
Crick, Francis 339
Crosbie, George 199

Daly, Frank 226
Darley, George 405
Debye, Peter 290
Deutsch, Helene 56
Dielenz, Franz 68, 72–74, 211, 213–16, 218, 382–83
Dielenz, Marie, née Wurb 68, 73–74, 213–14, 218, 382–83
Dillon, James 105, 186
Dillon, Matthew 162, 176
Dillon, Myles 309
Dillon, Theobald W. T. 58–59, 82, 89, 93, 112, 119, 124, 129, 134, 136, 162, 176, 178, 275–76, 303–04, 310, 320–21, 345
Dillon, Thomas 302–03
Dirac, Paul 325, 337
Ditchburn, Robert W. 123, 127, 129, 275–81, 297, 300, 345
Donath, Robert 34–35, 114, 299–300
Doorly, Edward 179
Doorly, Mary Rose 5
Douglas, Harold 262
Douglas, James G. 108–09, 113–14, 262, 300
Dowley, Joseph 199
Drechsler, Frantisek (Frank) 72, 213–14, 259, 366
Drechsler, Friederike, née Schmolka 65, 72
Drechsler, Hanus 72, 213–14, 259, 367
Drechsler, Josef 65, 72
Dreyer, Andreas-Günter 180
Dubsky, Robert 35, 180, 237, 260, 366, 387–88
Duff, John 302
Duffy, Colum Gavan 136, 146, 162
Duffy, George Gavan 146–47
Dunne, Mr 210
Durcan, Paul 210
Dziewientnik, Siegfried 356
Dziewientnik, Teresa 187

Eason, Keith 77
Eddington, Arthur 337
Edwards, Hilton 265

Ehrenberg, Victor 273, 310–12, 345
Ehrlich, Paul 283–84
Eichenstein, David 245
Eichmann, Adolf 54
Eichmann, Ruth 14
Einäugler, Ernst 153, 155, 239, 243, 357–58
Einstein, Albert 9, 270–72, 290–92, 324, 334, 339, 404
Eisenstaedt, Wolfgang 80, 82, 161–63, 165, 372
Emanuel, Wilhelm 23
Endeveld, Mathilde 222
Enright, James 223
Evans, Bryce 4
Ewald, Peter Paul 273, 290, 292, 336–38, 344

Fabian, Julius 102
Fäsenfeld, Georg 253
Fahy, Frank 119, 124, 135
Falk, Otto Michael 248, 260, 362, 370
Farkas, Ludwig von 307
Farnan, Robert 282
Fearon, William 298
Feric, Stefan 35–36, 39, 57–58, 112, 237, 254, 260–61, 303–04, 330, 367, 385
Ferriter, Diarmaid 4
Finck, Franz N. 305
Finkel, Joan 393
Fischer, Emanuel (Ishmael Fisher) 116, 244–47, 249, 390
Fischer, Erika (Erica) 56, 164, 258, 376
Fischer, Georg 56
Fischer, Lisa 56, 164, 258–59, 376
Fitzpatrick, T. 160
Flynn, Jude 203
Forell, Friedrich 53
Forell, Hans 23, 78, 82, 166, 354
Forrest, James 169
Frankel, Fanny, née Mukacevo 246
Frankel, Israel 116, 246–47
Frankl, Bernhard 80, 82, 138, 171–72, 237–38, 373
Frankl, Gerd 138, 171–73, 373
Frankl, Heinz 82, 138, 171–72, 373
Frankl, Margarete, née Burkhard 82, 138, 171–72, 373

Freedman, Norman 394
Freilich, Blima 246
Freilich, David 140, 245–47, 390
Freilich, Dina, née Anabacher 246
Freilich, Joseph 246
Freilich, Nandor 140, 245–47, 249, 390
Freud, Sigmund 49
Friedjung, Gerhard P. 58, 180
Fröhlich, Herbert 334
Fuchs, Annaliese 170, 256
Fuchs, Lothar 33, 170, 235, 256, 372
Fuchs, Melanie 170, 256, 376
Fuchs, Richard 290
Fuchs, Stephanie 170, 256
Furlong, George 321

Garbarz, D. 245
Gahr, Hilda, née Goldstein 154
Gahr, Peter 154, 357
Gardiner, Alan 307, 309
Garner, Steve 147
Gelpke, Rhenus 53
Georgi, Walter 284
Giersch, Anny, née Polesie 218, 376, 383
Gildemeester, Frank van Gheel 59–60
Gittleson, Abraham 245
Glaser, Otto 58, 252, 256, 260, 367, 387, 395
Glasersfeld, Ernst von 94–95, 233–34, 238, 256, 265–66, 369
Glasersfeld, Helena von 94, 96, 233, 256
Glasersfeld, Isabel, née Yves 95, 256, 265, 369
Glasersfeld, Leopold von 94, 96, 233, 256
Glass, Else, née Hirsch 67, 213, 382
Glass, Ernst 65, 67, 72, 211, 213–15, 382
Glass, Sidney 67, 218, 383
Glass, Vera 67, 218, 383
Glenavy, Lord (Gordon Campbell) 225–26, 265
Goebl, Alois 45, 207–09, 379, 385, 395
Goebl, Pauline, née Lintner 45, 205, 207–09, 385, 395
Goertz, Hermann 388–89
Gogan, Liam 319
Goldberg, Marcel 185
Goldschmidt, Ferdinand 241, 249, 291, 294–95

Goldschmidt, Sidonie 241, 249, 291, 294–95
Goldstein, Friederike 154
Goldstein, Sidney 292
Goldstone, Katrina 118, 128
Grelling, Kurt 288
Griffin, George 269
Griffith, Arthur 147
Griffith, William 239, 373
Grüttner, Michael 270
Gudansky, Abraham 121
Gwynn, E.J. 276

Haas, Robert 23–24
Hähnlein, Viktor 23–24
Hainbach, Fritz 49–50
Hainbach, Heinrich 49
Hainbach, Isabella, née Coutts 220, 222–23, 377
Hainbach, Kurt 35, 49–50, 220–23, 358, 377, 397
Hainbach, Mark 223
Halifax, Lord 276
Hamill, John B. 163, 180
Hamilton, Deirdre, née Sinclair 1
Hamilton, Hugo 5
Hamilton, James 337
Hansel, Grete, née Schmolka 65
Harant, Gerhard 133, 354
Harris, Nick 248
Hearne, Michael 206, 380
Hedenquist, Göte 53–55
Heilfron, Charlotte, née Russ 83, 249, 253, 288
Heilfron, Curt 79, 83, 243, 249, 253, 288
Hein, Katharina 61, 187
Heinsheimer, Eva Maria 168–69, 376
Heinsheimer, Ludwig 32, 168, 177–78, 262, 371
Heinsheimer, Risa, née Löw Beer 33, 168, 177, 374
Heitler, Annerose 335, 374–75
Heitler, Hans 335
Heitler, Ottilie 375
Heitler, Walter 254, 273, 333–38, 343, 347, 375, 398, 403–04
Hempel, Eduard 118, 266, 318
Henderson, Denis 385

Hengstenberg, Jochen (Heston, John) 173, 252, 257, 370
Hengstenberg, Reiner (Brian) 173, 252
Hengstenberg, Trude 252
Henlein, Konrad 67, 71
Hennig, Claire, née Meyer 254–55, 268, 288, 389
Hennig, Gabriele 255
Hennig, John 178, 180, 235, 254–55, 265–66, 268, 275, 288, 299, 347, 389, 399
Hennig, Monica 255
Hepner, Wolfgang 337
Heron, Agnes 233
Heron, Barney 225, 233, 238
Heron, William 233
Hertz, Rudolf 319
Herzfeld, Karl 333
Herzog, Isaac 100, 105, 118, 144
Hetherington, George 17
Heymann, Hermann 247, 249, 356
Hill, A.V. 271
Hillery, Michael 221–23
Hipwell, Catharine, née Hunt 164
Hipwell, William 164
Hirsch, Elsa, née Rosenberg 45, 207, 256, 379
Hirsch, Emil 32–33, 36, 41–46, 48, 183, 203, 205–08, 256, 379
Hirsch, Ernst 52, 155, 160–61, 165, 236–37, 259–60, 365, 387
Hirsch, Friedrich 33, 52, 152, 155, 160–61, 225, 239, 268, 373
Hirsch, Fritz 39, 153–58, 160–61, 165–66, 236–37, 259–60, 366–67, 387
Hirsch, Marie 52, 152, 155, 160–61, 239, 373–74
Hirsch, Robert 36, 42, 45, 206–07, 264, 395, 397
Hirschberg, Gerhard 92–94, 166–68, 240–41, 299, 354, 372
Hitchman, Hana 196–97, 200, 379, 393
Hitchman, Paul 70, 379
Hitler, Adolf 6–7, 15–16, 27, 32, 67, 72, 106, 108, 116, 143, 148, 270, 273, 278, 285, 307–08, 312, 322, 380, 387
Hitschman, Carlos 199, 379
Hitschmann Albert 70, 199, 379

Hitschmann (Hitchman), Fritz (Fred) 70–71, 197–201, 379, 393
Hitschmann, Irma, née Reich 70, 199–201, 379
Hitschmann, Karl 70
Hitschmann, Richard 33, 70, 197, 199–201, 379
Hoek, Kees van 286–87, 289
Höfer, Annemarie (Mimi) 59–60, 254, 376
Hoffmann, Conrad 22–23, 53–55, 82, 109, 112, 117, 137, 166, 168, 242, 352
Hogan, Patrick 240
Holländer, Bernhard 115–16, 235, 245–49, 390–91
Holländer, Gertrud, née Croner 116, 235, 246–49
Holländer, Jürgen 21, 173–74
Honig, Else, née Popper 187, 247, 249, 378
Honig, Fritz 85, 249, 378
Honig, Theodor 33, 187, 249
Hopf, Alice, née Goldschmidt 89, 249, 291, 293–96, 297–98, 375
Hopf, Arnold 291–92, 296–97
Hopf, Dieter 291–92, 296–97
Hopf, Hans 291, 296–97
Hopf, Liselore 249, 258–59, 291, 293–96
Hopf, Ludwig 89, 249, 252, 273, 282, 289–98, 307, 324, 334, 339, 345
Hopf, Peter 291, 296–97
Horwitz, Anselm 61–62, 158–59, 163, 182, 223–27, 253, 262, 397
Horwitz, Hugo Th. 61
Howard, Emma 133, 172
Huggard, Kathleen 56, 59, 112, 130, 167, 172, 231, 236, 240, 257, 357, 386
Humboldt, Wilhelm von 306, 402
Hwan-Wu Peng 337
Hyde, Douglas 28–29, 318

Infeld, Leopold 404
Innitzer, Theodor 57, 110, 320
Iveagh, Lord 276

Jacob, Charles 133, 189
Jacob, Stella 133, 189
Jakobovits, Immanuel 391
Jakobi, Erwin 247, 361–62

Jammet, Louis 240
Janossy, Lajos 403
Johnston, Denis 265
Jones, David 209
Joyce, James 4, 95, 191
Jung, C.G. 291

Kafka, Franz 65
Kahn, Felix S. 240, 249
Kalman, Adolf 33
Kalman, Beile 33
Kalman, Josef 32–34, 48, 188, 192, 254, 373, 379
Kalman, Lucie 61, 254, 373, 379
Kalman, Saul 48
Kaplan, Franz 394
Kappeler, Alice, née Kobler 38, 154, 241, 385
Kappeler, Richard 38, 154, 241, 244, 263, 360, 385
Karfunkelstein, Irma 256
Kármán, Theodore von 290, 295
Karrach, Emilie, née Nathan 231, 249, 359, 373
Karrach, Ferdinand 32, 231, 249, 359, 373
Karrach, Herbert 37, 257, 259, 261, 368
Karrenberg, Gisela 89, 249, 252
Karrenberg, Ludwig 89, 127, 234, 249, 260
Kavanagh, Patrick 265
Kawerau, Einhart 20, 23–24, 113, 127, 134, 237, 252, 259, 261, 298, 368, 371
Kawerau, Siegfried 20, 81
Kawerau, Sigurd 20, 113, 237, 260, 369, 371
Keane, Sir John 153, 157
Kelly, S. 194
Kende, Adolphine, née Hirsch 45, 207, 249
Kende, Erika 45, 207, 376
Kende, Ludwig 45, 207, 249
Keogh, Dermot 3
Kidney, R.J. 131
Kinas, Sven 270
Kingston, Lucy 113–14, 133
Kingston, Samuel 113–14
Kirchhoff, Johanna, née Faulhaber 15
Kirchhoff, Paul 15
Klaar, Ernst 31–32, 39, 44–45, 48, 50, 356
Klaar, Georg (see Clare, George)
Klaar, Stella, née Schapira 31, 44–45, 76

Klemperer, Victor 85
Klepper, Margarete, née Heller 67, 213, 215, 381–82
Klepper, Siegfried (Fred) 65, 67, 72, 211, 213, 215–16, 218, 381–82
Kobler, Rosa 38, 154
Kohlseisen, Hans 37, 58, 180
Kokotek, Jakob 393
Kolb, Annette 15–17
Königsberger (Kingshill), Ernst W. 84–85, 87–88, 201–203, 385
Königsberger, Gertrud, née Sachs 85, 87–88, 201–203, 375, 385
Königsberger, Konrad 88
Königsberger (Kingshill), Peter 19, 88
Konirsch, Fritz 65, 67, 211, 213–16
Konirsch, Gertrud 67, 213–14, 376
Konirsch, Margarete, née Feldmann 67, 214, 216, 375
Koppel, L.B. 397
Kraus, Kurt 163, 367
Krehl, Ludolf von 285
Kröner, Albert 74–75, 219–20
Kröner, Beate, née Franke 74–75, 219–20
Kröner, Leo 74–75, 219, 221
Krotoschin, Alice, née Hettmann 27, 79, 84, 193–94, 249
Krotoschin, Heinz 27, 79, 84, 193–94, 248–49
Kurz, Benjamin 33, 350, 355
Kurz, Diana 350, 355
Kurz, Golda 350

Lamb, Bernard 133
Lancy, Rosa de 15
Landauer, Gustav 28
Lederer, Friedrich 35, 60, 275, 373
Ledermann, Hans V. 21, 180, 260–61, 352
Lemass, Seán 44, 70–71, 103, 149, 181, 183–84, 186, 190, 204, 213, 227, 395
Lendt, Stefan 39, 355
Lentaigne, Vida 59–60, 136, 160–61, 165, 238–39, 373
Lentin, Louis 5
Leslie, Shane 169
Leszynski, Else 139
Leventhal, A.J. 293

Lewin, Walter 256, 352
Lewis-Crosby, Ernest 112
Lewy, Ernst 111, 230, 249, 273, 275, 304–10, 317–18, 347, 376, 400–402
Lewy, Georg 249, 305, 309, 376
Lewy, Hedwig, née Ludwig 249, 305–06, 308–09, 376
Leydon, John 225
Libin, Arnold 185
Liddell, Max 298
Liepmann, Leo 311
Liffmann, Rosa, née Silber 85–87, 249, 375
Liffmann, Siegmund 84–87, 233, 249, 253, 371
Lincoln, Siobhan 156
Lindemann, Frederick 324–25, 334
Lintner, Hedwig 45, 206–08
Lisowski, Friedrich 27–29, 230–31, 371
Lisowski, Käte (see Müller-Lisowski, Käte)
Lisowski, Peter 29, 134, 166, 173, 230–31, 260, 368
Liss, Georg 95–96, 168, 357–58
Litera, Julia 69
Litera, Vaclav 69
Loewenkopf, Hermann 152
Loewenkopf, Wetty 152
London, Fritz 334, 336
Londonderry, Lord 276
Lönhardt, Marianne 256
Lowy, Hans 48, 188, 192, 379–80
Lowy, Helena (Hene), née Kunstler 33, 48, 192, 379
Lynch, Mr 210

McDyer, James 397
MacEntee, Seán 140
Macken, Mary 310
MacLiammóir, Micheal 265
MacNeill, Eoin 319
MacRory, Joseph 57, 110, 135
Mandl, Hans 194–96, 362, 378
Mandl, Ines, née Hochmuth 34, 194–96, 362, 377
Mann, Wilhelm 303
Manswort, Margit 222
March, Arthur 325
March, Hilde 325, 328

March, Ruth 325, 328
Marckwald, Fritz 85, 87, 189–91, 209, 378, 385
Marckwald, Maria, née Guradze 85, 87, 187, 189–91, 374, 378, 385
Margulies, Frieda, née Promuschkin 26, 90, 246–47
Margulies, Inge 26, 90, 247
Margulies, Leib 26, 90, 104–05, 117, 233–34, 246–48, 397
Mark, Hermann 280
Marsh, Arnold 173–74, 402
Martin, Thomas 226
Marx, Richard 89, 93, 260, 360
Masaryk, Jan 380
Masaryk, Tomas 63
Maston, Lord 276
Mautner, Friedrich 344
Mautner, Richard 44–45
McCauley, Leo T. 100–102
McCrea, William 331, 337
McDermott, John 188
McEllin, John 71, 103, 183, 185, 203, 206, 212, 219–20, 280
Menkes, Hans (John) 35, 61, 247, 257, 356, 361
Menkes, Karl 38, 61, 247, 356, 361
Menkes, Valerie, née Tupler 33, 61, 247, 356, 361
Meyer, Eduard 311
Meyer, Kuno 311, 332
Michel, Kurt 14–15
Michel, Leo 14–15
Miretinsky, Josef 185
Moddel, Garret 390
Moddel, Paula, née Margulies 26, 90, 235, 247, 374
Moddel, Philip 90–91, 140, 235, 245–49, 263, 390–91
Montgomery, R. 171
Morgenstern, Hans 52–53, 166–67, 172, 240–41, 357–59
Mortl, Berta 187
Mott, Nevill 334–35
Motz, Hans 273, 279–81, 345
Muchitsch, Wolfgang 3
Mulcahy, Richard 105–06

Mulchrone, Kathleen 319
Müller-Lisowski, Käte 27–29, 175, 230–31, 374
Mündheim, Adolf 85, 88–89, 247, 249, 361–62
Mündheim, Siegfried 88–89
Murphy, James 212
Murphy, Kathleen 389

na gCopaleen, Myles (Brian O'Nolan / Flann O'Brien) 337
Nachmann, David 79, 83–84, 89, 132, 231, 243, 247, 249, 251, 361–62
Nachmann, Thomas 173, 248, 251, 361
Nagle, Austen 343
Nathan, Walter 101–102
Nelki, Otto 23–24
Neuman(n), Marianne, née Heilfron 83, 249, 253, 368
Neuman(n), Rudi 83, 249, 253, 389, 393
Ney, Katharina 75, 219–20
Ney, Paul 75, 219–20
Nicholson, Joyce F. 166–67
Noyk, Michael 121
Nugent, Alison 167–68
Nugent, Sir Oliver 167–68
Nugent, Lady Catherine 167–68

O'Brien, Conor Cruise 299
O'Connell, Daniel 14
O'Connor, Siobhán 4
O'Dea, L.E. 185
O'Donnell, Peadar 15
O'Driscoll, Jeremy 222
O'Dwyer, Dermot 212
O'Faoláin, Seán 2
O'Grada, Cormac 3
O'Kelly, Seán T. 406
O Máille, Tomas 300
O'Suilleabhain, Proinnsias 389
O'Sullivan, Donal 129
Oberer, Florian 48, 189, 192, 379
Odell, Mary 156
Orbach, Henri 26, 144, 184–85

Pächt, Otto 321–22
Pappenheim, Wolfgang 259, 368

Peres, Alfred 322
Petersen, Carl 267
Philipson, Serge 26, 144, 184–85, 188, 264, 378
Philipson, Sophie, née Orbach 26, 144
Philipson Levy, Rachel 144, 184
Pick, Eva Maria 22, 56, 82, 110–12, 258, 260, 305, 354, 376
Pick, Georg 22, 56, 82, 110–12, 257, 259–60, 305, 354, 386
Pius XI 127, 136
Pius XII 136
Planck, Max 273, 322, 324, 334
Pokorny, Julius 318–19
Polesie, Karl 68, 211, 212–14, 216, 218
Polesie, Marie, née Taussig 213–14, 216, 218, 383
Pollak, Johanna, née Dittrich 254, 341–43
Pollak, Leo 74, 254, 273, 339–43, 347, 402–03
Porges, Walter 65, 67, 211, 213–16, 219, 383
Power, Sheila 337
Price, Stanley 245
Priebatsch, Erich J. 84, 237, 247–48, 372
Priebatsch, Eva-Agnes 84
Priebatsch, Johanna, née Breit 84
Proctor, William C. 252
Pückler, Hermann Fürst von 286

Reichelt, Franz 201
Reinert, Edeltraut 23, 127, 256, 260
Reisman, Arnold 347
Reiss, Hans 253, 257–59, 261, 265, 299, 369
Reynell, Louise 171
Reynell, Richard 171
Richards, Shelagh 265
Riegner, Gerhart 147
Roche, Stephen A. 104, 106, 110–11
Rosanowsky, Jacob 246–47
Rosenberg, Else, née Pietrkowski 126, 247
Rosenberg, George (Hymen) 233, 360
Rosenberg, Gerhard 126–27, 247, 260
Rosenberg, Marianne 126
Rosenberg, Michael 126
Rosulek, Anastasia, née Chojkova 185, 379
Rosulek, Karl 185, 379
Rothschild, Anthony de 151

Rund, Hedwig, née Segal 83, 247, 249, 371–72
Rund, Max 80, 83, 231, 247, 249, 371–72
Rutherford, Ernest 271, 275
Ryan, John 248
Ryan, Maura 215

Sachs, Charlotte, née Grelling 249, 253, 283, 285–86, 288, 375
Sachs, Hans 249, 252–53, 263, 273, 275, 282–89, 294–95, 297, 307, 318, 345
Sachs, Ilse 288
Salazar, Antonio de Oliveira 152
Samter, Else 79, 83, 242, 249, 253, 286, 362, 371, 375
Scheff, Dietrich 256, 259
Schenk, Leopold 232
Scheyer, Ernst 23, 84, 249, 253, 263, 275, 299, 361–62, 389, 392–93
Scheyer, Heinz 23–24, 84, 259, 261, 360, 362
Scheyer, Marie, née Epstein 23, 84, 249, 253, 332, 361–62
Scheyer, Renate 84, 258–59, 261, 369, 377, 393–94
Schlesinger, Olga 354
Schlesinger, Percy 173
Schloss, Elisabeth, née Wetzel 194–96, 253
Schloss, Gerhard 194–96
Schmeltz, Stefan 180
Schmolka (Smolka), Erika, née Wilka 211, 380–81
Schmolka (Smolka), Franz 66–70, 74, 76, 211–16, 380–81
Schmolka, Fred 65, 74, 211, 213–14, 381, 393
Schmolka, Hans 65, 213
Schmolka, Paul 65, 213
Schmolka, Peter 259
Schmolka, Steffka, née Heumer 74, 213–15, 381, 393
Schmutzer, Josef 136
Schnitzler, Karl 23, 247
Schnitzler, Paul 23, 247
Schönberg, Karola 56
Schonfeld, Solomon 122
Schrödinger, Annemarie, née Bertel 254, 325–28, 330, 332, 343, 406

Schrödinger, Erwin 254, 266, 268, 271, 273, 275, 295–96, 310, 322, 323–39, 343–45, 347, 398, 403–06
Schrötter, Fridolin 201
Schulhof, Alfred 39, 53, 139, 180, 254, 260
Schüller, Robert 219, 369
Schulz, Ignaz 32, 176–77, 262
Schulz, Käte 21, 173
Schulze, Wilhelm 305
Schumpeter, Josef A. 320
Schwab, Gertrud 356
Schwab, Julius 356
Schwarz, Berta 242, 249, 370, 375, 389
Schwarz, Eva 75, 219–20, 243
Schwarz, Gertrud(e) 259
Schwarz, Kurt 56, 173, 175, 367
Schwarz, Ottilie 56, 256, 259
Schwarz, Peter 242, 257, 259, 261, 369–70
Schwarz, Rudolf 75, 219–20, 232
Schwarz, Walther 44–45
Schwarz, Werner 92–94, 166, 172, 174, 240–41, 360
Schwenk, Mathilde 185, 189, 379
Scott, Michael 265
Segal, Doris, née Klepper 67, 72, 213, 215, 217–18, 372, 376, 381
Serff, Eric(h) 89, 236, 254, 359
Setälä, Emil N. 307
Shea, Margaret 190
Sheehy, Edward 265
Sheehy-Skeffington, Hanna 15
Shemeld, Jack 174
Sherry, Francis 220
Shillman, Bernard 118
Siebeck, Richard 285
Silber, Julius 85–86, 253, 357
Simon, Walter 60, 240, 247, 356, 361
Simpson, Esther 271, 311
Sinclair, Frances, née Beckett 1–2
Sinclair, Peggy 1
Sinclair, William 1–2
Singer, Alfred 352
Singer, Oscar 351–52
Sitte, Hedwig 322
Sitte, Kurt 322
Slattery, Maud 124, 130, 132, 152, 190, 223
Smallbones, Robert T. 286

Smyllie, R.M. 266
Snyder, Timothy 33
Sokolov, Nahum 100
Somerville-Large, Philip 133
Sommer, Ernst 23–24, 115
Sommerfeld, Arnold 9, 290–92, 324, 332–34, 406
Sonnenschein, Elisabeth, née Stückgold 45, 207, 209–10, 379
Sonnenschein, Ernst 32, 41, 44–45, 205, 207–10, 379
Sousa Mendes, Aristides de 151
Staples, Hetty 159
Starkie, Walter 109
Staudt, Kurt 158, 162–63, 170–72, 357–58
Stein, Aaron 356, 361
Stein, Josefa 38, 60, 249, 260, 360
Steiner, Karl 260, 357–58, 360
Steiner, Robert 58, 260, 360
Steinitz, Wolfgang 305, 400
Stephenson, Father 190
Stiegwardt, Elise, née Koppel 159, 163, 170–72, 236, 352
Stiegwardt, Kurt 52, 158–59, 163, 170–72, 236, 352, 357–58
Stiel, Elias 249
Stockley, Germaine 16
Stockley, William 16
Stoney, Robert V. 168
Stoney, Theffania, née Nugent 168
Storch, Alice 247
Storch, Walter 61, 247, 361–62
Storm, Else, née Petersilka 38, 133, 187, 378
Storm, Josef 187, 378
Strauss, Herbert A. 270
Strunz, Erwin 35, 40, 51–52, 114, 134, 153, 155, 157, 160, 239, 264, 373
Strunz, Georg 369
Strunz, Liesl, née Pardovici 40, 51–52, 134, 153, 155, 157, 160, 239, 264, 373–74, 385
Strunz, Peter 173, 367
Sweetman, Dom John (Francis) 162
Synge, John L. 403
Synge, John Millington 405
Szilard, Leo 271
Szöllösi-Janze, Margit 270

Taylor, Geoffrey I. 292–93
Teichmann, Bertha 144, 242, 252
Tenison, Gerald E.F. 168–69
Thrift, W.E. 293
Thurneysen, Rudolf 319
Ticher, Ellen, née Teichmann 252–53, 288, 299, 393
Ticher, Kurt 226, 252–53, 288, 299, 393
Ticher, Peter 252–53
Ticher, Ruth 252
Ticher, Thomas 252–53
Tierney, Mark 178
Tierney, Michael 331
Topper, Konrad 53, 354
Trafford, Siegbert 162
Tuchmann, Anna Maria 21–22, 258, 260–61, 360
Tuchmann, Hans Sigmund 22
Tuchmann, Marianne 22

Unger, Herbert K. 80–81, 158, 162–63, 170, 172, 237–38, 260, 357–58, 367, 385, 390
Unger, Klaus 390
Unger, Ursula 80
Ussher, Arland (Percy Arnold) 157

Valera, Éamon de 4, 100, 107, 110–12, 122, 126, 138, 144, 146, 161, 183, 226, 276, 282, 301, 310–11, 315, 318, 323–24, 327–33, 336, 338–39, 347, 406
Vasmer, Max 307
Vere O'Brien, Elinor 166
Vere O'Brien, Flora 165–66
Vere O'Brien, Hugh 166
Vogt, Paul 53

Wallach, Richard 36–37, 39, 166, 354
Walshe, Joseph 104, 106, 110–11, 144, 315, 320
Warburg, Max 17–18
Warnock, William 199
Warnock, William A. 138
Watson, James D. 339

Weil, Robert 78, 83, 173, 259, 261, 369, 393
Weil, Renate (see Scheyer, Renate)
Werner, Klaus Peter 159, 163
Werner, Kurt 157, 163–64, 377
Werner, Lilli, née Robert 159, 163, 377
Wessely, Paul 155, 352
Westphal, Otto 285
Whelan, Robert E. 226
Whittaker, E.T. 327, 333
Wicklow, Joseph 133
Wiedmann, Elisabeth, née Hermann 241–43, 377
Wiedmann, Franziska 231, 254, 377
Wiedmann, Fritz 32
Wigham, E.M. 113
Wilkins, Maurice 339
Wilmersdörfer, Hans 356, 361
Wills, Clair 4, 264
Winkler, Wilhelm 39, 57, 319–21, 345
Wirsberger, Mr 245
Wissmann, Wilhelm 401
Wittgenstein, Ludwig 17
Witztum, Abraham 47
Witztum, Arnold 33, 35, 47, 232
Witztum, Deborah, née Künstler 48
Witztum, Feiga 47
Witztum, Marcus 33, 44–48, 60–61, 71–72, 75, 103, 144, 182–88, 192, 198, 203, 205–06, 208, 211–12, 219–20, 232, 380, 383
Witztum, Naftali 33, 47, 249
Wizniak, Abraham 247
Wizniak, Sabina 5, 376
Wolfgarten, Josef 260, 360
Woodward, Guy 150
Woolfson, William Lewis (Wolf) 234–35

Yeats, William Butler 405

Zawisch, Carla 310–11, 315, 317–18
Zeiler, Wolf 33, 185
Zimmer, Heinrich 305
Zuckmayer, Carl 36

Index of Places

Aachen 282, 290–94
Alpbach/Austria 406
Amsterdam 27
Antwerp 47–48, 185, 192
Ardmore, Co. Waterford 131, 153–60, 239
Ardnacrusha, Co. Clare 14
Athlone, Co. Westmeath 164, 204, 377

Balla, Co. Mayo 183
Ballina, Co. Mayo 75, 180, 219
Balrath Bury, Co. Meath 166–67
Bamberg/Bavaria 22
Barcelona 47, 308
Bayreuth/Bavaria 277
Basle/Switzerland 399
Belfast 109, 256, 273, 292, 313–14, 336–38, 344, 358, 361
Belmont, Co. Offaly 172
Bennettsbridge, Co. Kilkenny 172
Berlin 7–9, 21–23, 26–28, 44, 48, 54, 57, 62, 72–73, 76–77, 80–83, 100–101, 105, 111, 115–16, 118, 126, 152, 171, 246, 251, 283, 290, 293, 298, 304–09, 311, 318–20, 324, 327, 333–34, 358, 365, 374, 384, 389, 400–01, 403
– Charlottenburg 27, 77
– Kreuzberg 80
– Lichtenberg 102
– Lichterfelde Ost 79
– Mariendorf 126
– Reinickendorf 77
– Schöneberg 77, 79
– Wilmersdorf 27, 77, 93
Besançon/France 280
Birmingham 337
Bobowa/Poland (formerly Austrian Empire) 115
Bolzano/South Tyrol 94
Bonn 90, 319
Bray, Co. Wicklow 27, 171, 176, 230, 235, 254
Bremen 242
Breslau/Silesia 21, 115, 283, 305, 324
Brighton 23
Bristol 334–35

Brno 65, 71, 73–75
Buchenwald 89, 322
Burgstädt/Saxony 19, 85, 87

Cabinteely, Co. Dublin 230
Cambridge 275, 292–93, 312, 325, 334, 337, 403
Canberra 354
Cappagh, Co. Waterford 131, 157–60, 163, 170, 223
Carlisle/Cumbria 312
Carrick-on-Suir, Co. Tipperary 71, 181, 197–201, 379
Carrickmacross, Co. Monaghan 69
Castlebar, Co. Mayo 9, 71–74, 181, 183, 206, 211–19, 378, 378–81, 383
Chemnitz/Saxony 85
Chicago 58
Chichester/West Sussex 314
Clairefontaine/Belgium 314
Clogham, Co. Offaly 172
Cobh, Co. Cork 62
College Park/Maryland 9
Cologne 15, 89–91, 180, 384
Columbus/Ohio 334
Copenhagen 309, 333–34
Cork 16, 28, 118, 121, 123, 154, 182, 194–96, 226, 275–76, 300–01, 311–12
Cracow/Poland 46
Croydon 87, 341

Dachau 37, 82
Dalkey, Co. Dublin 256
Darmstadt 20
Delvin, Co. Westmeath 171, 389
Divišov (Diwischau)/Bohemia (formerly Austrian Empire) 70
Donamon Castle, Co. Roscommon 89, 178–79
Dresden/Saxony 85–87
Drogheda, Co. Louth 60, 160
Dublin 1–2, 7–9, 15, 18, 20, 22–24, 32, 44, 55–56, 58, 61–62, 72–74, 77, 83–84, 87, 89, 91, 93, 95, 99–103, 105–06, 112,

115–16, 118, 121–25, 127, 129, 134–35,
137, 141–44, 163, 167–68, 171–73,
177, 180, 182–83, 188, 190–91, 194,
198, 205–11, 213–214, 223, 225–26,
228–69, 272, 275–76, 278–82, 286,
288, 293–94, 296–98, 300–01, 303–05,
310–12, 315–17, 323, 327–28, 330–33,
336–38, 343–47, 355, 357, 359, 362, 367,
375–82, 388–90, 392–93, 399–400,
403, 405–06
– Clontarf 254, 330, 336, 343, 377, 406
– Dunsink 402
– Rathfarnham 305, 317, 393
– Rathgar 113, 229, 245, 248–49, 251, 256
– Rathmines 245–46, 248–52, 260, 286,
    294, 305
– Stillorgan 154
– Terenure 247, 315, 382
Dun Laoghaire, Co. Dublin 244, 254, 335, 399
Dunleer, Co. Louth 163

Edinburgh 127, 327–28, 337–38, 369, 398
Eidlitz (Údlice)/Sudetenland 68
Eiwanowitz/Moravia (formerly Austrian
    Empire) 33
Elphin, Co. Roscommon 179
Ennis, Co. Clare 165
Enniskerry, Co. Wicklow 160
Ennistymon, Co. Clare 304–05
Enzensdorf/Austria 219
Erdeborn (near Halle)/Saxony Anhalt 192
Erkner/Brandenburg 82
Evian/Switzerland 108, 110–11

Farrenconnell, Co. Cavan 163, 167–68
Fishguard/Wales 154
Foynes Island, Co. Limerick 166
Frankfurt/Main 25–26, 90–91, 115, 246,
    283–84, 286
Freiburg/Baden 283, 319
Fribourg/Switzerland 313
Fürth/Bavaria 356, 383

Galway 44, 164, 181, 182, 184–94, 203, 206,
    209, 219, 238, 275–76, 300–302, 305,
    311–12, 319, 332, 337, 374, 378, 394

– Salthill 191
Gdynia/Poland 73
Geneva 107–08, 112, 328
Ghent 328
Gladbeck/Westphalia 115
Glasgow 400
Glasslough, Co. Monaghan 89
Glencolmcille, Co. Donegal 397
Glencree, Co. Wicklow 160
Gmünd/Austria 37
Göpfritz/Austria 41–42, 209
Gorey, Co. Wexford 162
Gort, Co. Galway 164
Göttingen 311, 333–34
Graz 46, 188, 326–28, 405
Guildford/Surrey 360

Hadzor/Worcestershire 179
Halle/Saxony Anhalt 85, 88
Hamburg 17, 28, 62, 80, 91, 109, 168, 311,
    346
– Altona 91, 311
– Eimsbüttel 109
– Wandsbek 109
Haulbowline Island, Co. Cork 195
Heidelberg 281–82, 284–88, 300, 302, 399
Hirschberg/Silesia 84

Innsbruck 53

Jena/Thuringia 324
Jerusalem 9

Kanturk, Co. Cork 226
Karlsruhe/Baden 25, 333
Kassel/Hesse 1
Kattowitz/Upper Silesia 283
Kilternan, Co. Wicklow 233, 265
Kingsfort, Co. Meath 170–71
Kitzingen/Main 85
Komotau (Chomutov)/Sudetenland 9, 63–74,
    213, 216, 380–81

Ledeč 70
Leeds 91
Leipzig 77, 85, 283, 305

Leitmeritz (Litomerice)/Sudetenland 69–71, 199
Leixlip 238
Levico/South Tyrol 340
Liegnitz/Silesia 23, 84
Limerick 3–4, 175, 177, 342
Little Bray, Co. Wicklow 154
Liverpool 351
London 8, 17–18, 25, 44, 49, 51–53, 55, 82–83, 102, 109, 114, 116, 126–27, 134, 141–42, 144, 149–50, 154, 168, 195, 197, 222, 231, 241, 253, 271–73, 281, 286, 293, 296, 312, 321–22, 325, 341, 346, 368, 382, 387, 392–93, 397, 403, 406
Longford 9, 181, 183, 203–10, 374, 379, 395–96
Lough Bawn, Co. Westmeath 168
Lviv (Lemberg, formerly Austrian Empire) 33
Lyck/East Prussia 92

Magdeburg/Saxony Anhalt 101
Manchester 334, 403
Mannheim/Germany 299, 302
Mantua, Co. Roscommon 180
Maynooth, Co. Kildare 235, 300, 399
Melbourne 344
Meran/South Tyrol 94–96
Middletown, Co. Armagh 169
Milan 92
Millisle, Co. Down 150, 361–62
Miltown Malbay, Co. Clare 49, 180, 220–22, 358, 377
Moscow 334, 387
Moynalty, Co. Meath 170
Mullach, Co. Meath 298
Mullagh, Co. Cavan 167, 170
Mullingar, Co. Westmeath 171
Mulranny, Westport, Co. Mayo 168
Munich 9, 67–68, 74–75, 94, 277, 290–91, 305, 313, 324, 333–34, 356, 400
Murroe, Co. Limerick 175–76

Naas, Co. Kildare 180
Naumburg/Saxony Anhalt 21
Nenagh, Co. Tipperary 193
Neudorf/Moravia (formerly Austrian Empire) 33

New York 53, 196, 213, 223, 272, 346, 352, 372
Newbliss, Co. Monaghan 52, 155
Newcastle 74, 312, 360
Newport/England 88
Newtown, Co. Waterford 9, 21, 29, 83, 113, 134, 171, 173–74, 230
Newtownards/Northern Ireland 361
Nuremberg 19, 22, 103, 105–06, 290, 382–83

Odenkirchen/Rhineland 85
Offenbach/Main 14, 25, 102
Ontario 397
Oranienburg/Brandenburg 28
Oslo 73
Oxford 9, 311, 324–25, 328, 334

Paris 15–16, 21, 26, 32, 48, 95, 184, 314
Plotyeze (formerly Austrian Empire) 33
Pilsen 65, 69, 72
Podebrady/Bohemia 69
Potsdam 29
Pozna/Poland 90
Prague 65, 70–74, 199, 273, 290, 311–12, 322, 339–40
Pressburg/Slovakia 33
Princeton/USA 324–25, 344, 346, 400
Prossnitz/Moravia (formerly Austrian Empire) 33
Przemysil (formerly Austrian Empire) 33, 48

Rakonitz/Bohemia 73
Regensburg/Bavaria 277
Remscheid/Rhineland 14, 93
Rome 92–93, 135, 298, 307, 328
– Vatican 93
Rotterdam 77

Sachsenhausen 76, 83, 86, 88–89
Salzburg 313
San Sebastian 307
Sasava/Bohemia 73
Schneidemühl/Pomerania 116, 248
Schönschornstein/Brandenburg 82
Sisak/Croatia 65, 74
Sligo 164
Spanish Point, Co. Clare 220
St Augustin/Rhineland 89–90

Stanislau/Galicia (formerly Austrian Empire) 33
Stary Sambor/Galicia (formerly Austrian Empire) 33, 47
Strzelbice/Galicia (formerly Austrian Empire) 33
Stuttgart 324
Suhl/Thuringia 103
Svetla/Bohemia 73
Sydney 355

Tapolcsan (formerly Austrian Empire) 33
Tarnobrzeg (formerly Austrian Empire) 26
Termonfeckin, Co. Louth 60, 160–61, 165
Tipperary, Co. Tipperary 88, 181, 197–203
Torino 93
Toronto 376, 403
Tralee, Co. Kerry 181, 182, 223–26, 253, 397
Tramore, Co. Waterford 189
Trento/South Tyrol 340
Tuam, Co. Galway 394
Tübingen/Germany 313

Utrecht/Holland 82, 136

Valentia, Co. Kerry 343
Verona/Italy 93

Verviers/Belgium 72, 184, 211–12
Vichy 144
Vienna 7–9, 23, 31–62, 65, 67, 70, 76, 82, 94, 114, 138, 154, 161, 176, 180, 182, 185, 187–88, 192, 195, 199, 205–06, 219, 222, 226, 228, 231, 238, 244, 273, 279–80, 304, 313, 319–20, 326–27, 339, 344–45, 356, 379, 403, 406
– Hietzing 46
– Josefstadt 33
– Kagran 51, 54, 58, 120, 163
– Leopoldstadt 33, 38, 70, 187
– Meidling 49
– Stadlau 51, 54

Waidhofen/Austria 37
Walzenhausen/Switzerland 53
Warsaw 26
Waterford, Co. Waterford 134, 154–55, 158, 173
Weiden/Bavaria 277
Wojnilov/Galicia (formerly Austrian Empire) 33–34

Zagreb 176
Zurich 53, 55, 92, 94, 290, 324, 327, 333, 404

www.ingramcontent.com/pod-product-compliance
Lightning Source LLC
Chambersburg PA
CBHW022103290426
44112CB00008B/525